COHERENT JUDAISM

CONSTRUCTIVE THEOLOGY, CREATION, & HALAKHAH

COHERENT JUDAISM

JUDAISM

CONSTRUCTIVE
THEOLOGY,
CREATION,
& HALAKHAH

SHAI
CHERRY

Library of Congress Cataloging-in-Publication Data

Names: Cherry, Shai, author.
Title: Coherent Judaism : constructive theology and halakhah / Shai Cherry.

Description: Boston : Academic Studies Press, 2020. | Includes index. |
Summary: "Coherent Judaism begins by excavating the theologies within the Torah and tracing their careers through the Jewish Enlightenment of the eighteenth century. Any compelling, contemporary Judaism must cohere as much as possible with traditional Judaism and everything else we believe to be true about our world. The challenge is that over the past two centuries, our understandings of both the Torah and nature have radically changed. Nevertheless, much Jewish wisdom can be translated into a contemporary idiom that both coheres with all that we believe and enriches our lives as individuals and within our communities. Coherent Judaism explains why pre-modern Judaism opted to privilege consensus around Jewish behavior (halakhah) over belief. The stresses of modernity have conspired to reveal the incoherence of that traditional approach. In our post-Darwinian and post-Holocaust world, theology must be able to withstand the challenges of science and history. Traditional Jewish theologies have the resources to meet those challenges. Coherent Judaism concludes by presenting a philosophy of halakhah that is faithful to the covenantal aspiration to live long on the land that the Lord, our God, has given us"-- Provided by publisher.
Identifiers: LCCN 2020037137 (print) | LCCN 2020037138 (ebook) | ISBN 9781644693407 (hardcover) | ISBN 9781644693414 (adobe pdf) | ISBN 9781644693421 (epub)
Subjects: LCSH: Judaism.
Classification: LCC BM562 .C54 2020 (print) | LCC BM562 (ebook) | DDC 296.3--dc23
LC record available at https://lccn.loc.gov/2020037137
LC ebook record available at https://lccn.loc.gov/2020037138

ISBN 9781644693407 (hardback)
ISBN 9781644693414 (adobe pdf)
ISBN 9781644693421 (ePub)

Book design by Lapiz Digital Services.
Cover design by Ivan Grave, artwork by Joel Moscowitz, reproduced by permission.

Published by Academic Studies Press
1577 Beacon Street
Brookline, MA 02446, USA
press@academicstudiespress.com
www.academicstudiespress.com

To Tehila Yona, Rina Zimra, and Shalev David

Kinder, reach beyond coherence
כי לעולם חסדו

Contents

Book Three: Philosophies of Halakhah

Acknowledgments

One of the very few advantages of being an underemployed adjunct professor was having spare time.

A friend, Jonathan Lapin, asked me a question on Shabbat Toledot. "Why didn't Isaac just take back the blessing he had given to Jacob and give it to Esau?" My answer to Jonathan elicited the following response: "That's stupid!" I could have just agreed with Jonathan and saved myself seven years of work. But as previously noted, I had some spare time.

The middle book of *Coherent Judaism* was inspired by a Time Magazine story promoting what would become Robert Wright's forthcoming title, *The Moral Animal: The New Science of Evolutionary Psychology.*[1] At the time, I was studying in Jerusalem at the Hebrew University, and a guest professor from UCLA, Neil Malamuth, happened to be teaching a course on evolutionary psychology. Upon my return to Brandeis University, I recruited our historian of science and overall mensch, Silvan Schweber (*z"l*), to keep me honest on the science while I wrote my dissertation on the Jewish responses to Darwinism. Arthur Green supervised the thesis, patiently helped me acquire the tools of the trade, and went on to write far too many letters on my behalf. My debt to them both is deep and ongoing.

In the acknowledgements from my dissertation, I was able to thank a few people from my slog through graduate school who were supportive when I needed it most. I am delighted to be able to thank them, again, in print: the Raphael family, the Bornstein Stacks family, Marsha Slotnick, and my in-laws, Susan and Joseph Milstein. With a wink to the Talmudic tradition that it takes three to make a person (mother, father, and God),

---

1   New York: First Vintage Books, 1994.

I dedicated my dissertation to my folks (z"l) and my sister Roxanne. My parents showed me what relentless love looks like. My sister led the way for making Judaism and Israel central parts of my life.

In the middle of writing my first book, it became clear to me that my ignorance of Jewish law was preventing me from doing the kind of research I wanted to do. My family's former congregational rabbi, Bradley Shavit Artson, had become the dean of the Ziegler School of Rabbinic Studies in Los Angeles. His gracious cooperation, along with that of Cheryl Peretz, the Associate Dean, was instrumental in negotiating a path toward ordination where I could focus my attention on Talmud with Aryeh Cohen and *halakhah* with Elliot Dorff. Both Aryeh and Elliot gave generously of their time and talent.

Many friends have contributed their precious time to help make this text more intelligible to the non-specialist. Sol Kempinski, Todd Kobernick, and Michael Marks were part of the minyan at Congregation Beth Am in San Diego where this project took root. Other friends in San Diego, Alina Levy and Bard Cosman, patiently waded through many of the early chapters and offered very helpful feedback. The Copley Library staff of the University of San Diego was both generous and instrumental in facilitating my research during my four years there.

In the Spring of 2019, as I was concluding the manuscript and thinking about my next project, a rabbinic position opened up in Elkins Park, Pennsylvania. The process of writing *Coherent Judaism* had opened me up to the possibility of becoming a congregational rabbi. I have been serving Congregation Adath Jeshurun since the summer of 2019. I am blessed to be part of this community, and I look forward to a deep, rich, and enduring relationship. Adath Jeshurun members Skip Atkins, David Seltzer, Allan Freedman, and Meryl Sussman each read sections of the manuscript and offered helpful advice. I am grateful.

Rabbis and/or Doctors Leon Wiener Dow, Abraham Havivi, Avner Ash, and Jonah Rank each gave of his subject matter expertise and read sections of the manuscript in its final stages. They did their best to warn me of my missteps. I am very appreciative of their comments and concern.

Although not without asterisks, my life has been charmed. I met my wife when she was twenty-one and asked her to marry me before she knew any better. Best decision of my life. Although, truth be told, my mother did push. In the following pages, my wife appears as a muse, a travel companion, and a sage. That's about right.

Coherent Judaism is dedicated to our children at a moment when paying attention is painful. The health of our nation is under siege by a microscopic virus; our democratic institutions are being bludgeoned; our civil discourse coarsened; our relationship with Israel is unstable; and our planet is increasingly inhospitable. We repeat to our children, with waning conviction, "This is not normal." We listen to their despair and struggle to honor their perceptions while not conceding the future, their future. We, as a people, have trekked through this valley of dry bones more than once. It was there that our ancestors first abandoned hope—*avda tikvateinu* (Ezekiel 37:11). Ezekiel encouraged us, and we carried on sowing with tears. Although not without asterisks, our harvest has been bountiful.

SC
Congregation Adath Jeshurun
Elkins Park, Pennsylvania
Rosh Hodesh Elul 2020

List of Abbreviations

b.   Babylonian Talmud, also known as the Bavli. All Talmudic references are to the Bavli unless otherwise noted.

h.   halakhah. A specific halakhah from RaMBaM's Mishneh Torah (M. T.)

m.   mishnah

M. T.   Mishneh Torah by RaMBaM, 1180

O. H.   Orach Hayim, one of the four major sections of the halakhic works by Rabbi Yakov ben Rabbeynu Asher (author of Arba'ah Turim) and Yosef Caro (author of Shulchan Arukh)

S. A.   Shulchan Arukh by Yosef Caro, 1565

t.   tosefta

y.   Jerusalem Talmud, also known as the Yerushalmi

Y. D.   *Yoreh De'ah*, one of the four major sections of the halakhic works by Rabbi Yakov ben Rabbeynu Asher (author of Arba'ah Turim) and Yosef Caro (author of Shulchan Arukh)

Timeline of Important Events

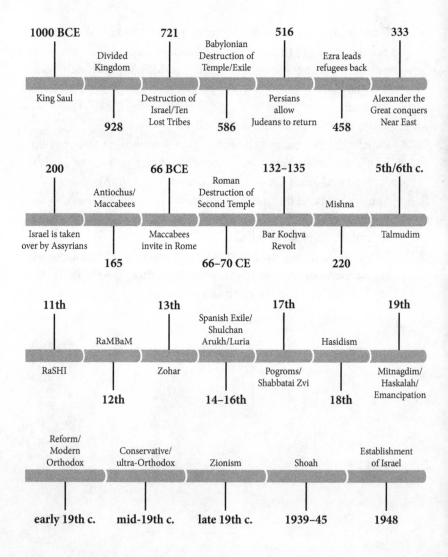

1000 BCE		721		516		333
	Divided Kingdom		Babylonian Destruction of Temple/Exile		Ezra leads refugees back	
King Saul		Destruction of Israel/Ten Lost Tribes		Persians allow Judeans to return		Alexander the Great conquers Near East
	928		586		458	

200		66 BCE		132–135		5th/6th c.
	Antiochus/ Maccabees		Roman Destruction of Second Temple		Mishna	
Israel is taken over by Assyrians		Maccabees invite in Rome		Bar Kochva Revolt		Talmudim
	165		66–70 CE		220	

11th		13th		17th		19th
	RaMBaM		Spanish Exile/ Shulchan Arukh/Luria		Hasidism	
RaSHI		Zohar		Pogroms/ Shabbatai Zvi		Mitnagdim/ Haskalah/ Emancipation
	12th		14–16th		18th	

Reform/ Modern Orthodox		Conservative/ ultra-Orthodox		Zionism		Shoah		Establishment of Israel
early 19th c.		mid-19th c.		late 19th c.		1939–45		1948

Introduction

The Incoherence of the Philosophers. No, that was not my original title for this book. That title was taken about 1,000 years ago by the Persian theologian Al-Ghazali (c. 1058–1111) for his critique of Aristotelian philosophy (which included science). *The Incoherence of the Philosophers* generated opposition. The following century, Ibn Rushd (also known as Averroes, 1126–1198) published *The Incoherence of* The Incoherence.

In the past fifteen years, celebrated authors have published books with similarly provocative titles ranging from the belligerent to the dismissive: *The God Delusion (2006), Breaking the Spell* (2007), *God is not Great* (2008), *Religion without God* (2013), and *Outgrowing God* (2019). Some of these authors are called New Atheists. Parallel to Ibn Rushd, they were motivated to attack popular religion because of the pernicious influence that, from their perspective, religious leaders wield over scientific education and culture in the United States. One difference between our medieval Muslims and the New Atheists is that only the Muslims were experts in theology. The New Atheists tend to parrot the blather of tele-evangelists. One goal of *Coherent Judaism* is to educate my contemporaries on the history, diversity, and sophistication of Jewish theologies.

Coherent Judaism is a less antagonistic title vis-à-vis science and philosophy than *The Incoherence of Philosophy*. By my own criteria listed below, there can be no coherent theology without recognizing and accommodating the truths of history and science. But my title does implicitly charge contemporary expressions of Judaism with being less than coherent. Here are my three criteria for any coherent Judaism:

1) Judaism must be *internally* coherent and remain faithful to its overarching values of compassion, righteousness, and

stewardship, beginning with our own tribe, but like love, radiating outward;

2) Judaism must *cohere* with what we know to be true about reality. A critical embrace of all disciplines, particularly history and science, enhances our ability to bring to light more divinity in our world;

3) Judaism must cohere, in the most robust form consistent with the first two principles, with *traditional* Judaisms.

Conservative Judaism, the movement with which I identify, is not internally coherent because it continues to privilege Torah law over rabbinic law even though it admits that they are both equally human (principle number 1). This privileging leads to hypocrisy and legal fictions which are unbecoming and self-sabotaging.

Orthodox Judaism, in its rejection of critical biblical scholarship, does not cohere with what we know to be true about the composition of the Torah (principle number 2). Such willful ignorance leads to legal outcomes, specifically vis-à-vis women and homosexuals, which are immoral.

Reform Judaism, in its rejection of the binding force of *Halakhah* (Jewish law), does not cohere with a fundamental principle of historical Judaism that obliges us to certain behaviors (principle number 3). The exclusion of the language of obligation within Reform, because of its emphasis on personal autonomy, promotes individual religious feeling at the expense of group identity and solidarity.

Each of the three major American denominations violates a criterion for coherence. My primary goal in *Coherent Judaism* is to offer a vision of God and God's relationship to creation, combined with a posture for our response to that vision, that is internally consistent, coheres with everything else we know to be true about reality, and draws deeply and abundantly from the wells of our ancestors. Hence, *Coherent Judaism* is divided into three books: theology, theology of creation, and the philosophy of Halakhah.

The category of *constructive theology* is not a native term to Judaism. For reasons that will be discussed in the third chapter of book one, the rabbis who wrote the Midrash and Talmud foregrounded halakhic practice over theology. Consequently, throughout my academic career, Christians have informed me that Judaism has no theology. Since my doctorate is in Jewish thought and theology, I feel obligated to engage.[1] "What you may mean," I suggest gently, "is that Judaism has no *systematic* theology or *dogmatic* theology as does Christianity." The rabbis agreed to disagree about theology for the sake of agreeing about practice. Hence the rhyme: Judaism is more about deed, and Christianity more about creed.

In the Christian world, theology has a privileged history. The two universities where I taught each had divinity schools. Vanderbilt University's Divinity School shares faculty and cross lists courses with the Department of Religious Studies, where I was housed for four years. University of San Diego, a Catholic university, features a single department for both theology and religious studies. Historically, Christians write theology and have institutional homes in which to do so. The Jewish world is more compartmentalized.

For the most part, rabbinical schools train rabbis for the pulpit, and graduate programs train scholars for the academy. Although questions of personal meaning and theological truth were not out of place in rabbinical school, as they were in graduate school, such questions were not usually encouraged. The unspoken assumption in both institutions was that we needed to get our bellies full of traditional texts before we were entitled to think theologically for ourselves.

One problem with that model is that it doesn't stimulate new theological thinking because there is neither an institution nor an association dedicated to the task. In 2013, Brill published the first in a series of books called *The Library of Contemporary Jewish Philosophers*. The editors, Hava Tirosh-Samuelson and Aaron W. Hughes, introduced the series by making a distinction between Jewish philosophy as an academic discipline and Jewish philosophy as constructive theology.[2] Part of their hope, articulated at the end of their introduction, is that the series will function

---

1 "Jewish Thought and Theology" is the name of the department at the Hebrew University of Jerusalem where the faculty for Jewish philosophy, mysticism, and related fields are housed. At my *alma mater*, Brandeis University, the Jewish thought and theology program is housed in the Near Eastern and Judaic Studies Department. It was decided to label the department "Jewish Thought and Theology" at the Hebrew University to make its area of study absolutely clear.

2 Hava Tirosh-Samuelson and Aaron W. Hughes, "Editors' Introduction to the Series," in *Menachem Fisch: The Rationality of Religious Dispute*, ed. Hava Tirosh-Samuelson and Aaron W. Hughes (Leiden: Brill 2016), xiii.

as a virtual association to encourage thinking and debate.[3] Notice that the title of the series—*The Library of Contemporary Jewish Philosophers*—avoids the term *theology*. The editors explain that Jewish theology is only one category of Jewish philosophy, and in this series they are casting a wide net.

Until the twentieth century, Jews didn't usually describe what they wrote as *theology*, even when it was. In the Middle Ages, when Jews mimicked their Muslim neighbors and wrote what we today would call theology, they did not use that word. Those Jews were writing in Judeo-Arabic—Arabic words but with the Hebrew alphabet. The word *theology* existed in medieval Arabic, but it wasn't used in Jewish works or in their Hebrew translations. The term doesn't exist because in the Jewish worldview, theology (what we think about God) is not separable from religion (what we do based on our theology). Indeed, there's no word for *religion* in biblical or rabbinic Hebrew, either. Both elements were intertwined in Jewish identity. Furthermore, those "theologies" from the Middle Ages were not accepted by all Jews, perhaps because we have no central authority.

In summary, rabbinic religiosity did not foreground theology; no single theology was universally accepted when Jews did begin writing theology; theology, as a discrete discipline, was not a distinct category for Jews until modernity; and the gap between studying traditional texts and writing Jewish theology has still not been bridged institutionally or organizationally. Even when Solomon Schechter published a book on rabbinic theology in 1909, he called it *Some Aspects of Rabbinic Theology*, as a way of distinguishing his work from Christian models of such thinking. Schechter disavows any pretense of systematic or dogmatic theology in both his preface and introduction. It is, therefore, at least understandable why some Christians think Judaism has no theology.

Given that books one and two of *Coherent Judaism* comprise an extensive survey of Jewish theology from the Torah to today, I found the term suitable. Appending the adjective *constructive* to modify *theology* signals that I am not offering a Jewish version of systematic or dogmatic theology, but neither am I engaged in an exclusively academic analysis. I am, self-consciously, constructing anew. In Christian circles, constructive

---

3 Ibid., xv.

theology as a *model* comes closest to what Judaism has always been and what Jewish theologians have always written. The first description that Jason A. Wyman, Jr. offers in his *Constructing Constructive Theology* is that "Constructive theology is pluralistic and dialogical."[4] Judaism's foundational texts, the Torah, the Midrash, and the Talmud, lend themselves to such a characterization, particularly the rabbinic literatures of Midrash and Talmud.

Judaism is a text-centered enterprise which places interpretation as a vital element of its theology. Michael Fishbane, one of the few Jewish academic theologians, speaks of "hermeneutical theology."[5] My first book *Torah through Time: Understanding Bible Commentary from the Rabbinic Period to Modern Times* presents a series of case studies in hermeneutical theology. Christian constructive theologians adopt a similar posture in their own work. "The human element of interpretation and theological construction, in polyphonic, pluralistic, historicized complexity, characterizes constructive theology."[6] Without making the claim that the rabbis were post-modernists, certain aspects of their theology sit comfortably within the post-modern matrix.

Constructive theology for Christians promotes what has been integral to Judaism since the Torah: a vision of a messianic future that demands our commitment to just and righteous behaviors. The politics and economics of Torah and Talmud are concrete expressions of the commitment to those values. "Constructive theology is a critically conscious integration of interdisciplinarity and activism/advocacy."[7] Much of the focus of Christian constructive theology is grounded in the Torah's liberation motif.[8]

Where constructive theology can energize Judaism is in the application of Halakhah to the domain of *tikkun olam* (social justice). The Talmud is our foundational model for such applications, but the impulse to generate new Halakhah has atrophied as its scope has narrowed in

---

4   Jason A. Wyman, Jr., *Constructing Constructive Theology: An Introductory Sketch* (Minneapolis: Fortress Press, 2017), vii.

5   Michael Fishbane, *Sacred Attunement: A Jewish Theology* (Chicago: University of Chicago Press, 2010).

6   Wyman, *Constructing Constructive Theology*, xxvi.

7   Ibid., 73.

8   Ibid., 127–29 and 147–48.

modernity.[9] "The distinctive variety of engaged, activist theology that constructive theology embraces is always based in critical insights derived from other fields expanded into a theological zone, and put toward causes of justice."[10]

In 2014, for example, Rabbi Shmuly Yanklowitz publicly withdrew his support from factory farmed meat, poultry, and dairy because the unethical treatment of animals violates Halakhah.[11] More concerning, from the perspective of human health, are the dangers from zoonotic (animal-borne) disease. When rabbis spotlight the practices of bad actors and the dangers of their practices, the likelihood of effecting change increases. We should not minimize our potential impact through our actions at the consumer level or our innovations in the fields of husbandry and health. A *takkanah*, a noun form of *tikkun*, in its original halakhic context means a legal remedy. Ultimately, as I will argue in the conclusion, we should amend government regulations that oversee the food industry. Constructive Jewish theology leverages the wisdom of the tradition to remedy the ills of society. That's what we see in the Torah, and that's what we see in Midrash and Talmud. Thus, constructive Jewish theology recovers and reactivates traditional Judaism's activism and advocacy.

Lest I give the misperception that marrying Halakhah and *tikkun olam* is solely a function of traditional, premodern Judaism, both nineteenth-century Reform and neoorthodox leaders in Germany deployed the rhetoric of ethical progress. As we will see toward the end of book one, *Bildung* (edification) became a surrogate religion for German Jews in the era of Emancipation. Since our major denominations emerged from Germany, it is logical that they all promoted ethics as the summit of piety. Here is the father of neoorthodoxy in 1838, Rabbi Samson Raphael Hirsch, rousing all Jews to be in the vanguard of progressive change. For Hirsch, being a light unto the nations is not enough. He wants us to lead the charge with torches.

---

9   Eliezer Berkovits, *Not in Heaven: The Nature and Function of Jewish Law* (New York: Ktav Publishing House, 1983), 86.

10 Wyman, *Constructing Constructive Theology*, 120.

11 See https://www.wsj.com/articles/shmuly-yanklowitz-why-this-rabbi-is-swearing-off-kosher-meat-1401404939.

> Picture every son of Israel a respected and influential priest of
> righteousness and love, disseminating among the nations not specific
> Judaism—for proselytism is forbidden—but pure humanity.[12]

Hirsch constructed a Judaism for post-Emancipation German Jewry; I
hope to help frame a Judaism for the twenty first century.

When I wrote *Torah through Time*, I wrote as a theologically sensitive academic who was teaching in Vanderbilt University's Department
of Religious Studies. Even then, I couldn't keep my theological self separate from my academic self and included several comments under the
alias of the unknown Torah commentator Meshi. *Meshi* is an acronym
of my first two names, Michael Shai. As the author of *Coherent Judaism*,
I have pivoted into a new identity as an academic theologian. As such, I
have written as myself, in my own voice, prepared to share some of my
own experiences. Academic protocols have been superseded by my passion to persuade you. I feel an urgency to enlist you in Judaism's primary
objective: to live long on the Land, the world, that the Lord, our God,
has given us. The survival of Judaism requires leaders of each generation
to excavate and reinvigorate aspects of our ancient traditions which will
enrich our lives and offer guidance for our increasingly perilous future.
The survival of our species depends on advancing an agenda with which
Jews, a self-described "surviving remnant" since the days of the Torah, are
familiar. We are in a unique position to lead the charge of pure humanity.

Although *Coherent Judaism* is not addressed to an exclusively academic audience, I have stocked the text with primary sources, secondary
literature, and footnotes. As a text lover, I want to give others the chance
to fall in love. Although paraphrasing is often easier, you should meet the
sources yourselves and have the references to see them in their own contexts if you so choose. As a generalist in Jewish thought, I have included
many of my expert colleagues' analyses to assuage my "imposter complex" and to fortify your faith in my narratives. By *narratives*, I wish to
convey my awareness that I am constructing a narrative arc in each of
the three books. I choose what to include, how to present and interpret
what I include, what to omit, and how to connect the data points. The

---

12 Samson Raphael Hirsch, *The Nineteen Letters on Judaism*, trans. Bernard Drachman
     (Jerusalem: Feldheim Publishers, 1969) letter 16, 108.

footnotes are primarily for scholars who want to look more closely at the sources.

Book one of *Coherent Judaism* is a history of Jewish thought and theology beginning with two mutually exclusive theologies, both in the Pentateuch. Some of the disputes in the rabbinic period are best explained by conflicts between these two biblical theologies. As a generalist, I believe I have seen a pattern in rabbinic Judaism that has escaped others who focus more narrowly in specific periods. Specifically, I will show that the goal of the Torah and the rabbis is one and the same: to live long on the land.

The second half of book one examines the literary and theological developments of rabbinic religiosity from the Middle Ages until today. The rise of the Talmudic commentary and law code, the clash between philosophy and mysticism, and the emergence of contextual biblical commentary dominated the Middle Ages until the exile from Spain in 1492. Shortly thereafter, Lurianic Kabbalah emerged, and the eclipse of philosophy was near total for 200 years. Only with the Emancipation and Enlightenment did Kabbalah begin to suffer setbacks, and then only in western Europe. The politics of eastern European Jewry precluded emancipation, so the revival movement there, Hasidism, remained within the four cubits of the Halakhah. The final chapter in book one examines how the threads of law, philosophy, mysticism, and Torah have been rewoven since the Shoah.

The theologies of book one lay the groundwork for *Coherent Judaism* and the intelligibility of books two and three. Book two takes us from discussions of God to discussions of God's relationship with the world. This book presents theologies of creation from Genesis One to today. Particularly in the first chapter of book two, my language attempts to capture the poetry, the song, of creation that was placed at the head of the Torah. I was inspired by the constructive theologian Catherine Keller to reflect the face of the deep.[13] To use conventional prose to describe the mystery and miracle of creation strikes me as a category mistake. The first chapter will demonstrate how the rabbis reimagined creation,

---

13 Catherine Keller, *Face of the Deep: A Theology of Becoming* (New York: Routledge, 2003).

against the plain sense of the Torah, to mirror their own theology: a rabbinic theology of creation.

Creation, as it happens, was the most controversial topic of the Middle Ages. Chapter Two describes the major debates and players. Lurianic Kabbalah's myth of creation, which reappears in modern theologies of creation, both Jewish and Christian, is described in detail. Chapter Three introduces the challenge of Darwinism and responses to evolution through the beginning of World War II. The final chapter in book two brings evidence of mass extinctions in the history of the planet – a dramatic challenge to divine providence corresponding to the near extinction of European Jewry. The first incarnation of book two was my doctoral dissertation written under the supervision of Professor Arthur Green. His subsequent writings on evolution are featured in the conclusion of the book.

Book three is unlike the previous two books because it is less a survey of philosophies of Halakhah than a long argument in support of my own favored approach to Halakhah. The categories in book three are legal interpretation, adjudication, and legislation. I begin by highlighting the rabbinic *tendenz* and the rabbinic method of midrash. Subsequent chapters show how and why the dynamism of rabbinic Halakhah became neutered by legal codes and bloated with the accretion of laws and stringencies. In the Conclusion, after summarizing a coherent Jewish theology, I will demonstrate its implications for Halakhah. I will offer a critique of the Conservative movement's response to homosexuality, as well as the burdensome observance of the second day of holidays.

Coherent Judaism is a deliberately challenging text. It should not be the first, or second, or even third book one reads about Judaism. Its topics include theology, philosophy, science, and law, each with its own jargon. To complicate matters more, each of the three books covers over 2,000 years. There is also the issue of languages. Some readers will want to know the original terms in Hebrew or Aramaic, which may mean directing others to the glossary at the back of the book. As a Jewish educator, I also want to teach particular words to enrich one's Jewish vocabulary. In addition to the glossary, there are also a timeline and two indices that I hope will make the text more understandable. Judaism is sophisticated, and in this era of Bible-thumping fundamentalists, Judaism deserves a full and nuanced hearing. (In terms of bibles, I have consulted the New

Jewish Publication Society *TANAKH* for my translations. All other translations are my own unless otherwise noted.)

I have undoubtedly missed, misrepresented, and/or mangled a few facts in my desire to create these narratives. I apologize in advance. Particularly in the final chapter of book two, I am cognizant of my deficits. Rabbi Elliot Dorff, whose presence at the Ziegler School of Rabbinic Studies at American Jewish University was my primary motivation to attend, was wont to remind his students not to allow the perfect to be the enemy of the good.[14] I hope that *Coherent Judaism* lives up to that more modest standard.

---

14 Elliot N. Dorff, *For the Love of God and People: A Philosophy of Jewish Law* (Philadelphia: Jewish Publication Society, 2007), 235.

Book One

Book One

A Partisan History of Jewish Theologies

Preface

Rebecca, for whom I was awash with unprecedented emotion, had planned our "WEekend" for that month on Nantucket. Since she had begun medical school, we saw each other less frequently than in the first nine months of our love, so we took turns planning what we called our "WEekends." It was my final year of coursework for a doctorate in Jewish thought, and I was serving as a teaching assistant to Professor Arthur Green for a class on the Zohar, the "bible" of medieval Kabbalah. The ferry brought us in with time to check into the bed and breakfast, change for Shabbat, and walk to a stretch of beach. It was early fall, just after the High Holidays.

The moon rose before the sun set. The two great lights sharing an expanse, foregrounding the passionate hues and cloudy streaks of sunset. The grains of sand, the rhythmic sweeping of the waves, the endless horizon of shimmering sea, the crisp ocean breeze, and the feminine divine at my side. The one who gives love unstintingly and the one who, like no one else before, draws love from me, like a limitless well.

It was a mystical moment for me, a moment in which I felt permeated, surrounded by, and connected to the divine presence. "In the time of Isaac our father [and in my time], the name of the Shechinah was Rebecca."[1] Swirling in my consciousness were those natural elements that I knew were kabbalistic signs for different aspects of divinity. My past experiences with Rebecca were symbolized in the constellation of emanating sun, reflecting moon, fiery palette, infinite ocean, and bracing breeze. I felt our future descendants numerous as sands on the shore of eternity. With the evening wind, *ruach* in Hebrew, on my face, I *experienced ruach's* alternate Hebrew meaning: spirit. Flashing on a textual tradition associated with my rabbinic patron saint Reish Lakish, who said that we are blessed with an extra spirit on Shabbat (Ta'anit 27b), I felt my soul swell. My engagement with Judaism prepared me for that moment (and my subsequent engagement to Rebecca).

On the shores of Nantucket, in the fall of 1996, I experienced what I will call a mystical montage. My past and future converged through a heady combination of textual tradition, sensory perception, and body chemistry. Religion's emphasis on the ethical is both crucial and necessary, but it is not sufficient. *Religion reaches toward transcendence.* Otherwise it is merely functional without being true, a distinction which we will see both medieval philosophers and mystics embrace. Today, unlike in the Middle Ages, there can be no dissembling about religion. (Although, discretion is still advisable.) What we say and do must cohere with what we believe. While belief must incorporate knowledge, it needn't be restricted to what the scientific method can demonstrate. Religion is no less true for being beyond a method to measure.

In this first book of *Coherent Judaism*, I will explore traditional Jewish theologies. I will distinguish between two different belief systems,

---

1   Joseph Ibn Gikatilla, *Gates of Light*, trans. Avi Weinstein (San Francisco: HarperCollins Publishers, 1994), 204.

both found in the Torah, and follow their development through the Middle Ages and into modernity. Both biblical theologies were coherent in their initial setting, but as they combined into a single document (the TaNaKH/Hebrew Bible), and, later, a single rabbinic Judaism, there were ideological incongruities that must have been less important than the social and political value of communal unity. We will see those tensions play out in the disputes of the rabbinic period when the reasons for the commandments become obscured. The fourth chapter of this book shows how those biblical voices reemerged in the writings of medieval mystics and philosophers, but with a rabbinic accent.

The final two chapters in this book track the theological shifts in modernity. Enlightenment, emancipation, and the Shoah have left us in a relatively barren landscape. *Torah from Sinai* has died the death of a thousand qualifications. Furthermore, while humanity may be the most intelligent species, Stephen Jay Gould, in Charles Darwin's name, assures us that there is no "golden barrier" which essentially separates humans from other animals. Not only has the content of our knowledge changed, but thanks to Immanuel Kant our very claim to knowledge must now be qualified. Democratic pluralism has challenged our pride of chosenness. And the Shoah has effectively buried whatever was left of our beliefs in divine providence and omnipotence. The resulting theology may be relatively thin, but thin is infinitely greater than null.

We begin this book with a guided tour through priestly religion, primarily in the books of Genesis through Leviticus. We begin with the priestly Torah not only because it is presented first within the biblical canon, but because it represents a full theology of creation in which how God created the world determines how Israelites should act in that world. In other words, the Israelite priests connect theology (how they understood God) to religion (how we should act given our understanding of God). In the language of secular philosophy, the Israelite priests connected ontology (the branch of metaphysics dealing with the nature of being) to ethics. In Hebrew, I would say that the priests connected their worldview to their *halakhah* (law).

The second belief system we will focus on, that found in Deuteronomy, is *reactive* to the priestly Torah. Deuteronomy is less concerned with theology per se and places more emphasis on affairs of the state and society. While not reducing religion to the political and ethical, Deuteronomy has less overt interest in accessing and experiencing the divine presence than did the priests. Deuteronomy's Torah is less robust in terms of a complete theological system that links ontology, the way the world is, to ethics and politics, how we should be in the world. In other words, the priests linked theology to religion in a systematic way that we do not see in Deuteronomy precisely because the authors of the latter were responding to and tinkering with priestly religion rather than articulating their own system *de novo*.

Whatever ethical or political system we embrace should cohere with how we understand reality. A religion's reality includes divinity. Thus, if there is to be a Judaism that coheres maximally to usable elements of its past, the holiness mandated by the priestly Torah is essential to recover. A life dedicated to the goal of holiness is also the best preparation for the experience of the Holy.

Chapter 1

Priestly Religion

A leading candidate for Judaism's most unsuccessful midrash attempted to quash theological speculation based on the shape of the Torah's first letter: a *bet* (ב), a poor bet. Rabbi Levi, reading from right to left in good Semitic fashion, noted that the *bet* is blocked upwards towards the heavens, downwards towards Sheol (the realm of the dead), and backwards towards the beginning—a one-way letter pointing forward in this world (Genesis Rabbah 1:10). Rabbi Levi believed that the Torah's focus on worldly concerns, so unlike the Israelites' neighboring cultures, behooved his own contemporaries to follow suit. I take solace that his midrash appears between two midrashim which ignore his advice. With all due respect to Rabbi Levi, it is time, again, to violate your teaching.

The priestly world, conjured into existence through divine speech, was one of separations and distinctions. The priestly cosmogony (a story depicting the creation of cosmos) of Genesis 1 provides the etiological myth for the priestly ontology we see unfold later in Torah. In the priestly cosmogony God organizes the chaos into a cosmos. An ancient rabbinic *havdalah* (separation) liturgy, to be performed at the conclusion of the Sabbath and other holy days, is recorded as follows: "[God] separates/distinguishes between the holy and the mundane, between light and darkness, between Israel and the nations, between the seventh day and the six days of creation, between ritually impure and ritually pure, between the ocean and the dry land, between the upper waters and the lower waters, and among the Priests, Levites, and Israelites" (P'sachim 104a).

Mircea Eliade, in his classic work *The Myth of the Eternal Return*, begins with a description of what he calls *archaic ontology*: "Obviously, the metaphysical concepts of the archaic world were not always formulated in theoretical language; but the symbol, the myth, the rite, express, on different planes and through the means proper to them, a complex system of coherent affirmations about the ultimate reality of things, a system that can be regarded as constituting a metaphysics."[1] The priestly ontology or metaphysics was shot through with bright lines distinguishing each according to its kind and marking gradations of holiness at all levels of reality.

When God Began Creating

The first verb, and second word, of Genesis 1 is *bara'*, a verb which we usually translate as *create*, but is better envisioned as cutting off, separating, or dividing.[2] When we translate *bara'* as *create*, we tend to think of *material* creation which links us to the *post*-biblical notion of *creatio ex nihilo* (creation out of nothing), and we lose the initial, ordering impulse of Genesis 1. Genesis 1 is simply not concerned with the creation of matter. God is the author of creation, and authors don't create their own alphabets (nor, usually, their own words).

The second verse describes the earth as initially (eternally?) in a state of *tohu va'vohu*: chaos and confusion, wild and waste, higgledy-piggledy.[3] Whatever the translation, note the rhyme (*higgledy-piggledy*), the alliteration (*chaos and confusion* and *wild and waste*), and, most importantly, the concatenation of open vowels—*tohu va'vohu*—that forces the speaker to mimic God's wind/spirit (*ruach*) sweeping over the face of the waters.

The first thing God speaks into existence is light, which God then separates from the primordial darkness, calling the light *day* and the darkness *night*. Then begins the chorus of creation: *there was evening, there was morning.* . . . The Hebrew word for *evening* (*erev*) is etymologically connected to *jumbled*, as when day and night *even* out because they are jumbled or mixed together. The word for morning, *boker*, is

1   Mircea Eliade, *The Myth of the Eternal Return*, trans. Willard R. Trask (Princeton: Princeton University Press, 2005), 3.
2   See Numbers 16:30, Ezekiel 21:24 and 23:47, and Joshua 17:15. Abraham ibn Ezra makes this point in his twelfth-century commentary.
3   *Chaos and confusion* is the translation of my teacher Arthur Green; *wild and waste* is from Everett Fox's biblical translation; *higgledy-piggledy* is from William Wordsworth. My thanks to Rabbi Michael Bernstein for that last reference.

etymologically connected to *distinguish*.[4] The morning is what separates or distinguishes nighttime from light-time and when we can begin to distinguish the world around us. Thus, the chorus of creation can be understood etymologically as: "it was all mixed up, but it got a bit clearer" in each of the successive days of creation. Without even looking at what God does throughout Genesis 1, the narrator's language (*bara'*, *erev* and *boker*) sets the stage for the emergence of cosmos out of chaos by means of separation and distinction. What Genesis does, literarily and literally, is to cut away, divide, and order the chaos that is already present on the stage of creation as the curtain rises.

Before leaving day one, let us focus on God's pronouncement of *ki tov* in regard to the creation of light (Genesis 1:4). That phrase, too, becomes part of the chorus of creation as God proclaims most every day the creations of that day to be *ki tov* (Genesis 1:10, 12, 18, 21, and 25). *Tov* means *good*, and we understand from this refrain that creation was good in the eyes of God. But the phrase *ki tov* appears nowhere else in the book of Genesis. It is a term of creation. The next instance of the term is in the book of Exodus. There it is not a description of what God sees, it is a description of what Yocheved/Jocheved sees (Exodus 2:2). When she looks at her infant she sees he is *ki tov*. Every translation gets it wrong. Could the Torah possibly be telling us that Yocheved sees that her baby is good, or good-natured, or good-looking? What mother doesn't think that about her creation? *Ki tov* is a literary marker that points the reader back to Genesis 1. The Torah is telling us that Yocheved perceives that this child is *ki tov*, the next phase of the unfolding creation process, the one who will draw out the people of Israel from slavery in Egypt (and the Red Sea) and separate them from the rest of the nations. Yocheved's son is Moshe/Moses.[5] The rabbis of the Talmud understood what contemporary translators don't: Yocheved is not a doting mother—she's a prophetess (Sotah 12a).

---

4   Abraham ibn Ezra and Moses Nachmanides, known as RaMBaN, point this out. See Leviticus 27:33.

5   Moshe is so named because "from the water I drew him" (Exodus 2:10). See Robert Alter, *The Art of Biblical Narrative* (New York: Basic Books, 1981), 57–58.

Mayim, Mayim: *The Waters of Salvation*

On day two, God makes an expanse in the midst of the waters and separates or divides the waters vertically into upper waters and lower waters. When someone describes a heavy rain as "the sky opening up," she is using a linguistic fossil of the image of waters above the sky. Now back to Moshe: "Then Moshe held out his hand over the [Red] sea and . . . the waters were split" (Exodus 14:21–22). God split the waters vertically at creation and then horizontally at the salvation of the Israelites, with some prompting by Moshe and his raised hands. The final image of this literary triptych is Yehoshua/Joshua (whose name might be translated as *savior*) leading the Israelites across the Jordan River whose flow has been miraculously arrested (Joshua 3:13–17). Waters first part at the creation of the cosmos, then at the redemption from Egyptian slavery, and finally at the border of what will become the Land of Israel. Biblical literature is not merely (or always) chronological; it operates at different scales of reality, from the cosmic to the national to the personal, from the primordial waters, to the sea, to the river, and tells the story from creation to the asymptote of redemption.

On day three, God gathered the lower waters into one area to allow dry land to surface. Once there was dry land, God called on the earth to bring forth vegetation. It is precisely the products of the plants and trees that later became available for humans to consume (Genesis 1:29). Indeed, in the priestly worldview, all the animals were originally herbivorous (Genesis 1:30). When Isaiah prophesizes about a future time when the wolf will dwell with the lamb (Isaiah 11:6), he was echoing the idyll of creation. We will see where the day three diet went awry, but it is a central feature of the priestly Torah. Indeed, diet's centrality is emphasized by its very inclusion in the opening chapter of Genesis which deals, almost exclusively, with creation.[6]

Day four is rich, and we shall shall return to the fourth day in the conclusion. But, for now, let us simply emphasize the division and separation that is attendant to the creation of sun and moon as "signs for the appointed times" (Genesis 1:14). Although day and night were named by God on day one, the signs by which *we* measure time awaited day four.

---

6   This curiosity was noted by Edwin Firmage, "Genesis 1 and the Priestly Agenda," *Journal for the Study of the Old Testament* 24, no. 82 (1999): 104.

Later in Leviticus 23, those "appointed times" are enumerated, beginning with the first lunar month of the spring.

From Zebrafish to Adam

On days five and six, God populated the distinct domains of the sea, the air, and the earth. Although we humans did not receive our own discrete day of creation, we are separated from the rest of the animal kingdom by being created in the divine image and receiving dominion over other animals. This dominion, however, does not include the prerogative to consume them.

On the seventh day, God ceases all work of creation. Apparently, blessing and sanctifying are not considered work since God blesses the seventh day and makes it holy (Genesis 2:3). Into the fabric of time, Shabbat is weaved; it is ontologically distinct. The Israelites will later be commanded to imitate God's sabbath in the revelation at Mount Sinai (Exodus 20:8–11). Although God rests on the seventh day, God has no earthly resting place until the Israelites finish building the tabernacle at the beginning of year two of their desert sojourn. Just as the second day saw the creation of a heavenly expanse within an undifferentiated abyss, the second year of the Israelite's Sinai sojourn saw the creation of holy space, the tabernacle, amidst the unending desert dunes. Just as God had "finished the work" of creation (Genesis 2:2), Moshe "finished the work" overseeing construction of the divine dwelling within God's creation (Exodus 40:33). Literarily, the priestly language indicates that the tabernacle serves as the resolution of and climax to creation.[7]

The continued presence of God in our midst, according to the priestly worldview, is contingent upon compliance with the divinely revealed laws. God will only abide in our midst if our holiness is compatible with His own. God's presence assures us of material blessings and protection. When we do err, animal sacrifices afford us the mechanism to expiate our transgressions, at least most of them. Before we look at animal sacrifices, though, let us shift our focus to the laws of animal consumption.

---

7   See also Exodus 39:43 and Jon D. Levenson, *Creation and the Persistence of Evil: The Jewish Drama of Divine Omnipotence* (Princeton: Princeton University Press, 1988), 78–99.

When Noach/Noah and his family disembarked, the dietary restrictions that had reigned in the antediluvian period were jettisoned. Humanity had proven to be violent and bloodthirsty (Genesis 6:11). After the flood, God gave humanity the license to indulge its appetite as it wished, with but one caveat: do not consume flesh with its lifeblood in it (Genesis 9:4). "It is the divine remedy for human sinfulness, which hitherto had polluted the earth and necessitated its purgation by flood. . . . Man must abstain from blood: human blood must not be shed and animal blood must not be ingested":[8]

> Obviously, the Bible felt it even more essential to a stable world than the Decalogue (which legislates only for Israelites). The latter is merely a credo; but for the Bible and for Judaism, a credo that purports to curb the imbruted nature of man is doomed to failure unless rooted and remembered in a regularly observed ritual, one which will intrude into the home, adhere to the family table, and impinge daily on the senses, all the while penetrating the mind and conditioning the reflexes into habitual patterns of behavior.[9]

Jacob Milgrom, one of the pioneers in the study of Leviticus, insists that the laws of *kashrut* (keeping kosher) serve an ethical function.[10] The violent bloodspilling which precipitated the Flood must be stanched, so the Torah mandates the draining of bloodlust even toward the animal kingdom.[11] Moreover, the animals which Israelites are permitted to eat are all herbivorous. Yet, as we move into the Israelites' restrictions on animal consumption, particularly land animals, ethics is just one part of the priestly worldview.

---

8   Jacob Milgrom, *The Anchor Yale Bible Commentary: Leviticus 1–16* (New York: Doubleday, 1991), 705.

9   Idem, *Studies in Cultic Theology and Terminology* (Leiden: E. J. Brill, 1983), 117.

10 Mary Douglas in "The Forbidden Animals in Leviticus," *Journal for the Study of the Old Testament* 18, no. 59 (1993) enhances Milgrom's emphasis on ethics by showing how the dietary laws not only prohibit ingesting animal predators but also protect the most vulnerable creatures which has parallels to the interpersonal laws found in Leviticus 18 and 19.

11 The context of Ezekiel 7:23's use of the word *hamas*, found also as an explanation for the Flood in Genesis 6:11, suggests that the violence of Noah's generation involved bloodshed. See Tikva Frymer-Kensky, *Studies in Bible and Feminist Criticism* (Philadelphia: Jewish Publication Society, 2006), 60–64.

In 1966, Mary Douglas took an anthropological approach to the forbidden animals of Leviticus. She mapped the dietary restrictions of Leviticus 11 onto the creation story. She posited that eligible animals need to be "equipped for the right kind of locomotion in its element."[12] Anomalies, like lobsters which live in the water but have legs, defy the clean-cut categories of creation, and are therefore not appropriate for a diet of holiness which requires "keeping distinct the categories of creation."[13] Although she subsequently recanted a few of her initial suggestions, she captured something essential about the priestly worldview.

In Milgrom's work on the dietary laws, he concurs with Douglas' insight from Emile Durkheim that "animal taxonomy is a mirror of human society."[14] In a 1990 essay, Milgrom presents three Venn diagrams that extend this insight to include sacred space. Within the human circle, moving from smallest to largest, there are priests, Israelites, and humans;[15] within the animal circle, there are animals that are eligible to be offered as sacrifices to God, animals eligible to be eaten by Israelites, and all animals; within the space circle, there is the sanctuary, the Land of Israel, and the earth.

Douglas penetrates even more deeply into the priestly worldview when she suggests that the forbidden suet dividing the anatomy of a sacrificial animal is parallel to the cloud of incense in the tabernacle which itself is parallel to the dense fog surrounding the sacred space on Mount Sinai.[16] "A projectible universe constantly reconstituting itself in objects and places is the essence of its [Leviticus'] microcosmic thinking."[17] The priests imagine that reality itself, according to the creation narrative, is structured hierarchically, with a fractal-like quality, around the axis of holiness. Ontology mirrors cosmogony.

---

12 Mary Douglas, *Purity and Danger* (New York: Routledge Classics, 2002), 69. Douglas subsequently retracted much of what she wrote in that chapter. See her preface to the Routledge Classics edition of *Purity and Danger*, xiii–xvi.

13 Ibid., 67.

14 Milgrom, *Anchor Yale Bible Commentaries*, 720.

15 Ibid., 722. The distinction of the Israelite male is the separation of his foreskin, see Genesis 17:14 and Leviticus 12:3.

16 Mary Douglas, *Leviticus as Literature* (Oxford: Oxford University Press, 1999), 79, 195, and 228.

17 Ibid., 230–31.

The requirements for a kosher land animal are that it chews the cud and has cloven hooves. At least as far back as Aristotle, the ancients understood that chewing the cud allows animals to feed on vegetation that is indigestible by humans.[18] As one scholar has recently observed: "Thus the ruminants have two very important traits in nutrient physiology: they are able to utilize the lowest grade of vegetable food available and they have the highest nitrogen efficiency found in mammals. Therefore, they make the best possible use of the limited resources in semiarid countries."[19] If this explains why the Torah requires eating only ruminants, then it very much accords with an ecological sensibility concerned with the conservation of resources. The prohibition of *bal tashchit*, do not destroy, prohibits cutting down fruit trees even in a time of war (Deuteronomy 20:19–20). *Bal tashchit* finds its positive counterpart in the incentive to raise only ruminants which maximizes the efficient utilization of Israel's limited resources at all times.[20]

The requirement that land animals have split hooves returns us, I suspect, to the priestly worldview. Douglas contended that kosher land animals were equipped for proper locomotion on the ground. But, given that split hooves are the only visible sign of a kosher animal, I offer a different explanation very much in Douglas' spirit. We have emphasized in our description of Genesis 1 that a primary motif, both linguistically and conceptually, is that of separation. The requirement of split hooves is an anatomical instance of the priestly theme of separation. The Hebrew for *split hooves* is not found in Genesis 1, which is why, I suspect, scholars have not made the connection. (Although, the word for cloven-hoofed land animals is *bakar*, orthographically identical to *boker*, morning.) But, in Leviticus 1:17 we do find one of our cloven hoof terms, *shesa*/cleave, coupled with the word for separation/*yavdil* that appears throughout Genesis 1. Thus, we see that *cloven* and *separated* share the same semantic

---

18 Aristotle, *Parts of Animals*, 3:14, in *The Complete Works of Aristotle*, vol. 1, ed. Jonathan Barnes (Princeton: Princeton University Press, 1984), 1051.

19 Aloys Huttermann, *The Ecological Message of the Torah: Knowledge, Concepts, and Laws which Made Survival in a Land of "Milk and Honey" Possible* (Atlanta: Scholars Press, 1999), 72. Huttermann, like Douglas, also sees the taboos on certain animals as protecting them in order that they may fulfill their ecological function, 72–77. For Huttermann, ecology replaces ethics. See Douglas, "Forbidden Animals": 21–23.

20 This theme resurfaces in the rabbinic prohibition on raising sheep in Israel. See Baba Kamma 7:7 and Baba Kamma 80a.

field in the priestly mind. Here is Robert Alter explaining the force of repetition in biblical literature:

> What we find, then, in biblical narrative is an elaborately integrated system of repetitions, some dependent on the actual recurrence of individual phonemes, words, or short phrases, others linked to the actions, *images*, and ideas that are part of the world of the narrative we "reconstruct" as readers but that are not necessarily woven into the verbal texture of the narrative.[21]

What is differentiated or separated is more holy. (The centers of Milgrom's Venn diagrams are holier than the peripheries.) Anatomically, what distinguishes humans from all other animals in the biblical environment is fingers. It is, of course, true that monkeys and apes have fingers and opposable thumbs, although they do not rotate as ours do, but these creatures seem to be unfamiliar to our priestly authors. Monkeys do make a cameo appearance in I Kings 10:22 (with a reprisal in Second Chronicles 9:21), but they are described as exotic animals imported periodically for the king's menagerie. In ancient Mesopotamia, there is not a single artistic image of a nonhuman primate.[22] Even in the rabbinic period, monkeys were so unusual that they warranted a blessing of wonder (Brachot 58b).

In the entire Pentateuch, the only fingers that are explicitly mentioned belong to either God or the priests. Indeed, God's fingers are linked to both creation (Psalm 8:4) and the legislation of the Decalogue (Exodus 31:18). The semiotics, the visual cue, of Aharon/Aaron the High Priest raising his hands while dedicating the tabernacle (Leviticus 9:22), suggests that his fingers may have been spread out, although it is not explicit. Both ancient and modern commentators have speculated that there is a direct connection between Aharon's act and the priestly blessing of Israel described in Numbers 6:24–26.[23] In the rabbinic tradition, the priestly blessing is conducted not only with outstretched arms, but

---

21 Alter, *Art of Biblical Narrative*, 95. My emphasis.
22 Catherine Breniquet, "Animals in Mesopotamian Art," in *A History of the Animal World in the Ancient Near East*, ed. Billie Jean Collins (Leiden: Brill, 2001), 145–68.
23 Sifra, Shmini 30 and Baruch A. Levine, *Anchor Yale Bible Commentaries, Numbers 1–20* (New Haven: Yale University Press, 1993), 243–45. Notice, too, that just as God blesses in Genesis 1, the priests continue that role as intermediaries who imitate God.

with some separation between the fingers (Sotah 39b). The earliest reference to (an ancestor of) Aharon spreading out his fingers is from the third/second century BCE Aramaic Levi Document (3:2). Whether it is simply a natural position for the fingers or a recurrence of the theme of priestly separation we cannot be sure.[24] My contention, nevertheless, is that cloven hooves, the separation of human fingers particularly as they are deployed within the priestly tradition, and references to God's own finger are anatomical homologies of the separation motif of Genesis 1's priestly ontology.

For some, it may have been shocking to first discover that the biblical God was imagined to be embodied. That body, particularly the divine countenance, emanated light. The prophet Habakkuk describes God as radiating a brilliant light from all sides (3:4).[25] The priestly blessing from Numbers refers to the illuminating face of God (6:24–26), but the idea of light radiating from God, as we have in Habakkuk, is a key text because it provides a linguistic link to Moshe whose encounter with God on Mount Sinai (the second time) caused his own face to radiate light (Exodus 34:29–35). Moshe's illumination struck fear into the Israelites, and he was forced to wear a veil in their presence to cloak his luminosity. Psalm 90 describes Moshe as *ish ha-elohim*, a man god or a man of God, and in that psalm, there is another reference to the light of God's face (Psalm 90:8). The rabbis later connected the biblical dots and understood that Moshe gained what the first human, Adam, had lost.

Within the rabbinic tradition, there are several stories depicting Adam as emanating light. One rabbi described Adam's heel as outshining the sun (Leviticus Rabbah 20:2 see also Genesis Rabbah 20:12 and Baba Batra 58a).[26] Alon Goshen Gottstein brings several rabbinic texts that link Adam's luminosity and Moshe's (Deuteronomy Rabbah 11:3 and Midrash Tadshe 4).[27] These links suggest that for some reason humans devolved to the point where they no longer radiated; Moshe's experience

---

24 Gedaliah Alon, "The Cohens' Spreading of the Fingers during the Raising of the Hands," *Tarbitz* 12 (1941): 55–57.

25 Mark S. Smith suggests that the light created on day one is actually a revelation of the divine in his *The Priestly Vision of Genesis I* (Minneapolis: Fortress Press, 2009), 71–79.

26 For a full treatment of this issue, see Alon Goshen-Gottstein, "The Body as Image of God in Rabbinic Literature," *Harvard Theological Review* 87, no. 2 (1994): 178–86.

27 Ibid.: 182–83.

with God restored the lost luster. Indeed, at the likely scene of the crime, in the Garden of Eden after the transgression, God is said to have made for Adam and Eve garments or coats "of skin" (Genesis 3:21). While one reasonable interpretation of these garments is that they are animal skins, that is, leather, to cover human nakedness, perhaps the first couple received an epidermis of their own since they no longer were pure light beings in the divine image. Rabbi Meir seems to say that the epidermis was indeed to clothe their initial garments of light (Genesis Rabbah 20:12). I believe Rabbi Meir's suggestion that the first humans radiated light is literally what the Torah meant.[28]

Recently, Yitzhaq Feder has demonstrated the semantic origins and conflation of *purity* and *radiance*.[29] When Adam and Eve lost their purity through disobedience, they lost their radiance as well. Just as God radiated light, so, too (originally), did humanity, since male and female were created in the divine image.[30] Although human illumination was initially intrinsic, another caste of characters was commanded to apply a divine shine when functioning as divine intermediaries: the priests.

The Priestly Image

Priestly vestments, prescribed in chapter 28 of the book of Exodus, are bedecked in gold, akin to ancient sequins. When moderns read about the gold *ephod*, breastplate, crown, frontlet (*tzitz*), bells, chains, and

28 To be more exact, I think that was the intention of the biblical redactor but not the story's author.

Naftali Herz Wesseley used the term *deep peshat* to characterize seemingly outlandish rabbinic comments that point toward the true explanation of a verse. In my opinion, rabbinic midrashim stating that light filled the room when Moshe was born, which triggered his mother to exclaim *ki tov*, and Rabbi Meir's play on skin (pronounced *or* with an *ayin*) and light (pronounced *or* with an *aleph*) are examples of deep peshat. For more on Wesseley, see my *Torah through Time* (Philadelphia: Jewish Publication Society, 2007), 27–28.

29 Yitzhak Feder, "The Semantics of Purity in the Ancient Near East: Lexical Meaning as a Projection of Embodied Experience," *Journal of Ancient Near Eastern Religions* 14, no. 1 (2014): 87–113. See Exodus 24:10 where the same root for *ritually pure* also means *brilliant*.

30 Rabbi Meir, like the biblical redactor, conflates the two creation stories. My sense is that Genesis 1 and the priestly worldview link God's light to humans created in God's image.

rings we may think of monetary value rather than brilliance. But, as the Psalms describe it, "his crown will sparkle (*yatzitz*)" (Psalm 132:18). Additionally, the High Priest is anointed with oil, which makes his countenance shimmer in the sun (Exodus 29:7). "In short, one cannot fully appreciate the relationship between radiance, purity and holiness without understanding the awe evoked by these lustrous substances in the ancient world. . . . A similar power was attributed to fine oil, particularly due to the fact that its glowing quality could be transferred to the skin through anointment."[31] Indeed, the priestly Torah designates a particular oil compound as sacred and to be used only for consecration (Exodus 30:22–32). The priest's shining aura is a visual allusion to the glow of the first human and mirrors God's own radiance.[32] The priestly image is the shadow of the divine image.

In Hebrew, the same root for *rays* of light is used for *horns, karnayim*. It is not that the Israelites confused the two, but they perceived them as being homologous and there was a natural association between the two.[33] They both, to use an English word, radiated. "The conceptual connection between horns and light was in fact a common feature of the international Near Eastern cuneiform high culture of the early first millennium BCE."[34] In Sumerian, the language of the southern Mesopotamian region, the same word means both *horn* and *shine*. We can now return to earlier on the sixth day to appreciate the mental montage at the moment of animal sacrifice.[35]

God radiated light; Moshe radiated light; at creation, humans radiated light; priests sparkled; and, all the species of land animals eligible for sacrifice on the altar had horns—which in Hebrew is the identical word to *radiating light*.[36] The Bible, Aristotle, and the rabbis all recognized that the

---

31 Feder, "Semantics of Purity": 109.

32 For the priest as a divine representative, see Michael D. Swartz, "The Semiotics of the Priestly Vestments," in *Sacrifice in Religious Experience*, ed. Albert I. Baumgarten (Leiden: Brill, 2002), 76–78.

33 See Alter, *Art of Biblical Narrative*, 95 and John H. Walton, *Ancient Near Eastern Thought and the Old Testament* (Grand Rapids: Baker Academic, 2006), 25.

34 Seth L. Sanders, "Old Light on Moses' Shining Face," *Vetus Testamentum* 52, no. 3 (2002): 403.

35 Douglas, herself, used the image of a montage in her description of Leviticus. Douglas, *Leviticus as Literature*, 53.

36 Many readers may be thinking of Michelangelo's Moses in which Moshe is horned based on Jerome's Latin translation of the Torah. As it happens, we Jews have a

kosher animal species eligible for sacrifice were horned.[37] Furthermore, the sacrificial altar's corners were not called *corners* but *horns*, and they were covered with shiny copper (Exodus 27:2 and 38:2). Milgrom has commented that the horns "are emblems of the gods."[38] Not only did the Israelites worship golden calves (Exodus 32 and I Kings 12:28), but the Bible retains ancient Near Eastern imagery of God as a bull.[39]

Lest I be misunderstood, I am not suggesting that God has horns. I am reconstructing the cognitive environment of the Israelites, particularly at the moment of animal sacrifice when the altar's shining horns are soon to be bloodied with the pulsating life force of a horned animal by a glittering priest. The visual image of the spurting blood and the animal's draining life must have affected the witnesses viscerally. That blood, for many sacrifices, is expiation for the transgressions that we humans, who once radiated light, committed.[40] (Indeed, according to both biblical and rabbinic law, the slaughter of the animal sacrifice could be done by the sinner himself.)[41] As Feder has recently reminded students of the Torah, "One of the major contributions of cognitive linguistics has been to illuminate the relationship between human experience and semantic structure."[42] The resonance among *dam* (blood), *adam* (human), and being created according to God's *d'mut* (*likeness* from Genesis 1:26) stimulates a cognitive conflation that intensifies the concept of substitutionary

tradition of Moshe being horned, as well. See Rimon Kasher, "The Mythological Figure of Moses in Light of Some Unpublished Midrashic Fragments," *Jewish Quarterly Review* 88, nos. 1–2 (1997): 19–42.

37 Psalm 69:32; Aristotle, *Parts of Animals*, 3:14; Gittin 6:9 and Hullin 59b.
38 Milgrom, *Leviticus 1–16*, 234.
39 Genesis 49:24, Numbers 24:8, Isaiah 49:26, and Psalms 132:2. These sources are gleaned from Oded Borowski, "Animals in the Religions of Syria-Palestine," in Collins, *A History of the Animal World*, 405–24.
40 See Stephen A. Geller, "Blood Cult: Toward a Literary Theology of the Priestly Work of the Pentateuch," *Prooftexts* 12, no. 2 (1992): 112–13, and Ithamar Gruenwald, "Sacrifices in Biblical Literature and Ritual Theory," *Review of Rabbinic Judaism* 4, no. 1 (2001): 1–44, esp. 40.
41 Leviticus 1:4-5 and Brachot 31b; cf. Ezekiel 44:11.
42 Feder, "The Semantics of Purity in the Ancient Near East": 89.

sacrifice.[43] But for the grace of God, our transgressions should be expiated by our own blood.[44]

In the instant that it takes the priest to sacrifice the bull or the ox at the altar, the priestly montage flashes before the eyes of the anxious Israelites standing in the Near East heat, redolent of the smells of the carcasses' burning flesh. The Israelites share something fundamental with the innocent animals whose life is ebbing away on the altar—they are both creations of the sixth day. Those sacrificial victims are distinguished from other animals by their cloven hoofs and horns. They received the divine pronouncement of *ki tov*. And we humans were charged with shepherding them, not killing them.

We have separated fingers but no longer radiate light. Later on that sixth day, after humans were created, there was no divine pronouncement of *ki tov*, that we humans were good. As the medieval philosopher Joseph Albo suggested, the animals do what God expects of them; but our goodness is only potential since we can indulge our beastly appetites and reject God's instruction. God, who radiates light, graciously permits vicarious sacrifice to atone for such transgressions.[45] The guiltless animal dies for our sins. At the moment of the animal's death, we are to see *our* lives flash before our eyes. The radiating priest sacrificing the horned/rayed animal is *not* a vision of the God of Justice, the radiating God, making the lightless human sinner lifeless; the vision is of the God of Mercy accepting a vicarious sacrifice and giving repentant sinners one more chance.

The cinematographic technique of a fast-cut montage is a staccato series of flashback images often used to help viewers understand how a character has discovered the truth or why she decides to act in a certain way.[46] The priestly tradition has created a literary version of a fast-cut montage which conflates ritual, literary tradition, cultural memory, and sensory stimulation to conspire to elicit a fresh, determined commitment,

---

43 Although humanity (*adam*) was named in relationship to the earth (*adamah*) in the second creation story (Genesis 2:7), in the Genesis 1 account we received our name because we are like (*domeh*) God. Naphtali Zvi Yehuda Berlin, in his Torah commentary, *Ha'amek Davar*, makes this point. See Genesis 9:6 for the *dam/adam* resonance.

44 RaMBaN on Leviticus 1:9.

45 Joseph Albo, *Book of Principles*, 3:2. See also my *Torah through Time*, 60.

46 My thanks to my friend Jason Rosenbaum for this term.

a *conversion*, to holiness.[47] "Be holy to Me, since I, YHWH, am holy, and I have separated you from the peoples to be Mine" (Leviticus 20:26). The priestly methods are separation and imitation of God; the priestly goal is holy *behavior* in order to enjoy God's presence. The messianic hope is not to continue cutting animals into pieces, but to cut a covenant of peace with the animals (Hosea 2:20). No longer shall fear and dread be the default posture between animals and humans (Genesis 9:2). The priestly Torah has us aspire to a level of holiness whereby we will once again radiate divine light as the result of our holy behavior.[48] The priestly drama, and concession, of animal sacrifice was designed to elicit repentance which has, as a necessary condition, the oral recognition of past wrongdoing (Leviticus 5:5).[49] As the rabbis understood, "We accept sacrifices from sinners of Israel in order that through them they will reorient towards repentance" (Hullin 5a). Creating a new cosmos, for the priests, begins with intention and speech. Repentance recapitulates cosmogony:

> The most fundamental principle of all is that man must create himself. It is this idea that Judaism introduced into the world. . . . Repentance, according to the halakhic view, is an act of creation—self-creation. The severing of one's psychic identity with one's previous "I," and the creation of a new "I," possessor of a new consciousness, a new heart and spirit, different desires, longings, goals—this is the meaning of that repentance compounded of regret over the past and resolve for the future.[50]

---

47 Although I usually translate *teshuvah* as *reorientation*, I am thinking of the etymology of *conversion* when I use the term here. *Vertere*, in Latin, means to turn, precisely the meaning of *shuv* in Hebrew.

48 See my comments in *Torah through Time*, 45.

49 Milgrom has pointed out that one would not bring a sacrifice unless one had already begun the process of repentance by suffering from pangs of conscience. David A. Lambert disputes this, but, to my mind, overinterprets the lack of explicit evidence in the Bible for guilt. Lambert, *How Repentance became Biblical: Judaism, Christianity and the Interpretation of Scripture* (New York: Oxford University Press, 2016), 60. Milgrom condenses decades of research in his 1991 *Anchor Yale Bible Commentaries*, 373–78, and "The Priestly Doctrine of Repentance," *Revue Biblique* 82, no. 2 (1975). Although I rely largely on his scholarly analysis, our religious and psychological insights about sacrifice sometimes differ.

50 Halakhah refers to Jewish law and practice. Joseph B. Soloveitchik, *Halakhic Man*, trans. Lawrence Kaplan (Philadelphia: Jewish Publication Society, 1983), 109–10.

Separation/Division in the Priestly Torah

Etymological	Bara'—cut away, divide	Gen. 1:1, 21, and 27
	Erev/boker—jumble/clarify, distinguish, separate	Gen. 1:5, 8, 13, 19, 23, and 31
Cosmological	Light/darkness	Gen. 1:4
	Day/night	Gen. 1:5
	Upper waters/lower waters	Gen. 1:7
Terrestrial	Waters/land	Gen. 1:9
	Mt. Sinai/tabernacle	Ex. 19:12 and 40:33
Flora	Flora according to its kind	Gen. 1:12
	No hybridization	Lev. 19:19
Temporal	Sun/day and Moon/night for appointed times	Gen. 1:14
	Seventh day	Gen. 2:2–3
Animals	Water, air, and land animals according to their kinds	Gen. 1:21, 24
	No cross breeding	Lev. 19:19
Anatomical	"Pure" land animals with split hooves	Lev. 11:4
	Priests and God with separated fingers	Lev. 4:6, Ex. 31:18
Humans	Gentiles from Israelites through male circumcision	Gen. 17:14 and Lev. 12:3
	Males and females	
Israelites	Priests, Levites, and laymen	Ex. 28:1, Num. 3:6–7
Sexuality	Prohibitions against incest, male-male sex, and bestiality	Lev. 18
	Prohibition against adultery	Lev. 20:10
Marriage	Jews and Gentiles	Ezra 9:2
Clothing	Prohibition against mixing cloths	Lev. 19:19

Priests' goal: holiness for all Israelites
Method: separation and imitation of God
Remedy for transgressions: remorse, verbal confession, animal sacrifice, and repentance
Motive: preserve God's protective presence in the camp

Divine Responsiveness

Until now, we have considered the function of animal sacrifices, central to priestly religion, from the perspective of human psychology. We will now shift perspectives. The covenant between God and the Israelites is mutual, and the priestly understanding of animal sacrifice is that it not only affects our psychology but nonhuman reality itself. "Rituals, and particularly sacrifices, exist in order to avert existential entropy."[51] The priestly ecosystem, unattended, moves toward disorder. According to Jonathan Klawans, "The daily offering not only attracts the divine presence, but the proper performance of the offering also maintains the presence within the community."[52] Klawans is referring to the daily offerings, *not* to the compensatory sin or guilt offerings. Existential entropy rules irrespective of Israelite behavior. The priests do not live on a level playing field.

Each individual is exposed to a constant cascade of evil urges (Genesis 6:5). When we violate the divine order, even inadvertently, we drive away the divine. Our actions have real consequences for both God and the Israelites. "A ritual act [i.e., sacrifice] reconstitutes a reality that has been disturbed, damaged, or gravely unbalanced, even by the tiniest thought."[53] Ritual redress is required because, as Jon D. Levenson has pointed out in his analysis of the *chaoskampf* (struggle against chaos) lurking behind the priestly cosmogony of Genesis 1, "The world is not inherently safe; it is inherently unsafe. Only the magisterial intervention of God and his eternal vigilance prevent the cataclysm."[54]

Milgrom, like other biblical scholars, has shown that there are stark similarities between the Israelite religion and other ancient Near Eastern religions. Among them is the notion that the sanctuary is in

51 Ithamar Gruenwald, *Rituals and Ritual Theory in Ancient Israel* (Leiden: Brill, 2003), 193.
52 Jonathan Klawans, "Pure Violence: Sacrifice and Defilement in Ancient Israel," *Harvard Theological Review* 94, no. 2 (2001): 152.
53 Gruenwald, *Rituals and Ritual Theory*, 171. See also Jonathan Klawans, *Purity, Sacrifice, and the Temple: Symbolism and Supersessionism in the Study of Ancient Judaism* (New York: Oxford University Press, 2009), 71.
54 Levenson, *Creation and the Persistence of Evil*, 17. I have recently treated this theme in the context of the redemptive motivations for rabbinic halakhah: see https://zeramim.org/wp-content/uploads/2020/02/Cherry-Camouflage-Motive.pdf.

need of constant purification lest it be abandoned by its resident god.[55] Throughout the ancient Near East, the abandonment of the deity from his shrine meant a withdrawal of that deity's "protective presence."[56] One purpose of the biblical sacrifices was to attract the potent Presence of God.[57] While sacrifices clearly fulfilled a psychological function for the individual and nation, the metaphysical or ontological result of those sacrifices provided for the national prosperity and security of the Israelites: sacrifices attracted and maintained the potent and protective divine presence within the community.[58]

Yet, according to priestly religion, even sacrifices were unable to protect the Israelites against certain transgressions that ultimately repulsed God's very presence from the land. As Klawans has recently outlined, "moral impurity" leads to exile:[59]

> Moral impurity results from committing certain acts so heinous that they are considered defiling. Such behaviors include sexual sins (e.g., Lev. 18:24–30), idolatry (e.g., Lev. 19:31; 20:1–3), and bloodshed (e.g., Num. 35:33–34). These "abominations" (תועבות) bring about an impurity that morally—but not ritually—defiles the sinner (Lev. 18:24), the land of Israel (Lev. 18:25, Ezek. 36:17), and the sanctuary of God (Lev. 20:3; Ezek. 5:11). This defilement, in turn, leads to the expulsion of the people from the land of Israel (Lev. 18:28; Ezek. 36:19).[60]

Klawans notes elsewhere that the "Divine Presence cannot or will not abide in a land defiled by idolatry, murder, and sexual sin."[61] Israel

---

55 Jacob Milgrom, *Leviticus: A Book of Rituals and Ethics* (Minneapolis: Fortress Press, 2004), 15.
56 Michael Fishbane, *Biblical Myth and Rabbinic Mythmaking* (New York: Oxford University Press, 2005), 78.
57 Baruch A. Levine, "On the Presence of God in Biblical Religion," in *Religions in Antiquity*, ed. Jacob Neusner (Leiden: Brill, 1968), 71–87.
58 Indeed, the efficacy of even human sacrifice by Israelite *enemies* is narrated in 2 Kings 3:26–27.
59 While murder, rape, and incest are obviously moral transgression, idolatry is less obvious. The Torah's conception of idolatry often assumed sexual acts and human sacrifice.
60 Klawans, *Purity, Sacrifice, and the Temple*, 55. See the similar list in Frymer-Kensky, *Studies in Bible*, 341–42.
61 Jonathan Klawans, *Impurity and Sin in Ancient Judaism* (New York: Oxford University Press, 2004), 132–33.

Knohl sharpens the point: "The punishment for the violation of the commandments is described as a necessary consequence of sin, rather than the act of a personal God who punishes those who transgress his will."[62] Because the Israelites violated the categories of holiness (separation) within the realms of family (sexual transgressions), human life (bloodshed), and the covenant (idolatry), God was, necessarily, crowded out of His creation. When the land is morally defiled, it "vomits out" its inhabitants (Leviticus 18:25). Vomiting is not volitional. The Israelites first exile God *and* God's protective presence; then the Land of Israel, with the help of the Babylonians, exiled the Israelites in 586 BCE.

Returning from Exile

After the destruction of the First Temple, several prophets envisioned the rebuilding of the temple as a necessary precondition for the return of Israel's deity to the land and better times.[63] "Thus said the Lord of Hosts: Consider how you have fared. Go up to the hills and get timber, and rebuild the House; then I will look on it with favor and I will be glorified—said the Lord" (Haggai 1:8-9). As Levenson contends, "it is through the cult [of animal sacrifice] that we are enabled to cope with evil, for it is the cult that builds and maintains order, transforms chaos into creation, ennobles humanity, and realizes the kingship of the God who has ordained the cult and commanded that it be guarded and practiced."[64]

God's potent, protective presence is understood by the priestly authors to be a *sine qua non* for the national well-being of the Israelites.[65] Thus, Benjamin Sommer's claim is given a motive: "Indeed, *a central theme of priestly tradition—perhaps, the central theme of priestly*

---

62 Israel Knohl, *The Sanctuary of Silence* (University Park, PA: Eisenbrauns, 2007), 140.

63 Gary A. Anderson, *Sacrifices and Offerings in Ancient Israel: Studies in their Social and Political Importance* (Leiden: Brill, 1987), 91-99. See also Klawans, *Purity, Sacrifice, and the Temple*, 69.

64 Levenson, *Creation and the Persistence of Evil*, 127. Levenson emphasizes this notion of entropy and cites Brevard Childs: "The present world order established by a victory in the past does not continue automatically. It must be constantly reactivated in the drama of the cult." (Childs, *Myth and Reality in the Old Testament*, 20. Cited in *Creation and the Persistence*, 103).

65 Jon D. Levenson, "The Jerusalem Temple," in *Jewish Spirituality*, vol. 1, ed. Arthur Green (Chestnut Ridge: Crossroad, 1986), 46-51.

tradition—is the desire of the transcendent God to become immanent on the earth this God had created."[66] For the Torah as a whole, national security was the single greatest extrinsic motivation to perform commandments.[67] The trajectory of the Hebrew Bible concerns getting the Israelites into, keeping them inside, and getting them back to the Land of Israel. The final line of the entire Hebrew Bible envisions returning to the Land and rebuilding the temple (II Chronicles 36:23) National security required God's immanence, and immanence required holy behavior as well as daily and compensatory sacrifices.

The Priestly Legacy

As we exit the stage of priestly religion, predicated on human hierarchies, priestly intermediaries, and animal sacrifice, I am surprised by how much I find deeply attractive about it. As we rummage for elements of a usable past, the priestly theology's assumption that God's Presence is sensitive and responsive to human deeds is compelling. Unlike Aristotle's God who is the unmoved mover, the priestly God is the most moved mover.[68]

I am, also, particularly impressed by the priestly notion that it was moral turpitude rather than ritual impurity that was responsible for attracting or repulsing the divine presence. As Milgrom has pointed out, the ethical demands of Leviticus 19, including not standing idly by the blood of your neighbor, not hating your kinsfolk in your heart, not taking vengeance, and not even holding a grudge, represent a significant raising of the bar to lead a holy life. And then there's Jesus' and Rabbi Akiva's favorite *mitzvah* (commandment): love your fellow as yourself (Leviticus 19:18). (That commandment, by the way, implicitly includes

---

66 Benjamin D. Sommer, *Bodies of God and the World of Ancient Israel* (New York: Cambridge University Press, 2003), 74. His emphasis.

67 There are certainly other motivations, as well. See Elliot N. Dorff and Arthur Rosset, *A Living Tree: The Roots and Growth of Jewish Law* (Albany: State University of New York Press, 1988), 93–109.

68 The expression, associated with Abraham Joshua Heschel, was coined by Fritz Rothschild. See Edward K. Kaplan, *Spiritual Radical: Abraham Joshua Heschel in America, 1940–1972* (New Haven: Yale University Press, 2009), 414–15.

loving yourself.) If this *mitzvah* remains unfulfilled, the fullness of God's presence remains unrealized.[69] Although animal sacrifice is irredeemable, I must admit that the drama of the sacrificial ritual may be a more effective catalyst for repentance than a daylong fast. More importantly, though, the presupposition that we are capable of repentance combined with providing a mechanism to repent is an incentive to righteousness and preempts any excuse that righteous behavior is unobtainable. As Milgrom has pointed out, "For the first time in history, perhaps, man is assured that his repentance is both desired and required by God."[70] We are not inveterate sinners. We can change our ways. As the curtain drops, on both the Pentateuch and the whole Hebrew Bible (II Chronicles 36:23), the Israelites stand at the threshold of the Promised Land. How long will be our tenure on the land that the Lord our God has bequeathed to us? Our acts will determine our unscripted future, and repentance can redeem our past.

On the literary level, as Douglas has observed, ethics are framed by ritual. Specifically, the ethical aspirations of Leviticus (centered in chapter 19) are preceded by the laws of kashrut (Leviticus 11) and followed by the calendar of sacred times (Leviticus 23). More importantly, sexual safeguards buttress ethical holiness on both sides (Leviticus 18 and 20). The frame supports and highlights the art within.[71] The priestly frame for an ethical life is supported by laws concerned with daily nourishment, which themselves have an ethical component, and the cycle of holy times that punctuate the year. It is not that I believe that *this* particular framework is the best; but having a ritual framework to support a life that strives for holiness is essential. The first month celebrates liberation from slavery (Passover), and the seventh month the trek through the wilderness (*Sukkot*). Logically, the twelfth month should commemorate salvation with the entrance to the Promised Land. But there is no such biblical holiday. Nor does Moshe reach the Land of Israel. Through omission, the Torah focuses our attention on the never-ending journey through the wilderness rather than the destination in the Promised Land.

---

69 Leviticus 19 has been recognized by both the rabbis and modern scholars as based on the Decalogue. Leviticus Rabbah 24:5 and Moshe Weinfeld, *The Decalogue and the Recitation of the "Shema"* (Tel Aviv: Hakibbutz Hameuchad, 2001) [Hebrew], 18–21.

70 Milgrom, *Anchor Yale Bible Commentaries*, 378.

71 Douglas, *Leviticus as Literature*, 229.

There is one further literary aspect that I find intriguingly appealing. The priests perceived that the world as a whole is animated at multiple levels by the same structure.[72] Scholars use terms like microcosms, homologies, fugues, and typologies to try to capture this aspect of priestly religion that unifies their cosmos. The word I prefer is *fractal*.[73] Coined by a Jewish refugee from Poland who spent World War II hiding in Nazi-occupied France, Benoit Mandelbrot invented a word with brokenness at its root. One of the most illustrious mathematicians of the past fifty years, Mandelbrot discovered order in seeming chaos by recognizing that similar structural patterns repeat themselves at different scales of reality.

As one who advocates a robust dialogue between science and religion, I am fascinated by fractals, what they represent in nature, and how priestly religion, in its own way, offers a similar understanding of reality through its literature. Consider this story from the fourteenth-century French sage, Moses of Narbonne:

> Be it known that there is testimony concerning Mount Sinai that drawn upon its stones is the image of the Burning Bush (*sneh*). Hence, this mountain is called Sinai, after the bush, from within which the Lord revealed Himself to Moses. One of the worthies of Barcelona, a son of Ben Hasdai, brought back one of these stones and showed it to me, and I saw a very definite representation of a bush on it. It is a Divine representation. When I broke the stone in half, the image of the bush appeared on each half. I then broke each of the parts, in turn, in half, and the image of the bush appeared all the way through. And so on, a number of times, until the fragments were the size of peanuts; and yet the bush still appeared on them. And I marveled at this.[74]

Lest we miss the literary fractal, the *sneh* (bush) is a mini Mount Sinai, both of which point to God's presence. I, too, marvel at this.

---

72 Chapter 11 of *Leviticus as Literature* is entitled, "Inside the House/Book of God." Douglas shows that the structure of the book of Leviticus maps on to the structure of the Tabernacle. Thus, as Jews read the Torah annually, the text becomes akin to a pilgrimage site.

73 David W. Nelson writes about God as a fractal. Nelson, *Judaism, Physics, and God: Searching for Sacred Metaphors in a Post-Einstein World* (Woodstock: Jewish Lights Publishing, 2006), 111–15.

74 Cited in *Present at Sinai: The Giving of the Law, Commentaries Selected by S. Y. Agnon* (Philadelphia: Jewish Publication Society, 1993), 158.

Chapter 2

Mosaic Religion

Moshe/Moses was a prophet without precedent (Deuteronomy 34:10), a shepherd, a military leader, a law giver, and a judge; what he wasn't was a priest. Although priestly concerns are present in Deuteronomy, the foundational text of what I am calling the Mosaic Torah, they are overshadowed by other themes of the text. The *torah*—the *teaching* and the *text*—of Deuteronomy, is a mosaic reflecting the varying interests of the entire people, from wood chopper to water carrier (Deuteronomy 29:10), more than those of the priesthood.[1] Even when the Mosaic Torah references the priests, it usually labels them *Levitical priests*, thus blurring the bright lines between Levites, which Moshe *was*, and Cohens (priests), descendants of Moshe's brother, Aharon/Aaron. With the exception of the last few verses describing Moshe's death, the entire book of Deuteronomy is ascribed to Moshe speaking to the Israelites during the last days of his life on the east side of the Jordan River. The book of Joshua, which immediately follows Deuteronomy and continues its narrative, refers to Deuteronomy as *Torat Moshe*, Moshe's Torah. Thus, the name *Mosaic Torah* points to both Moshe's reputed identification with Deuteronomy and the text's varied, extra-priestly interests which this chapter will explore.

Given Deuteronomy's position as the fifth and final book of the Pentateuch, it is not surprising that there is no full-bodied account of creation. Its references to creation are associated neither with the seven days of Genesis One nor the Garden of Eden from Genesis Two, but with

---

1   William M. Schniedewind, *How the Bible Became a Book* (New York: Cambridge University Press, 2005), 113.

the literary genre known as wisdom literature. As Moshe Weinfeld has pointed out, one of the characteristics of Deuteronomy is the conflation of two previously discrete traditions: law and wisdom.[2] Much like the Greek conception of natural law, the Mosaic Torah bridges God's revelation of laws in Jewish history with God's revelation of wisdom in creation. "Observe them [laws and rules] faithfully, for that will be proof of your wisdom and discernment to other peoples, who on hearing of all these laws will say, 'Surely, that great nation is a wise and discerning people'" (Deuteronomy 4:6). The laws are in harmony with creation. This is what a coherent Judaism should be.

At the beginning of Deuteronomy, Moshe recaps the Israelites' experiences since arriving at Mt. Sinai. (In the Mosaic Torah, the name of the mountain of revelation is Horev.) Moshe relates that he requested wise men from each tribe to serve as judges for disputes among the people. Later, when describing the judicial process for homicides, assaults, and civil laws, the Mosaic Torah has the individuals appear before those judges and/or the Levitical priests (Deuteronomy 17:9). Priestly religion nowhere assigned a judicial role for priests who were primarily involved with the sacrificial altar and issues of ritual purity. In reassigning the priests, the Mosaic Torah shifts their function within the Israelite community and the readers' understanding of their role. "They shall teach Your laws to Jacob and Your teachings to Israel. They shall offer You incense to savor and whole offerings on Your altar" (Deuteronomy 33:11). Notice the sequence: first they teach, then they service the altar. What in the priestly Torah was marginal (Leviticus 10:11), has become their primary function. The Levitical priests become teachers of the Mosaic Torah.[3]

The responsibility for education, however, is too important to leave to only one group of people. After all, it is through education that the Israelites will be knowledgeable about God's laws. The assumption is that if the Israelites know and understand the terms of the covenant, and the consequences of fidelity and infidelity, there will be no better motivation to meticulously keep to those terms. Teaching, thus, becomes a

---

2   Moshe Weinfeld, *Deuteronomy and the Deuteronomic School* (University Park, PA: Eisenbrauns, 1972), 255–56.

3   Bernard Levinson, *Deuteronomy and the Hermeneutics of Legal Innovation* (New York: Oxford University Press, 2002), 98–143. My thanks to Russell Fuller for this reference.

central activity in the Mosaic Torah. Although the designation of Moshe as *Moshe Rabbeynu*, Moshe our teacher, awaits the rabbinic period, he teaches his way through Deuteronomy.[4] Yet, the primary teaching relationship, according to the Mosaic Torah, is between parents and children (Deuteronomy 6:7). Indeed, in a revealing piece of etymology, *torah* (which literally means *teaching*), *teacher* (*morah*), and *parent* (*horah*) all derive from the same Hebrew root letters (*yod, resh, hey*). Abraham Joshua Heschel once chided American Jewry by saying that the Torah commands parents to teach their children "diligently, not vicariously."[5]

Before Moshe died, he instructed the priests and the elders to read the book of Deuteronomy every seven years. Moshe chose Sukkot, the most joyous of the pilgrimage festivals, as the occasion to read in front of the men, women, and children. (I point out this gender parity because in the priestly Torah, the Decalogue is addressed only to men [Exodus 19:15]). The expectation of this dramatic reading was "that they may hear and so learn to revere the Lord your God and to observe faithfully every word of this Teaching" (Deuteronomy 31:10–13). The gravity of the laws was such that even the King had to have his own copy of Deuteronomy, and read it daily, "so that he may learn to revere the Lord his God, to observe faithfully every word of this Teaching as well as these laws. Thus he will not act haughtily toward his fellows or deviate from the Instruction to the right or to the left, to the end that he and his descendants may reign long in the midst of Israel" (Deuteronomy 17:19–20).

> Israelite society was not connected to YHWH in a hierarchical way, with laypeople answering to priests who alone had access to cosmic texts held within a Temple [or tabernacle]. Sidelining this older dynamic, the written divine voice was available widely to all through the *torah*.[6]

In addition to this emphasis on teaching and learning Torah, there is palpable anxiety that the teaching will stray from the script. Several times

---

4   Timo Veijola, "Deuteronomistic Roots of Judaism," in *Sefer Moshe: The Moshe Weinfeld Jubilee Volume*, ed. Chaim Cohen, Avi M. Hurvitz, and Shalom M. Paul (University Park, PA: Eisenbrauns, 2004), 472.

5   Abraham Joshua Heschel, *The Insecurity of Freedom: Essays on Human Existence* (New York: Farrar, Straus and Giroux, 1966), 54.

6   Marc Leuchter, *The Levites and the Boundaries of Israelite Identity* (New York: Oxford University Press, 2017), 173.

the Mosaic Torah warns us not to add to or subtract from the commandments (Deuteronomy 4:2) nor to deviate to the right or the left. Stephen
Geller has called this a "nonalteration formula." "In effect, Deuteronomy
4 here offers the essential definition of canon: text that is absolutely not
to be altered."[7] The text is fixed and intelligible (Deuteronomy 30:11), and
the stakes could not be higher.

Not all biblical laws offer an explicit incentive. However, in the
Mosaic Torah we find a disproportionate percentage of motivational
clauses which promise well-being and longevity. Of biblical laws which
might be considered ethical or humanitarian, more than half are incen-
tivized by a motive clause.[8] For ritual laws, the proportion is roughly
half of that.[9] There are about a dozen, discrete instances in the book of
Deuteronomy of national security motive clauses attached to ethical
or humanitarian laws. For example, "You must have completely honest
weights and completely honest measures, if you are to endure long on the
soil that Lord your God is giving you" (Deuteronomy 25:15). More often,
the sermonizing of the Mosaic Torah incorporates all of the mitzvot and
ties them to national security:

> I call heaven and earth to witness against you this day: I have put before you
> life and death, blessing and curse. Choose life—if you and your offspring
> would live—by loving the Lord your God, heeding His commands, and
> holding fast to Him. For thereby you shall have life and shall long endure
> upon the land that the Lord swore to your ancestors, Abraham, Isaac, and
> Jacob, to give to them. (Deuteronomy 30:19–20)

Although the motivation for compliance is the same for both priestly
religion and the Mosaic Torah—living long on the Land that the Lord has
given to them—there are two important differences. The first is that the
Mosaic Torah articulates a broader and deeper array of social *mitzvot*
(commandments). The priestly Torah focuses attention on issues of ritual purity and animal sacrifice though without marginalizing the ethical heart of the Holiness Code in Leviticus 19. We will return to how

---

7   Stephen A. Geller, *Sacred Enigmas: Literary Religion in the Hebrew Bible* (New York:
     Routledge, 1996), 45.
8   Rifat Sonsino, *Motive Clauses in Hebrew Law* (Williston: Society of Biblical Literature,
     1980), 223. My thanks to David Bernat for bringing this source to my attention.
9   Ibid., 99.

the Mosaic Torah treats those priestly concerns shortly. But, the second major difference concerns reward and punishment. For priestly religion, national prosperity is a natural consequence of holy behavior, and exile is a natural consequence of our transgressions which drive away God's protective presence. For the Mosaic Torah, national prosperity is a divine reward for compliance to the covenant's terms, and exile is a divine punishment for violating those terms. For both the priestly Torah and the Mosaic Torah, obedience to the laws affect reality. For the priestly Torah, our actions directly, immediately affect reality through our behavior's effect *on* God; while for the Mosaic Torah, our behavior indirectly affects our reality through the rewards and punishments *from* God.

Due to its presence in Jewish liturgy, many Jews are familiar with the passage in Deuteronomy that proclaims the reward for covenantal obedience is rain which in turn provides for food. Disobedience, on the other hand, causes drought (Deuteronomy 11:13–17). Drought weakens the Israelites by depleting their stores of food and makes them vulnerable to internal wrangling and foreign domination. After continued transgressions, and many warnings, the divine wrath will be unleashed. "The Lord was incensed at Israel and He banished them from His presence. . . . So the Israelites were deported from their land to Assyria" (2 Kings 17:18 and 23).

The effects of drought take time to manifest. Prophets are dispatched. The nation will be punished for transgressions, but there is a known mechanism to avert the ultimate punishment. Drought is the call to repentance, or what will later be called *teshuvah. Teshuvah,* in its most narrow sense, means *turning.* Although it is often translated as *repentance,* I prefer the term *reorientation. Repentance* lays emphasis on remorse and regret—emotions. *Reorientation* is a more dynamic term— it necessitates movement. *Teshuvah* is reorienting oneself from pursuing one's own immediate, narrow self-interests to dedicating oneself to God's will. Although the noun *teshuvah* is not found in the Hebrew Bible, the verbal form appears repeatedly.[10] In Deuteronomy 30, Moshe encourages the Israelites to return to God even after being chastised with punishments. Only then will God turn and bless His covenantal partners in

---

10 The verb appears, as in Deuteronomy, throughout the book of Jeremiah, especially chapters three and four. The nominalized form, *teshuvah,* appears only later, e.g., in Mishnah Yoma 8:9.

love (Deuteronomy 30:3). The need for a sacrifice to effect teshuvah goes unstated. For the Mosaic Torah, teshuvah is psychological and behavioral; no priests are mentioned.[11]

The priestly worldview understood blood to be an intrinsically powerful substance, the liquid of life, and a required element to remedy the effects of life-negating transgressions. Not so the Mosaic Torah. For nonsacrificial purposes, blood may be poured on the ground like water and left exposed (Deuteronomy 12:16 and 24). In Leviticus, the blood must be covered with dust (Leviticus 17:13). As Weinfeld points out, "Sanctity is not a taboo that inheres in things which by nature belong to the divine realm but is rather a consequence of the religious intentions of the person who consecrates it."[12] Not blood, but tears effect teshuvah. When Weinfeld speaks of sanctity and taboo, he is translating biblical terms that have no precise English equivalent in part because they belong to an archaic ontology. The priestly Torah *reifies* certain types of purity and defilement. It turns them into things (*res* in Latin.) The word *miasma* might describe the dynamics of defilement. Death and bodily fluids ooze their contagion through contact or even by proximity with the source of the contagion. Practically speaking, being ritually impure precludes one from approaching the sanctuary until a certain period of time has elapsed and a purifying ritual, usually immersion in water, has been performed.

Holiness is also contagious in the priestly Torah. It is not only that certain people (priests) may enter certain precincts, or that improper contact with the realm of the sacred can be lethal (Leviticus 15:31), holiness spreads like a vapor or gas (Exodus 30:26–30).[13] (Interestingly, the word *gas* was coined by a seventeenth-century Flemish chemist, J. B. van Helmont, to echo the uncontainable and unpredictable qualities of *chaos*.) Shamma Friedman thus uses the expression "elemental cosmic humor" to describe the dynamics of both defilement and holiness.[14] Another scholar has helped clarify the shift in meaning between the

---

11 In the scenario described by Deuteronomy 30, sacrifice is precluded because the Israelites have been exiled from the Land of Israel and have no access to the Temple.

12 Weinfeld, *Deuteronomy*, 215.

13 Milgrom, *Anchor Yale Bible Commentaries*, 443–56.

14 Shamma Friedman, "The Holy Scriptures Defile the Hands: The Transformation of a Biblical Concept in Rabbinic Theology," in *Minhah le-Nahum: Biblical and Other Studies Presented to Nahum M. Sarna in Honour of his 70th Birthday*, ed. Marc Brettler and Michael Fishbane (Sheffield: JSOT, 1993), 127.

priestly and Mosaic Torahs concerning the issue of ritual purity. As we will see in the next chapter, the shift between our two *torahs* will have far-reaching halakhic consequences.

> The priestly system of holiness is a cosmic system. It presupposes a certain divine cosmic order. The covenant between God and the People of Israel is inherent in this cosmic system, and the People of Israel have a central place in the spectrum or pyramid of holiness. However, this system is not static and uninterrupted. Under certain circumstances it might be threatened, such as by pollution and sin. Indeed, one means of protection in this dynamic system of holiness is ritual. In contrast, according to the Deuteronomistic concept of holiness, the cosmos and nature are irrelevant. The holiness of Israel derives from God's will. It is a legal status with no implications on other aspects of the world order, and it is not affected by ontological or cosmic situations. . . . If ritual is practiced, it is only because God has ordered so![15]

Sacrifices happen in the Mosaic Torah, but they are inconsequential to God. "God has no need of the sacrifice itself; it is only an expression of gratitude to the Deity, and this constitutes its entire significance."[16] For the priestly Torah, sacrifices offer a pleasing aroma that draws God in. God may still be responsive to our pleas in the Mosaic Torah (Deuteronomy 26:15), but our actions do not "naturally" attract or repel Him as they do in priestly theology. Just as holiness is inherently dynamic for the priests, so, too, is God. God is affected, moved by the actions of the Israelites. In the Mosaic Torah, holiness is imputed or designated by God; divine actions are, correspondingly, determined by God and God alone. God promises to respond according to specific behaviors, but that reflects the carrot and stick of covenantal faithfulness. It is not a natural consequence. For the Mosaic Torah, being holy is an ascribed status irrespective of our behavior; for the priestly Torah, being holy is a goal contingent upon our behavior. The Mosaic Torah has offered a moral covenant; the priestly Torah has created a moral universe.

Consider the rationales for the observance of Shabbat. Initially, in the priestly Torah, we are to observe Shabbat because God finished the

---

15 Eyal Regev, "Priestly Dynamic Holiness and Deuteronomic Static Holiness," *Vetus Testamentum* 51, no. 2 (2001): 258.

16 Weinfeld, *Deuteronomy*, 212.

work of creation on the seventh day, and its sanctity is built into the structure of the cosmos (Exodus 20:11). Thus, Shabbat violations are worthy of death because they disrupt the cosmic order (Exodus 31:14). When the Decalogue is repeated in Deuteronomy, the rationale for observing Shabbat is to remember that God liberated us from slavery in Egypt. Thus, in imitation of God, work is prohibited by the entire household: parents, children, strangers, and even beasts of burden. Israelites are also prohibited from working "so that your male and female slave may rest *as you do*" (Deuteronomy 5:15). The equal treatment of slaves and masters, in any respect, is radical.[17] In Deuteronomy, the rationale for observing Shabbat is ethical, not ontological.

Deuteronomy, more than any other book in the Pentateuch, emphasizes love. Not only are we commanded to love God, we are also repeatedly commanded to love the stranger, the resident alien in our midst, because we experienced his vulnerability and subjugation when we were slaves in Egypt (Deuteronomy 10:19).[18] Perhaps this law was written when Judea was flooded by emigrants from the northern Kingdom of Israel after its destruction by Assyria in 721 BCE. If so, the strangers in question would be estranged cousins, once part of the united Kingdom of David and Solomon. Alternatively, just as there was one God and one sacrificial center, there was one law, one attitude, toward strangers and natives alike. The priestly Torah makes this explicit, and it seems as though the Mosaic Torah only enhances the strangers' position in society (Leviticus 24:22 and Numbers 15:16). Richard Elliot Friedman has recently pointed out exactly how exceptional, indeed revolutionary, such a posture was: "In the whole ancient Near East, in all those lands, through several millennia, we have found fifty-two references to equal treatment of aliens, and all fifty-two are in the first five books of the Bible. . . . The experience of

---

17 The rabbis continue this revolutionary approach towards slavery. See my *Torah through Time*, 101–31.

18 Leviticus 19:34 also has the stranger as the object of our love. The prepositions, however, are different between Leviticus 19:34 and Deuteronomy 6:5. Leviticus may have us treat the neighbor and stranger lovingly while Deuteronomy enjoins us to love God and the stranger. (See RaSHBaM on Leviticus 19:18.) Even if the prepositions lack significance, treating the stranger as you would God (as in Deuteronomy) trumps treating the stranger as you would your neighbor (as in Leviticus).

being aliens, of being oppressed, apparently led Israel's clergy and teachers, the Levite priests, to say, 'You must never do that.'"[19]

Scholars have emphasized that there is a theme of unity in the Mosaic
Torah that demands the Israelites' exclusive worship of the one God with
the totality of their being: "You shall love the Lord, your God, with all
your heart, with all your soul, and with all your might" (Deuteronomy
6:5). The love for God is to be all consuming. The conventional translation, cited above, does not convey the full force of the Hebrew. In
classical Hebrew, *heart* is the seat not only of emotions, but also of the
intellect. The biblical soul is not a discrete component of humans distinct
from the material body. That's a Greek notion, Platonic dualism, which
enters Judaism later. When the Torah uses *soul* (*nefesh*) it means one's
entire being, and can have a very physical sense (e.g., Genesis 14:21).
The Hebrew word translated above as *might* is opaque. Both Onkelos, the
earliest translator of the Torah into Aramaic (first/second century), and
the earliest rabbinic writings (third century) believed that it should be
understood as material wealth. If so, that means you should start loving
God with everything "inside" of you, emotional and intellectual; then
love God with your entire physical being and strength; and, finally, you
should love God with all your external resources. Love exudes by radiating outward.

In the priestly Torah, sacrificial altars might be anywhere in the land.
The Mosaic Torah, through a daring legal innovation, requires all offerings to be brought to a single altar at a place which is later identified
as Jerusalem. The priestly Torah insisted that *all* animals be slaughtered
at an altar, even those strictly for human consumption and nonsacrificial purposes (Leviticus 17). But once the Mosaic Torah eliminated local
altars, it was necessary to allow profane slaughter for dietary consumption everywhere in the Land of Israel (Deuteronomy 12:20–25).[20] The
Mosaic Torah explicitly makes this accommodation in part because of
the distance from Israelite population centers to the Jerusalem Temple.
The laws of the Mosaic Torah reflect a sense of practicality and a humanitarian concern.

---

19 Richard Elliot Friedman, *The Exodus* (New York: HarperOne, 2017), 203.
20 Levinson, *Deuteronomy*, 31–34.

Among the sacrifices that were no longer to be offered outside of Jerusalem were the sin and guilt offerings. Thus, the Mosaic Torah's shift in emphasis from sacrifice to teshuvah implicitly acknowledges that the trek to the capitol may have been an obstacle for potential penitents. As we will see below, concern for the ease of teshuvah will animate subsequent rabbinic legal innovation, as well. The rabbinic effort to provide functional equivalents to animal sacrifice in the post-Temple era was anticipated by Deuteronomy's promotion of teshuvah following the centralization of priestly activity in Jerusalem.

The final aspect to this theme of oneness is that of one people, the holy people. The Israelites are God's treasured possession, chosen from among all peoples to be holy to God (Deuteronomy 7:6). In the Mosaic Torah, the Israelites are a holy people not in their essence, but by divine fiat. They are not holy, they are holy *to God*. There is nothing ontologically distinctive about them. The priestly Torah, however, is predicated on an archaic ontology that perceives differences among the essences of humans. The priests are ontologically separate from regular Israelites who, themselves, are ontologically separate from gentiles.

In comparison to priestly religion, some scholars have described the Mosaic Torah as rational. Such a characterization reflects the Mosaic Torah's relative neglect of priestly concerns such as sacrifice and ritual purity. The archaic ontology has, for the most part, been left behind through benign neglect and conscious reinterpretation. What strikes so many moderns as irrational, namely animal sacrifices and the contagion of elemental cosmic humors of purity and impurity, are either bracketed or reinterpreted within the Mosaic Torah. Thus, the Mosaic Torah is understood to be relatively less irrational.

Leaving rationality aside, many of the themes of Deuteronomy have become fundamentals of subsequent Jewish identity, certainly in modern American Jewish culture. The shift in the primary leadership criterion from priestly pedigree to wisdom leveled the field for future leaders. Theoretically, anyone could study enough to become a wise judge and leader of Israel. It is not so much democratization as aristocratization.[21] All Israel is holy, not just the priests. Even the king is cautioned against

---

21 Reuven Kimelman, "Leadership and Community in Judaism," *Tikkun* 2, no. 5 (1987): 31. Kimelman there is speaking about the rabbinic program, the seeds of which are in the Mosaic Torah.

being haughty toward his subjects. Thus, the Mosaic Torah offers a counterbalance to the priestly Torah's archaic anthropology.

For much of Jewish history, the Mosaic Torah's emphasis on love and social justice has been instrumental in preserving a dispersed people with neither a common land nor common language. Cancelling debts every seven years, providing interest free loans, liberating an indentured servant after six years with resources to restart life, and not returning escaped slaves are all features of Deuteronomy designed to prevent anyone from sinking into a state of permanent poverty. "Justice, justice you shall pursue" (Deuteronomy 16:20). This rallying cry continued to be trumpeted in the prophetic literature. Distributive justice was a *sine qua non* for a society to reflect God's blessings. "There shall be no needy among you—since the Lord your God will bless you in the land that the Lord your God is giving you as a hereditary portion—if only you heed the Lord your God and take care to keep all this Instruction that I enjoin upon you this day. For the Lord your God will bless you" (Deuteronomy 15:4-6). Yet, the next paragraph demands generosity to those in need since poverty will never be fully eradicated. Edward Greenstein describes this as a "modest utopia in which all people will bless each other for being kind."[22] Scholars have noted how radically innovative such a vision was in its day: "What the Torah proposes is the Western tradition's first prescription for an economic order that seeks to minimize the distinctions of class based on wealth, and instead to ensure the economic benefit of the common citizen. . . . [The *maaser ani* is] the first known program of taxation legislated for a social purpose (Deut. 14:28-29)."[23] Such programs have informed Jewish sensibilities for millennia, and these laws are frequently invoked by contemporary Jewish activists in their pursuit of social and economic justice.

Perhaps the most important inheritance from the Mosaic Torah is the concept of *teshuvah*: "the essence of the religious and ethical ideal in Judaism."[24] As we saw in the previous chapter, the idea of reorientation

---

22 Edward Greenstein, "Bible: Biblical Law," in *Back to the Sources: Reading the Classic Jewish Texts*, ed. Barry W. Holtz (New York: Touchstone, 1984), 100.

23 Joshua Berman, Ani Maamin: *Biblical Criticism, Historical Truth, and the Thirteen Principles of Faith* (New Milford: Magid, 2020), 176-77.

24 Ehud Luz, "Repentance," in *Contemporary Jewish Religious Thought*, ed. Arthur A. Cohen and Paul Mendes-Flohr (New York: Free Press, 1987), 785.

is one of the purposes of animal sacrifice. But Deuteronomy describes it, and in doing so prefigures a concept that not only survives the destruction of the Temple, but becomes Judaism's greatest gift. The concept of *teshuvah* undergoes change within the Hebrew Bible and beyond, but the possibility, the invitation, and the benefits of reorientation are constants. The rabbis even claimed that teshuvah was created before the world in recognition that the world could not endure without it (Genesis Rabbah 1:4). Thus, much of the Mosaic Torah anticipated the needs of future Jewish communities to this very day: education, meritocracy, social justice, and reorientation without animal sacrifice.

The Mosaic Method

In addition to the bequest of content from the Mosaic Torah, there is also the inheritance of the method of recontextualizing the priestly Torah. This process of recontextualizing Torah is called *midrash* and is pioneered in the Mosaic Torah. Given Deuteronomy's anxiety of alteration, the midrashic method of the Mosaic Torah is a particularly ironic legacy. The rabbis, who were very close readers of the Torah, certainly noticed discrepancies between the priestly and Mosaic Torahs. Different rabbis approached those discrepancies with different assumptions. But, the precedent of rewriting Torah became a hallmark not only of the Hebrew Bible, but of subsequent Jewish literature.

> The concern of [the authors of the Mosaic Torah] was to implement their own agenda: to effect a major transformation of all spheres of Judean life— cultically, politically, theologically, judicially, ethically, and economically, The authors of Deuteronomy had a radically new vision of the religious and public polity and sought to implement unprecedented changes in religion and society. Precisely for that reason, the guise of continuity with the past became crucial. . . .
>
> Deuteronomy's reuse of its textual patrimony was creative, active, revisionist, and tendentious. It functioned as a means for cultural transformation. Comparable is the work of the Chronicler during the Judean restoration.[25]

---

25 Levinson, *Deuteronomy*, 16.

Levinson points to how Chronicles rewrites biblical history and notes that Second Temple and rabbinic literature carry on the tradition.[26] In other words, the Mosaic Torah is proto-midrash. As we will see, midrashic recontextualization does not stop with the rabbis. Thus, in Deuteronomy we have the seeds for both the method and content of much subsequent Jewish thought: a nonhierarchical anthropology, Near Eastern wisdom, judges selected on the basis of wisdom rather than lineage, an emphasis on teaching and the text of the Torah, a robust system of social and economic laws intended to support the most vulnerable, the promotion of teshuvah, all held together by the love of God.

A Covenant, Not a Contract

"Covenant really must become a form of wisdom if an immutable text is to become its ultimate authority."[27] Given the nonalteration formula of that immutable text, the ability to interpret and/or recontextualize the Torah for the future becomes paramount (Deuteronomy 17:11). The promulgation of wisdom and the requirement to study the laws of God's covenant demand a nation of educators and judges. A culture of learning becomes a necessity for survival. As the Mosaic Torah says, "One cannot live by bread alone; one lives by everything that the Lord *says*" (Deuteronomy 8:3). As one bible scholar has observed, "Deuteronomy's elevation of verbal revelation as the epitome of divine self-disclosure [as opposed to the visual revelation of the priestly Torah] has significant repercussions. Perhaps most importantly, it leads inevitably to a spirituality revolving around the inspired word."[28] Learning Torah aloud is not only practical, it is ritual. Learning Torah becomes a way to God.

Divine love and divine intimacy are pursued through the performance of God's *mitzvot*: walking in God's ways (Deuteronomy 28:9). If one does not pay close attention, one will stray or stumble off the path and then need to reorient oneself. The Mosaic Torah assumes you can

---

26 Ibid., 34, 47–48.
27 Geller, *Sacred Enigmas*, 50.
28 Stephen Cook, "God's Real Absence and Real Presence in Deuteronomy and Deuteronomists," in *Divine Presence and Absence in Exilic and Post-Exilic Judaism*, ed. Nathan MacDonald and Izaak J. de Hulster (Tubingen: Mohr Siebeck, 2013), 135. His italics.

choose, successfully, to walk in God's ways, but it requires a singleness of purpose. We are to love God with all our everything. Everything we do must be consistent with our commitment to walk in God's ways. We are to teach our children as we walk on our way. We, too, have the capacity to be gracious and merciful. Through our acts of grace and mercy toward others, we approach an encounter with the divine. In the felicitous words of Tikva Frymer-Kensky, "The *halakhah* is the path of God in the world and the path of the world to God."[29]

> For I command you this day, to love the Lord your God, to walk in His ways, and to keep His commandments, His laws, and His rules, that you may thrive and increase, and that the Lord your God may bless you in the land you are about to enter and possess. (Deuteronomy 30:16)

Love leads to marriage. The metaphor of marriage to describe the Mosaic covenant is not uncommon in the prophetic literature. In the rabbinic period, Moshe becomes the best man leading the bride, Israel, to the groom, God, under the *chuppah* (wedding canopy) of Mount Sinai. The wedding contract or *ketubah* is the Torah.[30] As we excavate the tradition in search of a usable past, it is important to remember that although the Israelites, as the bride, were to maintain an exclusive commitment to God, the exclusivity of the covenant is not mutual. In the biblical and rabbinic periods, men could have multiple wives. The Mosaic Torah depicts God giving tokens for other peoples to worship (Deuteronomy 4:19). The prophet Amos, while recognizing a unique covenant with Israel (Amos 3:2), also acknowledges that the Israelites are just like the Ethiopians, Philistines, and Arameans to God (Amos 9:7). God is in unique relationships with those peoples, as well. Anticipating a medieval Ashkenazi understanding of Christianity, one could say that God has ordained a covenant with them through intermediaries.

The sign of the covenant between God and *all* people is the rainbow, in all its polychromatic glory (Genesis 9:17). On the High Priest's breastplate were twelve different colored stones, each reflecting a different tribe of Israel (Exodus 28:15–21). Just as the Israelites were comprised of twelve tribes, God's universal covenant, the rainbow, is comprised of

---

29 Frymer-Kensky, *Studies in Bible*, 259.
30 Pirkei d'Rabbi Eliezer 40.

many colors. Each religion refracts its own arc of the rainbow. A coherent Judaism might disagree with elements of other religions; but it would never deny the possibility that other religious traditions could have an authentic relationship with God and express that relationship through a coherent religion of their own.[31]

St. Paul, for instance, imagined walking on the path of halakhah as a death march (Romans 8:3–8). The Mosaic Torah imagines it as a love stroll. A covenant, as Louis Newman has reminded us, is not just a contract between parties with terms to be fulfilled. A covenant is a contract plus a relationship between partners to be nurtured.[32] The Mosaic Torah, with its emphasis on loving God, imagines the covenantal partners walking hand in hand. Upon our hand, the Mosaic Torah prescribes we bind a symbol of our commitment to God (Deuteronomy 6:8). The rabbis understood that verse to command tefillin, which some Jews still don every morning except Shabbat and holidays. We bind ourselves, daily, to God with the following words of devotion: "I will betroth you to Me forever: I will betroth you to Me with righteousness and justice, and with mercy and compassion, and I will betroth you to Me in faithfulness. And you will know the Lord" (Hosea 2:21–22). Human partners are not "betrothed" forever. *Betrothed* does not mean married, it means engaged. It's the moment when love takes the leap into commitment, when love bubbles over.[33]

---

31 "In the Torah the nations are held guilty for what they do in the name of their religion, but not for what they worship." Jeffrey H. Tigay, *The JPS Torah Commentary: Deuteronomy* (Philadelphia: Jewish Publication Society, 1996), 435–36.

32 Louis E. Newman, *Past Imperatives: Studies in the History and Theory of Jewish Ethics* (Albany: State University of New York Press, 1998), 59-62.

33 See also Sifre Deuteronomy 33 to Deuteronomy 6:6.

	Priestly Torah	**Mosaic Torah**
Anthropology	Priests, Levites, Israelites, gentiles	Status is ascribed, not intrinsic
Theology	God is repulsed and attracted by our actions	God rewards and punishes us according to our actions
Purity System	Real/cosmic system Moral universe	Ascribed Moral covenant
Religion	Mitzvot	Mitzvot
Reason for Commandments	To maintain God's protective presence in the camp	To create a modest utopia through laws protecting the vulnerable
Leadership	High Priest, priest, Levite	Levitical priests and judges
Sacrificial Altars	All through the Land	Only in Jerusalem. Consequence is that teshuvah becomes uncoupled from sacrifices

What these two Torahs have in common is their commitment to a life of mitzvot as the way of God and the way to God.

Chapter 3

Rabbinic Religiosity

The previous two chapters were devoted to two discrete religions. Each religion built its laws and rituals upon its understanding of God, its theology. One's religion should cohere with one's theology. Again, to phrase this idea in philosophical terms, one's ethics should cohere with one's metaphysics. This chapter is not entitled "Rabbinic Religion" precisely because the rabbis shifted theology to the background. It is not that the rabbis did not care about theology or did not write about theology. Rather, given the collective enterprise of rabbinic literature, they emphasized and collaborated upon what they agreed about, namely, the centrality of halakhah. On issues of theology, however, they allowed individuals to enjoy what Rabbi David Hartman has called *cognitive autonomy*. Believe what you will, but behave according to our norms.

Rabbinic religiosity could privilege deed over creed, in large measure, because the goals for each inherited creed were identical. Priestly and Mosaic religions were easy to combine, or at least juxtapose, because they both maintained that covenantal obedience would result in their mutual goal of national prosperity and security. What may have been an incidental byproduct of redaction for the Hebrew Bible, a sort of theological pluralism, nevertheless became an essential component of rabbinic ideology.

The American philosopher Richard J. Bernstein coined the expression "engaged fallibilistic pluralism" to suggest the appropriate posture for philosophical and political dialogue. Bernstein comes out of the school of American Pragmatism founded by such thinkers as Charles Pierce, William James, and John Dewey. It was Pierce who first made fallibilism an explicit element in his philosophy. Bernstein elaborates on this principle by suggesting "we actually think that we might learn something from our interlocutor. One tries to see the strength of the thinker's position and what is insightful about it."[1] In some important ways, rabbinic religiosity anticipates the ideas of Pragmatism and engaged fallibilistic pluralism. The debates between the Houses of Shammai and Hillel, two schools of halakhic philosophy and practice during the late Second Temple period, offer such an illustration at the very foundation of rabbinic religiosity.

It is known that when the schools dispute, the halakhah usually follows the opinion of the School of Hillel. Why? One reasonable, but erroneous, answer might run along the lines that the School of Hillel had sharper students or that their arguments were more persuasive. The Talmud, however, endorses both schools as proffering the living words of the God. So, why decide according to Hillel? The School of Hillel taught the School of Shammai's position before their own, and they were self-consciously fallible to the extent that they were persuaded by their opponents to change their positions in roughly fifteen percent of their disputes (Eruvin 13b). In other words, the School of Hillel constructively engaged with the House of Shammai and demonstrated their own fallibility by occasionally adopting the position of their rivals.[2] How radical! We honor those who can admit they are wrong. The Mishnah explicitly promotes such fallibility as a model for future generations (m. Eduyot 1:4). The House of Hillel was not pluralistic in the contemporary sense of an "anything goes" relativism, but the inclusion of multiple and contradictory viewpoints, and the rabbinic designation of them both as living words of God, point toward a worldview that rejects the Aristotelian notion that mutually exclusive positions cannot be simultaneously valid. Light behaving like a wave and a particle could both reflect the living words of God.[3]

---

1   Richard J. Bernstein, "Engaged Fallibilistic Pluralism," 5. Address given to the Columbia Pragmatism Group. https://columbiapragmatism.files.wordpress.com/2014/10/engaged-fallibilistic-pluralism.pdf.

2   Reuven Kimelman, "Judaism and Pluralism," *Modern Judaism* 7, no. 2 (1987): 131–50. See also Menachem Fisch, *Rational Rabbis: Science and Talmudic Culture* (Bloomington: Indiana University Press, 1997), 210–11n17.

3   *Divrei Elohim chaim* can be translated as both *the words of the living God* and *the living words of God*. I prefer the latter translation since *the living God* strikes me as redundant.

Editors are magicians, or they can be. An editor can arrange a text in such a way as to plant an idea that the author of the text had never intended to sow. When we discuss the Hebrew Bible, there are multiple authors, and we use the term *redactor* to describe the potential magician who compiled the various texts. It is difficult, and sometimes impossible, to determine whether the redactor is acting as an anthologist of conflicting voices or as a harmonizer of conflicting voices. When the creation narrative of Genesis 1 patently contradicts that of Genesis 2, for example, did the redactor intend to present two distinct narratives, or did he want his readers to read Genesis 2 in light of Genesis 1? The ancient rabbis harmonize. They imagine that the Adam of Genesis 1, described as both male and female (1:26), was the single individual created in Genesis 2 (2:7). Thus, for (many of) the rabbis, that individual was a hermaphrodite.[4] Is that how the redactor intended us to understand the creation of humanity? We cannot be sure. What we can be certain about, is that there was a rabbinic view that read the two consecutive biblical stories as different perspectives of the same event. An alternative, taken up by Rav Joseph B. Soloveitchik in *The Lonely Man of Faith*, is that the Torah presents us with two distinct types of human beings.

Benjamin Sommer addresses the same phenomenon from a different angle. "What had seemed like new concepts in post-biblical tradition, concepts that apparently came out of nowhere, turn out to have a basis in scripture, since they resurrect ideas present in the biblical text but obscured by the process of redaction."[5] Although this chapter focuses on how the disparate biblical voices were treated in the rabbinic period, the process of juxtaposing, recontextualizing, and integrating the priestly and Mosaic Torahs is already in evidence in the late biblical period. The rabbis will later argue whether minority traditions have been preserved for future rehabilitation or eternal marginalization (m. Eduyot 1:5, 6). For this dispute to be meaningful in the biblical context, we must know what those individual traditions were. Moreover, as Sommer argues, "Surely the anonymous redactors can make no special claim to authority, at least no claim stronger than that of the anonymous authors whose work they

---

4   See Genesis Rabbah 8:1 and my *Torah through Time*, 49–51.
5   Benjamin Sommer, "The Source Critic and the Religious Interpreter," *Interpretation: A Journal of Bible and Theology* 60, no. 1 (2006): 10.

used."[6] Rehabilitating biblical traditions that had been obscured by the redactor, intentionally or not, unwinds rabbinic Judaism's assumption that the Torah had a single author with a singular purpose.

Not long after the Babylonians destroyed the Temple and exiled the Judeans (586 BCE), the Persians conquered the Babylonians (539 BCE). The Persian King Cyrus was hailed by Isaiah as a messiah, an anointed king who will bring redemption to the Jews (Isaiah 45). (Although the designation of *messiah* accretes different meanings in later Jewish history, I will be using the term in the sense of a king of a politically autonomous Israel.) Upon the return of some refugees to Jerusalem in 458 BCE, Ezra, as priest and scribe, read *Torat Moshe* to men, women, and children (Nehemiah 8:2 and RaLBaG). The scribe was a new model of leadership that signified the growing influence of the written word and its interpretation. After reading the Hebrew scroll, both a translation into Aramaic and an explanation were required so the returning Judeans could make sense of this Mosaic Torah. Just as the priests of old had explained God's will through the oracular devices of the Urim and Tumim (Exodus 28:30 and Numbers 27:21), the new scribe interpreted the Torah to explain God's will (Ezra 7:10). The Torah became a proxy for God. To put it plainly, the Torah became a textual incarnation of the divine. When Ezra unscrolled the Torah, all the people stood up. "Ezra blessed the Lord, the great God, and all the people answered, 'Amen, Amen,' with hands upraised. Then they bowed their heads and prostrated themselves *before the Lord* with their faces to the ground" (Nehemiah 8:6).

The Second Temple had already been started by Zerubavel in 515 BCE, yet it is the Torah that is described as the access point to God. The author of Psalm 119 composed a paean to *torah* in which she is not only glorified, she is deified.[7] While the Mosaic Torah has us cling to God (Deuteronomy 4:4), our psalmist clings to God's decrees (119:31). As James Kugel has written, "The divine commandments become an embodiment, a hypostasis, of God's presence on earth. . . . God is, as it were, manifest in divine law."[8] Although the Mosaic Torah had been

---

6   Ibid.: 12.

7   David Noel Freedman, *Psalm 119: The Exaltation of Torah* (University Park, PA: Eisenbrauns, 1999), 88.

8   James L. Kugel, *The Great Poems of the Bible: A Reader's Companion with New Translations* (New York: The Free Press, 1999), 270.

readily intelligible (Deuteronomy 30:11), *torah* becomes something mysterious, like God himself, and it requires divine wisdom to interpret (Psalm 119:18).

The priests of old were alone able to determine if a skin lesion or a mark on a wall was ritually pure or impure. The High Priest alone controlled the Urim and Tumim. In the wake of the Temple's destruction, it is the Torah scribe who deciphers and determines the meaning of the Torah which embodies divine wisdom. The *torah* of Psalm 119 assumes the divine attributes of mystery and perfection. The scribe, an office open to all men regardless of priestly pedigree, is now the keeper of the keys to Torah. By the time of the book of Chronicles, "'The word of YHWH,' has been transformed from the oral word of God spoken by the prophets into the written word of God."[9] To be sure, not all Jews believed that the Torah was God's primary or exclusive access point. But after the destruction of the Second Temple in 70 CE, the rabbis, slowly and haltingly, emerged as the leaders of the Jewish community, and their idiosyncratic religiosity became Judaism.

The books with the latest settings in the biblical canon—Ezra, Nehemiah, and Chronicles—depict the Jews returning to their land and rebuilding their Temple. It was unimaginable that national life could continue without the presence of God's sanctuary in their midst. Animal sacrifices featured prominently at the Temple site even prior to construction (Ezra 3:6). Nevertheless, from the initial return of the repatriates to the conclusion of the book of Nehemiah, "The center of gravity moved from the Temple to Torah."[10] Reward and punishment in Chronicles are doled out in response to compliance with the covenant, just as in the Mosaic Torah. Shabbat observance was enforced under threat of violence (Nehemiah 13:21). The stakes were too high to tolerate anything less than complete compliance. This second chance was far too precious to squander. King David's words in Chronicles must have had special resonance for the repatriated Judean community: "And now, in the sight of all Israel, the congregation of the Lord, and in the hearing of God, [I say]: Observe

---

9   Schniedewind, *How the Bible Became a Book*, 188.
10 Bustenay Oded, "The Time of Zerubbabel vis-à-vis the Time of Ezra: Between 'Holy People' and 'Holy Seed,'" in *Built by Wisdom, Established by Understanding: Essays on Biblical and Near Eastern Literature in Honor of Adele Berlin*, ed. Maxine L. Grossman (University Park, PA: Eisenbrauns, 2013), 247.

and search all the commandments of the Lord your God in order that you may possess this good land and bequeath it to your children after you forever" (1 Chronicles 28:8).

Post-Second Temple Judaism allows us to see how elements of the priestly and Mosaic Torahs were modified, combined, and marginalized. The literature of the rabbis often minimizes, deprecates, or polemicizes against priestly privilege and activities.[11] Learning becomes paramount: "Better a learned bastard than an ignorant High Priest" (m. Horayot 3:8). Ezra the scribe, a transitional figure to the rabbis, is a descendant of Hilkia, the priest responsible for finding a lost scroll of teaching in the First Temple (2 Kings 22:8). That lost scroll, according to bible scholars, is associated with the book of Deuteronomy, the Mosaic Torah. It is the Mosaic Torah that emphasizes teaching, learning, and Torah as text. Thus, both genealogically and conceptually, there is much that coheres between the Mosaic Torah and rabbinic religiosity.[12]

As we saw in the first chapter, priestly religion maintained an ontological halakhah where our actions affect Creator and creation. Priestly religion is based on an archaic ontology in which the invisible infrastructure of reality is reflected in the divinely revealed law. Our actions have an impact on that invisible infrastructure as well as on the invisible architect. Law in the Mosaic religion, on the other hand, tracked on to creation but did not affect it. The wisdom of the law, in the Mosaic Torah, is similar to the Greek concept of natural law whereby our behavior should conform to the nature of reality as we perceive it. The general drift from biblical law to rabbinic law is away from the ontological halakhah of the priests.[13] Priests considered themselves ontologically superior to other Israelites merely by virtue of their lineage. Among the first Israeli scholars to highlight this shift in legal metaphysics was Daniel Schwartz:

---

11 Peter Schafer, *Origins of Jewish Mysticism* (Tubingen: Mohr Siebeck, 2009), 224.

12 Veijola, "Deuteronomistic Roots of Judaism": 459–78. The Talmud cites a tradition that had the Torah not been received through Moses it would have been received through Ezra (Sannhedrin 21b).

13 Aharon Shemesh, *Halakhah in the Making: The Development of Jewish Law from Qumran to the Rabbis* (Berkeley: University of California Press, 2009), 135, and Vered Noam, "Ritual Impurity in Tannaitic Literature: Two Opposing Perspectives," *Journal of Ancient Judaism* 1 (2010): 65–103.

My basic thesis is that there is a symmetry between the respective natures of priests and rabbis themselves, on the one hand, and the natures of their respective attitudes toward law, on the other. Priests (in Judaism) are created by God, or by nature, if you will, and seem typically to have ascribed great authority [and responsiveness] to God or nature in the legal process. Rabbis, in contrast, created themselves, and even prided themselves on the lack of importance of pedigree among them; it is noteworthy that their approach to law leaves God and nature on the sidelines, objects of debate but not participants in it.[14]

As an example of the shift away from ontological halakhah, let's look at *kashrut*, the laws for keeping kosher. A Camp Ramah chef is preparing a very large meat stew.[15] A gentile employee, eating a shredded pork sandwich, slips on the freshly mopped kitchen floor. Eyewitnesses testify that some pork shreds flew into the meat stew, but there is no way to extract them once they entered the stew, which was on a high boil. Those of us who keep a kosher kitchen know that the stew is still kosher to eat. But, why?

Priestly religion forbids pork. There are no exceptions in the Torah, only mechanisms for expiation if pork were *unintentionally* consumed. Indeed, according to the Tosefta (an early legal compilation similar in structure to the Mishnah), this entire stew has been irreparably contaminated and cannot be consumed by Jews (Hullin 7:7). But, in the majority opinion of the early sages, as long as the taste of the pork has been overwhelmed by the kosher meat, the entire stew is edible (m. Hullin 7:5). At a later time, a ratio of one-part non-kosher food to sixty parts kosher food was ordained as the standard (Avoda Zarah 68b/69a and Rashi on Hullin 97b, *m'sha'arinan*). The Tosefta's prohibition on consumption reflects an ontological halakhah. Knowingly consuming pork would be a violation of our covenant, and the ontological consequence would be that God is weakened or distanced from us.[16] But, under the one-sixtieth rule, the

---

14 Daniel Schwartz, "Law and Truth: On Qumran-Sadducean and Rabbinic Views of Law," in *The Dead Sea Scrolls: Forty Years of Research*, ed. Devorah Dimant and Uriel Rappaport (Leiden-Jerusalem: Brill, 1992), 239–40.

15 Camp Ramah runs a network of camps throughout North America and is often described as the crown jewel of Conservative Judaism.

16 This could be an issue of legal interpretation rather than an issue of the philosophy of law. I take up this issue in book 3.

halakhah is simply a fiat without metaphysical consequences. Thus, even though we knowingly eat the pork that has been absorbed into the beef stew, since the pork's presence was inadvertent, there was no intention of violating the covenant. *B'tayavon!* (*Bon appetit!*)

Not only does rabbinic halakhah shift away from the ontological, it also contains polemics against the priestly mode of unmediated revelation. Consider the familiar midrash in which we are rerouted from following after God, for He is a consuming fire, and we are advised to follow in certain of God's more rabbinically sanctioned ways.[17]

> R. Hama son of R. Hanina further said: What does the text mean: *You shall walk after the Lord your God?* (Dt. 13:5) Is it, then, possible for a human being to walk after the Shechinah; has it not been said: *For the Lord thy God is a devouring fire?* (Dt. 4:24) But [the meaning is] to walk after the attributes of the Holy One, blessed be He. As He clothes the naked, for it is written: *And the Lord God made for Adam and for his wife coats of skin, and clothed them,* so should you also clothe the naked. The Holy One, blessed be He, visited the sick, for it is written: *And the Lord appeared unto him [Abraham] by the oaks of Mamre,* so should you also visit the sick. The Holy One, blessed be He, comforted mourners, for it is written: *And it came to pass after the death of Abraham, that God blessed Isaac his son,* so should you also comfort mourners. The Holy One, blessed be He, buried the dead, for it is written: *And He buried him [Moshe] in the valley,* so should you also bury the dead. (Sotah 14a)

In terms of method, it is not unusual for a rabbi to take two unrelated verses out of context and throw them against one another to make his point. That is a classic method of midrash. In this case, there is a wink to the rabbinic audience who recalls that Moshe began his prophetic career by witnessing a bush on fire that was *not* consumed (Exodus 3:2). The rabbis must have also appreciated that we are to follow only in God's merciful attributes and not his retributive ones. No smiting wicked cities, for example. Yet, in addition to promoting kindness, this midrash also argues against attempting to reach God directly. It is incendiary.

---

17 An earlier parallel is found in Sifre, Deuteronomy 49, which cites Daniel 7:9, and is a more explicit polemic against mysticism.

In the Hebrew Book of Enoch [second century CE] there is an account of the description given by the Patriarch to Rabbi Ishmael of his own metamorphosis into an angel Metatron, when his flesh was transformed into "fiery torches." According to the "Greater Hekhaloth," every mystic must undergo this transformation, but with the difference that, being less worthy than Enoch, he is in danger of being devoured by the "fiery torches."[18]

Uninitiated dilettantes risk death (Hagigah 13a). The Mishnaic restriction on expounding *maʾaseh merkavah*, the revelation of God on His celestial chariot (Ezekiel 1 and 10), and the stories of the early rabbis attempting mystical experiences with disastrous consequences, were also part of the rabbinic polemic against early Jewish mysticism.[19] As Rachel Elior has shown, there is a sturdy conceptual bridge between the dispossessed Zaddokite priests, who fled to Qumran by the Dead Sea following the Hasmonean usurpation of the priesthood (162 BCE), and the later authors of Merkava (chariot) and Heichalot (palaces) mystical literature.[20] Just as the High Priest had access to the Holy of Holies, the "Descenders on the Chariot," as some of the mystics called themselves, sought visual access to God in His chamber room. Unlike the Mosaic Torah which emphasizes aural revelation, the priestly Torah offered a more graphic visual component (e.g., Exodus 24:10). The rabbis do not deny the possibility of mystical visual revelation after the destruction of the Second Temple; but they do emphasize the danger of operating outside the halakhic system. Such provisos reveal that there were Jew doing just that.

Both Rachel Elior and Arthur Green suggest that what has been represented as mainstream, rabbinic Judaism in relation to a marginal, mystical tradition may be an artifact of scholarly prejudice and the availability

---

18 Gershom Scholem, *Major Trends in Jewish Mysticism* (New York: Schocken Books, 1946), 52.

19 M. Hagigah 2:1, t. Hagigah 2:1–7, y. Hagigah II:1 (77 a/b), and Hagigah 11b–15a.

20 Rachel Elior, *The Three Temples: On the Emergence of Jewish Mysticism*, trans. David Louvish (Oxford: Littman Library of Jewish Civilization, 2004), 1–37. Ithamar Gruenwald focuses on the ontological power of Heichalot hymns in the first chapter of his revised *Apocalyptic and Merkavah Mysticism* (Leiden: Brill, 2014).

of historical records.[21] It may have been that these two approaches, which may loosely be called the Mosaic and priestly approaches, were alive, well, and rubbing shoulders in the late Second Temple period. Much scholarship has shown the connections among the halakhah of the Qumran community, the Sadducees, and the House of Shammai.[22] We also know that Heichalot mysticism and the rabbinic liturgy bear certain family resemblances.[23] While it is true that the rabbinic institutions of learning Torah, practical halakhah, prayer, and teshuvah are in line with Mosaic religion, and that the destruction of the Temple precluded priestly animal sacrifices, rabbinic religiosity intentionally allows for a plurality of theological infrastructures to support their halakhic practices. Thus, before we concede that rabbinic Judaism is basically a post-Temple manifestation of the Mosaic Torah, we should look more closely at where the influences of the priestly Torah, and its ontological halakhah, might be discerned.

Priests in Moshe's Garb?

More than fifty years ago, Abraham Joshua Heschel isolated a series of rabbinic statements revealing an impaired deity in need of our help. From where will that help come? From Jews engaged in commandments and prayer. "The idea of God being in need of man is central to Judaism and pervades all the pages of the Bible and of Chazal, of Talmudic literature, and it is understandable in our own time."[24] This tradition, which Heschel associates with Rabbi Akiva and his disciples, resonates with priestly theology in the sense that our actions have an impact on God.[25]

---

21 Arthur Green, *Keter: The Crown of God in Early Jewish Mysticism* (Princeton: Princeton University Press, 1997), 85–87.
22 Scholars in this field include Yochanan Silman, Yakov Sussman, Vered Noam, Aharon Shemesh, and Eyal Regev.
23 Green, *Keter*, 12–19. Ruth Langer, To Worship God Properly: *Tensions Between Liturgical Custom and Halakhah in Judaism* (Cincinnati: Hebrew Union College Press, 1998), 199.
24 Abraham Joshua Heschel, *Moral Grandeur and Spiritual Audacity* (New York: Farrar, Straus and Giroux, 1997), 159. Cited in Reuven Kimelman, "Abraham Joshua Heschel's Theology of Judaism and the Rewriting of Jewish Intellectual History," *The Jewish Journal of Thought and Philosophy* 17, no. 2 (2009): 220.
25 The first volume of Heschel's magnum opus on rabbinic theology *Torah Min HaShamayim BeAsplaqariah Shel HaDorot* appeared in 1962. In 2005, Gordon Tucker

In the Torah, the sins of the Israelites drive God away, and the sacrifices bring God back. In rabbinic expressions of an inherently responsive God, we also see that covenantal obedience augments God's power. (Strengthening God through human action is called *theurgy*.)

- The essential home of the Shechinah is in the lower worlds. But when Adam sinned, it was removed to the first heaven. When Cain sinned, it went to the second heaven and so on until the seventh heaven. But Abraham [brought it down] from the seventh to the sixth . . . and Moses brought it down to the lower world (Genesis Rabbah 19:7).
- Whenever Israel acts according to God's will, they add strength to the Power (*g'vurah*) (*Pesikta de-Rav Kahana, Slichot*, pis. 25:1, to Deuteronomy 32:18 and Psalm 60:14).

Already in 1949, Heschel wrote: "Thus man's relationship to God should not be that of passive reliance upon His Omnipotence but that of active assistance. 'The impious rely on their gods . . . the righteous are the support of God.' The Patriarchs are therefore called 'the chariot of the Lord.' The belief in the greatness of man, in the metaphysical effectiveness of his physical acts, is an ancient motif of Jewish thinking."[26] As the following midrashim illustrate, metaphysical effectiveness is a double-edged sword. Just as we can strengthen God through our deeds, so, too, can we weaken Him:

- When Israel fulfills God's will, He builds the chambers of heaven; but when Israel does not fulfill God's will, God's vault, as it were, founders on earth (Amos 9:6) (*Sifre, Habrechah*, pis. 346 to Deuteronomy 33:5).[27]
- When Israel does the will of the Omnipresent, they make the left hand into the right hand [thereby increasing God's strength]:

and Leonard Levin published a translation entitled *Heavenly Torah as Refracted through the Generations* (New York: Continuum, 2006).

26 Abraham Joshua Heschel, "The Mystical Element in Judaism," in *The Jews: Their History, Culture, and Religion*, ed. Louis Finkelstein (New York: Harper & Bros., 1949), 605 citing Bereshit Rabbah 69:13 to Genesis 28:13 and 82:6 to Genesis 35:9.

27 Translation from Tucker and Levin, *Heavenly Torah*, 109.

"Your right hand, Lord, glorious in power. Your right hand, Lord, shatters the enemy" (Exodus 15:6). But when the Israelites do not do the will of the Omnipresent, as it were, they make the right hand into the left hand: "He has withdrawn His right hand" [thereby weakening God] (Lamentations 2:3; Mekhilta, Beshallah, Shira 5).

Heschel does not, however, address the benefit to the Jewish people of engaging in the mitzvot within the rabbinic paradigm. Notice in the Mekhilta's midrash above that when Israel does the will of God, there is salvation and rejoicing at the crossing of the Red Sea, but when Israel does not do the will of God, there is catastrophe and lamentation after the First Temple's destruction. The same nationalistic urge that motivated compliance with the covenant in the priestly and Mosaic Torahs is in evidence amongst the rabbis, as well. The pervasive concern with national security and the burning desire to be a free people did not disappear along with Jewish political sovereignty in 63 BCE, or the razing of the Second Temple in 70 CE, or even the suppression of the Bar Kochva Revolt in 135 CE. There was a theurgic, redemptive myth of divine restoration and sovereignty which undergirded one stream of rabbinic thought in the wake of the Second Temple's destruction.[28]

Biblical sacrifices certainly offered the psychological function of atonement for the individual and the nation, but there were rabbis who shifted *both functions* of priestly sacrifices, psychological and national security, into the substitutes for sacrifices endorsed by the rabbis. In the Mosaic Torah's rabbinic incarnation, there was no need to identify a functional replacement for sacrifices, since what animated the biblical Mosaic Torah was text, prayer, and teshuvah. The insistence on a replacement for sacrifices emerges from requirements of the priestly Torah. Rabbinic insistence on the practice of Torah, prayer, and teshuvah (obedience to the terms/mitzvot of the covenant) effectively merged the means and ends of the Mosaic Torah with the ontological presuppositions and theology

---

28 For an academic treatment of this claim, see Shai Cherry, "The Camouflaged *Ta'am* (Motive): Redemptive Implications of Rabbinic Theurgy," *Zeramim* 4, nos. 1–2 (2019–20), https://zeramim.org/current-issue/volume-iv-issue-1-2-fall-winter-2019-2020-5779-5780/the-camouflaged-taam-motive-redemptive-implications-of-rabbinic-theurgy-shai-cherry/.

of the priestly Torah. Those functional equivalents to sacrifice could then serve as vehicles to restore God's presence and empower divine sovereignty allowing the people of Israel to rule again in their occupied, ancestral, and divinely promised land.

Ta'amei Hamitzvot—Rationales for the Commandments

The biblical material inherited by the rabbis demanded obedience to ritual laws and interpersonal mitzvot in order to protect domestic tranquility and ensure the national security of the Israelites. All agreed that the covenant between God and the Israelites was reciprocal, if not necessarily symbiotic. Israelites performed the mitzvot, and God protected the people. Once the Second Temple was destroyed and the people exiled, what becomes the motivation for the Israelites/Jews to maintain the covenant? Not only may there have been a suspicion of God's impotence, but the egocentric question emerged in full force—what's in it for me?

One possible response is that Jews keep the mitzvot because they are decrees from God, our Sovereign, and we are forbidden to violate them.[29] There were pious Jews who accepted such reasoning and divine fiat, even in the face of humiliating defeats by the Romans. This motive for covenantal obedience is novel, and this attitude toward compliance is associated with a philosophy of halakhah called nominalism. We should obey because God "named" the commandments which comprise the covenant, *not* because they map on to reality either with ontological force (priestly) or through the wisdom of natural law (Mosaic). "The corpse does not defile nor does water purify. This is a decree of the Holy One, blessed be He, who says, 'I have legislated a law and decreed a decree, and you are not free to violate my decrees'" (Pesikta de-Rav Kahana, *Parah 'adumah*, pis. 4:6, to Numbers 19:2). "Don't say pork isn't yummy—it *is* yummy! But what can I do? God so decreed" (Sifra, Kedoshim 10:11).

This variety of legal nominalism, *an innovation of rabbinic Judaism*, shifts the reason for ritual mitzvot from ontology or wisdom to relationship. We comply with God's requests for no other reason than to nurture the relationship between us and God. We are, nevertheless, rewarded for our compliance. But when we unintentionally transgress the terms of the

---

29 E.g., Sifra, *Kedoshim*, par. 2:4, to Leviticus 9:19 and Yoma 67b.

relationship, God does not respond with strict justice. As an act of loving kindness, God does not insist that we discard the pork-infused beef stew.[30] A healthy relationship can withstand errors as long as they were not committed with intentional malice.

Another incentive to maintain the mitzvot in the post-destruction era was the promise to acquire the land that is purely good and eternal in duration—the world to come after one has died.[31] Indeed, already in late biblical material, we see this venue vaguely introduced in the book of Daniel (12:2). This innovation not only protected God's omnipotence, it offered a reward to the downtrodden. God's strength and love are obscured in this fleeting existence but will be transparent for the remainder of eternity—for those who merit God's beneficence. The importance of this innovation cannot be overstated. While it is true that there was no rabbinic attempt to systematize the various and contradictory claims of heaven, hell, resurrection, immortality of the soul, and messianic days— another example of cognitive autonomy—many rabbis simply could not countenance the thought that there was nothing more to reality than the strikingly unjust existence on this orb of spit and dust.

If the Mosaic Torah's doctrine of reward and punishment were to be maintained in the wake of the Hasmonean Revolt, the Great Revolt, and the Bar Kochva Revolt, then a new world had to be created, *ex nihilo*. In the rabbis' world, as Job had already testified, the virtuous are not necessarily victorious nor are the wicked necessarily vanquished. Blaming the victim, the official theology of the prayer book, might prompt introspection and be empowering. After all, if we brought on this suffering through our own deeds, perhaps we can effect a remedy through our own deeds, as well. But, during these revolts, Jews were being killed for being Jews. Death has no remedy, at least, not in this world. The only reward that compensates for everlasting death in this world is everlasting life in the world to come.

Yet another rationale for the mitzvot centered on ethical behavior. Such behavior affords humans benefit in this world, structurally analogous to the rationale within the Torah itself. In the commonly understood language of the rabbis, the mitzvot "refine" us. Certainly, the emphasis on

---

30 Although one could still sell the stew to gentiles, if it were being prepared prior to the onset of Shabbat, one may not have time to prepare another stew before sundown.
31 M. Sannhedrin 10:1, m. Avot 4:16, and Kiddushin 39b.

ethics in both the priestly Torah and Mosaic Torah are consonant with such a claim. The classic midrashic source for such a contention, however, has almost certainly been misinterpreted.

> Rav said: The mitzvot were given only in order that humanity might be refined through them. For what does the Holy One, blessed be He, care whether a man kills an animal by the throat or by the nape of its neck? Hence, its purpose is to refine humanity. (Genesis Rabbah 44:1)[32]

In Maimonides' *Guide of the Perplexed* (c. 1190), he described this midrash as "very strange."[33] Maimonides then goes on to interpret "refine" as related to ethical refinement. If Maimonides' reading were correct, what *would be* very strange is that neither Saadia Gaon nor Bahya ibn Pakuda, both of whom wrote on ethics prior to Maimonides, cites this midrash.

The expression in Hebrew, *letzaref* (or *litzrof*) *bahen 'et habriyot*, literally means to refine humanity through them (the mitzvot), and the verb comes from metallurgy. Specifically, the process of refining a metal involves separating out the ore from the metal. This process, called *cupellation*, is mentioned in Jeremiah 6:28–30.[34] Although slaughtering a cow by slicing its jugular vein is less painful to the cow, does it refine humanity? It may make Jews more sensitive to the pain of other sentient creatures, but the rest of humanity is unaffected by the laws of kashrut. In Midrash Tanhuma, this rationale of "refining humans" is associated with Rabbi Akiva and the issue is circumcision. There is no compelling argument that circumcision morally refines humans (or even Jewish men!), although Maimonides tried to make exactly that argument (*Guide*, 3:49, 609).[35]

A more reasonable reading of this midrash, in keeping with a prevailing rabbinic value, is that the mitzvot were given to *separate humanity*, Jews (e.g., silver) from non-Jews (lead). Certainly, the laws of

---

32 I deal extensively with this midrash in "The Camouflaged *Ta'am*," 15–18.

33 Moses Maimonides, *Guide of the Perplexed*, trans. *Shlomo* Pines (Chicago: University of Chicago Press, 1963), 3:26, 508.

34 Dan Levene and Beno Rothenberg, *A Metallurgical Gemara: Metals in the Jewish Sources* (London: Thames & Hudson, 2007), 11.

35 See also Isaac Heinemann, *The Reasons for the Commandments in Jewish Thought from the Bible to the Renaissance*, trans. Leonard Levin (Boston: Academic Studies Press, 2008), chapter 4.

kashrut and the mitzvah of circumcision had such a separating effect. For Maimonides, being ethical was of primary importance, while being separate was problematic. He served in the sultan's palace as a physician, and many Jews interacted daily with their Muslim neighbors in Cairo. (In Maimonides' day, ninety percent of Jews lived under Islamic rule.) What Maimonides did, and which we will see again, is to *derash*, or recontextualize, an earlier tradition, creating a new reading that, *to this day*, has replaced the author's intention.

We saw in the first chapter how embedded the idea of separation is for the priestly Torah. Moreover, the prohibition on intermarriage with specific peoples in the Mosaic Torah is universalized upon return from Babylonian captivity. "The general ban on intermarriages, which is a clear self-segregation approach, is appropriate for a minority in exile as a strategic means to preserve self-identity by intensifying social and religious boundaries in order to maintain . . . cultural survival and to foster cohesion."[36] Rabbinic aspersions of Roman immorality animated harsh legislation against non-Jews and exacerbated the chauvinistic attitude already present at the beginning of the Second Temple period.[37] Far from promoting ethics, our midrash aimed at a survival strategy for the Jewish remnant.

There is a glorification of *gmilut chasadim*, bestowing deeds of loving kindness, throughout rabbinic literature. The introduction to the Mishnah Avot envisions that deeds of loving kindness are one of the three pillars upon which the world rests; the Mishnah also incentivizes deeds of loving by qualifying them both for immediate reward and future benefit (Peah 1:1); and Rabbi Simlai frames the entire Torah as beginning and ending with God's deeds of loving kindness, a God whom we are to imitate (Sotah 14a). Encouragement, however, is not a rationale. As central as ethics are to the rabbinic enterprise, that centrality is an inheritance of the Torah, and the rabbis add relatively little.

The rabbis promoted a life of mitzvot, including *gmilut chasadim*, for Jews of the post-Temple era. Some believed that the punishments from past transgressions would be truncated and their condition returned to the status quo ante akin to what transpired after the destruction of the

---

36 Oded, "The Time of Zerubbabel": 261–62.
37 T. Baba Metzia 2:33.

First Temple. There were rabbis, from the moment of the destruction, who worked within the biblical paradigm that religious observance leads to national security. After all, the surviving remnant of Second Temple Judaism needed nothing more acutely than protection and national restoration. The introduction of the world to come for *individuals* of Israel never eclipsed the central importance of this world for the *nation* of Israel.

When we encounter rabbinic statements that explicitly claim that God will be strengthened by the performance of mitzvot, we must ask ourselves what is it that God cannot do now that He will be able to do once strengthened? Furthermore, we know from late Second Temple literature that apocalyptic and messianic impulses were running high. Did they completely disappear after the Great Revolt and Bar Kochva Revolt?[38] Or, did those redemptive impulses become sublimated? Given the centrality and function of the sacrifices in priestly religion, our discussion will soon take us to prayer as a functional substitute for the sacrifices. Before we can most profitably discuss prayer, however, we need to better understand the power of language.

The Power of Language

Within the priestly Torah, we have seen the power of words manifest both in the creation narrative and in the process of teshuvah where confession is a mandatory prerequisite for the re-creation of the self.[39] Isaac Rabinowitz describes words as "concentrations of powers." He cites examples where certain "strong-souled" people in the Bible "invested [speech] with extracommunicative power."[40] For our present purposes,

---

38 William Horbury, *Jewish Messianism and the Cult of Christ* (Norwich: Hymns Ancient & Modern Ltd., 2012), 36–108 and William Horbury, *Messianism Among Jews and Christians: Biblical and Historical Studies* (London: T & T Clark, 2003), 35–122. We see the reemergence of militaristic messianism in post-Tannaitic sources. See Lawrence Schiffman, "Messianism and Apocalypticism in Rabbinic Texts," in *The Cambridge History of Judaism*, vol. 4, *The Late Roman-Rabbinic Period*, ed. Steven T. Katz (New York: Cambridge University Press, 2006), 1065–70.

39 Soloveitchik, *Halakhic Man*, 109–10.

40 Isaac Rabinowitz, "'Word' and Literature in Ancient Israel," *New Literary History* 4, no. 1 (1972): 120–21.

it is critical to recognize that for the Israelites, oral formulations "could conform realities to their verbal semblances."[41]

> All created realities are, in their first manifestation, words: the words are incompletely developed forms, presentiments, signs of realities which, God willing, will come to their full scope. To use words to say that something has occurred, even though it may not have occurred, is thus to introduce a preliminary form of this reality into the world, and, in effect, to invite God's willingness to bring it to fulfillment.[42]

Isaac could not retract his blessing to Jacob even though he had intended it for Esau (Genesis 27:37); Jepthah could not retract his vow even though it meant sacrificing his daughter (Judges 11:35); and King Ahashverosh could not retract his decree to have the Jews killed even after he had decided otherwise. He had to issue another decree (Esther 8:8). Their words created a new reality. It is true that just because the Torah empowered language with extra-communicative potency, it does not necessarily mean its rabbinic heirs did the same. But they did—at least some of them.[43]

Consider this dispute between the Mishnah and the Tosefta. The Mishnah (Hagigah 1:8) accords the power to dissolve an oath to the rabbinic sages, a power the rabbis admit is beyond what is found in the Torah. The Tosefta (Hagigah 1:9), on the other hand, explains that the sages are wise enough to find loopholes in order to invalidate the vow. This tosefta is priestly. It acknowledges that once a vow has been properly made, it cannot be undone.[44] Indeed, we see no mechanism for loosening a vow in the Temple Scroll (54:5) of the Qumran community where they also maintained an ontological halakhah.[45] In the rabbinic laws of betrothal, as well, language creates the essential condition for the new reality to be effected. In this case, *intention is irrelevant* (Kiddushin 49b/50a).

---

41 Ibid.: 133.
42 Ibid.: 138–39.
43 See Exodus 1:10 and Sotah 11a for a particularly fascinating example.
44 Moshe Benovitz, *Kol Nidre: Studies in the Development of Rabbinic Votive Institutions* (Atlanta: Scholars Press, 1998), 149–52.
45 See Jeffrey L. Rubenstein, "Nominalism and Realism in Qumranic and Rabbinic Law: A Reassessment," *Dead Sea Discoveries* 6, no. 2 (1999): 108.

According to the Mishnah, a man was once able to nullify a writ of divorce he had sent to his wife merely by convening a court of three men and *declaring* the writ nullified—even without her knowledge (Gittin 4:1)! The words of certain formulae effect a new reality and status which have serious legal ramifications both for the individuals involved and their subsequent offspring. The likeliest explanation for this mishnah about divorce is that there is an extra-communicative power to language in the minds of some rabbis. It is also worth remembering that the ontological reality of speech is built into the Hebrew language: the word for *word* is the same as the word for *thing* (*d'var*).

In a discussion of the Mishnah's statement that one does not force a woman to take an oath concerning the prior collection of her *ketubah* (the monetary settlement upon divorce or the death of her husband), the Talmud asks why that would be the case. It answers with a story of a woman who took an oath which caused the death of one of her sons. Although the woman believed her oath to be truthful, she was mistaken in a *very* minor way. "When the sages heard of the incident they remarked: If such is the fate of one who [intends to] swear truly, what must be the fate of one who swears falsely?!" (Gittin 35a)[46] Thus, the mishnah (Gittin 4:3), at least as interpreted by its gemara, accords lethal power to oaths irrespective of intention. God is designated as the One who spoke the world into existence. As beings created in the divine image, we can correspondingly destroy the world through speech.

Most would agree that speech can affect our perceptions of reality, which in turn can affect our behavior. The philosophy of language which we are describing, however, claims that language affects reality itself; language is ontologically transformative. (This is akin to the Roman Catholic doctrine of transubstantiation: during the sacrament of the Eucharist the bread and wine are ontologically transformed into the body and blood of Christ through the oral formula of the priest.) This conception of language is the product of a priestly, ontological halakhah in which legal categories reflect the structure of creation. That archaic ontology is the foundation of priestly religion.

---

46 Rabbinic literature acknowledges, using the phrase from Ecclesiastes 10:5, that even misspoken words possess extracommunicative, and lethal, power. See, in particular, Moed Katan 18a, but also K'tubot 62b, and Bereshit Rabbah, *Va'yetze*, par. 74:14, to Genesis 31:3.

Prayer and Blessings

For the leaders who sought to restore God's Presence to Israel after the destruction of the Second Temple, the method of sacrifice was no longer a possibility. What, then, became the functional replacements for sacrifices? The commonplace that prayer replaced sacrifices has also been nuanced over the past decade, again in keeping with Heschel's assessment fifty years ago.[47] "In sum, Temple associations were appropriated to create a religious continuum [between sacrifices and prayer] without creating a religious equivalency."[48] Although we will examine other substitutes for the sacrifices, prayer is paramount precisely because of its temporal and legal parallels as well as its explicit goal to "restore God's presence to Zion."[49]

As James Kugel has pointed out, already within the book of Psalms there is an assimilation of praise to animal sacrifices: "Let my prayer be as incense before You, the raising of my hands as the evening offering."[50] By the time of the rabbis, and the destruction of the Temple, there are numerous statements which raise the value of prayer *above* that of sacrifices (Brachot 32b).[51] Texts such as these have long been highlighted by scholars, but there has been no explicit connection drawn between the biblical *function* of sacrifices and the rabbinic *motivations* for prayer. This biblical function, I am arguing, is present for some rabbis who harbor a redemptive ideology even/especially after the failed revolts of the first and second centuries. This redemptive ideology is neither apocalyptic nor dependent on Jewish militarism; God alone is the Redeemer.[52] This

---

47 Tucker and Levine, *Heavenly Torah*, 88.
48 Reuven Kimelman, "Rabbinic Prayer in Late Antiquity," in Katz, *The Cambridge History of Judaism*, 593. See also *Liturgy in the Life of the Synagogue: Studies in the History of Jewish Prayer*, ed. Ruth Langer and Steven Fine (University Park, PA: Eisenbrauns, 2005), 5–14; Klawans, *Purity*, 208–11; and Stefan C. Reif, *Problems with Prayers* (Berlin: De Gruyter, 2006), 180.
49 From the rabbinic *Amidah*. Reif, *Problems with Prayers*, 162.
50 James L. Kugel, *In Potiphar's House: The Interpretive Life of Biblical Texts* (Cambridge, MA: Harvard University Press, 1990), 125. Psalms 141:2.
51 For similar statements, see Heschel, *Heavenly Torah*, 87–88.
52 See Jeremiah Unterman, "The Social-Legal Origin for the Image of God as the Redeemer of Israel," in *Pomegranates and Golden Bells: Studies in Biblical, Jewish, and Near Eastern Ritual, Law, and Literature in Honor of Jacob Milgrom*, ed. David P. Wright, David Noel Freedman, and Avi Hurvitz (University Park, PA: Eisenbrauns, 1995), 399–405, esp. 404–5.

version of redemption seeks to restore the Temple and divine sovereignty through the augmentation of divine power. Rabbi Isaac claimed that Israel was redeemed from Egypt, and the Temple built in Jerusalem, as a reward for their worship—a not-so-subtle incentive for the Jews of his own day to emulate the deeds of their ancestors for the same end.[53]

Reuven Kimelman has emphasized the theme of divine sovereignty that wends its way through Jewish prayer. "What covenant was to biblical theology, the acceptance of divine sovereignty became for rabbinic theology."[54] Kimelman makes the point that the Shema liturgy, for example, is not descriptive as much as it is performative.[55] "The worshipper finds him/herself praying for, if not actually announcing, the future redemption."[56] Among the earliest rabbinic understandings of the central verse of the Shema, Deuteronomy 6:4, is that our God will only attain universal recognition in the messianic future.[57] The subsequent biblical/liturgical verses, the V'ahavta (Deuteronomy 6:5–9), then predicate that divine sovereignty on observing the mitzvot. Given the ontological force of language, the performance of the Shema liturgy may have been designed to augment divine power to bring ancient Jews closer to the world to come and divine sovereignty. But, even if the Shema's effect is only on the pray-er, its rhetoric is that of national redemption.

The Amidah itself, the central prayer of the liturgy, is modeled after the sacrificial cult.[58] There are petitionary blessings for material prosperity, national restoration, the return of the divine Presence, the rebuilding of Jerusalem and the Temple, culminating with the coronation of a Davidic savior. Again, Kimelman: "The distinctive contribution made by this liturgy to the idea of national redemption lies in the particular linguistic formulation, in the sequence of events, and in the uncompromising emphasis on divine involvement, all of which converge to make

---

53 Bereshit Rabbah, Va-yer'a, par. 56:2, to Genesis 22:5.
54 Kimelman, "Rabbinic Prayer," in Katz, *The Cambridge History of Judaism*, 609.
55 Reuven Kimelman, "The Shema and Its Rhetoric: The Case for the Shema' Being More than Creation, Revelation, and Redemption," *Jewish Thought and Philosophy* 2 (1992): 132.
56 Ibid.: 129.
57 Sifre Devarim, V'etchanan, par. 31, to Deuteronomy 6:4. Sifre Devarim, Ha'azinu, par. 313:10, to Deuteronomy 32:10, "admits" that prior to Abraham, God was not sovereign on earth.
58 Kimelman, "Rabbinic Prayer," in Katz, *The Cambridge History of Judaism*, 580–86.

the point that God alone is the redeemer as opposed to any human redeemer."[59]

The element of prayer specifically associated with divine coronation is the Kedusha. In fact, some versions of the Kedusha reflect daily divine coronation.[60] In Arthur Green's work on the divine crown, he brings together complementary passages illustrating that just as the smoke of the sacrifices rises to heaven, the prayers of Israel rise up and crown God.[61] "Depicting themselves as the daily offerers of God's crown places Israel in a position of great mythic power, one that makes them nearly equals in the economy of divine/human powers on which the world is based."[62]

Green then cites a midrash that allocates the three "holies" of the Kedushah (Isaiah 6:3 and Leviticus Rabbah 24:8). One "holy" crowns God and two crown Israel. "Here we have a rabbinic prototype for the sort of circular exchange of sacred energy between God and Israel that will stand at the very heart of later kabbalistic religion."[63] Supernal need might be the proximate cause for prayer and performance of the mitzvot, but there is a felicitous corollary *which crowns Israel*. Multiple times daily, divine sovereignty is announced or performed in a medium which stands in a continuum with biblical sacrifices, the purpose of which was to attract God's protective presence. The return of the divine presence is the prerequisite for Israel to crown her own Davidic king.

One final thought on the relationship between sacrifices and prayers: both are highly choreographed and constrained. The stage directions for the priests were very specific. When Nadav and Avihu violated the instructions, they were killed (Leviticus 10:1–2). According to the Talmud, if sacrifices were performed out of order, they were inconsequential (Sannhedrin 49b). Similarly, if one prays out of order, one has not fulfilled one's obligation (m. Brachot 2:2). One is also forbidden

---

59 Reuven Kimelman, "The Messiah of the Amidah: A Study in Comparative Messianism," *Journal of Biblical Literature* 116, no. 2 (1997): 313–24.

60 Green, *Keter*, 12.

61 Ibid., 33–43.

62 Ibid., 35.

63 Ibid., 36. Mekhilta de-Rabbi Yishmael, par. *Beshallach* 6, to Exodus 15:18 also features mutual coronation.

to recite a blessing unnecessarily or to modify an established blessing (Brachot 33a and t. Brachot 4:5).[64]

Unlike prayer which has three set times per day corresponding to the biblical sacrifices, blessings were designed to be verbal responses to punctuate specific experiences throughout the day. Rabbi Meir insisted we should say 100 blessings each day based on a verse with ninety-nine letters. The verse includes the exclamation *ma* meaning *what*. The medieval Talmudic commentary, Tosafot, suggests that if one adds the letter *aleph* to the middle of the word *ma*, one gets *meʾah*, which means 100, and also gives the verse 100 letters (Menachot 43b and Tosafot, op. loc.) This movement from language to halakhah is a wonderful example of an organic and coherent worldview where interrelationships reflect a unified creation.

Scholars of prayer emphatically reject the notion that blessings empower God. Although the first two (Hebrew) words of most blessings are "Blessed are you," scholars insist the phrase is *not* to be understood that as a result of those words or the ensuing action, God is "blessed" in the sense of being more powerful, more complete, or more in control than prior to the blessing.[65] Yet, as Rabinowitz reminds us, in the biblical world, words can bless. Moreover, we have a scene in the Talmud where God explicitly asks for a blessing (Brachot 7a).

A recent treatment of blessings which also rejects the notion that God can benefit in the theurgic sense through being blessed, nevertheless emphasizes that of all the verbs employed to praise, laud, and exalt God, only *b-r-ch* is used in circumstances of covenantal reciprocity whereby the blessings (*brachot*) are mutual.[66] God never praises, lauds, or exalts humans. But we bless and are blessed, and God blesses and is blessed.[67] Measure for measure. Once we disabuse ourselves of the Greek notion that the biblical and rabbinic God is omnipotent, immutable, impassible, and autarchic, then the conceptual obstacles to blessing God, in the

---

64 Langer, *To Worship God Properly*, 28–29.

65 Howard L. Apothaker, "On Blessing and Being Blessed in Early Rabbinic Liturgy," *Conservative Judaism* 60, nos. 1–2 (2007–2008): 102n55 and 114. See also Moshe Idel, *Kabbalah: New Perspectives* (New Haven: Yale University Press, 1988), 160–61.

66 Apothaker, "On Blessing": 100.

67 See Levenson's analysis of Psalm 134, *Creation and the Persistence*, 38. Note, too, that in Psalm 134 humans bless the Lord before God reciprocates.

plain sense of the word, vanish. As Janowitz concludes in her discussion of Merkavah mysticism, "to say the word *blessed* is to bless."[68] Once we recognize the worldview that performance of mitzvot strengthens God, why is it any more difficult to accept that we can also bless God, in an ontological sense, through the recitation of blessings? There is biblical precedent (as in Psalm 134), and it is the most natural reading.

Mitzvot, Repentance, and Redemption

Throughout rabbinic literature, the question is asked: What did our ancestors do to merit redemption from Egypt?[69] The assumption underlying the question is that the Israelites did *something* to merit redemption. Behind their persistent questioning is not historical curiosity, but existential angst. What can *we*, the rabbis of occupied Palestine née Judea, do to merit redemption? The answer, for many rabbis, could be reduced to one word: mitzvot.

As we saw above in our discussion of the Shema, the sequencing of the passages suggests a causal connection between accepting divine sovereignty, performance of the mitzvot, and redemption.[70] The Talmud offers a tradition that if Israel keeps the laws of Shabbat for two consecutive Shabbats, they would be redeemed immediately (Shabbat 118b). By observing mitzvot, God will redeem the Jews vis-à-vis the Romans just as God did with the Israelites vis-à-vis the Egyptians. When a scholar of rabbinic Judaism writes that "several times we hear that repentance and observance of the Law are the keys to bringing the messiah," we now must ask ourselves if this is a divine reward for being faithful covenantal partners (as in the Mosaic Torah), or if this reflects the consequence of God's enhanced ability to fulfill His covenantal responsibilities (as in the priestly Torah).[71]

68 Naomi Janowitz, *The Poetics of Ascent: Theories of Language in a Rabbinic Ascent Text* (Albany: State University of New York Press, 1989), 104.
69 Y. Ta'anit 1:63/4a; Mekhilta de-Rabbi Ishmael, Beshallach 6; Bereshit Rabbah, *Va-yer'a*, par. 56:2, to Genesis 22:5; and Pesikta de-Rav Kahana 11.
70 Reuven Kimelman, "The Rabbinic Theology of the Physical: Blessings, Body and Soul, Resurrection, and Covenant and Election" in Katz, *The Cambridge History of Judaism*, 968.
71 Schiffman, "Messianism and Apocalypticism in Rabbinic Texts," in Katz, *The Cambridge History of Judaism*, 1068. Michael Fishbane raises this same issue in

In an ancient midrash we find: "If you perform what is required of you, then I, too, will perform what is required of Me: 'The Lord will dislodge before you all these nations' (Deuteronomy 11:23)" (*Sifre Dvarim, Ekev, pis.* 41, to Deuteronomy 11:23). As Steven Fraade explains, "human action, as informed by Torah study, can trigger divine action."[72] Although Fraade is not suggesting a theurgic myth, it takes little imagination to see such a myth behind his description. Indeed, I am suggesting that there is much halakhah and aggadah (non-halakhic texts) that could easily be read both ways, "traditionally" or theurgically. Heschel's paradigm shift is thus more of an expansion. Statements like we have discussed might be read conventionally, that redemption is a reward for covenantal obedience (Mosaic Torah), or theurgically/ontologically, that redemption is the desired byproduct of strengthening God through mitzvot (a variation of the priestly Torah's understanding that our actions draw in God's protective presence).[73] As a result of Heschel's scholarship, a greater level of indeterminacy now enchants many rabbinic traditions. Thus, although the superstructure of rabbinic Judaism more closely resembles the Mosaic Torah than the priestly Torah, the same cannot be said with certainty about the infrastructure.

The rabbinic mitzvah par excellence is Torah study (*Talmud Torah*).[74] Already by the time of Ezra and Psalm 119, the Torah had taken on aspects of divinity. When the Second Temple was destroyed, God had no other address than the Torah. The divine's comforting presence continued to be felt through the study of Torah. The latent divinity within Torah was activated through its study: "When even one person sits and engages in Torah, the divine Presence therein dwells" (m. Avot 3:6). In the rabbinic mind, Talmud Torah is far more than the mere process in which scholars engage to determine a course of action in a specific setting. There is nothing *mere* about the process of Talmud Torah. The process is precisely

---

his *The Exegetical Imagination: On Jewish Thought and Theology* (Cambridge, MA: Harvard University Press, 1998), 79.

72 Steven D. Fraade, *From Tradition to Commentary: Torah and Its Interpretation in the Midrash Sifre to Deuteronomy* (Albany: State University of New York Press, 1991), 90–91.

73 Idel makes the distinction between these different types of theurgy in his *New Perspectives*, 173–99.

74 M. Peah 1:1 and Sifre, Deuteronomy 41.

what is essential. Menachem Fisch aptly describes rabbinic Judaism as a "Covenant of Learning."[75]

There are even accounts of rabbis for whom the process of Talmud Torah bursts beyond an intimation of the divine indwelling to visual revelations—but not of God. Shimon ben Azzai was drashing the Torah and a ring of fire flared around him (Shir Hashirim Rabbah 1:2).[76] In his analysis of this midrash, Daniel Boyarin writes: "Ben-Azzai . . . read in such a way that he reconstituted the original *experience* of revelation [as recorded in Deuteronomy 4:11 where fire engulfs Mt. Horev] . . . [Midrash] is re-citing the Written Torah, as in Ben-Azzai's wonderful experience, recreating a new event of revelation."[77]

As Heschel, and later Fishbane[78] have pointed out, the function of the Temple and the sacrifices have also been absorbed by the ritualistic study of Torah (Megilah 16b and Eruvin 63b). "When a sage sits and *derashes* to the congregation, Scripture accounts it to him as if he had sacrificed fat and blood upon the altar" (Avot d'Rabbi Natan [A] 4:18). "Whoever is occupied with the teaching of the sin offering is as if he were offering a sin offering; and whoever is occupied with the teaching of the guilt offering, is as if he were offering a guilt offering" (Menachot 110a). When one offers a sin or guilt offering one does not only attain atonement on a personal level—one prevents the departure of, or attracts the protective, divine Presence. After all, if one were solely concerned with personal atonement, Yom Kippur (or death) was believed to be effective for repentance (m. Yoma 8:8–9). Since personal atonement was available without sacrifices, is there more that these traditions about sacrifices promise?

---

75 Fisch, *Rational Rabbis*, part 2.

76 Hagigah 14b also contains such a legend.

77 Daniel Boyarin, *Intertextuality and the Meaning of Midrash* (Bloomington: Indiana University Press, 1994), 110.

78 Michael Fishbane, "Aspects of Transformation of Sacrifice," in *Sacrifice, Scripture, and Substitution: Readings in Ancient Judaism and Christianity*, ed. Ann W. Astell and Sandor Goodhart (Notre Dame: University of Notre Dame Press, 2011), 114–39.

Messianism

In the Passover Haggadah, we find that anyone who expatiates on the exodus from Egypt is praiseworthy.[79] The Haggadah is the annual rehearsal of redemption, and the script minimizes Moshe's personal role in the process. Scholars also see the Haggadah as an encoded challenge to the Roman occupation of Israel. Long ago, Judah Leib Maimon suggested that the RoMAns are the ARaMeans of the Haggadah who were trying to "destroy my father, Israel."[80] Thus, the Haggadah itself becomes a weapon to thwart their designs. The Haggadah, *the telling*, is not promoting messianic militarism, a point made by many, but divine sovereignty through unleashing the salvific power of the word.

Rabbi Akiva's redemptive posture is on full display in his blessing for the second cup of wine at the seder: "[As You redeemed our ancestors in Egypt] so, too, Lord, our God and God of our ancestors, bring us to future holidays and festivals in peace, happy in the building of Your city and joyous in Your worship. May we eat there from the different sacrifices, the blood from which will reach the wall of Your altar and please You." As we have seen, the power of the word to precipitate changes in the world is found throughout rabbinic literature. Rabbi Akiva's redemptive posture is not militaristic: it is part and parcel of a theurgic restoration myth. God *will* redeem the Jews just as God *did* redeem the Israelites. According to the Talmud, Rabbi Akiva is arrested for teaching Torah in public and executed as he performs the Shema (Brachot 61b).[81] Torah and prayer are his weapons. If a *derasha* can reactivate revelation, why not redemption?

Gershom Scholem sorts rabbinic Judaism into three forces: conservative/halakhic, restorative vis-à-vis Jewish sovereignty, and utopian. Scholem's claim is that the conservative forces of halakhah "have no part

---

79 Although there is no evidence that this phrase is rabbinic, it does cohere with the rabbinic claim that associates lengthening one's prayer with efficacy (Brachot 32b).

80 Judah Leib Maimon, *Yovel ha-Mizrahi: kovets torani, mada'i, sifruti le-yovel ha-hamishim* (Jerusalem: Irgun Ezra-Nehemyah be-tokh histadrut ha-Mizrahi be-siyua Mosad ha-Rav Kuk, 1952), 209–16 and Midrash Tanaim on Deuteronomy 26:5.

81 Rabbi Akiva's purported support of Bar Kochva as a messiah is a later interpolation into the Talmud Yerushalmi. See Cherry, "The Camouflaged *Ta'am*": 42 and Peter Schäfer, "R. Aqiva and Bar Kokhba," in *Approaches to Ancient Judaism*, vol. 2, ed. William Scott Green (Ann Arbor: Scholars Press, 1980), 113–130.

in the development of messianism." Rather, messianism is the collision of restorative and utopian thinking.[82] Furthermore, according to Scholem, messianism is neither developmental nor progressive. "Classical Jewish tradition is fond of emphasizing the catastrophic strain in redemption."[83] My claim is that there is a neglected strain of rabbinic thought which neutralizes the catastrophic element in messianism precisely by combining the conservative/halakhic forces with the restorative.

The sound and fury of catastrophic, apocalyptic messianism, which we find *in abundance* in the late Second Temple period, gives way in the Tannaitic material to what Schiffman has described as a "sort of quietism . . . punctuated primarily by restorative, naturalistic, messianic tendencies."[84] By quietism, Schiffman means the lack of any discernible encouragement of a military messianism, the likes of which had met with catastrophic results in the generations prior to the emergence of the Tannaitic works of Mishnah, Tosefta, and midrash halakhah.[85]

Numerous scholars have pointed out the Mishnah's seeming lack of interest in the messiah. One scholar accounts for the lull not only because of the recent messianic debacles, but also because the Mishnah is primarily concerned with halakhah.[86] My contention is that the very focus of the Mishnah with halakhah may be intrinsically, and intensely, messianic—not in the sense of a military messiah like Bar Kochva, but redemptive in the sense of Moses in Egypt. David Kraemer suggests that "the Mishnah represents the early rabbinic vision of a restored, Torah-perfected, 'messianic' world." Yet, he footnotes his quotation of *messianic* to qualify and dilute its meaning.[87] With an ontological halakhah, *messianic*, in the sense of redemptive, should be emphasized not qualified.

The climactic finale of Mishnah Sotah (9:15) offers a causative sequence of virtuous personality traits stemming from the eager performance of the mitzvot and culminating in the return of the holy spirit,

82 Gershom Scholem, *The Messianic Idea in Judaism and Other Essays on Jewish Spirituality* (New York: Schocken Books, 1971), 3.
83 Ibid., 38.
84 Schiffman, "Messianism and Apocalypticism," in Katz, *The Cambridge History of Judaism*, 1062.
85 Ibid., 1060–61.
86 Robert Goldenberg, "The Destruction of the Jerusalem Temple: its Meaning and Its Consequences," in Katz, *The Cambridge History of Judaism*, 201.
87 David Kraemer, "The Mishnah," in Katz, *The Cambridge History of Judaism*, 313.

the arrival of Elijah the prophet, and the resurrection of the dead. Jacob Neusner uses this mishnah, in particular, to advance his theory that in the Mishnah salvation arises by sanctification through the mizvot.[88] Neusner has been consistent over the years in his assertion that the rationale for the mitzvot within the Mishnah is the coming of the messiah. By virtue of keeping the laws explicated in the Mishnah, the Jews help bring the messiah. Neusner claimed that through the study of Torah, the observance of mitzvot, and the performance of good deeds, each Jew would be transformed into a rabbi, "hence into a saint."

> When all Jews had become rabbis, they then would no longer lie within the power of history. The Messiah would come. So redemption depended on the "rabbinization" of all Israel, that is, upon the attainment by all Jewry of a full and complete embodiment of revelation or Torah, thus achieving a perfect replica of heaven. When Israel on earth became such a replica, it would be able, as a righteous, holy, saintly community, to exercise the supernatural power of Torah, just as some rabbis were already doing. With access to the consequent theurgical capacities, redemption would naturally follow.[89]

My friendly amendment to Neusner's claim involves his understanding of theurgy and history. Given Heschel's contribution that for some rabbis the performance of mitzvot strengthens God, it is not that Jews will rise *above* history, it is that God will become sovereign *in* history, ushering in messianic times. The refrain which punctuates mishnah Sotah 9:15 three times is: "We have no one to rely upon other than our Father in heaven."[90] God will, through our eager performance of mitzvot, become King. Although the ideas of human messianism and divine sovereignty may seem to be in tension, "a heavy emphasis on God's own action was fully compatible with recognition of the activity of a king or messiah."[91] Indeed, the biblical God is sometimes described as the God

88 Jacob Neusner, "Mishnah and Messiah," in *Judaisms and their Messiahs at the Turn of the Christian Century*, ed. Jacob Neusner, William S. Green, and Ernest Frerichs (New York: Cambridge University Press, 1987), 265–82.
89 Jacob Neusner, *There We Sat Down: Talmudic Judaism in the Making* (Brooklyn: Ktav Publishing, 1982), 78–79.
90 See Isaiah 10:20.
91 Horbury, *Jewish Messianism*, 83.

of Hosts, which is an English euphemism for God as the general of an army of angels.[92] In the Psalms, we have an account of God building His temple (Psalm 78:69-70). If God is chief of staff who also built the First Temple, along with King David's son, then regaining political sovereignty and rebuilding the Third Temple is merely a recycling of those motifs.

Rabbi Abbahu said: "Every salvation that comes to Israel, belongs [also] to the holy One, blessed be He, as it says, 'I am with him in distress . . . and show him *My* salvation' (Psalm 91:15-16)" (Tanhuma [Buber], Acharei Mot, 18). Rabbi Abbahu transforms the salvation wrought *by* God to the salvation *of* God. The covenant between God and the Jewish people is mutual; the question is, is it reciprocal? God has needs, and some rabbis are not shy about acknowledging that. The theurgic myth of divine sovereignty, in which Torah-observing Jews can augment or enhance divine power, has a redemptive coda. "[God said:] My Torah is in your hands and the time of redemption is in My hands. Each of us needs the other. If you need Me to bring the redemption, I need you to observe My Torah and bring about sooner the rebuilding of my House and of Jerusalem" (Psikta Rabbati 31:5 to Psalm 137:5).

The Rabbinic Survival Strategy: Emphasize Deed Over Creed

This chapter has emphasized the legacy of the priestly religion within rabbinic religiosity. I specifically used those terms because the priests had a religion based on a particular theology and archaic ontology. Rabbinic religiosity, however, was predicated not on theology, but on the power of halakhah. Particularly in the Mishnah, there seems to have been a conscious editorial effort to downplay issues of theology and the reasons for the commandments while promoting the "overlapping consensus" on the importance of the fulfillment of the mitzvot.[93] A recent treatment draws a similar conclusion: "a detailed study of the entire Mishnah shows that ostensibly doctrinal matters are consistently addressed in the language

---

92 See 2 Samuel 5:22-25, Isaiah 13:1-22, and Patrick D. Miller, Jr., "Cosmology and World Order in the Old Testament: The Divine Council as Cosmic-Political Symbol," in *Horizons in Biblical Theology* (Leiden: Brill, 1987), 422-44, esp. 433.

93 Richard Claman uses this term, borrowed from John Rawls, in "Mishnah as the Model for a New Overlapping Consensus," *Conservative Judaism* 63, no. 2 (2011): 49-77.

of praxis."[94] Although I have been emphasizing the theurgic, redemptive tradition in rabbinic thought, there were competing philosophies and theologies within rabbinic circles. The overlapping consensus was on the value of the mitzvot and their consequences in the post-Temple world— regardless of their rationale.

For those Jews who neared despair in the aftermath of the Temple's destruction, the rabbis ensured that there was no shortage of equivalents for the sacrifices irrespective of their perceived function.

- Fasting is like offering your fat and blood on the altar (Brachot 17a).
- Prayer *is* worship/service of the heart (Sifrei Devarim, *'Ekev, pis.* 41, to Deuteronomy 11:13).[95]
- Talmud Torah is greater than building the Temple (Megilah 16b).
- One who repents is considered as if he went up to Jerusalem, built the Temple and the altar, and made *all* the sacrifices in the Torah (Vayikra Rabbah, *Tzav, par.* 7:2, to Leviticus 6:2)!

For Rabbi Yonatan, teshuvah brings redemption near (Yoma 86b). When rabbinic literature speaks of teshuvah, it is no longer a reorientation toward or return to God, as it is in the Bible, but a return to God's ways as expressed through rabbinic halakhah (Deuteronomy 4:30 vs. m. Yoma 9:7). Teshuvah is, ultimately, directed toward doing God's will, and we have a rich vein of theurgic myth that explicitly reveals the consequence.[96] "Whenever Israel acts according to God's will, they add

---

94 David M. Grossberg, "Orthopraxy in Tannaitic Literature," *Journal for the Study of Judaism* 41, no. 4/5 (2010): 519.

95 "Prayer is an essential component of authentic penitence that will bring an end to the exile." Marc J. Boda, "Confession as Theological Expression: Ideological Origins of Penitential Prayer," in *Seeking the Favor of God: The Origins of Penitential Prayer in Second Temple Judaism*, vol. 1, ed. Marc J. Boda, Daniel K. Falk, and Rodney A. Werline (Atlanta: Society of Biblical Literature, 2006), 27. See also Rodney Alan Werline, *Penitential Prayer in Second Temple Judaism: The Development of a Religious Institution* (Atlanta: Scholars Press, 1998), 11–64, esp. 25n50.

96 Yohanan Silman, too, deals with repentance in "The Source of the Validity of Halakhic Instructions: A Meta-Halakhic Inquiry," in *New Studies in the Philosophy of Halakhah* [Hebrew], ed. Avraham Ravitzky and Avinoam Rosenak (Jerusalem: Magnes, 2008), 16–24.

strength to the Power (*g'vurah*)" (*Pesikta de-Rav Kahana, Slichot, pis.* 25:1, to Deuteronomy 32:18 and Psalm 60:14). Yet, we also have the indeterminate: "The Land of Canaan is yours if you act according to God's will; if not, you will be exiled from it" (Sifrei Devarim, *'Ekev, pis.* 38, to Deuteronomy 11:1). Do we receive the Land of Canaan as a reward for our obedience or as a byproduct of enhancing God's strength? In the theurgic reading, God's strength must be augmented in order for Him to fulfill His covenantal obligations. Heschel reminded us that God cannot do it alone. The theurgic myth of redemption *explains* what it is that God cannot do: attain sovereignty. And without divine sovereignty, God is incapable of restoring political sovereignty to the Jews in the Land of Israel. Given the myth of an ontological halakhic, we should not assume that the perceivable shift toward halakhic nominalism among the rabbis, as in kashrut and the loosening of oaths, applies in cases where the underlying legal infrastructure is indeterminate.

In the aftermath of the Temple's destruction, a series of failed revolts, and the land's desolation, the rabbis sought both an explanation of their plight and a restoration program that would not provoke the Romans. Their strategy was to create a Torah-rooted religion in which their national aspirations were sublimated into what a contemporary psychologist might deem "mitzvah-mania"—excessive enthusiasm for the performance of mitzvot. Even while the restoration remained unrealized, the Jews survived in their native habitat of Torah by keeping themselves separate from gentile culture (Brachot 61b). In the wake of catastrophe, there was no despair; only accommodation to what was hoped would be a very brief caesura in the potent Presence in and divine sovereignty over the Land of Israel (Baba Metzia 21b-22b and m. Tamid 4:3).[97]

Contemporary Uses of Rabbinic Religiosity

Rabbi Ishmael advised extreme caution to Torah scribes since one minor error could destroy the world—even given rabbinic hyperbole, the faithful replication of Torah, both Written and Oral, was taken very seriously.

---

97 See also Paul Mandel, "The Loss of Center: Changing Attitudes towards the Temple in Aggadic Literature," *Harvard Theological Review* 99, no. 1 (2006): 17-35, and Adiel Schremer, *Brothers Estranged: Heresy, Christianity and Jewish Identity in Late Antiquity* (New York: Oxford University Press, 2010), chapter one.

As Gruenwald has advised us: "Nobody can claim with absolute certainty that what to a modern reader of a text looks as ordinary or metaphorical forms of expression, which allegedly relate to fictional experiences and realities, were also treated as such by the ancient readers. The opposite could well be the truth."[98] The pervasiveness of the idea that the Torah and her observance preserve the world, wedded to an ontological halakhah which incontrovertibly exists during the rabbinic period, suggest to me that such a worldview is more than metaphor. Statements such as Rabbi Ishmael's could reflect a magical reality, an archaic ontology, which has been muffled by subsequent rabbis and is relatively unknown outside the academic and ultra-Orthodox worlds. Most modern Jews know of and prefer the Maimonidean interpretations of rabbinic texts which rely on metaphor. But when the Mishnah, for example, makes the distinction between a charlatan and a sorcerer, who is actually able to manipulate reality, the curtain is lifted on their archaic ontology (m. Sannhedrin 7:11).[99]

I do not believe, as Rabbi Ishmael might have, that the world will be destroyed as a result of a scribal error in the Torah. I don't believe it for two reasons: the first is that there have been scribal errors; the second, and more significant, is that I have a different worldview. Ritual law has *no* ontological consequences in my worldview. None. A ritual framework can support an ethics that does have ontological and theological force, but the details of those rituals are relatively inconsequential. As Maimonides, whom we will formally meet in the next chapter, will say in a related context, "All those who occupy themselves with finding causes for something of these particulars are stricken with a prolonged madness" (*Guide*, 3:26, 509).

98 Ithamar Gruenwald, "Reflections on the Nature and Origins of Jewish Mysticism," in *Gershom Scholem's Major Trends in Jewish Mysticism 50 Years After*, ed. Peter Schafer and Joseph Dan (Tubingen: Mohr Siebeck, 1993), 47.

99 Moshe Idel sketches the attempts at distinguishing magic and mysticism in "On Judaism, Jewish Mysticism and Magic," in *Envisioning Magic*, ed. Peter Schafer and Hans G. Kippenberg (Leiden: Brill, 1997), 195–214. Idel points to the magical nature of blessings and mitzvot (ibid., 203). See also the fascinating article about the differences between the *Bavli* and *Yerushalmi* on magic in Joshua Levinson, "Enchanting Rabbis: Contest Narratives between Rabbis and Magicians in Late Antiquity," *Jewish Quarterly Review* 100, no. 1 (2010): 54–94. Since there were rabbis comfortable using magic against *minim* as Levinson showed (y. Sannhedrin 7:19 [25d]), why not theurgy against the Romans?

Ritual mitzvot, as many rabbis recognized, were designed in part to separate Jews from non-Jews. Notice that these ritual mitzvot have their source in the priestly Torah whose operating principle is that of separation. For the vast majority of American Jewry, such a principle is untenable. Kashrut, for example, should not be about keeping Jews and gentiles from breaking bread together. Neither should kashrut be about only a list of proper ingredients or the final moment of an animal's life. Kashrut, in our American context, should be about conscious consumption, an element of traditional kashrut that merits promotion in our current environment. Who is involved in the food production chain, and how are they being treated? How are the animals being raised?[100] What is the impact on the health of individuals and the health of our planet? The bogeyman of intermarriage is not lurking in non-kosher restaurants. On the contrary, promoting conscious consumption in our multiethnic society will cause gentiles, and uninformed Jews, to say, "What a wise and understanding people is this great nation" (Deuteronomy 4:6)! In this case, the Mosaic Torah and its heirs in the rabbinic period, can be our teachers: "'You shall love the Lord, your God,' [Deuteronomy 6:5] means that through you, [your actions, and your values], God's name will become beloved" (Yoma 86a).

As we saw with the one-sixtieth rule, the rabbis were not averse to shifting from an ontological halakhah to a nominal halakhah. That was the trend. Thus, even a piece of pork can be called "nullified" when it is overwhelmed by sixty times the amount of permitted food. Yet, in many cases of personal status, the rabbis maintained an ontological understanding of language and identities which has had devastating consequences. A wife whose husband refuses to issue a *get*, a writ of divorce, is functionally "anchored" to that man until he says, "Write a *get*." The recalcitrant husband can, according to rabbinic tradition, be physically abused until he says those words, and once he says those words, everyone can put on headphones so they do not hear him screaming to recant his coerced statement (Gittin 34a)! Such is the power of language (and headphones).

The law of not wearing wool and linen together (*shaatnez*) is rooted in the same priestly Torah, but it does not ruin lives. Hence, I am very particular about the materials in my clothing. Preventing a woman from receiving a divorce because of an archaic ontology, however, approaches the demonic.[101] If ancient rabbis could have had recalcitrant husbands beaten, contemporary rabbis can have a *get* written under the rabbinic principle that we can benefit a person without their knowledge (m. Gittin 1:6). We assume that Jews want to do the right thing, including bitter husbands, even when their passions temporarily blind them from recognizing it (Maimonides, h. Gerushin 2:20).

Doing the right thing, however, is no guarantee of external reward. Although the Mosaic Torah's reward and punishment scheme remains on the books for purposes of public consumption and liturgical recitation, "we were exiled from our land for our sins," the rabbinic mind is far more complicated. In the rabbis' own ironic manner, they create a scene in which Moshe time travels to the world of the rabbis and is flabbergasted to witness the disconnect between one's deeds and one's rewards (Menachot 29b). We moderns are not surprised. Nor do we tend to look to the afterlife for justice to prevail. Like the Torah, we modern Jews focus our efforts on this world—and, therein, lies the greatest single barrier to rabbinic religiosity.

Like the Hebrew Bible, the goal of rabbinic religiosity is the national redemption of the Jews in the Land of Israel. Whether that goal is attained as a reward or as a byproduct, the overlapping consensus between the Mosaic and priestly Torahs is that prayer, Torah, and teshuvah will lead to the Jews being sovereign in their own land. The overwhelming majority of Western Jews, over 100 years ago, acknowledged that Judaism was not dependent on political Zionism. Rabbinic religiosity may be theoretically coherent with some Zionist agendas, but not for Diaspora Jews living in a world where Israel is again a living reality.

All Jews should support the existence of a thriving, democratic Jewish state where Judaism can find its fullest national expression, but Zionism is not reason enough to be or stay Jewish. Regardless of the place

101 Shai A. Wozner, "Ontological and Naturalist Thought in Talmudic Law and in Lithuanian Yeshivot," *Diné Israel* 25 (2008): 90–91 [Hebrew] and Yair Lorberbaum, "Halakhic Realism: Conceptual, Phenomenological and Methodological Remarks," *Diné Israel* 30 (2015): 75–77.

that Israel holds for contemporary American Jews, one's religiosity is not primarily motivated by a desire to secure the Jewish national homeland. We must admit that the aim of rabbinic religiosity is both anachronistic and too parochial. In other words, it is incoherent with our values. The land we hope to live long upon is no longer the Jewish sliver on the eastern Mediterranean coast, but the big, blueish planet we call home.[102] Nevertheless, many of the methods, insights, and laws of rabbinic religiosity continue to be incredibly powerful for a contemporary, coherent Judaism. They will be the focus of our discussion on a contemporary philosophy of halakhah.

The rabbinic survival strategy of mitzvah-mania has outlived its usefulness. "Since the day the Temple was destroyed, the Holy One, blessed be He, has in this world nothing other than the four cubits of halakhah" (Brachot 8a). Like the Jews, God was caged in exile.[103] The fullness of the whole world was no longer His glory. Jews may see Jewish national redemption as necessary for redemption writ large, but it is far from sufficient. Yet, rabbinic religiosity has so much to offer the process of divine redemption. Indeed, the whole concept of "religiosity" is extremely important for American Jews. The way I am using the term signifies different theologies or metaphysics that form the subterranean foundation or infrastructure for religious practice. Regardless of your metaphysics, you may choose to enter or stay in this structure called Judaism. Atheists are welcome, too. That is the whole point of religiosity—it *subsumes* theology. What keeps you in the structure has to do with your actions (deeds), not the belief system that forms the foundation (creed).

I began this chapter with a nod to engaged fallibilistic pluralism. The anthological style of much midrash and the Talmud reflects a comfort with multiple voices. The ideology of some rabbis explicitly demands an accommodation to multiple, conflicting views: "Make yourself a heart of many rooms and bring into it the words of the House of Shammai and the words of the House of Hillel, the words of those who declare unclean and the words of those who declare clean" (t. Sotah 7:12). Shammai would never have uttered such a statement, and that is exactly why we

---

102 See Bradley Shavit Artson, "Our Covenant with Stones: A Jewish Ecology of Earth," *Conservative Judaism* 44 (1991–1992): 25–35.
103 Heschel, *Heavenly Torah*, 105–21.

incline toward the House of Hillel. The rabbis were pioneers of engaged fallibilistic pluralism.

There are many rooms in this structure we call Judaism. Some rooms face outside, and others are deep in the interior. One of those outside-facing rooms, with a *required* window, is for prayer (Brachot 31a). (In other words, prayer must be related to what is happening in the world.) At the same time, one must face toward the place of the ancient Temple in Jerusalem, the historical face of intimacy between God and the Jewish people (m. Brachot 4:5 and 6). In our metaphorical palace of Judaism, the throne room is in the center. To enter the palace, you need to go through one of the external rooms. Those are rooms of Talmud Torah, halakhah, deeds of lovingkindness, Israel, and prayer. And there are internal, interior spaces, as well.

Some people enter the palace with hopes of getting to the center, and others have no such intention. It is relatively easy to imagine an atheist entering the room of Talmud Torah or environmental halakhah or deeds of lovingkindness, but would an atheist enter the room of prayer? The Talmud actually acknowledges three different reasons to be in the prayer room. One reason is to give God glory and strength; another is to strengthen one's relationship with God; but the third is to muster the inner strength to stand upright and move forward in a world that sometimes feels crushing and disorienting (Brachot 28b). That last reason could certainly work for an atheist, and she would then be in a community with other people who value the deeds practiced by those in the other exterior rooms.

Those exterior rooms offer what Max Kadushin called "normal mysticism." It is a relationship with God, much like in the Mosaic Torah, by walking in God's ways. It is, in other words, halakhic Judaism. The mystics of the period, whose writings have been preserved in the Heikhalot and Merkava texts, found this halakhically mediated, "normal mysticism" too tepid for their temperaments. They wanted to storm the King's chamber. Within Talmudic religion, however, Talmud Torah was the recommended route to enter the inner chamber. But unlike the detailed prescriptions for the mystical initiate, engaging in Talmud Torah is unscripted and idiosyncratic. As if to underscore the pluralism of individuals' theological perceptions and devalue any single theological vision or mental icon, the rabbis frequently described the revelation at Sinai as tailored to the predispositions and capacities of each individual (Pesiqta de-Rav Kahana 12:25). God reveals Godself differently to each of us. When the Shechinah dwells among those engaged in Talmud Torah, the divine presence will not only appear differently for each person, but it will change for the same person at different points in her own lifetime.

We have the same rooms in our palace as they did 2,000 years ago, but our furniture has changed. The content of today's halakhah cannot and should not be that of the rabbis. It is hard to imagine how one could express creativity and innovation in prayer when the template of prayer is understood to be fixed like the sacrifices (Brachot 29b). Even for those who believe prayer produces consequences beyond the pray-er, it beggars the imagination that such consequences are predicated on specific oral formulations, a claim of the medieval German Pietists whom we will meet in the next chapter.

Some mystics from the rabbinic period tried to reach the throne room through the recitation of different holy names. There is precedent in the Mosaic Torah to invoke God's name to invite God's presence. But *abra k'dabra* belongs to a premodern world with an archaic ontology. Speech *can* change our consciousness and shift our perceptions. In that sense, words can create new realities, because our reality is at least partially determined by our consciousness. But the notion that certain words or formulas will necessarily unlock and open the interior doors of perception for all who utter them is, I believe, utter nonsense.

So, how might one for whom normal mysticism is insufficient attempt to penetrate the inner chamber? I do think liturgical flexibility is helpful. Experimenting with different metaphors for God is also helpful. Although thinking about God as king might resonate for some on Yom Kippur, the sovereignty metaphor does not usually speak to us post-monarchical Jews. My teacher, Arthur Green, tries to rehabilitate the image of our patriarchs digging wells deep into the earth to find flowing water. We, too, dig deep into our inner selves to experience the sublime.

Recall that Rabbi Meir said we should recite one hundred blessings each day based on the following verse: "And now, O Israel, what [*mah*] does the Lord your God demand of you? Only this: to revere the Lord your God, to walk in all His paths, to love Him, and to serve the Lord your God with all your heart and soul" (Deuteronomy 10:12). Rabbi Meir drashed the first half of the verse as, "And now, O Israel, the Lord, your God demands of you: *mah*." Rabbi Meir focused on *mah* and deciphered the divine code he assumed was embedded within. Since there are ninety-nine Hebrew letters in this verse, one shy of a round number, Rabbi Meir added the letter aleph to the middle of *mah*. In doing so, he arrived at 100 letters *and* the word *me'ah* which means 100. Since the last half of the verse, "serving the Lord your God with all your heart," was understood by the rabbis to mean prayer (Mekhilta d'Rabbi Shimon bar Yochai 23:25), Rabbi Meir made the connection: the Lord demands 100 blessings daily. Rabbinic religiosity deploys halakhah to consecrate the quotidian.

Our next chapter deals with changes to rabbinic religiosity in the Middle Ages. One medieval mystic, Joseph ibn Gikatilla, cites Rabbi Meir's *derash* and links it to the 100 sockets of the portable Tabernacle's frame.[104] In other words, the expression of blessings should build a consciousness of God's indwelling presence, akin to the function of the Tabernacle, throughout the day, every day. Another medieval tradition holds that there were one hundred Jews dying daily until King David established the standard of saying 100 blessings per day. In this tradition, blessings ward off death, and one is in mortal danger by saying fewer than the prescribed number.[105] And yet another tradition, this time from a medieval philosopher, says that 100 is just a rough estimate, and there is no obligation to reach precisely one hundred blessings each day.[106] They all agree, more or less, that we should say 100 blessing a day. But the rationale for the halakhah—that's up to you. The story of medieval Judaisms is, in large part, the reclamation of the priestly Torah for the mystics and the Mosaic Torah for the philosophers. But each of those Torahs will have percolated through rabbinic religiosity.

---

104 Gikatilla, *Gates of Light*, 17–18. My thanks to Reuven Kimelman for this reference.
105 David Segal, *Turei Zahav*, Orach Hayim 46:3.
106 Abraham ibn Ezra, *Yesod Morah*, Second Gate.

Chapter 4

The Medieval Centrifuge

The Jewish Middle Ages, which for our purposes encompasses the millennium between the canonization of the Babylonian Talmud (seventh century) and Spinoza's cannonball at the divine authorship of the Torah (seventeenth century), acted as a centrifuge for rabbinic religiosity. Nearly all of the literary genres to crystallize in the Middle Ages had precursors in the rabbinic era, but they were interwoven into the fabric of rabbinic literature, Talmud and midrash, rather than isolated in discrete texts. For the first time in the Middle Ages, we have documents written by a single thinker as opposed to anthologies and redactions. Although there is a clear tendency for mysticism to operate with a priestly metaphysics and for philosophy to rely on the Mosaic ontology, medieval Jews inherited rabbinic versions of those biblical worldviews. This chapter's challenge is to see how rabbinic religiosity, with its overlapping consensus on mitzvah-mania, became "genrefied." If the mitzvot remain the visible superstructure, the Middle Ages offers a variety of invisible infrastructures that provide contrasting religious and theological rationales for the mitzvot. The medieval centrifuge spins apart what may justifiably be described as medieval Judaisms.

Halakhah

We begin with halakhah precisely because of its centrality to rabbinic religiosity. Although the third book of *Coherent Judaism* will be dedicated to the philosophy of halakhah, this section will provide a skeletal survey of the various subgenres devoted to halakhah in the Middle Ages. Medieval halakhah is, obviously, an outgrowth of the Talmud.

Surprising though it may be, however, in the centuries after the sealing of the Talmud there was controversy over what the Talmud actually was. In North Africa and Spain, the Talmud was the repository of *authoritative Jewish law*. In Babylonia (the home of the Babylonian Talmud), on the other hand, the Talmud was the repository of *authentic Jewish legal reasoning*.

The leadership of Babylonian Jewry would often receive questions of Jewish law from the four corners of the Jewish world. Responsa literature captures how individual rabbis drew from the legal tradition and applied those traditions to the unfolding legal challenges of a geographically dispersed Jewry. According to a recent study by Talya Fishman, for the Babylonian leaders, the geonim, "[legal] authority did not reside in the texts of tradition, but only in its living tradents."[1] In other words, just because a law seems to have been settled in the Talmud, which rarely happens in any case, the law is not binding unless a legal authority has acknowledged that such a law is in force. The geonim of the Babylonian academies had greater deference toward the traditions of the Mishnah than those of the Gemara, but practical halakhah still required the corroboration of a living sage. When Sherirah Gaon (tenth century) discovered that rabbinic students in Tunisia were deriving law exclusively from the Talmud, he was sharply dismissive of their approach.[2]

At the same time as the responsa literature grew, scholars also penned Talmudic commentaries, Talmudic digests, and inventories of the 613 mitzvot. The Talmud records a tradition that there were 613 mitzvot given to Moshe at Sinai. Rabbi Simlai breaks them down into 248 imperatives for each of the 248 parts of the body and 365 prohibitions corresponding to the days of the solar year (Makkot 23b). Without justifying Rabbi Simlai's knowledge of anatomy, I understand him to be saying that each of us should be walking Torahs, or if you will, incarnations of Torah/God's will, all the time. But, beginning with Saadia Gaon in tenth-century Baghdad, mitzvah hunters spilled much ink on counting and defending their choices of the 613.

Also in the geonic period, halakhic codes began appearing, though not without opposition. The most important codes influenced the content

---

1   Talya Fishman, *Becoming the People of the Talmud: Oral Torah as Written Tradition in Medieval Jewish Culture* (Philadelphia: University of Pennsylvania Press, 2011), 36.
2   Ibid., 47.

and structure of the sixteenth-century Shulchan Arukh by Joseph Caro with interspersed annotations by Moshe Isserles. In most instances, Caro relied on three earlier sources and when two out of three agreed on a certain law, that position became codified. The three authoritative sources for Caro were Rabbi Yitzhak Alfasi (RIF, 1013–1103) of Algeria and Andalusia, Rabbi Moshe ben Maimon or Moshe Maimonides (RaMBaM, 1138–1204) of Andalusia and Cairo, and Rabbeynu Asher ben Yehiel (RoSH, c.1250–1327) of Cologne and Toledo. The format of Caro's code was based on the code of Rabbi Yakov ben Asher (1269–1343, Cologne and Toledo), the son of the RoSH.

The Tosafot were Talmudic scholars in Ashkenaz during the twelfth and early thirteenth centuries beginning with the grandsons of the great Torah and Talmudic commentator, Rabbi Shlomo ben Yitzhak (RaSHI, 1040–1105). According to Haim Soloveitchik, the First Crusade of 1096 marks a transition between the commentary work of RaSHI, explaining the meaning of the Talmudic text on the individual page, and the dialectical work of the Tosafot in which they bring together passages from different parts of the Talmud to resolve seeming inconsistencies.[3] When Rabbeynu Asher and his son Rabbi Yakov abandoned an increasingly inhospitable Germany, the Tosafot period came to an end.

Opposition to this new style of dialectical study was voiced by the *Hasidei Ashkenaz* (German Pietists), who both championed more traditional learning and worried about the spiritual consequences of caviling over legal minutiae.[4] The Tosafot prevailed. In the process, two related but distinct phenomena coalesced around the study of Talmud, both pernicious. The first is that some of the Tosafot argued that the study of Talmud should not only be the primary focus of the Jewish curriculum, it should be the exclusive focus. One of the great Tosafot, Rabbeynu Tam (1100–1171), went so far as to suggest that the Talmudic requirement to study the five books of Moses could be fulfilled through the study of Talmud since individual biblical verses are cited therein.[5]

---

3   Haym Soloveitchik, "Catastrophe and Halakhic Creativity: Ashkenaz: 1096, 1242, 1306 and 1298," *Jewish History* 12, no. 1 (1998): 79.

4   Fishman, *Becoming the People*, 182–217.

5   Ephraim Kanarfogel, *Intellectual History and Rabbinic Culture* (Detroit: Wayne State University Press, 2013), 14.

The second negative consequence involves not curriculum but juris-prudence. Although we saw a tendency among those in North Africa and Spain to adjudicate halakhah on the basis of the Talmud alone, by the end of the Tosafot period, this style of legislation had won wide currency. What the geonim had dismissed as juvenile and invalid was quickly becoming the norm throughout the Jewish world.

> The tosafist enterprise transformed the Talmudic text from a collection of legal and nonlegal traditions into a prescriptive blueprint for Jewish life. Within a matter of generations, it was hard for northern European Jews to imagine that the Talmud had ever been regarded as anything but the definitive reference to be consulted when deciding applied Jewish law. Indeed, by the thirteenth century, northern European Jewish scholars (like earlier rabbis of Sefarad [Spain] and Provence) expressed astonishment that Babylonian geonim could have knowingly deviated from Talmudic teachings.[6]

The mitzvah-mania of rabbinic religiosity evolved into the "Talmudocentrism" of medieval Judaism.[7] Halakhists quickly under-stood that such fealty to Talmudic decisions, as opposed to its logic or principles, would strait jacket the development of Jewish law. Beginning in the fourteenth century, Ashkenazi authorities imbued new meaning to the Talmudic principle, *the law is like the most recent ruling*, and applied it to post-Talmudic decisions. Ultimately, by the fifteenth century, this rule was applied to contemporary courts.[8] Although the principle that the law accords with the decisions of the latest authorities became the legal norm, even after the appearance of the Shulchan Arukh, Rabbi Shlomo Luria (1510–1574) wrote a reactionary code based on "Talmudic sources as he understood them. . . . [He did not] recognize any inherent authority in the views of the post-Talmudic scholars."[9]

6   Fishman, *Becoming the People*, 147–48.
7   "Talmudocentrism" was coined by Isadore Twersky. See ibid., 310n19.
8   Israel Ta-Shma, *Creativity and Tradition: Studies in Medieval Rabbinic Scholarship, Literature and Thought* (Cambridge, MA: Harvard University Press, 2007), 163.
9   Lawrence Kaplan, "Rabbi Mordekhai Jaffee and the Evolution of Jewish Culture in Poland in the Sixteenth Century," in *Jewish Thought in the Sixteenth Century*, ed. Bernard Dov Cooperman (Cambridge, MA: Harvard University Press, 1983), 269.

Biblical Exegesis

A resurgence of interest in the Torah, in part for polemical purposes, contributed to some remarkable shifts in Jewish religiosity. At the turn of the millennium, roughly ninety percent of all Jews lived in the Islamic world. (By way of contrast, in contemporary North America, about ninety percent of Jews trace their ancestry to the Ashkenazi areas of Christian Europe.) While it is true that Islam spread beyond the lands of Arabia, the Arabic language had pride of place and was the intellectual lingua franca from the African shores of the Atlantic to the steppes of central Asia. Muslims considered Arabic to be the divine language in which the Koran was transmitted through a heavenly intermediary to the prophet, Mohammed. Grammatical and linguistic works by Muslim scholars on Arabic shed light on Hebrew grammar and linguistics, as well. Saadia Gaon translated the Torah into Arabic and was among the first to write a running biblical commentary. This genre of biblical commentary, dedicated to the contextual meaning of Torah (*peshat*), reached its climax in twelfth-century France among the Tosafot.[10]

For our purposes, biblical exegesis remains an important development in the history of Jewish thought for several reasons. Without a doubt, the two most important reasons are the precedent it established for intellectual honesty and explicitly treating the Torah as religious literature. The influence of Greek rationality, mediated through Islamic philosophy and absorbed by Jewish thinkers, encouraged Saadia Gaon to acknowledge that "a reasonable person must always understand the Torah according to the simple meaning of its words . . . except for those places in which sense perception or reason contradicts the well-known understanding of an expression."[11] Saadia is channeling the Mutazilites, an Islamic school of thought which purged the more irrational elements and crass anthropomorphisms of God from Islamic teaching.

More than a century later, in northern Spain, Bahya ibn Paquda adds two more essential components to our understanding of scripture—both

---

10 Cherry, *Torah through Time*, 17–26.

11 Saadia, *Introduction to Commentary on Torah*, 17-18, as cited in Robert Brody, *The Geonim of Babylonian and the Shaping of Medieval Jewish Culture* (New Haven: Yale University Press, 1998), 305, translation slightly modified. The rabbis, too, treated the Torah as religious literature, but their approach was unself-conscious. The medievalists were systematic in their interpretive methods.

of which, once again, come from Islamic thought. "Bahya distinguishes between the literal interpretation (Arab. *zahir*) and that based upon the 'inner' or hidden dimension (Arab. *batin*) of the biblical text."[12] The two-tiered Torah becomes a staple for both Jewish mystics and philosophers. The exoteric meaning for the masses is the Torah's facade of stories and mitzvot, while duties of the heart, secrets of Kabbalah, and philosophical truths form the esoteric foundation. We will explore these different esoteric readings of Torah below, but it is significant that the Jewish paradigm of the two-tiered Torah emerges through the influence of Koranic exegesis by Muslims.

Bahya's second contribution complements his first by endorsing the superficial reading of the Torah for the masses. Bahya offers a novel interpretation of the Talmudic statement that the Torah was written in human language (Brachot 31b). In the Talmud, that expression refers to the interpretation of a specific grammatical form that involves a doubling of the Hebrew verbal root. Some rabbis drashed (expounded) each of the two verb forms, while others acknowledged that the doubling is nothing more than a grammatical convention and should not be exploited to generate a derash. Bahya deploys the dictum to explain that the *entire* Torah was written in language that the average person understands—and that language was not philosophy.

Another Spanish exegete, Abraham ibn Ezra (1089–1164) brought his international travel experience and rational explanations to bear on his Torah commentary. The first population explosion recorded in the Torah was facilitated by two midwives, Shifra and Puah. Ibn Ezra points out that there must have been at least 500 midwives to coach all the fertile Israelite women through birth. Shifra and Puah must, therefore, be the names of two different supervisors who each had hundreds of midwives in their charge. Ibn Ezra then mentions that he has seen this system in many places (ibn Ezra on Exodus 1:15). Ibn Ezra similarly relies on his travel experience on the seas to explain the plague of darkness. He claims to have witnessed, many times, a thick darkness that eclipsed the sun lasting for five days—two more than the Egyptians had to endure (ibn Ezra on Exodus. 10:22).

---

12 Sara Klein-Braslavy, "The Philosophical Exegesis," in *Hebrew Bible/Old Testament: The History of Its Interpretation*, vol. I/2, *The Middle Ages*, ed. Magne Saebo (Gottingen: Vandenhoeck & Ruprecht, 2000), 307.

A particularly daring medieval phenomenon was the admission that not all rabbinic interpretation, even when related to halakhic issues, is the plain sense of Scripture. The most famous *peshat* seeker, or *pashtan*, is one of RaSHI's grandsons, Rabbi Shmuel ben Meir (RaSHBaM, 1085–1158). "Even though the halakhah is what is essential, that is not what I have come to explain. . . . I have come to explain the contextual sense (peshat) of the biblical verses according to common parlance."[13] RaSHBaM concludes his programmatic statement by shifting attention to a rabbinic statement that the law can uproot the Torah (Sotah 16a.) In its context, the Talmudic statement was quite narrow, but RaSHBaM pried it wide open to justify the potentially subversive audacity of his enterprise.

A final example of the lengths to which some medieval commentators went to demonstrate their commitment to reason and truth is exemplified by ibn Ezra. Although he was dedicated to defending the rabbinic (or rabbanite) interpretation of Scripture against the Karaite Jews, who rejected rabbinic authority, he was willing to wink to those careful readers who saw evidence that Moshe was not the sole author of the entire five books of Torah. A verse in Genesis (12:6) tips off the close reader that it had been written *after* the Israelites conquered the Land of Canaan (and, therefore, long after Moshe's death), although the setting of the verse is during the days of Avraham. After offering a weak explanation, ibn Ezra requests that those who understand the secret to remain silent. In the seventeenth century, as Benedict Spinoza argued that the entire Torah was written by human beings, and that much of it was composed after the time of Moshe, he was sure to acknowledge his precursor Ibn Ezra.[14]

Among the sages with the greatest literary sensitivity was Rabbi Moshe ben Nachman or Nachmanides (RaMBaN, 1194–1270, Barcelona-Israel).[15] RaMBaN may be best known for his allusions to Jewish mysticism sprinkled throughout his Torah commentary. As we will see below, medieval mysticism resonates with the priestly Torah. One of the characteristics of the priestly ontology was to see the world as an integrated

13 RaSHBaM on Exodus 21:1.
14 Benedict de Spinoza, *A Theologico-Political Treatise*, trans. R. H. M. Elwes (New York: Dover Publications, Inc., 1951) book 8.
15 Yaakov Elman, "Moses ben Nahman / Nahmanides (Ramban)," in Saebo, *Hebrew Bible/Old Testament*, 416–32.

system of homologous structures operating on different scales of reality. In the chapter on priestly religion, I used the term *fractal* to describe their worldview. RaMBaN popularized the rabbinic notion that the deeds of the ancestors prefigure later history when stories repeat themselves on different scales.[16] RaMBaN sees this literary fugue at work, for instance, when Avram (Avraham's early name) voluntarily travels to Egypt to escape famine in the Land of Israel (Genesis. 12:10). For showing a lack of faith in God's providence, Avram's progeny, who similarly travel to Egypt during a famine, will be punished by being forced to stay there as slaves.[17] On the cosmic level, the six days of creation map onto the 6,000 years of the world's existence, and just as the seventh day signifies rest, the seventh millennium will signify messianic redemption.[18] For Jewish mystics, fractals exist in both space and time. Furthermore, knowledge of their existence can help us understand the Torah and God's ways.

The medieval approach to Torah exegesis promotes (and provides precedent) for honesty, reasonableness, and literary sensitivity. Equally significant is RaSHBaM's model of fearlessly interpreting the Torah even when it contradicts halakhic norms. These elements converge in Maimonides' discussion of the world to come. He explained that within the Talmud there was no shortage of aggadic traditions promising rewards in the afterlife for behaving well in this world. He compared such incentives to how we train a child to succeed academically. Until they acquire their own sense of the joy of learning and its intrinsic rewards, we bribe them with treats to study and behave. That, according to Maimonides, explains rabbinic descriptions of rewards in the world to come where there is, in truth, no dark chocolate, only the divine radiance in which to bask.[19]

Maimonides then outlines three different approaches to aggadic statements that contradict reason. The first is to believe such statements literally. RaMBaM thinks such people are "truly pathetic. . . . As God

---

16 Genesis Rabbah 40:8, for example.

17 RaMBaN on Genesis 12:10. See also Nina Caputo, "'In the Beginning'...: Typology, History, and the Unfolding Meaning of Creation in Nahmanides' Exegesis," *Jewish Social Studies: History, Culture, and Society* 6, no. 1 (1999): 54–82.

18 RaMBaN on Genesis 2:3 and Scholem, *Major Trends in Jewish Mysticism*, 178–79.

19 Bahya ibn Paquda anticipates RaMBaM's comments in his *The Book of Direction to the Duties of the Heart*, trans. Menahem Mansoor (Oxford: Littman Library of Jewish Civilization, 1973), 258–59.

lives, this approach destroys the glory of the Torah and dims its radiance. It distorts and perverts God's Torah."[20] Roughly forty percent of Americans believe that the world was created in six days because the first story in the Torah seems to say so. Maimonides would consider them "truly pathetic."

The second posture RaMBaM describes is also that of a literal reading of such irrational texts in our religious literature, but the literalism leads to a blanket rejection. Maimonides describes people who hold this position as those who "see themselves as clever men of wisdom and philosophers. . . . They are even more foolish and inane than those who follow the first approach."[21] Contemporary scientists and intellectuals unschooled in theology, led by Richard Dawkins and Daniel Dennett, are examples of this group. Yet, if the first group did not exist, *and intervene in the scientific education of our children* (!), this second group would have less reason to raise their hue and cry.

The stance which Maimonides champions is to avoid literalism when it would result in absurdities. "The gates of figurative interpretation [are never] shut in our faces."[22] Take, for example, the Garden of Eden story featuring a talking serpent. That defies reason! So, toward the very beginning of RaMBaM's *Guide of the Perplexed*, he explains the Garden of Eden as an allegory about form, matter, intellect, and imagination.[23] Not only does Maimonides offer an Aristotelian reading of the intellectual and psychological nature of humanity, but in so doing, he dislodges Eden from any historical or geographical moorings. Eden isn't about our past or our creation; it is an allegory that explains our life's purpose of striving for intellectual perfection—RaMBaM's version of paradise.

As we will see in subsequent chapters, the Torah was interpreted in many ways, often influenced by the interpreter's worldview and contemporary events.[24] As ubiquitous as Torah is in all genres of medieval Jewish

---

20 Maimonides, Pirkei Avot *with the Rambam's Commentary*, trans. Eliyahu Touger (New York: Moznaim Publishing Corporation, 1994), 161.

21 Ibid., 162.

22 *Guide*, 2:25, 327.

23 Ibid., 1:2. See the analysis by Marvin Fox in his *Interpreting Maimonides: Studies in Methodology, Metaphysics, and Moral Philosophy* (Chicago: Chicago University Press, 1990), 152–98.

24 My book *Torah through Time* offers five studies on the multiplicity of interpretations of a single story.

literature, bible study *qua* bible study is rarely championed in Europe for centuries after the heyday of the *pashtanim* in the twelfth century. As Kanarfogel tersely concludes, "Study of the biblical text for its own sake was apparently not the norm in Ashkenaz."[25] There are laments both within the Ashkenazi and Sephardic spheres about such neglect. Perhaps the greatest champion of the Torah, Profayt Duran (Spain, d. c. 1414) charges Jewish scholars of his day, and in generations prior, both in Sefarad and Ashkenaz with "show[ing] great disdain for biblical studies."[26] When Duran made his indictment, however, he had already lived for years as a Christian. By the fifteenth century, the Torah had largely been relegated to Christianity. Yet, as we will see, the mid-sixteenth century experienced something of a resurgence of Torah piety, particularly in the mystical center of Safed where Torah became a vehicle for divine communion.[27] Subsequently, the tools of literary interpretation introduced by the medieval exegetes would be dusted off by the pioneers of modern Judaism, and in our own time, rabbinic midrash would come to be appreciated for its parallels with contemporary literary theory.

Mysticism and Kabbalah

Although Kabbalah is Jewish mysticism, not all Jewish mysticism is Kabbalah. Kabbalah is a species of mysticism that uses the language of *sefirot* to describe the inner life of God (i.e., theosophy). Although the term *sefirah* (singular of *sefirot*) appeared in an earlier non-mystical text, Sefer Yetzirah, the term is appropriated by Sefer Ha-Bahir in the twelfth century. By the end of the thirteenth century, the Zohar, which was to become the central kabbalistic text for centuries, employs the image of ten sefirot, or character beacons, to describe the dynamism of the divine image. Well before the sefirot began to dominate mystical literature, there were Jewish mystics, influenced by the Islamic mystics, the Sufis, who sought an intimate relationship with God unmediated by mitzvot.

---

25 Ephraim Kanarfogel, *Jewish Education and Society in the High Middle* Ages (Detroit: Wayne State University, 2008), 79.

26 Ibid., 85n140.

27 Mordechai Pachter, "The Concept of Devekut in the Homiletical Ethical Writings of 16th Century Safed," in *Studies in Medieval Jewish History and Literature*, vol. II, ed. Isadore Twersky (Cambridge, MA: Harvard University Press, 1984), 171–230.

Bahya ibn Paquda's *The Book of Directions to the Duties of the Heart* (c. 1100) inaugurates the medieval shift from external action to awareness of the divine. For Bahya, the shift was from deed to devotion.

The title of Bahya's book is based on an Islamic (Mutazilite) distinction between duties of the limbs and duties of the hearts. Keep in mind that when Bahya uses the term "heart," the head is included. Ancient and medieval usage bundled emotions and intellect into the same organ. The Torah, of course, has commandments that seem to target the heart: loving God, respecting parents, not coveting your neighbor's Tesla, and so forth. But the rabbis were uncomfortable leaving the content of such commandments to individual discretion. They legislated, for example, what they believed was required to *show* respect to one's parents. How else could you know if you were fulfilling the commandments?

Bahya is not uncomfortable with the mitzvot; he sees them as a superstructure demanding a foundation or an infrastructure. Duties of the heart serve as that infrastructure for duties of the limbs. Paul Fenton explains Bahya's motivation to write such a book: "In an effort to remedy the ritual formalism and religious desiccation of his fellow Jews, Bahya devised an individualistic, inward itinerary, guiding the soul through contemplation and love to union with the 'supernal light,' based on the progressive spiritual stages of the path as set out in Sufi pietistic manuals."[28] Bahya describes the love of God as "the yearning of the soul, the desire of its very substance to be attached to God's supreme light."[29]

In Bahya's introduction, one immediately senses a shift from the way in which inwardness (*kavannah*) had been discussed by the rabbis in terms of the mental accompaniment to the performance of a mitzvah or the commission of a transgression. In rabbinic literature, *kavannah* can be translated as *intention*. Not so for Bahya.

> Inward obedience, however, is expressed in the duties of the heart, in the heart's assertion of the unity of God and the belief in Him and His book, in constant obedience to Him and fear of Him, in humility before Him,

28 Paul B. Fenton, "Judaism and Sufism," in *The Cambridge Companion to Medieval Jewish Philosophy*, ed. Daniel H. Frank and Oliver Leaman (New York: Cambridge University Press, 2003), 204.
29 Bahya, *Duties*, 427. See also 261.

love for Him and complete reliance upon Him, submission to Him and abstinence from all things hateful to Him.[30]

Bahya's emphasis, like the Sufis', is on constant devotion. Menahem Mansoor, who translated Bahya from the original Arabic into English, points out how innovative Bahya was: "Generally speaking, ideas of the primacy of inward purity and of the secondary importance of external obedience to the laws are not new to Jewish tradition, for they appear in the Prophets. Nevertheless, Bahya's way of expressing these ideas is *not Jewish* because he replaces the distinction between intention and deed with a distinction between kinds of duties."[31]

Once Bahya made such a distinction, however, it *became* Jewish. But there are two different types of kavannah being discussed in Bahya. So far, we've been talking about duties of the heart, those duties which affect no one else. There is also the traditional, rabbinic kavannah. The degree to which devotion dominates Bahya's system results in a reversal of the rabbinic preference for deeds: "When intentions are defective, deeds are not acceptable to God, numerous and insistent as they may be."[32] In Bahya's introduction, he draws out the logical implication of his beliefs about kavannah: "The thought of a good deed by a true worshipper and his desire to carry it out, even if he prove unable to do so, may be balanced against many a good deed carried out by others."[33] According to Joseph Dan, it is for these reasons that "in many respects Bahya's ethics can be regarded as the most radical and revolutionary in Jewish ethical-philosophical literature."[34]

Although the distinction between duties of the limbs and duties of the heart is of Mutazalite origin, the outline of Bahya's book owes much to al-Ghazali and the Sufis. (The Mutazilites were more invested in the use of reason for religious purposes than were al-Ghazali and the Sufis.) Al-Ghazali, the theologian who wrote *The Incoherence of the Philosophers*, emphasized the concept of *dhikr*, a cognate to the Hebrew word *zakhor*,

---

30 Ibid., 89.
31 Ibid., 31. Emphasis mine.
32 Ibid., 97.
33 Ibid., 99. See Monsoor's "Introduction" to Bahya's *Duties of the Heart* where he describes Bahya's attitude as "not Jewish," 55.
34 Joseph Dan, *Jewish Mysticism and Jewish Ethics* (Northvale: Jason Aronson Inc., 1996), 26.

remember. The aim is to constantly remember God's presence and majesty. More than remembering, the goal is attunement. The Sufi master Yahya ibn Muadh (ninth century) wrote that God is always on the lookout. Bahya uses this image to describe the state of attentiveness that we must obtain to be on the lookout for God and to sense that God is on the lookout for us.[35]

Bahya is what we might call an intellectual mystic. He was also a judge, which might help to explain his comfort in exploring motivations which, sometimes, have legal consequences. He believed we could see traces of God in creation, and it is our responsibility, to the best of our ability, to be on the lookout for such traces.[36] Bahya also maintained that we should not accept religious doctrines on blind faith, but we should study philosophy and science to the extent possible in order to understand how God manifests his wisdom in this world.[37] Bahya's combination of pietistic devotion and appreciation for natural philosophy, embodied in a judge committed to halakhah, makes him a renaissance man centuries before the Renaissance.

The next mystical expression within Judaism, and a transitional form to the Zohar's Kabbalah, is represented by the German Pietists, *Hasidei Ashkenaz*, a small movement centered around three members of the Kalonymos family. Ancestors of Shmuel the Elder (fl. mid-twelfth century) moved to the Rhineland from Italy around the turn of the millennium. There is evidence that texts promoting Merkava (chariot) and Hekhalot (palaces) mysticism, liturgical piety, and theosophic speculation were then circulating in Italy.[38] Even before the First Crusade of 1096, Jews were composing liturgical poems (*piyyutim*) with strong mystical themes.[39]

---

35 Lobel, *A Sufi-Jewish Dialogue*, 10.

36 Bahya, *Duties of the Heart*, 153.

37 Ibid., 114 and 154-58.

38 Elliot R. Wolfson, "The Theosophy of Shabbetai Donnolo, with Special Emphasis on the Doctrine of Sefirot in *Sefer Hakhmoni*," *Jewish History* 6 (1992): 285. Haym Soloveitchik, "The Midrash, *Sefer Hasidim* and the Changing Face of God," in *Creation and Re-Creation in Jewish Thought: Festschrift in Honor of Joseph Dan on the Occasion of his Seventieth Birthday*, ed. Rachel Elior and Peter Schafer (Tubingen: Mohr Siebeck, 2005), 175.

39 Kanarfogel, *Intellectual History and Rabbinic Culture*, 383.

Bahya's *Duties* was translated to Hebrew in 1161 by Yehuda ibn Tibbon (1120–c. 1190) who fled from Andalusia to France after the Islamic Almohades wrested control of the region from the more tolerant Almoravids. (RaMBaM's family abandoned Andalusia at the same time but remained within the Islamic orbit by migrating south to Morocco. Yehuda ibn Tibbon's son, Shmuel, became the translator of RaMBaM's *Guide of the Perplexed* from Arabic to Hebrew.) In Sefer Yirah, a short work by the patriarch of Hasidei Ashkenaz, Shmuel the Elder, we see echoes of Bahya's radical innovation in the heart of Ashkenaz. "A man should perform every religious commandment that he can, and what he cannot perform, he should think of performing. . . . This is the case of a man who had no Torah and no good deeds. Yet he merely thought of performing good deeds and God counted it as a great thing. For 'the Merciful One desires the heart.'"[40]

A constellation of elements from the rabbinic period coalesce in the work of Yehuda he-Hasid (d. 1217), a son of Shmuel the Elder. His most famous work is Sefer Hasidim, a pietistic handbook which charts a course for personal salvation by "striv[ing] to discover limitless new obligations hidden in Scripture. . . . All aspects of the pietist's life are to be lived in total dedication to serving God, comparable to the burnt offering that was totally consumed on the Temple altar."[41] In the aftermath of the Crusades, when many Rhineland Jews were distraught over the ostensible divine wrath that had ravaged their communities, the Hasidei Ashkenaz assumed—as the Mosaic Torah suggests—that they had been punished for their sins. If so, then the road to redemption would be paved by renewed dedication to a life of divine service.[42]

Devotion, as well as asceticism, are found in Bahya, too. Although both features are more pronounced in the thinking of Hasidei Ashkenaz, they are not different in kind, only in degree. It is in the realm of language that we begin to see a major departure from Bahya and a rehabilitation of

---

40 Sefer Ha-Yirah, 4–6, as cited in Ivan G. Marcus, "The Devotional Ideals of Ashkenazic Pietism," in Green, *Jewish Spirituality*, 364, with slight changes. The internal quotation is from Sannhedrin 106b and RaSHI, ad. loc.

41 Marcus, "Devotional Ideals," in Green, *Jewish Spirituality*, 357-58.

42 Soloveitchik, "The Midrash, *Sefer Hasidim* and the Changing Face of God," in Elior and Schafer, *Creation and Re-Creation in Jewish Thought*, 147-63. See also Dan, *Jewish Mysticism*, 68-69.

concepts previously associated with the priestly Torah.[43] First, let us consider prayer. The requirement of kavannah during prayer is to be expected. However, the requirements of the pray-ers and the consequences of the prayers represent a fusing of medieval piety and the priestly Torah.

> The impact prayer has on the celestial powers depends by and largely [sic] on the special spiritual capabilities of the praying person. Those capabilities consist of a number of qualities chief among them being moral integrity and holiness, which the Hasidic writers viewed as the ideal of the Fear of God. But there is also something that emerges from out of the very knowledge of the secrets incorporated in prayers. Those secrets are the inner dynamics that turn words into active spiritual entities.[44]

One scholar of Hasidei Ashkenaz contends that by the mid-thirteenth century there "is the apotheosis of language as a divine and creative power."[45] The third member of the Kalonymos family, Rabbi Eleazer of Worms (d. c. 1230), who was the main student and cousin of Rabbi Yehudah he-Hasid, maintained that language is the golden barrier between humans and animals. Language, properly deployed, allows humanity to actualize their divine image.[46]

But that language must be exact. "Rabbi Yehudah was horrified by small variations in the text of prayers as said by the Jews of France and England."[47] If the prayer has been slightly modified and no longer has the correct words or the correct number of words, or if the pray-er is not knowledgeable about the secrets of prayer and worthy of such prayer, then the theurgic efficacy of the prayer is nullified. In the words of the

---

43 In a recent treatment of Hasidei Ashkenaz, David I. Shyovitz notes their retrieval of a Sadducean halakhah. He ascribes the halakhic reversal to the object of the halakhah, excrement; the reversal may be due, however, to the Pietists' worldview which has affinities with the Sadducean and priestly worldviews. David I. Shyovitz, *A Remembrance of His Wonders: Nature and the Supernatural in Medieval Ashkenaz* (Philadelphia: University of Pennsylvania Press, 2017), 166–67.

44 Ithamar Gruenwald, "Social and Mystical Aspects of Sefer Hasidim," in *Mysticism, Magic and Kabbalah in Ashkenazi Judaism,* ed. Karl Erich Grozinger and Joseph Dan (Berlin: de Gruyter, 1995), 114.

45 Karl Erich Grozinger, "Between Magic and Religion—Ashkenazic Hasidic Piety," in Grozinger, *Mysticism, Magic and Kabbalah in Ashkenazi Judaism*, 43.

46 Ibid., 36.

47 Joseph Dan, "The Ashkenazic Hasidic Concept of Language," in *Hebrew in Ashkenaz: A Language in Exile*, ed. Lewis Glinert (New York: Oxford University Press, 1993), 21.

founding father of the academic study of Jewish mysticism Gershom Scholem: "The enormous concern shown for the use of the correct phrase in the traditional texts, and the excessive pedantry displayed in this regard reveals a totally new attitude towards the function of words. . . . A renewed consciousness of the magic power inherent in words."[48]

Beyond the domain of prayer, the Hasidei Ashkenaz elevated ethics to an unprecedented level. Ethics had always been important, but ethical ideals had been "beyond the line of the law."[49] Halakhah sets the standard, and the pious (*hasidim*) will act above and beyond. Rabbi Eleazer of Worms wrote Sefer Rokeach, a halakhic text which "makes an attempt to codify the Hasidic ideal in Halakhic terms."[50] As Gruenwald has pointed out, "practicing the Hasidic law means adapting an inner spiritual orientation that transforms the Law into a Pietistic act. Allegedly, that Pietistic act has a number of personal and cosmic reverberations."[51]

An unprecedented, and unorthodox, component of Ashkenazi piety was an obsession with penance. Apparently influenced by Christian monastic traditions, excessive asceticism was perceived as a way to atone for known and unknown transgressions.[52] Sefer Hasidim references Isaiah's suffering Messiah, a cornerstone of Christian theology. Vicarious atonement, the notion that one's sins can be absolved by others, provides an opportunity for the Hasidim to atone for the sins of others. Specifically, the Pietists' way of life was imagined to atone for the sins which were responsible for the Christian Crusades in the Rhineland that ravaged local Jewish communities from the late eleventh to thirteenth centuries. What Sefer Hasidim also claims is that no one else should have to atone for the sins of Hasidim—both a programmatic statement for Hasidim and a jab at their Christian neighbors who rely on the vicarious atonement of Christ.[53]

In the theology of Hasidei Ashkenaz, God reveals His *Kavod*, his glory, to those who are worthy. For Eleazar of Worms, this Kavod is the

---

48 Scholem, *Major Trends*, 101.
49 Brachot 7a, among many others.
50 Scholem, *Major Trends*, 95.
51 Gruenwald, "Social and Mystical Aspects," in Grozinger, *Mysticism, Magic and Kabbalah in Ashkenazi Judaism,* 113.
52 Scholem, *Major Trends*, 104.
53 Sefer Hasidim, Par. 1556, cited in Scholem, *Major Trends*, 106.

second sefirah of Sefer Yetzirah. (The relationship between God and God's created Kavod is first articulated by Saadia Gaon.)[54] God's Kavod appears on the throne of the chariot as a confirmation to the Hasidim that they are not being deceived by demons. "[Nevertheless], the real object of mystical contemplation, its true goal, is the hidden holiness of God, His infinite and formless glory, wherefrom there emerges the voice and the word of God."[55] The mysticism of Hasidei Ashkenaz aspires to recapitulate revelation, a goal far more ambitious than Bahya seeking traces of divine fullness.

The divine immanence which animates creation, according to the Hasidei Ashkenaz, finds its personal corollary in the soul of the individual. In an act of mystical exegesis, the Torah's assurance that God is on the Israelites' side, "in your midst" (Deuteronomy 7:21), is explained by the insight that divinity is within each individual; God dwells within each of our souls.[56] Through prayer, penance, and devotion, the Hasid can access an unmediated experience of God's majesty. In the yearning for God's presence, the restraint of reason has been loosened and the door to kabbalistic mysticism has been opened. By the end of the twelfth century, certain Hasidei Ashkenaz behaviors were being adopted by outsiders. In central and eastern Europe, they had "a fairly significant impact on Ashkenazic *minhagim* [customs]."[57] More influential than specific customs, however, may be the resurgence of the priestly idea that there are theurgic consequences to Jewish acts. Jews may be unable to control their own destiny, but with the emergence of Kabbalah they have unprecedented influence over God's destiny.

The Zohar

The theosophy of sefirot traces its origins to two sources. The first is Sefer Yetzirah which is not a mystical text, but rather a treatise on cosmogony

---

54 Saadia Gaon, *Book of Beliefs and Opinions*, trans. Samuel Rosenblatt (New Haven: Yale University Press, 1948), 130.
55 Scholem, *Major Trends*, 116.
56 Ibid., 110. Members of the Pietistic circle adumbrated notions of pantheism and acosmism. See Shyovitz, *Remembrance of his Wonders*, 176–78.
57 Ephraim Kanarfogel, *"Peering through the Lattices": Mystical, Magical, and Pietistic Dimensions in the Tosafist Period* (Detroit: Wayne State University, 2000), 114.

(the creation of the cosmos). Sefer Yetzirah uses the term *sefirah* with the likely meaning of a natural number in a Pythagorean sense of a building block of the cosmos. In addition to the ten numerals, Sefer Yetzira opens its discussion by including the twenty-two letters of the Hebrew alphabet which sum to thirty-two "wondrous channels of wisdom."[58] The importance of numbers, in addition to the fundamental components of language, the alphabet, was seen already in the worldview of Hasidei Ashkenaz. "Therefore, every God-fearing person should be careful not to add or subtract any word from what our forefathers have established because all depends on the measurement [amount] of words."[59]

The "measurement of words" cited above by Yehudah he-Hasid can mean the number of words, but it can also refer to the gematria of words. Gematria, the assignation of numbers to letters of the alphabet (*gamma* is the *third* letter of the Greek alphabet), was a common tool of the ancient world. It is found in the Talmud, but in the minds of Hasidei Ashkenaz, it is mystical corroboration that the natural numbers found in creation have counterparts in the Hebrew language which must, therefore, be every bit as natural and integral to the cosmos as are numbers. Once those natural numbers, the sefirot, become associated with God's own being, then the universe becomes a manifestation of the divine rather than a creation of the divine. However daring previous flirtation with radical divine immanence was, the theology of sefirot provides the framework for effacing the metaphysical boundary between Creator and creation, and facing the glory of God that is the fullness of the world (Isaiah 6:3).

Besides kabbalistic commentaries on Sefer Yetzirah, the other source for sefirot is the twelfth-century book, The Bahir. Edited in Provence, and bearing the influence of Merkavah mysticism, The Bahir merges notions of theurgy with the vocabulary and imagery of sefirot. The Bahir asks the question why a sacrifice, *korban*, has the same three letter root as *bringing near*, *karev*. The answer is through sacrifice, the Israelites bring near to one another the holy forms, a reference to the sefirot.[60] The Bahir then cites a verse from Ezekiel (37:17) where God commands Israel to perform

---

58 Sefer Yetzirah 1:1.
59 Yehudah he-Hasid, Ms. Kauffman A3999, fol. 50r; cited in Kanarfogel, *"Peering through the Lattices,"* 88.
60 The Bahir, 109, and Daniel C. Matt, "The Mystic and the Mizwot," in Green, *Jewish Spirituality,* 383-84.

acts of unification: "Bring for you each one near to one other, to be one tree; and they will be unified through your hands." The sefirotic sapling has been planted and will flourish as the sefirotic tree of the Zohar.

Before entering the lush landscape of the Zohar, let us look back on the terrain covered so far. The intellectual mysticism of Bahya ibn Paquda brings to the fore the problems with a religion by rote. His emphases on intention and devotion adjust, for many, the focus of Judaism from duties of the limbs to duties of the heart. Traditions of Merkavah mysticism are brought with the Kalonymos family from Italy to the Rhineland. The literature of Hasidei Ashkenaz promotes a pietistic notion of mystical revelation, reveals the secrets of proper prayer, and expounds upon the benefits for the entire Jewish community of the ascetic, atoning behavior practiced by the pietistic elite. Finally, commentaries on Sefer Yetzirah and The Bahir set the stage for a theosophic Kabbalah based on the sefirot.

Into this northwest Mediterranean region intrudes a southeastern Mediterranean, Sephardic import: the RaMBaM. His strident, philosophical rationalism, front and center in both his halakhic code, Mishneh Torah (c. 1170), and in *The Guide of the Perplexed* (c. 1180), rankled many Ashkenazim, among them Rabbi Avraham ben David of Posquieres (1125–1198). His son, Rabbi Yitzhak the Blind (1160–1235), is among the first kabbalists we know by name. As he was transmitting kabbalistic ideas to his students, who then brought these notions to Spain, Shmuel ibn Tibbon's translation of RaMBaM's *Guide*. Rabbi Yitzhak the Blind and his students admitted RaMBaM's conception of the deity, only to immediately shove it offstage, and then reintroduce the familiar attributes of the rabbinic, personal God as emanations from behind the curtain.

The Zohar emerged toward the end of the thirteenth century in northern Spain (Castile). The God of the Zohar had two aspects: the Maimonidean *Eyn Sof* and the sefirot. *Eyn Sof* literally means *there is no end, limitlessness, infinitude*. According to one of Rabbi Yitzhak the Blind's students: "Know that one cannot attribute to *Eyn Sof* will or desire or intention or thought or speech or deed, although there is nothing beyond it, and one can say nothing of it that implies its limitations."[61] The

---

61   Rabbi Azriel, cited in Isaiah Tishby, *The Wisdom of the Zohar*, trans. David Goldstein (Oxford: Littman Library of Jewish Civilization, 1991), 235.

personal God of the rabbis and Sholem Aleichem's Tevye is nowhere to be found in the *Eyn Sof.* This is the aspect of God that defies our ability to capture anything that bears any resemblance to the truth.

RaMBaM had earlier urged precisely this use of a language of negatives:

> Know that the description of God, may He be cherished and exalted, by means of negations is the correct description—a description that is not affected by an indulgence in facile language and does not imply any deficiency with respect to God.[62]

For RaMBaM, any attribution we make of God merely describes our perception of God's actions, not God's essence.[63] God is not essentially merciful; the workings of God's world may, however, appear to us as (sometimes) merciful. For the kabbalists, RaMBaM's "negative" theology had negative consequences on Jewish observance. His theology, while not wrong, was incomplete. It had to be complemented by theosophy, a description of the inner life of God: the *Eyn Sof* coupled with the sefirot. *Hesed*, the characteristic of mercy, is one of the names of the sefirot precisely because there *is* an aspect of God's very essence that radiates mercy. That is (part of) who God is. If we are not feeling the blessings of divine mercy, then we have it in our power to clear the supernal channels to allow divine mercy to flow towards us. That power derives from leading a pious life of Jewish observance.

In most books dealing specifically with Kabbalah you will find the sefirotic tree. Each sefirah has a cluster of names that tries to capture facets of its core character as it relates to the rest of the sefirotic world. In Kabbalah, everything is in relationship. And all healthy relationships share a certain structure that serves as a matrix to all scales or dimensions of reality. The names of the different sefirot come from nature, the family, and the Torah. The kabbalists saw these homologous matrices at work anatomically, psychologically, among biblical characters, in nature, in the heavens, and within the Godhead (another way to talk about God's inner life.) Above, I referred to the sefirot as *character beacons.* The term's first word alludes both to the characters and characteristics that inform the

---

62 *Guide,* 1:58, 134.
63 Ibid., 136.

names of each sefirah. The image of a beacon is something that illumines and calls forth. The word *zohar* means radiant illumination. Beneath the etymological surface of sefirah is sapphire, a gem that appears to contain heavenly light, and the facets of the sapphire are akin to the different faces of God. Like our own personalities, different divine characteristics surface depending on context. Like our own personalities, the sefirot are in constant flux—what my teacher Arthur Green calls a dynamic unity.[64]

All metaphors are imperfect, which is why the Zohar and other theologians keep adding to the storehouse. Nevertheless, we can abstract a few salient elements of the Zohar's theology from their metaphors. For our purposes, the most important theological contribution is the idea of mediated monism. The self-revelation of God through the emanation of sefirot culminates with the tenth sefirah, designated both as the *community of Israel* and the *Shechinah*. (In the rabbinic period, the Shechinah referred to God's immanence.) The name sharing of this sefirah alludes both to its function as conduit between the upper and lower worlds, (between the Shechinah as the last sefirah and the community of Israel in the world) *and* the mysterious identification of the community of Israel with this aspect of God. In the words of Scholem, "Theogony [the creation of God] and cosmogony represent not two different acts of creation, but two aspects of the same."[65]

> Everything is linked with everything else down to the lowest ring on the chain, and the true essence of God is above as well as below, in the heavens and on the earth, and nothing exists outside Him.—Moshe de Leon, Sefer HaRimon 47b[66]

Another name for this last sefirah is *all*. Notwithstanding passages like the one immediately above, the Zohar retreats from explicitly identifying *all* of reality as divine. "While the inner logic of the kabbalists' emanational thinking would seem to indicate that *all* beings, including the physical universe, flow forth from the *Shekhinah*, the medieval abhorrence of associating God with corporeality complicates the picture,

---

64 Arthur Green, *A Guide to the Zohar* (Stanford: Stanford University Press, 2003), 36. See also Scholem, *Messianic Idea*, 107.

65 Scholem, *Major Trends*, 223.

66 Cited and translated in ibid., 223.

leaving Kabbalah with a complex and somewhat divided attitude toward the material world."[67]

As we learn more about the interactions between Christians and Jews during this period, it is worthwhile recalling the fundamental Christian claim that Christ is both fully divine and fully corporeal. In the rabbinic period, Torah served as the embodiment of God's will, and, indeed, another name for the tenth sefirah is Torah. Given the popular aphorism of Ben Bag Bag, "Turn it [Torah], turn it, for *all* is in it" (Avot 5:22), one can only speculate how the richly associative mentalities of the mystics understood their place, the place of the community of Israel, in the All of the Shechinah. As Green observes, "the *sefirot* may be viewed not as hypostatic 'entities' but as *symbol clusters*, linked by association, the mention or textual occurrence of any of which automatically brings to mind all the others as well."[68] Perhaps the Zohar's conflation of names for the final sefirah is also a response to Christianity: you Christians claim that the Chosen One, Christ, is divine; but we claim that the entire community of Israel, the chosen people, is divine! Or, more radically, all is divine.

According to the kabbalists and others, historical and psychological interpretations for the mitzvot offered by philosophers like the RaMBaM, were contributing to a laxity in Jewish observance. The kabbalistic program identified the performance of mitzvot as the key to the smooth flowing of the sefirotic system. As a result of transgressions, of both omission and commission, the channels linking the sefirot become clogged. The bounty of divine beneficence that flowed among the sefirot, the *shefa*, can no longer reach the final sefirah which serves as the aperture through which the *shefa* cascades into the lower world. In the sexual imagery of the Zohar, the feminized Shechinah is not in a secure bond with the sefirah representing male sexuality. As a result of this erotic and sefirotic isolation, the Shechinah becomes vulnerable to the powers of "the other side," the *sitra achra*, which is parasitic on human transgressions. "The powers of uncleanness burst out of the darkness and the deep in their desire to get near the realm of holiness and feed on it, and they lie

---

67 Green, *Guide*, 53.
68 Ibid., 56. Hartley Lachter, *Kabbalistic Revolution: Reimagining Judaism in Medieval Spain* (New Brunswick: Rutgers University Press, 2014), 57.

in ambush near the Shechinah."[69] In the Zohar's myth, the Shechinah is raped by those diabolical forces and conceives demons that catapult the Jewish world into chaos.

Although the various mythical images of the *sitra achra* are not irrelevant to our discussion, I want to focus on the other side of the *sitra achra*. While it is true that the performance of mitzvot is the key to the sefirotic system, performance alone is insufficient to prime the sefirotic pump—kavannah is required. "Thought is obviously the organ of influence upon this theosophic structure."[70] In consonance with Bahya and Hasidei Ashkenaz, *and in direct opposition to the rabbinic rejection of kavannah as a requirement for most mitzvot*, the kabbalists demand it. "Ritual acts and speech have no effect on the upper world and do not draw a man closer to the Holy One, blessed be He, unless they are accompanied by kavannah."[71]

In our discussion of priestly religion, we used the metaphor of entropy, the notion that the world was inclined toward a state of disorder and required the active intervention produced by the priestly sacrifices. Within the world of Kabbalah, the playing field is similarly askew.[72] Although mitzvot require kavannah to have a cosmic impact, transgressions do not. This double standard of intentionality is in evidence in the realms of both ritual and ethics. Prayer can be outwardly perfect, but if the pray-er does not "know how deep the power of prayer is, and from which place it begins and to which it emanates forth as a chain," the sefirot will not be united.[73] "If one does not know the secret of a mitzvah, one cannot fulfill it properly."[74] In terms of transgressions, however, intention is not required. The Zohar is extremely disapproving of anger, for example, and throwing objects in anger is considered like presenting offerings to the *sitra achra*.[75] Although it takes intention to not become angry, it takes no intention to react angrily. Even transgressions as obviously inadvertent as nocturnal emissions are described as unleashing satanic forces.[76]

---

69 Tishby, *Wisdom*, 373.
70 Ibid., 54.
71 Ibid., 953. Zohar 3:183b. See Brachot 13a.
72 Green, *Guide*, 153.
73 Gikatilla, *Gates of Light* 1:167. Cited in Lachter, *Kabbalistic Revolution*, 131.
74 Galya Raza, 65. Cited in Matt, "The Mystic," in Green, *Jewish Spirituality*, 395.
75 Tishby, *Wisdom*, 1333.
76 Ibid., 1365–67 and accompanying notes.

For both benefit and harm, actions by Jews can affect the super-nal realm and the very being of God. It is no coincidence, as many have noted, that Kabbalah gives Jews tremendous metaphysical power in a time and place where their lack of political power was a source of shame.[77] Christians and Muslims were fighting over the Land of Israel with the Jews far off on the sidelines, fearful, insecure, and dependent on the mercurial whims of the leaders and subjects of their host nations. The Zohar, however, places God's fate in Jewish hands. Even divine actions are understood as reactions to what Jews do. "Deeds above are aroused by deeds below."[78]

Medieval mysticism, in general, held gentiles in very low esteem. To put it bluntly, Jews were quite willing to concede that the Christian doctrine of original sin and the subsequent depravity of humanity was true—for Christians. For Jews, the covenant at Sinai removed the snake's "pollution."[79] To put it more bluntly, "Non-Jews possess only a *nefesh hayyah*, 'living soul' or 'animal soul,' created from the earth rather than the Godhead. . . . Non-Jews are like animals, and Jews are like God."[80]

Mordechai Kaplan, the founding father of Reconstructionist Judaism, said the entire concept of the chosen people "is haunted by an inferiority complex!"[81] Granted. While I reject any ontological distinc-tion between Jews and gentiles, let us remember the historical context. "The Christian supersessionist theology of the age claimed tirelessly that Judaism after Christ was an empty shell, a formalist attachment to the past, lacking in true faith. . . . In this context, the Zohar may be viewed as a grand defense of Judaism, a poetic demonstration of the truth and superiority of Jewish faith."[82] "Kabbalistic discourse concerning the cen-trality of Jews constitutes a rejection and inversion of such [pernicious] Christian depictions of Jewishness."[83]

The geographic epicenter of the Jewish inferiority complex was Jerusalem, the earthly city. The locus and focus of Jewish power is in the

---

77 Matt, "The Mystic," in Green, *Jewish Spirituality*, 397.
78 Zohar 3:38b.
79 Zohar 1:126a/b and see Yevamot 103b.
80 Lachter, *Kabbalistic Revolution*, 98.
81 Mordecai M. Kaplan, *The Meaning of God in Modern Jewish Religion* (Detroit: Wayne State University Press, 1995), 94.
82 Green, *Guide*, 88.
83 Lachter, *Kabbalistic Revolution*, 93.

supernal realms of the Godhead. After centuries of yearning to secure, retain, and return to a homeland, at some point prior to the Spanish exile of 1492, the Land of Israel receded to the background of the Jewish imagination. As Green points out, the Jerusalem Temple becomes a symbol of inner, spiritual experience.[84] Prayer had already replaced the sacrifices for the rabbis, and the kabbalists rendered unto prayer the same function. "Such a doctrine attenuates the negative implication of exile, insofar as Jews retain the same theurgic role by different means."[85] The political and military nationalism of rabbinic messianism had atrophied. Nevertheless, Scholem's description exaggerated the extent of the shift. "Redemption becomes a spiritual revolution which will uncover the mystic meaning, the 'true interpretation' of the Torah. Thus a mystic utopia takes the place of the national and secular utopia of the early [rabbinic] writers."[86]

Moshe Idel has challenged Scholem's articulation of this issue. Medieval mysticism did not *replace* national redemption with spiritual redemption, rather it foregrounded spiritual redemption and added novel terminology. What fascinates the Zohar is the inner workings of God, the sefirot, and how everything in the world and in the Torah reflect and participate in those relationships. Nevertheless, the goal of the priestly version of rabbinic religiosity, national redemption, was identical for some of the most influential streams of medieval mysticism.

> By following some earlier [rabbinic] traditions, however, many Kabbalists developed a theory that assumes the existence of a linkage between the national redemption and the redemption of the divine power that participates in the vicissitudes of the Jewish people, the Shechinah. This approach is found in the theosophical-theurgical Kabbalah [i.e., the Zohar], where the unification of the feminine divine presence with the male divine powers was considered to be part of the process of redemption of both the divine realm and the world.[87]

---

84 Green, *Guide*, 138.
85 Lachter, *Kabbalistic Revolution*, 135.
86 Scholem, *Messianic Idea*, 40.
87 Moshe Idel, "Multiple Forms of Redemption in Kabbalah and Hasidism," *Jewish Quarterly Review 101*, no. 1 (2011): 33.

Since kabbalists maintained that the inner workings of God are on display in the Torah, it makes sense that the Zohar's literary form is that of a Torah commentary. Although there were earlier rabbis who compared the Torah to an eternal bride, the Zohar's approach to the Torah is qualitatively distinct. The eroticism of rabbinic religiosity has been both intensified and projected onto the sefirotic world.

> The hermeneutical premise of the Zohar, namely, that the relationship between the student and the text is not that of a subject and an object but rather of two subjects—and an erotic one at that—opens up many avenues regarding what constitutes awakening to the Torah and its study, as well as the nature of the student's activity when engaged in interpreting and innovating Torah.[88]

To recite the Shema (Deuteronomy 6:4) is not to declare God's unity, but actually to unite the uncoupled sefirot within the Godhead.[89] The mitzvah to know God is understood by the kabbalists as knowing the theosophic secrets of Kabbalah and how the sefirot map onto the divine reality.[90] To cleave to God (Deuteronomy 4:4 and 10:20), a phrase worshippers declare immediately prior to reading Torah in synagogue, "is to awaken in the reader a mystical consciousness."[91] When Isaiah describes Israel as God's servant "in whom I [God] glory (et'paar)" (Isaiah 49:3), the Zohar understands that we serve God in the sefirotic world by drawing together the "left side" of justice with the "right side" of grace into the golden mean of compassion (tiferet, etymologically related to et'paar).[92] The preposition bet (ב) can mean in ("in whom I glory), but it can also mean through. In the Zohar's mystical reading of Isaiah, God's polarities converge into glory, tiferet, through the thoughts and deeds of Israel, God's servant. We serve as the escorts and matchmakers bringing together the different divine attributes including the male and female.

---

88 Melila Hellner-Eshed, *A River Flows from Eden: The Language of Mystical Experience in the Zohar*, trans. Nathan Wolski (Stanford: Stanford University Press, 2009), 162.

89 Lachter, *Kabbalistic Revolution*, 151–58.

90 Ibid., 79-80; also Hellner-Eshed, *A River Flows from Eden*, 320-21. To know God is the very first, logically, of RaMBaM's commandments, M. T., h. Fundamentals of the Torah 1:1.

91 Hellner-Eshed, *A River Flows from Eden*, 291.

92 Zohar 1:11a.

The sefirah with which the community of Israel has the greatest interaction is the tenth sefirah, variously labeled Shechinah, community of Israel, moon, among others. The moon has no light of its own, it reflects the light of the sun. In medieval physiology, a woman contributed nothing to the formation of a human. She merely served as the incubator for the fetus. The tenth sefirah is a passive receptacle and the most mercurial of the sefirot. The Shechinah, which is grammatically female in Hebrew, takes on gendered feminine attributes only in the Middle Ages. The moon, associated with a woman's menstrual cycle, waxes and wanes. As we saw above, sometimes the Shechinah serves as the spigot of divine blessing into this world, yet at other times, she becomes Satan's consort who is responsible for the pandemonium in the Jews' world. As a contemporary theologian, what interests me most about this aspect of God that "faces" the world is not its flux, per se, but its constant adaptations to novel contexts.

> Come and see: at first, she is green like a calla lily whose leaves are green. Afterwards, like a star lily (*shoshanah*), red with shades of white. Shoshanah, with six (*shesh*) leaves. Shoshanah, who changes herself (*ishtaniat*) from shade to shade, and changes (*shaniat*) her shade. Shoshanah, first a calla lily. When she desires to couple with king, she is called calla lily. Afterwards, she has cleaved to the King through those kisses, she is called Shoshanah because it is written, "His lips are like star lilies" (Song of Songs 5:13). "A star lily of the valleys" for she changes her shades, sometimes for good, sometimes for evil, sometimes for mercy and sometimes for judgement.[93]

Three different sets of metaphors are braided in this brief passage. We have the personal experience of transitioning from the nervousness of anticipating a first kiss with a true love, to being flushed and blushing upon a kiss which leads to more. Botanically, we go from green and unripe, to red and ripe. In the Land of Israel, this shift is seen between the calla lilies and the star lilies. What in the context of the *Song of Songs*, the mystics' favorite biblical book, refers to two different flowers is read by the Zohar as the same flower but in two different phases. The eroticism of the Song of Songs' characters is but a symbol of the relationship between

---

93 Ibid., 1:221a.

the Community of Israel and the Godhead. What the Community of Israel/Shechinah must do is unite with the six (*shesh*) upper sefirot in the upper world, not counting the very top triad, which will culminate in goodness and mercy flowing into the lower world. To my point, one of the names of the Shechinah is *shoshanah*, or lily, precisely because she changes (*shinah*) depending on the behavior of the Community of Israel in the lower world. The divine planes of language, creation, and Torah merge in the mystical consciousness into a three-dimensional dynamic unity.

Rabbinic tradition emphasizes the notion of continuous revelation. Since revelation for the mystics involves divine disclosure and divine self-revelation, that is also continuous. Rabbi Asher ben David, one of the students of Rabbi Yitzhak the Blind who traveled from France to Spain with kabbalistic traditions, wrote:

> "A river *issues* from Eden to water the garden" (Gen 2:10). The meaning of a river (*nahar*) is from the word for light in Aramaic (*nehora*). That is the inner light which continuously comes from Eden. Therefore, it says "issues" and does not say "issued," because it does not cease and is spreading all the time among the attributes.[94]

What may be the earliest use of the word *zohar* in the composition bearing the same name refers to the soul's descent into the body.[95] Hellner-Eshed traces the word throughout the text and suggests *zohar* means "the flow of sparkling colors that erupts from the river of divine plenty, the power that creates and sustains reality. . . . It is the potentiality that bursts forth from the divine river."[96] Given this image of the flow of vitality, it is perhaps easier to understand how a disruption in that flow could induce dis-order. For the mystics, disorder results not only from transgressions, but from making a "molten image" of the divine dynamic by allowing one particular instantiation of past divine representations to

---

94   Cited in Hellner-Eshed, *A River Flows*, 232.
95   Pinchas Giller, *The Enlightened Will Shine: Symbolization and Theurgy in the Later Strata of the Zohar* (Albany: State University of New York Press, 1993), 22. See Zohar 1:116a.
96   Hellner-Eshed, *A River Flows*, 263.

become one's one and only god.[97] The cardinal sin of religion is *reifying* a metaphor.

Although there were scores of kabbalistic texts produced in the decades surrounding the composition of the Zohar, nothing—not even texts written by the same authors as the Zohar—rivals its brilliance and influence. Yet, the Zohar is anything but an accessible and systematic text. In contrast, Joseph ibn Gikatilla's book *Gates of Light* (Sha'arei Orah) invites the uninitiated through the gates toward the light. Unlike the Zohar which takes the form of Torah commentary, Gikatilla (1248–c. 1305) arranges his gates of light according to the sefirot. The Jewish body becomes central in the theurgy of Spanish Kabbalah through a mystical understanding of God's creation of humanity corresponding to the divine image. "Know and believe that there is a special quality to the essence of the purity of limbs that allows for man to cleave to the Shechinah even though it is a consuming fire. It is also a fire that warms and comforts those who cleave to it with a pure soul that is known as the 'light of God.'"[98] Whereas the rabbis warned their community against the unmediated approach to the consuming fire, Gikitilla invites his readers closer through the portal of the tenth sefirah, the Shechinah.

> The kabbalistic dictum that "one limb sustains—or strengthens—another [supernal] limb" became a widespread statement by the end of the thirteenth century. . . . This is part of a more comprehensive theory, whose sources are rabbinic, which established a correspondence between the 613 limbs of the human body and the same number of commandments, both positive and negative. It is hard to overestimate the contribution this correlation makes—that envisages the anatomy of the body in the light of ritual—to the development of the theosophical-theurgical Kabbalah.[99]

Foregoing phylacteries during morning prayers has cosmic consequences. And that is "only" a sin of omission! Kabbalah has been called reactionary precisely because of the dramatic repercussions

---

97 Ibid., 179–80. My analysis differs slightly from Hellner-Eshed's.

98 Gikatilla, *Gates of Light*, 45.

99 Moshe Idel, "On the Performing Body in Theosophical-Theurgical Kabbalah: Some Preliminary Remarks," in *The Jewish Body: Corporeality, Society, and Identity in the Renaissance and Early Modern Period*, ed. Maria Diemling and Giuseppe Veltri (Leiden: Brill, 2009), 253–54.

which threaten God as a result of Jewish neglect of the commandments. Although we have encountered antecedents of theurgy in the priestly Torah, the medieval centrifuge has isolated and concentrated this tradition. Thus, Spanish Kabbalah is both reactionary *and* a reaction to the perceived threat to Judaism by philosophic and rational explanations for the commandments. The translation of RaMBaM's *Guide of the Perplexed* at the beginning of the thirteenth century into Hebrew from Arabic has long been considered a precipitating factor in the emergence of kabbalistic literature. Menachem Kellner convincingly argues that RaMBaM was moved to write *The Guide* because of the mystical ideas he had already encountered, and deemed blasphemous, in the twelfth century.

In the previous chapter, I suggested that there is a closer relationship between mysticism and halakhah than has been generally acknowledged. A similar, but gentler critique of scholarly and academic compartmentalization applies to medieval philosophy and Kabbalah. The terms themselves (philosophy and Kabbalah) do not lend themselves to nuance, yet there are several prominent Jewish thinkers who straddle these classic distinctions. RaMBaM may be considered a mystic, of the Sufi variety, who rejects the ideas of divine need and divine immanence. Gikatilla does not denigrate philosophy, he simply devalues it as a source of wisdom in comparison to the revelatory secrets of Kabbalah that have been passed down through oral transmission. Indeed, by the end of the fourteenth century, we see figures like Hasdei Crescas who use philosophical argumentation against the regnant Maimonidean Aristotelianism, yet seem to reflect a kabbalistic worldview.[100] By the fifteenth century, the medieval centrifuge winds down, and philosophy has largely been overwhelmed and piously subsumed by Kabbalah.

Beginning in 1391, life for Spanish Jews became increasingly perilous. Anti-Jewish riots in that year claimed the lives of thousands of Jews, including Hasdei Crescas' only son. At roughly the same time, philosophy and Kabbalah became less distinct, and magic and astrology became part of the intellectual mix.[101] Although conceptual similarities and ritual parallels between Kabbalah and Christianity have been noted for some

---

100 Warren Zev Harvey, "Kabbalistic Elements in Hasdei Crescas' *Light of the Lord*," *Jerusalem Studies in Jewish Thought* 2 (1982-1983) [Hebrew]: 75-109.

101 Moshe Idel, "The Magical and Neoplatonic Interpretations of the Kabbalah in the Renaissance," in Cooperman, *Jewish Thought in the Sixteenth Century*, 186-242.

time, recently there has been increased attention paid to the role of *conversos* and returning Jews in innovations in Jewish thought.[102] Ironically, the increased importance of inwardness for both philosophers and mystics provided a protected niche for crypto-Jews in Spain. Consider Profayt Duran who was forcibly converted to Catholicism in 1391 upon threat of death.

> By adopting kavannah as the defining factor in Jewish identity, Duran had solved his own circumstantial problem as well: for him, too, the outer form of a nominal Christian does not signify the inner truth. By stamping mechanical observance of the commandments as not only insufficient but indeed potentially pernicious and harmful, he has leveled the playing field between Jew and *converso*: the performance of a few commandments with full and passionate intention by a *converso* becomes superior to the perfunctory performance of many commandments by an unconverted Jew.[103]

Duran, who had marginalized Talmud study while still an unconverted Jew, ultimately championed the ideal of cleaving to God through the Torah, its memorization, and constant contemplation—as opposed to the performance of mitzvot. Historically, we saw the more extreme Tosafot, like Rabbenu Tam, championing Talmud at the expense of Torah, and in Duran we see something of a distorted mirror image. For our purposes, as we move toward the Kabbalah of Safed after the Spanish exile of 1492, it is worth noting a theory associated with Shlomo Alkabetz of Safed (1500–1576): "For she [the Torah] brings us to a state of Devekut [cleaving] to Him, may He be exalted, because when we cleave to her, we also cleave to our Creator, since He and His wisdom are one."[104]

Hoping to avoid what Isadore Twersky has called "the pitfalls of precursorism," I am not drawing a straight line between Duran and

---

102 Arthur Green, "*Shekhinah*, the Virgin Mary, and the Song of Songs: Reflections on a Kabbalistic Symbol in Its Historical Context," *Association of Jewish Studies Review* 26, no. 1 (2002): 1-52; Shaul Magid, *From Metaphysics to Midrash: Myth, History, and the Interpretation of Scripture in Lurianic Kabbala* (Bloomington: Indiana University Press, 2008); and Maud Kozodoy, *The Secret Faith of Maestre Honoratus: Profayt Duran and Jewish Identity in Late Medieval Iberia* (Philadelphia: University of Pennsylvania Press, 2015).

103 Kozodoy, *Secret Faith*, 159-60.

104 Alkabetz, Ayelet Ahavim 42a. Cited in Pachter, "Concept of Devekut," in Twersky, *Studies in Medieval Jewish History and Literature*, 178.

Alkabetz. Nevertheless, there are other scattered points linking the intellectual world of Duran and that of Alkabetz. The invention of movable type combined with the influence of Martin Luther's *sola Scriptura* of 1517 represent bold points on our scatter graph. The increased availability and emphasis on Torah allowed Duran's ideas, and writings, to enjoy a dramatic technological and cultural boost. The presence of a *converso* community in Safed is another point on the "best fit line" between Duran and Alkabetz because the conversos in Spain and Portugal had been well positioned to privilege the Torah over the public performance of the commandments. Towards the end of this chapter we will meet Baruch Spinoza (1632–1677), a descendant of Portuguese conversos who had fled to Amsterdam and there reestablished their Jewish identities. What a shattering notion it must have been to those whose religious faith focused on the divinity of the Torah to argue explicitly, as Spinoza would, that the Torah is an all-too-human document and should be treated like any other book.

Shattering it must have been, as well, to suffer the ignominy and hardships of exile. After hundreds of years on the Iberian Peninsula, faring relatively well, and in some cases, exceptionally well, between 1492 and 1498 the Jews of Spain and Portugal were given the ultimatum to flee or convert to Catholicism. Although many did opt for conversion, with varying degrees of sincerity, hundreds of thousands of Jews abandoned their homes to preserve their identities. Not since the destruction of the Temple and the catastrophic culmination of the Bar Kochvah Revolt had there been such a challenge to Judaism. Messianic rumblings bubbled to the surface among Sephardic refugees of the northeastern Mediterranean and the Balkans. Particularly after the successes of the Ottoman Empire against Byzantine Christianity from 1453–1517, both Ashkenazi Jews and Sephardic refugees began to settle in the Land of Israel.[105] By the middle of the sixteenth century, the mountaintop village of Safed became home to a group of mystics who would forever change Judaism.

Rabbi Yitzhak Luria (1534–1572), known as the holy *Ari* (lion), was born in Jerusalem and spent his final years in Safed articulating a new theology, along with its religious implications, to an elite group of

---

105 Isaiah Tishby, "Acute Apocalyptic Messianism," in *Essential Papers on Messianic Movements and Personalities in Jewish History*, ed. Marc Saperstein (New York: New York University Press, 1992), 259-86.

disciples. One of those disciples, Hayyim Vital (1543–1620), wrote down the Ari's radical new vision, and it is largely through Vital that we know of the three stages of creation that together may be the most powerful constellation of ideas in Jewish thought: *tzimtzum*, the shattering of the vessels, and *tikkun*.[106]

In broad strokes, the Ari opens the drama of creation with the Infinite light, *Eyn Sof*, the unknown, unknowable, undifferentiated divine in its place, in every place, absent from no place. For reasons to be discussed below, the thought arises in the divine will to create that which is other than God. In a physical metaphor for the metaphysical, the *Eyn Sof* withdraws its luminescence from a point and continues to withdraw until there is a spherical space, a vacuum, that is void of the infinity of divinity. This 360-degree withdrawal of the divine into the divine, this equidistant contraction away from the initial point of evacuation, this finite expansion of nothingness within the divine infinite is the process of *tzimtzum*.

There is something of a consensus among Kabbalah scholars that the impetus for *tzimtzum* was cathartic.[107] There are multiple and contradictory articulations of Luria's Kabbalah which have come down to us through his students. I find helpful Elliot Wolfson's explanation of Vital's rendition of Lurianic Kabbalah: "The purpose of the initial withdrawal of light was to crystallize the latent forces of judgment within the Infinite to form the *bosina' de-qardinuta'*, the hardened flame, which serves as the instrument of judgment that gives shape and measure to the emanations that [will] proceed from *Eyn Sof*."[108]

What was initially described as a withdrawal was not complete. There remained in that space a trace of the evacuated divine light. This trace, the residue of the infinite luminescence (*reshimu*), crackles with the remnant of "light with the power of judgment, which is the root of the strong judgment, and all of the trace and judgment are mixed together, and as soon as the mercy is withdrawn the judgment is revealed. Since the

---

106 Dan, *Jewish Mysticism*, 107.

107 In addition to Scholem's essay on Lurianic Kabbalah in *Major Trends of Jewish Mysticism*, 244–86, see Isaiah Tishby, *The Doctrine of Evil and Shells in Lurianic Kabbalah* [Heb.] (Jerusalem: Magnes Press, 1942); and Elliot R. Wolfson, "Divine Suffering and the Hermeneutics of Reading: Philosophical Reflections on Lurianic Mythology," in *Suffering Religion*, ed. Robert Gibbs and Elliot R. Wolfson (New York: Routledge, 2002), 101–62.

108 Wolfson, "Divine Suffering," in Gibbs and Wolfson, *Suffering Religion*, 130.

trace in only a vestige [*roshem*], it belongs to judgment, and it is mixed together with it."[109]

Attendant to the divine thought of *tzimtzum* was a concentration of the force of judgement or restraint (*din*), which was associated in rabbinic literature and the Zohar with justice. (This aspect of justice in earlier mystical literature has a destructive edge when untempered by mercy.) What was intentionally left behind, abandoned, purged, or even exiled after the *tzimtzum*, therefore, had a higher concentration of *din* than had been present in the undifferentiated *Eyn Sof* prior to the *tzimtzum*. In Vital's description below, *tzimtzum* results in the remaining, "denser" elements forming an amorphous mass within the surrounding "lighter" vacuum created by the withdrawn light of *Eyn Sof*.

> In this manner was the contraction of the light that gathered above as the place [below] remained vacant. Then all the coarseness and thickness of the judgment that was in the light of *Eyn Sof* as a drop in the great ocean is clarified and separated, and it descends and is gathered in that vacated space, and an amorphous mass (*golem*) is made from the coarseness and thickness of the aforementioned power of judgment. This amorphous mass is surrounded by the light of *Eyn Sof* from above, below, and the four sides.[110]

Before offering a different perspective on *tzimtzum*, we need to understand its consequences: the breaking of the vessels. The second movement of the Lurianic symphony begins with an emanating ray of light from the post-withdrawal *Eyn Sof* into the relatively empty center. The ray refracts through the vestiges of the withdrawn light, the amorphous mass which twinkles imperceptibly through concentrations of *din*/judgement. Ten roughhewn vessels of containment, called sefirot, coalesce from the first burst.[111] As the light continues to emanate from *Eyn Sof*, the vessels fill with its light.

The vessels, however, had not coalesced equally. The first three vessels, corresponding to the upper three sefirot, were able to contain the

---

109 Yosef ibn Tabul, *Derush Hefsi Ba*, 1c; cited in Wolfson, "Divine Suffering," in Gibbs and Wolfson, *Suffering Religion*, 120-21. See also Scholem, *Major Trends*, 263.

110 Vital, *Liqqutim Hadashim*, 17-18. Cited in Wolfson, "Divine Suffering," in Gibbs and Wolfson, *Suffering Religion*, 128.

111 Tishby, *The Doctrine*, 23.

vibrancy of light from *Eyn Sof*. As light spilled over from the third to the fourth vessel, the ability of the lower vessels to contain the light deteriorated, and the lower seven vessels spider webbed and ultimately shattered. The now uncontained light returned to its source in *Eyn Sof*, as well as some of the "light" that had comprised the vessels. That initial stream of light from the undifferentiated *Eyn Sof* had some aspects of *din*/judgement. When the vessels shattered, differentiation ensued. The aspects of *din* accreted and remained in the not-quite-empty space while the unalloyed light returned to its source in the *Eyn Sof*. As a result of the shattering of the vessels, then, the concentration of *din* increased yet again, and the cataclysm became a catalyst. In the language of metallurgy, the silver was separated from the dross. What had been the roots of judgment now became the roots of evil. In Luria's mythical language, the shattered vessels now became shards, shells, and husks (*klipot*). To be sure, sparks of divine light were still present in the klipot, for if not, they would cease to exist. But there was now an activated element of impurity or evil that had coalesced.

Scholem noted that in the process of *tzimtzum*, exile is the primordial act of the Father which is then recapitulated repeatedly by the sons, most recently by the exiles from Iberia. In priestly religion, in the rabbinic world, and in the Zohar, we exiled God;[112] in Lurianic Kabbalah, God exiled Godself as a prerequisite for the creation of that which is not God. In the Zohar, the *Sitra Achra* crystallizes when judgment, untempered by mercy, establishes its own dominion.[113] Because of this long-standing association between judgment and evil, and the then recent trauma of exile from Spain, Kabbalah scholars have tended to interpret *tzimtzum* as a purging of potential evil, the roots of judgment, from within the *Eyn Sof*. In the second phase of creation, the emanation from *Eyn Sof* and the consequent shattering of the vessels, the roots of *judgment* break their bonds with divine mercy and compassion, and with that uncoupling they transmute into the roots of *evil*. It is in this world of *klipot* which our creation has emerged. Thus, the exile of the Jews from the Iberian peninsula,

112 The Zohar, 1:53b. See "Adam's Sin," in Daniel Chanan Matt, *Zohar: Book of Enlightenment* (Mahwah: Paulist Press, 1983), 54, and *The Zohar: Pritzker Edition*, vol. 1, trans. with commentary by Daniel C. Matt (Stanford: Stanford University Press, 2003), 297–98.
113 Green, *Guide*, 44.

along with the rest of the travails of Jewish history, can be explained by the forces of evil that are the substrate of our reality.

Both Scholem and Dan discuss how the reality of evil so deeply resonated with both the refugees and other Jews who witnessed from afar the explosion of Spanish Jewry. *Tzimtzum* depicts a Godless world; the breaking of the vessels imagines something like negatively charged divine ions that propagate negativity unless counteracted—that is, redeemed, through mitzvot. Just as in the priestly Torah, the powers of uncleanness are contagious.

Nevertheless, there were alternatives to this version of Lurianic Kabbalah, particularly from Moshe Cordovero (1522–1570), that diluted the divinity of the demonic. "The truth is that above, in the world of the divine emanations," writes Cordovero, "no evil thing descends from heaven, for up there everything is spiritual."[114] For Cordovero, worldly evil is the corruption of divine goodness which awaits purification through teshuvah. "He does not deny the actual existence, or even the ferocity, of earthly evil; he just denies that it is really, constantly bad. Evil is ephemeral, while good is eternal."[115] Dan explains why Luria's depiction of evil, rather than Cordovero's, lodged itself in the Jewish psyche:

> When Luria explained the power of the gentiles as derived from the power of Satan [*Sitra Achra*], his ideas were much more easily accepted than theories explaining that the tortures inflicted by the gentiles on the Jews sprang from God's eternal love for the people of Israel. . . . Lurianic myth became the dominant Jewish ideology because it succeeded in creating a harmony between its symbols and Jewish reality, while destroying the harmony in the divine worlds and postulating that evil did indeed descend from heaven.[116]

In the Zohar, Adam's transgression in the garden was the earthly manifestation of creation gone awry. Evil emerged in the process of creation, not as a precondition for creation. "According to Lurianic theology, the source of evil is completely independent of human action. . . . *Evil is*

---

114 Cited in Joseph Dan, "'No Evil Descends from Heaven'—Sixteenth-Century Jewish Concepts of Evil" in *Jewish Thought in the Sixteenth Century*, ed. Bernard Dov Cooperman (Cambridge, MA: Harvard University Press, 1983), 91.
115 Ibid., 100.
116 Ibid., 103.

one of the basic potentialities of the eternal Godhead."[117] The Torah contains textual fossils of great sea creatures that challenged God's supremacy. Those myths were elaborated upon in aggadic literature. Luria unleashes those evil forces of rabbinic Aggadah *and gives them autonomy.* They are no longer parasitic on human evil as in the Zohar. They are negative divine ions, divine atoms which have had their positive charge, which kept the atom in equilibrium, stripped away. In the Zohar, human transgressions fed evil. In Lurianic Kabbalah, mitzvot are required to starve evil by redeeming the divine sparks that would otherwise quicken the *klipot.* Given the dualism of Luria, it seems to me that monotheism has blinked. We now live in a much scarier universe. But, like Cordovero, I would like to offer a different reading of Luria and highlight certain texts that have been somewhat marginalized.

Tzimtzum is not a singularity in the Lurianic universe; it is the first step in a continuous, two-step process which leads to emanation. "Every new act of emanation and manifestation is preceded by one of concentration and retraction. . . . The whole of Creation constitutes a gigantic process of divine inhalation and exhalation."[118] If the cathartic view of *tzimtzum* is our only view, then we are left with the image of the perpetual purging of unalloyed judgment from the deepest recesses of the Godhead. We have seen how an immoral universe is explicable on such a reading, but emphasizing exile and purgation obfuscates a crucial alternative. I concede the possibility that I am reading Lurianic Kabbalah through my post-Darwinian spectacles; yet, I will also note that Tishby and Scholem may have read the same material through their emigrant, European, and post-Shoah lenses.[119]

Luria's task of *tikkun* centers on the uplifting of the sparks which had adhered to the *klipot*/shards. Vital writes that the shards were animated "in order to be returned and redeemed."[120] We are not only redeeming the sparks, we are also redeeming the *klipot*! The sparks attached

---

117 Ibid., 91. My emphasis.
118 Scholem, *Major Trends*, 261 and 263.
119 Gerhard Scholem was born in Berlin in 1897 and emigrated to the Land of Israel in 1923 as the Nazi Party was forming. Isaiah Tishby, Scholem's student, was born in Hungary in 1903 and emigrated to the Land of Israel in 1933. The annihilation of European Jewry may have influenced their decisions about which of the competing explanations for *tzimtzum* they favored.
120 Vital, Etz Chayyim. Cited in Tishby, *The Doctrine*, 36.

themselves to the shards so that the shards could be detected and not be permanently abandoned.[121] The commander does not abandon his fallen soldiers, however disabled, on the battlefield. The sparks animating the shards are beacons to integrate and harmonize all the divine forces in our capacity.

Tishby cites several passages where Luria acknowledges that the *klipot* can be converted, as it were. More precisely, through the power of our teshuvah, we are able to convert the *klipot* back into forces of judgment that add to God's holiness rather than oppose it.[122] That's akin to what Reish Lakish said in the Talmud: teshuvah transforms intentional transgressions into merits (Yoma 86b). Moreover, it seems that the *klipot* themselves can be redeemed through prayer and mitzvot, not only teshuvah. Although there has been a dominant reading of Luria whereby the uplifting of the sparks starves the shards of their vitality rather than redeems them, I believe there are grounds for this alternative reading.

Redemption, Tishby tells us, is not to purify the impure, but to destroy it. (Tishby first published this work, in Jerusalem, in 1942. It is difficult to hear the language of *destroying the impure* and not think of Nazi Europe.) He continues, however, to qualify his assertion: "We have already seen that as a result of the forces of holiness coming together with evil, evil can be transformed to goodness prior to redemption. But this style of tikkun is impermanent, and if there is a subsequent shifting of forces, that goodness can be transformed back to evil."[123] Nothing is irredeemable. On the other hand, all progress is vulnerable to backsliding. The price of progress is eternal vigilance.

Rewinding through Luria's phases of creation, we can reframe the dominant reading of a cathartic *tzimtzum,* too. Tishby offers several possible explanations for the crystallization of the roots of judgment consequent to *tzimtzum.* Among those Tishby rejects is a suggestion by Hayyim Vital that the roots of judgment are the necessary by-products of existence outside *Eyn Sof.*[124] As Scholem noted, it would have been obvious to all that "a perfect world cannot be created, for it would then be

---

121 Ibid., 35–6.
122 Ibid., 81–2. Cordovero emphasizes this point. See chapter four of his *The Palm Tree of Deborah* (Brooklyn: Menucha Publishers, 2012).
123 Tishby, *The Doctrine*, 141.
124 Ibid., 56.

identical to God Himself, who cannot duplicate Himself, but only restrict Himself."[125]

Here are two reasons for foregrounding the "necessary by-product" explanation which still, it must be noted, explains the presence of radical evil in the world. One of the many names of God in the Torah is El Shaddai. In rabbinic literature, that name is associated with God's word, *dai*, which constrains the creative process. "It was I [God] who said to the world, 'Dai!' [Enough!] and to the land, 'Dai!" Had I not said, 'Dai!' to both the heavens and the earth, they would still be stretching forth even now."[126] Infinity withdrawing into itself is, to be charitable, a paradox. Withdrawing from infinite light with the intention of subsequently emanating discrete quanta of that infinite light *requires* a force to constrain the emanating infinity from reuniting with the withdrawn infinity. *Tzimtzum*, to be effective, had to leave a residual of Dai. Once we enter this paradoxical myth of the Infinite withdrawing into itself, it strikes me as nearly necessary to insist that the infinite, divine creative capacity be checked by some equally powerful force. The rabbis intuited this and attributed the name Shaddai to that function. Although the roots of judgment/restraint/containment do manifest when isolated from the divine equilibrium of *Eyn Sof*, they also serve the necessary function of preserving the boundary between *Eyn Sof* and its subsequent emanations.

My suggestion is that the goal of *tzimtzum* was not to purify *Eyn Sof* from the roots of judgement. Exporting those roots was a necessary and *desired* by-product of *tzimtzum*. My reading of the holy Ari is that the act of *tzimtzum* was precipitated by an existential aloneness that shaded into loneliness. In the Torah, God comes to understand that it is not good for the human to be alone (Genesis 2:18). Given philosophical descriptions of an infinite God, and Crescas' argument that a vacuum is not irrational, as Aristotle had insisted, Luria carved out a place for the One, infinite God to assuage His loneliness. It is not good for God to be alone. As the poet wrote, "*One* is the loneliest number."[127] The goal of *tzimtzum* is relationship.

125 Gershom Scholem, *On the Mystical Shape of the Godhead: Basic Concepts in the Kabbalah,* trans. Jonathan Chipman (New York: Schocken Books, 1991), 84.
126 Genesis Rabbah 5:10. The Zohar also cites this midrash and provides a sefirotic interpretation, 3:11b.
127 Harry Nillson, "One": 1968.

In Plato's *Timaeus*, creation occurs because the creator wants or needs to share. There is goodness in the creator, but that goodness is incomplete if not enjoyed by others. Luria's God is in pain like a heifer who needs to nurse and like a lover who needs to love (P'sachim 112a). The God of the mystics, ultimately and fundamentally, is a god of relationship. With maturity comes the capacity to love; with maturation comes the need to love. The absence of someone, or something, to love is painful; and that pain, almost involuntarily, creates the space for the other to occupy. According to one version of Vital, "When the thought arose in the divine will to create worlds *for the good of the other*, He withdrew His Shechinah and removed His light upwards."[128] Martin Heidegger and Jim Morrison would both agree that "into this world we're thrown." Exile is the human condition, the deed of the Father that becomes paradigmatic for the children. But, the cure for the isolation of exile is the invitation to enter into relationship, and I propose *that* invitation is the deed of our ancestor that resounds through the dimensions of our universe.

The final, ongoing phase of creation is that of *tikkun*, the process of reintegrating the fallen sparks, and to the degree possible, the shards, too. As we have seen, the process is arduous. Although this reading of Luria vitiates a full-blown dualism, the unlevel playing field of the priests and the Zohar has become more like the slope of Sisyphus. Entropy reigns, and the neutral has been nullified.

> The only weapon in the hand of man when he tries to assist the divine power in its mythological war against evil are the ethical and religious commandments, those listed in the halakhah, those described in ethical works like Sefer Hasidim, and the many new demands and customs introduced by the Safed community. . . . Every good deed always frees a spark, and every sin always strengthens evil. . . . Idleness and idle thoughts certainly strengthen evil.[129]

Before leaving the realm of Lurianic Kabbalah, it is necessary to clarify the redemption for which medieval mystics yearn. While it is true that there was messianic speculation in the fifteenth and sixteenth centuries, we do not see active messianism amongst the Safed kabbalists. As

---

128 Perush Ha'Ari, Hadrat Hamelekh 43a; cited in Tishby, *The Doctrine*, 24. My emphasis.
129 Dan, *Jewish Mysticism*, 107–9.

counterintuitive as it may be, these mystics living in the Land of Israel were focused on metaphysics, not politics. The goal of *tikkun* was to return exiled souls to God, not exiled bodies to the Land of Israel. As Wolfson has noted, "Restoration entails the elevation of the worlds to the Infinite rather than the constitution of a perfect world in space and time. . . . The eschatological task is to be redeemed from rather than in historical time."[130]

Lurianic Kabbalah was, and remains, a contested expression of Jewish mysticism. In the years following Luria's death, several thinkers attempted systematic presentations for both beginners and more advanced students. Digests became available for those seeking an abridged presentation. A life of asceticism and penitence was promoted for all, not just the rabbinic and mystical elite. Since life is a cosmic battle between the forces of good and evil, one can strengthen the forces of holiness even without having had personally committed a prior transgression.[131] In other words, vicarious atonement for the sins of others now becomes invested with cosmic significance. The ethics promoted by Bahya ibn Pakuda merge with the theurgy of the Zohar and get applied to the ascetic ideals of Hasidei Ashkenaz. Moshe Cordovero's *Palm Tree of Deborah*, published in 1588, is the first ethical handbook designed to expose the uninitiated to this world of Lurianic Kabbalah.

As we approach the final scene of medieval mysticism, it behooves us to note the world-changing events that contributed to the advent of what historians generally call the early modern period. Movable type and the proliferation of printing following Guttenberg's invention of his press in 1456 allowed for an unprecedented ease of access to new texts and ideas. One can think of it as a democratization of ideas, as books moved from universities, monasteries, and libraries into the marketplace. Not long after, Martin Luther took advantage of the proliferation of Bibles with his demands for reformation in 1517. His rallying cry of *sola Scriptura* relied on individuals' appropriation of the Bible from the monopoly previously

---

130 Elliot R. Wolfson, "The Engenderment of Messianic Politics: Symbolic Significance of Sabbatai Sevi's Coronation," in *Toward the Millennium, Messianic Expectations from the Bible to Waco,* ed. Peter Schaefer and Mark R. Cohen (Leiden: Brill, 1998), 212 and 216. As noted above, Idel has qualified this assertion, but Wolfson captures the thrust of mystical attention.

131 Dan, *Jewish Mysticism,* 91.

enjoyed by the Catholic Church. The shift in authority of biblical meaning toward the individual was mirrored by the shift away from the individual in cosmic meaning with the heliocentric theory of Copernicus
(1543, Poland) and discoveries of Galileo (1632, Italy).

The Spanish exile and dispersion of 1492 was tantamount to a major
shifting of Jewish tectonic plates. The legal code published in Safed by
Yosef Caro in 1563 also contributed to the democratization of halakhah by
allowing laymen to consult with an authoritative text rather than a living
authority. The broad dissemination of Safed Kabbalah, with its emphasis
on *tikkun*, began with Cordovero's *Palm Tree of Deborah* in 1588 and continued its dramatic rise in popularity through the publication of *The Two
Tablets of the Covenant* by Isaiah Horowitz (c. 1570–1626) in 1649. Roughly
150 years after the expulsion of the Jews from the Iberian Peninsula, the
next antisemitic spasm erupted in Ukraine. The Khmelnytskyi Revolt
against Polish rule by the Cossacks (1648–1649) led to the destruction of
hundreds of Jewish villages and the massacre of tens of thousands of Jews.

Within a generation after the Khmelnytskyi Revolt, the Jewish world
was ripe for redemption. Onto the scene came the mentally unstable
Shabbatai Tzvi with his prophetic publicist Nathan of Gaza. From March
of 1665 to September of 1666, a messianic frenzy seized Jews in large
swaths of Europe, North Africa, and the Middle East. Attracting the
attention of the Sultan of the Ottoman Empire, Shabbatai was arrested
and given the choice between death or conversion to Islam. Shabbatai
converted. The apostasy of their ostensible messiah did not prevent many
thousands of his followers from remaining faithful to him, and many of
those converted to Islam.

The theological subtleties and disputes within the world of
Sabbatianism need not long detain us. For our purposes, there are just a
few points necessary to emphasize. Divine immanence, the presence of the
divine pulse beating within all reality, serves as the metaphysical bedrock of
both Lurianic Kabbalah and Sabbateanism. Sabbateanism is an antinomian
(law-rejecting) interpretation of Lurianic Kabbalah, the latter of which had
become quasi-normative throughout the entire Jewish community.[132] In
Sabbateanism, it is the messianic redeemer alone who has the capacity to

132 Gershom Scholem, *Sabbatai Sevi: The Mystical Messiah*, trans. R. J. Zwi Werblowsky
(Princeton: Princeton University Press, 1976), 291.

lower himself into the abyss in order to redeem those holy sparks impris-oned in impurity.[133] "The ingathering of the exiles" once applied to Jews in the messianic era; Lurianic Kabbalah took that image as a symbol of the ingathering of exiled divine sparks.[134] Luria imagined the ingathering through mitzvot; Shabbatai Tzvi through "holy" transgressions.[135]

We have already mentioned the doctrine whereby repentance by Ploni can atone for the transgression of Almoni.[136] Vicarious atonement is the theological presupposition for both the Torah's animal sacrifices and the crucifixion of Jesus. For crypto-Jews or conversos, vicarious atonement would have been a familiar religious notion from their time in church. The acceptance of divine immanence, though not unique to Kabbalah, is another commonality between medieval Judaism and Christianity. Scholem acknowledged how Sabbatianism may have found fertile ground among the community of crypto-Jews from Spain and Portugal. Like them, Shabbatai Tzvi seemed outwardly to have adopted a new religion, but inwardly still professed a commitment to Judaism.[137]

It is noteworthy that for those Jews still committed to Sabbatianism even after their messiah's apostasy, what remains of their Judaism is "pure faith, unaccompanied by specific works."[138] Scholem is undoubtedly cor-rect in associating this posture with St. Paul's doctrine of faith, but we have also seen a movement toward inwardness within different expressions of medieval Judaism, particularly the mystical elements. It is true that no other Jewish expression became antinomian, but the seeds of inwardness were sown not just by St. Paul, but by Sufi mystics as well. Indeed, if we think of rabbinic religiosity as excluding the requirement of inwardness, Sabbatianism excludes the requirement of outwardness.[139] God "desires

---

133 Scholem, *Major Trends*, 302.

134 Scholem, *Messianic Idea*, 94.

135 Scholem, *Sabbatai Sevi*, 318.

136 "Ploni Almoni" is the Hebrew name for a generic man. See, e.g., Ruth 4:1. In this case, I am dividing the names to indicate two generic men. In English, we might say, "Peter and Paul."

137 Scholem, *Major Trends*, 309. Magid develops this theme in *From Metaphysics to Midrash*, chapter two.

138 Scholem, *Sabbatai Sevi*, 322.

139 The bracketing of inwardness by rabbinic religiosity may have been, in part, a response to Pauline Christianity. Yet, I believe that the reasons presented in the previous chapter offer a fuller explanation.

the heart/mind" (Sann. 106b) is an old rabbinic adage. Some elements within medieval Judaisms stressed that God wants the heart/mind even more than the performance of mitzvot. Sabbatianism took that notion to a logical conclusion: God wants only the heart/mind and not the mitzvot.

Philosophy

The most famous of the pre-Maimonidean philosophers is Saadia Gaon (882–942), a leader of one of the two rabbinic academies in Babylonia. His philosophic defense of Judaism, informed by the Islamic rationalistic theology of Kalam, is *The Book of Beliefs and Opinions* (933). Jeffrey Macy offers a helpful description of those like Saadia, the rationalistic theologians:

> The Rationalistic Theologians are, at least on the surface, much more open to the use of human reason in the attempt to attain true knowledge than were the Fundamentalistic Theologians. Central to the position of the Rationalistic Theologians is the premise that both reason, properly used, and divine revelation lead to the same unitary truth.[140]

The first question of all medieval philosophers was, "How do we know?" Greek philosophy answered that question without recourse to divine revelation. But the Abrahamic traditions had prophets and scriptures whose claims *seemed* to be in tension with what reason, as mediated through ancient Greek philosophy, *seemed* to prove. The job of the rationalistic philosophers was to unstitch one of those "seems." They employed either figurative biblical interpretation to accord with reason or resorted to philosophy to bolster religious propositions and/or undermine philosophical ones. In other words, and this is really the point, for theologians, be they "Fundamentalistic" or rationalistic, revelation is a source of true knowledge. Indeed, Saadia's first chapter of his *Book of Beliefs and Opinions* answers the questions of how we come to know and argues that revelation is such a source.

Rabbi Moshe ben Maimon (1138–1204), the RaMBaM, was not, in my estimation, a rationalist theologian. He was what Macy has termed a

---

140 Jeffrey Macy, "'True Knowledge' in Medieval Islam and Judaism," *Cultural Traditions and Worlds of Knowledge: Explorations in the Sociology of Knowledge* 7 (1988): 89.

"religious" philosopher. For this category, the Mulsim philosopher Abu Yusuf Ya'kub al-Kindi (c. 801–c. 873) is the prototype. Al-Kindi, like RaMBaM, rejects revelation as a source of knowledge, but values religion for the function it plays in society.[141] Here, I must explicitly acknowledge a lack of scholarly consensus due to RaMBaM's *intentionally* ambiguous writing style. He tells his readers in the introduction to *The Guide of the Perplexed* that he will sometimes contradict himself, i.e. lie, about his true beliefs in order not to upset the mental habits of the unlettered masses. His legacy is, therefore, contested because we are simply unsure of what RaMBaM truly believed.

In his discussion of prophecy, all agree that he brazenly redefines the prophetic event from God reaching out to someone with a specific communication to a person attaining a high degree of intellectual, moral, and imaginative perfection. That combination of endowments should allow such a person, a prophet, to translate their knowledge into symbolic speech that will ideally help move the masses toward intellectual refinement. That is how RaMBaM understands Moshe's revelation at Mount Sinai.[142] RaMBaM's first goal for *The Guide* is also precisely such intellectual refinement: the first thirty-six chapters are dedicated to disabusing Jews of the blasphemy of believing in divine corporeality.[143] Both divine speech and God's outstretched arm are examples of the Torah's figurative language.[144]

Scholars describe this approach toward prophecy as naturalistic. Although there is no unanimity, there does seem to be a consensus among Maimonides scholars that the prophetic event does not add to the prophet's knowledge.[145] The only way in which one's fund of knowl-

---

141 Ibid.: 90.

142 *Guide*, 2:33.

143 It is also a commandment for RaMBaM to understand, to the best of one's capacity, that God is incorporeal (M. T., Fundamentals of the Torah 1:7).

144 *Guide*, 1:65.

145 Lenn Evan Goodman, *Rambam: Readings in the Philosophy of Moses Maimonides* (New York: Viking Press, 1976), 398–403; Moshe Halbertal, *Maimonides: Life and Thought*, trans. Joel Linsider (Princeton: Princeton University Press, 2014), 321–29; Micah Goodman, *Maimonides and the Book that Changed Judaism: Secrets of* The Guide for the Perplexed (Philadelphia: Jewish Publication Society, 2015), 17–39; cf. David B. Blumenthal, "Maimonides' Philosophic Mysticism," *Daat: A Journal of Jewish Philosophy & Kabbalah* 64-66 (2009): v-xxv and M. T., Fundamentals of the Torah 7:1. Note that the description of prophecy in the Mishneh Torah does

edge can be increased is the old-fashioned way—diligent, focused, and systematic study of science and philosophy. In both Maimonides' halakhic work and his philosophic presentation, he redefines the commandment to love God as a commandment to understand God's actions in nature.[146] The more one knows of God's actions, the more one loves God. For this reason, the study of Aristotelian physics and metaphysics cannot be haphazard. RaMBaM concludes the first book of his legal code, the *Book of Knowledge*, with the following demand: "Therefore, one must seclude oneself to understand and intellectually internalize the wisdom and insights which make the Creator known to him according to one's capacity to understand and comprehend."[147] Maimonides made the study of science and philosophy a mitzvah.[148]

As we will see, the journey toward intellectual perfection animates much of RaMBaM's work. His glorification of the intellect, his reliance on Aristotle and Muslim philosophers, and his rewriting of biblical history and its commandments obscure what David Blumenthal calls RaMBaM's "post-cognitive piety." There is a mystical vein in the RaMBaM's sober philosophy that demands we see beyond the exterior to acknowledge the ultimate goal of worship. Scholars like Paul Fenton and Diana Lobel have also helped us place RaMBaM more comfortably in the Islamic world in which he lived. As one scholar has recently reminded us, he may have been called up to read Torah in synagogue as *Rav Moshe ben Rav Maimon ha-Dayyan* (the judge), but his friends called him "Musa," the Arabic name for Moses. RaMBaM was an Arab Jew, and the language of Sufi mysticism, once you are on the lookout, permeates his writings. Blumenthal contends that the "post-cognitive piety" that RaMBaM holds out as the ultimate goal of religious worship could just as well be called philosophic mysticism. RaMBaM's concluding chapters in the *Guide* limn this ideal.

not indicate that the prophet's store of knowledge increases, *per se*, but that his understanding from his knowledge increases. It is the imagination that synthesizes the prophet's knowledge in a dream or dream-like state that constitutes the prophetic experience.

146 Maimonides, M. T., Fundamentals of the Torah 2:2 and *Guide*, 3:28.
147 Maimonides, M. T., h. Teshuvah 10:6.
148 Herbert A. Davidson, "The Study of Philosophy as a Religious Obligation," in *Religion in a Religious Age*, ed. S. D. Goitein (Cambridge: Association for Jewish Studies, 1974), 53–68.

There may be an individual who, through one's apprehension of the true realities and one's bliss in what one has apprehended, achieves a state in which one talks with people and is occupied with one's bodily necessities while one's intellect is wholly turned toward Him, may He be exalted, even while outwardly one is with people—in the sort of way described by the poetical parables that have been invented for these notions: "I sleep but my heart is awake," "The voice of my beloved knocks," and so on. . . .

The philosophers have already explained how the bodily forces of man in his youth prevent the development of moral principles. In a greater measure this is the case as regards the purity of thought which man attains through the perfection of those ideas that lead him to an intense love of God, may He be exalted. For it is impossible that it should be achieved while the bodily humors are in effervescence. Yet in the measure in which the faculties of the body are weakened and the fire of the desires is quenched, the intellect is strengthened, its lights achieve a wider extension, its apprehension is purified, and it rejoices in what it apprehends. The result is that when a perfect man is stricken with years and approaches death, this apprehension increases very powerfully, joy over this apprehension and a great love for the object of apprehension become stronger, until the soul is separated from the body at that moment in this state of pleasure.[149]

The religiosity of such an author cannot be in doubt. I emphasize this point because RaMBaM's rationalism strips away so much myth that for those who equate myth and religion it may seem like RaMBaM is nothing but an atheist wrapped in a rabbi's *tallit* (prayer shawl). RaMBaM's God is not the rabbinic God, but that does nothing to disqualify RaMBaM's theology from informing our own. RaMBaM's Judaism was coherent precisely because he articulated a theology which served as the foundation for his halakhic code of behavior. That is why the Mishneh Torah, his halakhic code, *begins* with *The Book of Knowledge*—that is, statements of God's existence, unity, and incorporeality. Put in philosophical terms, he articulated a metaphysics for his ethics. Given that God and God's relationship to the world are x and y, we should behave in a way that conforms to x and y. Remember, what rabbinic religiosity did was to

---

149 *Guide*, 3:51, 623, and 627. Translations modified by Blumenthal in "Maimonides' Philosophic Mysticism": xiii-xv.

bracket the metaphysics of mitzvot so that it did not matter why one engaged in the commandments. RaMBaM restores the theological basis that we last saw in the priestly and Mosaic Torahs. Although between the two, RaMBaM more often gestures toward the Mosaic Torah, he offers an Aristotelian reading, or derash, of the Mosaic Torah. His methods of midrash were no different than that of the rabbis. To cite rabbinic scholar David Stern out of context, RaMBaM was simply "driven, as it were, by a different set of anxieties."[150] It is worthwhile to cite RaMBaM's opening halakhah which, although written in Hebrew, is pure Greek: "The foundation of all foundations and the pillar of wisdom is to know that there is a primary being who brought into being all existence. All the beings of the heavens, the earth, and what is between them came into existence only from the truth of His being."[151]

The goal of humanity is to strive for intellectual knowledge. Intellectual perfection requires a long, dedicated, and organized course of study. That's tough to do when you're indigent, or a soldier, or managing a financial empire. Enter the mitzvot. For RaMBaM, the commandments are about regulating society, from individuals to institutions, in a way that will maximize the possibility that people will have the opportunity to engage in this long, dedicated, organized course of study. RaMBaM divides the mitzvot into two categories: those for the welfare of the body and those for the welfare of the intellect. The goal for both types is to provide a well-ordered society in which the greatest possible number of people will be afforded the opportunity to pursue intellectual perfection.

Welfare of the body is achieved by eliminating wrongdoing between members of society and promoting morality. Welfare of the intellect is achieved by commanding correct beliefs and abolishing false beliefs. So far, so good. Unlike the God of the kabbalists (and the priestly Torah), the God of the philosophers has no needs. Again unlike the God of the kabbalists, God is radically transcendent so nothing that humans do affects God. For the kabbalists and the priestly Torah, performing ritual mitzvot affected God in a positive way. For the Mosaic Torah, ritual mitzvot did not affect God per se, but the Israelites were rewarded with rain and national security. RaMBaM rejects both of those theologies. His

---

150 David Stern, "Midrash and Midrashic Interpretation," in *The Jewish Study Bible* (New York: Oxford University Press, 2004), 1872.
151 Maimonides, M. T., Fundamentals of the Torah 1:1.

transcendent God has no needs, so the priestly Torah's theology is not even recognized by RaMBaM as anything other than figurative language. In the process of explaining anthropomorphic terms in the first thirty-six chapters of the *Guide*, RaMBaM also demythologizes the priestly language of God's movement and passions.[152] But the religion of reward and punishment, the Mosaic Torah, was more difficult to explain away.

In Aristotle's cosmos, as in RaMBaM's, the world goes according to its custom. If by a miracle, one means the violation of natural laws, there are no miracles. God does not change the weather according to the level of obedience of the Israelites. Rain and drought are independent of compliance with the covenant. The *deus ex machina* of biblical literature is more than a literary device, however: it is both a noble lie and a paradigm for religious writings.

RaMBaM serves as an historian of religion and reminds his readers that at the time the Israelites were freed from slavery in Egypt, everyone in their world offered animal sacrifices to their gods in the expectation of receiving a divine bounty.[153] Next, RaMBaM serves as a psychologist: "A sudden transition from one opposite to another is impossible. And therefore man, according to his nature, is not capable of abandoning suddenly all to which he was accustomed."[154] His conclusion is that the biblical connection between obedience and reward is a noble lie which allows the Israelites to continue doing what everyone had been doing while merely changing the address of the sacrifices to avoid the cardinal transgression of idolatry. The ideal, "meditation without any works at all," was unattainable immediately after the exodus from Egypt.[155]

One implication of God not withholding rain as a result of disobedience is that individual suffering should not be seen as a product of divine punishment. That is not how God works.[156] Humans bring suffering on themselves through their own ignorance, stupidity, and cupidity.[157] There are no evil forces in the world, be they autonomous or parasitic, scanning

---

152 *Guide*, 1:10, 18, 19, 21, 35, and 36.
153 Ibid., 3:30.
154 Ibid., 3:32.
155 Ibid.
156 In RaMBaM's interpretation, Job learns that one should not take suffering personally. See Robert Eisen, *The Book of Job in Medieval Jewish Philosophy* (New York: Oxford University Press, 2004), 65.
157 *Guide*, 3:12.

the horizon for opportunities to entrap us unsuspecting dupes. Our wounds are more often than not self-inflicted. RaMBaM also ascribes suffering to how we treat one another. And, least frequently, suffering occurs because of our physical constitution which is required for purposes of birth and death. If one enjoys a stroke of luck, one may live a long life; without luck, it's just a stroke.

Disconnecting God from human suffering also has implications for prayer. In his psychologically penetrating analysis of RaMBaM and prayer, Marvin Fox points out that for RaMBaM, God cannot be moved to action in any substantive way as a result of our prayer (or anything else). Furthermore, since God is radically transcendent, there is no relation between God and humans. "How, given such a view of God, can He either be praised or petitioned? What do we know of Him that would make such praise in any sense possible or such petition in any way sensible?"[158] Allow me to sharpen the questions—Does God know or care what we do?

A later philosopher, Rabbi Levi ben Gershon (RaLBaG), wrote explicitly that God does not know human acts. Robert Eisen summarizes RaLBaG's argument:

> [RaLBaG] reasons that if God's thought cannot change, His knowledge of the world is necessarily limited. Through self-intellection, God can have cognizance of the essences that are responsible for all that exists, since these are immutable objects of knowledge. However, God cannot have knowledge of particulars, because they are in constant flux. Nor, by corollary, can He have knowledge of historical events, since these by their very nature also undergo constant change.[159]

What RaLBaG maintains explicitly, RaMBaM believed and encrypted in his writings. God has no knowledge of particulars, of individuals, of history on a grand scale, or of what I did yesterday that I am struggling not to do again tomorrow. God does not know my prayers, nor does God care. One of my intellectual heroes, Hans Jonas, in comparing ancient gnostics to contemporary existentialists, reflects

---

158 Fox, *Interpreting Maimonides*, 307.
159 Robert Eisen, *Gersonides on Providence, Covenant, and the Chosen People: A Study in Medieval Jewish Philosophy and Biblical Commentary* (Albany: State University of New York Press, 1995), 14.

something of the dichotomy between the medieval kabbalists and the Aristotelians. "Gnostic man [like the kabbalists] is thrown into an antagonistic, anti-divine, and therefore antihuman nature, modern man [like the Aristotelians] into an indifferent one. Only the latter case represents the absolute vacuum, the really bottomless pit."[160]

If my description of RaMBaM's theology is accurate, we are left with the following:

- God is radically and exclusively transcendent which precludes relationships.
- To the degree that we can say anything affirmative about God, God is pure intellect in a constant state of thinking all essences, called forms, into existence.
- God is responsible for the motions of the heavenly spheres but does not interfere with the customary course of nature for purposes of human reward or punishment.
- God has no needs.
- God does not undergo change.
- God can neither hear nor respond to prayer.
- God's knowledge does not include the actions of individuals.
- God does not speak, hence revelation and prophecy emerge from the prophet's intellect and imagination.

Given such a God, it may be easier to understand why I began our discussion of the towering figure of medieval Jewish philosophy with a description of his idiosyncratic version of intellectual mysticism. The traditionalists who branded Maimonides a heretic had cause.[161]

There is one additional aspect of RaMBaM's theology that has recently garnered the attention of Maimonides scholars. Although Shlomo Pines was the first modern scholar to zero in on RaMBaM's epistemology—what we can claim to know and how it is we know it—Micah

---

160 Hans Jonas, *The Gnostic Religion* (Boston: Beacon Press, 1958), 338.
161 Gregg Stern, "Philosophy in Southern France: Controversy over Philosophic Study and the Influence of Averroes on Jewish Thought," in Frank, *Cambridge Companion to Medieval Jewish Philosophy*, 281-303, and Moshe Halbertal, *Concealment and Revelation: Esotericism in Jewish Thought and its Philosophical Implications*, trans. Jackie Feldman (Princeton: Princeton University Press, 2007), 120–34.

Goodman offers a terse, if unsettling, summation: "After a long, complex, and sometimes dry discussion that extends over many chapters of the *Guide*, the reader who has successfully followed the arguments recognizes that he does not know how the world came into existence and cannot even have certainty about the existence of God."[162]

Upon reflection, why describe RaMBaM's conclusions as "unsettling"? Why not "courageous" with his unflinching honesty, and "prophetic" for our contemporary reality that similarly acknowledges no successful proof for the existence of God? What RaMBaM offers us is the first Jewish critique of rationalism. Intellect can take you only so far in your goal, your purpose in this life, "to be with the ruler in the inner part of the habitation."[163] Toward the end of the *Guide*, where readers find the parable of one who approaches the ruler in his palace, the journey to the ruler's inner sanctum is strewn with comments like: "to the extent possible," "everything that may be ascertained," and "close to certainty."[164] "We are fated to live in the space between the *eros* that yearns for absolute knowledge and the limits of our minds, which can approach that knowledge but never reach it."[165] Yet, as Blumenthal and others have highlighted, RaMBaM holds out the possibility of bliss even for us intellectually imperfect creatures of flesh and blood.

It is ironic that RaMBaM's greatest philosophical success, disabusing Jews of divine corporeality, is that which I will attempt to temper in the next section. (Although, hard as it may be to believe, there were forteenth-century Tosafists for whom the question of divine corporeality was not yet settled.)[166] Much of what RaMBaM failed at convincing the Jewish world, at least at the time, are those aspects which motivate many of us today to consider him our prophet and pioneer. Moshe Halbertal concludes his study of RaMBaM by highlighting three of his legacies that, from my perspective, must characterize any coherent Judaism. The first element is that the Torah is religious literature, not to be read

---

162 Goodman, *Maimonides and the Book that Changed Judaism*, 185. See also Shlomo Pines, "The Limitation of Human Knowledge According to Al-Farabi, ibn Bajja, and Maimonides," in Twersky, *Studies in Medieval Jewish History*, 82–109.

163 *Guide*, 3:51, 619.

164 Ibid.

165 Goodman, *Maimonides and the Book that Changed Judaism*, 203.

166 Kanarfogel, *Intellectual History and Rabbinic Culture*, 525–29.

literally but literarily. The Garden of Eden is not historical, God did not call Abraham from Ur of the Chaldees, and Job never lived. These stories are allegories meant to be instructive to the masses.[167] Shmuel ibn Tibbon (1150–1232), who translated the *Guide* from Arabic to Hebrew, suggested that as wisdom spreads, the need for camouflaging the Torah's truths in allegory will diminish.[168] Eight hundred years later, it appears as though ibn Tibbon was unduly optimistic. The enduring fanaticism of religious fundamentalists suggests RaMBaM's approach was more psychologically savvy.

The second element Halbertal highlights as RaMBaM's legacy is "the focus on the causal order and the wisdom inherent in it as the most substantive revelation of the divinity."[169] In other words, it is nature and not Mount Sinai that more accurately reveals God's will and wisdom. Revelation of God's will by the prophets is a function of their intelligence *and* imagination. Nature has no imagination with which to distort God's wisdom. RaMBaM, however, does not engage in what we will later call *natural theology* which moves from our understanding of nature and allows us to make truth claims about God. In an extended discussion of God's thirteen attributes (Exodus 33), RaMBaM explains that these characteristics of God's management of the cosmos *do not* describe God, Godself. Rather, God "performs actions [in nature] resembling the actions that in us proceed from moral qualities."[170]

Finally, the third element of RaMBaM's legacy is the elevation of the study of science and philosophy to a mitzvah.[171] The rabbis were flummoxed by the command to love God. Does it mean to follow the mitzvot lovingly? Does it mean to act like a mensch and cause others to love God by keeping the mitzvot?[172] RaMBaM said that to love God means to understand how God works in the world; and the more knowledge, the more love. We will never know God in God's essence, but studying nature will allow us to understand more of God's will and wisdom. In our

---

167 Halbertal, *Maimonides*, 358.

168 Frank Talmage, "Apples of Gold: The Inner Meaning of Sacred Texts in Medieval Judaism," in Green, *Jewish Spirituality*, 322.

169 Halbertal, *Maimonides*, 358.

170 *Guide*, 1:54, 124.

171 Halbertal, *Maimonides*, 359.

172 Cherry, *Torah through Time*, 17

study of nature, as RaMBaM emphasizes, "one should accept the truth from whatever source it proceeds."[173] The delicious double entendre is that RaMBaM lifted that very line from an Arabic source, his predecessor as a religious philosopher: al-Kindi.[174]

Two additional factors, one of which I have already mentioned, are prerequisites for a coherent Judaism. The first is coherence between what we understand about God and reality to conform to how we think and behave. RaMBaM's unprecedented introduction to his halakhic code with philosophy and science illustrates that coherence. "In Hilkhot Yesode ha-Torah we are commanded to study the sciences in order to fulfill the commandments related to the knowledge of God; and in Hilkhot De'ot we are commanded to act morally as a result of that knowledge."[175] The second factor, about which I will have more to say in the third book, is that RaMBaM insisted that every single commandment, though not every detail, had a purpose in the over-arching goal of helping humanity move toward intellectual refinement. Indeed, it is this insistence, which protects the rationality of the Torah's legislation, that motivated RaMBaM to interpret the classical aggadah of legal nominalism—why animals are slaughtered at the front of the neck rather than the back—as "the commandments were only given to refine humanity."[176]

Both Moshe Idel and Menachem Kellner agree that RaMBaM was reacting to the proto-Kabbalah of his day, as represented by Yehudah HaLevi's *Kuzari*.[177] Kabbalah has far more in common with the theology of the priestly Torah than RaMBaM does with any previous Jewish theology. "Though it was possible to point out a relatively organic development that produced most of the forms of Jewish mysticism, the new commencements of Jewish philosophy were the results of encounters with alien types

---

173 Introduction to RaMBaM's commentary on Avot.

174 Daniel H. Frank, "Maimonides and Medieval Jewish Aristotelianism," in Frank, *Cambridge Companion to Medieval Jewish Philosophy*, 155n11.

175 Warren Zev Harvey, "Ethical Theories among Medieval Jewish Philosophers," in *The Oxford Handbook of Jewish Ethics and Morality*, ed. Elliot N. Dorff and Jonathan K. Crane (New York: Oxford University Press, 2013), 94.

176 *Guide*, 3:26 and "Rabbinic Religiosity" above.

177 Menachem Kellner, *Maimonides' Confrontation with Mysticism* (Oxford: Littman Library of Jewish Civilization, 2006), 3-4.

of speculation."[178] Thus, as Halbertal suggests, RaMBaM can be considered so rare a religious reformer as to constitute a religious *founder*.[179]

We have already seen that in the kabbalistic cosmos, the RaMBaM's God is accounted for in, and relegated to, the realm of the *Eyn Sof*. The kabbalists absolutely agree that there is an aspect of God beyond our ability to comprehend in any way. In the mysticism of Abraham Abulafia (1240–1291), we find a version of Maimonidean intellectual piety using the vocabulary of the sefirot which are reworked as Aristotelian Separate Intellects.[180] By the end of the fourteenth century, the more impious elements of Aristotelianism were increasingly under attack in Spain, particularly after the anti-Jewish riots of 1391. Hasdei Crescas composed a very sophisticated critique of Aristotle and Maimonides. The language of the critique, it must be noted, was that of philosophy. While other thinkers branded philosophy as a product of the *sitra achra* with philosophy being fundamentally flawed, Crescas pressed philosophical argumentation into service for his own religiously motivated critique.

Crescas undermined the validity of Aristotle's arguments that space and time were continuous quantities; that space and time were dependent on physical objects; that space is finite; and that a vacuum is impossible. In arguing against these propositions, Crescas was instrumental in bringing down the Aristotelian worldview that had dominated natural philosophy for centuries.[181] The eclipse of Aristotle allowed for metaphysical possibilities that had previously been precluded. Into this newly created space, as it were, Crescas posited a God of boundless love who creates in order to share that love.

Crescas' God of creation resembles Plato's craftsman who is good and has not a trace of envy.[182] Indeed, Crescas' God is so loving, and so perfect in that love, that God creates an infinite number of worlds to

---

178 Moshe Idel, "Jewish Philosophy and Kabbalah in Spain," in *Sephardic and Mizrahi Jewry: From the Golden Age of Spain to Modern Times*, ed. Zion Zohar (New York: New York University Press, 2005), 130.

179 Halbertal, *Maimonides*, 4.

180 Hava Tirosh-Samuelson, "Philosophy and Kabbalah: 1200–1600," in Frank, *The Cambridge Companion to Medieval Jewish Philosophy*, 232–36. Abulafia's influence continued for centuries in Italy.

181 Warren Zev Harvey, *Physics and Metaphysics in Hasdai Crescas* (Amsterdam: J. C. Gieben, 1995), 3–30.

182 *Timaeus* 29d.

maximize the recipients of the divine bounty.[183] The Neoplatonic images of continuous overflow and continuous creation, as well as references to kabbalistic notions, suggest that Crescas was influenced by Kabbalah. Zev Harvey presents a strong case for the likelihood that Crescas, like the kabbalists, understood an aspect of God to be immanent in the world.[184] There is, to be sure, no necessary equivalence between divine immanence and Spinoza's conception of divine extension, but, as Carlos Fraenkel has recently pointed out, the ideas do share a family resemblance.[185]

We have seen that for RaMBaM the love of God includes the intellectual joy of increasing knowledge. RaMBaM, however, would never discuss God's own love for God's creatures, because RaMBaM's God has no passions. Crescas' God, and Crescas' universe, pulsates with love in all directions. But according to Zev Harvey, when Crescas attributes love and joy to God, "he attributes them to Him not as *passions*, but as *actions*."[186] God loves humanity by bringing us love and joy. "Thus, the causative joy of God and the affective joy of His creation are ultimately one and the same joy but described from two different standpoints."[187] As a philosophic concept, I understand that Crescas is refraining from imputing passion and change to God. As a father of three, when I provide opportunities for my children to experience glee or pride or love, it gives me deep gratification. Depriving God of gratification may be metaphysically sound. But, it is a reminder that the philosophical emergence from myth does not come without growing pains.[188]

Another element of the exposure to rationalism, and another legacy of RaMBaM, is Crescas' admission that we have no ironclad proof for the existence of God. To anticipate the phrase of Blaise Pascal (1623–1662), "The heart has its reasons which reason does not know." Be they Aristotelian, rabbinic, or Maimonidean, "physical proofs can at best give one an inclination. True knowledge of God is not achieved

---

183 Or HaShem 2:6 and Harvey, *Physics and Metaphysics*, 111.
184 Harvey, "Kabbalistic Elements": 91–96.
185 Carlos Fraenkel, "Hasdei Crascas on God as the Place of the World and Spinoza's Notion of God as *Res Extensa*," *Aleph: Historical Studies in Science and Judaism* 9 (2009): 77-111.
186 Harvey, *Physics and Metaphysics*, 106. His italics.
187 Ibid., 107.
188 The rabbinic God experiences gratification. See Baba Metzia 59b, the story of the oven of Achnai.

by philosophers, but by prophets."[189] And the medium of prophecy for Crescas is not intellect, but love.

We conclude our survey of medieval Jewish philosophers with Spinoza (1632–1677). Harry Wolfson, the great twentieth-century scholar of Jewish philosophy, quipped that Baruch Spinoza was the last medieval Jew and Benedict Spinoza the first modern Jew. While again trying to navigate around the "pitfalls of precursorism," I must say that for the purposes of Jewish thought, Spinoza is the least interesting of the philosophers we will examine. He treats the Torah as religious literature. So did the RaMBaM. Spinoza considers reason to be the only source of true knowledge. RaMBaM anticipated him there, as well. Spinoza attributes extension to God. So did many of the kabbalists who treated the sefirot as the emanated essence of God.[190] I am admittedly doing a disservice to the depth of Spinoza's metaphysics. But whatever his metaphysics—and it is still the subject of dispute—they were not any more of a challenge to Judaism than were his medieval predecessors' theologies and metaphysics.

Spinoza's affront to Judaism, and the reason why his philosophy is often marginalized in the study of Jewish thought, is his historicism. Simon Rawidowicz called him the "first peshat-Jew of modern times."[191] When RaMBaM employed history to understand the Torah, even if he explained certain mitzvot as responses to idolatrous conditions no longer present, he never suggested that the mitzvot in question could now be discarded. For Spinoza, it was only during the period of Israelite and Judean statehood that any of the commandments were in force.[192] Since the loss of political sovereignty in 70 CE, the rabbis have had no legitimate power over the Jews. When Spinoza was summoned by the Jewish leaders of Amsterdam in 1656, he did not recognize their authority over him. He never appeared. Indeed, according to Spinoza's political philosophy, none of the religious establishments of the seventeenth-century Dutch Republic should wield political power.

---

189 Harvey, *Physics and Metaphysics*, 65.
190 Tirosh-Samuelson, "Philosophy and Kabbalah," in Frank, *The Cambridge Companion to Medieval Jewish Philosophy*, 224–27.
191 Simon Rawidowicz, "On Interpretation," in *Simon Rawidowicz: Studies in Jewish Thought*, ed. Nahum N. Glatzer (Philadelphia: Jewish Publication Society, 1974), 109.
192 For the record, Moses Nachmanides, RaMBaN, cites a parallel rabbinic comment. See Nachmanides' *Commentary on the Torah*, Lev. 18:25 and Sifrei, Ekev 43. Even this claim of Spinoza was not innovative.

[B]y naturalizing the Torah and the other books of the Bible and reducing them to ordinary (though morally valuable) works of literature, Spinoza hopes to undercut ecclesiastic influence in politics and other domains and weaken the sectarian dangers facing his beloved Republic.[193]

In the next chapter, when we enter Jewish modernity, we will see how rejecting divine authorship of the Torah was used by reformers to undermine rabbinic authority. Spinoza was their trailblazer. Juda-ism was the law of the land when the Judeans lived in Judah. Perhaps, Juda-ism could even be the law of the land if Jews were to return to the Land of Israel and reestablish their state. But in Spinoza's time, Juda-ism was an anachronistic legal system. Of course, his ideas had ramifications for the academic study of the Bible, but identifying Judaism with law, which was echoed by Moses Mendelssohn (1729–1786), became a trope within the modern Jewish world. "It was Spinoza who injected into Jewish thought the idea that Judaism is not a religion but a legal system, and this doctrine courses through the body of modern Jewish thought like venom."[194]

Concluding the Middle

Love was in the air for medieval thinkers. Halbertal notes that RaMBaM's crescendo in the *Guide* does not point toward intellect, as did his first halakhah in the Mishneh Torah, but toward engaging in acts of loving-kindness in imitation of God.[195] Two centuries later, Crescas' universe pul-sates with love. "Its infinite worlds are generated in love, sustained in love, and perfected in love."[196] The following century, Isaac Abarbanel, the great statesman who was exiled from Spain, agreed with Crescas that God cre-ated the world out of love and out of a desire to share His divinity with His creatures.[197] His son, Judah Abarbanel (c.1465–c.1521), writing under the name Leone Ebreo, wrote the first Jewish dialogue on love.[198] If my reading

---

193 Steven Nadler, *A Book Forged in Hell: Spinoza's Scandalous Treatise and the Birth of the Secular Age* (Princeton: Princeton University Press, 2013), 111.
194 Heschel, *Heavenly Torah*, 4.
195 *Guide,* 3:54 on Jeremiah 9:22–23 and Halbertal, *Maimonides*, 308.
196 Harvey, *Physics and Metaphysics*, 113.
197 Seymour Feldman, *Philosophy in a Time of Crisis: Don Isaac Abravanel: Defender of the Faith* (New York: Routledge, 2003), 55.
198 Ibid., 173.

of Luria is correct, he, too, envisioned God withdrawing from the Infinite in order to share his love with the finite. I suspect that just as Spanish Kabbalah influenced Crescas, Crescas influenced Luria.[199] For Elijah de Vidas (1518–1592), a kabbalist from the Land of Israel, love is a cosmic principle that is the vehicle for communion with God: "One's deeds, enthusiastically performed from one's heart and soul, are the outstanding signs of love . . . [and] Devekut [cleaving to God] grows organically out of love."[200]

The rabbis had already understood the commandment to love God as meaning to perform commandments lovingly. Love-centered religion, whether the ultimate goal be uniting uncoupled sefirot or cleaving to the divine presence, relied on actions as the vehicle for love.[201] The outlier here is Spinoza who rejected the force of the Torah's commandments. Nevertheless, even for Spinoza the love of God, which is identical to the intellectual knowledge of God (*amor Dei intellectualis*), becomes the ultimate goal of life.

Although there remained Jewish philosophers committed to the Aristotelian ideal of intellectual perfection, by the end of the fifteenth century, they were an endangered species. Tellingly, even in Maimonides' own family, there was a dramatic shift from Aristotle to Sufism.[202] For those dedicated to undermining the Aristotelian framework, there was an increasing tendency to depict God in more familiar terms by restoring traditional notions of omniscience and providence. In the competition for the hearts and minds of medieval Jewry, Kabbalah, if not in name then in ideology, won the day. Philosophy was not only vanquished by the seventeenth century, it was demonized. Yet both metaphysical systems shared one important element, in addition to the promotion of inwardness, that combined to create a powerful legacy for modernity.

---

199 Crescas was "preeminent" in the field of theology during his time. Idel, "Magical and Neoplatonic Interpretations," in Cooperman, *Jewish Thought in the Sixteenth Century*, 210. Moreover, Spinoza not only knew Crescas well, but he was seventeen when Horwitz's *Two Tablets of the Covenant* was published in Amsterdam in 1649. Thus, it is extremely likely he was familiar with kabbalistic notions of divine immanence which may well have informed his own philosophy.

200 Pachter, "The Concept of Devekut," in Twersky, *Studies in Medieval Jewish History and Literature*, 210–11.

201 For a few of our thinkers, such as Duran and Alkabetz, clinging to the divine presence can also be effected primarily through the Torah and its devotional study.

202 Fenton, "Judaism and Sufism," in Frank, *The Cambridge Companion to Medieval Jewish Philosophy*, 204.

As Tirosh-Samuelson points out, by the seventeenth century both theologies had neutralized the political messianism of rabbinic religiosity:

> Finally, both programs regarded their privileged knowledge to be the exclusive path toward religious perfection, culminating in the bliss of immortality in the afterlife. Thus both philosophy and kabbalah contributed to the interiorization of Jewish religious life by shifting the focus of Jewish messianism from collective, political redemption to personal salvation of the individual soul.[203]

Like a centrifuge, the Middle Ages spun apart the theologies of Kabbalah and philosophy from the amalgam of rabbinic religiosity. Kabbalah demonstrated a stickiness, a viscosity, that was able to maintain a bond with the mitzvot. Rational philosophy, on the other hand, slipped away to become the basis for the Enlightenment. It is true, nevertheless, that in the seventeenth century the challenge to rabbinic authority came not only from Spinoza but also from Shabbatai Tzvi's antinomianism. The specter of the latter explains the suspicion of and scrutiny endured by the early Hasidim who will be a focus of the next chapter.

Although a halakhic code is pernicious in that it freezes the halakhah on the printed page and creates what the Zohar would call a molten image, it has the advantage of making the mitzvot accessible to everyone. Mitzvah observance could then be grounded in Aristotelian philosophy, á la RaMBaM's Mishneh Torah, or in Kabbalah, á la Eliyahu Horwitz's *Two Tablets of the Covenant*. Modernity can be seen as a contest between these two medieval worldviews. I am grateful to be the heir of both worldviews because neither one alone does justice to a contemporary and coherent view of reality. A giant of Orthodox thought, Rav Joseph Soloveitchik, held the same belief about the two creation stories in Genesis. They are mutually exclusive—but we need them both to capture the complexity of who we are. Medieval philosophy and mysticism are mutually exclusive, as well. The common denominator of medieval Judaisms, however, is their commitment to mitzvot.

Although the Mishnah mandated a minimum level of *kavannah* or mental accompaniment when engaged in prayer, the gemara did its best

---

Tirosh-Samuelson, "Philosophy and Kabbalah," in Frank, *The Cambridge Companion to Medieval Jewish Philosophy*, 252.

to undermine that minimum (M. Rosh Hashana 2:1 and 13a). Rabbinic Judaism, though promoting the ideal of inwardness and devotional posture, crafted a religiosity that allowed kavannah, or its lack, to reflect individual preferences—cognitive autonomy (M. Rosh Hashana 5:1). But in the Middle Ages, the influence of both the Muslim Mutazilites and Sufis brought duties of the heart and devotion to the fore. Once northern Spain was conquered by the Catholics, new public rituals involving Mary flourished and influenced the feminization and near obsession with the Shechinah in nascent Kabbalah.[204] Jews became increasingly exposed to the centrality of belief within Catholicism. By the middle of the thirteenth century, Rabbeynu Yonah of Catalan (1200–1263) qualified the geonic position by requiring kavannah when performing mitzvot involving speech, such as prayer.[205] Thus, it seems that the Jewish appropriation of inwardness in the Middle Ages owes something to both Islam and Christianity.

By 1700, the mitzvot that comprised Judaism were, primarily, the mitzvot according to Yosef Karo's Shulchan Arukh and Moshe Isserles' Mapa, published together in Cracow in 1580. Within 100 years of its publication, the text became the "preeminent restatement of the law, outdistancing its rivals and silencing its rather harsh critics. In the seventeenth century a brilliant array of rabbinic jurists chose Shulchan Arukh as the focus for their own extensive legal commentary, which now appears in the printed text along with the Karo-Isserles rulings."[206] Caro legislated that reciting the Shema requires kavannah.[207] Among the brilliant array of commentators printed along with the Shulchan Arukh was Avraham Gombiner (c.1635–1682). His note of clarification there is that only biblical laws require kavannah, not rabbinic laws.[208] Disputes for the sake of heaven will continue—on to modernity.

---

204 Green, "Shekhinah, the Virgin Mary, and the Song of Songs": 27.

205 Rabbeynu Yonah on the Rif, Brachot 6a.

206 Stephen M. Passamaneck, "Toward Sunrise in the East," in *An Introduction to the History and Sources of Jewish Law*, ed. N. S. Hecht et. al. (Oxford: Oxford University Press, 1996), 340-41.

207 O. H., Kiryat Shema 60:4.

208 Magen Avraham, ad. loc.

Chapter 5

The Modern Mix

The late eighteenth century was, for European Jewry, the push, pull, and lurch from the Middle Ages to modernity. There were small steps toward civic amelioration, edicts of nominal tolerance, and the occasional recognition that universal rights should, in theory, include even the Jews. Christian Europe hoped that by extending some rights to Jews, their otherness would diminish. Jews, for their part, adopted a variety of strategies to respond to the uneven welcome they were receiving from the different countries of Western and Central Europe. Those emerging Judaisms, which developed throughout the nineteenth century, are roughly the Judaisms that we have today.

> Jewish modernity most simply defined represents the dissolution of the political agency of the corporate Jewish community and the concurrent shift of political agency to the individual Jew who became a citizen of the modern nation-state.[1]

Although our focus remains on theology, the politics of emancipation in Western Europe make the artificial separation between theology and politics untenable. As we survey theological innovations, from East to West, over the past three centuries, there will be the inevitable winnowing of important details. My goal in this chapter is to offer the student of Jewish thought some of the essential insights of our greatest thinkers as they encountered the unprecedented opportunities of post-Enlightenment Europe until World War II. Many of their theologies' components

---

1   Leora Batnitzky, *How Judaism Became a Religion: An Introduction to Modern Jewish Thought* (Princeton: Princeton University Press, 2013), 4.

will be familiar to us from previous chapters. As we conclude this chapter, we will be in a position to see how contemporary theologians have woven together the strands of Judaisms past.

The Hegemony of Kabbalah on the Eve of Modernity

The classical texts of medieval Jewish philosophy were largely ignored from 1650–1750. RaMBaM's *Guide of the Perplexed* was not published in eastern Europe even once during the seventeenth or eighteenth centuries. Although there were pockets of resistance to Kabbalah, Central and Eastern Europe were largely held under its sway from the sixteenth century through the emergence of the Haskalah, the Jewish Enlightenment, beginning in the eighteenth century.[2] Books like Moses Cordovero's *The Palm Tree of Devorah* (1588), Isaiah Horowitz's *The Two Tablets of the Covenant* (1649), and, later, Pinchas Hurwitz's *Book of the Covenant* (1797) successfully disseminated kabbalistic ethics and theology to Ashkenazi Jewry. David Sorkin, a contemporary scholar of the Haskalah, reports that two of the four defining characteristics of Ashkenazi Jewry by the mid-eighteenth century were the stigmatization of medieval Jewish philosophy and the penetration of Kabbalah deep into the fabric of Jewish theology.[3] Thus, we will begin this chapter by explaining the surprising fortunes of Kabbalah by the end of the eighteenth century.

Although the countries of Eastern Europe did not extend national rights to their Jewish communities, those communities were affected by the European and Jewish Enlightenments. Concepts of democracy and individualism drifted eastward and met with the halakhic democratization created by the wide-spread availability of the Shulchan Arukh. The reputed, if unintentional, founder of the spiritual revival movement, Hasidism, was Israel ben Eliezer, known to posterity as the Baal Shem Tov (1700–1760). The role of a *baal shem*, a master of [God's four-letter]

---

2   Moshe Idel, "Differing Conceptions of Kabbalah in the Early 17th Century," in *Jewish Thought in the 17th Century*, ed. Isadore Twersky and Bernard Septimus (Cambridge, MA: Harvard University Press, 1987), 137–200; David B. Ruderman, *Jewish Thought and Scientific Discovery in Early Modern Europe* (New Haven: Yale University Press, 1995), 118-52.

3   David Sorkin "The Early Haskalah," in *New Perspectives on the Haskalah*, ed. Shmuel Feiner and David Sorkin (Oxford: Littman Library of Jewish Civilization, 2004), 10.

name, was the utilization of charms for the benefit of individuals in need. The rabbis of the Talmud reportedly engaged in magic, and that tradition became institutionalized. Immanuel Etkes describes the tasks of these folk doctors as writing amulets and adjuring oaths. "The 'operations' these amulets and oaths were meant to effectuate included: overpowering demons, conversing with spirits of the dead, 'travel hops,' an ability to see without being seen, injury to enemies, restoration of stolen property, assistance for women in pregnancy and release of the imprisoned from jail."[4]

Contrary to the romantic image from the tales of the Baal Shem Tov, the information we have on *baalei shem* (pl. of *baal shem*) indicates that they were members of the scholarly and religious elite.[5] Etkes suggests that there was a presumption, not necessarily universal, that *baalei shem* relied on their knowledge of Kabbalah in order to manipulate reality. Thus, many were community rabbis who engaged in practical Kabbalah as part of their official duties. The Baal Shem Tov's own master, Rabbi Yoel, from whom the Baal Shem Tov received his "charm book," began traveling from village to village. The Baal Shem Tov was enabled to gather a small coterie of likeminded mystics in part because of his itinerant occupation.

Academic treatments of Hasidism are not unanimous in treating the movement as essentially a mystical movement, although that is certainly the consensus.[6] Nor is there unanimity concerning the right historical time period to slot Hasidism within. My teacher, Arthur Green, considers Hasidism a "late postmedieval phenomenon. Its theological assumptions and limitations are unapologetically (for the last time in Jewish history) those of the classic rabbinic-medieval world: the authority of Scripture, the inviolability of halakhah, the mysterious truth hidden in the teachings and parables of Talmudic sages."[7]

---

4   Immanuel Etkes, *The Besht: Magician, Mystic, and Leader*, trans. Saadya Sternberg (Waltham: Brandeis University Press, 2005), 26.

5   Ibid., 27.

6   E.g., Mendel Piekarz, "Hasidism as a Social-religious Movement," in *Hasidism Reappraised*, ed. Ada Rapoport-Albert (Oxford: Littman Library of Jewish Civilization, 1996), 225-48.

7   Arthur Green, *The Heart of the Matter: Studies in Jewish Mysticism and Theology* (Philadelphia: Jewish Publication Society, 2015), 227-28.

I have placed the discussion of Hasidism in the chapter of modern Jewish thought and theology because I understand Hasidism as a transitional movement whose goal, as opposed to assumptions, is quite modern. In some ways, Hasidism is the reform movement of Eastern Europe that remains within the four cubits of halakhah, unlike the Reform movement of Western Europe. In both movements, there is an emphasis on individual piety and spirituality. Personal salvation, as opposed to national redemption, is the goal of each Hasid.[8] For Hasidism, trends within classical and medieval Judaisms emphasizing personal piety combined to form a powerful revival movement that challenged the hegemony of Talmudic erudition and cognitive dexterity. Intellectual virtuosity was no longer considered the prime virtue of a leader. In keeping with the Zeitgeist, Green understands Hasidism to be a movement of "spiritual democratization."[9]

Key legacies from the Kabbalah of Safed were transmitted by Horwitz in his *Two Tablets*, among them the Cordoverian image that each letter of the Torah corresponds to a living Jewish soul. Only the bearer of that individual soul has the capacity to energize the latent divinity within his letter of the Torah.[10] The first published Hasidic work, *Tol'dot Yakov Yosef* by Jacob Joseph of Polonnoye (1780), emphasized the unique ability of each Jew to rescue the divine sparks within the material world corresponding to that individual's soul-root. Every Jew has a piece of the puzzle necessary to complete the messianic picture. This emphasis on the individual resonates with the general ethos of the European Enlightenment and represents a shift in Jewish thought. The shift is not in the novelty of the concept of individual piety, but in the centrality of its role in this revival movement.

Hasidism also foregrounded the theology of divine immanence that Horwitz transmitted to the Baal Shem Tov and his circle. "Divine

---

8 Morris M. Faierstein, "Personal Redemption in Hasidism," in Rapoport-Albert, *Hasidism Reappraised*, 214–24. See also Rachel Elior, *Paradoxical Ascent: The Kabbalistic Theosophy of Habad Hasidism*, trans. Jeffrey M. Green (Albany: State University of New York Press, 1993), 14.

9 Arthur Green, "Teachings of the Hasidic Masters," in Holtz, *Back to the Sources*, 362.

10 Bracha Sack, "The Influence of Cordovero on Seventeenth-Century Jewish Thought," in Twersky, *Jewish Thought in the 17th Century*, 368.

vitality penetrates all existence because only thus are they able to exist."[11] If we think of Lurianic Kabbalah as beginning with divine withdrawal and absence, Hasidism emphasizes "the equal presence of God in every place."[12] The world itself is a phantasm that subsists only through the reality of God's existence. This metaphysics of acosmism, the rejection of the independent reality of the visible world, gains full articulation in the writings of the founder of HaBaD Hasidism, Shneur Zalman of Liadi (1745–1813). "There is truly nothing beside Him. The visible worlds appear to be an entity and something separate in itself only to our eyes because of the concealment and the great number of withdrawals. . . . Everything is only His divinity."[13]

The ontology of the early Hasidic masters invited two, distinct religious responses. If divinity is present in all things, then one could worship God *through* all things. The Hasidim termed this approach to devotion, "worship through corporeality." The Baal Shem Tov avoided asceticism precisely because God is accessible even in the pleasures of this world. Moreover, we can leverage those pleasures for spiritual elevation, for both ourselves and for the world.[14]

Logically prior to worship through corporeality was the recognition of the divine within the corporeal. Thus, contemplation (*hitbonenut*) took on increased importance for the Hasidim as the vehicle to this expanded state of consciousness. The goal of contemplation was to endow the Hasid "with a conceptual structure for interpreting the whole range of his experience and to provide him with an intellectual horizon beyond the borders of his normal consciousness and sensory perception."[15] Just as Immanuel Kant was driving a wedge between perception and reality in Western Europe, the Hasidim of Eastern Europe were rehabilitating the kabbalistic language of husks and garbs to explain the difference between perception and reality. All of existence pulses with a constant flow of divine energy cloaked behind the husks and garb of corporeality.

11 Sack, "The Influence of Cordovero," in Twersky, *Jewish Thought in the 17th Century*, 369.
12 Elior, *Paradoxical Ascent*, 17. See also Etkes, *Besht*, 136.
13 Likkutei Torah, Shir ha-Shirim, 41a; cited in Elior, *Paradoxical Ascent*, 50. Translation slightly modified.
14 Etkes, *Besht*, 140–44.
15 Elior, *Paradoxical Ascent*, 159.

Overcoming the illusion that corporeality is intrinsically autonomous, as opposed to a veil to be seen through, is our *primary* religious goal.[16]

Given the metaphysics of acosmism or panentheism (the former emphasizes the illusion of a godless world while the latter emphasizes the all penetrating and all-encompassing divine presence of the world), the function of prayer is to consciously integrate one's self into the divine matrix in which each of us is a part. Rachel Elior describes the metaphysics behind prayer: "According to HaBaD psychology, the divine soul's yearning toward its source and its desire to cling to its root are the source of the very possibility of *bittul* [overcoming the sense of a discrete and compartmentalized self that is distinct from the divine]. The service of *bittul* begins with *hitbonenut* ("contemplation"),—rational, intellectual speculation on the finite and the infinite, of being and nothingness."[17]

> At the psychological-devotional root of this entire complex of ideas stands the experience of the negation or transcendence of self, and the discovery, in the wake of that experience, that it is only God who remains.[18]

Leadership within the revival movement was initially predicated on charisma rather than Talmudic erudition or dynastic succession. (Hasidic dynasties emerged in the third generation of Hasidism.) Furthermore, in many expressions of Hasidism, joy was praised and to be pursued. Scholars caution us against making generalizations about Hasidism. It is true that each tzaddik, each leader of a Hasidic sect, stamped his own idiosyncratic traits on his Hasidim. (Indeed, one of the more salient controversies within the world of Hasidism involved *hitbonenut*.[19]) Nevertheless, at least for late eighteenth-century tzaddikim, there was a consensus that overcoming one's ego was a prerequisite for attaining communion with God (devekut). In addition to removing the obstacle of the ego, one also had to pursue piety, live in joy, and immerse in prayer. For many tzaddikim, the immanent fullness of earthly divinity awaited discovery through paradigm shifts within our own consciousness. "Often

---

16 Ibid., 14
17 Rachel Elior, "HaBaD: The Contemplative Ascent to God," in *Jewish Spirituality: From the Sixteenth-Century Revival to the Present*, vol. 2, ed. Arthur Green (Chestnut Ridge: Crossroad, 1987), 182.
18 Green, *Heart of the Matter*, 244.
19 Elior, *Paradoxical Ascent*, 167–72.

Schneerson [the last Rebbe of HaBaD (1902–1994)] expressed this point by utilizing a time-honored play on words, especially cherished by HaBaD thinkers, the world (*ha-olam*) is a place of concealment (*he'lem*), for the divinity is hidden within the cloak of corporeality."[20]

In the following book on creation theology, I will have much more to say about divine immanence as it expressed in HaBaD thought. In particular, we will see how HaBaD teachings on leaps were employed by Rav Avraham Yitzhak Kook (1865–1935) in his musings on biological evolution and speciation. In many ways, Hasidism has been home to the most sophisticated theological writings within the Jewish world. In addition to theology, Hasidic masters have also penned Torah commentaries that bracket the historicity of the bible in order to focus on issues of devotional posture and religious psychology. Yet, for all their merit and utility for modernity, they tend to be frozen within the medieval world of divine dictation, innate Jewish superiority, and female submissiveness. Although we will return to the insights of HaBaD and other ideologies arising out of the circle of the Baal Shem Tov, as well as those opposed to Hasidism, those Judaisms are fundamentally flawed by their unwillingness to contend with the full truth about the origins of the Torah, humanity, and the cosmos.

The first communal expression of opposition toward Hasidism came as a writ of excommunication in 1772. There were allegations of liturgical innovations and impious behavior, neither of which would have provoked the Vilna Gaon (Elijah ben Solomon Zalman, 1720–1797), the greatest rabbinic authority of his day, to sign the decree. Although this ban can be examined from a variety of different perspectives, our vantage point is theological. In the writ of excommunication, the authors refer to this group not as Hasidim, but as *hashudim*, the suspected ones. The Hasidic emphasis on divine immanence set off alarm bells in Vilna because of its Sabbatian echoes.

The theology of Shabbatai Tzvi similarly had emphasized divine immanence. Sabbatianism drove that claim to antinomian conclusions. If everything is ultimately divine, why should there be any prohibitions at all? If we are engaged in liberating divine sparks from corporeality,

20   Elliot R. Wolfson, *Open Secret: Postmessianic Messianism and the Mystical Revision of Menachem Mendel Schneerson* (New York: Columbia University Press, 2009), 52.

they are trapped also in what is halakhically impure—why is that not part of our divine mission? The theology of uplifting sparks, as held by the Maggid, Dov Ber of Mezeritch (1704–1772), did set corporeality and spirituality in opposition, and the Maggid of Mezeritch had disciples who continued that line of thought. Shnuer Zalman, however, articulated a worship *through* corporeality *to* divinity, not a redemption *of* divinity *from* corporeality.[21] The Vilna Gaon and his colleagues, who come to be known as the *Mitnagdim* or opponents, suspected that this emerging group would go the way of the Sabbatians. Thus, the Mitnagdim excommunicated the Hasidim.[22]

By and large, though, the Hasidim were unoriginal in their halakhic practice. Their innovations were in the fields of theology and psychology, and even there they were less innovators than proliferators. Rachel Elior entitled her book on our subject *The Paradoxical Ascent to God: The Kabbalistic Theosophy of Habad Hasidism*. The foundation of that paradox is precisely the truth of the Sabbatean theology—panentheism. HaBaD and other Hasidic groups, therefore, struggled all the more to avoid Sabbatian conclusions in this climate of suspicion. Yes, the world is divine; no, not everything is permitted. "It is forbidden to believe that creation is merely an illusion, for all of Torah and mitzvot are performed within corporeal, material reality as it is; yet we are also obliged to believe that the cosmos is literally void and nothingness!"[23] The Mitnagdim rejected the paradox, perhaps because they feared our inability to live in paradox. Indeed, even within Hasidism, the concept of worship through corporeality became controversial enough that it was relegated to the spiritual elites.[24]

The theology of immanence is a legacy of Kabbalah. Both Hasidim and the early Mitnagdim were heirs to that kabbalistic tradition, and *both accepted the theology of immanence*. Furthermore, neither accepted the literal sense of *tzimtzum*. God did not contract Himself to create a

---

21 Rivka Schatz Uffenheimer, *Hasidism as Mysticism: Quietistic Elements in Eighteenth Century Hasidic Thought*, trans. Jonathan Chipman (Princeton: Princeton University Press, 1993), 268–71.

22 Allan Nadler, *The Faith of the Mithnagdim: Rabbinic Responses to Hasidic Rapture* (Baltimore: Johns Hopkins University Press, 1997), 34–35.

23 Aaron Ha-Levi, *Avodat Ha-Levi*, Be-ha'alotkha, 21b; cited in Elior, "HaBaD," in Green, *Jewish Spirituality*, 198. Elior's translation.

24 Uffenheimer, *Hasidism as Mysticism*, 52.

vacuum void of divinity for purposes of creation. There can be no place void of divinity. God is all and everywhere. According to both Hasidim and Mitnagdim, *tzimtzum* is what we designate as the *human inability to perceive the divine* from within the fullness of God. *Tzimtzum* is not out there in reality; it is in our heads. *Tzimtzum* describes our inability to recognize or know the divine. Our contracted consciousness is an issue of epistemology or psychology, not ontology.

The dispute between the Hasidim and the Mitnagdim, represented by HaBaD versus the Vilna Gaon and his protégé Rav Hayim of Volozhin, respectively, was *not* based on whether *tzimtzum* was literal or figurative. Both groups agreed it should be understood figuratively—thus, one essential aspect of Lurianic Kabbalah does not enter modernity unreconstructed. For HaBaD, *tzimtzum* was psychological; for the Mitnagdim, it was epistemological. In other words, God's immanence is an accepted inheritance from medieval Kabbalah, primarily that of Moshe Cordovero. The source of that knowledge is tradition, i.e., Kabbalah. For the Hasidim, we can overcome God's figurative withdrawal from our perception through contemplation. Not so for the Mitnagdim. There is nothing humans can do to pierce the veil and perceive divine immanence. The barrier is epistemological. We simply lack the capacity.[25]

Allan Nadler explained that Mitnagdic epistemology precludes unmediated mystical experiences.[26] For Rav Hayim of Volozhin, one is not even permitted to *contemplate* divine immanence.[27] There is, however, one single exception where divinity erupts into our world and consciousness: Torah. For the Vilna Gaon, the Torah is the unique point of immanence in this world. Mount Sinai was a singularity in which the divine fullness burst through our epistemological barriers. In his 1797 condemnation of Hasidism, the Gaon ridiculed them for seeing divinity in "every tree and every rock."[28] As Rabbi Phineas ben Judah, one of the

25 Nadler, *Faith of the Mithnagdim*, 22. See also Tamar Ross, "Two Interpretations of the Theory of Tzimtzum" [Heb.], *Mehkarei Yerushalayim Be-Machshevet Yisrael* 2 (1982): 153–69.
26 Nadler, *Faith of the Mithnagdim*, 163.
27 Shaul Magid, "Deconstructing the Mystical: The Anti-Mystical Kabbalism in Rabbi Hayyim of Volozhin's Nefesh Ha-Hayyim," *Journal of Jewish Thought and Philosophy* 9 (1999): 52.
28 Eliyahu Stern, *The Genius: Elijah of Vilna and the Making of Modern Judaism* (New Haven: Yale University Press, 2013), 85–95.

early, prominent Mitnagdic polemicists, wrote: "Do not imagine that you can arrive at devekut or ethical perfection except via Torah study. . . . Torah study constitutes the true devekut."[29]

For the Vilna Gaon, prayer was not a vehicle for cleaving to God, it was just another mitzvah. More importantly, since devekut was impossible through anything other than Torah study, those other activities that Hasidism engaged in were a waste of the precious opportunity to study more Torah. Since you can't get there (to God) from here (our minds), don't waste your time! Indeed, in the original ban of 1772, there was the charge that the Hasidim "belittled Torah study."

Nadler contends that the Mitnagdim held a lower opinion of humanity than did the Hasidim. "The most prominent and consistent teaching of Mitnagdism was the impotence of the human spirit."[30] Was the Mitnagdic contention that we are unable to overcome our cognitive deficiencies a product of that generally pessimistic conception of humanity? Even if Nadler is correct, we should point out that such pessimism is far clearer in the theology of the Baal Shem Tov's great grandson, Rebbe Nachman of Bratslav (1772–1810).[31] Rebbe Nahman warned that there are questions which have no answers because they seemingly come from a place where God's presence has been removed. Recognition of human limitations strikes me as less of an admission of impotence than an acknowledgement that humans are not omnipotent.

An alternative explanation to Nadler's is that the Vilna Gaon and Rav Hayim had read or heard of Kant through Pinchas Hurwitz's incredibly popular Sefer Habrit (1797). They latched on to Kantian epistemology which posited an impenetrable barrier between our perception of things and the things themselves. As Kant himself wrote in the preface to the second edition of the Critique of Pure Reason (1787), "I have therefore found it necessary to deny knowledge in order to make room for faith." (David Ruderman, in his analysis of Hurwitz, was explicit: "Hurwitz,

---

29 Keter Torah, 10a; cited in Nadler, Faith of the Mithnagdim, 156-57.
30 Nadler, Faith of Mithnagdim, 175; see also p. 77.
31 For a discussion of Rebbe Nachman's critique of rationalism, see Arthur Green, Tormented Master: The Life and Spiritual Quest of Rabbi Nahman of Bratslav (Woodstock: Jewish Lights Publishing, 1992), 285–336, and more recently Alon Goshen-Gottestein, "Speech, Silence, Song: Epistemology and Theodicy in a Teaching of R. Nahman of Breslav," Philosophia 30, nos. 1-4 (2003): 143–87.

like Kant, was denying the human pretension to knowledge in order to make room for faith.")[32] It may be that Kant's epistemology was initially deployed as a weapon against the Hasidic program of perceiving divinity through the garb of corporeality. Panic-stricken at the thought of a resurgence of Sabbateanism, the leaders of traditional Eastern European Judaism grasped at Kant's epistemology to thwart worship through corporeality and its potential antinomianism.

In terms of ontology, both the Hasidim and Mitnagdim agree on the radical nature of divine immanence. The Vilna Gaon was, after all, perhaps the leading kabbalist of his generation.[33] Interestingly, although there is a popular conception that the Hasidim are more faithful to Kabbalah, in the sphere of mitzvot and theurgy, the opposite is the case. The Vilna Gaon, Rav Hayim of Volozhin, and Rabbi Pinchas of Polotsk all agree that performance of the mitzvot affects the supernal realms much in the way we saw with medieval Kabbalah. "Every deed you perform has repercussions in the loftiest heights and affects the brilliance of the spiritual lights above."[34] Due to our cognitive handicaps, the precise relationship between our deeds and the supernal sefirot will remain forever obscure, but we can be confident of our deeds' impacts.

The Hasidic tzaddikim, on the other hand, interpreted the sefirot as intellectual and emotional stages within each person's religious and mystical journey. Rather than only a top-down description of divine emanation and theosophy, the Hasidic sefirot plot points on the individual's ascent toward a mystical consciousness.[35] Thus, for much of Hasidism, prayer, contemplation, and the mitzvot have primarily a psychological effect on the Hasid and secondarily an ontological impact on divinity—which, given the theology of panentheism, an impact on humans is, by definition, an impact on the divine, as well.[36] Thus, by the end of the eighteenth century, the theosophy of medieval Kabbalah had largely been bracketed by the Mitnagdim and psychologized by the Hasidim.

32 David B. Ruderman, *The Best-Selling Hebrew Book of the Modern Era: The Book of the Covenant of Pinhas Hurwitz and Its Remarkable Legacy* (Seattle: University of Washington Press, 2014), 70.
33 Nadler, *Faith of the Mithnagdim*, 36.
34 Rav Hayim of Volozhin, Nefesh Ha-Hayim, ch. 4.
35 Yoram Jacobson, *Hasidic Thought*, trans. Jonathan Chipman (Woodstock: Jewish Lights Publishing, 2000), 52–55.
36 Elior, *Paradoxical Ascent*, 154.

Perhaps the greatest marker of Hasidism is the "institutionalization" of the tzaddik.[37] Some tzaddikim insisted that their followers struggle themselves to find their own way to self-realization and expanded consciousness.[38] Other tzaddikim were proponents of vicarious or transitive devekut—the Hasid attaches to the tzaddik and the tzaddik attaches to God and brings the Hasid along with him. The priestly Torah's ontology of holy contagion is pressed into service for this conception of a tzaddik: "'Every male among the children of Aaron may eat of [the meal offering] . . . whatever touches it shall be holy' (Leviticus 6:11). The Torah here indicates how great is the merit of clinging to scholars and the tzadikkim of the generation. . . . Everything that is joined to what is pure becomes pure itself."[39]

Joseph Dan, a leading scholar in this field, suggests that the innovative period of Hasidism has long been over. "Not only are new ideas apparently absent, but the old spiritual teachings are giving way to a new emphasis on the external features of Jewish life."[40] We can see the translation and modernization of Hasidic fundamentals in the writings of Hillel Zeitlin, Abraham Joshua Heschel, and Arthur Green—all of whom, significantly, are writing with at least one foot outside of the traditional world of Hasidism.

Before shifting our attention to Western Europe, we must note one other movement to emerge in the nineteenth century from the Mitnagdic world of Eastern Europe. Cleary, the Hasidic masters emphasized ethics and personal piety. The Mitnagdim also wrote about the importance of ethics, but relatively little time was accorded to ethical literature in Rav Hayim of Volozhin's yeshiva.[41] The haskalah, the Jewish enlightenment, posed a challenge to the yeshivah curriculum which Rav Hayim met with

---

37 Arthur Green, "Early Hasidism," in Rapoport-Albert, *Hasidism Reappraised*, 445.

38 Immanuel Etkes, "The Zaddik," in Rapoport-Albert , *Hasidism Reappraised*, 159–67; Arthur Green, "Typologies of Leadership and the Hasidic Zaddiq," in Green, *Jewish Spirituality*, 127–56. Elliot Wolfson in *Open Secret* claims that the late Lubavitch Rebbe did not appoint a successor to foist that responsibility on each individual Jew.

39 Solomon Rabinowitz of Radomsk (1803–1806); cited in Piekarz, "Hasidism as a Socio-Religious Movement," in Rapoport-Albert, *Hasidism Reappraised*, 248.

40 Joseph Dan, "Hasidism: The Third Century," in Rapoport-Albert, *Hasidism Reappraised*, 422.

41 Shaul Stampfer, *Lithuanian Yeshivoas of the Nineteenth Century: Creating a Tradition of Learning* (Oxford: Littman Library of Jewish Civilization, 2014), 42.

stalwart resistance. Thus, the emergence of the Mussar movement, dedicated to the highest level of personal propriety, which is true piety, is yet another link connecting modern Judaisms.

The most distinctive element of the Mussar movement, which took root in the 1840s, was their method of ingraining ethical reflexes to the challenges of living an ethical life.[42] The psychology of Mussar and its curricular implications reflect the shift in religiosity from theocentric Kabbalah to anthropocentric piety.[43] For Rabbi Israel Salanter (1810–1883), the founder of the Mussar movement in the mitnagdic heart of Vilna, piety is attained not through contemplation, nor through Torah study *per se*, but through ethical self-perfection. As Salanter himself wrote, "It is easier to become expert in the entire Talmud than it is to correct a single stubborn character trait."[44]

Like Hasidism, Mussar was not geared toward the intellectual elite, nor was it exclusive to men, unlike the world of the yeshiva. Mussar was for everyone.

> Learning Mussar is not like other kinds of learning. There is no other study which imposes its obligation upon all the people: women are exempt from Torah study; there is considerable latitude to exempt [from Torah study] those who endure suffering or who are lacking in intellect or who are in acute distress, heaven forbid; each one according to his particular situation may be exempt from this obligation. . . . *But not so this study [of Mussar], which is an obligation that embraces every person without exception.* For the battle against the *yetzer harah* [the evil inclination], with its cunning ruses, envelopes every rational being"[45]

Rabbi Salanter's leading disciple, Simcha Zissel Ziv (1824–1898) focused on crowding out opportunities to succumb to temptation by "seeking opportunities for lovingkindness each day, even in small ways,

42 Immanuel Etkes, "Rabbi Israel Salanter and his Psychology of Mussar," in Green, *Jewish Spirituality*, 211.
43 Ibid., 209–210.
44 Pechter, Kitvei, 202. Cited and translated in Immanuel Etkes, *Rabbi Israel Salanter and the Mussar Movement* (Philadelphia: Jewish Publication Society, 1993), 122.
45 Pechter, Kitvei, 204–205. Cited and translated in Etkes, *Rabbi Israel Salanter*, 110–11. Translation slightly modified.

whether using body, money, or speech."[46] Salanter had been critical of
Jews who were more meticulous in ritual observance than in interpersonal ethics.[47] Hurwitz's influential Sefer Habrit, particularly the second edition published in 1807, was emphatic that the commandment
of neighborly love trumped all other commandments, including Torah
study, and extended to non-Jews! More surprisingly, Hurwitz claimed
that both the Talmudic rabbis and Hayyim Vital understood that commandment in the same way.[48]

Thus, Salanter's disciple strives to cultivate a character of lovingness
to all: "As God bestows particular abundance upon human beings, providing for their physical and spiritual needs, we are called to love other
people by attending to both their bodies and souls."[49] Although relatively
few people had the discipline and commitment to dedicate themselves
to the Mussar movement, by the end of the nineteenth century, Mussar's
values had seeped into Lithuanian culture. When the Slobodka Yeshiva
opened in 1881, the curriculum reflected that "musar (ethics) was an
essential attribute of a Torah scholar."[50] As we shift our focus to the
West, we will notice a parallel promotion of individual piety and ethical
self-perfection as well as a marginalization of classical Kabbalah.[51]

The Haskalah

"The early Haskalah [1720–1770] was first and foremost an attempt to
broaden the curriculum of Ashkenazi Jewry by reviving knowledge of
neglected strands of the [Jewish] textual tradition while also engaging with the larger [non-Jewish] culture."[52] The early Haskalah over-

---

46 Simcha Zissel Ziv, Kitvei HaSabba Mi'Khelm, 193; cited and translated in Geoffrey
Claussen, "Sharing the Burden: Rabbi Simhah Zissel Ziv on Love and Empathy,"
Journal of the Society of Christian Ethics 30, no. 2 (2010): 153.
47 Etkes, *Rabbi Israel Salanter*, 173.
48 Resianne Fontaine, "Love of One's Neighbour in Pinhas Hurwitz's Sefer ha-Berit," in
Studies in Hebrew Language and Jewish Culture, ed. Martin F. J. Baasten and Reinier
Munk (Doredrecht: Springer, 2007), 271–95.
49 Claussen, "Sharing the Burden": 156.
50 Stampfer, *Lithuanian Yeshivas*, 255.
51 Leora Batnitzky emphasizes the centrality of individual spiritual quests in early
modern Judaism in chapter six of *How Judaism Became a Religion*.
52 David Sorkin, "The Early Haskalah," in Feiner, *New Perspectives on the Haskalah*, 10.

lapped with the European Enlightenment of the eighteenth century. The philosophical and political implications of equality, progress, and inherent individual rights slowly worked their way into the regimes of Western and Central Europe. The Eastern European Haskalah lagged behind its Western counterparts, not beginning until the 1820s, and manifested politically in quite different ways. Just as Spinoza's philosophy cannot be fully understood without knowledge of his historical context and political agenda, the same is true for the early maskilim (advocates of the Haskalah). They reconstructed Jewish tradition in anticipation of the political emancipation which marks the Jewish transition to modernity.

Moses Mendelssohn (1729–1786) holds pride of place in any discussion of the Haskalah and the beginnings of modern Jewish thought. Alexander Altmann calls him the "patron saint of German Jewry."[53] He was respected by German gentiles for his command of Western philosophy and literature. He was a legend within German Jewry for his proud defense of Judaism as both rational and superior to Christianity precisely because of Judaism's rationalism.[54] As many historians have noted, the best way for Jews to become German citizens was to uncouple citizenship from a shared, ethnic history. The Enlightenment's emphasis on both vocational and moral education, what Mendelssohn calls *Bildung*, puts Germans and Jews on the same playing field.[55] If Jews wanted to become German without renouncing their Jewishness, then there had to be an expression of Judaism compatible with German citizenship.

> Jewish commitment to the humanistic ideal of *Bildung* was based on the correct perception that only through transcending a German past, which the Jews did not share, could Jew meet German on equal terms. . . . Similarly, the concept of respectability was based upon a moral order and not dependent upon shared historical roots.[56]

---

53 Alexander Altmann, "Moses Mendelssohn as the Archetypal German Jew," in *The Jewish Response to German Culture: From the Enlightenment to the Second World War*, ed. Jehuda Reinharz and Walter Schatzberg (Hanover: University Press of New England, 1985), 18.

54 Ibid., 26

55 Amos Morris-Reich, "*Bildung* and German-Jewish History: Idea and Ethos," in *The German Jewish Encounter: Sixty Years after the War*, ed. Ben Mollov (Ramat Gan: Bar Ilan University Press, 2006), 38.

56 George Mosse, "Jewish Emancipation: Between *Bildung* and Respectability," in Reinharz, *The Jewish Response to German Culture*, 14.

Mendelssohn claimed that Judaism was nothing more than publicly revealed legislation between God and the Israelites. It was not *religion* in the Christian sense of the term because it dealt with actions not beliefs. For Mendelssohn, moral behavior was the essence of religion. As Nathan Rotenstreich has observed, "What strikes us as new [in modern Jewish thought] is the insistence on the primacy of ethics in the sphere of faith; traditional religion is divested of its beliefs in transcendence, and pressed into the service of morality."[57] Once Mendelssohn identifies Judaism as a legal system, as had Spinoza, the way is open to become a German who is loyal to both the civil laws of Germany and the ritual laws of Judaism. But Arnold Eisen has pointed out the consequences of Mendelssohn's compromise with emancipation:

> [T]he scope available for Jewish behavior in obedience to divine commandments would henceforth be severely constricted. It had already been progressively limited during centuries of existence in exile. . . . Emancipation was about to contract that domain still further, sweeping away Jewish courts, Jewish schools, Jewish languages, Jewish public spaces. Only the "four ells" of synagogue, on the one hand, and "home," on the other, would remain. . . . Ceremony—ritual—was virtually all that the Jews had left.[58]

As Mendelssohn wrote in *Jerusalem*, "the ceremonial law itself is a kind of living script, rousing the mind and heart, full of meaning, never ceasing to inspire contemplation and to provide the occasion and opportunity for oral instruction."[59] Bildung as education, morality, and respectability was the legacy that Moses Mendelssohn bequeathed to his nineteenth-century heirs struggling to articulate what Mendelssohn did not—if Jews can be integrated into the nations in which they live, and religion is fundamentally about the universalist commitment to ethical behavior, then why remain Jewish with its attendant liabilities?

---

57 Nathan Rotenstreich, *Jewish Philosophy in Modern Times: From Mendelssohn to Rosenzweig* (New York: Holt, Rinehart and Winston, 1968), 6.

58 Arnold M. Eisen, *Rethinking Modern Judaism: Ritual, Commandment, Community* (Chicago: University of Chicago Press, 1998), 40.

59 Moses Mendelssohn, *Jerusalem: Or on Religious Power and Judaism*, trans. Allan Arkush (Hanover: University of New England Press, 1967), 102–03.

The modern approach to the Hebrew Bible as a text composed by multiple authors over hundreds of years had its champions already in the seventeenth century. Throughout the eighteenth century, it became increasingly acknowledged that human authorship of the Torah posed a near insurmountable challenge to traditional rabbinic interpretations based on premodern assumptions. If the Torah had multiple authors, then repetitions within the Pentateuch were not fodder for midrash halakhah, they were just repetitions. More than that, what signaled to the Talmudic rabbis two different commandments was nothing more than emphasis. For instance, in one of the many injunctions concerning the fair treatment of the foreigner, the Torah commands to "not *wrong* a stranger or *oppress* him" (Exodus 22:20). Nahum Sarna, a modern Bible scholar steeped in Jewish commentary, acknowledges that the two verbs "heighten the stringency of the prohibition."[60] The rabbis, however, linked the first verb to verbal and emotional abuse and the second verb to financial fraud.[61]

Linking law to the Torah is not *necessarily* deriving law from the Torah. The rabbis of the Talmud may have just used the idiosyncrasies of the Torah's language as a mnemonic to trigger their recall of the Oral Torah that, according to the rabbinic myth, was given at Sinai parallel to the Written Torah. This dispute about whether the Oral Torah is derived from the Written Torah through designated interpretative rules, or whether the oral Torah is an independent source of law, crystallized in the Middle Ages.[62] Mendelssohn and his allies devised various strategies to defend the autonomy of Oral Torah from the onslaught of historical criticism of the Written Torah. Reformers, on the other hand, saw history as their ally.

By the middle and late decades of the nineteenth century, the Jewish battles in Western and Central Europe focused on the authority of halakhah. Again: Does midrash halakhah actually generate laws, or is it merely

60 Nahum M. Sarna, *Jewish Publication Society Torah Commentary on Exodus* (Philadelphia: Jewish Publication Society, 2003), 138.
61 Mekhilta, Nezikin 18.
62 Moshe Halbertal, *People of the Book: Canon, Meaning, and Authority* (Cambridge, MA: Harvard University Press, 2007), 54–72; and Jay M. Harris, *How Do We Know This? Midrash and the Fragmentation of Modern Judaism* (Albany: State University of New York Press, 1994), 73–101.

a mnemonic for an independent Oral Torah handed down at Sinai? The application of new historical and literary standards was not favorable to either possibility. Rabbinic midrashim, on their face, often seemed to be implausible. Furthermore, if the Written Torah was not given at Sinai, all the more so the Oral Torah was not! Thanks to this unprecedented challenge to the divine integrity of the Written and Oral Torahs, we have been blessed with exquisitely creative and insightful bible commentary from the likes of Jacob Zvi Mecklenberg (1785–1865), Samuel David Luzzatto (1800–1865), Meir Loeb ben Yehiel Michael (Malbim, 1809–1879), and Samson Raphael Hirsch (1808–1888). Their losing battle to defend the coherence of traditional Judaism should not detract from their contributions to philology, grammar, literary theory, and religious psychology.[63] At roughly the same time, Jewish thinkers who acknowledged the historical influences on the development of Jewish law began to formulate the ideology of the Positive-Historical School, which was the ideological forerunner of Conservative Judaism. But the emergence of the Positive-Historical School awaited the perceived excesses of early Reform.

Undermining the Torah's divine authorship undermined the authority of the entire Jewish tradition. Thus, it was predictable that as Jews were emancipated, there would be certain reforms that emerged unencumbered by the traditional halakhic method. Abraham Geiger (1810–1874), both a historian and a rabbi, argued in 1835 that "the principle of tradition, to which the entire talmudic and rabbinic literature own their emergence, is nothing other than the principle of constant advance and timely development."[64] Samuel Holdheim (1806–1860) famously wrote, "The Talmud speaks out of the consciousness of its age and for that time it *was* right; I speak out of the higher consciousness of my age and for this age I *am* right."[65] This higher consciousness, in the context of Germany, emphasized a universal rationalism and morality that demanded decorum in the synagogues, a sermon in proper German (not Yiddish) promoting ethical behavior, an abandonment of prayer for the return to

---

63 In addition to Harris, *How Do We Know This?*, chapters 7 and 8, see Cherry, *Torah through Time*, 27–30 and 122–24.
64 Cited in Harris, *How Do We Know This?*, 158.
65 Samuel Holdheim, *Das Ceremonialgesetz*, 50; cited in Michael A. Meyer, *Response to Modernity: A History of the Reform Movement in Judaism* (Detroit: Wayne State University Press, 1988), 83.

Israel and the rebuilding of the Temple, conducting confirmations, and the ultimate expression of national commitment—advocating military service for Jews.[66]

The use of Maimonides and Immanuel Kant was nearly a necessity in the late eighteenth- and early nineteenth-century Jewish thought of Western Europe. Mendelssohn wrote of his love for Maimonides, the greatest Jewish philosopher of the Middle Ages, even though he seemingly demurred from Maimonides' insistence that Judaism has dogmas.[67] The early maskilim undoubtedly yoked themselves to RaMBaM because of his dedication to rationalism. As Arthur Cohen has pointed out, "Intolerant supernaturalism had first to be disdained before the reign of reason and humanist culture could be realized."[68] The logic of emancipation was predicated on the reign of reason.

In Mendelssohn's version of Judaism, designed to invite offers of political emancipation, religion has no coercive power. The reformers who followed in his wake were equally adamant that Judaism was a voluntary association that encourages ethical behavior, but religious acts are expressions of the individual will and not externally imposed. The reaction against Kant's criticism of Jewish heteronomy, the idea that God commands Israel, is transparent in early Reform Judaism's insistence on individual autonomy. Jews choose the commandments that they find ennobling. Although individual autonomy is associated with Reform, we find the logic in Mendelssohn.

> Whatever may have been Mendelssohn's innermost thoughts, the practical ramifications of his ruminations are clear. They provide a rationale for the dissolution of what we might call Judaism's coercive, collectivist dimension and the transformation of the Jewish religion into an entirely *voluntary* matter. Mendelssohn was the first Jewish thinker to declare it entirely up to the individual Jew, and not his rabbi or his communal leaders, to

---

66 Michael A. Meyer, *The Origins of the Modern Jew: Jewish Identity and European Culture in Germany, 1749-1824* (Detroit: Wayne State University Press, 1967), 130–37.

67 Michael A. Meyer, "Maimonides and Some Moderns: European Images of the Rambam from the Eighteenth to the Twentieth Century," *CCAR Journal: A Reform Jewish Quarterly* (1997): 4–6.

68 Arthur A. Cohen, *The Natural and the Supernatural Jew: An Historical and Theological Introduction* (New York: Pantheon Books, 1962), 20.

determine whether he would fulfill his duty to live in accordance with its demands. He thus showed, for the first time, how one could render the Jewish religion fully compatible with liberalism.[69]

Before we continue with nineteenth-century Jewish thought, let us pause to reflect on the magnitude of emancipation's ramifications. The modern individualism of the Enlightenment severed "the inherent link between Jewish persons and the Jewish people."[70] By 1820, most Jews in Western Europe no longer looked first toward the Jewish community for their values, esthetics, or their place on the intellectual horizon. What had been primary receded to the background; gentile society was now the cultural juggernaut. The fiddler had fallen off the roof. Modernity changed everything, forever.

Although there had been harsh critics of RaMBaM, his promotion of reason, rationality, and secular education overlapped very conveniently with Mendelssohn's understanding of Bildung. "For many German Jews who wished to remain Jewish but who were no longer religiously observant, Bildung came increasingly to be considered as a 'substitute Judaism.' . . . Here the ideal of Bildung and the ethical interpretation of Judaism were in every respect compatible."[71] The promotion of RaMBaM went hand in hand with the marginalization and repudiation of the mystical tradition. The Reform Rabbi Samuel Hirsch (1815–1889), for instance, rejected mystical divine immanence as well as any inkling of original sin that had penetrated medieval Jewish thought since the Protestant Reformation and Catholic Counter-Reformation's emphasis of the doctrine at the Council of Trent (1546 to 1563).[72]

---

69 Allan Arkush, "The Liberalism of Moses Mendelssohn," in *The Cambridge Companion to Modern Jewish Philosophy*, ed. Michael L. Morgan and Peter Eli Gordon (Cambridge: Cambridge University Press, 2007), 46–47.

70 Mervin F. Verbit, "Emancipation, Modernity, and Jewish Identity in America," in *Contention, Controversy, and Change—Evolutions and Revolutions in the Jewish Experience*, vol. 1, ed. Simcha Fishbane and Eric Levine (New York: Touro College Press, 2016), 313.

71 Morris-Reich, "*Bildung* and German-Jewish History," in Mollov, *German-Jewish Encounter*, 44.

72 For example, the concept of original sin is found in both kabbalistic sources like Horwitz's *Two Tablets of the Covenant* and Shlomo Ephraim of Lunschitz's Torah commentary Kli Yakar. See Alan Cooper, "A Medieval Jewish Version of Original Sin: Ephraim of Luntshits on Leviticus 12," *Harvard Theological Review* 97, no. 4 (2004): 445–59.

Significantly, it was in Italy, a country without Reform Judaism's apotheosis of rationality, where we see a discriminating reappropriation of the kabbalistic tradition. Italy, in more than one way, differed from the German model of Enlightenment. Not only was Kabbalah not universally stigmatized, but the application of a historical consciousness toward halakhah was *accepted* as early as the seventeenth century by Leone de Modena (1571–1648). Subsequent Jewish thinkers held views that will be later perceived as inconsistent. Isaac Samuel Reggio (1784–1855), for example, argued for the necessity of a historical consciousness vis-à-vis halakhah and rejected his father's commitment to Kabbalah, but he also believed that "Hebrew words do not resemble those of any other language, for they are alive, and God is in them."[73]

Samuel David Luzzatto was a critic of Maimonides' approach to Judaism, but he, like Reggio and his enlightened German colleagues, rejected Kabbalah as an obstacle to true Judaism. Luzzatto also repudiated the idea that Judaism should tether its theology to any particular scientific paradigm since religion's goal was essentially ethical. Elijah Benamozegh (1823–1900), of Moroccan descent, argued vehemently for the authenticity of Kabbalah. He also qualified the place of ethics within Judaism. Benamozegh, much like Maimonides, believed that intellectual perfection, understanding the unity and coherence of all knowledge, was the ultimate goal for which ethics was the necessary means.

> Hebraism does not confine itself to knowledge which is immediately useful to man, which helps in the discipline of his will, but devotes itself also to metaphysical knowledge, to the law of Being and Understanding. . . . Thus science and religion, the law of the universe and the law of man, Wisdom and Torah, are declared identical. . . . All knowledge becomes religious knowledge, all understanding is sanctified, and the intellectual act is a moral act.[74]

---

73 Isaac Samuel Reggio, preface to Torat Elohim, 17; cited in Alessandro Guetta, *Philosophy and Kabbalah: Elijah Benamozegh and the Reconciliation of Western Thought and Jewish Esotericism*, trans. Helena Kahan (Albany: State University of New York Press, 2009), 72.

74 Maxwell Luria, ed., *Elijah Benamozegh: Israel and Humanity* (Mahwah: Paulist Press, 1995), 226–227. See also pages 93-94.

Benamozegh, though persuaded by the fundamental truths of Kabbalah, nevertheless rejected the version of pantheism articulated by some contemporary German philosophers. As we will see in the next book in our discussion of evolution, Benamozegh could acquiesce to a teleological transmutation of species because his panentheism links immanence with divine transcendence. The Kabbalah's emanationist schema provides Benamozegh the framework to reconcile more than just Darwin with Judaism. Here is how Alessandro Guetta, a leading scholar on Benamozegh, puts it:

> Matter is not lowly and contemptible, verging on nonbeing as held to be the case by the most extreme Platonic doctrine, but it had dignity; nature deserves the love due to realities from which God has not divided himself. Idealism and empiricism are both true and are reconciled in the Kabbalistic emanationist doctrine Benamozegh considered "complete Judaism."[75]

Benamozegh, however, was no naive kabbalist. He was quite willing to strip away the myth and racism of the Kabbalah. There was already an Italian tradition that Kabbalah had become distorted over the centuries and its teachings needed to be purified for the modern world. "This was exactly the aim of Benamozegh, who considered himself to be ridding the ancient science of the 'rust of centuries.' Benamozegh was therefore the heir to an Italian kabbalistic culture which had already begun to embrace the challenges of modernity."[76]

Benamozegh championed the seven Noahide laws and believed that the arrival of the messianic era was dependent upon more people understanding and committing themselves to their observance. (The seven Noachide laws are: no worship of false gods/idolatry; no blaspheming the true God; no sexual immorality; no murder; no thievery; no unnecessary cruelty to animals; and the establishment of a court system to administer these laws.) Benamozegh amplified the positive notes that we saw in Hurwitz's Sefer Habrit concerning gentiles. He expressed gratitude toward the mixed multitude coming with the Israelites out of Egypt for the divine sparks which they brought with them, and for other proselytes

---

75 Guetta, *Philosophy and Kabbalah*, 56.
76 Ibid., 154.

and gentiles who continue to elevate these fallen sparks. These acts help redeem the exiled Shechinah. In the language of nineteenth-century philosophy, they close the gap between the ideal and the real.[77] Part of Benamozegh's greatness is his selective combinations of philosophical and kabbalistic ideas, distilling the truths and wisdom embedded in the totality of the Jewish tradition. He reformulates rather than rejects many of Judaism's central values, particularly those that resonate with the Jews' new position in society.

Progress, perfectibility, and universal brotherhood, themes at the very heart of French Enlightenment philosophy, were presented by Benamozegh in a kabbalistic key.[78] We will see this again in his discussion of biological evolution. In his attempt to root Kabbalah in rabbinic Judaism, what he calls Pharisaic Judaism, he makes the following observation that has not been fully appreciated even today. "The Pharisees even accomplished the miracle of lending respectability to a word which in any other religion is synonymous with heterodoxy: *hiddush*, change or innovation."[79] Given his theology, as humans (both Jews and gentiles) partner with God in the ethical progress for which our world yearns, we inevitably affect the aspect of God, the *Shechinah*, who is within this world. God, too, progresses.[80]

As our story of Jewish thought and theology moves in to the twentieth century, the religious philosophy of Hermann Cohen (1842–1918) serves as the pivot. Cohen is identified as the founder of Neo-Kantianism because he attempts to clarify what he perceives as the nineteenth-century misreadings of Kant's epistemology and metaphysics, including that of Georg W. F. Hegel (1770–1831). Given that there is no scholarly consensus on the interpretations of the philosophies of Kant, Hegel, or Cohen, and given that there is development in each of their thought throughout their careers, far be it from me to attempt the quixotic and diagram their intellectual relationships. Therefore, in plotting Cohen's role in the development of Jewish thought, I will confine my comments to Cohen's focus

---

77 Benamozegh, *Israel and Humanity*, 71–77.
78 Benamozegh, writing in French at the end of his career, saw himself within the French intellectual orbit. Guetta, *Philosophy and Kabbalah*, 66.
79 Benamozegh, *Israel and Humanity*, 171.
80 Guetta, *Philosophy and Kabbalah*, 31; and Benamozegh, *Israel and Humanity*, 190–204.

on the individual subject. Parenthetically, however, I must re-empha-
size the conceptual parallel between the German philosophical debates
concerning the relationship between ontology/epistemology or subject/
object, and the theological debates within Eastern European Jewry on
epistemological limitations.

As Steven Schwartzschild has pointed out, "no ontological claims
about God or man or the world are made" in Cohen's primary Jewish
work, *Religion of Reason out of the Sources of Judaism* (published posthumously in 1918).[81] Cohen's philosophy of idealism, much like that of
Kant, *posits* God as a transcendent *idea*, the guarantor of ethics. Since
God cannot be proven empirically or rationally, Cohen postulates, i.e.
assumes, the existence of a moral God.

> Nature and morality are not one and the same, yet both have their origin in,
> and are vouchsafed by, the unity of God. But though nature and morality
> are and must remain different, they interact and are conjoined at a certain
> point: in man. For when I live in accord with moral concepts, I am no
> animal, no mere creature of nature, but a member of a moral universe.
> It is however, only the idea of God which gives me the confidence that
> morality will become a reality on earth. And because I cannot live without
> this confidence, I cannot live without God.[82]

One may look to nature in vain to find conclusive evidence of an
ethical God; the religion of the Hebrew prophets is the source for such a
God. The God of philosophy addresses humanity at large, and the message is ethical. But the God of the prophets addresses the individual, and
the message is compassion.

> Prophetism depicts God almost always as loving not only the stranger
> but also the orphan and widow; they are therefore seen as victims of
> social oppression from which they will be liberated through God's
> justice. . . . God compassionately takes pity upon the poor; and man must
> compassionately discover his fellow man in the poor.[83]

---

81 Steven Schwartzschild, "How to Read *Religion of Reason*," in Hermann Cohen,
   Religion of Reason out of the Sources of Judaism, trans. Simon Kaplan (Atlanta:
   Scholars Press, 1995), 15.
82 Hermann Cohen, *Reason and Hope: Selections from the Jewish Writings of Hermann
   Cohen*, trans. Eva Jospe (New York: W W Norton & Company, Inc., 1971), 46.
83 Ibid., 71.

Arthur A. Cohen suggested that Cohen took reason as far as it could go and then "ended the contribution of philosophical idealism to Judaism."[84] Even before World War I, the optimistic philosophies of German idealists had begun to be eclipsed by the darker hues of Arthur Schopenhauer (1788–1860) and Friedrich Nietzsche (1844–1900). And in the real world of 1908 Bialystok, a three-day pogrom left seventy dead and even more seriously wounded. Cohen may have lived into the twentieth century, but he was a nineteenth-century philosopher of religion. Although uncharitable, Eliezer Berkovits' assessment is not incorrect: "Cohen's interpretation of Judaism and Israel is, of course, a philosopher's attempt to lend scholarly dignity to the typical assimilationist ideology of German reform Jewry of his generation."[85] More to the point, and more sympathetically, is the assessment by Kenneth Seeskin: "In a nutshell, people became dissatisfied with infinite tasks [of ethical progress] and transcendental presuppositions. The existentialists wanted to break out of the circle of ideas and concentrate on lived experience."[86] By the end of Cohen's literary career, which coincided with the end of The Great War, the blood-soaked soil had been well prepared for the existentialists Martin Buber (1878–1965) and Franz Rosenzweig (1886–1929).

As a graduate student at Brandeis University studying with Arthur Green in the late nineties, I remember my teacher saying that in the rabbinic period, the focus was on redemption; in the medieval period, creation; and in the modern period, revelation. Nowhere do we see that more clearly than in the writings of and dialogue between Buber and Rosenzweig. Both theologians shifted the Jewish discussion from epistemology to psychology. God did not need to be saved from the academic disciplines of philosophy and science; God needed to be experienced and loved. Buber came to his theology as a student of Hasidism, and Rosenzweig through his confrontation with German thought and theology.

84 Cohen, *The Natural and the Supernatural Jew*, 79.
85 Eliezer Berkovits, *Major Themes in the Modern Philosophies of Judaism* (New York: Ktav Publishing, 1975), 25.
86 Schwartzschild, "How to Read *Religion of Reason*," in Cohen, *Religion of Reason*, 40.

Much of my presentation of Martin Buber leans on the essay by Paul Mendes-Flohr entitled, "Martin Buber's Conception of God."[87] Mendes-Flohr understands Buber as a metaphysical minimalist due to his consistent resistance at engaging in speculation about God's self. Buber's God was one of relationship. As Buber wrote in his 1922 classic *I and Thou*, "God is the Being that . . . may properly only be addressed, not expressed."[88] Philosophically, Buber remained under the sway of idealism which precluded his ability to speak of God's noumenal essence. Our sole portal to experiencing God is through recognizing and experiencing the authenticity of the other who becomes, for that fleeting moment, a thou. A philosophy of dialogue and relationship with other humans serves as the foundation of Buber's ethics and theology.

In a thorough rejection of the mysticism of his youth, Buber contends that "man cannot approach the divine by reaching beyond the human."[89] An I-Thou attitude provides a glimpse of the Eternal Thou and discloses the unity that lies beyond all seemingly discrete objects. In the language of Jewish mysticism, the world of separation is revealed to be an illusion when one shifts one's consciousness, what Buber calls one's attitude, to one of I-Thou. The Hasidic term for this state of consciousness might be *gadlut*, or perceiving things with an expansive mind. The difference between Buber and Hasidism on this score is that for Buber the only port of entry to the world of *gadlut*, the world of unity, is through the thou of your neighbor.

That evanescent moment of revelation is unconditioned by the past. Revelation, in other words, is atemporal. Time in the world of I-It relations "is a fixed sequence from one moment to the next, with each moment bearing the impress of that which preceded it. The I-Thou attitude frees time from the determinative coefficient of the past; the moment in which the I-Thou attitude prevails is temporally autonomous."[90] Before explaining what Buber infers from his description of I-Thou time, I want

---

87 Paul Mendes-Flohr, *Divided Passions: Jewish Intellectuals and the Experience of Modernity* (Detroit: Wayne State University Press, 1991), 237–82.

88 Martin Buber, *I and Thou*, trans. Ronald G. Smith, 2nd ed. (New York: Charles Scribner's Sons, 1958), 80–81; cited in Mendes-Flohr, *Divided Passions*, 237.

89 Martin Buber, *Hasidism and Modern Man*, trans. Maurice Friedman (New York: Harper Torchbooks, 1958), 42–43; cited in Mendes-Flohr, *Divided Passions*, 245.

90 Ibid., 247.

to express my sympathetic understanding. Time may be linear, but it is not uniform. I imagine we have all had experiences where "time flies." I hope we all have experienced a love which, when finally checking the time, is shocked to discover the hour. Moments of I-Thou do take us out of ordinary, uniform time. What I am suggesting is that even without experiencing a peak I-Thou moment, we can understand Buber's claim through our own experience that the rate of time is not constant. When the medieval mystics emerged from their mystical state of consciousness they did not know if it was day or night.[91]

The content of revelation for Buber is always the same for everyone: nothing. The experience of revelation, however, is sui generis. Each of us will have a unique response to the experience of the Thou glimpsed through the thou. That response is the basis of our responsibility to the other. Mendes-Flohr calls it "the metaethical moment of all genuine moral (and political) judgment."[92] But, because the metaethical moment is a moment outside of time, there is no necessary continuity between that metaethical moment and one in the past or future. Halakhah, however, requires some degree of continuity. Furthermore, my response and your response to the same metaethical moment may differ, again impeding the possibility of a uniform, collective response in the form of communal halakhah. Thus, Buber rejects traditional halakhah, and the rejection is consistent with his understanding of revelation.

> [In revelation] man receives, and he receives not a specific "content" but a Presence, a Presence [that confirms] meaning. . . . The meaning that has been received can be proven true by each man only in the uniqueness of his being and the uniqueness of his life. As no prescription can lead us to the meeting, so none leads from it.[93]

Moreover, that metaethical moment of dialogue is symbiotic. The I-Thou "relation is mutual. My Thou affects me, as I affect it."[94] Here is yet another pillar of kabbalistic thought. The metaethical moment, otherwise known as revelation, has the potential to be mutually transformative. God beckons us into dialogical responsibility. As a result of taking

---

91 Hellner-Eshed, *A River Flows*, 300–02.
92 Mendes-Flohr, *Divided Passions*, 249.
93 Buber, *I and Thou*, 110.
94 Ibid., 15

increasing responsibility, "man's deed affects God's destiny on earth. . . . Whether God is 'transcendent' or 'immanent' does not depend on Him; it depends on man."[95] In one of Buber's scholarly works on Hasidism, he similarly notes "the principle of the responsibility of man for God's fate in the world."[96]

Buber depicts God as becoming present in the realm of the dialogic between. The mishnah in Avot portrays the divine presence as dwelling between two people who are studying Torah (3:3). Buber extends the image to two who are relating to one another with the attitude of I-Thou. Just as Talmud Torah was a sacrament for the rabbis, genuine dialogue is a sacrament for Buber.[97] "When two stand side by side on an equal footing and are open to each other without reservation, there God is."[98]

As Mendes-Flohr explains, Buber's God is experienced as an "independent, autonomous Being [who] 'addresses' each of us dialogically, personally to our Thou; and this address is sounded anew in the ever evolving 'here and now.'"[99] In each encounter, whether between people or a person and another of God's creatures, there is the potential to experience the eternal Thou through the particular thou before us. Buber maintained that Hasidism's appropriation of Lurianic holy sparks was not a metaphysical doctrine about redeeming the divinity within corporeality, but a "*metaphor* for the hallowing of the world . . . when one relates to the world as a Thou."[100]

Although Buber's assessment of Hasidism has been widely rejected, not altogether fairly in my opinion, Hava Tirosh-Samuelson recognizes that "there is no doubt that Buber interpreted the Hasidic sources in

---

95 Martin Buber, "Jewish Religiosity," in *On Judaism*, ed. Nahum N. Glatzer, with foreword by Roger Kamenetz (New York: Schocken Books, 1995), 85-86, originally published in 1923.

96 Martin Buber, "Spirit and Body of the Hasidic Movement," in *The Martin Buber Reader: Essential Writings*, ed. Asher D. Biemann (New York: Palgrave Macmillan, 2002), 64; originally published in 1935.

97 Buber, *I and Thou*, 76; cited in Mendes-Flohr, *Divided Passions*, 259.

98 Buber, *Hasidism and Modern Man*, 250.

99 Mendes-Flohr, *Divided Passions*, 262.

100 Jerome Gellman, "Early Hasidism and the Natural World," in *Judaism and Ecology: Created World and Revealed Word*, ed. Hava Tirosh-Samuelson (Cambridge, MA: Harvard University Press, 2002), 373. My italics.

the image of his own philosophy of dialogue."[101] Thus, if divine sparks are metaphorical and not metaphysical or ontological, then describing Buber's God as panentheistic is inappropriate.[102] For Buber, creation is not divine. Rather, creation serves as a thou through *whom*, not *which*, we may merit an intense, inner-experience of the world's inner-unity. In Buber's own words: "Every particular *Thou* is a glimpse through to the eternal *Thou*."[103]

Rosenzweig's *The Star of Redemption* came out in 1921, two years before Buber's *I and Thou*. Rosenzweig's thought represents something of a caesura in Jewish thought. Rosenzweig's primary interlocutors seem to be German philosophers and Protestant theologians, and his explicit engagement with post-biblical Jewish sources is thin. Peter Eli Gordon recently remarked that Rosenzweig's *Star* "was not in any obvious way continuous with prior traditions in Jewish religion."[104] Indeed, in 1925, Rosenzweig himself conceded that *The Star* was not a "Jewish book."[105]

Whether Rosenzweig intended to write a Jewish book or not, his theology certainly fits in the horizon of modern Jewish thought, and, in crucial ways, is easier to assimilate into Jewish thought than was Buber's. For example, in addition to Buber's wholesale rejection of authoritative Jewish law, Norbert Samuelson describes the philosophical problem with Buber's theology:

> [Buber] says nothing about the God of creation. . . . Buber is a phenomenologist, which is to say a thinker who limits the domain of his speculation to what can be deduced about reality from what we as human beings can experience, and the origin of the universe in general

101 Hava Tirosh-Samuelson, "Response. The Textualization of Nature in Jewish Mysticism," in Tirosh-Samuelson, *Judaism and Ecology*, 399. Both Gellman and Tirosh-Samuelson have overlooked the resonances between Buber's scholarly claims and the theology of HaBaD. Schatz Uffenheimer and Wolfson agree that in HaBaD, from the very beginning, divinity is to be perceived *through* materiality, not liberated *from* materiality. Schatz Uffenheimer, *Hasidism as Mysticism*, 268–71, and Wolfson, *Open Secret*, 150

102 Cf. Mendes-Flohr, *Divided Passions*, 263–64.

103 Buber, *I and Thou*, 75; cited in Mendes-Flohr, *Divided Passions*, 255.

104 Peter Eli Gordon, "Franz Rosenzweig and the Philosophy of Jewish Existence," in Morgan, *Cambridge Companion to Modern Jewish Philosophy*, 123.

105 Franz Rosenzweig, *The New Thinking*; cited in Gordon, "Franz Rosenzweig," in Morgan, *Cambridge Companion to Modern Jewish Philosophy*, 123.

does not fall within this domain. . . . If there is no [account of] creation, God cannot be [assumed to be] a creator, and if God is not a creator, there is no radical separation between God and everything else in the way that Buber claims there to be.[106]

Rosenzweig offers this critique from a different angle: "For us, Idealism had proven to be in competition, not with theology in general, but only with the theology of creation."[107]

One of the differences between Buber and Rosenzweig in their account of revelation is that for Buber, revelation is universal and continuous. "The revelation at Sinai is not this midpoint [between creation and redemption] itself, but the perceiving of it, and such perception is possible at any time."[108] For Buber, revelation beckons us, always. For Rosenzweig, revelation cannot be taken for granted. As Robert Erlewine describes, "God's love does not proceed in all directions; it is not predictable and is completely unforeseeable 'except for the one certainty that the love will one day seize even that which has not yet been seized.'"[109] Rosenzweig's God has a dynamic quality, inscrutable to humanity, whereby the moment of being graced and embraced by divine love is beyond our control. We can prepare, but we cannot precipitate.

When God does disclose Himself to us, again unlike Buber, there is content to the revelation: love God.[110] For Buber, God's revelation is nothing more than that—the experience of divine disclosure. That overwhelming sense of pure love attendant to the experience, for Rosenzweig, calls forth God's command to reciprocate that love. God's love for an individual precedes and precipitates that individual's love. It is easier to say, "I love you," when the object of your love has already revealed their love for you. Like the sequence in the Jewish prayer book, God proclaims love

106 Norbert M. Samuelson, *Revelation and the God of Israel* (Cambridge: Cambridge University Press, 2002), 60–61.

107 Franz Rosenzweig, *The Star of Redemption*, trans. William W. Hallo [from 2nd edition of 1930] (Notre Dame: University of Notre Dame Press, 1970), 188.

108 Martin Buber, "The Man of Today and the Jewish Bible," in Biemann, *Martin Buber Reader*, 54. See also Mendes-Flohr, *Divided Passions*, 268.

109 Robert Erlewine, *Judaism and the West: From Hermann Cohen to Joseph Soloveitchik* (Bloomington: Indiana University Press, 2016), 70; citing Rosenzweig, *Star*, 164–65.

110 Rosezweig, *Star*, 178.

for Israel prior to the commandment to love the Lord.[111] More than what Buber will allow himself to say, Rosenzweig claims God desires relationships with His creatures. God is not an island of autarchic self-sufficiency.[112] In this sense, as well others, Rosenzweig is the one who strikes a kabbalistic note.

"Only the soul beloved of God can receive the commandment to love its neighbor and fulfill it. Ere man can turn himself over to God's will, God must first have turned to man."[113] The individual's reciprocity of God's love can be expressed *only* through the love of "the nighest, the neighbor."[114] There is nothing we can do for the parent (God) except to love her children. Again, Erlewine emphasizes the distinction between Buber and Rosenzweig on this count. For Buber, one moves from the *it* to the *thou* to the *Thou*. One arrives at a glimpse of God through relating authentically to God's creatures. For Rosenzweig, the love of the neighbor is a consequence of one's reciprocated love for God. God's love comes first, then our reciprocated love of God, and then, finally, our expression of love for God's creatures. "The neighbor is not valued for who he or she is but only as 'a representative; he is not loved for himself, he is not loved for his beautiful eyes, but only because he is just there, because he is just my neighbor. In his place—in this place that is for me the one neighboring on me—there could just as well be another person.'"[115] Just as in Kabbalah where one's primary intention is to unify the divine world, the benefits in our world are (merely?) a felicitous byproduct. On the issue of revelation, there is a note of irony: the theology of Rosenzweig, who wrestled primarily with German Idealism and Protestantism, upon closer examination seems less alien to traditional Jewish thought than the theology of the scholar of Hasidism, Buber.[116]

---

111 I first heard this insight from Reuven Kimelman as a graduate student at Brandeis University. Recently, Jon D. Levenson has pointed out the same sequence within the master narrative of Exodus, as well. God shows love to the Israelites by redeeming them from slavery and then requests love in return through the covenant at Sinai. Jon D. Levenson, *The Love of God: Divine Gift, Human Gratitude, and Mutual Faithfulness in Judaism* (Princeton: Princeton University Press, 2016), 61.

112 Rosenzweig, *Star*, 114.

113 Ibid., 215.

114 Ibid., 241.

115 Erlewine, *Judaism and the West*, 70; citing Rosenzweig, *Star*, 218.

116 In a chapter entitled "Franz Rosenzweig and Kabbalah," Moshe Idel calls Rosenzweig's thought one of the most Jewish produced in the twentieth century. See *Old Worlds,*

Before temporarily taking leave of our German-Jewish thinkers, it is important to note that they accepted the fundamental tenets of biblical criticism – multiple authors over many centuries—*and* that they took the Torah very seriously.[117] The Torah's power lay not in its authorship but its content. Cohen saw in the biblical prophets not divine revelation, but the foundation for the ethical concern of the vulnerable. For Cohen, this ethical concern for the other, who becomes a thou, is the prerequisite for the claim that God loves man.

> It is not clear whether Cohen means that man attributed to God his own experiences or that the love of man is an attribute of God as the Creator of man. . . . After God is conceived as loving man, we can understand man's love of God. The circle of love is completed in three steps—the love of man for his fellow man, which is kindled by suffering and poverty; the love of God for man; and, after the position of the fellow man has been defined, the love of man for God.[118]

Cohen gleans this circle of love from his reading of the biblical prophets. Note that his student, Rosenzweig, begins the circle with God loving the human – that is how Rosenzweig reads the message of biblical prophecy. Buber is closer to Cohen on the origin of love than is Rosenzweig. For Buber, too, one experiences God through one's attitude toward another person who becomes a thou. In that experience of revelation, God's presence is between the I and the thou. For Rosenzweig, unbeholden to any shred of German idealism unlike Buber, "the voice of God sounds forth directly from within [the prophet], God speaks as 'I' directly from within him."[119] As Rivka Horwitz puts it, Rosenzweig's prophet "becomes a vessel of God."[120] For Buber, God is between the humans; for Rosenzweig, God, for a moment, becomes human. (One senses Rosenzweig's sympathy towards Christianity here.)

New Mirrors: On Jewish Mysticism and Twentieth-Century Thought (Philadelphia: University of Pennsylvania Press, 2012), 167.

117 Rivka Horwitz, "Revelation and the Bible According to Twentieth-Century Jewish Philosophy," in Green, *Jewish Spirituality*, 352.
118 Rotenstreich, *Jewish Philosophy in Modern Times*, 76-77f.
119 Rosenzweig, *Star*, 178.
120 Horwitz, "Revelation and the Bible," in Green, *Jewish Spirituality*, 359.

Buber and Rosenzweig were so invested in the religious value of the Torah that they translated it into German. Buber maintained that the Bible, while not a record of revelation, is superior to all other texts in that it models the demand to be in authentic relationship with others and God. Buber believes the Bible preserves a verbal trace of the experience between the Israelites and God which disclosed the purpose of creation: redemption. "Man of today resists the Scriptures because he cannot endure revelation. To endure revelation is to endure this moment full of possible decisions—to respond to and to be responsible for every moment."[121] Buber recognizes that to hold ourselves open to the claims of faith is terrifying. As Michael Fishbane notes:

> Beyond all dogmatism and fixed commandments, the Bible is for Martin Buber the rescued and ever-hearable speech of the living God. It is a Teaching which simply points out an ongoing way. . . . Thus the Bible releases the primal forces of Sinai—of response and commitment—to those who hear in it the voice of divine Instruction. "Untransfigured and unsubdued," says Buber, "the biblical word preserves the dialogical character of living reality."[122]

To where does the biblical word point us? As voyeurs, we see various responses in the Torah. Buber, however, claims that mimicking those responses allows us to dodge our own authentic responses.

Buber and Rosenzweig conducted a dialogue in which Rosenzweig further developed his formulation of revelation. Yet, already in *The Star* Rosenzweig is far less concerned with the historical revelation of Sinai than on the biblical paradigm of revelatory love: The Song of Songs.[123] In *The Star*, Rosenzweig seems to insist, if we read him literally, that there is propositional content to revelation, namely, to love God. In his dialogue with Buber, he either clarifies or retracts such a claim. "The primary content of revelation is revelation itself."[124] The Torah's *description*

---

121 Buber, "Man of Today," in Biemann, *Martin Buber Reader*, 54.
122 Michael Fishbane, *Garments of Torah: Essays in Biblical Hermeneutics* (Bloomington: Indiana University Press, 1989), 98 and 83-84; citing Martin Buber, *On the Bible: Eighteen Studies by Martin Buber*, ed. Nahum N. Glatzer (New York: Schocken Books, 1967), 215.
123 Rosenzweig, *Star*, 202.
124 Letter to Buber dated June 5, 1925, in Franz Rosenzweig, *On Jewish Learning*, ed. N. N. Glatzer (New York: Schocken Books, 1955), 118.

of revelation is human interpretation. I suspect Nathan Rotenstreich is correct when he claims that revelation, for Rosenzweig, is "an ever-recurrent event in the inner life of man . . . not an objective, historical event in the past but a constant reaffirmation of such an event in man's subjective experience."[125]

The experience of revelation, when it breaks forth, is not a neutral event. To claim that there is no propositional content to revelation does not necessarily contradict the claim that God's revelation commands us love to God. Any presence provokes a response, all the more so the divine presence. I concur with Rosenzweig's position in *The Star* that the experience of revelation generates the command to love God. Although a fuller discussion of this theology awaits our final book on the philosophy of halakhah, I do want to suggest here that Rosenzweig's exclusive emphasis on love is more Christian than Jewish. As our biblical prophets repeatedly attest, revelation also elicits awe. God is one, but our response to God's presence is not unalloyed.

My final comment regarding Rosenzweig involves his claim that revelation is not constantly accessible but comes unaware like a lost object (Sannhedrin 97a). Rosenzweig is more comfortable using personal anthropomorphic language to describe God than am I. "What separates [God's] love from an 'all love' is only a 'not yet'; it is only 'not yet' that God loves everything besides what he already loves. His love traverses the world from an always new impulse."[126] Rosenzweig resorts to this image of traversing love to explain why revelation is not always a live possibility. For me, the image is problematic because it seems to place God in the position of deciding where God's love is directed "from an always new impulse." Here I side with Buber—the new impulse comes from the human side. God is not haphazardly volitional.

Rosenzweig's sense that revelation is not always accessible resonates with my own experience, but that is the result of *my* state of consciousness and *my* circumstances. We sometimes say that something felicitous happened because "the stars aligned." In our context, the image is helpful to use as a way of picturing God's presence penetrating our consciousness when external circumstances and our internal state of mind are attuned.

---

125 Rotenstreich, *Jewish Philosophy in Modern Times*, 199.
126 Rosenzweig, *Star*, 164–65; cited in Erlewine, *Judaism and the West*, 70.

From God's side, as it were, revelation is always a possibility; it is only from our side that there may be impediments. Once those impediments are removed, Rosenzweig's theology introduces, or better, rehabilitates, a central feature of mysticism and Kabbalah: creator and creature may enjoy an intimate and sustained relationship which can be described as a covenant of love. Toward the end of his life, Rosenzweig acknowledged the difficulty of "draw[ing] so rigid a boundary between what is divine and what is human."[127] As Scholem remarked on the occasion of the 1930 edition of *The Star of Redemption,*

> The seductive illusion of man's moral autonomy determined the theology
> of Jewish liberalism [i.e., Reform thinkers, Cohen, and Buber], which had
> its origins essentially in [German] idealism. From here no path lay open,
> except for a radical reversal in direction, back toward the mysteries of
> revelation that constituted the basis of Rosenzweig's new world, which
> turned out to be the most ancient world of all.[128]

For Scholem, Rosenzweig had succeeded in overcoming, at least conceptually, what had plagued Jewish thought since the advent of modernity: "Kabbalah-phobia."[129]

Prior to World War II, the greatest concentration of world Jewry was in Eastern Europe. This Jewish population had been exposed, to varying degrees, to secular culture through the Haskalah. While for our German Jewish thinkers, Jewish thought was essentially a second language in which they achieved various levels of fluency, for Eastern European Jews, Jewish thought was still the mother tongue. Rav Avraham Yitzhak Kook (1865–1935), born fewer than one hundred miles northeast of Vilna, is the epitome of the ideological confluence of Eastern European Jewish thought. His mother was raised within the world of HaBaD Hasidism while his father was a classic Mitnaged who studied at the Volozhin Yeshivah. Kook, too, was a student at the Volozhin Yeshivah, and his early, formal education was predominantly influenced by the Mitnagdim. When Rav Kook took a position in a small Russian town at the age of twenty-four, he began studying Kabbalah with Rabbi Solomon Eliashev of Shavell. Six years later, he accepted a position in Lithuania, where he

---

127 Rosenzweig, *On Jewish Learning,* 119.
128 Scholem, *The Messianic Idea,* 322.
129 Ibid., 321.

was confronted and forced to contend with, for the first time, Jewish youth influenced by the Haskalah. Thus, by 1904, when Rav Kook immigrated to the Land of Israel, he was both deeply learned in all aspects of Jewish thought and conversant in secular philosophy and science. Rav Kook will feature in all three sections of our work, but we begin with the elements of his theology that will help bridge the worlds of traditional Jewish thought and post-Shoah theology.

An ancient dispute between Greeks, Parmenides and Heraclitus, pits the views of stasis against dynamism, respectively. Along came Plato and offered a compromise: in the supernal world of forms, all is perfect and immutable; but in the lower world where we live, all is imperfect and in flux. Fast forward a few millennia and we have Spinoza taking up a version of Parmenides' argument, and a French Jew, Henri Bergson (1859–1941), arguing for progressive change in the fashion of the Enlightenment philosophes. Rav Kook translated the argument into kabbalistic terms. The *Eyn Sof* represents a static perfection, while the world of sefirot, including our world, is in the process of perfecting itself. This dichotomy serves to provide a direction, a goal for the process of betterment: everything which emanated from the *Eyn Sof* seeks to return to its source. In the language of Judaism, that return is called teshuvah. The process of teshuvah is no longer only about returning to God's will as expressed in the halakhah, but the return and reunification of all divine sparks to the divine origin.

Rav Kook suggests that perfection necessarily includes the opportunity for improvement. Where there does not exist the possibility of betterment, perfection is incomplete. The creation of the lower worlds, which in classical Kabbalah was widely considered a cathartic act by God to purge the roots of judgment from within *Eyn Sof*, was for Rav Kook the manifestation of a fuller perfection because it allowed for the possibility of betterment.[130] One may call the content of emanation from

---

130 This process is briefly described in an article by Tamar Ross, "The Elite and the Masses in the Prism of Metaphysics and History: Harav Kook on the Nature of Religious Belief," *The Journal of Jewish Thought and Philosophy* 8, no. 2 (1999): 362, and its implications are laid out by Yosef Ben Shlomo in *Poetry of Being: Lectures on the Philosophy of Rabbi Kook* (Woodstock: Jewish Lights Publishing, 1997), 59–61. Their Hebrew works contain fuller expositions. See Tamar Ross, "Rav Kook's Concept of Divinity" Da'at 8 (1982): 124–26, and Yosef Ben Shlomo, "Perfection and Betterment in Rav Kook's Teaching on Divinity," *Iyyun* 33 (1984): 296–303.

Eyn Sof "the roots of judgment" but that would be a one-sided designation. Those roots enjoy the capacity for future perfection *which requires current imperfection*. Our goal in life is to engage in the work of seeing ourselves as part of the divine unity of the cosmos. That effort offers a messianic return.

> It is only through the great truth of returning to oneself that the person and the people, the world and all the worlds, the whole of existence, will return to their Creator, to be illumined by the light of life. This is the mystery of the light of the Messiah, the manifestation of the soul of the universe, by whose illumination the world will return to the source of its being, and the light of God will be revealed.[131]

In Rav Kook's reworking of the kabbalistic myth, which bears strong resemblance to that of HaBaD Hasidism, Luria's vessels become a metaphor for our perception. The shattering of the vessels is not an ontological event, it is a psychological status. We only perceive fragments and shards. Holiness will be effected by overcoming the perception of atomization and compartmentalization to achieve a vision of unity. In the priestly Torah, and continuing through rabbinic halakhah, holiness was all about separation. But as Bible scholar Samuel Balentine reminds us, separation does not mean estrangement.[132] And as James Jacobson-Maisels writes, "We should not, however, mistake the path for the goal."[133] For Rav Kook, separation in this world of fragmentation will dissolve into an all-embracing unity through the collective process of teshuvah, of returning to a state of consciousness before the kabbalistic original sin when Adam severed the roots of the Tree of Life from the roots of the Tree of Knowledge.

Although we will more closely examine Rav Kook's ideas about halakhah in our final section, what we can assert now is that morality is the single most important feature of teshuvah. "Ethics is the corridor to the

---

131 Abraham Isaac Kook, *Lights of Penitence*, 15:10. Translation slightly modified from *Abraham Isaac Kook: The Lights of Penitence, the Moral Principles, Lights of Holiness, Essays, Letters, and Poems*, trans. Ben Zion Bokser (Mahwah: Paulist Press, 1978), 117.

132 Samuel E. Balentine, *The Torah's Vision of Worship* (Minneapolis: Fortress Press, 1999), 87.

133 James Jacobson-Maisels, "Non-dual Judaism," in *Jewish Theology in Our Time: A New Generation Explores the Foundations and Future of Jewish Belief*, ed. Elliot J. Cosgrove (Woodstock: Jewish Lights Publishing, 2010), 39.

palace of holiness."[134] Yehudah Mirsky, a recent biographer of Rav Kook, explains: "The goal of ethics is holiness, the total transformation of the person and the world, the fusion of body and soul."[135] If sin thrusts one into the world of fragmentation and compartmentalization, teshuvah reveals the world of unity. Although Rav Kook held that the mitzvot were given as a means of refining Jews, there is an even higher "moral Torah" available to all.[136] Moral perfection involves both the cleansing of one's character traits and the "purification of the intellectual presuppositions that condition action."[137] Raising rabbinic Judaism's requirements, Rav Kook demands not only ethical behavior, but ethical behavior for the right reasons. The contested value of intention (*kavannah*) among the Talmudic rabbis is glorified within the medieval, mystical tradition and the Hasidic world from the Maggid of Mezeritch to Rav Kook. "Intention is everything. The revival of intention is the revival of the world."[138]

At some point in the individual's process of teshuvah, she attains a level of consciousness that comprehends the divine unity behind our perception of an atomized world. The distinctions we make between ourselves and others, and ourselves and God, are mirages. All is God, and all is good. "The more deeply rooted teshuvah is, the more there recedes the fear of death until it stops altogether. . . . The individual identity continues to expand, it becomes part of the general being of the people in a very real fusion, and from there it is absorbed in the general existence of the whole world."[139] Both Hugo Bergman and Tamar Ross have emphasized that Rav Kook takes the sting out of death precisely by declaring our perceived reality to be an illusion. Death has lost both its dread and finality. "He will welcome [death] because he will be capable of regarding it as the

---

134 Kook, *Lights of Holiness*, 3:14.

135 Yehudah Mirsky, *Rav Kook: Mystic in a Time of Revolution* (New Haven: Yale University Press, 2014), 109.

136 Kook, *Abraham Isaac Kook: The Lights of Penitence*, 292.

137 Ibid., 92.

138 Ibid., 211. See also Schatz Uffenheimer, *Hasidism as Mysticism*, 136 for her discussion about the continued importance of kavannah for the Maggid of Mezhirech. Wolfson discuss kavannah for Rebbe Menchem Mendel Schneerson in his *Open Secret*, 192.

139 Kook, *Abraham Isaac Kook: The Lights of Penitence*, 80. Although Bokser takes liberties with the translation, he captures Rav Kook's sentiment.

happy occasion for advancing into a higher form of existence."[140] We die into God. Issues of providence and theodicy simply dissolve.

So much of what I find appealing about Rav Kook, the panentheism, our cognitive capacity to see through this world of compartmentaliza- tion, the emphasis on kavannah, and even the death of death, is also to be found in the theology of HaBaD.[141] But there's an emphasis on unity, ethics, and renewal (including the Zionist renewal) in the writings of Rav Kook that makes him especially attractive. His *Lights of Holiness* offers a vision of the cosmos in which absolutely everything shimmers, though with different degrees of radiance. If God's light or energy or munificence stopped informing anything for even a moment, it would cease to exist. It is precisely Kook's commitment to divine unity and renewal that makes the theory of evolution so amenable to him, as we will see in the next book. Of course, his appreciation for science does not blind him to its limitations.

> As long as one is immersed in one's senses and their narrow confinements, he will not be able to know fully the spiritual dimensions of life, only faint shadows thereof will be discernible through them. And if he should relate to these shadows as though they were the true reality, then these shadows will turn for him into a heavy burden and they will diminish both his physical and spiritual vigor. . . . There is only one escape from the shadows and that is through augmenting the light through one's intuition of divine faith. Through this faith we attain the climactic reach of knowledge and of feeling that links one's spiritual life, in its existential functioning, with the ultimate spiritual reality.[142]

---

140 Tamar Ross, "Immortality, Natural Law, and the Role of Human Perception in the Writings of Rav Kook," in *Rabbi Abraham Isaac Kook and Jewish Spirituality*, ed. David Shatz and Lawrence Kaplan (New York: New York University Press, 1995), 248. See also Rav Kook, *Lights of Holiness*, 1:40 and Samuel Hugo Bergmann, "Death and Immortality in the Teachings of Rabbi Kook," *Judaism* 7, no. 3 (1958): 245.

141 See Wolfson, *Open Secret*, 165, esp. footnote 17, for a discussion of Schneur Zalman and death.

142 Kook, *Abraham Isaac Kook: The Lights of Penitence*, 287; Bokser's translation, slightly modified. German idealism, until Rosenzweig, relied on the self-authenticating truth of intellectual intuition. This *deus ex machina* was not exclusively the trump card of theologians. See Terry Pinkard, *German Philosophy 1760–1860: The Legacy of Idealism* (Cambridge: Cambridge University Press, 2002), 110–11. and Benjamin Pollock, *Franz Rosenzweig and the Systematic Task of Philosophy* (New York: Cambridge University Press, 2009), 269–75.

Metaphors of light and shadow flow throughout Rav Kook's writings. He makes explicit that he is not at all reluctant to use even anthropomorphic similes in discussing theology. Just as one requires intuition for faith, one also requires intuition to understand theological language. I find his use of shadows in the above citation to be particularly apt. It is not only in Plato's cave that people mistook shadows for reality. Rav Kook articulates the fundamental theological critique of scientism, the conceit that science is not just a method of pursuing truth, but that its findings are the only truths there are. For Rav Kook, "Science seeks to simply describe partial and discrete aspects of the physical world as they appear phenomenally; its vision is therefore exclusive and limited."[143]

Yet, Rav Kook also understood that there were times when science *should* precipitate changes within Judaism in order to achieve coherence.[144] Rejecting or ignoring scientific and academic advances turns shadows into a plague of darkness. Although one of Rav Kook's expositors, and seeming disciples, valiantly attempts to jerry rig an argument that would allow Rav Kook to not necessarily reject the findings of biblical criticism, her attempt is unsuccessful. Tamar Ross' liberal usage of "may" and "perhaps" cannot stand up to the hard fact that Rav Kook only agreed to speak at the inauguration of The Hebrew University of Jerusalem on the condition that the school not teach biblical criticism.[145] In the end, like his Hasidic ancestors, Rav Kook was far more radical in theory than in practice. Ross has artfully applied her craft to the question of religious coherence and the contribution that Rav Kook's mystical theology might make. She has articulated the conundrum, particularly for the Orthodox who either continue to believe in a naïve literalism of the biblical or rabbinic accounts of revelation or to pretend that they do.

---

143 Tamar Ross, "The Cognitive Value of Religious Truth Statements: Rabbi A. I. Kook and Postmodernism," in *Hazon Nahum: Studies in Jewish Law, Thought, and History Presented to Dr. Norman Lamm on the Occasion of His Seventieth Birthday*, ed. Yaakov Elman and Jeffrey S. Gurock (New York: Yeshiva University Press, 1997), 69.

144 Tamar Ross, "Science and Secularization in the Service of Faith: Rabbi A. I. Kook's Theory of Truth," in *Streams into the Sea: Studies in Jewish Culture and Its Context: Dedicated to Felix Posen*, ed. Elchanan Reiner and Ruth Freudenthal (Tel Aviv: Alma College, 2001), 182–83; and Ross, "Cognitive Value," in Elman and Gurock, *Hazon Nahum*, 69.

145 Mirsky, *Rav Kook*, 187–88.

It is obvious that developing the means for disseminating a theology which takes the relative nature of any truth-claim [e.g., the source of Torah] into account with complete intellectual integrity, while leaving religious fervor intact and undiluted, may turn out to be the greatest religious challenge of our age.[146]

Historically, when the Torah's divine authorship had been rejected, or even nuanced, religious authority was undermined, and the religious fervor necessary for a life of halakhic observance suffered. Yet, Judaism, and the mystical tradition in particular, has resources to promote halakhic observance without falling back on incoherent myths of divine authorship and authority. The rabbinic doctrine that the voice of Sinai goes on forever coupled with the Baal Shem Tov's innovation of worship through corporeality can serve as a foundation for halakhah that transcends the contents of the Shulchan Arukh.

As we close our discussion of pre-Shoah Jewish thought, it is appropriate to introduce the United States. A senior scholar of Jewish history once asked me what I intended to study in graduate school. At the time, I was considering focusing on American Jewish thought. The scholar, who spoke English with an English accent, sniffed and replied, "Oh, how derivative!" It is to those derivations that we now turn in this book's final chapter on post-Shoah theology.

---

146 Ross, "Cognitive Value," in Elman and Gurock, *Hazon Nahum*, 85.

Chapter 6

Covenantal Judaism

Even if writers don't explicitly engage with the cataclysm, there is no way to escape its overshadowing presence. My oldest child, born in 2001, visited Auschwitz as a teenager knowing that her grandfather likely avoided the destination by a matter of days. Strangely, although the founding of Israel in 1948 may be experienced by her generation as "history," the Shoah has not yet receded to that category. In this, our final chapter focusing on theology, we need to distinguish between Holocaust theology and what I am calling post-Shoah theology. The former is an explicit grappling with the radical evil that lay behind a continent's dehumanization and decimation of two-thirds of its Jews. Thinkers like Eliezer Berkovits, Irving Greenberg, and Richard Rubenstein may justly be considered Holocaust theologians. This chapter examines the works of none of them.

The word *holocaust* is itself a religious term. For those not familiar with certain English translations of the Septuagint, or the chilling short story by Nathaniel Hawthorne, *holocaust* means a "wholly burnt offering." The Torah references this sacrifice, an *olah*, roughly three hundred times. The idea that a human being could be a sacrifice to God is Christian; the idea that six million human beings could be a sacrifice to God is an abomination. *Shoah* means *catastrophe* in Hebrew. The post-Shoah theologians examined in this chapter, none of whom is known primarily as a Holocaust theologian, all wrote after the Shoah.

An immediate qualifier: our first two thinkers also wrote before the Shoah, although they continued writing well afterwards. Mordecai M. Kaplan (1881–1983) is the perfect bridge figure from Eastern European thought to American Jewish thought. He was born in Lithuania to a pious family whose father, Israel Kaplan, received rabbinic ordination from two luminaries at the Volozhin Yeshiva. The father also fell sway to the influence of Rabbi Israel Salanter's Mussar movement. When Mordecai was eight years old they relocated to New York City. Although Mordecai's father was the young boy's principal teacher, there were *maskilim* who frequented the Kaplan's home who also left their intellectual marks on the maturing youth. One of the earliest and most enthusiastic Jewish respondents to Darwinism (in 1875!), Joseph Lev Sossnitz, was hired by Rabbi Israel to teach his son RaMBaM's *Guide of the Perplexed*. In his family home, young Mordecai was also exposed to theories of biblical criticism that challenged the Mosaic authorship of the Pentateuch.

Kaplan received his bachelor's degree from City College in 1900 and master's degree in philosophy from Columbia University in 1902. From his secular studies, Kaplan internalized the cutting-edge scholarship that would frame his religious writings for the next seven decades, although it wasn't until his publication of *Judaism as a Civilization* in 1934 that his publishing career began in earnest. There was a single criterion that all contemporary theologians had to accept: the modern temper will no longer accommodate supernatural ideas about miraculous, divine intervention whether they concern personal revelation or communal redemption. Reform Judaism's Pittsburgh Platform of 1885 met that standard, but Kaplan was among the first non-Reform rabbis to explicitly break with those traditional assumptions.[1]

This interlocking set of ideas—of a supernatural God, ahistorical sources, authoritarian approaches to religious truth, the elevation of a tradition's past, and convictions of chosenness or uniqueness—became problematic in the modern world. They no longer embodied interpretations of reality that twentieth-century persons could easily espouse. Kaplan mounted his attack against this complex of ideas on several fronts. In particular, he argued that such ideas failed in light of the findings of modern science and the historical disciplines. Moreover, they stood in contradiction to the democratic and equalitarian commitments of modern American life.[2]

1   Leora Batnitzky, "Mordecai Kaplan as Hermeneut: History, Memory, and His God-Idea," *Jewish Social Studies: History, Culture, Society* n.s. 12, no. 2 (Winter 2006): 88–98.
2   Shelia Greeve Davaney, "Beyond Supernaturalism: Mordecai Kaplan and the Turn to Religious Naturalism," *Jewish Social Studies: History, Culture, Society* n.s. 12, no. 2 (Winter 2006): 73–87, 76.

Although many of the ideas and propositions that we find in Kaplan had previously been articulated by Reform thinkers in both Germany and the United States, the clarity and insistence with which Kaplan rejects supernaturalism in all its guises is distinctive. Moreover, even Reform Judaism did not surrender the concept of chosenness. To be sure, the sentiment was domesticated, but the language was preserved. Kaplan believed that the whole idea of a chosen people smacked of an inferiority complex! There is no personal God who singles out a people to be something special; chosenness breeds smugness among Jews and resentment among gentiles; and it is neither egalitarian nor democratic. For Kaplan, chosenness was beyond reconstructing.

For reasons that are somewhat mystifying, otherwise competent thinkers have elided Kaplan's rejection of supernaturalism to a rejection of metaphysics. Some have criticized him for not having a metaphysics, and others have criticized him for *having* a metaphysics since he claimed to reject supernaturalism! A particularly grievous example of the latter is offered by Steven Katz who calls Kaplan "a near total failure as a philosopher of Judaism."[3] Kaplan was not, however, a philosopher of Judaism; he was a theologian.

Kaplan was heavily influenced by thinkers who emphasized the function of religion. So, in discussing God, much like RaMBaM and the nineteenth-century English literary critic Matthew Arnold, Kaplan described the consequences of belief rather than expatiating on God's unknowable essence. What Kaplan sought to avoid was nihilism. He understood that ethical behavior depended on metaphysical assumptions about the nature of reality. "What can exercise a more blighting effect upon all moral endeavor than the notion that there is no meaning or purpose to the world. . . . "[4] Kaplan made a deeply religious assumption about the relationship between God and the world. But, consequent to that foundational assumption, Kaplan refrained from further metaphysical speculation. In that sense, he was a metaphysical minimalist. But the difference between something, even something minimal, and nothing is infinite and infinitely meaningful. The attitudes of functionalism and

---

3   Steven T. Katz, "Mordecai Kaplan's Theology and the Problem of Evil," *Jewish Social Studies: History, Culture, Society* n.s. 12, no. 2 (Winter 2006): 116.

4   Mordecai M. Kaplan, *Judaism as a Civilization: Toward a Reconstruction of American Jewish* (Philadelphia: Jewish Publication Society, 1981), 98.

pragmatism dissuaded Kaplan from saying any more about God than was required by his demand for an ethical anchor. His reticence to go beyond the metaphysical minimum is also a nod to the diversity of theologies that have characterized Judaism since the redaction of the Torah. Jews are free to supplement his ever-changing formulations of God's function. Here is the foundation he offers:

> Faith in life's inherent worthwhileness and sanctity is needed to counteract the cynicism that sneers at life and mocks at the very notion of holiness. . . . Belief in God as here conceived can function in our day exactly as the belief in God has always functioned; it can *function* as an affirmation that life has value. It implies, as the God idea has always implied, a certain assumption with regard to the nature of reality, the assumption that reality is so constituted as to endorse and guarantee the realization in man of that which is of greatest value to him. If we believe that assumption to be true, for, as has been said, it is an assumption that is not susceptible of proof, we have faith in God. *No metaphysical speculation beyond this fundamental assumption that reality assures both the emergence and the realization of human ideals is necessary for the religious life.*[5]

Katz denounces Kaplan for his "pious, a priori assumption [because] Kaplan invests nature and history with a purpose no less metaphysical and grand . . . than classical theism."[6] But that "pious, a priori assumption" is not a postulate of reason by an idealist philosopher, a la Kant, it is a declaration of faith by a rabbi. Demonstrating a disappointing lack of theological sophistication, Katz suggests that Kaplan's brand of metaphysical minimalism is as grand as classical theism. But, classical theism posits a personal God who exercises His superlative attributes with singular purpose. Kaplan repeatedly and explicitly rejects such a God.

> Of course, this involves a radical change in the traditional conception of God. It conflicts with that perception of God as infinite and perfect in His omniscience and omnipotence. But the fact is that God does not have to mean to us an absolute being who has planned and decreed every twinge of pain, every act of cruelty, every human sin. *It is sufficient that*

---

5   Kaplan, *Meaning of God,* 29. My italics.
6   Katz, "Mordecai Kaplan's Theology": 120.

> *God should mean to us the sum of the animating organizing forces and relationships which are forever making a cosmos out of the chaos.*[7]

For classical theism, God is a personal being; for Kaplan, God is an impersonal force.[8] Nevertheless, Kaplan's contention that God is the force which makes a cosmos out of the chaos leaves too much unaccounted for. Kaplan rejected *creatio ex nihilo* and had a nearly Gnostic view of nature as "infinite chaos . . . uninvaded by the creative energy."[9] Jacob Staub's criticism of Kaplan's God idea is right on the mark.

> In firm Jewish tradition, the Kaplanian perspective chooses to identify the divine with a prophetic and rabbinic ethics rather than with an all-inclusive embrace of the totality of all things—even at the expense of an account of the world that makes complete sense.[10]

Kaplan's critics at the other extreme were those, like Kaplan's own student, Rabbi Milton Steinberg, who charged him with having a "theology without a metaphysics."[11] "The actuality of God is brought into question. Does God really exist or is he only man's notion?"[12] How are we to understand the dipolar critiques against a man who struggled for decades to hone a theological formulation that was not obnoxious to reason but still served as a metaphysical foundation for ethical behavior? Perhaps part of the answer is precisely that he wrote for decades, in different contexts and with evolving notions, and the variety of language triggered very different responses among readers. Eliezer Schweid, however, offered a different explanation. "Kaplan prefers to mask his faith in camouflaging scientific colors in order to make it attractive to those

---

7   Kaplan, *Meaning of God*, 76. Italics in original.

8   Ibid., 25.

9   Mordecai M. Kaplan, *The Religion of Ethical Nationhood: Judaism's Contribution to World Peace* (New York: Macmillan Publishers, 1970), 51 and 72–73. Kaplan, *Judaism as a Civilization*, 98. See also my "Three Twentieth-Century Jewish Responses": 275–76.

10 Jacob Staub, "Kaplan and Process Theology," in *The American Judaism of Mordecai M. Kaplan*, ed. Emanuel S. Goldsmith, Mel Scult, and Robert M. Seltzer (New York: New York University Press, 1990), 292.

11 Steinberg, "Theological Problems," 378–79, cited in Simon Noveck, "Kaplan and Milton Steinberg," in Goldsmith, *The American Judaism of Mordecai M. Kaplan*, 165.

12 Milton Steinberg, *Anatomy of a Faith* (New York: Harcourt, Brace, 1960), 183.

impressed by the importance of science in our time."[13] At times, that mask suffocates Kaplan's own piety. That observation helps explain why Katz does not think that Kaplan, given his rejection of supernaturalism, should have a metaphysics *and* why Steinberg questions Kaplan's faith.

Kaplan fancied himself something of a contemporary RaMBaM. Already in 1935, Kaplan published an article entitled, "How Maimonides Reconstructed Judaism."[14] There are, indeed, many parallels between RaMBaM and Kaplan, but there are also two critical differences, one theological and one religious. Although it may seem counterintuitive to those who do not know the writings of these two figures, Kaplan was the more traditional and pious. In terms of theology and metaphysics, the Maimonidean cosmos is not necessarily conducive to human salvation, however defined. RaMBaM explicitly rejects the kind of anthropocentric thinking that is the foundation of Kaplan's metaphysics (*Guide*, 3:12). Salvation for RaMBaM involved perfecting the intellect alone, as opposed to Kaplan's more holistic approach. Yet, throughout the *Guide*, RaMBaM acknowledges our intellectual limitations which preclude perfection.

In terms of religion, RaMBaM was the better psychologist. He understood that a "sudden transition from one opposite to another is impossible" (*Guide*, 3:32). RaMBaM's commitment to intellectual honesty demanded an esoteric writing style to preserve "necessary beliefs" for the masses. These necessary beliefs were untrue but promoted social welfare (*Guide*, 3:28). Kaplan had more faith in the American Jew of the twentieth century. He consistently applied the scalpel of functional demythologizing to Judaism's sacrosanct concepts. Kaplan's commitment to intellectual honesty precluded an esoteric writing style which would have allowed the masses the succor of their traditional myths. Kaplan considered the myths of supernaturalism to be religion's enemy. Kaplan was nothing but a cold shower. Well, a cold shower and a warm towel.

Kaplan was neither opposed to nor devoid of a mystical sense. Kaplan is often perceived as a one-dimensional, rationalist Litvak. But such a perception totalizes Kaplan's novelty while bracketing his traditionalism.

---

13 Eliezer Schweid, "The Reconstruction of Jewish Religion out of Secular Culture," in Goldsmith, *The American Judaism of Mordecai M. Kaplan*, 46.

14 Mordecai M. Kaplan, *The Reconstructionist* 1, no. 11 (April 5, 1935): 7–15. He significantly expanded on that article in *Judaism in Transition* (New York: Covici Friede Publishers, 1936), 185–205.

The intelligence to which religion must henceforth learn to submit its content is that inclusive process of thought which views each aspect of reality as part of an inter-related whole. Intelligence does not preclude either intuition or mysticism, but intuition should not be confused with supernatural revelation, nor mysticism with intellectual surrender.[15]

To my mind, one of the least appreciated of Kaplan's insights, and one that is usually associated with his foil at The Jewish Theological Seminary of America, Abraham Joshua Heschel, is the human need to be needed. "For there is something in the human being that craves giving itself to others in selfless devotion, some objective to live for beyond one's self, whereby one's life becomes integrated into the context of universal human life."[16] Several scholars have pointed out that there are Hasidic intimations in Kaplan's writings and we see that most clearly in his own liturgical poetry.[17] The following poem, published in 1936, resonates with the Hasidic emphasis on divine unity.

God is the oneness/ that spans the fathomless deeps of space/ and the measureless eons of time/ binding them together in act/ as we do in thought.

He is the sameness/ in the elemental substance of stars and planets/ of this our earthly abode/ and of all that it holds.

He is the unity/ of all that is/ the uniformity of all that moves,/ the rhythm of all things/and the nature of their interaction. . . .

God is the mystery of life,/ enkindling inert matter[18]/with inner drive and purpose. . . .

God is in the faith/by which we overcome/the fear of loneliness, of helplessness,/ of failure and of death.

---

15 Kaplan, *Judaism as a Civilization*, 308.

16 Kaplan, *Meaning of God*, 115–16. See S. Daniel Breslauer, "Kaplan, Abraham Joshua Heschel, and Martin Buber: Three Approaches to Jewish Revival," in Goldsmith, *The American Judaism of Mordecai M. Kaplan*, 246.

17 Arthur Green, "Neo-Hasidism and Our Theological Struggles," *Ra'ayonot* 4, no. 3 (1984): 11-17; Jack J. Cohen, *Guides for an Age of Confusion: Studies in the Thinking of Avraham Y. Kook and Mordecai M. Kaplan* (New York: Fordham University Press, 1999).

18 I understand this to be a translation of *m'chaye ha'metim*, which is usually rendered as "resurrection of the dead." In Kaplan's reconstruction, this term does not mean revivifying what had once been alive and then died; it means quickening that which had never been alive.

God is in the hope/ which, like a shaft of light, cleaves the dark
abysms/ of sin, of suffering, and of despair.
God is in the love/which creates, protects, forgives.
His is the spirit/which broods upon the chaos men have wrought,/
disturbing its static wrongs/ and stirring into life the formless beginnings/
of the new and better world.[19]

As a liturgist, Kaplan strives to evoke a sense of awe and mystery. As a
theologian, not only does he not disparage intuition and mysticism, he
extolls its virtues. In his 1937 work *The Meaning of God in Modern Jewish
Religion*, an entire chapter is dedicated to "God Felt As a Presence."
Kaplan, there, rejects the *idea* of God as inadequate; it is only the "actual
awareness of His presence" that sates the religious yearning to connect
with the Transcendent.[20] In a sentence that could have been lifted from
the writings of the first HaBaD rebbe's description of *bittul*, self-nullifica-
tion, Kaplan sounds every bit the rebbe: "It is as though by surrendering
our souls to God, we admit God into our souls and partake of his infinity
and eternity."[21] Kaplan's biographer, Mel Scult, also makes Kaplan's theology seem in line with Hasidic thought: "To the unschooled eye, the world
may seem variegated and diverse. To experience the world as one—as a
unity—Kaplan believed, is the primary challenge of the religious life."[22]

As much as I admire Kaplan's intellectual honesty, I do think that
camouflaging his piety and traditionalism behind contemporary philosophical and sociological doctrines was, in retrospect, excessive.[23] But,
shifting paradigms requires zeal, and Kaplan considered his rejection
of supernaturalism and emphasis on religious functions akin to the
Copernican revolution. What I attempted to do in the previous chapter, in part, was to highlight those aspects of Hasidism that also seem to

19 Kaplan, "Revelation of God in Nature: A Piyut for the First Benediction of the
    Evening Prayer," *The Reconstructionist* 1, no. 18 (1936): 1–13. Cited in Ira Eisenstein,
    "Kaplan as Liturgist," in Goldsmith, *The American Judaism of Mordecai M. Kaplan*,
    327–28.
20 Kaplan, *Meaning of God*, 244.
21 Ibid., 249.
22 Mel Scult, *Judaism Faces the Twentieth Century: The Biography of Mordecai M. Kaplan*
    (Detroit: Wayne State University Press, 1993), 173.
23 Ironically, Kaplan had a similar critique toward RaMBaM. See S. Daniel Breslauer,
    "Mordecai Kaplan's Approach to Jewish Mysticism," *The Journal of Jewish Thought
    and Philosophy* 4, no. 1 (1995): 42.

reject a personal God as part of their acosmic or panentheistic theologies. Thus, such a Copernican revolution was not an innovation of American Judaism. Yet, Kaplan's embrace of a democratic, honest, reasonable religiosity, is refreshing when coupled with the deep respect he shows for tradition. I wish I were as optimistic as he about the hospitality of the cosmos—I am not. In the next book on the theology of creation, we will delve deeper into Kaplan's theology of transnaturalism. What remains for this chapter is an exploration of the very few thinkers who were able to offer Kaplan's honesty, respect for tradition, and demand for coherence along with their own torah.

Although the Hasidic tradition had much to contribute to our theological discussion in the previous chapter, up to and including the teachings of the last Lubavitch rebbe, the post-Shoah *theology* to emerge from Modern Orthodox thinkers has been thin. Not only have the Holocaust theologians, Eliezer Berkovits and Irving Greenberg, offered nothing of novelty or cogency, but others like Joseph Soloveitchik, Yeshayahu Leibowitz, and David Hartman steered clear of the theological minefield altogether.[24] As Avi Sagi has noted, for both Soloveitchik and Leibowitz, "their shared crucial concern was how to preserve Orthodox religious commitment in a modern secular world."[25] For Hartman, I believe he was channeling and championing the model of rabbinic pluralism from the world of the Talmud.[26] What Hartman writes about Soloveitchik's ideal hero might as well be applied to himself: "[Halakhic man] shows no interest in metaphysical speculation."[27] Cass Fisher offers a compelling explanation, going back to Kant's bracketing metaphysical knowledge to make room for faith: "The academic study of Judaism emerged in an intellectual environment in which German idealism was de rigueur, and

---

24 Eliezer Berkovits emphasizes the hidden God and human freedom—nothing novel. Irving Greenberg's "Third Great Cycle of Jewish History," whereby Jews assume the proactive role in the covenant, makes for excellent sermons but poor philosophy.

25 Avi Sagi, "Contending with Modernity: Scripture in the Thought of Yeshayahu Leibowitz and Joseph Soloveitchik," *The Journal of Religion* 77, no. 3 (1997): 424.

26 David Hartman, *A Living Covenant: The Innovative Spirit in Traditional Judaism* (New York: The Free Press, 1985), 199–200. Even the name of his 1999 book reinforces this suggestion: *A Heart of Many Rooms: Celebrating the Many Voices within Judaism* (Woodstock: Jewish Lights Lublishing, 2001).

27 David Hartman, *Love and Terror in the God Encounter: The Theological Legacy of Rabbi Joseph B. Soloveitchik*, vol. 1 (Woodstock: Jewish Lights Publishing, 2001), 30.

contemporary Jewish studies draws most of its philosophical resources from Continental philosophy. It is no surprise, then, that the embrace of philosophies that launch serious critiques of metaphysics and ontotheology would result in depictions of Judaism in which theology plays little role."[28]

Lest I be misunderstood, as a student of modern Jewish thought I have been either educated or inspired by every one of the modern Orthodox thinkers mentioned above.[29] Nevertheless, their contributions to Jewish theology per se will not be their legacy. The only Orthodox thinker we will mention in this chapter, Tamar Ross, is herself so steeped in the theology of Rav Kook that the paucity of modern Orthodox theologians is glaring. Modern Orthodoxy is on the defensive, at least when it comes to theology. History is their bogeyman. In general, they do not accept that the Torah and halakhah are products of humans over time.[30] In response to a vapid critique of Arthur Green's *Radical Judaism* by a modern Orthodox rabbi, Green remarked that such reviews reflect the "theological bankruptcy" of modern Orthodoxy. Although I will have points of dispute with Green, at his assessment of Orthodoxy, I can only sigh in assent.

Since Kaplan and Abraham Joshua Heschel (1907–1972) taught at The Jewish Theological Seminary of America together for decades, there is a natural tendency to compare the two. Similarities between the two, given their distinctive theologies, help to better appreciate their historical and sociological contexts. Well before the Shoah, Kaplan expressed concern about the "blighting effect upon all moral endeavor [from] the notion that there is no meaning or purpose to the world. . . . "[31] Heschel put a more existentialist spin on that sentiment in his first essay published in America, "[a person] would feel wretched and lost without the

---

28 Cass Fisher, "Jewish Philosophy: Living Language at its Limits," in *Jewish Philosophy for the Twenty-First Century* (Leiden: Brill, 2014), 86.

29 In particular, the semester I spent studying with Rabbi Hartman at the Hebrew University of Jerusalem in 1995 shaped my understanding of rabbinic thought and gave me a deep appreciation for Rabbi Hartman. My appreciation for Rabbi Berkovits will be obvious below in our discussion of the philosophy of halakhah.

30 Exceptions to this generalization include many of the contributors to the website www.TheTorah.com.

31 Kaplan, *Judaism as a Civilization*, 98.

certainty that his life, insignificant though it be, is of some purpose in the great plan."[32]

Kaplan began building his theology with an axiom about the nature of the world, what I have called metaphysical minimalism. Heschel, a pedigreed prodigy born into the elite world of Hasidic leadership in Warsaw, constructs his theology beginning with our awe and radical amazement at the existence of ourselves, the existence of the cosmos, and the existence of ourselves within the cosmos. Arthur Green, one of Heschel's students and heirs, points out that in "recasting" Hasidic theology into an idiom intelligible to American Jews, Heschel avoided "alienating terminology."[33] Schweid might say that Heschel "camouflaged" his own mysticism *and* the mysticism Heschel sees as the fundamental operating system of Judaism. In the twentieth century, particularly after the Shoah, Jewish theologians were tasked with articulating a compelling anchor for ethical behavior that did not smack of an outdated divine dictator or run afoul of sovereign science. Although Kaplan did not minimize the human need to be needed, he was unwilling to rely on that feeling to form the foundation for his theology. Kaplan's commitment to the gracious hospitality of the cosmos is, somewhat ironically, more "traditional" than is Heschel's existentialist theology that radiates from the human outwards.

As a young university student in Berlin, Heschel wrote poetry in his mother tongues: Yiddish and radical divine immanence. As scholars have noted, the intense mysticism and monism of his poetry was tempered in his mature writings.[34] No doubt, the Shoah played a role. Heschel was no mere spectator to the genocide. On October 28, 1938, Heschel was awakened and arrested at his Frankfurt flat by agents of the Gestapo. After spending the night in jail, he was taken to the train station where,

---

32 Abraham Joshua Heschel, "An Analysis of Piety," *The Review of Religion* 6, no. 3 (1942): 293-307; reprinted as the final chapter in Abraham Joshua Heschel, *Man is Not Alone: A Philosophy of Religion* (New York: Farrar, Straus and Giroux, 1951), 273-96, and Heschel, *Moral Grandeur and Spiritual Audacity*, 317.

33 Arthur Green, "Three Warsaw Mystics," *Jerusalem Studies in Jewish Thought* 13 (1996): 49.

34 As Katz puts it: "One is tempted to speculate that more of his earlier years were spent in Mezbizh while the older he got the more he resided in Kotzk." Steven T. Katz, "Abraham Joshua Heschel and Hasidism," *Journal of Jewish Studies* 31 (1980): 92. See also Green, "Three Warsaw Mystics": 52.

as a Polish Jew, he was deported to Poland. After the three-day journey to the border in a rail car, Polish officials refused to allow Jewish Poles back into the country. The refugees were forced to remain in a no-man's land between the two countries. (Among the refugees was the family of a young man living in Paris, Herschel Grynszpan. When young Herschel received a postcard from his sister describing their family's plight, the seventeen-year-old was impelled to do something for his family. Days later, he walked into the German Embassy in Paris with the intention to assassinate the Ambassador. Missing the opportunity, Grynszpan assassinated a German diplomat and provided the Nazis with the pretext for two days of antisemitic frenzy, November 9–10, 1938, known as Kristallnacht.)

Within several days of Heschel's arrival at the border, he was able to cross into Poland and return to Warsaw. Several months later, in April of 1939, Hebrew Union College of Cincinnati invited Heschel to join their faculty, allowing his escape "just six weeks before the disaster began. . . . I am a brand plucked from the fire in which my people was burned to death."[35] His "people" included his mother and sisters who were murdered by the Nazi juggernaut. The trope of exile has punctuated Jewish life and literature. Heschel was familiar with such tropes as a student and scholar well before he, himself, became an exemplar of exile. His doctoral dissertation on biblical prophecy was completed in 1933 and served as the working draft of his 1962 work *The Prophets*. The essence of Heschel's insight about the prophet may well be understood in the shadow of Heschel's own history of exile and suffering.

> One must share the experiences, or similar experiences, in order to share the emotional reactions to them. Moreover, disillusionment is a

---

35 Abraham Joshua Heschel, "No Religion is an Island," *Union Seminary Quarterly* 21, no. 2, pt. 1 (1966): 117. Reprinted in Edward K. Kaplan and Samuel H. Dresner, *Abraham Joshua Heschel: Prophetic Witness* (New Haven: Yale University Press, 1998), 276. Biographical information is on p. 274.

An autobiographical note: my father, Lejb Dov Czeretynko, left Danzig, Poland, on the morning of August 24, 1939, a week before the Nazi invasion. He was twelve years old, with his two younger siblings and parents, traveling to the United States to reunite with his maternal grandmother who had emigrated from Rovno (now in Ukraine) earlier. Upon reaching this country, my father's name was changed to Louis Bear Cherry. As a result of the German blitzkrieg into Poland on September 1, his boat was the last to leave from Danzig for the United States until after World War II.

feeling the intensity of which is dependent upon the nature and depth of the emotional attitudes; one must have shared the love in order to share the disillusionment. Only a revival, one by one, of past happenings, together with the reactions they called forth, would enable the prophet to experience sympathy for the drama. For this purpose, the full story was reenacted in the life of the prophet, and the variety of divine pathos experienced and shared in the privacy of his destiny: love, frustration, reconciliation.[36]

In writing for a Jewishly estranged and uneducated community, Heschel begins not with theology, but with the sublime. Heschel defines the sublime as "that which we see and are unable to convey. It is the silent allusion of things to a meaning greater than themselves."[37] Translating this back into Hasidic terminology, we may say the sublime is the divine point or divine vitality responsible for the existence of every existent. Our response to the intimations and awareness of the sublime is in an attitude of wonder; and "indifference to the sublime wonder of living is the root of sin."[38]

Like Buber, Heschel is careful to say that God cannot be inferred from nature or history—only intimations can be sensed. God is not the sole Author of history.[39] Without revelation, there would be no way to distinguish the signal from the noise, to know which events reflect God's will and which are obstructionist. Perhaps in a nod to Kantian epistemology, Heschel identifies "a *preconceptual* faculty that senses the glory, the presence of the Divine."[40] This sense or awareness of the divine presence is the mystery of existence which Heschel labels an ontological category.[41] To summarize, Heschel begins with our feelings of wonder and radical amazement. He then argues that these feelings are a response to the sublime nature of material reality which conceals God's glory or presence.[42]

---

36   Abraham J. Heschel, *The Prophets*, vol. 1 (New York: Harper Torchbooks, 1962), 52.

37   Abraham Joshua Heschel, *God in Search of Man: A Philosophy of Judaism* (New York: Farrar, Straus and Giroux, 1955), 39.

38   Ibid., 43.

39   Heschel, *The Prophets*, 168.

40   Ibid., 108. Italics in original. Katz calls the presence of Kant in Heschel's writings "subterranean." Katz, "Abraham Joshua Heschel and Hasidism": 100.

41   Heschel, *God in Search of Man*, 57.

42   Ibid., 58.

In contrast to the more radical theologies within Hasidism, such as the acosmism of HaBaD, Heschel does not suggest that the world is an illusion. Nor is he a pantheist or panentheist. Corporeality is shot through with divinity, but there is a nondivine remainder. Heschel is not a monist. There is a transcendent God who both reveals and recoils. This mystery within and beyond corporeality serves as the metaphysical foundation for Heschel's *theology*. The circuit that Heschel closes between God and humans, Heschel's *religion*, also emerges from within each person's psyche.

"Revelation begins with a consciousness that something is asked of us."[43] According to Heschel, that revelation is universal: "It is a call that goes out again and again. It is a still small echo of a still small voice, not uttered in words, not conveyed in categories of the mind, but ineffable and mysterious, as ineffable and mysterious as the glory that fills the whole world."[44] In the eponymous chapter of *God in Search of Man*, Heschel begins his exposition that our sense of God calling to us, revelation, is a reflection of God's need for us to "bring God back into the world, into our lives. To worship is to expand the presence of God in the world."[45]

Shai Held has cogently argued that "self-transcendence is the axis around which all of Heschel's theology revolves."

> The God who limits His power in order to make space for humanity beckons humanity to restrain its own power in turn. Thus covenant becomes a process of mutual and reciprocal self-transcendence: the God of transitive concern seeks covenantal partners who will cultivate transitive concern; the God who engages in *tzimtzum* seeks partners who will engage in *tzimtzum*.[46]

Attendant to the idea of *tzimtzum*, what Heschel calls "restrained omnipotence," is divine incapacity to act unilaterally in history.[47] This theme of divine incapacity, as we have seen, is a motif that predates

---

43 Ibid., 162.
44 Ibid., 137.
45 Ibid., 156–57.
46 Shai Held, *Abraham Joshua Heschel: The Call of Transcendence* (Bloomington: University Press, 2013), 233.
47 Heschel, *God in Search of Man*, 377.

Luria's *tzimtzum* and rehabilitates rabbinic notions of restraint. As Held points out, Heschel's use of this trope has obvious implications for theodicy.

> God's self-limitation means that God is vulnerable to the decisions human beings make, so much so that God's immanence depends on human self-transcendence. Human beings have the terrifying power to drive God into exile, and to cause God to hide his face, but we also have the awesome potential to solicit and enable God's return. . . . Since a mitzvah, as we have seen, is "a prayer in the form of a deed," all acts of worship are, at bottom, attempts to reestablish God's immanence.[48]

Buber, too, maintained that divine immanence is dependent on us. Heschel draws much from his German-Jewish predecessors. Cohen emphasized the prophets and their ethical concerns. Buber emphasized that the way to encountering God is through other human beings, although through dialogue rather than deed. And Rosenzweig began his divine-human circuit with God's love for us. Heschel rearranges these three elements in his own idiosyncratic presentation of the divine-human circuit. We experience God's call and respond through a just and righteous deed. Through the "sacred deed we unseal the wells of faith. 'As for me, I shall behold Thy face in [or through deeds of] righteousness (Psalms 18:15)."[49]

When Heschel claims that "we have to love [God] in order to know [God],"[50] he stands RaMBaM on his intellectual head. For RaMBaM, as we saw, love of God is in proportion to one's knowledge of God, and knowledge is through the study of philosophy and science.[51] Heschel describes a God of pathos and a religion of sympathy. "Love of man is the way to the love of God."[52] Our love for God, through a leap of action to perform sacred deeds, is needed by God to assuage his disillusionment with humanity. God is unable to right human wrongs; that is *our* task, to be partners with God in the work of redemption.

---

48 Held, *Abraham Joshua Heschel*, 233.
49 Heschel, *God in Search of Man*, 282.
50 Ibid., 281.
51 Maimonides, M. T., Foundations of the Torah, 2:2.
52 Heschel, *God in Search of Man*, 375.

Reuven Kimelman, another student and heir of Heschel, and Green identified this sacred partnership as the key to Heschel's theology and his reading of Judaism in separate essays appearing in 2009.[53] Kimelman cites an address Heschel delivered in 1968 on Jewish theology: "God is in need of man. The idea of God being in need of man is central to Judaism and pervades all the pages of the Bible and of Chazal (the rabbis), of Talmudic literature, and it is understandable in our own time. . . . God is not going to do it [redemption] alone. He needs us."[54]

Green contributes three important points to this discussion. First of all, the sacred deeds that Heschel invites us to embrace are not the ritual mitzvot stressed by earlier kabbalists, but are interpersonal mitzvot.[55] Moreover, as Green notes, the sacred deeds that Heschel emphasizes are acts of love, compassion, and righteousness that are not necessarily enumerated in the medieval catalogues of the 613 mitzvot. Finally, as both Kimelman and Green note, the idea of commandments fulfilling a supernal or divine need (*tzorekh gavoah*) has biblical antecedents in the prophets' cries for righteousness and compassion.

> But the boundaries of good deeds are expanded beyond all limitation. Heschel has subtly turned around the order of priorities. Yes, the *mitzvot* are indeed divine need, he says, but it is in the first case these commandments—the life of goodness and justice—that God needs of us. In doing this, of course, Heschel is restoring the link between the Hasidic masters he knew and the prophets of ancient Israel. . . . Heschel sought to rescue the notion of *mitzvot tzorekh gavoah* from the obscurantism of the mystics and to bring it back to what he believed was its first source—the teachings of the prophets of Israel.[56]

In a subsequent essay on Heschel's theology, Green contends that Heschel "forcibly detached" the original, priestly sense of "commandments fulfilling

---

53 Kimelman, "Abraham Joshua Heschel's Theology": 226 and Arthur Green, "Recasting Hasidism for Moderns," *Modern Judaism* 29, no. 1 (2009): 73. Green significantly expands on this idea in a subsequent essay, "God's Need for Man: A Unitive Approach to the Writings of Abraham Joshua Heschel," *Modern Judaism* 35, no. 3 (2015): 247–61.

54 Reprinted in Heschel, *Moral Grandeur and Spiritual Audacity*, 159.

55 Green, "Recasting Hasidism": 74. Kimelman, "Abraham Joshua Heschel's Theology": 224–25.

56 Green, "Recasting Hasidism": 75–76.

a divine need" for purposes of his religion of sympathy.[57] What we have with Heschel, though, is less a detachment than a conflation. In *The Prophets*, Heschel repeatedly cites biblical verses that combine the great priestly transgressions of murder, idolatry, and sex crimes with sins of injustice.

1.   Your children have forsaken Me, Have sworn by those who are no gods. When I fed them to the full, they committed adultery and trooped to the houses of harlots. . . . They judge not with justice the cause of the fatherless. . . . They do not defend the rights of the needy. (Jeremiah 5:7 and 28, cited in Heschel, *The Prophets*, vol. 1, 109)

2.   There is no truth, no love, and no knowledge of God in the land; Swearing and lying, killing and stealing, and committing adultery, They break all bonds, and blood touches blood. (Hosea 4:1–2, cited in Heschel, *The Prophets*, vol. 1, 13)

3.   Woe to him who heaps up what is not his own. . . . Woe to him who gets evil gain for his house. . . . For the stone cries out from the wall, And the beam from the woodwork responds. Woe to him who builds a town with blood, and founds a city on iniquity! (Habakkuk 2:6, 9, 11–12, cited in Heschel, *The Prophets*, vol. 1, 7)

4.   The prophet directs his rebuke particularly against the "heads of the house of Jacob and the rulers of the house of Israel, who abhor justice and pervert all equity." It is because "they build Zion with blood and Jerusalem with wrong" (Micah 3:9–10) that Zion and Jerusalem will be destroyed. (Cited in Heschel, *The Prophets*, vol. 1, 98)

In each of these citations, Heschel offers his megaphone to prophets railing with righteous indignation. In the first two cases, the prophets group together the priestly cardinal sins of idolatry, adultery, and murder, with random acts of injustice towards society's vulnerable. In the final two examples, prophetic rhetoric conflates injustice and bloodshed. What Heschel does is to take the medieval, mystical concept of *tzorekh gavoah* and expand its scope to include unjust acts that the prophets, themselves, had coupled with the priestly causes for divine exile. Although the insights

---

57   Arthur Green, "God's Need for Man," *Modern Judaism* 35, no. 3 (2015): 254.

as Heschel expresses them are innovative, to be sure, they are also logical extensions of Judaism's pre-kabbalistic inheritance from the priestly Torah. As Heschel wrote, "Only he who is an heir is qualified to be a pioneer."[58]

As we saw in the chapter on rabbinic thought, once the Temple was destroyed the rabbis offered several functional substitutes for sacrifices, including deeds of lovingkindness. Heschel, in his treatment of the rabbis, brings the classic example of this idea along with its prooftext from Hosea. The midrash pictures two survivors of the Temple's destruction, Rabban Yohanan ben Zakkai and Rabbi Yehoshua, revisiting the ruins. Rabbi Yehoshua agonizes over the destruction of the Temple because it had been the place where Israel atoned for its sins. Rabban Yohanan comforts his colleague that they have an equally efficacious means of atonement, namely, acts of lovingkindness, as the prophet Hosea said, "I desire lovingkindness not sacrifice" (Hosea 6:6).[59] The rabbinic passage then explores examples of lovingkindness. In a surprising claim, our midrash declares that prayer is one such act. Some acts of lovingkindness are directed towards people and others towards God. Since prayer is the primary substitute for sacrifices in the rabbinic mind, and prayer is a form of lovingkindness, the category of deeds of lovingkindness (*hesed*) takes on increased significance as a vehicle for satisfying supernal needs.

Heschel argues that the prophetic critique of the priesthood is not an attack on animal sacrifice. "The prophets disparaged the [sacrificial] cult when it became a substitute for righteousness. It is precisely the implied recognition of the value of the cult that lends force to their insistence that there is something even more precious than sacrifice."[60] Heschel acknowledges that through animal sacrifice "something was released or cast away. The person was transformed, a communion vital to man and precious to God established."[61] Moreover, Heschel asserts that "prayer is not a substitute for sacrifice. Prayer is sacrifice."[62] And since sacrifice had the potency to effect such a communion, all the more so do righteousness and justice. "To do justice is what God demands of every man: it is

58 Abraham J. Heschel, *Who is Man?* (Stanford: Stanford University Press, 1965), 99.
59 Avot d'Rabbi Natan 4:5.
60 Heschel, *The Prophets*, 196.
61 Ibid.
62 Abraham J. Heschel, *Man's Quest for God: Studies in Prayer and Symbolism* (Santa Fe: Aurora Press, 1954), 71.

the supreme commandment, and one that cannot be fulfilled vicariously [as are sacrifices]."[63] Lest we think that justice, for Heschel, be blind and dispassionate, he assures us that "there is a point at which strict justice is unjust."[64] After all, one explanation for the destruction of the Temple was that the rabbis ruled with strict justice alone (b. Baba Metzia 30b). "Justice dies when deified, for beyond all justice is God's compassion."[65]

Heschel tells us that the prophets believed "that the primary way of serving God is through love, justice, and righteousness." Just as the prophets were not rejecting sacrifices, the priests did not reject acts of lovingkindness and justice. Leviticus 19, the heart of the priestly Holiness Code, overflows with admonitions against injustice, and it is framed by the prohibitions concerning idolatry and sexual immorality. The priests emphasized avoiding the transgressions where the consequences could not be counteracted by the sacrificial cult. The prophets foresaw the same consequence, exile, through perpetrating the cardinal sins of the priests as well as acts of injustice. The rabbis, yearning to restore both Jewish sovereignty and the Temple, claimed that just as sacrifice and teshuvah had brought God back into the Israelite camp during the days in the desert, prayer and deeds of lovingkindness will bring God back to the Land of Israel and Jerusalem. Heschel asks, "What is the way of true worship?" He answers by citing the famous lines from Micah 6:8: "What does the Lord require of you but to do justice, and to love kindness and to walk humbly with your God?" For Heschel, "worship is a way of living."[66]

After the Six-Day War in 1967, Heschel traveled to Jerusalem for the first time. At sixty years old, Heschel beheld the reality of Israel, the ancient city of Jerusalem, and the Wailing Wall. He had already written about righteous deeds being a form of prayer, a form of self-transcendence. But at the vision of the rebuilt city of Zion he exclaimed, "Hewing stones, paving roads, planting gardens, building homes, can also be carried out as prayers in the form of deeds."[67] Unlike Rosenzweig's literary organization of creation, revelation, and redemption, Green points out

---

63 *The Prophets*, 204.
64 Ibid., 215.
65 Ibid., 201.
66 Heschel, *Man's Quest for God*, xii.
67 Abraham Joshua Heschel, *Israel: An Echo of Eternity* (New York: Farrar, Straus and Giroux, 1967), 145.

that Heschel's nomenclature is different: creation, revelation, and deed.[68] Heschel concludes with deed precisely because it is through our deeds that we approach redemption.[69] Tsippi Kaufman links Heschel's theology to the Hasidic notion of worship through corporeality.[70] She cites several passages in *God in Search of Man* to demonstrate the totalizing effect of Heschel's application of this Hasidic idea. No deed is neutral; we are either aiding or undermining God. "In every act we either answer or defy, we either return or move away, we either fulfill or miss the goal."[71]

Whether the metaphor is God creating the world and the Torah with the same letters, or there being holy sparks in everything that exists, Kauffman understands that Heschel's theology is a contemporary expression of divine immanence.[72] As we saw with the theology of HaBaD, divinity is accessed or revealed through the deed. Unlike HaBaD, for Heschel the deed can be far more expansive than the catalog from the Shulchan Arukh, particularly concerning acts of justice and lovingkindness. But, more importantly, the encounter is not purely psychological. Heschel's theology is not acosmic and his world is not illusory. It is all too real. Sacred deeds do not disclose the divine presence for Heschel as much as they engage and activate the divinity that inheres only in potential within our world.

Heschel may be the most quotable theologian in Judaism. That Heschel learned English as an adult both humbles and inspires me. His poetry and linguistic mastery nearly overwhelm my critical faculties. Yet, even if Heschel's mapping of wonder to mystery to deed resonates with my own sensibilities, his universalizing the experience of revelation remains unconvincing. His description, although not always consistent, is of a God who "sues for our devotion, constantly, persistently, who goes out to meet us as soon as we long to know Him."[73] Really? I am so grateful to be a beneficiary of the wisdom and insights of Abraham Joshua Heschel whom this God, ostensibly, sued. I simply do not believe that

---

68 Green, "Recasting Hasidism": 72.

69 Heschel, *God in Search of Man*, 379–80.

70 Tsippi Kauffman, "Abraham Joshua Heschel and Hasidic Thought," [Hebrew] *Akdamut* 24 (2010): 137–55.

71 Heschel, *God in Search of Man*, 291. See chapter 4 in this volume for the medieval mystical precedent for valorizing even neutral acts.

72 Kauffman, "Abraham Joshua Heschel and Hasidic Thought": 141.

73 Heschel, *Man is Not Alone*, 76.

everyone was named in the suit. As a rhetorical device, as a declaration of inspiration, I can endorse the claim. I believe that Heschel was "penetrated by His insight."[74] But to then assert, as Heschel does, "there is no man who is not shaken for an instant by the eternal" falls somewhere between unjustifiable and untrue.[75]

Heschel's version of immanence, however, is compelling. Heschel was exiled, and Heschel was orphaned. Such experiences sensitized him to the suffering of others and to the pathos of God, both of which demonstrate the overwhelming need to *respond* to that suffering.[76] Heschel's understanding of prophetic religion as such a response is what he describes as a "science of deeds."[77] Heschel does not reduce Judaism to ethics, as Kauffman pointed out.[78] Although her Hebrew is more Heschelian than my translation: "The never-ending divine presence demands a never-ending human response."[79]

In our discussion of Rav Kook in the last chapter, I leaned heavily upon the scholarship of Tamar Ross. Ross (b. 1938), professor emerita of Jewish Thought at Bar Ilan University, stands out among the small but growing field of female Jewish thinkers precisely because of the depth of her knowledge within the world of Jewish thought. Well before she hesitantly entered the discourse of constructive Jewish theology, Ross had mastered the history of the field as well as contemporary philosophy and feminist theory. Nevertheless, she addresses traditional Judaism's tensions with modernity by drawing on native Jewish resources.

Like all the theologians featured in this chapter, Ross has acknowledged that the old model of Orthodoxy has failed. Her career was largely devoted to finding elements within the tradition to serve as a metaphysical foundation for her halakhic commitments. She does not offer a systematic or dogmatic theology. She tends to rely on the mystical tradition, as mediated through Rav Kook, to address the major stress points where tradition and modernity clash. Traditionalists are likely to be more sympathetic to her theology than Jews outside Orthodoxy. Yet, Ross' ability

---

74 Ibid., 78.
75 Ibid., 79.
76 Green, "Recasting Hasidism": 73.
77 Heschel, *God in Search of Man*, 281–92.
78 Kauffman, "Abraham Joshua Heschel and Hasidic Thought": 152.
79 Ibid., 145.

to translate Rav Kook's poetic, mystical insights into prose and philosophy, thereby carving out entry ways for Jewish feminists and skeptics, would delight Rav Kook.

Ross identifies the Lurianic fissure of *tzimtzum* as the harbinger of Kant's epistemological distinction between reality in itself and what can be known about reality from our own consciousness. The subsequent language of "from God's side" and "from our side" anticipates the Kantian distinction between noumena and phenomena.[80] We cannot hope to know anything about God's essence; our only knowledge emerges from our experience of relating to the divine.[81] Importantly, the dynamic interconnectedness and interdependencies among the sefirot correspond to feminism's emphasis on individuals being enmeshed in a web of relationships.[82]

Of course, the focus on relationships is not novel. Judith Plaskow, a pioneer in the field of Jewish feminist theology with her 1990 work *Standing Again at Sinai: Judaism from a Feminist Perspective*, emphasizes that the fundamental Jewish unit is not the individual but the community.[83] The philosopher of relation, Martin Buber, is, thus, widely promoted in feminist circles. But as Plaskow noted in a subsequent essay, Buber's default position is one of classically male instrumentality. Plaskow, citing a colleague, suggests that "while relation is key to both Buber's philosophy and feminist theory, it seems as though it enters their experience from opposite ends: Buber works toward relation, while feminists begin with relation."[84]

Plaskow understands that Jewish mysticism can be feminism's ally in certain respects, she just doesn't have command of the literature in the way that Ross does.[85] For example, Plaskow rejects the theistic God

---

80 Tamar Ross, "Religious Belief in a Postmodern Age," in *Faith: Jewish Perspectives,* ed. Avi Sagi and Dov Schwartz (Boston: Academic Studies Press, 2014), 178–83.
81 Ross, "Rav Kook's Concept of Divinity": 120.
82 Tamar Ross, *Expanding the Palace of Torah: Orthodoxy and Feminism* (Waltham: Brandeis University Press, 2004), 211–15.
83 Judith Plaskow, *Standing Again at Sinai: Judaism from a Feminist Perspective* (New York: HarperCollins, 1990), 18–21.
84 Judith Plaskow citing Lauren Granite, "Jewish Theology in Feminist Perspective," in *Feminist Perspectives on Jewish Studies,* ed. Lynn Davidman and Shelly Tenebaum (New Haven: Yale University Press, 1994), 68.
85 Plaskow, *Standing Again at Sinai,* 158.

of Greek attributes dwelling aloof in His omnipotence and immutability. She explicitly invokes the limited God of Process theology and explains one of the problems of divine omnipotence: "On the one hand, the notion of divine omnipotence encourages human passivity. On the other hand, images of human weakness and nothingness foster a self-abnegation that can paralyze the capacity to act."[86] Ross need not turn to Process Thought or feminist theory for such a concept.

> Indeed, R. Kook regards a strictly theistic model as inferior precisely because of the crippling effects that it can have on human initiative, tending to diminish a person's confidence in his or her own creative ability and value. In Lurianic Kabbalah in general, it is the notion of substantive connection between God and the world and their interdependence that emphasizes the responsibility of human beings for the cosmic state of affairs. . . . But God in no sense dominates or controls human beings. . . . Rather the relationship between God and human beings is one of mutual need and completion.[87]

Ross now speaks for herself: "God need not be thought of as transcending history or acting as an agent in history, but rather as a sacred force that is present within history, inspiring a vision of liberation that progresses from age to age."[88] Progress, a principal theme for Rav Kook, becomes central for Ross' understanding of revelation and halakhah. Book 3 will explore Ross' philosophy of halakhah, but her notion of cumulative revelation is our present concern. She posits three traditional assumptions that form the foundation for her theory: 1) revelation is a "dynamic unfolding of the original Torah transmitted at Sinai that reveals in time its ultimate significance"; 2) God's voice is heard through "rabbinical interpretations of the texts"; and 3) "although successive hearings of God's Torah sometimes *appear* to contradict His original message, that message is never replaced."[89] Ross is a careful writer. *Replacing* the revelation requires a time-travel machine; what some feminists are looking for is the *repeal* of certain pieces of legislation. What cumulative revelation gets Ross, as we will see in the final section, is the possibility that the

---

86 Ibid., 133–34.
87 Ross, *Expanding the Palace of Torah*, 215.
88 Ibid., 213–14.
89 Ibid., 197–98. Italics in original.

emergence of feminism is part of God's providential and revelatory inter-actions with humanity through which changes in halakhah will authen-tically follow.[90]

Like Rav Kook, Ross believes that history is another form of ongo-ing revelation, what she calls "surrogate prophecy."[91] She even suggests that the emergence of biblical criticism to challenge the puerile conceit of divine dictation was providential.[92] We are now intellectually sophis-ticated enough to understand that divine revelation does not occur orally. Without mentioning William James' similar notion, Ross cites Rav Kook's understanding that truth is a dynamic property of living and not a static, Platonic ideal. Truth is constantly developing in reaction to our changing world. "Truth grows from the earth" (Psalms 85:11). What makes something true, for Kook and Ross, is its coherence with the total-ity of our reality.[93] Such a perception of reality is one reason why Ross believes that postmodernism bears a closer family resemblance to mys-ticism than to philosophy.[94] Professor Ross says as little as possible about her own theology. In her own way, not so unlike Mordecai Kaplan, she is a metaphysical minimalist. "My interest," she acknowledges, "is no less in stimulating others to address this challenge than in promoting any specific suggestion of my own."[95]

Our final female thinker in this section, although not a Holocaust theologian, is a theologian who has applied feminist theory to the Shoah. Melissa Raphael begins her work *The Female Face of God in Auschwitz* with a critical analysis of the Holocaust theologians like Berkovits and Greenberg.[96] As feminists have pointed out for decades, strength is a dream of teenage boys. As men, they/we find it too easy to project that

90 Ibid., 210–12.
91 Tamar Ross, "Overcoming the Epistemological Barrier," in Tirosh-Samuelson, *Jewish Philosophy in the Twenty First Century*, 383.
92 Ibid., 384. See also Jerome Yehuda Gellman, *This Was from God: A Contemporary Theology of Torah and History* (Boston: Academic Studies Press, 2016).
93 Ross, "Overcoming," in Tirosh-Samuelson, *Jewish Philosophy in the Twenty First Century*, 378.
94 Ross, "Religious Belief," in Sagi and Schwartz, *Faith: Jewish Perspectives*, 183.
95 Ross, *Expanding the Palace of Torah*, 224.
96 See also Sandra B. Lubarsky, "Reconstructing Divine Power: Post-Holocaust Jewish Theology, Feminism, and Process Philosophy," in *Women and Gender in Jewish Philosophy*, ed. Hava Tirosh-Samuelson (Bloomington: Indiana University Press, 2004), 289–313, 299–302.

ideal in its superlative form on to God. For many male Holocaust theologians, God may be absent or hiding or restraining Himself, but that God is still the mighty warrior.

> There has been too much asking "*where* was God in Auschwitz?" and not enough "*who* was God in Auschwitz?" . . . While the conditions in Auschwitz were wholly non-ordinary, God-She may have been so 'ordinarily' present among women whose personhood was getting ever less perceptible that she herself was imperceptible. But that is not to say that she had deliberately hidden herself. If she seemed hidden it was by virtue of the non-numinousness of the medium of her presence, the depth of evil into which she was plunged, and her very soft tread.[97]

Although stories are not unusual in Holocaust theology, male theologians tend to use the stories as the Talmud does—to prove or disprove a point. The stories are embedded in a discursive, logical presentation. Raphael's approach is different. She wants the narratives and memoirs of the survivors to serve as primary theological sources. Her approach is more traditionally aggadic. "In these stories and fragments of stories, the face of Shekhinah shines dimly, almost imperceptibly, through the smoke clouds of Auschwitz."[98] The stories of women's support, concern, tenderness, and sacrifice are where we sense God's immanence. A scene of women, during an hours-long roll call, huddling together to prevent any of their ranks from collapsing—and thus becoming an immediate target for murder—is a scene of divinity.

Patriarchal power, by which I mean traditional understandings of divine omnipotence, is at odds with matriarchal compassion. "Informal, female power . . . is often the quiet, gentle power of sympathy, patience, care and support."[99] But, in Jewish mysticism, the ideal is not an either/or, but a balance between the two sides. Interestingly, Jewish mysticism places compassion and love on the male side while power and strict justice are on the female side. Perhaps this inversion will help us understand that these attributes are not inherently male or female. What feminist theory has reminded us all is that the one-dimensional depiction of God

---

97 Melissa Raphael, *The Female Face of God in Auschwitz: A Jewish Feminist Theology of the Holocaust* (New York: Routledge, 2003), 54.
98 Ibid., 124
99 Lubarsky, "Reconstructing Divine Power," 302.

as all/only powerful is a distortion both of Judaism and our experience. It is, after all, the biblical God who "wipes the tears from every face" (Isaiah 25:8).

What Jewish feminism offers is a more just, balanced approach to the "theology of presence" that is faithful to both our texts and experience. We are partners with God in creation, and it is through our sacred deeds that we make our contributions toward redemption. Resh Lakish offered the following midrash on the creation story: if the Israelites won't observe the commandments, God will return the world to chaos and confusion.[100] Melissa Raphael offers a gentler, more universalistic aggadah: "When the communal fabric of the world was being torn apart, human love was anticipating its renewal. That there were those, men and women, who stopped the world unravelling is, after all, the meaning of the word religion, from *religare*, to bind up."[101] My own teacher, and our next theologian, updated an ancient aggadah that has the messiah binding lepers' wounds at the gates of Rome while awaiting God's call to redeem the world. Arthur Green wrote, in 1992, "today we would be likely to find him in an AIDS hospice."[102] At a minimum, religion should prevent the unravelling of civilization. Ultimately, religion should bind together all of creation with the Divine.

The final two thinkers in our section on theology serve as the segue to the next book on creation. They both understand that creation *is* revelation. The traditional line between creation and revelation, dependent on an independent Creator communicating with a distinct creation, has been effaced. God's face has been revealed as the facets of the cosmos. Moshe cannot see God's face and live because one of God's facets is death. The radical immanence expressed by our final theologians allows us to anticipate our next book by treating issues of theology and creation in concert.

Arthur Green had been serving as President of the Reconstructionist Rabbinical College when he returned to Brandeis University as a professor of Jewish Thought. He had attended Brandeis as both an undergraduate and graduate student. I began my graduate studies at Brandeis the

---

100 See my *Torah through Time*, 62–63.
101 Raphael, *The Female Face*, 142.
102 Arthur Green, *Seek my Face, Speak my Name: A Contemporary Jewish Theology* (Northvale: Jason Aronson, Inc., 1992), 186.

same year he returned. Shortly after I completed my dissertation under Green's supervision, he returned to his vocation of educating rabbis as the founding Dean of the Rabbinical School at Hebrew College. (Green, himself, received rabbinic ordination from the Jewish Theological Seminary where he studied with Abraham Joshua Heschel.)

Over the past twenty-five years of theological reflection, several of Green's views have evolved.[103] I will only cite his most recent articulations of his theology. What stands out to me is his humility and commitment to intellectual honesty. Both in his latest writings and in a 2014 interview, Green was wont to say, "I don't know." This was not an admission of ignorance; it was an existential acknowledgement of personal experience. Green does not know of a God "out there," for instance, who chooses Israel for a special covenant.[104]

Like Heschel, Green unfolds his personal theology from his own sense of awe, wonder, and radical amazement.[105] Yet, unlike Heschel who seems to insist that we have all had flashes of mystical insight, Green's more modest claim is that we all have the potential for such experiences.[106] In describing himself as a neo-Hasidic, *mystical panentheist*, he telegraphs the pedigree of his thought. Yes, he is heir to the mystical panentheism of HaBaD and Rav Kook, but he is not struggling to keep assimilationist forces at bay. That dam has burst. Part of Green's *neo-Hasidism* is the acceptance of the fruits of academic research into history and science. Green is ready to *reframe* what scientists tell us about the nature of reality into religious myth.[107]

Green intuits that every existent shimmers with a divine vitality which is cloaked by the kaleidoscopic cascade of evolutionary history. Green's panentheism posits an underlying and integrating unity of the divine and the cosmos which points to two things: transcendence *within* immanence and the mysterious synergy of the One. "Transcendence means that God—or Being—is so fully present in the here and now of

---

103 Compare, for example, Green's shifts concerning the willfulness and telos of evolution from "A Kabbalah for the Environmental Age," *Tikkun* 14, no. 5 (1999): 33-40, reprinted in *The Heart of the Matter*, 319, to *Radical Judaism: Rethinking God and Tradition* (New Haven: Yale Press, 2010) 17, 27.

104 Green, *Radical Judaism*, 18 and 108.

105 Ibid., 4.

106 Ibid., 5.

107 Ibid., 20.

each moment that we could not possibly grasp the depth of that presence."[108] Being "is mysteriously and infinitely greater than the sum of its parts, and cannot be fully known or reduced to its constituent beings."[109] Since the Being that flows through all finite beings is infinite, it links and unites all *seemingly* separate beings. Here, Green is offering the Hasidic understanding of *tzimtzum* which is psychological rather than ontological or epistemological. "The illusion of cosmic fragmentation and distance from God is a 'gift' given to the human mind in order to enable us to engage in the labors of restoration."[110]

Restoring cosmic fragmentation is Green's idiomatic translation of *tikkun olam*. The restoration usually involves acts of compassion and lovingkindness. The response to our acts, however, can be unanticipated.

> The source of light may be so deeply hidden within us that we cannot see it, until we lose faith that it exists at all. Then another, whose light may be more visible to us than our own, shines forth in such a way that our own light is called out of hiding. This other may be a lover, friend, or teacher; the communication may take the form of mountain, well, or bolt of lightning. In our opening to one another, our two lights meet, casting forth a new light. This light is surely brighter and more widely seen that was the sum of our two faint lights as they had existed before our meeting.[111]

The dance between the two subjects generates a greater intensity of light, of divine vitality, than the simple combination of the individual lights. That is synergy. "Here is the great lesson of love: the more you give, the more you receive."[112] The feedback loop of love goes hand in hand with the realization that all of us are connected at the deepest possible level with one another and the rest of creation.

Green's interpretation of God's ineffable name, YHWH, involves a conflation of the three temporal tenses of the verb to be: was, is, and will be. "Y-H-W-H is a verb that has been artificially arrested in motion and

108 Ibid., 18.
109 Ibid.
110 Ibid., 68.
111 Green, *Seek My Face*, 182.
112 Green, *Radical Judaism*, 109.

made to function as a noun."[113] Green repeatedly makes the point that the four letter name of God, with letters rearranged, is the Hebrew word for being or existence, HWYH. "All beings are somehow manifestations of the same single Being. . . . When you think of those beings as individuals, they collectively make up existence and are HWYH, or *Havayyah*. But when you think of them as One they open to an infinite mystery, a dimension that was not seen before, and that HWYW becomes Y-H-W-H."[114]

One of Green's primary interests is promoting acts of love among humanity, thus he remains largely, though not exclusively, on the human/ divine plane. Although Green appreciates DNA as *"zecher lema'aseh bereshit*, 'in memory of the act of Creation,'" he rarely gestures toward the prehistoric or nonhuman.[115] But the love that he emphasizes as a manifestation within human history existed from the very beginning.[116] Hans Jonas, as we will see in book 2, calls that force the "cosmogonic eros." When Green expounds on the verse from Psalms (42:8), "deep calls unto deep," he imagines both depths as "aspects of consciousness, the highly complex human mind pushing and churning within itself" to attain deeper levels of understanding about the nature of reality.[117] Let me suggest that the same phrase can also be read back in our evolutionary history as different nonhuman individuals calling to one another from the depths of their own divinity, their own Being, to drive evolution forward. (Notice, I am not qualifying the word *forward* by wrapping it in quotation marks. Part of my faith is in the direction of evolutionary history.)

Green discusses transcendence in epistemological terms: "we could not possibly grasp the depth of that [divine] presence."[118] I understand transcendence as ontological. It is the divine overflow, what the mystics called *shefa*, that radiates beyond the discrete, individual unit to connect and attract all other units through their participation in the One of

113 Green, *Seek My Face*, 18. See also Arthur Green, *Ehyeh: A Kabbalah for Tomorrow* (Woodstock: Jewish Lights Publishing, 2003), 1–2.
114 Arthur Green, *Arthur Green, Hasidism for Tomorrow*, ed. Hava Tirosh-Samuelson and Aaron W. Hughes (Leiden: Brill, 2015), 235–36.
115 Green, *The Heart of the Matter*, 315.
116 Green approaches recognition of this fundamental force but, it seems to me, emphasizes the emergence of multiplicity from the One, rather than the dynamic interplay between the different manifestations of the One. *Radical Judaism*, 24–25.
117 Ibid., 75–76.
118 Ibid., 18.

Being. Since each discrete unit of existence participates in Being, it, too, radiates *shefa* that transcends itself in search of like energy. As the rabbis and mystics reread the biblical narrative by marinating it in the eros of Song of Songs, we can do the same to the evolutionary narrative.[119] In book 2, I will explore further these different emphases between Green's theology and my own.

Green's theology is coherent. The conundrum of theodicy is neutralized by his panentheism. God acts only through surrogacy. And surrogates always have the right of refusal. Green's goal is to preserve, reframe, and, dare I say, reconstruct, the mystical fundamentals of Jewish tradition while unapologetically abandoning that which flies in the face of contemporary knowledge and morality. But, as Tamar Ross has questioned, is the reconstructed deity worthy of worship? The answer depends in part on your definition of worship, which for Jews has historically centered around halakhah and prayer. The covenant is alive and well, for Green, even though the terms have changed.

Let's agree that lighting candles before sunset on Friday night will not cause God to reverse global warming. So, how does Green's theology benefit us?

> To open yourself to serve others as a channel of divine grace, to bring light and blessing into their lives, is endlessly rewarding. The more light you shine forth, the more comes pouring through. The inner Wellspring is one whose "waters do not betray" and never run dry. This is all I have by way of faith in reward. *And it is plenty.*[120]

Kindling flames on Friday night reminds us to be kind and shine our own light throughout the week. But faith bestows additional reward. I can tell Nietzsche's Madman that the god he proclaimed dead was an imposter. I don't feel seasick as our orb of spit and sand sails through the galaxy. Those who insist that there is nothing other than sound and fury are not idiots, but they are Epicureans who deny God's involvement with the universe. The Stoics knew how to respond to the Epicurean: the absence of divine intervention in no way diminishes the ubiquity of divine participation. The Stoics gave divine immanence more agency

---

119 Ibid., 55.
120 Ibid., 109. Emphasis in original. Quotation is from Jeremiah 15:18.

than do I; they called it logos, while I follow Jonas and call it eros. But the covenant gives me the ultimate *sh'lom bayit*, the peace that comes with feeling I'm at home. As Jorge Borges wrote about a justified world: "the universe suddenly usurped the unlimited dimensions of hope."[121]

Before we take leave of my teacher, he deserves acknowledgement in one more area that was touched upon above, namely feminism. In 1983, Susannah Heschel edited a reader entitled *On Being a Jewish Feminist*. Green was one of only two men who contributed. It was in that volume that Judith Plaskow wrote an essay that was an early installment of her *Standing Again at Sinai*. Green has been a consistent champion of women's roles in Judaism and academia. In two ways Green has anticipated both the contributions of feminism in general and those of Tamar Ross in particular. As we saw above, in theory and practice, feminists have sought to reclaim aggadah as a source of theology. Aggadah has always been central to Green. "Jewish theology in its most native form," he reminds us, "is narrative theology."[122]

Green, like Ross, recognized the potential contribution of Jewish mysticism to a feminist agenda. He also lamented that very few females were training in the field and encouraged women to enter the discourse. Finally, avoiding the essentialism that sometimes haunts attempts at egalitarianism, Green offers his own interpretation of the verse in Genesis describing God's creation of humanity as male and female: "In the deeper spirit of third wave feminism, all of us are both male and female, and we respond to images of both genders in complex and subtle ways."[123] Green, himself, will have the last word, a word able to be communicated only by one with mastery of the sources and profundity of heart.

> The real meaning of "male" and "female" in Kabbalistic language is what they call *mashpiah* and *mekabel*, giver and receiver, so-called active and passive partners, to use the metaphor of human sexuality, but those terms are hardly adequate. As lovers, we know that we are all both givers and receivers, indeed our own greatest pleasure may lie in giving to the other

---

121 Jorge Luis Borges, "Library of Babel," in *Ficciones*, trans. Anthony Kerrigan (New York: Grove Press, 1962): 79–88.
122 Green, *Heart of the Matter*, 347.
123 Ibid., 355. See also Cherry, *Torah through Time*, 52.

in ways that entirely blur the clarity of who is giving and who is receiving. Let us not be too embarrassed or prudish to learn from that lesson.[124]

Particularly in terms of offering a religious reframing of contemporary science and philosophy, Bradley Shavit Artson (b. 1959) complements the theological insights of Green. Artson, like Green, was ordained by the Jewish Theological Seminary. His first pulpit position was at my parents' synagogue, and he and I team-taught a group of unruly seventh graders in 1988–1989. Subsequently, he became the dean of the Ziegler School of Rabbinic Studies at the American Jewish University where I received ordination in 2009. Although Artson earned a doctorate in Hebrew letters, his contributions have primarily been for the general Jewish public rather than for the scholarly community.[125]

Artson has done more than anyone else to raise the profile of Process Thought, a metaphysical system associated with Alfred North Whitehead and Charles Hartshorne, in the Jewish community. Process Thought features many elements we have already encountered in our discussion of Jewish mysticism, namely: a God limited in power, a dynamic God affected by humanity, a relational God, and a panentheistic God immanent in creation but with a remainder.[126] (Green's similar theology is expressed in language indigenous to Jewish thought, a point to which I will return in the following book on theologies of creation.)[127]

Although Artson exaggerates the presence of Process ideas within classical Jewish literature, he does highlight many texts that are consonant with Process Thought.[128] In shifting the focus of relationships away from our understandable anthropocentrism, he describes how bees and

---

124 Green, *Heart of the Matter*, 356.
125 The exception is an excellent essay where Artson critiques what he calls the "dominant theological paradigm" using contemporary science, philosophy, and literary theory. Bradley Shavit Artson, "Life of the World: Beyond Mind/Body Dualism to Embodied Emergence," *Hebrew Union College Annual* 79 (2008): 193–254.
126 Alfredo Borodowski examines this overlap in his critique of Artson: "The Perfect Theological Storm: Process Theology and Mysticism in Spiritual America," *Conservative Judaism* 62, nos. 1–2 (2010–2011): 88–104. This entire issue of *Conservative Judaism* responds to Artson's treatment of Process Theology and Judaism.
127 See Ariel Evan Mayse, "Arthur Green: An Intellectual Profile," in Tirosh-Samuelson, *Arthur Green: Hasidism for Tomorrow*, 34.
128 It is unfortunate that Artson makes the unsupportable claim that "Process Theology offers the opportunity to . . . appreciate Judaism for what it was intended to be and

flowers, for example, co-evolve. Relationships are manifest in every aspect of creation, whether between two seemingly discrete elements or within a single system. And when relationships are symbiotic, synergy can result in emergence, the manifestation of properties not present in the discrete elements of the system, such as consciousness. "Emergence recognizes the supplemental relationship of nature's different levels of complexity. . . . Reality is not simply the mechanical sum total of its component parts, but an evolving, interacting, and self-surpassing process."[129]

Artson sees that forward-leaning, dynamic, divine drive reflected in God's self-description of *ehyeh asher ehyeh*, "I am becoming what I am becoming" (Exodus 3:14).[130] His articulation of the dynamic unfolding of the One echoes Green's: "Oneness is itself the expression of emergent, dynamic monism—contemplated and expressed through embodied metaphor. . . . [The] universe [is] growing toward greater complexity, experience, and awareness."[131] Green understands the four-letter name of God as "a verb ['to be'] that has been artificially arrested in motion and made to function as a noun."[132] Artson captured that sentiment when he writes that being is only a logical abstraction, but becoming is real.[133] In my own words, the tetragrammaton can be understood, then, as the jussive (the invitational or persuasive mood) of the verb *to be*: let being become.[134]

With Artson's addendum on relationships and emergence, our survey of Jewish theology concludes. To be sure, there are other voices that could have been featured in this chapter, particularly from the academic

---

truly is." *God of Becoming and Relationship: The Dynamic Nature of Process Theology* (Woodstock: Jewish Lights Publishing, 2013), xiv.

129 Bradely Shavit Artson, *Renewing the Process of Creation: A Jewish Integration of Science and Spirit* (Woodstock: Jewish Lights Publishing, 2016), 34. See also Green, *Ehyeh*, 1–3.

130 Artson, *God of Becoming*, 131.

131 Artson, *Renewing the Process of Creation*, 41.

132 Green, *Seek My Face*, 16.

133 Artson, *God of Becoming*, xiv.

134 The Y of YHWH can signify the jussive, as in Genesis 1, while HWH is the root of *being*. See Cherry, *Torah through Time*, 41. See also Ariel Evan Mayse, who cites a similar understanding expressed by the Hasidic master Rabbi Yitzhak Ayzik Yehudah Yehiel Safrin of Komarno (1806–1874.) Safrin understands the tetragrammaton as a *hiphil* or causative tense of the verb "to be." Mayse, "Setting the Table Anew: Law and Spirit in a Nineteenth-Century Hasidic Code," *The Journal of Jewish Thought and Philosophy* 27, no. 2 (2019): 233.

world. But they have made their decision to comment and coach from the sidelines of Jewish life, even if they occasionally enter the fray. Green likes to paraphrase Rabbi Ezra of Gerona: many in the academy have separated the Tree of Knowledge from the Tree of Life.

Intimations and adumbrations of a coherent, contemporary theology certainly predate the Shoah, but Auschwitz has become our meridian. Traditional notions of the omni-God that may have survived World War I were incinerated with so much else in the Shoah. Theodicy is no longer a question—divine *omni*potence is obscene. Our question is anthropodicy. Given that our faith in humanity's inherent goodness was unfounded, how do we best instill conditions to minimize the chance of a relapse? As for *omni*science, Gersonides was correct—God doesn't know the future until we make it. And even then, we need to footnote what we mean by God knowing anything.

The thinkers in this chapter no longer believe that Moshe acted as a stenographer at Sinai. It's all metaphor.[135] Chosenness has been dismissed or democratized into "distinctness."[136] Yet, incredibly, the covenant survives. Indeed, with the greater participation of women, our covenant has expanded and strengthened. According to Rav Kook, whatever increases in inclusivity enjoys a corresponding increase in holiness.[137]

RaMBaM had predicated the love of God on the knowledge of God primarily through the study of science and philosophy. How wonderful to be part of a tradition that understands that studying our world is a *religious* obligation! Heschel, then, reversed the RaMBaM's causal sequence. For Heschel, we need to love God in order to know God; and loving God requires a leap of action.[138] Although Judaism unabashedly demands compassionate deeds from its covenantal members, loving God entails an intimacy beyond morality. Devotion to the divine invokes a faithfulness usually reserved exclusively for lovers. Our impoverished language offers no better word to describe this devotional posture than *love*.

---

135 Maimonides, M. T., Foundations of the Torah 1:9.
136 Plaskow, *Standing Again at Sinai*, 105.
137 Tamar Ross, "Feminist Aspects in the Theology of Rav Kook," in *Derekh Ha-Ruach: A Volume Honoring Eliezer Schweid*, ed. Aviezer Ravitsky and Yehoyada Amir (Jerusalem: Hebrew University Press, 2005), 732–33.
138 Heschel, *God in Search of Man*, 281–83.

The theologies in this chapter comprise a mystical and philosophical tapestry whose threads spool from the Torah. Divine presence is the goal of the priestly Torah. God responds to our deeds, and we strive to keep God in our midst. When sacrifices are offered, God savors the scent. For the medieval mystics, mitzvot do not keep God near, they maintain God's unity. They bind the fractured Godhead. The Hasidic tradition understands that what is fractured is not God but our perception of God. When *tzimtzum* is understood psychologically, our essential obligation is to shift our consciousness to perceive and respond to the divine that shimmers within and around us. Through spiritual discipline and devotion, we have the capacity to arouse our awareness to God's presence in ourselves, in others, and in all that exists. Rav Kook links this awareness to the process of teshuvah, and piety is the single greatest factor in teshuvah. "Ethics is the corridor which leads to holiness."[139] Heschel closes the priestly circuit with the following piece of demythologization: God does not *respond to* our deeds; God is *revealed through* our deeds.

The threads from the Mosaic Torah will be more apparent in book 3. But the love that erupts in the Mosaic Torah overflows and saturates every subsequent expression of Judaism. Justice is a straight line; ethics bend; but, love leaps. *Hesed*/lovingkindness takes you beyond yourself, the leap into self-transcendence, and there's the potential to experience discontinuity from our normal state of consciousness. HaBaD theology and Rav Kook spoke of leaps within different levels of reality including *creatio ex nihilo* and revelation.[140] In our next book on theologies of creation, Rav Kook's teaching on leaps will apply to emergence and speciation. Not only will revelation recapitulate creation, but creation will be understood as divine self-revelation.

In concluding our survey of Jewish theology, my astonishment has not diminished. After so many years of rejecting everything priestly, I find myself in fundamental agreement with a demythologized priestly theology. The relationship between our deeds and our perception of God's presence is not a function of divine reward or punishment; the

---

139 Kook, *Lights of Holiness* 3:14.
140 Elliot R. Wolfson, "Achronic Time, Messianic Expectation, and the Secret of the Leap in Habad," in *Habad Hasidism: History, Thought, Image*, ed. Jonatan Meir and Gadi Sagiv (Jerusalem: Zalman Shazar Center, 2016): 45–86, esp. 53–55 and Ross, "Rav Kook's Concept of Divinity," *Da'at* 9 (1982): 43, 59–60.

relationship is organic. It's natural—Mordecai Kaplan might call it trans-natural. The relationship affirms Melissa Raphael's point: the question is not *where* was God, but *who* was God. More precisely, the question is not where is God, but who is making godliness perceptible in the world through their intentional deeds?

The destruction of the Temple, which precluded animal sacrifices by hereditary priests, cleared the path for rabbinic religiosity to preserve priestly theology while endorsing the Mosaic Torah's emphasis on prayer, deeds of lovingkindness, teshuvah, and Torah study as sacraments accessible to all. Each of us has the awe-inspiring power to make godliness perceptible through our faithful embodiment of Torah.

יגדיל תורה ויאדיר

Book Two: Jewish Theologies of Creation

Preface to Book Two

An argument could be made that *Coherent Judaism* should have begun with this book on theologies of creation. Indeed, much of the first book *did* discuss creation, especially the final chapters. Jewish theologies articulate our understanding of God and our relationship to God. Our relationship to God may or may not involve God's relationship to us. For RaMBaM, whose God is wholly other, the relationship is one-sided. But for the majority of Jewish theologies, God is in relationship, in a reciprocal covenant, with the Jewish people. And since the Jewish people are part of creation, in our discussion above about theology, creation was a necessary component.

This book is not about God's relationship to the Jews, in particular, but to creation as a whole. A theology of creation is similar to natural theology in subject matter, but the starting points are opposite. One of our Jewish Arab thinkers from the Middle Ages, Bahya ibn Pakuda, was the first Jew to develop the argument from design. There are harbingers of the argument from design in both biblical and rabbinic texts, but Bahya offers an extended metaphor. In English, we are familiar with William Paley (1743–1805), an Englishman during the Industrial Revolution, who stumbles upon a watch while walking on a heath. Bahya gives us a more Jewish simile:

> Everybody knows that things devoid of purposeful intention, even in their smallest parts, can show absolutely no sign of wisdom. Were a man

to spill some ink on a sheet of paper by accident, could it form itself into a book with readable lines and a well-arranged plan, like a book written with a pen?[1]

Natural theology relies on arguments from the structure and design of the world. The world is far more sophisticated than any book, so there must be an author. The world is far more intricate than any watch, so the world must have a designer. Natural theology begins with observations about the world and then reasons to a divine being. A theology of creation, on the other hand, begins with theology and then observes the world to seek evidence of the divine. We began with theology in the first book to best understand how a coherent Judaism might express a theology of creation. Already in the eighteenth century, philosophers like David Hume (1711–1776) and Immanuel Kant (1724–1804) had undermined the utility of natural theology for traditional religion. Hume, for example, pointed out that not only can't you infer a single god from the cornucopia of creation, neither can you infer a good god. The Gnostics would agree.

Our first chapter in this book will reference ideologies like Gnosticism, a general term to describe the dualistic belief in autonomous, opposing forces in the world. Monotheism emerged as a foil to such ideologies. Although Genesis 1 will occupy much of our attention, other creation narratives will be excavated, if not always rehabilitated. Unlike biblical theologians, I do not privilege the biblical text as a matter of principle. There is much wisdom to be gleaned from our oldest texts, but I am equally interested in how those texts have been reinterpreted and deployed throughout Jewish history. My goal is theological appropriation for a contemporary and coherent Judaism, not biblical fidelity.

The next chapter will focus on the Middle Ages, specifically comparing the philosophical and mystical worldviews. The third chapter examines Jewish reactions to Charles Darwin's *On the Origin of Species*, published in 1859. Darwin challenged natural theology and the argument from design in ways far more devastating than had Hume and Kant. But throughout the nineteenth century, most religious respondents to Darwinism focused not on the *mechanism* of evolution, natural

---

1   Bahya, *Duties of the Heart*, 121. A version of this argument can be traced back to Cicero in 45 BCE.

selection, but on the *premise* of the transmutation of species over deep time. Thus, the initial challenges from Darwinism tended to be textual by virtue of evolution's contradictions with the plain sense of Genesis One. Given Judaism's traditional rejection of biblical literalism, there is no theological novelty in early responses to biological evolution. More interesting is the reframing of evolution as evidence *for* Judaism.

The final chapter in this section turns, again, to Jewish theologies in the shadow of the Shoah. By chance (?), Darwin's mechanism of natural selection is rehabilitated in the years just before and during World War II. In traditional terms, what Darwin and the Shoah challenged was teleology and divine providence. One Jewish philosopher, Hans Jonas, came to understand that traditional Jewish theologies can address the challenges of both. That explains why there was so little theological novelty in Jewish responses to Darwinism. It also explains what is radically innovative: Christian theologians embracing elements of Jewish theology.

Just as the third chapter addresses Darwinism, the fourth chapter in this section responds to the Neo-Darwinian Synthesis and subsequent scientific theories. RaMBaM premised his argument for God's existence in the Mishneh Torah on Aristotle's notion of the eternity of the world. He later claimed he didn't really believe Aristotle, but he wanted to use the more difficult premise to argue his case. It turns out there were two problems with that approach. The first is that not everyone believed RaMBaM; the second is that, since the acceptance of the Big Bang, even fewer believe Aristotle.

Unlike RaMBaM in his day, I am not an expert in contemporary science. Although a dilettante, I am no charlatan. I admit my scientific ignorance. When I cite scientists in the fourth chapter, I acknowledge in advance that there are opposing views, particularly on the issue of speciation. I am citing well regarded scientists whose theories are more compatible to my theology. Like RaMBaM, I *could* make my argument based on a more difficult theory. I am not doing so for several reasons, the most important among them is that I am a writing as a theologian and not as a philosopher. My faith transcends the evidence. Just as Darwin expected that further discoveries in the fossil record would corroborate his theory, I expect that further advances in science will make theologies of creation more robust.

In recognition that chapters in this book might be read independently of those in the first book, I have repeated myself a bit. I included just enough background to be intelligible to those who did not read the first book. I do, however, recommend reading at least the chronologically corresponding chapter from the previous book to provide the best context. Given the focus on creation in this section, my frames and critiques have shifted accordingly. My hope is that by using different language in a different context, even those who have read the first section will be rewarded. As the Talmud says, "There is no comparison between what one understands after reviewing material 100 times and one's understanding after the 101st time."[2]

---

2 Hagiga 9b.

Chapter 7

A Rabbinic Theology of Creation: Biblical Visions and Rabbinic Revisions

The beginning was not smooth; poetic, but not smooth. *B'reishit bara*—those two initial b's in phonetics are called *plosives*, which is short for explosives. Literally and literarily, the first two words of Genesis are the Bible's Big Bang.

Without going into grammatical niceties, these words really don't belong together, at least not as traditionally vowelized. (Remember, there are no vowels in the Torah.) They are seemingly incompatible, yet there they are. As Tikva Frymer-Kensky has remarked: "The ambiguity of the phrase must be intentional. . . . An intentionally ambiguous phrase mirrors the mystery of creation."[1] That makes two things that Genesis 1 does not teach: grammar and science.

Scholars, both traditional and modern, have come to something of a consensus that however one translates the opening line of Genesis, the King James Bible (also know as the King James Version or the Authorized Version) got it wrong. In the beginning, God did not create the heaven and the earth. Neither historical parallels nor grammar support such a reading, even though that is exactly how the Greek Septuagint, the Vulgate, and the King James Bible have it.

---

1   Frymer-Kensky, *Studies in Bible and Feminist Criticism*, 373.

If those translations had it right, when God began creating the heavens and the earth, there would have been nothing on stage, not even the stage. But, if the rabbis and most contemporary Bible scholars are correct, *when* God begins creating the heavens and the earth in Genesis 1, not only is there a stage, but there's furniture on the stage: darkness on the face of the abyss and God's spirit/wind hovering over the face of the water. What that means theologically, is that one cannot rely on Genesis 1 alone to demonstrate (textually) that God is the exclusive Creator of all that exists. Jon Levenson writes that Genesis 1 is not about *creatio ex nihilo*, creation out of nothing, but "creation without opposition."[2] God bursts on to the stage of creation and orders the chaos into a cosmos.

Creatio ex nihilo is certainly part of later Jewish tradition, but the Torah itself was not interested in the origins of matter. In none of the biblical creation narratives do we sense such a concern. To phrase it differently, and more broadly, the Torah is not interested in what we now call science or natural history. The Israelites had a cosmology, a vision of their world that they shared with other cultures in the ancient Near East. They believed there were upper waters, which is where rain comes from, and lower waters, the oceans, separated by a heavenly expanse. The common cosmology amongst cultures in the ancient Near East was scientifically inaccurate—but that is not what is at stake in Genesis 1. The fact that Genesis *accepts* the common cosmology is the best evidence that cosmology is not the issue. In this age of benighted biblical fundamentalism, I want to reiterate the point: Genesis 1's agenda is not arguing for bad science because it is not arguing for any science.

Genesis 1 is interested in how we relate to God and God's other creations. It is about theology and religion. A key component of the Torah's concern for our relationship to God is promoting our exclusive fidelity. So, when Genesis 1 has God creating light on day one, while the sun awaits its appearance until day four, the ancient Israelites are meant to understand two things. First of all, our God is super-duper powerful and can create light without what we all know to be the source of light, the sun. And, more importantly, the sun is no god—it doesn't even have a name. Elohim, the creator God of Genesis 1, eclipses the sun god of

---

2   Levenson, *Creation and the Persistence of Evil*, 122.

ancient Babylonia and Egypt.[3] What the Torah is concerned about is idolatry.

As we saw in our discussion of Heschel and the prophets, idolatry is not "merely" a metaphysical error. Often, pagan rites included cultic prostitution and human sacrifice. Together, these comprise the three cardinal sins that appeared frequently in our first chapter on priestly religion. Thus, it should come as no surprise that the priestly creation story should feature a polemic against paganism. Were we to focus exclusively on the polemics of Genesis 1, however, we would miss its theology of creation.

Yet some modern scholars of the Hebrew Bible emphasize that the creation story is not even concerned with creation, per se. "In the ancient Near East, creation faith did not deal only, indeed not even primarily, with the origin of the world. Rather, it was concerned above all with the present world and the natural environment of humanity now. . . . In short, ancient Near Eastern cosmic, political, and social order find their unity under the concept of 'creation.'"[4] David Wright sums it up as follows: "[The priestly] portrayal of division at creation structurally anticipates the intellectual shape of its legal system."[5] Yes, Genesis 1 is coherent with the rest of the priestly Torah, but it also has something to say about creation itself.

Far more than other theologians of whom I am aware, Catherine Keller has developed a "theology of becoming" using the first two verses of Genesis 1. In her discussion of *tohu va'vohu*, the Torah's term for earth prior to God's creative activity, Keller comments: "*Tohu va'vohu* remains

---

3   The Sun God of Babylonia was *Shamash*. Jacob Milgrom points out that Genesis 1 avoids using the Hebrew word for sun, *shemesh*, to preclude any possible misidentifications between the sun, one of God's creations, *shemesh*, and the Sun God of Babylonia, *Shamash*. Jacob Milgrom, "The Alleged 'Hidden Light,'" in *The Idea of Biblical Interpretation: Essays in Honor of James L. Kugel*, ed. Hindy Najman and Judith H. Newman (Leiden: Brill, 2004), 42.

4   H. H. Schmid, "Creation, Righteousness and Salvation as Essential Aspects of Old Testament Theology," in *Creation in the Old Testament*, ed. Bernhard W. Anderson (Minneapolis: Fortress Press, 1985), 103 and 105.

5   David P. Wright, "Law and Creation in the Priestly-Holiness Writings of the Pentateuch," in *Writing a Commentary on Leviticus. Forschungen zur Religion und Literatur des Alten und Neuen Testaments 276*, ed. Christian Eberhart and Thomas Hieke (Göttingen: Vandenhoeck & Ruprecht, 2019), 89.

an indefinable singularity, invented for the sake of its alliteration."[6] In our earlier discussion of the priestly Torah, I, too, emphasized the expression's poetic qualities which include rhyme. *Higgledy-piggledy* and *hodgepodge* are translations of *tohu va'vohu* that seize on the rhyme. Those words, too, were invented for effect, like *super-duper*. While the second noun in our *tohu va'vohu* pair does seem to have been custom made for our verse, *tohu* appears throughout the Hebrew Bible. Its meaning, however, is as fluid as the deep (verse 2). Sometimes it seems to mean chaos, and sometimes it seems to mean a wasteland. Green's translation, *chaos and confusion*, turns *tohu vavohu* into poetic synonyms. Fox's *wild and waste* preserves both the poetry and the ambiguity.[7] *Chaos, confusion*, and *wild* describe multiple objects; but *waste*, in the sense of wasteland, conjures the image of unending desert dunes. No chaos, just monotony.

The grammatical conjunction that links our two nouns is distinctive. You wouldn't translate it as *and* as much as *'n*. It links words that are frequently paired like *peanut butter 'n jelly*. Sometime the pairs are synonyms, like grace *'n* mercy (*hen va'hesed*). But other times they are in opposition, like day *'n* night (*yom va'layla*) and good *'n* bad (*tov va'ra*.) Both King James and the New Jewish Publication Society offer translations of *tohu va'vohu* that emphasize opposition (and eliminate the poetry): "unformed and void." Unformed, by definition, refers to matter. Void, by definition, refers to an absence of matter. Well, which is it?

It may well be that our author had only one meaning in mind. Or, he may have intentionally played a term with poetic ambiguity. Then, he rhymed it with an artificially manufactured plosive (*bohu*) which becomes defused after the conjunction (*va*), muffling its explosivity but increasing its alliteration (*va'vohu*). The resulting phrase intensifies the initial indeterminacy of *tohu* and leads to the possibility that the rhymes are an oxymoron—unformed and void! We began our discussion suggesting that the first two words of Genesis, *bereshit bara*, are grammatically incompatible. I am now suggesting that the condition of the world prior to creation may have been a paradox: an incompatible couple,

---

6   Keller, *Face of the Deep*, 183.
7   S. Y. Agnon, "On One Stone," trans. Arthur Green in S. Y. Agnon, *A Book that Was Lost* (New York: Schocken Books, 1995), 136 and Everett Fox, *The Five Books of Moses* (New York: Schocken Books, 1997), 13.

bound to one another's opposing polarities in a swirling dance, awaiting divine impetus to break through the inertia of eternity.

A grammatical irregularity followed by a state of indeterminacy. What's next? Darkness. The word, however, is easier to translate than to understand. What is darkness? Is darkness the absence of light? Or, does darkness overwhelm and subsume light, preventing it from shining? In Yiddish, such a query might be called a *klutz kasheh*, a fruitless question. But, in our case, not only do we have evidence, though admittedly inconclusive, but if we embrace the evidence, it provides an interpretive key to the first day.

In the Torah, there is another word that looks identical to the word for darkness, but is pronounced *chasakh* rather than *choshekh*. *Chasakh* means to withhold, to hold back. If that literary or linguistic connection holds, the priestly mind understands darkness as holding back light. So when God says (to the darkness? from within the darkness?), "Let there be light" or "Let light be" in verse 3, rather than creating light *ex nihilo*, God's words serve as a catalyst. "Let light be" activates, energizes, and illuminates the embedded, but eclipsed, light from the darkness that is holding it back. Imagine a pitch-black night sky. God's words bring out the stars, they do not create them. The very next thing God does is to separate the newly visible light from within the darkness.

Before we call it a day, however, let us reexamine the primordial state. It is called *tohu va-vohu*, but it is described with the following two clauses: darkness on the face of the abyss (*tehom*) and the wind/spirit of God (*ruach Elohim*) hovering/fluttering on the face of the water.[8] I do not know if *abyss* and *the water* are referring to the same object. What I do sense are two faces. When confronted with darkness, the face is an abyss. When confronted with something divine, the face is water. The abyss, *tehom* in Hebrew, is not negative, although its depths are imponderable. The *tehom* is actually a source of blessing (Genesis 49:25). This is the chaos from which order emerges.

I am also unsure how to translate *ruach Elohim*. Is it a wind that God causes to blow, or is it part of God's own self? Allow me to offer this similarly ambiguous translation: the divine was fluttering on the face of

---

8 Alternatively, *tohu va'vohu* might not be the name of the primordial state: it might be part of the description.

the waters. But the conjunction is disjunctive: the earth was *tohu va'vohu*: darkness on the face of the abyss, *but* the divine was fluttering on the face of the waters. There's a face off. The darkness and the divine, the abyss and the waters. Creation may have been without opposition, as Levenson noted, but until God said the word, there was tension everywhere we look: grammatically, conceptually, linguistically, and facially.

To the degree that I have succeeded in describing the myth of the priestly precreation and the first moment of what Catherine Keller calls the "Big Birth," what might be its salvage value?[9] *Bereshit bara* and *tohu va'vohu* just shouldn't be. They defy the laws of logic and language as we know them. Keller said it, creation is a singularity. If the medium is the message, then creation is highly improbable. Stephen Jay Gould, even without the benefit of knowing the original language of the Hebrew Bible, described the pageant of evolution as "staggeringly improbable."[10]

Scholars have long drawn comparisons between the creation in Genesis 1 and the story of creation in one of Plato's dialogues, *The Timaeus*. In both texts, the creator uses preexistent material to order the chaos into a cosmos. In my translation of Genesis 1:2, however, there is something of the divine already in relationship with the primordial elements before the ordering process beings. Such a relationship does not exist in *The Timaeus*. In Genesis 1, God is there even before the beginning with which we begin. *And the spirit of God is fluttering*. The next occurrence of the term *flutter* in the Torah is part of a metaphor describing God as an eagle fluttering or hovering over its chicks, Israel, to protect them (Deuteronomy 32:11). This image of fluttering is frequently explained as "touching and/but not touching." Recall from the priestly worldview, worldview, that anything which touches something holy becomes holy itself. The priestly authors want their readers to understand that when God's spirit flutters, the face of the abyss lifts to become the face of the waters, and all that had been described as *tohu va'vohu* becomes divinely charged. In some intimate fashion, we now face the divine everywhere we look, even in the mirror. Perhaps that helps explain why the humans of Genesis 1 were meant to be vegans (Genesis 1:29). There is something heartless about slaughtering an animal whose face reflects the divine.

---

9   Keller, *Face of the Deep*, xv.
10   Steven Jay Gould, *Wonderful Life: The Burgess Shale and the Nature of History* (New York: W. W. Norton & Company, 1990), 14.

The next messages of Genesis 1 are that entropy is, indeed, the default, and organization takes energy and intention. More than that, light and darkness are not absolutes. There was no fall from perfection in Genesis 1. The world was already all mixed up before God began teasing the elements apart. If I phrase this just a bit differently, it will anticipate a much later version of creation. In Genesis 1, in order to separate light and darkness, God activated the light from within the primordial darkness. In Lurianic Kabbalah, light and darkness are understood metaphysically, and creation begins by purging the roots of judgment that become the source of evil (to which darkness is symbolically parallel). In Genesis, the preexisting light is imperceptible until God speaks; in Luria, the pre-existent roots of judgement are imperceptible until they are exiled and isolated. In both cases we have a mix of light and darkness.

It is tempting to say that the separation motif of Genesis 1 is the first installment of creation which awaits its second installment with Luria. Luria's overarching goal of unification heals the world of separation and division. As a contemporary bible scholar notes, "In the liturgy of creation *division does not mean estrangement.*"[11] Separation is a method, not a value.

"Let light be." *Y'hi or.* That is an invitation, not a command.[12] The grammar of Genesis 1 avoids imperatives. Throughout that chapter, God doesn't just invite, God empowers.

> We encounter in the classical creation texts *a rich description of the creature engaged in the activity of separating, ruling, producing, developing, and reproducing itself.* Not only God separates, but also the creature—including the firmament of the heavens, the gathering water, and the stars—assumes functions of separation (Gen. 1:6, 9, 18). Not only God rules, but also the creature—for example the stars—rules by the establishment of rhythm, differentiation, and the gift of measure and order (Gen. 1:14ff.). Not only God brings forth, but also the creature brings forth creature: animals of all species and plants in an abundance of species (Gen. 1:12, but also 11, 20,

---

11 Balentine, *The Torah's Vision of Worship*, 87. His italics.
12 William P. Brown, "Divine Act and the Art of Persuasion in Genesis 1," in *History and Interpretation*, ed. M. W. Brown et al. (Sheffield: Sheffield Academic Press, 1993), 19-32.

and 24!) And the creature develops and reproduces itself, as is recorded explicitly and in detail with regard to plants, animals, and human beings.

Repeatedly the creature's own differentiated activity is practically set parallel with God's creative action, without ceasing to be the creature's own activity. . . . The creature's own activity as a constitutive element in the process of creation is seen in harmony with God's action.[13]

As strong a case as Michael Welker makes above for co-creation, it is not strong enough. If we look closely at God's activity, his contributions become increasingly modest. On day two, God makes the heavenly dome which separates the upper waters from the lower waters. But the heavenly dome is not exactly a thing. It is an empty space between things. And there must have been some space above the primordial waters which allowed room for the divine to flutter. In other words, what God did was to stretch out what was already present when the curtain of creation lifted. Indeed, we have an example of this word used in its verbal form for precisely this action: stretching out the heavens (Job 37:18).

What is more interesting about making the heavenly dome is that the making (verse 7) is preceded by speech (verse 6). That means God's speech, at least in this case, is not effective by itself, unlike with the emergence of light (verse 3). So, on the third day when God says, "Let the waters beneath the heavens be gathered into one place and let dry land appear," there is no necessary reason to think that God's word itself effected the separation; perhaps, God's word invited or empowered the waters to separate themselves. Although Welker emphasizes the agency among creation, he also claims that God brings forth and rules. In terms of vocabulary, God does neither in Genesis. The entire narrative of Genesis 1 has God and creation, together, bringing forth order out of chaos. As for ruling, God delegates that duty to His final creation: humanity.

There is one activity that God does which is reserved for God alone—*bara*, create.[14] In the first chapter we discussed that this verb bears the sense of branching off or dividing. After the first instance of *bara* in the first verse, the verb appears only two other times in the creation

---

13 Michael Welker, *Creation and Reality* (Minneapolis: Fortress Press, 2000), 11 and 13. His italics.

14 In Genesis 1, only God bestows names. That exclusive divine prerogative of Genesis 1 is shared with humanity only in the Garden of Eden.

narrative—the creation of animals and the creation of humans (verses 21 and 27). Although God is active throughout Genesis 1, there are only three points at which God does something that only God can do: to begin the process of creation, to create animal life, and to create humanity. Perhaps it would not be too leading to translate *bara* as emerge, and the three uses of the predicate are the three fundamental instances of emergence: existence, animal life, and human consciousness.

What is of particular theological interest is the degree of interdependence. God's speech act in verse 20 establishes the possibility that the waters will swarm with living swarms and that winged ones will wing over the earth. But, unlike other speech acts, the text does not then say, "It was so." Not until the next verse does God *create* those things (and more). It is as if the water and sky creatures only exist *en potencia* until God vivifies them. But that potential originates within the primordial water which God did not create. What was God's contribution to life in this priestly cosmogony? God called forth creation by causing the building blocks of life to coalesce from the primordial elements. Let me be clear, I have no desire to shoehorn contemporary accounts of creation into Genesis 1. I have mocked such silliness.[15] Nevertheless, as I read the creation narrative of Genesis 1, I see the primordial elements being organized and activated to bring forth animal life by God.

On the sixth day, the interdependence between the elements and God rises to a new level. God still creates that which is invited to be made in the previous verse, namely humanity, but this time God invites collaboration even in the making. "Let us make humanity in our image after our likeness" (verse 26). In my book *Torah through Time* I run through the possibilities that rabbinic sages have proposed over the centuries to account for the plural.[16] To whom is God speaking? One reasonable guess is that God is speaking with other heavenly beings, be they lesser gods (Psalm 82) or angels (1 Kings 22:19–22), who have been edited out of the text to preserve its monotheistic purity. Given the interdependence noted with the emergence of the animals, it is also reasonable to imagine

---

15 Shai Cherry, "Crisis Management via Biblical Interpretation: Fundamentalism, Modern Orthodoxy, and Genesis," in *Jewish Tradition and the Challenge of Darwinism*, ed. Geoffrey Cantor and Marc Swetlitz (Chicago: University of Chicago Press, 2006), 166-87.

16 Cherry, *Torah through Time*, chapter two.

that God is speaking to what has emerged heretofore, namely, the *multiple* creations of the earth and the seas. Previous divine utterances were directed only to a single address, the waters or the land. Given the nature of biblical literature, the intensification of the interdependence of the fifth day may be exactly what we see on the sixth day.[17]

We are created in God's image, and we are to rule the other creations in the world. We rule, not God. Yet, the language of ruling in Genesis 1 that we are to exercise over the fish, birds, and land animals, is one of benevolent stewardship (Genesis 1:28). That is how Jewish tradition has always understood the charge, and it is consonant with the Torah's very next verse that we are not to exercise our dominion over animals by consuming them. Reading just a bit ahead into Genesis Two, we are expected to preserve the garden (Genesis 2:15). If we are to rule like God, then we, too, must extend our concern to "earlier" life forms and their domains. We will return to ecology in the next book, but it is clear from both creation stories of Genesis that God's very first charge to humanity involves caring for all of creation.

The creation narrative of Genesis 1 pauses on Shabbat (Genesis 2:2). But just as the narrative began with creative tension, so, too, does it conclude. The following verse, which according to some scholars closes the narrative, seems to have an extra verb appended to the very end. Richard Elliott Friedman preserves the awkwardness. "And God blessed the seventh day and made it holy because He ceased in it from doing all His work, which God had created."[18] That last clause seems as useless as the human appendix. Here is my translation: God blessed the seventh day and sanctified it, for on that day God ceased from all His work that God had created [for humans] to do. An elegant sentence, in any translation, it is not. But there is another anomaly on the seventh day that could support the clumsiness. Unlike every other day of the week, the seventh day has no coda: there was neither evening nor morning on the seventh day. By omission, by ceasing, it is as if God's cessation on the seventh day has no closure, which leaves all of creation's work undone

---

17   James L. Kugel notes this phenomenon of intensification in biblical poetry. See *The Idea of Biblical Poetry: Parallelism and Its History* (Baltimore: The Johns Hopkins University Press, 1981), chapter one.

18   Richard Elliott Friedman, *Commentary on the Torah* (New York: HarperOne, 2003), 15.

and awaiting us after Shabbat.[19] As a contemporary bible scholar suggests, "This taxonomic approach builds a creation model that highlights and then de-centers the one God, as the human being's relation to this environment mirrors God's relation to it. One salient feature of the role of human being in this environment is a further distancing of the deity from the field of action. . . . The fields of the earth are for human action, not so much for the divine."[20]

For readers familiar with classical Jewish literature, my comments on Genesis 1 may seem suspiciously familiar. Specifically, my claim that God was collaborating with the works of heaven and earth in the creation of humanity appears in a less robust form in Genesis Rabbah (8:3). Similarly, my understanding of creation's conclusion with the seemingly superfluous verb also has antecedents in medieval commentary and is explicitly found in a sixteenth-century biblical commentary by Moshe Alsheikh. I believe that these earlier sources got it basically right but without justifying their interpretations. My appreciation for their literary sensitivity has grown as I have matured as a reader. When I first read the Genesis Rabbah comment that the plural in "Let us make humanity" was directed at the earlier elements of creation, I smiled at the thought of the cartoon version of God's voice booming from the sky and the animated heavens and earth singing their assent. But, as has happened repeatedly, what I initially took as whimsy has subsequently generated wonder.

There is an eerie degree of consonance between Genesis 1 and the contemporary understanding of reality. Although I am intrigued by the blessings of the *tehom* (abyss), I hesitate naming chaos theory as that which lurks under its surface. I side with RaMBaM in describing the attempt to determine one-to-one correspondences from the symbols of religious literature a "prolonged madness."[21] Such psychosis is prevalent both among some Orthodox Jews and Protestant biblical literalists. The Big Bang, dark matter, chaos theory, and biological evolution are not cryptically encoded in the text of Genesis 1. Nevertheless, someone like the contemporary Bible scholar William Brown rightly refuses to abandon

19 Levenson, *Creation and the Persistence of Evil*, 109.
20 Kurt Anders Richardson, "Created Agencies of Creation in Genesis 1," in *Creation Stories in Dialogue: The Bible, Science, and Folk Traditions*, ed. R. Alan Culpepper (Leiden: Brill, 2015), 134.
21 *Guide*, 3:26.

the treasures of Genesis just because the text has been kidnapped by fearful fundamentalists who know their worldview is under siege:

> The ancient sages of Scripture, of course, had no inkling of such cosmic and biological agedness [13.7 and roughly 3 billion years, respectively]. But what they share with modern science is a fundamental awareness that the universe took time to develop to what it is now, that it began with an initial defining event characterized by a cosmic effusion of light, the emergence of time, the structuring of space, and eventually the formation of life.[22]

More than what Brown has noted, the collaboration on the sixth day between God and the animal kingdom to create humankind is downright prescient. Psalm 8 places humans a little lower than the angels. I would expect as much from an anthropocentric text. But Genesis 1 links humans to the rest of the animal world. We don't even get our own day! What becomes reaffirmed in Genesis 2 is that humans and animals are made from the same stuff (Genesis 2:7 and 19). In Genesis 1, the animals which preceded us on the earth contribute to our making (Genesis 1:26); in Genesis 2, the earth is our mother before Eve claims the title.

The seven-day creation narrative establishes a priestly heptagon that serves as the pattern for future divine activity. The Jerusalem Temple, the divine domicile, is also associated with seven. King Solomon dedicates the Temple during the seven-day holiday of Sukkot in the seventh calendar month (1 Kings 8). The Temple's literary prototype, the Tabernacle, contains linguistic echoes of the creation narrative. The architect, Betzalel, has even been graced with *ruach Elohim*, the spirit of God that had earlier hovered over the face of the waters (Exodus 31:3 and Genesis 1:2). Jon Levenson, in concluding his presentation of the parallels between creation and the tabernacle/temple, observes: "The Temple was conceived as a microcosm, a miniature world. But it is equally the case that in Israel . . . the world . . . was conceived, at least in priestly circles, as a macro-temple, the palace of God in which all are obedient to his commands."[23]

---

22 William P. Brown, *The Seven Pillars of Creation: The Bible, Science, and the Ecology of Wonder* (Oxford: Oxford University Press, 2010), 60
23 Levenson, *Creation and the Persistence of Evil*, 86.

As we saw in the previous book, the priestly theology is one of homologies. So, the parallels between creation and revelation in the Tabernacle/Temple, or between our earthly home and God's earthly home fit into that worldview. Once we have introduced creation and revelation, redemption cannot be far behind, conceptually if not chronologically. The archetypal story of redemption from the house of bondage in Egypt is celebrated annually during the seven-day holiday of Passover. At the decisive moment, when the Egyptian chariots are closing in on the Israelites, redemption recapitulates creation: the waters divide, and dry land appears.

A theology of creation, by definition, links creation and revelation. So, if the exodus from Egypt has literary ties to creation, one would expect the future redemption to tie together the creation and the Israelites worshipping God at their Temple in freedom. The prophet known as second Isaiah does not disappoint. His words unite the language and themes of creation, revelation, and redemption.

> For as the rain or snow drops from the heavens
> And returns not there,
> But saturates the land
> And causes her to bear and to sprout,
> Yielding seed for sowing and bread for eating,
> So is the word that exits from My mouth:
> It does not come back to Me empty,
> But does what I desire,
> Succeeds in what I sent it.
> For in joy, you shall exit [the Babylonian exile] and be led in safety.
> Before you, mount and hill shall shout aloud,
> And all of the trees of the field shall clap their hand....
> I will bring them to My sacred mount
> And let them rejoice in My house of prayer. (Isaiah 55:10–12 and 56:7)[24]

Encapsulated in just a few verses, Isaiah offers a theology of creation in which God's unity is refracted at different levels of divine activity. God's

---

24 Thomas M. Mann explores the connection between creation and redemption in "Stars, Sprouts, and Stream: The Creative Redeemer of Second Isaiah," in *God Who Creates: Essays in Honor of W. Sibley Towner*, ed. William P. Brown and S. D. McBride, Jr. (Grand Rapids: Eerdmans, 2000), 135-51.

word organizes the heavens and the earth to generate bread for our physical nourishment and food security; and God's word reveals His will to
generate our political and religious redemption.

There are other creation narratives in Hebrew Scriptures, but none is
as dominant within the Bible or as influential for subsequent Jewish literature as Genesis 1. Since this book is focused not on creation, *per se*, but on
theologies of creation, we will now leap over the rest of the Hebrew Bible
as well as the Pseudepigrapha's book of Jubilees found in the Catholic
Bible. The remainder of our chapter will explore rabbinic revisions of creation emerging primarily from Genesis Rabbah, a fifth-century aggadic
text from the Land of Israel, and the siddur, the prayer book which offers
us a rabbinic consensus on both theology and creation. The rabbinic theology of creation to emerge will owe its shape and unity, though not its
contents, to the priestly Torah's worldview which sees divine activity in
creation as homologous to divine activity in revelation.

Rabbinic Revisions of Creation

Although we are looking at later texts in the rabbinic period than we were
in Genesis 1, the setting of our first text is earlier. According to the rabbis, in the very beginning, God created the Torah. Not until 2000 years
later did God create the heavens and the earth through the agency of the
Torah.[25] In terms of a theology of creation, this image of the Torah as
an intermediary between God and creation *guarantees* that creation and
Torah will be in synch. One might be able to understand that the addressee
of God's speech in Genesis 1, for the rabbis, was the Torah. "Hey, Torah,"
says God, "light it up!" This midrash on the primordial Torah relies on
a verse from Proverbs (8:22) that personifies Wisdom, who is described
as having been made in *the beginning*. The rabbis identify Wisdom with
Torah, and they link *the beginning* to the very first word of Genesis 1.
Thus, they arrive at: in (or through) beginning (that is, Wisdom/Torah),
God created the heavens and the earth.

Philo of Alexandria (25 BCE–50 CE) had a similar understanding of
Genesis 1 based on his reading of the Greek Septuagint. For Philo, such a
reading parallels the classical notion of natural law.

---

25 Midrash Tehillim 90:12 and Genesis Rabbah 1:1.

As he [Philo] states in the account in the *Life of Moses*, the lawgiver wanted to demonstrate two essential doctrines, first that the Father and Maker of the cosmos ... [were] also its true lawgiver, and second that the person who observes the laws will live in accordance with the ordering of the universe, so that there will be a profound harmony between his words and his deeds.[26]

Natural law, like natural theology, starts with nature. Law and theology must conform to what we know about the ways things are in the world. But the rabbis began from the other side in their search for harmony. However God operates in creation must conform to how God operates in revelation. The Talmud contains scattered references to creation, but the first catalog of rabbinic ideas about creation is recorded in Genesis Rabbah. The text was compiled in the Land of Israel by the end of fifth century, though it likely contains earlier material. To describe the text as a *catalog* emphasizes the historical fact that not each and every rabbi agreed with each individual statement. Ultimately, we cannot know if what we are reading is something of a consensus or an outrageous howler by a lone wolf. If we are looking for something reliably representative of rabbinic thought, check the halakhah and the *siddur* (prayer book).

Fortunately, our first element of a rabbinic theology of creation offers evidence from both realms. In the Mishnah's discussion of blessings, the final chapter includes a list of experiences which demand that we recognize God's ongoing renewal of creation. Earthquakes and comets shock us precisely because they are so infrequently perceived. Yet, the same mishna has us recite a blessing for mountains, oceans, and deserts. Although the blessings are different, both use the same grammatical form to characterize God's relationship to creation regardless of whether the phenomenon in question is ephemeral or enduring, at least enduring from our vantage point.[27] In the gemara's discussion of these blessings, we encounter the blessing found on the cover of this book, what I call

---

26 David T. Runia, "Cosmos, Logos, and Nomos: the Alexandrian Jewish and Christian Appropriation of the Genesis Creation Account," in *Cosmologies et cosmogonies dans la littérature antique: Huit exposés suivis d'une discussion et d'un epilogue*, ed. Michael Erler, Therese Fuhrer, and Pascale Derron (Vandoeuvres-Geneva: Foundation Hardt, 2015), 185. Runia is citing Philo, *Life of Moses*, 2:48.

27 M. Brachot 9:2.

Darwin's blessing: Blessed are You who varies creatures.[28] The animal on the cover is a mandrill—and our gemara says to make the blessing when seeing a monkey.

It is, of course, true that the idea of ongoing creation, or what we will call continuous creation, has biblical precedent.[29] Yet, the creation story that enjoys pride of place is explicit: God ceases (Genesis 2:2). At least on the level of God's unique contribution to creation, expressed with *bara*, God stops. Nevertheless, rabbinic Judaism emphasizes that God's creation is continuous. By insisting we recite a blessing over both natural landscapes, ostensibly created long ago, and current experiences of God's power and creativity, the rabbis conflate the original act of creation with every act of nature.

> Creation, we are taught, is not an act that happened once upon a time, once and for ever. The act of bringing the world into existence is a continuous process. God called the world into being, and that call goes on. There is this present moment because God is present.[30]

Within the siddur, the notion of continuous creation becomes nothing less than doctrinal. In the morning prayer service, we rise as we say: "Blessed is He who *spoke* and the world came into being; Blessed is He. Blessed is He who maintains creation. Blessed is the One who *says* and does." My translation is pale; but the point I wish to emphasize is the transition from the past tense to the present. We see the doctrine explicitly later in the morning service when we recite, "In His goodness, He renews each and every day the act of creation." Lest we become jaded, within the Amidah, the central prayer service recited three times a day, every day, we acknowledge and thank God "for Your miracles that are with us every day." Creation, each and every day, is a miracle.

In the Torah, God stops. God stops creating, *and* God stops revealing. The Mosaic Torah could not be clearer: God spoke those words and no more (Deuteronomy 5:19). And, incidentally, do not add or subtract from what God said (Deuteronomy 13:1)! Richard Elliot Friedman wrote a book titled *The Disappearance of God* where he shows how God's

---

28 Brachot 58b and T. Brachot 6:3.
29 Abraham Joshua Heschel emphasizes this point. See *The Sabbath* (New York: Farrar, Straus and Giroux, 1951), 118n9.
30 Ibid., 100.

character disappears as one reads through the biblical narrative. But a strange thing happens on the way to the rabbis: God's voice returns. In an ancient Aramaic translation of the Torah, Onkelos (35–120) translates our verse that says God spoke those words "and no more" as God spoke those words "and did not stop." Midrashically, these polar opposite readings are obtained from the same letters with different vocalization.

Continuous revelation becomes parallel to continuous creation within our rabbinic theology of creation. The move that the rabbis make to achieve this consonance is to replace prophecy with the interpretation of Torah. "Rabbi Avdimi of Haifa said: Since the day when the Temple was destroyed, prophecy was taken from the prophets and given to the sages."[31] The primary mission of the sage was to search Torah. "Just as one finds new figs on a fig tree each time one searches, so too does one find new meanings in the Torah each time one searches."[32] Figs, as our rabbis knew, have not one, but two crops per year. Thus, they imagined that the figs are ever-ripening. Similarly, those called up to the Torah each Monday, Thursday, and Shabbat, conclude their blessing with, "Blessed are You, Adonai, who *gives* the Torah."[33]

Continuity manifests in worldly creation, in communal revelation, and in one's own personal religious journey. The rabbinic decision to canonize the Pentateuch, rather than the Hexateuch, guarantees that we, along with Moshe, will never quite reach the Promised Land. After Moshe's death, Joshua continued to write the Torah in the Land of Israel (Joshua 24:26). The rabbis resisted entry. Each year on Simchat Torah we rewind the Torah scroll just when Moshe is at the border, on the threshold of redemption. He can see it. And with the vision, comes his death (Deuteronomy 34:4–5). As voyeurs, we have no time to mourn Moshe. We see Moshe seeing the whole of the Land, and the very next Torah reading thrusts us back to the beginning as if to say, "Remember, it's not about the destination, but the journey. And the journey never ends."

---

31 Baba Batra 12a. See also Elliot N. Dorff and Arthur Rosett, *A Living Tree: The Roots and Growth of Jewish Law* (Albany: State University of New York Press, 1988), 188–93.
32 Eruvin 54 a/b.
33 The Hebrew is ambiguous. "Giver of the Torah" is an equally plausible translation.

The Seed Principle of Instantaneous Creation

Continuous creation and continuous revelation speak to the present moment. A second aspect of the rabbinic theology of creation deals with their historical emergence. Consider the following argument between two second-century sages living in the Land of Israel. Rabbi Yehuda makes the seemingly obvious claim that creation was sequential and discrete. God created new things on each day according to Genesis 1. Rabbi Nehemia leverages the seam stitched between our two creation narratives to arrive at a radically different understanding of creation. A literal-leaning translation reads like this: "These are the generations of the heavens and the earth when they were created; on the day that the Lord God made earth and heavens" (Genesis 2:4). Many scholars understand the first half of the verse as the coda of Genesis 1 in which God creates over seven days, while the second half of the verse is the introduction to the Garden of Eden narrative in which the Lord God *makes* but does not *create*. Rabbi Nehemia focuses on the time element of the second story, *on the day*, but applies it to the first creation story: the generations of the heavens and the earth were created, in potential, on the day. Rabbi Nehemia offers a now-familiar simile: "They were like pickers of figs, each one appeared in its own time," that is, when the figs would ripen.[34] Because there is an ambiguity about whether the fig pickers are appearing or the ripened figs are appearing, the midrash immediately continues: "Rabbi Berechia interpreted similarly to Rabbi Nehemia. 'The earth brought forth' something that had already been deposited within."

Both Aristotle and the Stoics expressed a similar idea before the rabbis. St. Augustine (354–430) then applied those early philosophical ideas to Genesis:

> In the seed then, there was invisibly present all that would develop in time into a tree. And in this same way we must picture the world, when God made all things together, as having had all things which were made in it and with it when day was made. This includes not only heaven with sun,

---

34 Genesis Rabbah 12:4.

moon and stars…but also the beings which water and earth produced in potencia and in their causes before they came forth in the course of time.[35]

Employing a similar seed principle, Rabbi Nehemia argues for instantaneous creation. There was an instantaneous singularity "in the beginning," and all subsequent creation is an unfolding or emergence of that initial sowing of divine creativity. For Rabbi Yehuda, what was created on day one and what was created on day four have no necessary connection—each was a discrete creation. But for Rabbi Nehemia, they share a family history; they are the *generations* of the heavens and the earth.

There seems to be tension, however, between continuous creation and instantaneous creation. If, according to instantaneous creation all that eventually emerges was present in potential from the beginning, what more is there to do which requires God's continuous creativity in the present? It may be that these ideas stand in contradiction to one another. Nevertheless, we see a similar development vis-à-vis revelation that will be enable us to better understand the implications of instantaneous creation.

In the Torah, just as creation is sequential and discrete, revelation happens at different times and different places. The most famous revelation is at Mount Sinai, but the book of Leviticus begins with God speaking to Moses from the Tent of Meeting, and later during their sojourn God speaks to Moses on the plains of Moav (Numbers 35:1). Although sequential revelation is as obvious as the sequential creation of Genesis 1, there were rabbis who, for some reason, denied both. Rabbi Akiva maintains that the Torah's first verse includes the creation of the sun, the moon, the stars, trees, grass, and even the Garden of Eden.[36] Similarly, Rabbi Akiva insisted the entire Torah, generalities and specifics, were given at Sinai and merely repeated in the tent of Meeting and on the plains of Moab.[37] Even more startling is Rabbi Akiva's belief, recorded in the Mishna, that the Song of Songs was also given at Sinai.[38] By the time

---

35 Augustine, *The Literal Meaning of Genesis*, 2 vols., trans. J. H. Taylor (New York: Newman, 1982), 175.
36 Genesis Rabbah 1:14.
37 Sota 37b and Heschel, *Heavenly Torah*, 378–80.
38 M. Yadayim 3:5.

of the Talmud, we have the maximalist claim that the entire Talmud was given to Moses at Mount Sinai.[39]

To be sure, there were also rabbis who accepted the straightforward biblical account of multiple revelations with different content. But, there were rabbis, like Akiva, who collapsed revelation into a singularity. Within this school of thought, though, there were two different conceptions about the content of that instantaneous revelation. The first is that God gave both the Written and the Oral Torahs to Moses on Mount Sinai. That version appears as the first chapter of Mishnah Avot which justifies the authority of the Mishnah's laws. They have exactly the same authority as the Written Torah because they have exactly the same source—from God at Mount Sinai.

The second understanding of a singular, instantaneous revelation is that the Written Torah was given along with its principles of interpretation. These principles allow future sages to generate new understandings and revelations of God's will which are called Oral Torah. In this model, the sages have the agency to generate Torah. Their method is the process of midrash which links novel insights to biblical verses. In Rabbi Ishmael's introduction to the Sifra, the earliest midrashic collection on the book of Leviticus, he enumerates thirteen principles of interpretation which rabbis use to generate Oral Torah. Midrash coordinates the historical Torah of Sinai with the ever-changing exigencies of society to allow Torah to be a "tree planted by waters, sending forth its roots by a stream . . . its leaves are ever fresh . . . and it never stops making fruit" (Jeremiah 17:8). In extolling the benefits and beauty of midrash, Simon Rawidowicz suggests that midrash "is Israel's *creatio continua*."[40]

Both rabbinic understandings of instantaneous revelation reflect, at least partially, Rabbi Nehemia's seed principle. The idea that both the

39 Brachot 5a, Y. Peah 17a, and Heschel, *Heavenly Torah*, 563–68.
40 Simon Rawidowicz, *Studies in Jewish Thought*, ed. Nahum N. Glatzer (Philadelphia: Jewish Publication Society of America, 1974), 25. Azzan Yadin-Israel has made two extensive studies of rabbinic midrash and concludes that within the Tannaitic school of Rabbi Ishmael the sage "is not a partner in interpretation" (*Scripture as Logos: Rabbi Ishmael and the Origins of Midrash* [Philadelphia: University of Pennsylvania Press, 2004], 134). Yadin-Israel argues that generative midrash did not emerge until after the Mishnah. See *Scripture and Tradition: Rabbi Akiva and the Triumph of Midrash* (Philadelphia: University of Pennsylvania Press, 2015), especially pages 104–114.

Written and Oral Torahs were given at Sinai corresponds to the seed principle: God will create nothing more like God will reveal nothing more. With the seed principle, however, creation takes time to emerge. Not so for instantaneous revelation: "Even the question a student will ask his teacher was given to Moshe at Sinai" (Exodus Rabbah 47:1).

Fortunately, this version of instantaneous revelation, the one that has only a partial parallel to instantaneous creation, is ridiculous. Polemics prompted such silliness. Christianity's rise to power through the fourth century undoubtedly unnerved the leadership of rabbinic Judaism. Tethering rabbinic law to the Sinai was part of their response since both communities agreed about the divine authority of the Written Torah. The alternate version of instantaneous revelation avoids the silliness and provides a better parallel to the novel rabbinic theology of instantaneous creation.

This second model of instantaneous revelation, with the Written Torah and its interpretive principles given at Sinai, is generative or midrashic. This model sees the Torah and the rabbis as partners in the midrashic process which unfolds over time. Analogously, the elements of creation exercise their agency and con-spire (literally, breathe together) with God to breathe new forms of life into existence, to activate the inherent potential of all existents. The biblical model of creation in Genesis 1 was a co-creation between God and primordial elements that God had not created. As we will see, the final element of our rabbinic theology of creation is about those elements on stage at creation. Rabbi Nehemia is explicit that God sowed at the beginning the creation that later emerged. Although Rabbi Nehemia is silent about whether God created those elements on stage at the beginning, we will see that rabbinic Judaism is not comfortable with the plain biblical sense that God worked with what was available.

Instantaneous creation at the beginning and continuous creation are not contradictory, they are complementary. The seed principle of instantaneous creation links all of creation together from the origin and guarantees the unity of all that ever emerges. The balance, harmony, and interdependence among the constituent elements of the cosmos emerges from their common singularity. When the prayer book invokes the continuous divine renewal of creation, the term used for everything created during Genesis 1's six days is *ma'aseh bereshit*, the *act* of creation, in the singular. God renews creation as a unified whole, not as discrete, and potentially discordant, elements. God renewing creation, breathing divine vitality to preserve the cosmos, is continuous creation.

This is, I believe, a fair reading of some rabbis and their theology of creation. God and creation generate novelty in natural history analogously, or even homologously, to how God and the sages generate novelty in our understanding of God's will. An initial endowment of divinity unfolds over time in partnership with the autonomous agents which/who previously emerged from the same process. Since God is the author of the book of Nature and the book of Torah, His penmanship should be the same. I am not claiming that all rabbis had such a worldview. They did not. The ones who did, I believe, were influenced by the fractal paradigm of the priests. Since their theology demanded that revelation be instantaneous and continuous, they projected that model onto creation.

Sowing the Ground for Darwinism

Before addressing the final strand in our rabbinic theology of creation, I would like to point out that although the rabbis did not anticipate Darwinism, they did accept the components of Darwinism. Natural selection involves some of the variations within a species being or becoming advantageous. There is a lovely aggadah that has a nasty man trying to make Hillel lose his temper. One of the questions with which he peppers Hillel is, "Why do desert dwellers have slanted eyes?" Hillel responds in good adaptive fashion: "it helps keep out the sand." The man returns and asks Hillel why Africans have wide feet. Hillel responds: "because they live in marshy areas."[41] We would have been more impressed if Hillel were asked about the higher incidence of sickle cell anemia amongst Africans and answered that it provided a defense against malaria. Yet, Hillel does display a receptivity to the notion that variations provide advantages. I suspect that Hillel assumed that God created the Africans with wide feet to help them walk through swampy areas, but Darwin, too, began with a deep appreciation for the argument from design. (He wrote in a letter that he had nearly memorized William Paley's *Natural Theology*.)

---

41 Shabbat 31a.

With variations, some of which become advantageous as circumstances change, Darwin claimed that given enough time, one species would evolve or transmute into another. As we will see, there are several midrashim in Genesis Rabbah that allow for deep time. Such midrashim were dusted off in the eighteenth century as it became clear that the world must be older than the biblical chronology suggests. As for transmutation of species, we see that quite explicitly in the Garden of Eden— the crafty serpent loses its limbs and becomes a belly crawler (Genesis 3:14). A rabbinic midrash has the pre-punishment serpent shaking the Tree of Knowledge with his hands and feet until the fruit dropped in front of the unsuspecting woman.[42]

The literature cited above is fanciful. One rabbi even imagines that Adam was initially created with a tail![43] Yet, I do think it at least suggests that not all rabbis would have been opposed to the elements of Darwinism. One more example of "transmutation" will suffice. The Talmud contains a prison scene featuring Rabbi Akiva before his execution by the Romans. In this scene, he offers another prisoner a parable involving a fox and fish. The fox, angling for a meal, says to the fish: "Would you like to come up to the dry land and we can dwell together as our ancestors did?"[44] The fish does not reject the fox's historical memory, only the invitation. I am not sure what to make of fish and foxes living together on land, but it certainly speaks to a more fluid view of creation than what we have with the strict categorization of the priestly creation in Genesis 1.

A final example of the potential compatibility between rabbinic thought and Darwinism concerns extinction. In Greek philosophy and Christianity, extinction was irrational. Why would God create an animal species only to allow its demise? Rabbinic Judaism was not so rational. In particular, there was one species whose hide was used as a covering of the desert tabernacle (Exodus 26:14). According to rabbinic tradition, this uncertain species became extinct once its purpose in Jewish history had been fulfilled.[45] I am not making some silly claim that the rabbis understood the transmutation of species two thousand years ago. What

---

42 Avot d'Rabbi Natan 1:5.
43 Genesis Rabbah 14:10.
44 Brachot 61b.
45 Shabbat 28b.

I am suggesting is more profound. The ways in which some rabbis articulated their vision of how God interacts with creation turned out to be
fundamentally consonant with much of what we currently believe about
how the world operates. Moreover, that rabbinic revision of creation is
analogous to their theory of revelation which together create a coherent
rabbinic theology of creation. Some rabbis intuited a continuous overflow of divine energy, both on the level of Torah and creation, that helped
catalyze the potential within each. That divine pulse generated new revelations through the autonomy of rabbinic midrash and new creations
through the autonomy of natural agents.

Here is what Professor Moshe Greenberg, a Jewish Bible scholar,
says of new interpretations: "the meaning and significance of a passage
(an event, an utterance) may not be realized until activated by later circumstances or contemplation."[46] That is an apt description of midrash. If
we rephrase Greenberg's comment and give it an evolutionary frame, we
arrive at an apt description of speciation: the meaning and significance
of a heritable variation may not be realized until becoming adaptive by
later circumstances.

Inclining towards Creatio ex Nihilo

The final strand in our rabbinic theology of creation introduces the concept of *ex nihilo*, the claim that God is not only the author of creation, but
also the creator of the letters and alphabet. As discussed above, when the
curtain rises on Genesis 1 there were already elements on stage. Genesis
1 is silent about the origins of those elements. My assumption is that the
biblical author understood his audience to believe that the origin of those
pre-mundane elements was independent of God. Like an author, God
ordered preexisting words to create a narrative. Authors do not, generally, create their own words (or letters). *Nowhere* in biblical literature is
there an indication that God created the world out of nothing and, therefore, is the material cause of the world. (A carpenter is the efficient cause
of a wooden chair while a tree is the material cause.)

---

46 Moshe Greenberg, *Studies in the Bible and Jewish Thought* (Philadelphia: The Jewish
Publication Society, 1995), 239.

In Genesis Rabbah we see both a discomfort with the plain biblical sense and an attempt to provide the biblical reading with a back story that turns God into the material cause of creation. A midrash asks if denying God's ability to create out of nothing disparages His honor. The implicit answer is that indeed it does, but, nevertheless, Genesis 1 is explicit that God orders the primordial elements of the earth that were in a state of *tohu va'vohu*.[47] There may have been several reasons for the discomfort. Particularly given Hellenistic notions of omnipotence, to deny God as the material cause of the universe may have been perceived as an assault on God's power. Alternatively, if God did not create the pre-mundane elements, they may have been created by another god, or if they are eternal they may be divine themselves. Finally, and to my mind most plausibly, if God is not responsible for what we humans are made from, then that raises the possibility that we may be materially incapable of following God's commandments. The sprit may be willing, but if the flesh is weak—don't blame us. We're doing the best we can given the venality in our blood.

The most explicit confrontation in rabbinic literature regarding ex nihilo reveals the philosopher's faith that nothing comes from nothing, "*ex nihilo, nihil fit*." "Your God is a great artist, but he found [already present] good ingredients that aided him: *tohu va'vohu*, darkness, wind, water and the abyss."[48] The philosopher's interlocutor, Rabban Gamliel, unceremoniously tells him to drop dead. He proceeds to offer a series of biblical verses to support his claim that each element on the stage of Genesis 1 when the curtain rose had already been created, *ex nihilo*, by God. In this case, my suspicion is that Rabban Gamliel is less concerned with an excuse for human frailty than he is with an assault on divine sovereignty and power. Rabban Gamliel's midrash is farfetched even by the standards of rabbinic logic. For example, Gamliel references a verse in Isaiah, to which we will return, in which God *creates* evil (Isaiah 45:7). Rabban Gamliel then identifies *tohu va'vohu* with evil and concludes, therefore, that God created *tohu va'vohu*.

Although *creatio ex nihilo* approaches the status of a doctrine in the Middle Ages, it is in this single rabbinic midrash where we see the notion most clearly articulated. In other words, although we see the first halting

---

47 Genesis Rabbah 1:5.
48 Genesis Rabbah 1:9.

moves towards a theology of *ex nihilo* in rabbinic thought, its full expression awaits the Middle Ages. There is one text, Sefer Yetzira, the dating of which remains controversial, that also tries to account for those pre-mundane elements. Although Sefer Yetzira will be considered a mystical text by Jewish thinkers in the Middle Ages, in actuality it was a cosmogonic text. Joseph Dan emphasizes that "the sefirot are stages in the creation process which preceded the creation itself, which prepared existence for 'Let there be light,' the actual beginning of creation."[49] What remains inconclusive is whether those pre-mundane elements were created *ex nihilo* or emanated from God's essence, a reading which became popular among some medieval mystics.[50] What is unambiguous in Sefer Yetzira is the importance of language in the process of creation, thus forming an essential link from the priestly Torah to medieval Kabbalah. According to the introduction of Sefer Yetzira, God created the world through thirty two wondrous paths of wisdom: the 10 fundamental digits (0–9, called *sfirot* in Sefer Yetzira) and the twenty-two letters of the Hebrew alphabet—the same alphabet God used in speaking the world into existence.

Up to this point in our discussion of *ex nihilo*, we have looked at midrash outside of the consensus texts of halakhah and the siddur. In the prayer book, there is a modification of the aforementioned verse in Isaiah (45:7) which describes God as creating evil. In the morning service, the word *evil* is changed to *all*. God creates (*boreh*) all. Although in charting the shift toward *ex nihilo* I would prefer to use texts from the Siddur, I do not believe this text is evidence of that shift. Isaiah, in a polemical context, makes the following claim: "God forms light and creates darkness, makes peace and *creates evil*." Isaiah insists on monotheism as opposed to any hint of dualism. When the siddur modifies Isaiah's language and places the verse in the morning service, there is corresponding shift in emphasis from God's role in human history (peace and evil) to God's role in the natural world (light and darkness).[51] In this new context, mentioning evil would be a distraction and at odds with the liturgy's emphasis on creation's goodness which counters the claims of Gnostic dualists.

---

49 Joseph Dan, *The Ancient Jewish Mysticism* (Tel Aviv: MOD Books, 1993), 208.
50 Azriel on Sefer Yetzira 2:6, cited in Gershom Scholem, *Origins of the Kabbalah* (Philadelphia: Jewish Publication Society), 425.
51 See also Jakob J. Petuchowski, "The Creation in Jewish Liturgy," *Judaism* 28, no. 3 (Summer 1979): 310–11.

What we can say is that among the rabbis there were those who understood the implications of God creating the world from pre-mundane, eternal matter. What we don't see is the engagement of midrashic muscle, as there was with continuous creation and instantaneous creation, to excise the plain sense of Genesis 1. Nevertheless, when we look at the parallel to *ex nihilo* in the domain of Torah, we see a concerted rabbinic effort to drash away the peshat, the contextual meaning. Nowhere in the Pentateuch is the claim made that God is responsible for all the material within the Pentateuch. The Hebrew Bible, from Genesis to Chronicles, never makes a claim for the comprehensive divinity of the Pentateuch. That claim is rabbinic.

Consider the topic under discussion: creation. When God begins his relationship with Moshe, nowhere does the Torah record a parenthetical aside where God rewinds the tape and begins to explain to Moses how creation unfolded. As crucial to our identity and national narrative as the stories of the patriarchs and matriarchs are, nowhere does the Torah say that God recounted these stories to Moshe who then wrote them down as the prelude to the exodus. We see Moshe being told to write a tablet or two here, a song or poem there, but we have no record of anything close to divine dictation of the entire Pentateuch.

The book of Jubilees was not canonized in the Hebrew Bible. Jubilees was far more popular among the Jews living around the Dead Sea than it was among the rabbis who largely ignored it. Archeologists found more than a dozen copies of portions of *Jubilees* in the Qumran library, the oldest dating back to the second century BCE. Jubilees begins with the command for Moses to come up to Mount Sinai and receive Torah. But in the second chapter of Jubilees there is an angel delegated to dictate to Moshe the account of creation. The angel continues to retell the stories of the patriarchs and matriarchs with some fascinating differences from what we have in our Torah. For our purposes, it is instructive that this non-canonical text reworked the sequence of events in order to guarantee the divine authority of the account of creation.

The Mishnah, itself, tells us that the issue of divine authorship of the entire Torah was controversial. "These have no portion in the world to come: one who says that resurrection of the dead is not from Torah, or that Torah is not heaven, or an *epikorus.*"[52] The Mishnah's ambiguity as to

---

52 M. Sannhedrin 10:1.

the meaning of *Torah from heaven* is clarified in the gemara. "Even one who acknowledges that the entire Torah is from heaven except for this [one] verse that Moshe spoke himself and was not from the holy One."[53] The gemara concludes by including in the heavenly Torah not only the rules of rabbinic interpretation, but their specific applications, as well. The divine provenance of the entire Torah is not to be doubted.

Given the vehemence (though not unanimity) of the rabbinic claim that the entire Torah is of divine origin, I would expect the claims for *creatio ex nihilo*, that all elements of the world are of divine origin, to be more numerous. Our rabbinic theology of creation has consistently demonstrated parallel shifts from biblical concepts of creation and revelation to those of the rabbis. I have only one idea to account for the seeming lack of evidence of *ex nihilo* in rabbinic literature. Jonathan Goldstein had suggested this line of reasoning in a 1984 article, and then subsequently retracted under withering criticism from a colleague. Goldstein proffered that the doctrine of *ex nihilo* was, indeed, more widespread than surviving literature would suggest. Moreover, "creation *ex nihilo* is a polemical doctrine, invoked to defend the belief in bodily resurrection!"[54]

The claim is logical. If God can create out of absolutely nothing, then, all the more so can God refashion biodegraded flesh to resurrect the righteous. Consider the obverse: if God cannot create out of nothing, could God resurrect the decomposed dead? That is an open question. *Creatio ex nihilo*, although not quite a logical prerequisite for resurrection, is certainly the strongest possible evidence. Think back to our list of miscreants who do not make it into the World to Come. At the head of the list was one who says that resurrection of the dead was not from the Torah. For rabbinic Judaism, resurrection of the dead is as close to dogma as it gets. The prayer for resurrection is the focus of the Amidah's second blessing, and the Amidah is recited at least three times every day. Although the Amidah's invocation of resurrection likely applies to individuals, it recycles the biblical imagery of resurrection from Ezekiel (chapter 37) which deals with national restoration. In the first book I argued for the redemptive focus of rabbinic Judaism, and here we see the significance of the related theme of

---

53 Sannhedrin 99a.
54 Jonathan Goldstein, "The Origins of the Doctrine of Creation Ex Nihilo," *Journal of Jewish Studies* 35, no. 2 (1984): 134.

individual resurrection. The question then becomes, is there a connection between resurrection and creation? Indeed, there is.

The Talmud presents a discussion that begins with Caesar asking Rabban Gamliel how resurrection of the dead is possible. Once humans die and decompose, they turn to dust of the earth, argues Caesar. "Can dust come to life?"[55] Caesar may be aware of rabbinic doctrine, but, unlike the philosopher with whom we last saw Rabban Gamliel engage, he is a biblical illiterate. Of course dust can be animated—it says so right in the second creation story: "The Lord God formed Adam from the dust of the earth" (Genesis 2:7). The Talmudic passage then continues with a comment from the School of Rabbi Ishmael which seems to rely on the continuation of our verse from Genesis which has God blowing the breath of life into the inert earthling. Here the Talmud answers our question from above: If God can blow life into the dust that becomes Adam, there is no logical reason why God cannot blow life into the dust that had once been Adam.

The next example in this Talmudic passage is the strongest evidence for our understanding of a rabbinic theology of creation. A heretic challenges a rabbi about the possibility of resurrecting the dead. The rabbi responds with a parable: This may be compared to a human king who directed his servants to build a great palace in a place where there was no water or earth [to make bricks], and they built it! After some time, the palace collapsed. The King said to them: "Go and build the palace in a place where there is water and earth." They replied, "We can't!" The King was angry at them and said, "In a place where there wasn't water and earth you were able to build; so in a place where there *is* water and earth it should be even more doable!"[56]

This is the rabbinic logic of *creatio ex nihilo* without the explicit language: If God can create the world out of nothing, then it is even more doable to resurrect the dead since God has material with which to work. In the first two examples, God is creating something from the earth. In the third example, water is added to mix, which may hark back to Genesis 1 (or, as RaSHI suggests, may represent semen). But the point is that initially God commanded the palace to be built without any material substrate. His servants had neither earth nor water. The palace was built

---

55   Sannhedrin 90b.
56   Ibid. 91a.

from nothing. Although the specific language does not appear until the tenth century, this example describes *creatio ex nihilo*. And, as Goldstein pointed out, it serves as the logical underpinning for resurrection of the dead which may well be the most important theological innovation of rabbinic Judaism. Resurrection, on the personal plane, becomes a theodicy positing a venue beyond this inscrutable world where the righteous of Israel will be rewarded for their loyalty to their covenant with God. More importantly, on the national plane, resurrection of the people of Israel remains the single greatest rabbinic goal. We can believe that God has the power to effect resurrection on both planes precisely because God accomplished an even greater feat when He created the world out of nothing. Exactly what constitutes *nothing* is a medieval question.

As plausible as *creatio ex nihilo* is for us today, resurrection of the dead is equally implausible—at least for individuals. (The resurrection of the State of Israel makes Ezekiel's dry bones dance the hora.) Contemporary science is responsible for reinforcing one plausibility structure, *creatio ex nihilo*, and undermining the other, resurrection of the dead. Whether we label the beginning the Big Bang or the Big Birth, both science and Torah perceive its eruption as staggeringly improbable. Science calls it a singularity, an event in which the laws of nature as we know them do not apply. Analogously, the first two words of the Torah do not belong together grammatically, and the condition of the primordial world, *tohu va'vohu*, is indeterminate. We just don't know.

We do know, textually, that God's spirit was fluttering over face of the abyss. For the priestly author, holiness is contagious, thus the primordial waters become divinely charged. In other words, the primordial elements are not eternal gods themselves; they were touched by God. In this myth of contagious holiness, God creates all life with the participation of other, non-divinely created elements. The co-creation continues as God invites those co-created agents to contribute to the making of humanity, "in our image." Rabbis Nehemia and Berechia similarly endow creative agency to the earth and waters through their seed principle.

Amongst the smorgasbord of rabbinic comments on creation, several attained doctrinal status in the Middle Ages. The seed principle which views creation as the unfolding of an instantaneous endowment is one such midrash. Already in the rabbinic period, continuous creation, as opposed to a view of creation in which God's creative input had ceased, became the norm in both the siddur and the halakhah. As we explore medieval Jewish literature in the next chapter, we enter with an appreciation for the continuously unfolding nature of interdependent, divinely charged co-creation.[57][58]

Theologies of Creation

	Creation in Torah	Revelation in Torah	Creation in Rabbinics	Revelation in Rabbinics
Origins	Not all divine/ Primordial matter from Genesis 1:2	The Torah is not all divine	Discomfort with "Not all divine"[57]/ Leaning toward *ex nihilo* as logical basis for resurrection	Rejection of Torah being "Not all divine" as outside rabbinic Judaism
Emergence	Sequential and discrete	Sequential and discrete	Instantaneous and unfolding seed principle	Instantaneous and unfolding[58] 1) Oral Torah given at Sinai 2) Rabbis generate oral Torah from interpretive principles given at Sinai
Status	God is finished	God is finished	Continuous creation	Continuous revelation

---

57 See also Genesis Rabbah 1:5.
58 The relationship between what Christians traditionally call the Old Testament and the New Testament is discrete and sequential. Thus the rabbinic move to instantaneous and unfolding creation may reflect a polemical need to organically embed the Oral Torah in the revelation at Mount Sinai which both communities agreed was divine and authoritative. The New Testament's midrashic use of biblical verses exposes the same anxiety. What affords the new dispensation offered by Christ's crucifixion authority given its explicit novelty?

The rabbinic move to instantaneous and unfolding creation accords with the priestly worldview in which revelation recapitulated creation. If revelation needed to be instantaneous and unfolding for polemical purposes with the Christians, then creation was suitably re-viewed and revised.

Chapter 8

A Mystical Theology of Creation

Where, Lord, will I find you:
your place is high and obscured.
 And where
  won't I find you:
 your glory fills the world.

You dwell deep within—
 you've fixed the ends of creation.
You stand, a tower for the near,
 refuge to those far off.
You've lain above the Ark, here,
 yet live in the highest heavens.
 Exalted among your hosts,
 although beyond their hymns—
  no heavenly sphere
  could ever contain you,
 let alone a chamber within.

***

I sought your nearness.
 With all my heart I called you.
And in my going out to meet you,
 I found you coming toward me,

as in the wonders of your might
   and holy works I saw you.

                              ***

But could the Lord, in truth,
   dwell in men on earth?
How would men you made
   from the dust and clay
fathom your presence there,
   enthroned upon their praise?
The creatures hovering over
the world praise your wonders—
      your throne borne high
      above their heads,
   as you bear all forever.

—From Judah HaLevi, "Where Will I Find You?"[1]

You've lain above the Ark, here; yet live in the highest heavens. According
to Hillel Halkin, HaLevi's most recent biographer, "The paradox of a God
who is both transcendent and immanent, outside yet inside His creation, runs through Yehuda HaLevi's religious thought."[2] Both Halkin and
Leo Strauss imagine that HaLevi went through a philosophical phase.[3]
Certainly by the time he wrote his enduring defense of Judaism, *The
Kuzari* (1140), he had abandoned Aristotelian philosophy which, as we
saw in book 1, rejects the possibility of a God immanent in the world of
creation. For philosophers, God functions as the formal and final causes
of the world, both of which are terribly impersonal. The formal cause of a
chair, for example, is the arrangement or pattern of matter that allows for,
or causes, the chair to function as a platform for sitting. For Aristotelians,
like RaMBaM, the form of the human is our intellect because it allows
us to fulfill our function or goal (final cause) as a human, namely, to

---

1   Judah HaLevi (d. 1141) was born in Muslim-controlled Spain like RaMBaM.
    Also like RaMBaM, he was a doctor. There the similarities end. Translation by
    Peter Cole. https://www.poetryfoundation.org/poetrymagazine/poems/55427/
    where-will-i-find-you.
2   Hillel Halkin, *Yehuda Halevi* (New York: Schocken Books, 2010), 93.
3   Leo Strauss, *Persecution and the Art of Writing* (Chicago: University of Chicago Press,
    1952), 109 and Halkin, *Yehuda Halevi*, 157.

strive for intellectual perfection.[4] Similarly, the final cause of a chair, its function, is to provide a platform for sitting. The other two Aristotelian causes are more direct. The material cause of a chair might be wood or plastic. The efficient cause of the chair is the carpenter or manufacturer. For classic Aristotelian philosophy, God is neither the material nor the efficient causes of the cosmos.[5]

HaLevi was no Aristotelian; his worldview was influenced by elements of Neoplatonism, the philosophical infrastructure we saw in book 1 associated with Bahya ibn Pakuda.[6] Plotinus (204–279), the founder of Neoplatonism, described a series of overflowing concatenations cascading from the immaterial One to our tangible universe. The soul, the most pristine remnant of the One in our dimension, longs to return to its Source. "I sought your nearness. With all my heart I called you. And in my going out to meet you, I found you coming toward me." HaLevi's yearning for divine intimacy has become divine immanence, without humanity becoming divine. Nevertheless, HaLevi was certainly not an orthodox Neoplatonist. HaLevi combined rabbinic religiosity with select elements of Neoplatonism. HaLevi's God rewards and punishes as in Mosaic theology, but the reward is usually deferred to the rabbinic world to come.[7] Divine reward and punishment are not features of standard Neoplatonism. HaLevi's world is hierarchically structured both on the plane of anthropology and geography. Many scholars associate HaLevi's hierarchical worldview with Neoplatonism, but it is rooted in the hierarchies of the priestly Torah which reappear in kabbalistic theology. Yet, HaLevi was not a kabbalist who believed that God has needs which Jews engaging in mitzvot with the proper *kavannah* could fulfill. One might say that HaLevi is a non-kabbalistic, Neoplatonic rabbi.

HaLevi, and the few Jewish Neoplatonists who preceded him, helped set the spiritual stage for the Kabbalah to emerge in thirteenth-century Spain. What we do not find in the writings of these earlier Neoplatonists

---

4   *Guide*, 1:7.

5   Actually, God *is* the efficient cause, but through the indirect process of natural causality. When I say above that God is not the efficient cause, I mean that God is not the *proximate* cause which is the most recent cause in the series to effectuate the product.

6   Medieval Aristotelianism, itself, bore the influence of Neoplatonism. Two of the primary medieval sources for Neoplatonic thought were attributed to Aristotle.

7   *Kuzari*, 1:111.

is the language of sefirot, the mythical imagery of the Bahir and the Zohar, or the concept of divine need. This chapter will offer a medieval theology of creation after briefly examining the philosophical approach to nature, represented by the Aristotelians and most influentially articulated by RaMBaM. For our purposes, there are two major differences between Kabbalah and RaMBaM. The first distinction is that Aristotelian philosophy keeps God on the other side of the metaphysical barrier rejecting divine immanence, though with some significant qualifications. A mystical theology of creation, on the other hand, in-spires creation with divinity and perceives creation to be a self-revelation of God. The second distinction is that the philosophical approach preserves God's autonomy and autarchy—God is independent and without needs. Mysticism perceives reality as interdependent between creator and creation, mutually bound in a covenant, in which each has needs that can be fulfilled by the other. Using the image of a membrane, the philosophical membrane is semipermeable where God influences creation but not vice-versa; the mystical membrane separates creator from creation but allows *shefa/* divine energy to flow in both directions.

Legal literature does not generally concern itself with these explicitly theological issues. Yet, by the end of the Middle Ages, there was an innovation that speaks to the decisive victory of Kabbalah over philosophy. The author of *The Two Tablets of the Covenant* (written in 1623 and published in 1648) was an early adopter, if not the earliest, of insisting that the performance of mitzvot be preceded by the formula: "For the purpose of uniting the holy One, blessed be He, and His Shechinah, I will perform the mitzvah of . . . "[8] The holy One and His Shechinah are two sefirot representing the male and female energies within God. With the proper intention and the precise verbal formula, every Jew can play matchmaker for God by the performance of a mitzvah. Horowitz wrote his book for the masses—and they bought it! *The Two Tablets of the Covenant* "was not only one of the most popular rabbinic works of the last three hundred years, but had considerable influence on the thought of the early Hasidic masters."[9]

---

8   Horowitz, *The Two Tablets, Masechet Shvuot, Ner Mitzvah* 88.
9   Miles Krassen's Introduction to Horowitz, *The Generations of Adam* (Mahwah: Paulist Press, 1996), 33.

The other genre of Jewish literature in the Middle Ages, biblical commentary, was penned by kabbalists and philosophers alike. Indeed, the Zohar itself is structured as a biblical commentary. Several scholars have pointed out that the Muslim distinction between an outer and inner sense of the biblical text, *zahir* and *batin* in Arabic, was not only a hermeneutic for interpreting scripture.[10] It was also a worldview. Hava Tirosh-Samuelson sums it up best in her analysis of medieval science: "For the Jewish Aristotelians, science (i.e., natural philosophy) meant a causal explanation of the physical world on the basis of sensory perception and observation; for the kabbalists, in accord with the Platonic view, the physical world was only *a metaphor of reality*, a reflection of intelligible forms that cannot be perceived by the senses."[11]

Although RaMBaM did not write a biblical commentary, *per se*, he interpreted many Torah verses in his writings. A later philosopher, Rabbi Levi ben Gershom, or Gersonides (RaLBaG, 1288–1344), wrote both a commentary on the Torah and on Song of Songs. This erotic poetry, the favorite biblical text of medieval mystics, for Gersonides becomes an Aristotelian dialogue "between the human material intellect and the Active Intellect, a kind of conjunction with which is a human being's highest perfection and greatest felicity."[12] Not only did the philosophers and mystics write biblical commentary through their respective lenses, but within the school of *peshat* commentary (focusing on the literary and historical context), there was a reclamation of priestly Torah themes.

Hezekia ben Manoach, a thirteenth-century commentator, notes a parallel between the unfolding of creation and the construction of the Tabernacle. After the directions have been given to build the Tabernacle, the next set of instructions has to do with preparing the interior lamp. He comments, "We find the same in the creation account: after the land and its details were created, God prepared the light for them."[13] An earlier commentator, Abraham ibn Ezra, developed a rabbinic theme that

10 Joel L. Kramer, "The Islamic Context of Medieval Jewish Philosophy," in *The Cambridge Companion to Medieval Jewish Philosophy*, 61.
11 Hava Tirosh-Samuelson, "Kabbalah and Science in the Middle Ages," in *Science in Medieval Jewish Cultures*, ed. Gad Freudenthal (New York: Cambridge University Press, 2011), 497.
12 Menachem Kellner, *Commentary on* Song of Songs *by Levi ben Gershom* (New Haven: Yale University Press, 1998), xxi.
13 Hizkuni on Exodus 27:20.

the human is a microcosm of the world.[14] For ibn Ezra, the intermediate structure, and the mediating structure, between humanity and the cosmos is the Tabernacle.[15] These medieval Torah commentators are bringing to light a theology of creation rooted largely in the priestly Torah where patterns of time (the sequences of creation and the building of the tabernacle), space, and holiness emerge in homologous patterns. The mystical tradition will make the most of these three-dimensional fractals. But first, we must go down the paths not taken.

The Semipermeable Membrane of Medieval Philosophy

The function of a membrane is to partially separate two domains. In the case of medieval Jewish Aristotelianism, God and creation are entities whose relationship is confined to formal and final causality. Historians of Jewish thought have emphatically insisted on what they, anachronistically, term *divine transcendence* to describe the relationship between Creator and creation. In a provocative article, Dov Schwartz challenged this strict dichotomy between transcendence and immanence. He attributes the blurring of the boundaries to the conflation of Neoplatonism and Aristotelianism in the tenth century. In that hybrid philosophical system, every existent can trace its lineage back, through some path, to an emanation from the divine One. Moreover, the common origin of all beings allowed for the Neoplatonic assumption that all being was interrelated. "The Neoplatonists viewed the world as a uniform entity, in mutual sympathy with all its parts. Such concepts could not but impart a distinctly immanent tinge to the concept of the divine."[16]

There is a more subtle way in which divine immanence is acknowledged even by the most orthodox of philosophers. According to Aristotelian epistemology, one can be said to know something only when one has understood its pure, abstract form. Knowledge unifies

---

14 Tanhuma, Pikudei 3. See also David Mevorach Seidenberg, *Kabbalah and Ecology: God's Image In The More-Than-Human World* (New York: Cambridge University Press, 2015), 243–46.

15 Ibn Ezra on Exodus 26:1. See also the Zohar passage, 2:162b, that Seidenberg discusses in his *Kabbalah and Ecology*, 202.

16 Dov Schwartz, "Divine Immanence in Medieval Jewish Philosophy," *The Journal of Jewish Thought and Philosophy* 3, no. 2 (1994): 250.

the thinker's form (the intellect) with the form of the object of thought. According to RaMBaM, "The intellect (or intellectual cognition), the intellectually cognizing subject, and the intellectually cognized object are always one and the same thing in the case of everything that is cognized *in actu*."[17] While we humans flit from potential cognition to actual cognition (*in actu*) and back again, God cognizes all always. Or, in RaMBaM's terms, God *is* cognition *in actu* (actualizing the potential). RaMBaM might, thus, be described as a *formal* pantheist:

> God is an intellect *in actu* . . . and there is absolutely no potentiality in Him. . . . It follows necessarily that He and the thing apprehended are one thing, which is His essence. Moreover, the act of apprehension owing to which He is said to be an intellectually cognizing subject is in itself the intellect, which is His essence. Accordingly He is always the intellect as well as the intellectually cognizing subject and the intellectually cognizing object.[18]

In labeling RaMBaM a formal pantheist, I mean that he understands God to be the form of all forms.[19] Yet, his language in the citation above is either imprecise or ambiguous. He writes that "He and the thing apprehended are one thing, which is His essence." I understand RaMBaM to mean that He and the *form* of the thing apprehended are one thing— otherwise RaMBaM would be a material pantheist which runs afoul of RaMBaM's most fundamental premise—divine incorporeality. Yet, within this discussion, RaMBaM also acknowledges that the "universe exists in virtue of the Creator, and the latter continually endows it with permanence in virtue of the thing that is spoken of as overflow."[20] The Neoplatonic overflow endows all existents with the capacity for existence. There is no identification of the divine with matter, *per se*, but there is dependence of matter on the divine overflow to retain its form as something rather than no-thing. Dov Schwartz, in explaining Averroes' metaphysics (Averroes is a Muslim philosopher from RaMBaM's hometown of Cordoba), puts it as follows: "The essential identity of actual divine knowledge, on the one hand, and the existents, on the other, is not merely

---

17 *Guide*, 1:68, 164–65.
18 Ibid., 1:68, 165.
19 Ibid., 1:69, 167.
20 Ibid., 1:69, 169.

intellectual—it possesses a definite ontic dimension; the ontic status of the forms in the divine 'mind' is in fact a matter of 'existence' or 'being.'"[21]

This ontic dependence of creation on God is the medieval expression of what the prayer book describes: God daily renewing the act of creation. RaMBaM translated liturgical pieties into medieval philosophy. But by identifying the forms of all existents as an element of the divine form, everything, by definition, has a divine form. Labeling RaMBaM a formal pantheist reminds us that the distinction between form and matter is less stark than we often imagine.

RaMBaM demanded intellectual honesty even as he advocated and modeled discretion. We cannot deny that which has been demonstrated to be true. RaMBaM admits the possibility that if, in the future, philosophers prove the eternity of world as Aristotle argued, "the Law as a whole would become void, and a shift to other opinions would take place."[22] Although RaMBaM did not explicitly accept Aristotle's theory of eternity, neither did he believe that *creatio ex nihilo* had been proven. He maintained, therefore, that we should accept *creatio ex nihilo* on the basis of tradition. I do not know what RaMBaM believed in his heart, but he held reason to be the final arbiter. Toward that end, RaMBaM held the study of science and philosophy to be incumbent on Jews as the medium through which we come to know and, therefore, to love God. The Torah makes no epistemological claims—truth is derived exclusively through empirical and rational means.

As Schwartz noted above, a characteristic of Neoplatonism is that creation is a unity in which the parts interface harmoniously. RaMBaM concurs: "Know that this whole of being is one individual and nothing else."[23] When Moshe asks to see God's ways, RaMBaM interprets the request to mean that Moshe is asking God to help him understand the nature of all existents "and the way they are mutually connected so that he will know how He governs them in general and in detail."[24] One aspect of this organicity is the promotion of instantaneous creation which featured

---

21 Schwartz, "Divine Immanence": 255. In a footnote, Schwartz says that Averroes, who influenced RaMBaM, was aware that his formulation of divine knowledge shared concepts with Sufi mysticism.
22 *Guide*, 2:25, 330.
23 Ibid., 1:72, 184.
24 Ibid., 1:54, 124.

in the rabbinic theology of creation. "Everything was created simultaneously; then gradually all things became differentiated. They [the rabbis] have compared this to what happens when an agricultural laborer sows various kinds of grain in the soil at the same moment."[25] Thus the three themes of the rabbinic theology of creation are reinforced: instantaneous creation, continuous creation, and *creatio ex nihilo*. Indeed, though there are exceptions, these rabbinic notions attain near-doctrinal status in the Middle Ages in both philosophical and mystical circles.

The final aspect of RaMBaM's understanding of creation to explore is his approach toward the animal kingdom. Although RaMBaM maintains that humans are superior to all other animals, that does not mean that other animals were created for our benefit. They were not. RaMBaM is the first Jew of whom I am aware who rejects anthropocentrism.[26] (Averroes maintained this belief, as well.) Halakhah allows humans to use animals for our own purposes, but never to inflict gratuitous pain. To be sure, the definition of "gratuitous pain" is subjective, but RaMBaM does maintain that nonhuman animals feel physical pain and emotional suffering to the same extent as do humans.[27] RaMBaM actually suggests that humans who have developed their intellect will suffer *less* than non-rational animals. RaMBaM's interpretation of Job is that his initial suffering is the consequence of his intellectual deficits. When Job comes to true knowledge of the deity and his own intellectual constraints, which happen when God appears to Job in a tempest (Job 38–41), Job's suffering diminishes. Thus, for RaMBaM, one should be particularly solicitous regarding the pain and distress of nonrational animals since their suffering may be even greater than our own.

Whatever one can say about the contemporary utility of some of RaMBaM's insights, some of which were jarringly prescient, he had no theology of creation due to his insistence on our fundamental incapacity to know God. RaMBaM's approach would be better described as natural theology, whereby all we can know about God is through nature. But even that is more than RaMBaM will allow. God's management of the cosmos *does not* describe God, Godself. Rather, God "performs actions [in

---

25 Ibid., 2:30, 350.
26 Ibid., 3:13, 452.
27 Ibid., 3:48, 599.

nature] resembling the actions that in us proceed from moral qualities."[28] Nevertheless, understanding nature is a window into divine wisdom which is why RaMBaM's halakhic work begins with the laws of nature. Knowing nature's laws through one's own intellectual efforts, rather than accepting them on authority, is the ultimate goal of the commandments because it paves the only road available to know God to whatever extent possible. There is no better indicator of RaMBaM's failure as a religious reformer than the fact that no other halakhic code ever again began with philosophy or science—at least, not how RaMBaM had intended.

> [In the Levush Malkhut], we have here a bold attempt on R. Jaffe's [c. 1530–1612] part to incorporate the meta-halakhic disciplines of astronomy, philosophy and Kabbalah into the standard rabbinic curriculum whose basic text was to be his own work. . . . Here the trend of Jewish culture in Poland-Lithuania to include philosophy and Kabbalah as part of the rabbinic tradition reaches its climax.[29]

As Lawrence Kaplan, the author of the citation above, makes clear elsewhere, the philosophy of Rabbi Jaffe was no longer the radical Aristotelianism of RaMBaM. An anti-Maimonidean, *philosophical* swing began in the fourteenth century reaching its peak in the writings of Hasdai Crescas (1340–1410), Joseph Albo (1380–1444), and Isaac Abarbanel (1437–1508). Moreover, since RaMBaM considered astrology "stupid" and Kabbalah, or proto-Kabbalah, heretical, he would not have been a fan of Rabbi Jaffe's Levush Malkhut.[30] (*Nonphilosophical* anti-Maimonideanism began almost immediately with the legal glosses of Rabbi Abraham ben David of Posquieres (1125–1198) to the Mishneh Torah and in Rabbi Moses ben Nahman's (1194–1270) Torah commentary which contains kabbalistic references.) Beginning as early as the thirteenth century, radical Aristotelianism was largely defanged and devalued. Although we do find some science and philosophy in the Levush Malkhut, just a few decades later, Isaiah Horowitz prefaces his legal

28 Ibid., 1:54, 124.
29 Lawrence Kaplan, "Rabbi Mordekhai Jaffe and the Evolution of Jewish Culture in Poland in the Sixteenth Century," in *Jewish Thought in the Sixteenth Century*, 275.
30 See RaMBaM's "Letter on Astrology," in *A Maimonides Reader*, ed. Isadore Twersky (Springfield: Behrman House, 1972), 466, and Kellner, *Maimonides' Confrontation with Mysticism*, 25-30.

material in *The Two Tablets of the Covenant* with Kabbalah and only Kabbalah. Subsequent legal literature has avoided general discussions of science and philosophy altogether.

Although the study of science (but not philosophy!) was considered praiseworthy by some halakhic compendia of the late Middle Ages, it was not the exclusive way to know and to love God, as it was for RaMBaM.[31] For Joseph Albo, the true human purpose is not intellectual perfection, but engaging in acts of loving kindness that benefit others—*imitatio Dei*.[32] As for the kabbalists, to whom we now turn, our acts of loving kindness are, first and foremost, directed toward fulfilling the needs of the holy One, uniting the divided divine.

The Mediated Monism of Kabbalah

The microcosm/macrocosm analogy has deep roots both in Neoplatonism and Judaism. "Each of us is the intelligible world," Plotinus wrote in the third century.[33] At about the same time, Jewish sages wrote, "All that the holy One, blessed be He, created upon the earth, He created in humans."[34] We have also seen how the tabernacle was posited as an intermediary in the same pattern as both the cosmos and human. Finally, Hillel justified his trips to the Roman bath house by claiming to perform a mitzvah by scrubbing clean the divine image in which all humans were created![35] The divine, the human, the tabernacle, and the world all share homologous structures and relationships.

Kabbalah deepens the relationships. The sefirot, representing the inner life of God, are often depicted in the anatomical image of a human. But the connections are more than skin deep. Isaiah Tishby comments that "Kabbalistic cosmogony [the creation of the cosmos] . . . is really a framework for theogonic processes [the creation of God]."[36] Put differently, when Kabbalah describes the unfolding of creation, it serves as a

---

31 S. A., Y. D. 246. See also Ruderman, *Jewish Thought and Scientific Discovery*, 73–77.
32 Joseph Albo, *Book of Principles* 3:5, 48–49. Cited in Harvey, "Ethical Theories Among Medieval Jewish Philosophers," in Dorff, *Oxford Handbook*, 97.
33 Plotinus, *The Enneads*, 3:4:3.
34 Avot d'Rabbi Natan A, ch. 31.
35 Avot d'Rabbi Natan B, ch. 30.
36 Tishby, *Wisdom of the Zohar*, 549.

prism through which the unfolding of God is revealed. In terms of a theology of creation, Kabbalah presents us with a monism (the worldview that the world is essentially a single entity) centuries prior to Spinoza's identification of nature with God. Far more explicit and consequential than RaMBaM's formal pantheism is the monism, however mediated, that exists in Kabbalah. Elliot Wolfson describes the metaphorical "mirror of nature" that became popular in the twelfth century:

> That nature is a mirror of God signifies the symbolic participation of the immaterial spirit in the body of the universe. . . . [The kabbalists] viewed all things of the corporeal world as a reflection of an inner process within the divine reality. . . . The *sefirot* are not only the cause but the very substance of that which is real. The issue, then, is not merely the structural parallelism between the divine and the mundane, but their ontological conjunction, which facilitates divine omnipresence in both realms.[37]

There is another dimension in Kabbalah's theology of creation that brings to the fore the Jewish flavor of this otherwise Neoplatonic myth: time. Stuck in exile, Jews could not tolerate the thought that history was static or cyclical. "Redemption" may shift meanings, but the dream of redemption is required to stave off despair. "Those who sow with tears will reap with cries of joy" (Psalms 126:5). We see the conflation of creation, revelation, and redemption in the first Torah commentary to include Kabbalah, that of Moshe Nahmanides (RaMBaN, 1194–1270) of Gerona.

Nahmanides, in his opening comment on Genesis, reveals that there is a "deep mystery" about creation that is inaccessible from biblical verses alone, but was received through tradition (*kabbalah*) from Moshe. The first word of the Torah, according to this tradition, alludes to the creation of the world through the ten sefirot.[38] Since the sefirot "are really a framework for theogonic processes," as Tishby wrote, the account of creation in Genesis, read esoterically, is the self-revelation of God. To our present point, Nahmanides reads the seven days of creation as the seven lower sefirot. The final sefirah thus corresponds to the seventh day, Shabbat. In the Talmud, Shabbat is called a preview of the

---

37 Elliot R. Wolfson, "Mirror of Nature Reflected in the Symbolism of Medieval Kabbalah," in Tirosh-Samuelson, *Judaism and Ecology*, 305–6.
38 Nahmanides on Gen. 1:1.

coming world.[39] Incorporating elements of both a Talmudic midrash and an earlier kabbalistic tradition, Nahmanides takes each day to represent one thousand years. He then tracks each day's creation to the historical events of that epoch. The seventh 1000-year cycle cycle, corresponding to Shabbat, alludes to the coming world.[40] Thus for Nahmanides, esoterically embedded in the account of creation is not only revelation but also the promise of redemption.

In the Torah, the seventh year is associated with two different dimensions of freedom. In the seventh year of servitude, the Hebrew servant is released.[41] (For this reason, among others, this peculiar institution is not *slavery* as we normally use the term in the contemporary United States.) On the terrestrial plane, every seven years the entire land of Israel is to lay fallow and be released from agricultural productivity (*shemittah*). Personal debts, as well, are to be forgiven in the seventh year. Filing for bankruptcy is the American way of escaping the cycle of poverty and debt. The Torah offers a different mechanism, built into the system, which avoids social stigma in recognition that sometimes poverty happens through no fault of one's own. And, even if one bears fault, the Torah extends second chances on a regular basis.

Beyond the seventh day and the seventh year lies the longest unit of time in the Torah: the jubilee. Every fifty years is the celebration of the completion of seven full cycles of seven years. This celebration involves a homecoming both for individuals and for the biblical tribes. Hebrew slaves are released even against their will, and real estate that had been sold during the previous half century reverts to the seller. Thus, if someone had sold their property to pay off debts, the jubilee year was a reset. It also meant that the extended family would be reunited throughout their tribal territory.

In the twelfth century, Abraham bar Hiyyah notes a theory that when the seventh millennium arrives "all the creatures will be gathered

---

39 Sannhedrin 108b.

40 Nahmanides on Gen. 2:3. See also Sannhedrin 97a and Gershom Scholem, *Origins of the Kabbalah*, 471.

41 See my *Torah through Time*, chapter 4, for the history of Jewish interpretations regarding the Hebrew slave.

and passed out of existence."[42] Although Bar Hiyyah rejects the theory, a similar notion resurfaces in an anonymous fourteenth-century text, Sefer HaTemunah. "During the Jubilee everything will be destroyed, while during the thousand years of the end of each *Shemittah* only the vegetal, animal and human beings will disappear."[43] In addition to what can only be described as cycles of mass extinction, this cataclysmic view of history includes "global conflagrations, especially wars between empires."[44] Not surprisingly, there is an alternative, utopian account of the jubilee articulated by a fourteenth-century sage, Rabbi Shem Tov ibn Gaon. For Rabbi Shem Tov, with each subsequent *shemittah*, culminating in the jubilee, there is cosmic progress that is manifest on our plane by diminishing evil.[45] With the rabbinic material, we saw similar disputes regarding national redemption. Will it be apocalyptic or utopian? Within the world of medieval mysticism, this dispute has been projected on to the cosmos.

For our purposes, the mystical jubilee has provided images of change over time. Changes within the sefirotic world speak to the dynamic unity of God. The Aristotelians, of course, would reject any change in God. Less obviously, they would also reject any substantive change in the physical world. RaMBaM is explicit that in the days of the Messiah, the only difference will be that a descendant of King David will rule Israel. As much as the philosophers emphasize stasis, the mystics emphasize dynamism. What the mystics offer in their descriptions of the jubilee is familiar: the hope of progress or the threat of extinction.

The Battle of the Will

Orthodox Platonists, Aristotelians, and Neoplatonists agree on one thing: divine volition is a human delusion. God's nature is unchanging and to attribute will to the divine nature is as much a human projection as imagining God with an outstretched arm. Both anthropomorphism, attributing a body to God, and anthropopathism, attributing emotions

---

42 Megillat HaMeggaleh, 12, cited in Moshe Idel, "The Jubilee in Jewish Mysticism," in *Fins de Siecle—End of Ages*, ed. Yosef Kaplan [Heb.] (Jerusalem: Mercaz Zalman Shazar, 2005), 212.
43 Ibid., 233.
44 Idel, "Multiple Forms of Redemption": 50.
45 Idel, "The Jubilee in Jewish Mysticism," 222.

to God, are equally immature. Thus, as ancient Greek philosophy penetrated medieval religious thought, both Islam and Judaism were forced to grapple with the tension between divine will and divine wisdom, the latter sometimes being pious code for necessity. The stakes were high, as RaMBaM points out: "Belief in eternity the way Aristotle sees it—that is, the belief according to which the world exists in virtue of necessity, that no nature changes at all, and that the customary course of events cannot be modified with regard to anything—destroys the Law in its principle, necessarily gives the lie to every miracle, and reduces to inanity all the hopes and threats that the Law has held out."[46]

The key to understanding the philosophic and religious approaches boils down to the question of free will. Does God have it? Could nature have been any different than it is? Do human beings have free will—or is that also as much a delusion and projection as God's outstretched hand? RaMBaM certainly wrote laws that presume individuals have free will. He also explicitly encouraged the rejection of the eternity of the world the way Aristotle had described. But the philosophical challenge to theism, to the conviction of a responsive God, was not easily dismissed.

The emanationist metaphysics of the kabbalists may have been influenced by Isaac Israeli (c. 855–932). Israeli, himself, was influenced by Plotinus who, usually, described emanation as a *necessary* overflow from the One who, like Plato's craftsman, has no envy.[47] Israeli remains unclear about the initial movement from the One. He speaks of the "quality of the emanation of the light which is created from the power and the will." Alexander Altmann, one of the early academics in the field of Jewish thought, commented on this line: "Israeli's phrase 'by power and will' has an almost polemical ring when held against the background [of necessary emanation]. . . . It asserts that creation, as distinct from emanation, is not a necessary process following from the very essence of God and being expressive of his power alone but declares it to derive from both power and will."[48] Moreover, the use of both emanation and creation language is confusing.

---

46 *Guide*, 2:25, 328.
47 *The Enneads*, 5:1:6, but there is ambiguity in Plotinus about this core issue. See *The Enneads*, 2:18:12 and 17, and 6:8:6.
48 Alexander Altmann, *Essays in Jewish Intellectual History* (Hanover: University Press of New England, 1981), 7.

A similar ambiguity, or confusion, exists in the writings of Solomon ibn Gabirol, an eleventh-century poet from Saragossa. In one poem, "The Fountain of Life," he identifies divine will with divine wisdom; in another "The Royal Crown" he sets wisdom above will. I am uncomfortable putting myth and poetry under a microscope. It seems to me that such analysis risks the category mistake of interpreting poetry as prose or Platonic myth as Aristotelian discursive reasoning. One understanding of Platonic myth is that it is employed *because* of the limitations of reason. Given that myth and poetry rely on imagination and intuition, we would be well served to recall RaMBaM's warning not to subject the details of such literature to a fine-toothed analysis.[49]

Although I risk falling victim to my own admonition, there is an element of ibn Gabirol's poetry that anticipates a distinction within early Kabbalah that I believe is crucial for a theology of creation. According to Julius Guttman, another pioneering academic in Jewish thought, ibn Gabirol distinguishes between "two aspects of the divine will. As pure being, independent of any activity, it is identified with God; but it becomes distinct from him as it begins to function."[50] One of the teachers of Nahmanides, Azriel of Gerona (c. 1160–1238), translates the poetry of ibn Gabirol into the language of sefirot. For Azriel, divine will exists in an undifferentiated state within the *Eyn Sof*. The divine will coalesces or activates within the *Eyn Sof* as the emanation process begins. Thus, for Azriel, will is the first sefirah that then emanates the second sefirah of wisdom.[51] Gershom Scholem explains the influence of Azriel's insistence on the emanation process being a function of divine volition rather than necessity. "The discerning reader will find this idea present among all the representatives of the school of Gerona, including Nahmanides, and it appears to be part of the heritage this circle bequeathed to the author of the *Zohar*."[52]

Linking will and wisdom in this way has several consequences. The most obvious implication is that divine volition is no illusion. The

49 *Guide*, 3:26, 509.
50 Julius Guttman, *Philosophies of Judaism: A History of Jewish Philosophy from Biblical Times to Franz Rosenzweig* (New York: Schocken Books, 1973), 103.
51 See Scholem, *Origins*, 437.
52 Ibid., 438. It is not insignificant that *Bahir*, a proto-kabbalistic text, identifies the first sefirah with thought rather than will. See Green, *Keter*, 142.

various names of this first character beacon that exists eternally *in potencia* within *Eyn Sof* is Will, Nothing, and Crown. Thus, *creatio ex nihilo*, in addition to emanation from the divine Nothing is volitional creation. Without the divine will, there would be Nothing and only Nothing. In Green's treatment of crown symbolism in early Kabbalah, he notes that the first sefirah is the Upper Crown and the final sefirah is the Lower Crown which exist in concentric circles – this subverts the more common hierarchical ordering. The following is a text from a thirteenth-century kabbalist.

> All the crowns (i.e., all the *sefirot*) exist in triads, [standing] in relation to one another. But *keter 'elyon* [upper crown] is a world hidden unto itself; all the others receive of its flow. It alone is hidden and joined to the root of roots, which no thought can grasp. . . . The worlds are entirely internal, *triads that are encompassed by one another and encompass one another. [Each] surrounds the other but is also surrounded by it. Each is above the other, yet the other is also above it, each beneath the other yet the other is beneath it. All of them draw from one another. The first is the middle and the middle is the first; the middle is the last, and the last is the middle, all following the Supernal will, to show that they are all His creatures and were created following His desire and His will.*[53]

Passages like the one above help remind us that our familiar dichotomies of top/bottom, before/after, and inside/outside lack the subtlety required for metaphysical speculation. Good and evil is, also, too crass a distinction to be of much worth, as we will see. Another consequence of the divine will activating "before" divine wisdom is acknowledgement that what we perceive as the necessity of wisdom has been filtered through the prism of divine desire. For Hasdai Crescas, the greatest of the anti-Aristotelians in his day, creation is a volitional act because it is neither arbitrary nor is there anything external to God compelling God's action. "Crescas maintains that God created the world out of His goodness and grace, His desire to endow being to others. Indeed, since love is the chief attribute of God for Crescas, God creates out of love, the desire

---

53 Ibid., 155-56; Green's emphasis. This text is quoted in Shem Tov Ibn Gaon, *Baddey 'Aron*, f. 62a (122). Translation slightly modified.

to share being with something other than Himself."[54] Crescas, himself, writes that God's "will is nothing but the love of the willer for that which he wills."[55] For the Aristotelians, *imitatio dei* involves striving for intellectual perfection; for Crescas, it's responding to the loving God and, as a consequence, lovingly engaging in God's commandments.

"Tradition, according to [Crescas], is a guide only in matters theological; he does not employ it in deciding matters concerning the nature of things."[56] The Jewish philosophical tradition, thinkers like RaMBaM and Gersonides, forged that path. What Crescas accomplished better than his predecessors was to put his view of nature's truths into a rabbinic idiom that reframed Aristotelian necessity as *hesed*, lovingkindness. God *was* compelled to create, or emanate, but not in the sense that we generally use the word *compel* which refers to Ploni compelling Almoni. God's essence is such that God cannot withhold his unbounded love. Or, to reverse the image, an unbounded love that cannot but share itself is what Crescas calls *God*.

In book one's discussion of medieval theology, I claimed that love was in the air. As imperfect as such an anthropopathism as divine love might be, it is the price of admission for Jewish metaphysics. Love, itself, is imperfect. Perhaps that is what makes the anthropopathism fit. St. Paul wrote that "love is patient."[57] (If only he knew how many billions of years it took for humans to emerge to be able to utter such a truth!) Patience, however, is not an unalloyed good. Unalloyed patience allows evil to go unchecked just as unalloyed love invites corruption. Judaism insists on checks and balances in the form of laws. Our Torah bakes love into the laws to form a "modest utopia."[58] Yes, the Torah recognizes the reality of slavery, for instance—it was the law of most every land. But the Torah's laws of slavery demand that the master recognize that the slave, too, was

---

54 Seymour Feldman, "The Theory of Eternal Creation in Hasdai Crescas and Some of his Predecessors," *Viator* 11 (1980): 309. See also Harvey, *Physics and Metaphysics*, 98-118.

55 Or Adonai 2:2:4. Cited in Feldman, "Theory of Eternal Creation": 309.

56 Harry Austryn Wolfson, *Crescas' Critique of Aristotle: Problems of Aristotle's Physics in Jewish and Arabic Philosophy* (Cambridge, MA: Harvard University Press, 1971), 125.

57 1 Corinthians 13:4.

58 Greenstein, "Biblical Law," in Holtz, *Back to the Sources*, 100.

created in the divine image.[59] In our theology of creation, the universe runs according to laws. Those laws of nature, just like the laws of Torah, have divine love baked in. One of my heroes, whom we will formally meet in the final chapter of this book, called love-infused natural law "cosmogonic eros."[60]

St. Paul also wrote that love bears all things and is never ending. Unconditional, unstinting love. As parents, this is our aspiration towards our children; as children, this is our projection upon our supernal Parent. Crescas wrote the bulk of his philosophical work in the years immediately following the murder of his only son in the Spanish pogroms of 1391. When reading about God's unbounded love for His creation, one hears the unfulfilled dreams of a mourning father. As we move across the Mediterranean Sea to explore theologies of creation that develop from Lurianic Kabbalah, Crescas' legacy is twofold: love and law. Interestingly, in both realms he opposed RaMBaM. His approach to Jewish law will await our last section. But Crescas' understanding of natural laws, although fundamentally deterministic, reflects God's love for creation.[61] For RaMBaM, acquiring knowledge is how we show our love *of* God; for Crescas, deeds of lovingkindness are how show we show our love *for* God.

The chapter on medieval Judaisms in book one detailed competing interpretations of Lurianic Kabbalah. One understanding is that *tzimtzum* is a cathartic purging of the roots of judgment from within the *Eyn Sof*; another view is that *tzimtzum* is a divine contraction that intentionally left the roots of restraint to provide the capacity for circumscribing the subsequent re-entry of infinite divinity. Both Gershom Scholem and Isaiah Tishby, in explaining *tzimtzum* as purgation, argued that "God was compelled to make room for the world" and *tzimtzum* "was not a volitional act of God."[62] In following these earlier scholars of Kabbalah, David Biale emphasizes the point:

---

59 Exodus 21:20 and 26.

60 Hans Jonas, *Mortality and Morality: A Search for Good After Auschwitz*, ed. Lawrence Vogel (Evanston: Northwestern University Press, 1996), 173.

61 Seymour Feldman, "A Debate Concerning Determinism in Late Medieval Jewish Philosophy," *Proceedings of the American Academy for Jewish Research* 51 (1984): 15–54.

62 Scholem, *Major Trends*, 261 and Tishby, *Doctrine of Evil*, 57.

> In both cases [of *tzimtzum* and the subsequent breaking of the vessels], there is a strong undercurrent of determinism: God does not will either development, but is instead a captive of an inevitable process. . . . This creation is not willed by God, but is instead determined by laws over which he seemingly has no control.[63]

As we saw in book one, such a deterministic characterization does not apply to all understandings of *tzimtzum*. Withdrawal can be a prerequisite to allow for the creation of another with whom to be in relationship. Nevertheless, that there were *any* interpretations that sidelined divine volition regarding creation is counter-intuitive, at the least, for a theistic system. Earlier Jewish thinkers, both philosophers and kabbalists, recognized the inherent necessity of nature's laws; but what we have in this reading of Luria is a suggestion that those laws themselves were a function of necessity. *God had no choice.*

Even assuming God's initial act of *tzimtzum* was volitional, the subsequent breaking of the vessels was *prima facie* unintentional. From that moment, as it were, creation no longer unfolded according to the divine will. The relationship between divine judgment and lovingkindness became adversarial. An element of the intradivine dynamic turned renegade. It is difficult, therefore, to describe the Lurianic myth as one of "intelligent design" in the sense that the term is used today.[64] Of course, the same is true of the biblical creation that God, himself, acknowledged had not gone according to his desire: "The Lord saw how great was humanity's wickedness on earth. . . . And the Lord regretted that He had made humanity on earth, and His heart was saddened."[65] Divine design was woefully flawed.

---

63 David Biale, "Jewish Mysticism in the Sixteenth Century," in *An Introduction to the Medieval Mystics of Europe*, ed. Paul Szarmach (Albany: State University of New York Press, 1984), 324 and 323.

64 Gerald Schroeder has pointed this out. See his *Genesis and the Big Bang: The Discovery Of Harmony Between Modern Science And The Bible* (New York: Bantam Books, 1990), 170–71 and *The Hidden Face of God: Science Reveals the Ultimate Truth* (New York: Touchstone, 2001), 10–11.

65 Genesis 6:56.

The Medieval Arc of Creation

The medieval arc of creation began with *creatio ex nihilo* as an expression of divine volition by a transcendent deity as expressed by Saadia Gaon in the tenth century. By the sixteenth century, the medieval arc of creation concludes with Lurianic Kabbalah, a model of divine emanation and a semi-autonomous cosmos animated by a drama beyond God's control. God is both immanent within and captive to creation. In Luria's medieval myth, the Jews alone can redeem the captive (through the performance of mitzvot), restoring the damsel, the Shechinah, to her king.

It is no surprise that Spinoza's own metaphysics, as radical as it may have been for Western thought, has obvious precedents in Jewish thought in terms of divine immanence and determinism.[66] Over the past few decades, there has been growing awareness of Jewish influences on the breakdown of Aristotelianism and the emergence of a new approach to science in sixteenth-century Europe. In addition to Spinoza, both Crescas and Judah Abarbanel wielded influence over Renaissance philosophers Pico della Mirandola (1463–1494) and Giordano Bruno (1548–1600).[67]

The kabbalistic theology of creation that we find at the end of the sixteenth century is, however, neither exhaustively deterministic nor radically free. Luria's ontology might be compared to Michelangelo's Prisoners or Slaves who stand in Florence's Accademia Gallery. Within what appears to be inert matter, life struggles to break through. At one point in earth's history, when the circumstances were opportune, life did break through. Whatever we call the force or principle behind this break-through—*shefa*, *hesed*, cosmogonic eros—it is the love that quickens the laws of nature. This eros *responded* to its environment and exploited opportunities therein. This eros has a telos, and halakhah has a blessing for its success: "Blessed are You . . . who withheld nothing from His world, and created in it beautiful creatures and trees for humanity to enjoy."[68] From Crescas to Luria to Isaiah Horowitz in his *Two Tablets of*

---

66 Carlos Frankel, "Hasdai Crescas on God as the Place of the World and Spinoza's Notion of God as *Res Extensa*," *Aleph* 9, no. 1 (2009): 77–111.

67 Mauro Zonta, "The Influence of Hasdai Crescas's Philosophy on Some Aspects of Sixteenth-Century Philosophy and Science," in *Religious Confessions and the Sciences in the Sixteenth Century*, ed. Jurgen Hel and Annette Winkelmann (Leiden: Brill, 2001), 71-78.

68 Brachot 43b.

the Covenant: God desires, God needs, to share His irrepressible love. God delights in our joy.[69]

We noted above that RaMBaM rejected the anthropocentrism of earlier Jewish tradition. RaMBaM's vision of creation was holistic and symbiotic. "Know that the whole of existence is one being and nothing else."[70] He maintained that the ultimate purpose of the whole was "the bringing into being of everything whose existence is possible."[71] God withholds nothing from the world. What I have called "Darwin's blessing," after all, praises God for *varying* creation, not winnowing it. God's light brought forth that which had been withheld (*chasakh*) by dispelling the darkness (*choshekh*). That goal requires symbiosis, not "survival of the fittest," Herbert Spencer's term that Charles Darwin eventually employed. As we approach modernity, when we will unearth fossil remains of evolutionary dead ends, we understand with Isaiah (6:3) and Judah HaLevi that the unfurling of an interdependent and continuous creation, i.e, the fullness of the entire earth, *is* God's glory.

---

69 Krassen, *The Generations of Adam*, 28.
70 *Guide*, 1:72, 184.
71 Ibid., 3:25, 506.

Chapter 9

Nature Read in Truth and Awe

A decade prior to Charles Darwin's *On the Origin of Species* (1859), Alfred Lord Tennyson published a poem describing "nature red in tooth and claw." One of the questions of his poem, "In Memoriam," is the extent to which humans are distinct from or embedded within nature. By the nineteenth century, the fledgling sciences of embryology and paleontology cried insistently with such questions. Other fields of study, specifically philosophy, history, and geology conspired against the traditional understandings of the Bible. Friedrich Nietzsche championed the will to power over loving thy neighbor, and the divine authorship of the Torah was undermined by thematically similar, but older texts discovered in the Near East. Both of Francis Bacon's books, nature and the Bible, were being read with novel hermeneutics, and the challenges to human self-understanding had never been so acute.

The Western world inherited the "principle of plenitude" from the Greeks. Arthur Lovejoy defines the principle as follows: "The universe is a *plenum formarum* in which the range of conceivable diversity of kinds of living things is exhaustively exemplified."[1] In the previous chapter we saw this principle explicitly stated in RaMBaM's *Guide* as well as in the rabbinic blessings thanking God for varying creation and not withholding anything from creation. Christendom emphasized the additional principle, from Plato's world of eternal and unchanging Ideas, of the fixity of species which guarantees that all species to have ever been

---

1   Arthur O. Lovejoy, *The Great Chain of Being: A Study of the History of an Idea* (New York: Harper Torchbooks, 1965), 52.

created will always exist in their current form.[2] Thus, by the beginning of nineteenth century, when fossils of extinct mammoths and mastodons had been unearthed, the Great Chain of Being snapped. The teleology of creation and divine providence were challenged. Why would God create an entire species only to have it become extinct?

The French zoologist, Georges Cuvier (1769–1832), promoted a theory of catastrophism to account for the abrupt changes in fossils of adjacent strata. The competing geological theory of uniformitarianism, articulated and promoted by James Hutton (1726–1797) and Charles Lyell (1797–1875), held that the only forces currently observed, *and at their present intensity*, have been at work over long periods of time in the formation of the earth's crust. In the Christian world, there was a scramble to align the new geological data with "scriptural geology." As the scientific community reached a consensus that the world was far older than had been previously assumed, there were innovative strategies to shoehorn deep time into Genesis 1. Might there be a gap between the creation of other animals and humans (the Gap Theory)? Alternatively, perhaps each biblical day represents an eon (the Day-Age Theory)?

Within the Jewish orbit, accounting for deep time required no innovation. In a short essay entitled "The Light of Life," based on his Passover sermon of 1842, Rabbi Israel Lifschitz (1782–1860) cited rabbinic and medieval sources supporting the claim of deep time. The Mishnah had acknowledged that the creation narrative cannot be understood through a superficial reading. Other rabbinic midrash asserted that there were orders of time prior to the first day and that God had created and destroyed *worlds* prior to our own.[3] Lipschutz also cites the medieval tradition of *shmittot* found in Sefer Temunah.[4] As we saw in the previous chapter, Sefer Temunah describes cataclysms at the end of each sabbatical cycle. Rabbi Lipschutz associated those upheavals with Cuvier's catastrophes.

---

2   Although not normative in Jewish thought, RaMBaM also maintained such a position. *Guide*, 2:10, 272.

3   M. Hagiga 2:1, Genesis Rabbah 3:6.

4   See Aryeh Kaplan, *Immortality, Resurrection, and the Age of the Universe: A Kabbalistic View* (Brooklyn: Ktav Publishing House, 1993), chapter 1, and Raphael Shuchat, "Attitudes Towards Cosmology and Evolution Among Rabbinic Thinkers in the Nineteenth and Early Twentieth Centuries: The Resurgence of the Doctrine of the Sabbatical Years," *The Torah u-Maddah Journal* 13 (2005): 15–49.

For reasons both historical and hermeneutical, nineteenth-century Judaism was well equipped to deal with deep time and extinction. Regardless of Bishop Ussher's seventeenth-century dating of the beginning of the world to 4004 BC, or the second century's Seder Olam Rabbah's slightly later start date, the geologists' claim that the earth must be much, much older was not immediately problematic. Christians developed new strategies, and Jews recycled old ones. Extinction was more tricky since it challenged teleology and providence. Without resolving the issue, many rabbis simply pointed to the antiquity of the problem. Genesis Rabbah claims that God destroyed multiple worlds that were not to his liking prior to the creation of this world. Why? God only knows—but fossils of extinct animals could be attributed to those false starts.

As we have pointed out above, there is another reason why initial news of animal extinction was not faith shaking for traditional Jews. In the Torah's description of the desert tabernacle, it instructs the Israelites to use the skins of *t'chashim* (Exodus 25:5). The rabbis do not agree what sort of animal this might be, but they do agree that the animal is now extinct.[5] These animals served their purpose to be the covering of the tabernacle and they no longer exist—which is why we don't know precisely what type of animals they were. At least initially, this example of extinction, canonized in RaSHI's Torah commentary, may have helped assuage whatever theological concerns emerged in the interregnum between special creation of fixed species and widespread acceptance of transmutation.

Before we continue the advance of science with Darwin's theory of descent with modification, there is a far more pressing issue on the Jewish agenda with which to contend. At almost the exact moment that Darwin published *On the Origin of Species*, a thin volume entitled *Essays and Reviews* was published in London (1860). Modern biblical scholarship, for the first time, was exported from its German context and introduced to the English-speaking world in a series of essays edited by John William Parker. As Spinoza had contended 200 years earlier, the Bible must be approached and analyzed like any other text. The Torah must be seen within its ancient Near Eastern neighborhood; and the Christian Bible must be similarly contextualized and rationally interpreted. Within

---

5   Shabbat 28b.

two years, more than 22,000 copies of *Essays and Reviews* were sold. (By way of comparison, a decade after the publication of *On the Origin of Species*, only 10,000 copies had been sold.[6]

In Germany, as we saw in book one, modern biblical scholarship was embraced by early Jewish reformers. Indeed, the central theological dispute dividing the reformers and the traditionalists was the origin of the two Torahs, the Written and the Oral. In Germany, the home of Bible scholarship, the leaders of what became Reform, Conservative, and Orthodoxy were marking out their territories just as the new science of evolutionary biology was overthrowing the paradigm of the special creation of fixed species. As we wade into the evolutionary abyss, we must remember that the stakes for our Jewish theologians go well beyond any particular biological theory or mechanism. The dispute is over the future of Judaism itself. From the reformers' point of view, will Judaism be a tree of life or petrified wood? From the perspective of the traditionalists, will Judaism remain faithful to God's never-ceasing voice from Sinai, or repeat the mistake of the Sabbateans and abandon the traditions of the ancestors?

The Darwinian Revolution

Let us define our terms. Individuals of one animal species slowly morphing into another, over many generations, can be called *transmutation* or *descent with modification*. *Evolution* is also a term to describe such a process. Evolution contrasts with both special creation, that is, God calling each species into existence, and the fixity of species, that is, species never changing. Charles Darwin (1809–1882) was concerned with speciation, how new species emerge. Darwin did not, however, invent the notion of evolution. That concept can actually be traced back to Anixamander in the sixth century BCE.

Closer to Darwin's own day, the French *philosophes*, Jean-Baptiste Lamarck (1744–1829), and even Darwin's own grandfather, Erasmus, were speculating about evolution well before Darwin set sail on the HMS *Beagle* in late December of 1831. What Darwin realized during his years

---

6   R. B. Freeman, *The Works of Charles Darwin*, 44; cited in Thomas F. Glick, *The Comparative Reception of Darwinism* (Austin: University of Texas Press, 1974), 8.

on the *Beagle* was the *mechanism* for evolution which he called *natural selection*. (Empedocles, a fifth-century BCE thinker, adumbrated natural selection as well.) When Darwin finally published his work in 1859, more than twenty years after his initial insight, the full title was *On the Origin of Species by Means of Natural Selection* (hereafter *Origin*).

Speciation through descent with modification is *religiously* innocuous for Jews. To be sure, there are *textual* hurdles given the accounts of creation presented in the Torah. But, there is also textual precedent—the serpent in the garden originally had legs! Texts can be interpreted, and for Jews, unlike Christians, there is nothing doctrinally sacrosanct from the creation narratives. Furthermore, Jews have a long, storied history of nonliteral interpretation. The covenant between the Israelites and God centers around the commandments from Sinai. Historical studies, not evolutionary theory, challenge that narrative.

The good news of the new covenant between God and the Christians, however, is that the Israelites' commandments have been superseded. Jesus's sacrifice on the cross atones for the sins of humanity that have been passed down from the original sinners in the Garden. (In this way, the Catholic dogma of original sin has its parallel in Lamarck's theory of acquired characteristics!) But if *Homo sapiens* emerged from an earlier species, and there was no singular Adam to bequeath his original sin, for what did Jesus die? Christianity crafted multiple responses to evolutionary theory, but it was Darwin's mechanism of natural selection that was to present the greatest challenge to both Christianity and Judaism.

> As many more individuals of each species are born than can possibly survive; and as consequently, there is a frequently recurring struggle for existence, it follows that any being, if it vary however slightly in any manner profitable to itself, under the complex and sometimes varying conditions of life, will have a better chance of surviving, and thus be *naturally selected*. From the strong principle of inheritance, any selected variety will tend to propagate its new and modified form.[7]

Although Darwin's description lacks the jolt of a revolutionary's manifesto, with a one-two punch, he dropped design.

---

7   Charles Darwin, *On the Origin of Species by Means of Natural Selection, First Edition*, in Charles Darwin, *The Portable Darwin*, ed. Duncan M. Porter and Peter W. Graham (New York: Penguin Group, 1993), 110. Hereafter referred to as *Origin*.

To better appreciate Darwin's art and science, behold the scene from William Paley's *Natural Theology* (1802), a text which Darwin claimed to have committed to memory. *Natural Theology* opens with a gentleman strolling on a heath, happening upon a watch, and recognizing that the instrument, with its intricate mechanisms for telling time, must have had a designer. Paley then describes the intricate workings of the world and asserts that it, too, must have a designer. "The contrivances of nature surpass the contrivances of art, in the complexity, subtilty, and curiosity of the mechanism."[8] While Paley identified the designer of nature's contrivances as the providential God, Darwin had no use for that hypothesis. What appears as design in nature is an artifact of natural selection. In saying so, Darwin shakes the ground under Paley's heath. "But Natural Selection, as we shall hereafter see, is a power incessantly ready for action, and is as immeasurably superior to man's feeble effort, as the works of Nature are to those of Art."[9]

There are two implications to Darwin's mechanism of natural selection that have continued to haunt theological responses to evolutionary theory. The first looks backwards: creation had no preordained direction. As Stephen Jay Gould wrote, if we were to rewind the tape of history, the odds that anything like us humans would again evolve is staggeringly low. Which variations will prove to be adaptive in any given environment is unforeseeable. Only in retrospect can a naturalist reconstruct a plausible just-so story that attributes survival to a particular adaptation. But, a prospective teleology, looking forward to the emergence of certain extant species, including *Homo sapiens*, would be excluded by Darwin's mechanism of natural selection. More humbling is that what *Homo hubris* perceives as progress in nature, culminating in us, is nothing other than a felicitous artifact (from our perspective) of what happens to have been adaptive in evolutionary history. Science, qua science, does not identify what has been adaptive with what is superior mentally or physically. Darwin, himself, was at pains to deny that survival of the fittest was necessarily progressive.[10]

8   Paley, *Natural Theology*, 43.
9   Darwin, *Origin*, 108
10 James R. Moore, *Post-Darwinian Controversies: A Study of the Protestant Struggle to Come to Terms with Darwin in Great Britain and America, 1870–1900* (New York: Cambridge University Press, 1979), 155–59.

The second implication of Darwinism takes the concept of survival of the fittest, an expression of Herbert Spencer which Darwin did not use until the fifth edition of *Origin* (there were six), and projects it forward. If what has survived in evolutionary history is the fittest, does that not valorize competition over cooperation and struggle over kindness? We will see challenges to both implications, but in the aftermath of the opening salvoes of the Darwinian revolution, such was the gauntlet for whomever risked the run. Indeed, within the liberal Christian world where the axiom of progress was sacrosanct, accepting transmutation of species while ignoring or rejecting Darwin's mechanism was the prevailing strategy.[11]

True to Darwin's penchant for punctiliousness, he revised the *Origin* a total of five times, the sixth edition being published in 1872. Throughout the 1860s, European naturalists were overwhelmed by Darwin's evidence from related scientific fields. William Whewell, a philosopher of science, had coined the term *consilience* in 1840 and it was shortly thereafter applied to Darwin's strategy: evidence from independent, unrelated sources "jumping together" towards the same conclusion. Darwin was surprised that his theory of descent with modification was so quickly accepted on the European continent, although his mechanism of natural selection was not largely acknowledged until the late 1930s with the resurfacing of Mendelian genetics in the neo-Darwinian or Modern Synthesis.

Given Darwin's long argument in the *Origin*, he wisely deferred discussion of the place of humanity. Not until the scientific world had a decade to digest transformationism and its implications did Darwin publish the sequel *The Descent of Man* in 1871. He did not relish attributing the emergence of humanity to natural selection. He was a conservative British gentleman, married to an even more conservative British gentlewoman. They had lost three of their ten children, and he wished to cause his wife no further pain. Already in the 1840s, in the privacy of a letter to a colleague, he rued that arguing against providential design in nature felt like confessing to murder. The "murder" in the *Descent of Man* garnered far more attention than the presentation of evidence in *Origin*. Thus, although there are scattered references to Darwin and his theory of

---

11 Ibid., 236–41.

transmutation in Jewish sources during the 1860s, a sustained response from almost any theologian awaited the mid-1870s in the wake of *The Descent.*

Malbim: The Pivot from Medieval to Modern

Among the first traditional, Eastern European rabbis to wrestle with evolutionary theory was Rabbi Meir Loeb ben Yehiel Michael, known as Malbim (1809–1879). His Torah commentary, written from 1867–1876, never mentions Darwin, but does make the extraordinary claim that *transformationism is the proper understanding of Genesis 1.* Malbim's sensitive reading is primarily motivated by his commitment to defend the divine authority of Torah from the heretical claims of Reform rabbis and their acceptance of modern biblical criticism. In addition to defending the divine authorship of both the Written Torah *and* the Oral Torah, Malbim's commentary sought to demonstrate that, contrary to Reform charges of the historical development and change of Jewish law, the rabbinic derash was the plain meaning of the Written Torah.

Within Malbim's commentary on Genesis, there are discussions of anatomy, astronomy, biology, botany, geology, medicine, optics, and zoology. Malbim was familiar with German scientific texts and was trying to educate his readership who may have otherwise remained ignorant or received their scientific education from less pious sources. For instance, Malbim rejects the concept of deep time and geologists' arguments based on the fossil record of successive strata. He claims that the waters of Noah's flood and the chasms which opened from below shuffled the geological record rendering the geologists' claims specious.[12]

In his opening discussion of Genesis 1, Malbim argues for instantaneous creation citing the midrash of Rabbi Nehemia, as well as RaMBaM and Nahmanides. Given that Malbim also believes that all revelation was given at Mount Sinai and then unfolds through time, there is a parallel between creation and revelation. There are no discontinuities in either creation or revelation—*Torah non facit saltum*! The Torah does not jump!

The principle of plenitude informs the great chain of being. Aristotle had described nature as proceeding "little by little from things lifeless to

---

12 Malbim, Hatorah ve'Hamitzvah, on Gen. 7:23.

animal life in such a way that it is impossible to determine the exact line of demarcation, nor on which side thereof an intermediate form should lie."[13] Aristotle used the ascending scale of life for purposes of taxonomy; Malbim links God to the chain. "All of creation that was from pre-existing matter [from the initial burst of divine creativity], God said to it that it should shed its earlier form and take on a different form. For example, when the Torah says that the earth should sprout vegetation, it means that the earth should shed its inert mineral form and take on a vegetable form."[14] Malbim's greatest contribution to a modern theology of creation, however, is offering a *kabbalistic* great chain of being.

> In the creation of the world, creation began to emanate at the start from above to below, and everything that descended below materialized more and coarsened more until this lower, corporeal world emerged a great distance from the supernal light. . . . But after [this coarsened, thickened light] arrived at its material and turbid end, reality began to turn, to clarify itself and return to its supernal place.[15]

A kabbalistic great chain of being begins with the divine munificence cascading through "descending" dimensions, coarsening along the way, until it materializes in this world. That image, Neoplatonic in origin, animates medieval Kabbalah. Hasidism reversed the direction of the great chain of being to ascend toward the Source through spiritual discipline. The Hasidim transformed theosophy into religious psychology. Malbim transformed theosophy, the inner life of God, into panentheism, all reality is within the life of God. The emanation process is reversed to purify and spiritualize the gross corporeality of material existence. What Malbim then describes is how each link in the chain of being is incorporated in the return. "Previous steps of life are present *in their entirety* in

---

13 Aristotle, *History of Animals*, 8:1, 588b4.
14 Malbim on Gen. 1:3.
15 Malbim on Psalm 148:1 referenced in his comment on Gen. 1:25. There are echoes in this image of both Shlomo Alkebetz and Moshe Cordovero's *or yashar* and *or chozer*. See Joseph Ben-Shlomo, *The Mystical Theology of Moses Cordovero* [Hebrew] (Jerusalem: Bialik Institute, 1965), 268–74. For possible influence on Malbim from Cordovero, see Noah H. Rosenbloom, *Malbim: Exegesis, Philosophy, Science and Mysticism in the Writings of Rabbi Meir Lebush Malbim* [Heb.] (Jerusalem: Mossad HaRav Kook, 1988), 104 and 382–83. See also Moshe Idel, *Enchanted Chains: Techniques and Rituals in Jewish Mysticism* (Los Angeles: Cherub Press, 2005).

the succeeding steps. . . . All the products of the day were incorporated into the products of the following day. For example, when God desired to create the person, He included within him all the powers found in the animal kingdom which had been previously created."[16]

Rabban Gamliel's polemical derash against the philosopher concerning *creatio ex nihilo* reverberated through medieval biblical commentaries, particularly those of Nahmanides and Rabbi David Kimchi, RaDaK (1160–1235). They both, like Rabban Gamliel, asserted that *bara* signifies *creatio ex nihilo* while other "making" verbs involve recombinations of pre-existing material.[17] Their point is that human bodies are *made* from the same matter that existed prior to their emergence. What was created by God, *ex nihilo*, indicated by the use of *bara* in Genesis 1:27, was their intellectual soul and its capacity for free will. Malbim used Rabban Gamliel's linguistic distinction to differentiate soul creation from physical transmutation. The Malbim thus transformed Rabban Gamliel into an evolutionary!

Throughout Malbim's commentary on Genesis 1, he shows how the Torah and its rabbinic explanations actually anticipated the scientific discoveries of the nineteenth century. Special creation and fixity of species were never Torah truths. The Torah's usage of *bara*, as has been documented since Rabban Gamliel, is the unique divine creation from His "supernal wisdom."[18] "Supernal wisdom" is a kabbalistic marker for the second sefirah. Malbim used enough mystical terms to address the slice of his readership who was versed in Kabbalah, but he also wrote for those who were uninitiated. *Bara* indicates that all physical matter was created instantaneously, *ex nihilo*, and then unfolded over time. The ensoulment of animals (verse 21) and humans (verse 27) are the only other two instances of *bara* after the initial creation of matter. The Malbim here has done an impressive job of safeguarding the Torah from charges of being nothing more than an ancient myth by going on the offensive and claiming that the Torah anticipated the science of biological evolution. The Malbim's next move is particularly clever since it resolves textual oddities and furthers his argument that the Torah is scientifically prescient.

---

16 Malbim on Gen. 1:25. Malbim claims to be explicating Genesis Rabbah 8:2.
17 Nahmanides on Gen. 1:26 and RaDaK on Gen. 1:27.
18 Malbim on Gen. 1:25, section 5.

The Torah makes two claims that could be construed to be in tension. Genesis 1:31 concludes the sixth day and indicates that God reviews all that God has made. But then the text says that God finished His work on the seventh day and rested. The Torah does not indicate that God created anything on the seventh day, so why wouldn't God have completed His work on the sixth day? RaSHI, citing a rabbinic midrash, insists that the Torah means that God finished His work *by* the seventh day.[19] Malbim's resolution is evolutionary.

> Rabbenu Nissim (1320–1380) wrote that the reason why the Torah says, "And He rested on the seventh day," is that everything develops and changes and continues to develop even after the effecting agent is removed. A hen roosts on her eggs to change their disposition so that they take on the form of chicks. But there is no doubt that if the hen left in the middle of roosting, that the material in the egg would continue developing to take on the form of a chick and the development would not be arrested immediately upon the departure of the hen.
>
> And similarly, during the account of creation when God said, "Let the earth sprout forth vegetation" and "Let the waters swarm," even though the divine energy only generated each thing in its day, the earth was self-generating, and not from the activity of the Worker, for the next day or two.
>
> But as soon as the seventh day entered, God gave to the works of creation a tranquil and quiet nature and their self-propelling movement was stopped. Referring to this, when the Torah says, "The heavens and the earth were finished. God finished on the seventh day . . . " it means that their existence was completed on the sixth day but that their own self-propelling activity was not completed until God stopped that activity on the seventh day.[20]

This self-propelling movement is evolution. "During the days of creation, everything came into existence as a result of the destruction of a

---

19 Genesis Rabbah 10:9.

20 Malbim on Gen. 2:1. Zvi Faier has translated sections of Malbim's commentary into English. He translates *tnuatam hamitchayevet me'atzma* as "self-evolving activity." I have translated it as "self-propelling movement." *Malbim: Commentary on the Torah,* vol. 1, *Beginning and Upheaval,* trans. Zvi Faier (Jerusalem: Hillel Press, 1978), 174.

pre-existing form."[21] What God did, according to Malbim, was not to stop working on the seventh day, but to cause the heavens and the earth to stop working. (This grammatical move, to read *stopped* as *caused to stop*, is also found in Genesis Rabbah and mentioned by RaMBaM.)[22] According to Malbim, God's initial statements to the heavens and the earth implied that "the development should continue unceasingly all through the six days of creation."[23] It may reasonably be asked exactly how much evolution might occur within the course of a few days. Anticipating such a question, Malbim contends that the primordial light from day one, prior to the sun's emergence, was an emanation from God's great light and enveloped the earth on all sides simultaneously.[24] Moreover, the primordial light was "more efficient in generating life from the earth because it was unsheathed."[25]

One of the challenges to Darwinism was its alleged violation of the method of induction that had been championed by Francis Bacon and Isaac Newton. How could Darwin claim that species have evolved over deep time through natural selection if he has not witnessed a single example? To put the problem differently, but more sharply, *we* do not see speciation in nature. One of the earliest Jewish figures to comment on evolution was Abraham Geiger, a founding father of the German Reform movement. In 1864, Geiger wrote in the introduction to his *Judaism and its History*, a book whose thesis is the historical evolution of Judaism from the biblical period to modernity, that the natural world does not look like the one Darwin described.

> But this much we can see: species do exist, they do not change one into the other, they are apart and remain apart. The same force which created them at the beginning, one out of the other, as alleged, should necessarily continue the same process, should even at this time produce an animal out of the plant and perfect it to the higher organism. But the present world does not present to us such a phenomenon, each kind remains within its

---

21 Malbim on Gen. 1:5.
22 Genesis Rabbah 10:9 and *Guide*, 1:67, 162.
23 Malbim on Gen. 2:1.
24 Malbim on Gen. 1:5.
25 Malbim on Gen. 1:11. Noah Rosenbloom first suggested that the primordial light accelerated developmental processes. See his "A Post-Enlightenment Exposition on Creationism," *Judaism* 38 (Fall 1989): 474.

fixed limits, it continually begets individuals only of its own kind, and not one is transformed into another.[26]

The genius of Malbim's comment is that it affirms evolution *and* explains why it is not currently observable—God caused the evolution of nature to rest on the seventh day. The heavens and the earth were finished on the seventh day from continuing to be self-generating because God caused them to rest. Although the scientific salvage value of Malbim's commentary on Genesis 1 is slim, I do appreciate his ingenuity. Malbim will be among the last theologians to engage in such creative exegesis. Through a close reading of the Torah and the promotion of select midrashim, he resolves seeming tensions within the Torah itself and explains the usage of different verbs in light of the latest scientific advances. He presents himself as even more in tune with modernity than the founder of Reform Judaism while still "demonstrating" that the Torah, rabbinic tradition, and the Kabbalah were scientifically sound thousands of years before the Western world made such discoveries. For our purposes, Malbim will be credited as the first to explicitly apply the concepts of Kabbalah to evolutionary history, a strategy that has survived, with variations, until today.

American Reform (Mis)Appropriations

Americans were preoccupied through the 1860s with a civil war and the beginnings of Reconstruction. When the luxury arose to respond to the latest historical and scientific challenges to biblical religion, among the first to take up the cudgels against Darwinism was Charles Hodge (1797–1878). Hodge was the principal at the Princeton Theological Seminary. The president of Princeton University from 1868–1888, James McCosh, had seen how evolution made sense of so many different fields that there must be truth to it. McCosh was an early advocate of evolution, and Hodge responded with disproportionate force. His 1874 *What is Darwinism?* resounds throughout the remainder of the nineteenth century with his answer: Darwinism is atheism!

---

26 Abraham Geiger, *Judaism and Its History*, trans. Charles Newburgh (New York: Block Publishing Co., 1911), 17.

At roughly the same time, John William Draper published his *History of the Conflict between Religion and Science* effectively inaugurating a century of that misperception. One generation later, Andrew Dickson White published an even more influential polemic with an even more antagonistic title: *A History of the Warfare of Science with Theology in Christendom* (1896). White, the first president of Cornell University, wanted to carve out intellectual space for scientific studies unbeholden to any religious confession. Religious responses to Darwinian evolution in late nineteenth-century America were, therefore, framed by early Christian opposition and a nearly universal misperception that Christianity was historically hostile to scientific innovation. Jews were happy to exploit that image by aligning themselves with science. After all, there *was* a long-standing conflict between Christianity and Judaism, and the enemy of my enemy is my ally. By the time historians began correcting that polemical view of conflict between Christianity and science, Protestant fundamentalism had been born, reached maturity, and was challenging the teaching of evolution in America's schools.[27]

Although the first Jews arrived from Brazil to New Amsterdam in 1654, the American Jewish population was negligible until 1881. Within forty years, the Jewish population exploded from 250,000 to roughly 3,500,000. By the end of the 1890s, it was clear that Reform Judaism, born in Germany, would not attract the unemancipated emigrants streaming in from Eastern Europe. Until then, the founder of American Reform institutions, Isaac Mayer Wise, had hoped that his version of Reform would become American Judaism. When he opened the first Jewish seminary in 1875, he named it Hebrew Union College because he hoped that all "Hebrew" rabbis in America would be ordained there. Isaac Mayer Wise, beginning in late 1874, just after Hodge's book was published, gave a series of twenty-two lectures on evolution. In 1876, they were published under the title *The Cosmic God*.

Wise was born and educated in Germany. When he arrived in New York in 1846, he began calling himself rabbi and doctor, though historians have no evidence of such an extensive formal education. Wise was not the first rabbi to offer a sermon on Darwin or evolution, but his

---

27 For a history of this historiography, see David C. Lindberg and Ronald L. Numbers, "Beyond War and Peace: A Reappraisal of the Encounter between Christianity and Science," *Church History* 55 (1986): 338–354.

knowledge of the science was unparalleled amongst his peers and his treatment more sustained than any in the United States prior to 1887 when a member of Hebrew Union College's first class published *Evolution and Judaism*. The author, Joseph Krauskopf, affectionately dedicated the book to his teacher and mentor, Isaac Mayer Wise.

Wise rejected Darwinism and all other forms of materialist evolution that were popular in his home country of Germany.[28] Wise was not opposed to transmutation of species, per se, but rejected the mechanism of natural selection. "The evolutions were not external, they were internal in nature, with their cause in the vital force, hence in perpetual connection with the whole of nature."[29] Wise is presenting transmutation as the result of an inner, vital force, and not anything to do with the external environment or the survival of the species therein. Wise is positing an ideal type, through which the immanent, divine force "overcomes and metamorphozes matter gradually."[30] Repositioning the mechanism of evolution from the environment to within the organism was a favored strategy of Protestant thinkers in the 1870s as well. The immanence of the Word, or logos, was excavated from early Christian thought as a

28 Two articles by Marc Swetlitz and one by Naomi Cohen have laid the groundwork for all of us working in the field of American Jewish responses to Darwinism. My analyses, although occasionally diverging from Swetlitz, owe much to his pioneering research. Swetlitz was doing postgraduate work at Brandeis Univesity when I entered as a first-year graduate student. His encouragement and enthusiasm influenced my decision to pursue this topic further. See his "American Jewish Responses to Darwin and Evolutionary Theory, 1860–1890," in *Disseminating Darwinism: The Role of Place, Race, Religion, and Gender*, ed. Ronald L. Numbers and John Stenhouse (Cambridge: Cambridge University Press, 1999), 209-45, and "Responses of American Reform Rabbis to Evolutionary Theory, 1864–1888," in *The Interaction of Scientific and Jewish Cultures in Modern Times*, ed. Yakov Rabkin and Ira Robinson (Lewiston: Edwin Mellen Press, 1995), 103-25. See also Naomi Cohen, "The Challenges of Darwinism and Biblical Criticism to American Judaism," *Modern Judaism* 4, no. 2 (1984): 121-57.
29 Isaac Mayer Wise, *The Cosmic God: A Fundamental Philosophy in Popular Lectures* (Cincinnati: Office of American Israelite and Deborah, 1876) 116. Access to this book was kindly provided by Special Collections at Brandeis University through the Jacob Rader Marcus Collection. Swetlitz argues that Wise opposed all forms of evolution. "American Jewish Responses," 221 and "Responses of American Reform Rabbis," 118.
30 Wise, *Cosmic God*, 171. Wise's theory shared much with Robert Chambers' *Vestiges of the Natural History of Creation* (1844) as well as Ernst Haeckel's 1866 work on animal morphology.

response to Darwinism.[31] But what was novel in America was *de rigeur* in Wise's homeland.

Idealism, a name for a constellation of different philosophies circulating in Europe, posits that what is most real is not matter but the ideal form in which we perceive and experience matter to be embodied. A scholar from the period explains, "Religiously there is no difference between idealistic theism and immanent theism."[32] As Jon Roberts has noted, "In ascribing all causal efficacy to God, these [Protestant] thinkers were in effect according all power in the cosmos to intelligent Spirit rather than to matter."[33] That Spirit operates in and through biological organisms. For Hegel, another household name philosopher in Germany, that Spirit also works through history leading toward Hegel's own version of salvation. Thus, when Wise refers to an inner force, he is dragging the world of German philosophy behind him. "The vital force is perpetually and continuously at work to govern matter and liberate itself from matter, to become itself again, i.e., conscious and self-conscious in individualized lives."[34]

Although Wise remains committed to the divinity of the Torah, an anomaly within Reform Judaism, he makes no attempt to offer a scientific interpretation of Genesis. The closest he comes is breaking up the history of nature into seven phases. In the 1885 Pittsburgh Platform, Reform Judaism acknowledges that the creation narratives are "primitive ideas" that reflect the thinking of the ancient Near East. Wise also does not deal with providence and theodicy to the same extent that he deals with speciation. His emphasis is on immanence—and that emphasis is shared by popularizers like Herbert Spencer and John Fiske, as well as German philosophers and scientists.[35]

What Wise does accomplish, however, is significant. He distinguishes Judaism as a religion of reason that accepts demonstrated science compared to less progressive forms of Christianity. The defensiveness of

---

31 Jon H. Roberts, *Darwinism and the Divine in America: Protestant Intellectuals and Organic Evolution, 1859–1900* (Notre Dame: University of Notre Dame Press, 2001), 75 and 137.

32 Border Parker Browne, *Studies in Christianity* (1909), 286. Cited in Roberts, *Darwinism and the Divine in America*, 140.

33 Ibid., 140.

34 Wise, *Cosmic God*, 114.

35 Roberts, *Darwinism and the Divine in America*, 121–22.

Charles Hodge towards Darwinism and evolution is redirected by Wise. Evolution is a path, not a mechanism. Mechanisms are interchangeable. What Wise rejected was materialism—goal-directed Spirit was responsible for the progress in evolution and history plain for all to see. Wise's rejection of natural selection, acceptance of evolution, and benign neglect of Genesis 1 establishes a pattern that will be followed by generations of American rabbis.

Before turning to other early American rabbis, we should pause to reflect on the place of ethics in this discussion. We have seen how *Bildung* became something of an end in itself for German Jews in the nineteenth century. Outside of Germany, as well, ethics was considered the apogee of religiosity. What Wise found so profoundly objectionable in Darwin's natural selection was what he labeled "Homo-Brutalism."

> In a moral point of view the Darwinian hypothesis on the descent of man is the most pernicious that could be possibly advanced, not only because it robs man of his dignity and the consciousness of his pre-eminence, which is the coffin to all virtue, but chiefly because it represents all nature as a battle ground, a perpetual warfare of each against all in the combat for existence, and represents the victors as those praiseworthy of existence, and the vanquished ripe for destruction. . . . Peace in any shape is illegitimate and unnatural.[36]

Notice that the problems of natural selection for Wise are both descriptive of our past and prescriptive for our future. Darwin, himself, never took that step. That path was trod by Social Darwinists like Herbert Spencer who pressed survival of the fittest into service as public policy. Wise fell victim, here, to the naturalistic fallacy, namely that because something is natural it is virtuous or preferable. Wise might have accepted the winnowing work of natural selection in nature's past, while deeming it wholly inappropriate at this point in human history. The problem of materialism would still remain, but here is Lester Frank Ward in 1884, parrying the thrusts of Social Darwinism while accommodating natural selection.

> When a well-clothed philosopher on a bitter winter's night sits in a warm room well lighted for his purposes and writes on paper with pen and ink

---

36 Wise, *Cosmic God*, 51.

in the arbitrary characters of a highly developed language the statement that civilization is the result of natural laws, and that man's duty is to let nature alone so that untrammeled it may work out a higher civilization, he simply ignores every circumstance of his existence and deliberately closes his eye to every fact within the range of his faculties. If man had acted upon his theory there would have been no civilization, and our philosopher would have remained a troglodyte. . . . If nature progresses through the destruction of the weak, man progresses through the *protection* of the weak.[37]

Other early American Reform rabbis have been treated extensively by Marc Swetlitz. For our purposes, they are interesting primarily because of how they frame evolution. Generally, none of them bothers to learn the niceties of evolutionary theory. They take "Darwinism" as the divinely guided, progressive transmutation of species. Teleology is assumed or imposed, and theodicy bracketed. Their interest, with little exception, is demonstrating how Reform Judaism is the religious corollary of evolution in contrast to an atavistic Orthodox Judaism; and how Reform Judaism is an ally of scientific advance in contrast to a reactionary Christianity.

Already in January of 1874, a new American, Kaufman Kohler (1843–1926), delivered a sermon on religion and science to his congregation in Chicago. The sermon, like many in those days, was given in German. Kohler, a descendant of a long line of Orthodox rabbis, was born and educated in Germany and came to the United States in 1869 with both ordination and a doctorate. In 1903, Kohler became president of Hebrew Union College. But in 1874, he spoke to his congregation as a shepherd leading his flock through the minefield of modernity.

Beloved friends! Is this view of the world, which sets up progress and development as the law of nature and of spiritual life, and which says to man, "Strive upward and onward, seek victory over the lower world whence you sprang! Your paradise is not behind you, but before you"—is not this view of the world the highest and the best praise of the Creator? Does not this constant progress of all existence prove the control of a highest wisdom and goodness which leads everything on to completeness? Does

---

37 Lester Frank Ward, "Mind As A Social Factor," *Mind* 4 (Oct. 1884): 571–73.

not this idea of life perfectly harmonize with our religion, whose history is one of internal progress, and whose aim is the highest future ideal of humanity? Does is not harmonize perfectly with our comprehension of religion, which we do not recognize in form, but in reform, which has its living power in the internal remodelling of Judaism and its Messianic mission in progress toward completing humanity?[38]

At this point, Kohler's rhetorical moves should be readily discernible. His lack of familiarity with or commitment to Darwinism allows him to assume that evolution is progressive. Paradise is not behind us, as in the biblical account, it lies ahead in a messianic future. The "internal progress" of nature, controlled by "highest wisdom," is parallel to the "inward remodelling" of Judaism best exemplified by Reform. Progressive evolution meets progressive revelation. *QED.*

In 1874 America, Orthodoxy was not a threat to the hegemony of Reform—secularism was. Jews no longer had to identify as such in the new world. They could opt out of Judaism altogether, or, by 1877, they could associate with the Society for Ethical Culture, a church for expatriated Jews founded by the former Reform Rabbi Felix Adler. Alternatively, Jews might convert to the majority religion of America. Christianity was perceived as a threat, but a threat that could be neutralized through the alleged "conflict" between religion and science that had been declared by Draper in 1874. At the conclusion of Kohler's sermon, he highlighted the difference: "Let the 'Church' grow pale before the new science. It has declared that the views of Copernicus were heretical, since they deprived it of its heaven."[39] In grand polemical fashion, the Church pales in comparison to the adaptive Hebrew.

Emil Gustav Hirsch (1852–1923), another German American Reform rabbi, carries the Darwinian metaphor forward. Hirsch argues that "the survival of Jews and Judaism, according to the proposition of the new doctrine, testifies to the excellence of the religion of Israel."[40] Hirsch's point is that Christianity's *later* emergence gives it no inherent superiority over Judaism's *longer* development. Hirsch describes the remaining Jews as the remnant of Israel whose commitment to

---

38 Kaufman Kohler, "Science and Religion," *Jewish Times*, February 20, 1874, 821.
39 Ibid.
40 Emil G. Hirsch, *My Religion* (New York: Macmillan Co., 1925), 260-61.

continuous revelation harmonizes with Judaism's traditional doctrine of *creatio continua* and evolution. In Hirsch's entry on evolution in *The Jewish Encyclopedia*, published between 1901 and 1906, he wrote: "The philosophy of the Reform wing within Judaism, regarding Judaism as a growth, not a fixed quantity or a rigid law, and as still in the process of developing (tradition being its vital element), has even found corroboration in the theory of evolution."[41]

Hirsch was best known for his embrace of the Social Gospel and promoting its creed in the Pittsburgh Platform of 1885: "In full accordance with the spirit of the Mosaic legislation, which strives to regulate the relations between rich and poor, we deem it our duty to participate in the great task of modern times, to solve, on the basis of justice and righteousness, the problems presented by the contrasts and evils of the present organization of society." To this day, Reform Judaism leads the way amongst Jewish denominations in their dedication to causes of social justice, what is sometimes labeled as *tikkun olam*. Hirsch takes a less adversarial posture towards Christianity than did Kohler, in part, because he seeks allies with other religious liberals to create religions where "character and conduct, not creed, will be the keynote of the gospel in the Church of Humanity Universal."[42] As for the evolution of Judaism, Hirsch aspires not for "a dogmatic creed, but rather in the spirit of Deuteronomy, a philosophy of practical responsibilities, a religion of the deed, a life under the consecration of the passion for justice, righteousness, and love."[43] If a theory of evolution helps him advance that cause, he is happy to enlist its services. In that effort, Hirsch emphasizes an element of nature that our previous thinkers did not.

> Evolution reveals that life runs on through a process of interdependence. Whatever lives, lives through another and for another. Thus a new and deeper teleology or theory of purpose is suggested. There is in this long succession of evolving and enlarging life nothing but has an influence upon another. This truth may be formulated as follows: there is nothing that

---

41 Emil G. Hirsch, *Theology of Emil G. Hirsch*, ed. David Einhorn Hirsch (Wheeling: Whitehall, 1977), 165.

42 Emil G. Hirsch, "Elements of Universal Religion," in *The Dawn of Religious Pluralism: Voices From the World's Parliament of Religions, 1893*, ed. Richard Hughes Seager (Chicago: Open Court Publishing, 1999), 224.

43 Hirsch, *My Religion*, 260.

lives but serves an ulterior purpose. Moreover as through this interaction of one upon the other be it through natural selection or otherwise, the sum of life has even steadily increased and the quality of life has even so invariably been rendered more profound.[44]

Wise and Kohler both rejected survival of the fittest, accepted evolution, ignored Genesis 1 as a source of science, and emphasized divine immanence. What Hirsch adds is his dedication to the ethos of the Mosaic religion and the Hebrew prophets which articulates something akin to social safety net. The emphasis on interdependence operates on the societal level and on the animal level. Peter Kropotkin, a Russian naturalist whose essays on this topic were published between 1890 and 1896, argued that mutual aid and cooperation rather than competition were the mechanisms for speciation.[45] For Jewish mysticism, as we have seen, interdependence also operates within the covenant between God and the Jewish people. And, as we will see with our twentieth-century respondents, interdependence and symbiosis also characterize the biology of organisms.

The European "Counter-Reformation"

Our final nineteenth-century thinkers bring us back to Europe. Elijah Benamozegh, to whom we were introduced in the previous section, was likely the first Jew to cite Darwin in a Jewish context. *Origin* was translated into French in 1862, and Benamozegh's commentary on Deuteronomy was published the following year. In it he made extensive references to Darwin and the concept of species in discussing the prohibition of yoking an ox and ass together to plow one's field (Deuteronomy 22:10).[46] His treatment of Darwinism suggests that he had not properly understood the theory, nor would he have been likely to accept Darwinism even had he. Nevertheless, given his somewhat befuddled understanding, he did allow for the possibility that should Darwinism be scientifically confirmed and a teleological explanation given to the course of speciation,

---

44 Ibid, 251.
45 These essays were published in the British periodical *The Nineteenth Century*. They were collected and published as *Mutual Aid* in 1902.
46 Elijah Benamozegh, *Em L'Mikra* (Leghorn, 1863), 87a–88b.

"there no longer would be a contradiction between Darwin's view and that of the author of the Torah."[47]

By 1865, *Origin* was translated into Italian and was widely discussed in the following years. "Addressing the Italian Parliament in 1881, one MP remarked that the names of Darwin and Spencer had become so well known in Italy that mentioning them in conversation would not qualify one as intellectually sophisticated."[48] By 1877, the Italian Benamozegh was ready to pronounce judgement on evolution, if not on Darwin himself:

> I believe, as science teaches, that the forms of animals appear on earth always more perfect, whether this by revolutions and cataclysms, as stipulated by Cuvier, or by slow evolution, as stipulated by modern [scientists] such as Lyell, Darwin and others, [who ascertain that] species and genera always more perfect have followed up one another for millions of years on the face of the earth.[49]

Already in his Genesis commentary, he had cited Abraham ibn Ezra's medieval commentary arguing that biblical days could not be twenty-four hours.[50] Thus, Benamozegh has followed the now familiar pattern of discounting the literal text of *Genesis* while insisting on a progressive, divinely guided transmutation of species.

Although there was no Reform movement in Italy, Benamozegh responded to their claims that biblical criticism had divested the Torah of any relationship to the divine. While not a novel claim, Benamozegh emphasized that Genesis 1 and science both posit nature's progressive development. Benamozegh also shifts the Garden of Eden story to the future where it becomes a prophetic ideal rather than an account of the Fall. Benamozegh further emphasized the traditional understanding that God incorporated all of creation into the emergence of humanity thus establishing the unity of creation.

---

47   Ibid., 88a, and Jose Faur, "The Hebrew Species Concept and the Origin of Evolution: R. Benamozheg's Response to Darwin," *La Ressegna Mensile di Israel* 63, no. 3 (1997): 58.

48   Giuliano Pancaldi, *Darwin in Italy: Science Across Cultural Frontiers,* trans. Ruey Brodine Morellu (Bloomington: Indiana University Press, 1991), 152.

49   Elijah Benamozegh, *Teleogia Dogmatica e Apologetica,* vol. 1, *Dio* (Leghorn: Tipografia di Francesco Vigo 1877), 276. Cited in Faur, "Hebrew Species Concept": 45.

50   Benamozegh, *Em L'Mikra* on Gen. 1:5.

Benamozegh did his best to demonstrate that the Torah did not have to be the product of divine dictation to be divinely inspired. Moreover, according to Benamozegh, it is not only the Torah that is divine at root, but also the Oral Torah including the Kabbalah. According to Benamozegh's biographer, "Tradition, both in the general sense of oral teaching and Kabbalah proper, sheds light on the Scriptures: it does not create things, but renders them visible. The Scriptures taken alone, out of context, are ephemeral enough. For Benamozegh, true Judaism involves accepting the Bible, but as part of a larger whole by which it is overshadowed."[51]

Benamozegh's fidelity to the Written Torah is only a means to an end. Whether in terms of theology or halakhah, Benamozegh is far more interested in Jewish fidelity to the Oral Torah. Elements of Kabbalah, for purposes of theology, were particularly consonant with the idealist philosophy of late nineteenth-century Europe. Regardless of the mechanism of speciation, science could not explain the emergence of life, consciousness, and self-consciousness in the cosmos.

> Matter is not lowly and contemptible, verging on nonbeing as held to be the case by the most extreme Platonic doctrine, but it has dignity; nature deserves the love due to realities from which God has not divided himself. Idealism and empiricism are both true and are reconciled in the Kabbalistic emanationist doctrine Benamozegh considered "complete Judaism."[52]

Idealism in Europe and immanentism in America both serve the same function of explaining the origin of life and its development along divinely guided pathways. Kabbalah provides a traditional Jewish framework for a panentheistic theology that links transcendence and immanence through the Neoplatonic image of divine overflow or concentric circles which map on to *Eyn Sof* and the sefirot. Even though Benamozegh demythologized the Zohar and subsequent mystical literature, the idea that God was dependent on the performance of the mitzvot still held true for him. Thus, his commitment to halakhah, and his opposition to the antinomianism of Reform, was integral to Benamozegh's conception of Judaism.

---

51 Guetta, *Philosophy and Kabbalah*, 151.
52 Ibid., 56.

[W]e must accept the metaphor of religion as an organism, developing through all its phases from the seed to the fruit, always changing, but—like everything that lives—always identical in substance.

Indeed the rabbis adopted this hypothesis of religious evolution. The accusation made against them in the Gospel, that they elevated human traditions above the word of God, is enough to show that they were scarcely disposed to regard religion as unchanging. . . . Today, even the historical critic recognizes that the Pharisees represented change and religious progress at the very heart of Judaism. Yet we must not confuse the natural growth of an institution, its organic evolution, with changes which may be imposed in order to adapt the institution to new times and places. The first kind of change is proper, legitimate, in a word orthodox, whereas the second is false and injurious to the idea which it claims to serve.[53]

We see here the "Counter-Reformation" of Orthodox Judaism. If Reform emphasized growth and development, Orthodoxy would emphasize the slow tempo of such changes. If Reform ignored the scientific spirit of Genesis, Orthodoxy would emphasize the sometimes striking similarities between descriptions of nature and tendentiously selected biblical verses, midrashim, and kabbalistic cosmogonies. Another Eastern European Orthodox rabbi, Naphtali HaLevy, lionized Darwin from the start and offered an evolutionary midrash of creation. He too believed that the ancient sages "walked on the path of the scientific spirit."[54]

Eliyahu Stern recently published an important study on the ferment within Eastern European Jewish intellectual circles and the rise of materialist philosophies in the 1870s. One such intellectual is Joseph Lev Sossnitz (1837–1910). We will be focusing on Sossnitz's 1875 monograph, *Achen Yesh HaShem* (Indeed There Is a God). As we shall see,

---

53 Benamozegh, *Israel and Humanity*, 170. In the French edition of *Israel and Humanity* (1914), Benamozegh continues this paragraph noting that Reform is "anti-scientific" because in order to be adaptive, changes must happen slowly (320).

54 Naphtali HaLevy, *Toledot Adam* (Vienna: Spitzer & Holzwarth, 1875), 12. For more on this colorful figure and his relationship to Darwinism, see Ralph Colp, Jr. and David Kohn, "'A Real Curiosity:' Charles Darwin Reflects on a Communication from Rabbi Naphtali Levy," *European Legacy* 1, no. 5 (1996): 1716-27. See also Edward O. Dodson, "Toldot Adam: A Little-Known Chapter in the History of Darwinism," *Perspectives on Science and Christian Faith* 52, no. 1 (March 2000): 47–54.

Sossnitz decries materialism while accepting evolution. His strategy and sources anticipate the later response to evolutionary theory by Rav Avraham Kook. What Stern's research suggests is that as soon as Achen Yesh Hashem went to press, Sossnitz began reconsidering his position. He came to see Judaism as a materialist religion along the lines of Spinoza.[55]

By 1875, Sossnitz had been hired as the scientific editor of the Haskalah journal Ha-Tzefira. Sossnitz began Achen Yesh Hashem with a survey of natural history from Kant to Laplace. Eventually, Sossnitz arrives at Darwin and defends his theory against his critics. What Sossnitz emphasizes is that materialism as a biological account of nature must be inadequate because it cannot account for the emergence of life from inert matter.[56] Sossnitz then piously sanitizes Darwinism and translates natural selection as "The Natural Selector."[57] Sossnitz is aware that he is going beyond what Darwin himself would countenance in terms of teleology and progress. "This law [of progress] is fitting to add to Darwin's system, which he unintentionally hid inside his words. We find, in general, that . . . The Natural Selector prepared the accidental changes toward perfection."[58]

Sossnitz mentions that Darwin, especially in his later editions, highlights individuals of a species which sacrifice themselves for the benefit of the species. What comes to be known as inclusive fitness is seemingly in tension with a materialistic biology that should reward only what is good for the individual. Altruism, the ultimate expression of love for the other, made no sense from a materialistic perspective prior to the reemergence of Gregor Mendel's work in the early twentieth century. Sossnitz understood materialism to have a pernicious effect on the morality of youth.[59] Wise's Homo-Brutualism redivivus: "If God did not direct and

---

55 Eliyahu Stern, *Jewish Materialism: The Intellectual Revolution of the 1870s* (New Haven: Yale University Press, 2018), 85–113, esp. 107. I first wrote about Sossnitz in my 2001 dissertation. Fred Shaw, Sossnitz's great grandson, was kind enough to provide a copy of Sossnitz's own copy of Achen Yesh Hashem to me which I subsequently shared with Stern. The manuscript had Sossnitz's handwritten emendations that Stern convincingly argues show the shift in his thinking—see p. 104.

56 Joseph Lev Sossnitz, *Achen Yesh Hashem* (Vilna: Yehuda Leb Lipman Press, 1875), 15 and 30.

57 Ibid., 39–44.

58 Ibid., 44.

59 Ibid., 95.

rule, humans would swallow up the lives of their neighbors." The threat of materialism is that people will no longer fear God, will act immorally, and threaten the stability and progress of civilization. Sossnitz concludes, like RaMBaM, with an appeal to morality: "Reality and existence will teach one, more than a hundred teachers and seventy guides, to prepare his way and incline his being towards ethics."[60]

What distinguishes Sossnitz's response to Darwinism from others was his intimacy not with Kabbalah, per se, but with the Hasidic theology of HaBaD.[61] In the previous section, we described HaBaD's theology as acosmic, the view that the world has no true reality and is nothing more than a series of veils for God's dynamic presence. Within this model, divine energy jumps or leaps in a discontinuous fashion akin to a body attaining escape velocity from a specific orbit. Sossnitz applies this idea of leaping to explain speciation. Analogously, God leaped over the houses of the Israelites in Egypt prior to the exodus.[62] (The holiday name *Passover* is a translation of the Hebrew term for *passing over* or *leaping*, as in Isaiah 35:6.)

There are two points to be made here. The first is theological. Acosmism does not deny the existence of the physical world, per se; it denies its ultimate reality in comparison to the overwhelming, ultimate reality of God. Panentheism is a less mystical notion that combines pantheism with the intuition that divinity cannot be bound by physical reality. God constitutes the fullness of all which transcends the mere sum of material existents. To claim, as Stern does, that Sossnitz shifts from being something of a HaBaD Hasid to a materialist sounds like a complete reversal of his worldview. The shift, however, is more subtle.

> For more than a few modern Jewish thinkers, Habad would become a path toward philosophical materialism. According to the philosopher Elliot R. Wolfson, Habad places spirituality and materiality on par with each other. In Habad, empirical knowledge and reason are ultimately overwhelmed by the divine reality that fills the entire cosmos. All existence is perceived

---

60 Ibid., 97 and *Guide*, 3:54.
61 See Stern, *Jewish Materialism*, 96–106.
62 Sossnitz, *Achen Yesh Hashem*, 54. This analogy was crossed out in Sossnitz's manuscript suggesting, as Stern has argued, his rejection of such a belief. See Stern, *Jewish Materialism*, 105 and 231n86.

as an image, which is meaningless compared to its source in God. Human beings strive to understand the way God permeates the universe but in so doing eventually come to recognize the equality of all things and the ultimately illusory nature of the differences that exist in the physical world.[63]

By definition, the move from panentheism to pantheism, or acosmism to materialism, uses Ockham's Razor to slice away divine transcendence. But God's immanence, at least theoretically, remains for those so intoxicated. As Stern acknowledged, materialism did not necessarily equate to atheism.[64]

The second point relates to theodicy and providence. If creation and human history unfold within a divine reality, then every extinction and every massacre only appear evil from our limited, human perspective. From the divine perspective, there is no evil. All is divine. If God is radically immanent in creation, then theodicy and providence become inapplicable concepts. As people evolve and perceive the divinity of our reality, we will approach the messianic days.[65] Future respondents to evolution will invoke this worldview which imagines death as an absorption into a divine dimension of reality inaccessible from our own.

The final two theologians in this chapter, Avraham Isaac Kook (1865–1935) and Mordecai M. Kaplan (1881–1983), each worked out their theories of evolution prior to the cataclysm of the Shoah. Although Kaplan continued to publish after World War II, he was by then over seventy years old with the lineaments of his theology well marked out. Examining the two thinkers in tandem will show two different models of the relationship between religion and science. Kook is the last theologian we will examine whose perception of reality springs exclusively from Jewish tradition. Kaplan continues the American tradition of reforming Jewish theology in order to harmonize with science and secular philosophy. To revert to the biological metaphor, for Kook science and religion are separated by a semipermeable membrane allowing information to

---

63 Stern, *Jewish Materialism*, 97 citing Wolfson, *Open Secret*, 63.
64 Stern, *Jewish Materialism*, 185.
65 Ibid., 74.

flow from religion to science, but not vice-versa; for Kaplan, the membrane allows information to flow in both directions.[66]

Both Kook and Kaplan were born in Eastern Europe. Kook eventually made his way to Palestine and became the chief rabbi for the Ashkenazi community. Kaplan was taken by his parents to New York City as a youngster, and his education included the Jewish Theological Seminary, Columbia University, and private tutors—one of whom was Joseph Sossnitz. Thus, while Kook studied Talmud at the Volozhin Yeshiva and Kabbalah with Rabbi Shlomo Elyashiv, a renowned kabbalist, Kaplan studied Herbert Spencer, Emile Durkheim, and John Dewey. He also studied RaMBaM's *Guide* with Sossnitz. It is from these radically disparate stances that our two thinkers approach the theory of evolution. Here is Rav Kook's famous endorsement.

> The theory of evolution is increasingly conquering the world at this time, and, more so than all other philosophical theories, conforms to the kabbalistic secrets of the world. Evolution, which proceeds on a path of ascendancy, provides an optimistic foundation for the world. How is it possible to despair at a time when we see that everything evolves and ascends? When we penetrate the inner meaning of ascending evolution, we find in it the divine element shining with absolute brilliance. It is precisely the *Eyn Sof in actu* which manages to bring to realization that which is *Eyn Sof in potentia*.[67]

Like the other thinkers we have examined, Kook puts a progressive, ascending gloss on the picture of creation. He also explicitly relates to the theory as a philosophy and not as a science. Indeed, the biological mechanisms of speciation are of no interest to him. Kook is both too savvy and too mystical to anchor the concept of evolution to any particular mechanism. Scientific theories are fleeting. Ptolemy, Copernicus, and Galileo each had their moments in the sun before being eclipsed.[68]

---

66 I have compared these two thinkers, along with Yeshayahu Leibowitz, in "Three Twentieth-Century Jewish Responses to Evolutionary Theory," *Aleph* 3 (2003): 247–290.

67 Avraham Isaac Kook, *Orot HaKodesh*, 2:537.

68 Avraham Isaac Kook, *'Eder HaYakar* (Jerusalem: Mossad HaRav Kook, 1967), 38 and *Rav A. Y. Kook Selected Letters*, trans. Tzvi Feldman (Ma'aleh Adumim: Ma'aliot Publications, 1986), letter 91, 3-10.

There is no contradiction whatsoever between the Torah and the world's scientific knowledge. We do not have to accept theories as certainties, no matter how widely accepted, for they are like blossoms that wither. Very soon, scientific knowledge will be further developed and all of today's new theories will be derided and scorned. . . . But the word of God will endure forever.[69]

The progressive nature of evolution is metaphysically rooted in the *Eyn Sof* which actualizes the divinity latent in all phenomena. Traditional Kabbalah understands that the *Eyn Sof* is the realm of pure divine being that is always in a state of actualization. To speak of the *Eyn Sof in potentia* is both an innovation and a sign of Rav Kook's sympathies for the acosmism of HaBaD theology. The *Eyn Sof* is latent within the world of phenomena, and it is only the illusion of atomistic individuation that prevents us from perceiving the divinity of which we are a part and in which we have our existence. To phrase it differently, the shattering of the vessels was psychological. "The difference between individual finite existence and infinite existence is not ontological; it is a result of our limited understanding and defective vision that recognizes only particulars."[70]

As more of *Eyn Sof* is actualized, there is a concomitant development in material reality that manifests through the leap from mineral to vegetable, from vegetable to animal, and from animals to humans who have the capacity for self-consciousness and reflection. The metaphysical process of becoming is rooted in divine being. *Eyn Sof in actu is* the telos of creation.[71] Rav Kook terms the kabbalistic great chain of being that we saw with the Malbim as *teshuvah*, a return of all existents to a state of *Eyn Sof in actu* through humans developing an expanded consciousness of divine ubiquity. In part this process is driven by the individual's traditional teshuvah, or reorientation toward God.

---

69 Ibid.

70 Nathan Rotenstreich, "On Harmony and Return," in *Essays on the Thought and Philosophy of Rabbi Kook,* ed. Ezra Gellman (Rutherford: Fairleigh Dickinson University Press, 1991), 181–82.

71 Hermann Cohen develops a similar theory reconciling being and becoming. See his *Religion of Reason,* 35–70, and Samuel Hugo Bergman, *Faith and Reason: An Introduction to Modern Jewish Thought,* trans. Alfred Jospe (New York: Schocken Books, 1961), 46–51.

This process of teshuvah is not isolated to individual human beings. Rav Kook gives it biological, societal, and cosmic significance. Teshuvah has a metaphysical correlate, as well. "All of existence 'wants' to be perfect. . . . The internal, metaphysical meaning of this process is the spontaneous aspiration of everything that exists—beginning with the first *sefira*—to unite with *Eyn Sof*."[72] When Rav Kook claims that the *philosophy* of progressive evolution, and even certain theories of biological evolution, conform to Kabbalah, he is correct. Already in the sixteenth century, both Moshe Cordovero and Shlomo Alkabetz described the divine emanation from the *Eyn Sof* as a *straight light* and the divine energy that seeks to return to its source in the *Eyn Sof* as *returning light*. From Rav Kook's point of view, modern science, as expressed in evolution, is finally on the right track.

Although Rav Kook is frequently cited as an early supporter of evolution, he never accepted Darwinism. The transmutation of species over deep time was not a challenge to accommodate within traditional Jewish thought. The acosmism of HaBaD could have neutralized issues of providence. The psychological effects of higher consciousness, activated through teshuvah, allow one to understand that since all is God, providence is an illusion. As for theodicy, death is also, at its core, an illusion. One dies into God.

Had Rav Kook responded directly to Darwinism, there would be only two qualifications. The first, as we have seen, is the teleology of progressive ascent. The second qualification is that for Darwin, evolution is infinitesimally gradual; for Rav Kook, there are periodic leaps. "In general, the idea of gradual evolution stands at the beginning of its development. There is no doubt that it will change its form and give birth to visions which will include leaps to complete the vision of reality."[73] Sossnitz, as we saw above, depicted leaps within nature as responsible for the emergence of different species. Both Sossnitz and Kook took their Torah of Leaps from HaBaD. The founder of HaBaD described the initial emanation from *Eyn Sof* as being nonlinear.

---

72 Yosef Ben-Shlomo, "Perfection and Betterment in Rav Kook's Concept of the Divine": 299.
73 *Rav A. Y. Kook Selected Letters*, letter 134, 13-14.

It is impossible that there should be descent like this in the way of concatenation from cause to effect through gradation . . . but rather by way of a great leap, which is not through gradation at all, and this is [the import of] "Set out, my beloved, swift as a gazelle" (Song of Songs 2:17); that is, by way of analogy the movement of the gazelle is swift and in a great leap but not through any gradation, and so, too, is the aspect of the descent of light to be with Israel when they are in exile among the idol worshipers.[74]

Rav Kook believed in leaps on all planes of creation: metaphysical (*sfirot*), material, organic, animal, consciousness, and speech.[75] Revelation, repentance, and redemption also arrive by a great leap.[76] The clarity with which Kook insists that theories of evolution will change in the future to include leaps is audacious. I feel no need to validate Kook's assertion. Yet, I wonder if the theory of punctuated equilibrium would gain his assent. Punctuated equilibrium is the notion that for most of history, species have been relatively stable with long periods of stasis infrequently punctuated by relatively short bursts of speciation.

One half of the team that developed the theory, Stephen Jay Gould, provides a complementary data set that also might cohere with Kook's vision. "For 2.4 billion years after the Isua sediments [the oldest sedimentary rocks known], or nearly two-thirds of the entire history of life on the earth, all organisms were single-cell creatures of the simplest, or prokaryotic, design. . . . The time between the appearance of the first eukaryotic cell and the first multicellular animal is longer than the entire period of multicellular success since the Cambrian explosion [570 million years ago]."[77] Gould sums up his conclusion: "Modern multicellular animals make their first uncontested appearance in the fossil record some 570 million years ago—and with a bang, not a protracted crescendo. This 'Cambrian explosion' marks the advent of virtually all major groups of modern animals—and all within the miniscule span, geologically speaking, of a few million years."[78]

---

74 Shneur Zalman of Liadi, Torah Or, 116c. Cited and translated by Wolfson in "Achronic Time, Messianic Expectation, and the Secret of the Leap in Habad," 74.

75 Orot HaKodesh II:567-68; Eder HaYakar, 154, and *Rav A. Y. Kook Selected Letters*, letters 134 and 164, 11-15.

76 Wolfson, "Achronic Time," 77.

77 Gould, *Wonderful Life*, 58.

78 Ibid., 23-24.

Kook was a mystic. He intuited, as others had before him, the shape of history. We have a whole host of terms to describe discontinuous processes: escape velocity, tipping point, critical mass, phase change. Allow me to offer another, admittedly loaded, term for the leap: emergence. *Emergence* describes the phenomenon of a system's individual components to generate qualitatively novel properties that are neither derivable from nor reducible to the system's discrete elements. To phrase this in the language of the previous chapter, emergence is a con-spiracy.

The final thinker in this chapter viewed it as his responsibility to reshape Judaism through his knowledge of science and history. As we saw in book one, Mordecai M. Kaplan (1881–1983) brought his intellectual honesty to bear on the accretions of Judaism that he believed required excision. He attempted to sever the super from the natural. He accepted science while standing firm against scientism. And he replaced natural selection, with its ostensible assault on morality, with spiritual selection.

The Scopes Trial of 1925 quickly generated many responses in the Christian community; the Jewish community was less exercised by the Monkey Trial.[79] There was a certain schadenfreude in seeing various Christian groups struggle to survive evolution after there had been large scale acceptance of transmutation of species over deep time within the Jewish community.[80] It was not until after the Shoah that rightwing Orthodoxy began pushing back against evolutionary theory for fear that it would undermine Jewish commitment to tradition.[81] During the twenties and thirties, nineteenth-century concerns lingered about natural selection's implications for morality, namely Social Darwinism. What Kaplan hammered home with particular ferocity for the first generation of Americans, like himself, was that science did not and could not address religion's ultimate concerns. "Strictly speaking, there can be no conflict between science and religion as such. The function of science is merely to study the sequence of phenomena. . . . The moment science generalizes about the meaning of those sequences and tries to interpret

79 Rachel S. A. Pear, "Differences over Darwinism: American Orthodox Jewish Responses to Evolution in the 1920s," *Aleph* 15, no. 2 (2015): 343-87.
80 Pear, "Differences": 386.
81 Rachel S. A. Pear, "Arguing About Evolution for the Sake of Heaven: American Orthodox Rabbis Dispute Darwinism's Merit And Meaning in the 1930s–1950s," *Fides et Historia* 46, no. 1 (2014): 21-39.

them in relation to existence as a whole, it is no longer science but phi-losophy."[82] As we saw above, Kaplan was committed to ridding Judaism of supernaturalism as forcefully as RaMBaM was committed to ridding Judaism of anthropomorphism. There is no individual providence, pub-lic revelation, chosen people, or communal redemption by a personal God who intermittently intervenes to rearrange the cosmos according to His will. But rejecting supernaturalism does not require accepting natu-ralism as anything other than a method for conducting science. Kaplan emphasized the function of God and limned a belief system that would be necessary to provide such a function. One of Kaplan's earlier formula-tions of faith bears repetition:

> Faith in life's inherent worthwhileness and sanctity is needed to counteract the cynicism that sneers at life and mocks at the very notion of holiness. . . . Belief in God as here conceived can function in our day exactly as the belief in God has always functioned; it can function as an affirmation that life has value. It implies, as the God idea has always implied, a certain assumption with regard to the nature of reality, the assumption that reality is so constituted as to endorse and guarantee the realization in man of that which is of greatest value to him. If we believe that assumption to be true, for, as has been said, it is an assumption that is not susceptible of proof, we have faith in God. *No metaphysical speculation beyond this fundamental assumption that reality assures both the emergence and the realization of human ideals is necessary for the religious life.*[83]

In book one, I defended Kaplan's minimalist metaphysics from those who claimed he had none and from those who asserted he had no right to have one. In his 1934 magnum opus *Judaism as a Civilization*, he addresses evolution and complements the Homo-Brutalism critique of Isaac Mayer Wise. "What can exercise a more blighting effect upon all moral endeavor than the notion that there is no meaning or purpose in the world, and that it is soulless in its mechanistic perfection? We may accept without reservation the Darwinian conception of evolution, so long as we consider the divine impulsion or initiative as the origin of the process."[84] Social Darwinism and nihilism are enemies of Judaism. Kaplan, at this point, is offering a

---

82 Kaplan, *Judaism as a Civilization*, 37–38.
83 Kaplan, *Meaning of God*, 29. My italics.
84 Kaplan, *Judaism as a Civilization*, 98.

moral critique of Darwinism. Toward the end of *Judaism as a Civilization*, he articulates a theology of history that owes much to Bergson's *élan vital* while avoiding a supernatural design that dictates details.

> Ultimately, the forces for good that inhere in the world and in human nature will give rise to a just social order, one in which every human being will be able to achieve the full measure of self-realization and accord to his neighbor the same right and opportunity. The evolution of mankind, though marred by frequent and disheartening reactions, moves irresistibly in the direction of universal security and freedom. From the standpoint of the Jewish religion, ethical purpose does not emerge merely as an incident of social history, but is a directive and creative force.[85]

In comparing Kook to Kaplan, although both allowed for setbacks (like World War I), Kook's teleology has a specific target, while Kaplan's has a general direction. Kaplan's commitment to pragmatism, pluralism, and process-thought demands that the future be open-ended: direction without destiny. Both the path to the future and the particulars of that future are yet undetermined. But like Kook, we are in control of evolution's future through what Kaplan calls spiritual selection. "Man is not merely affected by evolutionary change; he participates in the process."[86] "That the world has not reached finality, but is continually being renewed by God and in need of improvement by man if it is to serve his ends, is a familiar Jewish idea. Likewise is the idea that man also is, in a sense, a creator, and therefore a collaborator with God."[87]

Several scholars have noted the affinities between Kaplan's thought and process theology. Emanuel Goldsmith identifies Kaplan as a process theologian influenced by process philosophy which "emphasizes both process, or becoming, and relations, or relativity. It contends that the entire universe is in a state of change or process and stresses the theme of relationship."[88] Kaplan's transnaturalism "sought to prove that ethical traits are the subjective expressions of objective processes in nature."[89]

---

85 Ibid., 477.
86 Kaplan, *Meaning of God*, 123.
87 Ibid., 76–77.
88 Emanuel S. Goldsmith, "Kaplan and Henry Nelson Wieman," in Goldsmith, *American Judaism of Mordecai M. Kaplan*, 204.
89 Ibid., 209.

The theory of reciprocal responsibility is the conscious human manifestation of the principle whereby everything in nature is both cause and effect of everything else. It corresponds with the universal law of polarity whereby everything in the universe, from the minutest electron to the vastest star, is both self-active and interactive, independent and interdependent.[90]

The God of process lacks omnipotence and evinces vulnerability. Kaplan finds theodicies, therefore, irrelevant.[91] The God of process is dependent on human deeds. According to one Kaplan scholar, Jacob Staub, "Such a theological framework represents a radical departure from both classical Jewish theology and from the popular beliefs on which most Jews have been raised. It requires a wrenching reorientation to begin to think of God as in perpetual process, involved in and substantially affected by the undetermined unfolding of concrete events."[92] Staub ignores the entire mystical tradition which is predicated on God being affected, continuously, by our deeds. Maimonides casts a long shadow.

Kaplan was not a Maimonidean rationalist, though rationalism was essential to his worldview. Kaplan "consistently affirms the superiority of the Jewish mystical tradition, the Kabbalah, to the teachings of the medieval Jewish philosophers."[93] Kaplan demythologized the theurgy of Kabbalah and was left with divine dependence on humanity. According to S. Daniel Breslauer, a scholar who focuses on Jewish myth, "The activism of Jewish mysticism appeals to Kaplan as a source for genuine religious insight. Such genuine religion calls upon human beings to take responsibility for their own lives, to act like members of a democratic society in which all citizens share the duties of government. . . . Jewish mysticism . . . [is] a religion in which humanity and the divine share responsibility."[94]

As much as Kaplan sought to avoid supernaturalism, a metaphysical naturalism was equally anathema. Transforming the methodological naturalism of the scientific process into metaphysical naturalism is what Kaplan labeled "sinister scientism."[95] Metaphysical naturalism, another

90 Kaplan, *Religion of Ethical Nationhood*, 34–35.
91 Ibid., 51–56.
92 Jacob J. Staub, "Kaplan and Process Theology," in Goldsmith, *American Judaism of Mordecai M. Kaplan*, 290.
93 Breslauer, "Mordecai Kaplan's Approach to Jewish Mysticism": 40.
94 Ibid.: 49.
95 Kaplan, *Future of the American Jew*, 21.

name for strict materialism, sealed off the "domain where mind, personality, purpose, ideals, values and meanings dwell."[96] Scientism stripped spirit from the cosmos, setting humanity adrift within an amoral universe. Transnaturalism was Kaplan's solution. Progress, identified with inexhaustible divine creativity, remains a religious axiom. It goes beyond methodological naturalism with its faith that the cosmos "is so constituted as to enable man to achieve salvation."[97]

Conclusion

Evolutionary theory was not the primary challenge for Jewish leaders in the late nineteenth and early twentieth centuries. Although there were conflicting strategies, the goal of most Jewish leaders was to keep Jews Jewish. It had never been so easy to opt out of Judaism, although as the 1935 Nuremberg Laws demonstrated, it was not as easy as many Jews had imagined. Jewish reformers were happy to seize on evolution's supposedly progressive development in consonance with Reform; Orthodox Jews were just as eager to emphasize the slow rate of evolution in consonance with Orthodoxy's approach to halakhic change. Both groups emphasized the primacy of ethics in Judaism as parallel to humanity becoming increasingly ethical over the "lower beasts." And, whenever possible, many Jewish respondents to evolutionary theory also took the opportunity to jab at Christianity's reputed hostility towards scientific advance.

Darwin's theory spread through Europe and the United States at the same time as the rise of Reform Judaism in Germany, the Haskalah in Eastern Europe, the spread of biblical criticism, and the institutionalization of Reform Judaism in America. There was a civil war in the United States and pogroms in Eastern Europe. On both sides of the turn of the century, there was the greatest exodus of Jews since the exodus, with the attendant Samsonian task of resettling those Eastern European Jews in America. By 1914, there was also a World War. In short, biological evolution was not on the front burner for most Jews.

Nevertheless, by the turn of the twentieth century, Jewish thinkers had largely accepted a progressive, immanent teleology responsible for

96 Kaplan, *Judaism without Supernaturalism*, 10.
97 Kaplan, *Meaning of God*, 26.

the transmutation of species over deep time. The sources to respond to evolution are present in traditional Jewish thought. Kabbalah provides an immanent God and a transcendent telos. The liturgy emphasizes *creatio continua*, which is what modern science demands. The Torah even describes creation over a period of time, a parallel with evolution that may have removed some urgency from any further reconciliation. The extent of mass extinctions had not yet been discovered. Moreover, the problem of theodicy may not have been, psychologically, any greater an issue for the vast majority of Jews than were previous occasions of death on a massive scale such as Jews experienced in late antiquity and in the Middle Ages.

In the 1930s, depression begins to set in. Darwin's natural selection is rehabilitated and married to Mendelian genetics with the crystallization of the Modern Synthesis by the mid-1940s. Natural selection's reliance on radical contingency becomes increasing difficult to ignore. Where is God in the process of the unfolding of nature? As the decimation of European Jewry was being recognized, so, too, was the decimation in the history of our planet. Beginning in 1946, the scientific community faced the Ediacaran fossil record that revealed more death than life. In 1962, fossils that had been previously unearthed in 1909 in the Burgess Shale were shown to defy a history of linear progression. By the 1980s, there emerged studies of extinctions by David Raup, among others, which claimed that ninety-nine percent of all species to have ever been present on the earth are now extinct. Moreover, there had been five major extinction events in the earth's history. The majority of species were killed not because of bad genes but because of bad luck.[98] Chalk one up for Cuvier.

Natural selection and cataclysms challenged divine providence. Natural history exacerbated that challenge and called into question divine benevolence. The Shoah sharpened the conundrum: how can God be both benevolent and omnipotent? How could the Shoah possibly be part of God's providential design? Kabbalistic and Hasidic theologies were pressed into service in the earliest responses to Darwinism. After the Shoah, contemporary varieties of those theologies slowly emerge to deal with what, in Darwin's understated words, "we may call chance."[99]

---

98 David M. Raup, *Extinction: Bad Genes or Bad Luck?* (New York: W. W. Norton & Company, 1991).

99 Charles Darwin, *The Correspondence of Charles Darwin*, vol. 8, *1860*, ed. Frederick Burkhardt et. al. (Cambridge: Cambridge University Press, 1993), 224. The letter is dated May 22, 1860.

Chapter 10

Omnicide as Threat and Theodicy

Heroes are in short supply. Hans Jonas (1903–1993) is a hero of mine. He wrote his dissertation on Gnosticism under the supervision of Martin Heidegger, left Germany for Palestine when Hitler came to power, fought for the Allies during World War II, returned to Palestine and fought in Israel's War of Independence, and, subsequently, constructed a philosophical biology to challenge the nihilism of Heideggerian ethics. His philosophical project was to create an ontological foundation for responsibility under the threat of omnicide. As both a philosopher of religion and a philosopher of science, he was in an excellent position to make the attempt. He understood that it would be easier to justify an ethical life using the traditional categories of religion, but he also knew that by relying on religion, he would be excluding many people who rejected anything related to the divine.[1] Not unlike Kaplan, but with greater philosophical expertise, Jonas' version of transnaturalism relied on metaphysical speculation to explain, and value, the phenomenon of life.

Although Jonas was Jewish *and* a philosopher, he was not a Jewish philosopher.[2] Usually, his categories of thought and discourse came from the world of western metaphysics. Nevertheless, he was not ignorant of Jewish thought. Jonas formally studied at the liberal Jewish seminary in

---

1   Hans Jonas, *Phenomenon of Life: Toward a Philosophical Biology* (New York: Harper & Row, 1966), 284, and his *Mortality and Morality*, 152.
2   Eric Lawee, "Hans Jonas and Classical Jewish Texts: New Dimensions," *Journal of Jewish Thought and Philosophy* 23, no. 1 (2015): 75-125.

Berlin for a brief time, was an expert on Gnostic myth, and ran in the same circle as Gershom Scholem while living in the Land of Israel. In the previous chapter, I hinted at something that Hans Jonas was the first to understand, and that is why we begin this final chapter in this section with his contributions. What Jonas discovered was that the theologies and theodicies that Jews developed since the destruction of the Temple to explain evil in Jewish history, particularly Lurianic Kabbalah, serve equally well to explain evil in the history of nature.[3]

In these pages, my task is not to explain Jonas' philosophical biology. The collection of Jonas' essays edited by Lawrence Vogel, *Mortality and Morality: A Search for the Good after Auschwitz* will reward the careful reader desiring more of Jonas' thought. My more limited task is to trace the genealogy of the myth that Jonas employs in his metaphysical speculations. Jonas tinkered with the wording of this myth throughout the 1960s. The version here is from a 1962 article based on a 1961 lecture he gave at Harvard University.

> In the beginning, for unknowable reasons, the ground of being, or the Divine, chose to give itself over to the chance and risk and endless variety of becoming. And wholly so: entering into the adventure of space and time, the deity held nothing back of itself; no uncommitted or unimpaired part remained to direct, correct, and ultimately guarantee the devious working out of its destiny in creation. On this unconditional immanence the modern temper insists. . . . Rather, in order that the world might be, and be for itself, God renounced his own being, divesting himself of his deity—to receive it back from the Odyssey of time weighted with the chance harvest of unforeseeable temporal experience: Transfigured or possibly even disfigured by it. . . .
>
> And then he trembles as the thrust of evolution, carried by its own momentum, passes the threshold where innocence ceases and an entirely new criterion of success and failure takes hold of the divine stake. The advent of man means the advent of knowledge and freedom, and with this supremely double-edged gift the innocence of the mere subject of self-fulfilling life has given way to the charge of responsibility under the disjunction of good and evil. To the promise and risk of this divine cause,

---

3   Shai Cherry, "Judaism, Darwinism, and the Typology of Suffering," *Zygon* 46, no. 2 (June 2011): 317–29.

revealed at last, henceforth finds itself committed; and its issue trembles in the balance. The image of God, haltingly begun by the universe, for so long worked upon—and left undecided in the wide and then narrowing spirals of prehuman life—passes with this last twist, and with a dramatic quickening of the movement, into man's precarious trust, to be completed, saved, or spoiled by what he will do to himself and the world. And in this awesome impact of his deeds on God's destiny, on the very complexion of the eternal being, lies the immortality of man.[4]

To avoid some of the mischaracterizations that the scholarly community has foisted upon Jonas, I will emphasize several points at the outset. That God cannot direct and ultimately guarantee an outcome does not mean that God cannot influence an outcome. A lack of omnipotence is not the same thing as impotence or powerlessness. Nor does a lack of omnipotence mean that God is absent.[5] God is fully immanent in Jonas' myth. From the same essay as the myth above, we find a Heschelian sensibility: "For the secret sympathy that connects our being with the transcendent condition and makes the latter depend on our deeds, must somehow work both ways—or else there would not even be that inward testimony for us to invoke on which our whole case for the eternal was grounded."[6]

Years after Jonas first offered this myth, he recycled it in the context of post-Shoah theology. At that point, *in retrospect*, he recognized his myth's similarity to Luria's *tzimtzum*.[7] In his retrospective analysis, Jonas claims that his myth pushes further Luria's myth.[8] I can understand why some scholars accept Jonas' claim at face value—even those who

4   Jonas, *Mortality and Morality*, 125 and 127.
5   Both Christian Weise and Sandra Lubarsky misrepresent Jonas' myth in *The Legacy of Hans Jonas: Judaism and the Phenomenon of Life*, ed. Hava Tirosh-Samuelson and Christian Wiese (Leiden: Brill, 2008), esp. 407–13 and 446–60. God cannot intervene or interfere, but God does influence. That is the function of the cosmogonic eros. Strangely, Lubarsky endorses this theology elsewhere, but she does not see it in Jonas. See Lubarsky, "Reconstructing Divine Power": 302 and 308.
6   Jonas, *Mortality and Morality*, 129–30.
7   Jonas, *Mortality and Morality*, 136. Originally published in Albert H Friedlander, ed., *Out of the Whirlwind: A Reader of Holocaust Literature* (New York: Schocken Books, 1968), 465–76.
8   Jonas, *Mortality and Morality*, 142.

recognize that Jonas was no scholar of Jewish thought.[9] But, Jonas was overstating his own originality.[10] In Luria's myth, as written, the uplifting of the divine sparks surrounded by the husks of evil depends on our deeds. God's fate is in our hands.[11] Luria's God, like Jonas', does not have the autonomy to operate independently in this world.[12]

One academic explanation of Luria's myth of *tzimtzum* was that it was a theodicy to explain the Jewish expulsion from Spain. God did not intervene precisely because God could not intervene. Regarding the Shoah, Jonas said the same: God did not intervene because God could not intervene. But such a myth suggests neither that God is absent, nor that God is powerless. God's influence, what makes Jonas' account one of transnaturalism, he calls *cosmogonic eros*.

Jonas lets God play dice with the universe, but the dice are loaded. "The very least that we must grant to matter that developed from the Big Bang, in regard to what ultimately emerged later on, is an original endowment with the *possibility* of eventual inwardness—not an endowment *with* inwardness, still long in coming, and not even an endowment *for* inwardness in the sense of being already prepared for it."[13] Jonas must be correct. We have self-consciousness. We have subjectivity. If all there was at the origin was stardust, that stardust must have had the capacity to eventually become self-conscious.

"This means that right from the beginning, matter is subjectivity in its latent form, even if aeons, plus exceptional luck, are required for the actualizing of this potential. Only this much about 'teleology' can

---

9   See, e.g., Christian Wiese, 'God's Adventure With The World' and 'Sanctity Of Life': Theological Speculations and Ethical Reflections in Jonas's Philosophy After Auschwitz," in Tirosh-Samuelson, *Legacy of Hans Jonas*, 459; Benjamin Lazier, *God Interrupted: Heresy and the European Imagination between the World Wars* (Princeton: Princeton University Press, 2009), 61; and Ron Margolin, "Hans Jonas And Secular Religiosity," in Tirosh-Samuelson, *Legacy of Hans Jonas*, 241.

10 Shoshana Ronen, "The Absolute Good or Omnipotence: God After Auschwitz in the Theology of Abraham J. Heschel and Hans Jonas," in *Abraham Joshua Heschel: Philosophy, Theology and Interreligious Dialogue*, ed. Stanislaw Kajewski and Adam Lipszyc (Wiesbaden: Harrassowitz Verlag, 2009), 137–44.

11 Tishby, *Doctrine of Evil*, 19–42, 63–64, and 105–6.

12 Dan, "'No Evil Descends from Heaven,'" in Cooperman, *Jewish Thought in the Sixteenth Century*, 89-105.

13 Jonas, *Mortality and Morality*, 172. Emphasis his.

be gleaned from the evidence of life alone."[14] When chance works in our favor, we call it luck. When staggeringly improbable chance works in our favor, some call it a miracle. Whatever the cause of subjectivity, of self-consciousness, its emergence is a biological fact that demands a philosophical explanation, even if the proposed theory is unscientific in the sense of not being falsifiable. Jonas reminds his readers that metaphysical naturalism is a worldview, a metaphysics as unscientific as any other metaphysical conjecture. Metaphysical naturalism, as opposed to the methodological naturalism of science, is a faith that in no way merits the name, or prestige, of science.[15]

> Whether and to what extent this teleological potency also played a role in the creation of those external conditions, i.e., of organic and especially cerebral evolution, or whether it can only wait for its heteronomous entrance, cannot be known. But, conjectures are permitted. A "yearning" for it *could* be causally *active*, and increasingly work toward its own fulfillment—from the first chances presented by matter and then exponentially with the accumulation of these chances. This is what I believe, as I already indicated when I admitted the concept of an eros.[16]

There is no sleight of hand with Jonas. He draws the line between science and philosophy, points out how many scientists have stepped over it without due acknowledgement, and then with full disclosure, steps over it himself. Honesty is heroic. Just as there is a line between science and philosophy, there is another separating philosophy and religion. In Jonas' writings *qua* philosophy, he is careful to stay on his side of the line. But when speaking as a philosopher who is also a Jew, he is willing to reframe his philosophic insights in Jewish terms. What I want to emphasize is that Jonas' introduction of his cosmogonic myth was offered in a secular setting dealing with issues of history of nature, metaphysics, and ethics. It was not until later, according to his own testimony, that he recognized the Jewish roots of his myth and its applicability to evil in human history.[17]

---

14 Ibid., 173. "Physicists should be aware of making their physics into a metaphysics, i.e., to pass off the reality known by them for the whole of reality" (ibid., 193).
15 Ibid., 163.
16 Ibid., 173–74. Emphasis his.
17 Immediately prior to offering his own myth in his 1961 lecture, he cited several gnostic myths that share a family resemblance with that of Isaac Luria. Jonas,

In an encouraging example of what Lenn Goodman might call "cross-pollination," Christian thinkers, beginning with German theologian Jurgen Moltmann, have incorporated the notion of *tzimtzum* into their own writings.[18] Christians using the Hebrew term *tzimtzum* and citing Isaac Luria feel like acts of interfaith flattery. Alas, what Jonas' work helped me to see was that given the Jewish need for theodicy to contend with the catastrophes that have punctuated Jewish history, those same theodicies can be applied to mass extinction in earth's history. Jewish history has become paradigmatic for our understanding of earth's history, *maʿaseh avot siman laʿvanim*. The consensus among these likeminded theologians is that our species and planet are staring unblinkingly at ecological, technological, and military threats that require a response that does not rely on a *deus ex machina*. Humanity is both a surviving remnant and an endangered species in whose hands God's fate rests. Omnicide is a true theat. The fundamental challenge of our time is biblical: how do we live long on the land that the Lord, our God, has given us? How do we prevent Jewish history from becoming a paradigm for the future of our planet?

Introducing Entanglement

A peculiarity of my biography is that I have spent roughly half my adult life learning with and from the thinkers whose theologies of creation we will now discuss. Bradley Shavit Artson was my family rabbi and later the dean of the Ziegler School of Rabbinic Studies where I received ordination; Arthur Green was my dissertation advisor at Brandeis University. The third thinker who merits mention in this chapter is Lenn Goodman. Goodman was on the search committee that hired me at Vanderbilt University, and we had a weekly study session for most of my four years

---

Mortality and Morality, 123–24. Interestingly, Scholem had previously pointed out there was a gnostic myth of divine withdrawal presented by Basilides in the second century CE. See Scholem, *Major Trends*, 264.

18 Jurgen Moltmann, *God in Creation: A New Theology of Creation and the Spirit of God*, trans. Margaret Kohl (Minneapolis: Fortress Press, 1993), 88; John F. Haught, *God after Darwin: A Theology of Evolution* (Boulder: Westview Press, 2009), 45–46 and 105–20. In Jurgen Moltmann's *The Spirit of Life: A Universal Affirmation*, trans. Margaret Kohl (Minneapolis: Fortress Press, 2001), he specifically notes Jonas' use of *tzimtzum* (319n29).

there. Goodman is a Jewish philosopher whose work, in many ways, updates that of Jonas. His *Creation and Evolution*, although having an abundance of Jewish sources, is less a Jewish theology of creation than a natural theology by a philosopher who is Jewish. Goodman's starting point is nature, and he moves from nature to values. Jonas did the same—it is the ontological move. "If nature's dynamism points to a deity, as I believe it does, it is by the possibilities for emergence opened by that dynamism."[19] With all deference to Goodman's contributions, we approach Sinai from opposite sides of the mountain.

It is the rational analysis of being and nature that constrains Goodman, philosophy, and natural theology; it is the subjective experience of being and nature that motivates Green and Artson, theology, and the theology of creation. Contemporary Jewish theologians like Green and Artson, and I include myself in this category, no longer pretend to first look to the Torah or tradition to determine what we need to "discover" in creation.[20] Intuition, experience, knowledge, and tradition come together to generate novel insight. That flash of comprehension should go *beyond* scientific knowledge but not *against* scientific knowledge. Thus, in seeking to articulate a robust Jewish theology of creation, while paying respect to and showing appreciation for the Jewish philosophical tradition, we hope to point to more than philosophy allows.

Arthur Green (b. 1941) identifies himself as a Neo-Hasidic, mystical panentheist. Compared to Goodman and Artson, Green cites relatively few philosophers and scientists. His theology, rooted in the acosmism of HaBaD, leads him to commence his "Neo-Hasidic Credo" with a claim that is so overtly unscientific that it minimizes science's potential contributions:

> There is only One. All exists within what we humans call the mind of God, where Being is a simple, undifferentiated whole. Because God is beyond

---

19 Lenn E. Goodman, "Value and the Dynamics of Being," *Review of Metaphysics* 61, no. 1 (2007): 38.

20 This approach is that of the fundamentalists featured in my "Crisis Management via Biblical Interpretation: Fundamentalism, Modern Orthodoxy, and Genesis," in *Jewish Tradition and the Challenge of Darwinism*, ed. Geoffrey Cantor and Marc Swetlitz (Chicago: University of Chicago Press, 2006), 166-87.

time, that reality has never changed. Our evolving, ever-changing cosmos and the absolute stasis of Being are two faces of the same One.[21]

Just as medieval Kabbalah distinguishes between *Eyn Sof* and the sefirot, Green distinguishes what we might call the Being of *Eyn Sof* and the Becoming of the sefirot, the two faces of the same One. Like HaBaD, Green's understanding of *tzimtzum* is psychological. "Human beings are capable of insight that comes from a more profound realm of existence."[22] Although Green says that theodicy is still an unresolved challenge for him, given his theology I do not understand why.[23] Both theodicy and providence lose their function within a world where God is all and individuality illusion. "At the psychological-devotional root of this entire complex of ideas stands the experience of the negation or transcendence of self, and the discovery, in the wake of that experience, that it is only God who remains."[24]

As for providence and teleology, Green identifies the self-consciousness that has emerged quite recently in evolutionary history as the telos of existence. "This Being, still in our evolutionary future, will fully know and realize the One that lives in all beings."[25] Part of our service to the divine is to cultivate such self-awareness. As Green's later work emphasizes, one consequence of increased consciousness will be to protect our threatened planet, thereby allowing self-consciousness to continue evolving. "We have emerged as partners of the One in the survival and maintenance of this planet and all the precious attainments that have evolved here. Without our help it will not continue to thrive."[26] More on the obligations that emerge from Green's theology will be discussed in the final book.

Green speaks of a synergy whereby "this whole is mysteriously and infinitely greater than the sum of its parts." It is here that Green discusses the traditional terms of immanence and transcendence: "Transcendence thus dwells *within* immanence. . . . There is no end to its unimaginable

---

21 Green, *The Heart of the Matter*, 271.
22 Ibid., 276.
23 Arthur Green, *Arthur Green: Hasidism for Tomorrow*, ed. Hava Tirosh-Samuelson and Aaron W. Hughes (Leiden: Brill, 2015), 237.
24 Green, *The Heart of the Matter*, 244.
25 Green, *Ehyeh*, 112.
26 Green, *Radical Judaism*, 27.

depth, but so too there is no border, no limit, separating that unfathomable One from anything that is."[27] Green's commitment to avoiding the duality of God and world motivates him to collapse transcendence into immanence. Although both Green and I recognize and value the poetic quality of religious language, I find this metaphor unhelpful. If divine immanence is within transcendence, then what's the divine remainder of transcendence? Isn't transcendence, by definition, meant to go *beyond* immanence? Am I guilty of taking religious language literally and distorting the meaning? Perhaps, but I just don't understand the poetry. Or, more likely, the mystical insights of acosmism are beyond me. Perhaps my understanding of God is more panentheistic in the sense that I cannot endorse, or even fully understand, the claim that reality is illusory. The fact that our present reality is ephemeral makes it no less real.

In the Talmud's account of the four who entered the *pardes*, paradise, the mystical orchard, Rabbi Akiva, the only one to enter and exit while maintaining his grip on reality, tells his colleagues "when you arrive at the stones of pure marble, do not say 'water, water'" (b. Hagiga 14b.) This is a pure Green aggada. In the heart of Green's orchard, what *looks like* water is in reality the entryway to the divine throne room. After the revelation at Sinai, there is a rare biblical description of what lies under God's feet: "the likeness of a pavement of sapphire, like the very sky for purity" (Exodus 24:10). Green, like Rabbi Akiva, believes the water is an illusion to be overcome. What looks like water are really shimmering pavers of translucent blue marble. In this aggada, it is Akiva whom we imagine walks on "water," across the stones of pure marble and into the divine throne room. In Green's orchard, in the center of the throne room, Akiva dissolves in divinity. That is acosmism. But, in the Talmudic aggada, Akiva returned. Perhaps, like Noah's sons, he approached the father by walking backwards to preserve His honor, and in that way preserved his own identity. Not even Moshe could see God's face and live. According to this aggadah, of the four who entered the orchard, only Akiva did not look.[28]

Where Green sees stone, stasis, and divine Being, I see waters, flux, and the *tehom*, the watery abyss of Genesis One. In *my* midrashic

---

27 Ibid., 18. His emphasis.

28 In the Bavli version, it does not say that Aher looked. The Toseftan version, however, does.

orchard, the *tehom* is no illusion. I warn my colleagues that the Lord is a consuming fire. The *tehom* encircles the radiant throne room like a moat, awesome and impassable, to mediate between Being and Becoming. I stand unsteadily at the tidal edge of tehom, touching and not touching, my senses overwhelmed by the synesthesia that caused the Israelites to "see the sounds" at Sinai (Exodus 20:15). Rays shooting from the throne room ricochet off the breakers, resounding like a plucked dulcimer. Turning from the radiance, I pivot and distinctly see the fruit, leaves, branches, trunk, bark, roots, and flowing sap of each tree in the orchard glimmering and pulsing with divine light. In my orchard, I approach the edge of immanence. What is beyond, by definition, is transcendent. That is panentheism.[29]

Our adventure in the orchard was intended to demonstrate the difference, using a traditional metaphor, between acosmism and panentheism. This was not an exercise in counting angels on the head of a pin. The difference between these theologies hinges on two elements: transcendence and relationship. Although the language of relationship is not absent from Green's work, if the discrete elements of reality are illusory and all "merely" different garbs of the One, then the coherence of relationships, as well as covenant, are somehow compromised.[30]

HaBaD's acosmism is described by Wolfson as: "all things in the created universe are nullified in the light that is the essence of the Infinite."[31] Although Green defines himself as a panentheist, he identifies with early

---

29 A traditional way to reconcile our orchards is by using Cordovero's distinction. Green's orchard is an aggada from God's perspective; my orchard is an aggada from the human perspective.

30 Ariel Evan Mayse contends that this is a tension in Green's writing. See his "Arthur Green: An Intellectual Profile", in *Arthur Green: Hasidism for Tomorrow*, 29. During a career that has spanned decades, there has also been development. In 1999, Green came down on the side that the ever-evolving one of Being was "a conscious and willful self." See "A Kabbalah for the Environmental Age": 319. At some point within the next decade, he shifted perspectives. "I do not affirm a Being or a Mind that exists separate from the universe and acts upon it intelligently and willfully." See Green, *Radical Judaism*, 17. Notice his careful language. He is admitting what he does not affirm; he is not affirming a rejection. He is also stipulating that the Being or Mind does not exist *separately* from the universe, not that it doesn't exist. What is at issue for me here, is whether there is something akin to Mind *within* Being that acts willfully. I believe there is, but, perhaps, I, too, will change my mind.

31 Wolfson, *Open Secret*, 93.

Hasidic theology which is closer to acosmism: "Nothing but God is real; there is no duality of God and the world, but only a false duality of God and illusion."[32] At this point, we can understand one distinction between acosmism and panentheism as an ontological border dispute. Green thinks there is no border; I think there is. I can't jump the moat. For Green, transcendence in immanence means there are no borders separating discrete elements in the cosmos; for me, transcendence beyond immanence allows for porous borders where individual integrity and interdependence entangle.

The second consequence of these two mystical theologies is the role of relationship. The final thinker in this section, Bradley Artson, emphasizes the centrality of relationships within his Jewish version of process theology. In ways reminiscent of RaMBaM's appropriation of neo-Aristotelian philosophy, Artson has done the same with process philosophy and theology. Ironically, Artson uses process thought as a tool to gut the Maimonidean synthesis that has dominated the Jewish scene since the Haskalah developed an allergy to all things mystical and mythical about two hundred years ago.

> What Process Theology offers is the opportunity to sandblast the philosophical overlay of Hellenistic Greece and medieval Europe off the rich, burnished grain of Bible, Rabbinics, and Kabbalah so that we can savor the actual patterns in the living wood of religion, the *etz hayyim* [tree of life], and appreciate Judaism for what it was intended to be and truly is.[33]

Among the legacies of that Hellenistic overlay was God's utter transcendence, impassibility (unable to experience emotion), and autarchy (self-sufficiency). God is an island, a never-changing island.

For RaMBaM, God is pure being. For Artson, being is but an abstraction and distraction. "Being on its own is a (mere) logical abstraction. It is only being in relationship to others, that is to say, becoming, that can be apprehended, that can enter into relationship."[34] Emil G. Hirsch and Mordecai Kaplan both emphasized interactive relationship, as we saw in

---

32 Green, *The Heart of the Matter*, 237. Note, this is Green's description of acosmism and not an explication of his own theology.
33 Artson, *God of Becoming*, xiv.
34 Ibid., 44.

the previous chapter. Artson's familiarity with contemporary sciences and philosophy allows him to update the discussion. His two books juxtaposing process theology and Judaism are valuable contributions to modern Jewish thought, notwithstanding the following critique.

My first question about Artson's books deal with process thought itself. It is not Artson's "whoring after foreign gods" that bothers me. Like Artson and Green, I find much of value in other religions, and I am delighted to incorporate "foreign wisdom" into my own theology and practice. I simply do not see what process adds to Judaism. Artson brings in the process concept of dipolarity, for example, and associates the *Eyn Sof* with the divine dimension "beyond becoming." Artson then describes a "process of becoming [that] is embodied, temporal, and dynamic. In such a mode, all is related to all, and lower orders emerge from higher orders."[35] But, if that's what the sefirot and *Eyn Sof* represent, what do we profit from process?

Process theology describes a continuous creation and a God who continuously influences and interacts with creation but is incapable of intervening in creation. Judaism had both those aspects well before Alfred North Whitehead, the founding father of process thought. What I find simply inaccurate is Artson's claim that process thought "is what [classical Judaism] was intended to be and truly is." The Mosaic religion, as opposed to the priestly, with its God who manipulates weather patterns as carrot and stick for Israelite behavior is not process oriented. Artson would be better served by the more modest claim, which he also makes, that there are strands of process thought within classical Judaism.[36] But, given that, what do we profit from process?[37]

More substantively, Artson introduces Whitehead's term "lure" to describe "the way God works on us, in us, and through us. . . . Creation, then, is the process of God luring emergent being into order, abundance,

---

35 Artson, *Renewing the Process of Creation*, 62. It is not clear to me how the *Eyn Sof* can be "beyond becoming" without becoming the abstraction of Being.

36 For the more modest claim, see Artson, *God of Becoming and Relationship*, xviii. For another example of the stronger claim, see Bradley Shavit Artson, "I Will Be Who I Will Be: A God of Dynamic Becoming," in *Jewish Theology in our Time*, ed. Elliot J. Cosgrove (Woodstock: Jewish Lights Publishing, 2013), 10.

37 For a positive perspective on the same facts, see Alfredo Borodowski, "The Perfect Theological Storm," *Conservative Judaism* 62, no. 1-2 (2010): 91–93.

diversity, and goodness."[38] And how do we know what the lure is? We just know it. "We know it intuitively because we prehend it, Whitehead's term for immediate, internal intuition. We do not have to be told; we are each connected to all and to the creative-responsive love that God offers."[39] To the degree that the lure aligns with Jonas' cosmogonic eros in prehuman life, I concur. But the denomination of Judaism that Artson represents, Conservative Judaism, could never endorse intuition as a sufficient reason for action. The anarchy unleashed by people following their idiosyncratic lures invites pandemonium.

Anticipating this argument, Artson asserts that "for Jews, the Torah represents the supreme distillation of this divine lure and human agency into words."[40] Artson has swung from the apotheosis of personal autonomy in Reform Judaism to the Orthodox dogma of an ontologically unique Torah. His middle ground is halakhically at home within Conservative Judaism, but his logic is tenuous.[41] If revelation is ongoing, as both Judaism and process theology assert, what makes one document more supreme than another? Why isn't midrash, or RaMBaM, or Artson supreme? In all candor, if I had to choose between the divine lure in the Torah and the divine lure in Artson's oeuvre, I'd go with Artson. (How is that for a backhanded compliment?) My point is that since Artson is writing for Jews who "cannot put on blinders and forget what their minds learned in science labs and history classes," he has done a better job for the science students than for the history students.[42]

In terms of the religion and science dialogue that Artson champions, one of his primary concerns is the issue of body/soul dualism. Green's monism pronounces the body/soul dualism deceptive from the start. For Green, even the human/divine dualism is illusory. "The 'radical otherness' of God, so insisted upon by Western theology, is not an ontological

---

38 Artson, *God of Becoming*, 18 and 25.
39 Ibid., 18. Artson apparently does need to tell us that what he deems to be negative urges are not God's lure, "but the addiction of *tohu va-vohu*." Artson, *Renewing the Process of Creation*, 163n11.
40 Artson, *God of Becoming*, 47.
41 Ibid., 55. In an issue of *Conservative Judaism* dedicated to Artson's theological proposals, Harold M. Schulweis offers a similar critique. *Conservative Judaism* 62, no. 1-2 (Fall–Winter 2010): 55–57.
42 Artson, *God of Becoming*, xix.

otherness but an otherness of perspective."[43] Artson, although he cites Rabbi Moshe Cordovero, never deploys his dipolar distinction of reality from God's perspective versus from our perspective.[44] That's not Artson's theology, it is Green's. Artson's process panentheism preserves an onto-logical distinction between God and creation, but not between body and soul.[45] Artson returns to a more biblical anthropology where humanity is an animated body or an embodied soul. Neither exists independently. As with Christian theologians referencing *tzimtzum*, it is both flattering and a sign of interreligious progress that Christians are recognizing the merits of the Torah's understanding of humanity. Here is one of the leading figures in the Christian world promoting a dialogue between religion and science, Arthur Peacocke:

> Christian anthropology has to return to the more Hebraic understanding of human beings as psychosomatic unities and not as the embodiment of naturally immortal souls—a notion imprinted on both academic and popular Christianity by centuries of the influence of Platonism on its philosophy.[46]

Within the Torah, there simply is no such thing as a separable, independent soul. Although a distinction emerges between body and soul in rabbinic literature, according to Alon Goshen-Gottstein, "the difference is not one of essence. Nowhere in rabbinic literature is the soul regarded as Divine. It may be of heavenly origin, but it is not Divine."[47] As Christianity struggles to refashion its image of humanity, one theologian asks a poignant question: "What *would* Christians have been doing these past 2000 years if there were no such things as souls to save?"[48]

If there are no separable souls, then there can be no problem of ensoulment. I am not speaking of the question as to when a zygote-fetus-infant becomes endowed with a soul; nor am I strictly speaking of the transition from prehuman to human. In the Greek taxonomy that

---

43 Green, *Radical Judaism*, 18.

44 Artson, *God of Becoming*, 15.

45 Artson, *Renewing the Process of Creation*, 60.

46 Arthur Peacocke, *Evolution: The Disguised Friend of Faith?* (West Conshohocken: Templeton Foundation Press, 2004), 241.

47 Goshen-Gottstein, "The Body as Image of God in Rabbinic Literature": 177.

48 Nancey Murphy, *Bodies and Soul, or Spirited Bodies* (Cambridge: Cambridge University Press, 2006), 27.

influenced medieval Jewish thought, there were three souls: human, animal, and vegetative. In other words, the leap from inanimate to animate could be described as ensoulment. One can imagine ensoulment as the moment when a separable soul is bestowed upon a soulless object.

Within the Hasidic theology we have discussed, souls are not bestowed from the outside, they emerge through a leap. That leap is neither triggered from the outside nor internally generated. The leap reflects a more complex dynamic that results from the relationship among systems internal to the organism *and* its surroundings. Creation, life, consciousness, speciation, self-consciousness, language, insights, and repentance are all functions of a leap. Admittedly it is not a very scientific term, but the more scientifically sounding *emergence* is equally metaphorical. Here is Wolfson's description of the leap within HaBaD theology. "Through the leap, then, one jolts to new ground that could not have been anticipated or foreseen, a radical irruption that signals inherent indeterminacy that proceeds from the 'sublimity of the essence of the infinite.'"[49]

That essence enlivens each existent and unites all existence. Coevolution happens when two different species, sometimes even an animal and a plant, adapt symbiotically to one another. Harold J. Morowitz, a biophysicist who specialized in the emergence of life, reminds us that "All evolution is coevolution."[50] God is evolving through the discrete aspects of godliness that fill the world and are the fullness of the world. Those discrete aspects are coevolving at every moment to further God's goals of freedom, diversity, and self-consciousness.

These three goals are values predicated on how Jews have understood God *and* how humans perceive reality. At Sinai, God introduces Himself to the Israelites as their Liberator—freedom is essential. There can be no covenant by coercion. From Heisenberg's Uncertainty Principle "on up," there is contingency, indeterminacy, unpredictability, free will, and chance woven into the fabric of the universe. If freedom is the warp, however, laws and constraints are the woof. We saw a similar dialectic with Lurianic Kabbala between the limitlessness of love and law-abiding justice. In nature, constraints lead to convergence: "from very different

---

49 Wolfson, "Achronic Time," 75, citing Dov Ber Schneersohn, Torat Hayyim: Bere'shit 72d.
50 Harold J. Morowitz, *The Emergence of Everything: How the World Became Complex*, (New York: Oxford University Press, 2002), 183.

starting points in the Tree of Life very much the same solution has evolved multiple times."[51] In society, constraints lead to harmony. Immediately after God's introduction, the laws begin.

The second goal, diversity, reflects a unity that is not uniformity. There are seventy nations in the Torah, twelve tribes of Israel, ten sefirot, and a rabbinic blessing that praises God for being *M'shaneh ha'briot*, the One who diversifies creation. Another blessing praises God for not withholding anything from the cosmic cornucopia. The "chance" inherent in Darwin's natural selection is no longer a stumbling block for many theologians. Arthur Peacocke explains how chance functions in his theology:

> The emergence of the immense variety of living forms manifests the potentialities of matter. That it does so through an exploration of all available possibilities by random molecular events does not seem to me to be in itself a sufficient basis for any apotheosis of "chance." Thus biological evolution no more qualifies for description as a "chance" process than any other.[52]

In order to generate new creation, to activate that potential inherent in creation, the elements of creation interact and con-spire (lit. breathe together) life into "endless forms most beautiful and most wonderful."[53] If an immense variety of living forms is a goal, *randomness is adaptive*.

The third goal, self-consciousness, is cultivating an awareness of our place within God and God's cosmos, what Jewish mysticism might describe as *within God's image*. This awareness has several aspects, and in the next book on halakhah we will explore the personal and communal obligations that emerge from this understanding of ourselves. In terms of a theology of creation, this awareness of our interconnectedness with all and All allows us to enhance and thicken our understanding of science. Toward the conclusion of an encyclopedic treatment of evolutionary convergence, Simon Conway Morris, an evolutionary biologist, opined: "In the final analysis, the only reason why evolution is of the remotest interest is neither that it is true (which any idiot can see) nor that it is

---

51 Simon Conway Morris, *The Runes of Evolution: How the Universe Became Self-Aware* (West Conshohocken: Templeton Press, 2015), 3.
52 Peacocke, *Evolution*, 55.
53 Darwin, *Origin*, final sentence.

fascinating (why else write this book?), but because it is the mechanism by which the Universe has become self-aware."[54]

In 1935, three physicists (yes, all Jewish!), crafted a counterintuitive theory called *entanglement*. Albert Einstein, Nathan Rosen, and Boris Podolsky claimed that once two particles had interacted with each other, they continued to influence each other even when separated. This influence, regardless of the distance, is causal. "What happens to the distant entity depends specifically upon what happens to the near one, so that the effect is genuinely causal and not merely epistemological, as if it just involved learning about something that was already the case."[55] As one of the leading figures in the religion and science field, John Polkinghorne, puts it: "Even subatomic particles, it seems, cannot properly be treated atomistically!"[56] Entanglement is a scientific pointer towards transcendence. When discrete, immanent aspects of godliness entangle in relationship, that is transcendence. (Allow me to rely on Ruth Page's disclaimer here: "I have used the word 'relationship' for this connection, although it is a human term and may not be right for nonhuman creatures. But it is the only word we have for the kind of valuable connection I wish to indicate."[57])

No man is an island, no religion is an island, not even an island is an island. All subatomic particles were once inchoate and in cahoots. Isn't that one of the unavoidable consequences of the Big Bang? If everything that exists now was together, in some way, at the beginning, in the Origin, then we should all be entangled, however attenuated. Not only does that help frame what Jung called synchronicity, but it might help explain what we call extrasensory perception. Some people are more attuned to entanglement than others. We each have a native endowment, and some cultivate that endowment while others leave it fallow. When Daniel Matt and Richard Elliott Friedman simultaneously write books

---

54 Morris, *Runes of Evolution*, 286.
55 John Polkinghorne, *Exploring Reality: The Intertwining of Science and Religion* (New Haven: Yale University Press, 2005), 31.
56 Ibid.
57 Ruth Page, "Panentheism and Pansyntheism: God in Relation," in *In Whom We Live and Move and Have Our Being: Panentheistic Reflections on God's Presence in a Scientific World*, ed. Philip Clayton and Arthur Peacocke (Grand Rapids: Eerdmans, 2004), 229.

describing the resonances between Big Bang cosmology and Kabbalah, that synchronicity might also be an example of entanglement.[58]

Karl Schmitz-Moormann, a Catholic theologian whose writings are redolent of those of his mentor, Teilhard de Chardin, coined the phrase *Creatio Appellata*, the called-forth creation. Although Schmitz-Moormann's panentheism is more willful than my own, his descriptions of *Creatio Appellata* track onto my understanding of entanglement and divine transcendence. "The innermost reality of anything would be conceived as the presence of God, [and therefore] as God's call to come to God."[59] God's immanence, informing all existence, radiates the call to connect. Schmitz-Moorman explains that his conception bears two aspects, one vis-à-vis humanity and the other vis-à-vis nonhuman creation. Here are the key elements of *Creation Appellata*:

Below are his key descriptors cited verbatim.

- This immanence of God calling from the inside of the elements leaves intact the integrity of the elements.
- God entices neighboring elements to unite. There is no outside pressure, only an inside tendency toward the neighboring element.
- On the level of human relations we have a name for this kind of accepting by the other, by offering oneself without imposing oneself: love.
- In an analogical way, this is applicable to all levels of union, where the other element must always be respected in its integrity and where both become more through union, coming in an infinitesimal way closer to the Creator.
- The loving call of God might thus, in theology, be considered the driving force of creation and so of evolution.

---

58 Daniel Matt, *God and the Big Bang: Discovering Harmony Between Science and Spirituality* (Woodstock: Jewish Lights Publishing, 1996) and Richard Elliot Friedman, *The Disappearance of God: A Divine Mystery* (New York: Little, Brown, and Co., 1995).

59 Schmitz-Moormann, *Theology of Creation in an Evolutionary World*, 123. I have emended the original sentence to better reflect my own theology. The original line is: "The innermost reality of anything would be conceived as the presence of God, or rather as God's call to come to God."

- This universe exists because it is held in existence and in its ongoing process of becoming by the creative call of divine love, infinitesimally present in all creatures.[60]

Your neighbor's godliness, immanence, exerts influence on you, and it is mutual: Buberian entanglement. The medium of that mutual influence, the entanglement of forces, is transcendence because it transcends the immanence within the discrete elements of the cosmos. Rather than the enticement *to unite*, I think a more helpful term for this divine activity might be *organize*. As Brian Swimme, a mathematical cosmologist has noted, "If we observe the universe over time we will find that the evolutionary process brings forth centers of activity that are differentiated, self-organizing, and interrelated."[61]

In his discussion of Crescas, Zev Harvey suggested love is the metaphysical correlate of gravity—it holds the world together. His student, Joseph Albo, wrote that our purpose on the planet is that of *imitatio Dei*, to engage in acts that benefit others, acts of lovingkindness.[62] This call of cosmogonic eros, this covenant between the pieces, operates throughout all creation, not just among animate creatures. The epitome of the inanimate is the rock, and yet the Torah describes God as a rock (Deuteronomy 32).[63] True, rocks are strong and secure, an appropriate metaphor for God. But, the Torah wallows in references to God's ability to get water from a rock.[64] *Water from a rock* is a coincidence of opposites—God can cause that which is life giving to emerge from what is lifeless. "Tremble, O earth, at the presence of the Lord, at the presence of the God of Jacob, who turned the rock into a pool of water, the flinty rock into a fountain" (Psalms 114:8).

---

60 Ibid., 123–24.
61 Brian Swimme, "Cosmic Directionality and the Wisdom of Science," in *Science and Religion*, ed. John F. Haught (Georgetown: Georgetown University Press, 2001), 95.
62 Harvey, "Ethical Theories," 97.
63 Michael P. Knowles suggests that the usage of rock in Deuteronomy 32:18 to describe God is "moral, or perhaps better, covenantal." See his "'The Rock, His Work is Perfect:' Unusual Imagery for God in Deuteronomy XXXII," *Vetus Testamentum* 39, no. 3 (1989): 311.
64 Isaiah 48:21, Psalms 78:20, and 105:41, in addition to the stories of Moshe striking the rock in Exodus 17 and Numbers 20. The story in Numbers uses a different word for rock, but the image is the same.

Not surprisingly, the kabbalists perceived this coincidence of opposites and projected it onto the sefirotic map. Ithamar Gruenwald discusses how these images were deployed by Joseph Gikatilla in his thirteenth-century kabbalistic work Sha'arei Orah. "Adonai is also referred to as *even* (stone), for it is the foundation for all the building in the world. All the world depends on it and its needs are fulfilled by it. It was called *Even ha-Ro'shah* [the first stone; Zechariah 4:7], from here came forth the celestial and earthly multitudes of Creation."[65] Gruenwald unpacks the kabbalistic imagery: one of the names of the tenth sefira, the portal between the earthly and divine realms, is stone or rock. "Through that sefira, the flow of the divine emanation into the lower world(s) becomes possible. In that sense, 'the world (really) depends on it.' . . . That 'stone' is viewed as a fountainhead of all the divine emanations that stream into the lower world."[66] When Schmitz-Moormann posits godliness as "infinitesimally present in all creatures," the kabbalistic tradition not only anticipated such a claim, but it zeroed in on the ultimate inanimate, the rock, to picture all of life streaming from that seemingly lifeless source.

My wife and I visited Mount Saint Helens sixteen years after its volcano erupted in 1980. Amidst the moonscape were filaments of life, green tendrils reaching for the sun. Scientists tell us the Big Bang happened 13.8 billion years ago. Theologians tell us God is beyond time. The former is difficult enough to conceptualize, but I definitely don't understand the latter claim. There are many videos on the internet helping to explain time scales. One video has earth's history divided into one hundred units and places significant events on a one-hundred-yard football field. Humanity appears a few inches from the goal line. God is described in the Torah as long suffering, but there is also the sense that we operate on different time scales. "For in Your sight a thousand years are like yesterday that has passed" (Psalms 90:4). In God's sight, the surface of Mount Saint Helens will be verdant tomorrow.

The results of yearning for life, freedom, consciousness, and self-consciousness has taken, as far as we know, all time and space. What Green calls the "greatest sacred drama" has become greater with each felicitous

---

65 Gikatilla, *Gates of Light*, 21; cited in Ithamar Gruenwald, "God the 'Stone/Rock': Myth, Idolatry, and Cultic Fetishism in Ancient Israel," *The Journal of Religion* 76, no. 3 (1996): 447.

66 Gruenwald, "'God the Stone/Rock'": 447.

step toward self-recognition and self-consciousness. Like Jonas, I do not believe that God is interventionist, but God is opportunistic. That was in evidence on Mount Saint Helens. "The exploitation of this opportunity for life shows that more than a neutral accident is at work. Life is its own purpose, i.e., an end actively willing itself and pursuing itself."[67] Here is where Kabbalah and Artson's emphasis on relationship and interrelationship enter.

Life is not atomistic. Darwin pointed us toward competition. But Green reminded us that the genius of Genesis 1 was to take the deified dragons of ancient Near Eastern battle myths and neuter them.[68] Post-Darwinian evolutionary biology has not neutralized the competition that was imagined to drive speciation, but it has reframed the struggle for survival. What we have seen since Kropotkin's emphasis on mutual aid is a deeper appreciation for the role of symbiosis. According to Lynn Margulis, a professor of Geosciences, "Long-term stable symbiosis that leads to evolutionary change is called 'symbiogenesis.' These mergers, long-term biological fusions beginning as symbiosis, are the engine of species evolution."[69] Symbiosis is the antiphonal call of the deep to the deep.

Since the 1960s, scientists have known that genes can be activated through their environments.[70] "Genes do not act all the time, but instead need to be turned on and off in response to specific stimuli."[71] Environments influence development at levels which would make Lamarck proud. Evelyn Fox Keller, a theoretical physicist, mathematical biologist, and historian and philosopher of science, explains that mapping the genome, as important as it is, is insufficient for the following reason.

> If the genes [among all animal phyla] are "essentially the same," what then is it that makes one organism a fly and the other a mouse, a chimp, or a human? The answer, it seems, is to be found in the structure of gene

67 Jonas, *Mortality and Morality*, 173.
68 Green, "A Kabbalah for an Environmental Age": 317.
69 Lynn Margulis and Dorion Sagan, *Acquiring Genomes* (New York: Basic Books, 2002), 12.
70 Evelyn Fox Keller, *The Century of the Gene* (Cambridge, MA: Harvard University Press, 2001), 64.
71 Ibid., 79.

networks—in the ways in which genes are connected to other genes by the complex regulatory mechanisms that, in their interaction, determine when and where a particular gene will be expressed. But unlike the sequence of the genome, this regulatory circuitry is not fixed: it is dynamic rather than static, a structure that is itself changing over the course of the developmental cycle.[72]

Fox Keller suggests, notwithstanding Richard Dawkins, that genes are not selfish. Genes are not the unit of selection, mature organisms are.[73] What some scientists call top-down causality or active information is "the way in which the network of an organism's relationships to its environment and its behavior patterns together determine in the course of time the actual DNA sequences at the molecular level present in an evolved organism."[74] This more interactive view of nature provides an example of the entanglement of relationships that, in some cases, generates leaps. We know that genetic material is, to a degree, plastic, and there has been plenty of time to experiment.[75] Japanese scientists observed that more trees in coastal areas lead to higher yields for fisheries and oyster growers. They concluded that leaves falling into adjacent streams leached acids that traveled into the oceans. Those acids stimulated the growth of plankton, "the first and most important building block in the food chain."[76] The kabbalists were fond of the image of an upside-down tree, with roots in heaven and fruits on earth. These Japanese trees have shown us that even dead leaves generate life.

Our ancient kabbalists would be intrigued to know that trees' root systems often extend twice as far as their crowns, and the roots of neighboring trees intertwine. A celebrity professor of forest ecology, Suzanne Simard, has demonstrated that fungal connections transmit signals from one tree's roots to the next. Simard calls the subterranean forest the "wood wide web."[77] Communication among the roots enables trees to nourish and protect an endangered individual. "A tree can only be as

---

72 Ibid., 100.
73 Ibid., 114–15.
74 Peacocke, *Evolution*, 70.
75 Margulis and Sagan, *Acquiring Genomes*, 11.
76 Wohlleben, *The Hidden Life of Trees: What They Feel, How They Communicate—Discoveries from A Secret World* (Vancouver: Greystone Books, 2016), 245.
77 Ibid., 10–11.

strong as the forest that surrounds it."[78] Conversely, when lighting struck a Douglas fir, although only one trunk absorbed the bolt, ten fir trees were electrocuted by their interconnected roots.[79]

Rounding up, one hundred percent of the species to have ever existed on our planet are now extinct.[80] To my mind, that fact of earth's history is the single gravest indictment of the omnigod who is imagined as simultaneously omnipotent, omniscient, and benevolent. The Talmud long ago redefined omnipotence from being all powerful to having complete self-restraint. As for omniscience, from the Torah to Gersonides, Jewish thought has rejected such a characterization of God. God's very first emotion, after all, was remorse after creating humanity because of our unimagined and unimaginable propensity for nastiness.[81] The Gnostics, of course, considered the ruler of this world to be evil. The history of nature and humanity can be read to support such a view. But, that's profoundly ungrateful. To chalk up our existence to an evil god, or sheer chance, is counter to both my intuition and Judaism's consistent affirmation that this world, *in its entirety*, is "very good" (Genesis 1:31). Admittedly, both my intuition and Judaism are fallible, but the relationship between reality and morality, for me, is a deal breaker. I can live as a Jew with a God who lacks omnipotence; indeed, for reasons that should now be clear, I prefer to do so.[82] But, I could not live *as a Jew* if I didn't believe that the world was good and had the capacity for improvement. One of our very earliest cosmogonic texts Sefer Yetzira posits that *morality is one of the dimensions of the universe.*[83]

At the end of the first work week, God reviews all of creation and proclaims it "very good." Samson Raphael Hirsch, in his biblical commentary, echoes RaMBaM: "Everything in existence, looked at in connection with everything else, is very good. That which is relatively bad only appears as bad when looked at alone, in isolation, compartmentalized in

---

78 Ibid., 17.
79 Ibid., 206.
80 See Raup, *Extinction*.
81 Michael Carasik, "The Limits of Omniscience," *Journal of Biblical Literature* 119, no. 2 (Summer 2000): 221–32.
82 "Rabbi Akiva and his cohorts believed that it is better to limit belief in God's power than to dampen faith in God's mercy." Heschel, *Heavenly Torah*, 119.
83 Sefer Yetzira 1:5.

time and space."[84] We are "in connection with everything else," without being the center of everything else. RaMBaM presciently rejected anthropocentrism; everything was created for itself, not for us. Our appearance just shy of the end zone on earth's football field of history is less of an issue if we are not the goal.

Over the course of a poplar tree's life, it might produce one billion seeds at a rate of about fifty-four million seeds per year. Perhaps *one* seed will take root and emerge into an adult poplar. One out of a *billion*.[85] That is one species of tree. For evidence of divine providence, that is a challenging ratio. Mass extinction events, where the vast majority of species become extinct, are particularly bad optics. There have been at least five such events. But, in the context of an evolving universe, they also seem a nearly inevitable byproduct once we release our grip on an omnipotent and omniscient deity who intervenes at will. "Moreover, the [exclusive] celebration of advance ignores or belittles the cost incurred en route."[86] Ruth Page, another Christian theologian active in the religion and science conversation, offers a theological reframing of extinction. Rather than a dead end, the emergence of a species for a finite interval is an expression of God's goal of "making beings-with-relationships possible."[87] Page adds another term to our theological lexicon: pansyntheism, God with everything. To be is to be with God.[88] What we witness in the universe is the full gamut of possibilities rather than a linear route to us. God's goal is diversity not efficiency. Although extinction events, "perhaps mediated by climate change, sweep the ecological board largely clean . . . when the dice are rolled again they seem to be loaded."[89] Evolutionary convergence points to a teleology of canalization towards consciousness and self-awareness.

A Jewish theology of creation cannot reject chance and randomness as a constituent element in the cosmos. But a Jewish theology of creation cannot see chance in isolation or as the lurking leviathan of the

---

84 Samson Raphael Hirsch on Genesis 1:31. Cited in Cherry, *Torah through Time*, 62.
85 Wohlleben, *Hidden Life of Trees*, 30.
86 Page, "Panentheism and Pansyntheism," in Clayton, *In Whom We Live*, 224.
87 Ibid., 228.
88 Heschel gifted us a different sense of being: "For man *to be* means *to be with* other human beings. His existence *is* coexistence." Heschel, *Who is Man?*, 45.
89 Morris, *Runes of Evolution*, 230.

tehom constantly challenging divine sovereignty. What Genesis 1 taught us is that the leviathan, contrary to what we had thought, is not a threat. Chance is not opposed to creation, it is essential for creation. But, randomness is in relationship, too. Biologists like Conway Morris are helping us see that chance gets channeled into outcomes of near inevitability: "To trace the paths that evolution actually chooses to take is of great interest, but more fascinating still is to see how the recurrence of design [convergence] points to deeper organizational principles. . . . Biological form transcends phylogeny."[90] Like the recurring patterns of the priestly worldview, these organizational principles manifest at different levels of reality. Conway Morris cites fellow biologist Gareth Jones who, in a discussion of molecular convergence in auditory genes related to echolocation in bats, porpoises, sperm whales, and dolphins, asserts that the results provide "a stunning insight into how gene and protein sequences can be subject to convergent adaptive evolution in similar ways to morphological characters."[91]

Rabbi Nehemia gave us the seed principle in which all that would ever emerge was sowed at the beginning. Abraham Joshua Heschel updates the botanical model: "The Bible is a seed, God is the sun, but we are the soil. Every generation is expected to bring forth new understanding and new realization."[92] A fig tree might produce two crops a year, but both crops are figs. The botanical model that Heschel offers introduces the element of generations of soil. Soil, as every farmer knows, affects the fruit. Soil changes over time, and seeds are blown to different soils. Heschel's botanical metaphor is radically evolutionary.[93] We are a product of our immediate environment and our historical tradition. Our new understandings and realizations emerge from our soil. Analogously, species emerge based on their own genetic endowment in relationship to their immediate environment. Our more interactive view of nature enhances the agency of all that coevolves. Activating genes based on environmental stimuli and generating midrash based on environmental stimuli share structures.

90 Ibid., 232. Heschel, *Who is Man?*, 33.
91 G. Jones, *Current Biology* 20, R62 (2010); cited in Morris, *Runes of Evolution*, 143.
92 Heschel, *God in Search of Man*, 274.
93 Cherry, *Torah through Time*, 189.

To return to the Shoah, I have no choice but to live as a human with our species' penchant for ignorance, indolence, sadism, and venality; but I do have a choice to live as a Jew. With a God who was a silent bystander to the Shoah, however, I could not live. I do not believe that God was silent, nor do I believe in a God who was capable of intervening but restrained himself. I reject the omnigod. Omnipotence and omniscience have been passé for centuries within Jewish thought. After omni-cide, what survives is a covenant of benevolence—*hesed*.

The rabbis who created the theodicy of omni-cide by identifying God's strength as self-restraint and describing God as mute in the face of insult, were promoting an image of God to imitate. Just as God is restrained, silent, and long suffering, so, too, should Jews be in the aftermath of the destruction of the second Temple and the Bar Kochva Revolt.[94] *Imitatio Dei* became a rabbinic tool for accommodationist politics with the Romans.[95] Perhaps that strategy preserved the surviving remnant. At the same time, it quietly interred the conceit of an omnigod capable of divine intervention. Luria's theodicy, which I have argued is a functional extension of these rabbinic ideas, is part of a coherent Judaism. The theodicy of omni-cide and insistence on divine immanence and interconnectedness is true to both our Jewish heritage and to everything I believe about the world. The divine image of the sefirot connecting to each other is an icon of entanglement and a mirror of coevolution. The lines of connection, the gravitational pull that keeps our universe together, are love. *Hesed*/lovingkindness survives as a model of *imitatio Dei*. We have the ability, and therefore the covenantal responsibility, to protect the divine image to prevent omnicide. How we protect that image is the function of halakhah.[96]

מלא כל-הארץ כבודו

---

94 Yoma 69b, Gittin 56b, and Ketubot 111a.

95 Catherine Keller offers a parallel insight concerning P's authorship of Genesis 1: "If the suffering of colonization and exile drove P to write a new beginning for the people, a recontextualization of their life in space and time, the narrative at minimum lets them grieve productively. It situates them in the only context large enough to contain their sense of displacement: the space-time of the creation" (Keller, *Face of the Deep*, 160).

96 Jonas, *Mortality and Morality*, 101–08.

Book Three: Philosophies of Halakha

Preface to Book Three

For the past several hundred pages, I have been using the term *halakhah* interchangeably with the English word *law*. Since our final section focuses on halakhah, it is time to lay out the distinctions. (In this book, I capitalize *Halakhah* when indicating the entire system and use lowercase to designate an individual rule.)

Halakhah means, minimally, a Jewish way of doing things. The English word *law*, and the historically antisemitic adjective, *legalistic*, are terms that simply don't translate well into Jewish culture. American law as a system can be understood as a social contract among members of society in which legislation and adjudication protect rights and preserve liberties of the members. The legal system comprises individual laws that further those goals and carry sanctions when violated. Halakhah is a concretization of the covenant between the Jewish people and God which obligates Jews to behave in a manner that optimizes *tzedakah umishpat* (righteousness and justice) among people and instills devotion toward God.[1] The legislative goal is to create and maintain "a modest utopia where people will bless each other for being kind."[2] In terms of adjudication, equity, as Aristotle defined it, is when laws need to be

---

1   Joshua Berman suggests that in the Torah *mishpat* often bears the meaning of "justice." *Ani Maamin*, 55. Onkelos translates tzedek in Deuteronomy 16:20 as *truth*, while some rabbis seem to understand it as a resolution closer to equity. E.g., Sannhedrin 32b.
2   Greenstein, "Biblical Law," in Holtz, *Back to the Sources*, 100.

modified in order to avoid an injustice in specific circumstances. Interpreting halakhah, when the goal is *tzedakah umishpat*, involves enhancing and extending equity.

While American law focuses on individual rights, Halakhah frames individual rights within a social context that not infrequently supersedes individual claims. When one is grieving the loss of a child, sibling, spouse, or parent, one can depend on the support of the community during *shiva*, the seven days of intense mourning following burial—unless there is a holiday which cancels the community's official responsibility toward the mourner (S. A., Y. D. 399:1). American law was created for rugged individualists; Halakhah for loving neighbors. The differing goals of the American legal system and Halakhah substantively affect new legislation, adjudication of specific cases, and legal interpretation. Using the word *law*, therefore, in our discussion is immediately misleading. Thus, we will not translate Halakhah. We will explain and explore.

Halakhah has movement at its root, from the word *l'lekhet, to go* or *to walk*. When the verb appears before the word *after*, it means *to follow*. We are to follow in God's rabbinically sanctioned ways. "Walking in all God's ways," according to the Mosaic Torah, demands that we "circumcise the foreskins of [our] hearts and stiffen [our] necks no more. . . . God deals justly with the orphan and the widow, and God loves the stranger by providing him with food and clothing. Love the strangers for you, too, were strangers in the land of Egypt" (Deuteronomy 10:12–19). Let us understand Halakhah, then, as an elliptical noun form of *walking in God's ways*.

Circumcising our hearts has come to mean increasing our sensitivity to the needs of others. I suppose we reasonably associate circumcision and sensitivity, but there is more to this biblical idiom than compassion. The *heart* in the Torah is also the seat of the intellect. Thus, *circumcising the heart* is to prevent our intellects from becoming coarsened through tired messaging. We are to keep an *open mind* and not allow past experiences or rumors to scar into prejudices and stereotypes. The medieval commentator Sforno explains that we are to remove the errors that generate "lying beliefs."

Stiffening our neck is an image of refusing to accept the yoke of the mitzvot. In the morning prayers, we ask God's help to subordinate our egoistic inclination in order to serve God's will. In the passage above from Deuteronomy, circumcising our hearts and not stiffening our necks seem to be preparatory for life in the covenant. Slavery also seems to have been a prerequisite, which might explain why Abraham did not challenge God's portent that the Israelites would be slaves in Egypt (Genesis 15:13). The Midrash points out that as Jacob was fleeing from his brother to a strange land, he asked God to provide him with food and clothing. God now demands we reciprocate to the strangers in our own midst (Genesis 28:20, Deuteronomy 10:18, and Genesis Rabbah 70:5). Biblical scholars emphasize that such solicitude for the resident alien was unprecedented in the ancient world.

In the previous two books, I have offered a survey of Jewish theology and Jewish theologies of creation. My goal in this book is more limited. Now that we have explored what Jews have thought about God and how God interfaces with creation, what should be our response? Is there a Jewish way of responding, a Halakhah, that is both a coherent response to today's realities and rooted in traditional Halakhah? In our search for a coherent Judaism, remember, we are seeking robust continuity with earlier expressions of Judaism. In terms of Halakhah, that continuity should be both formal and procedural. The forms of traditional Halakhah can be easily discerned by looking through codes and responsa literature. The process of halakhic legislation, adjudication, and interpretation requires more analysis. This book is devoted to those processes, what is called a philosophy of Halakhah.

Unsurprisingly, there are multiple philosophies of Halakhah throughout Jewish history. What distinguishes this book from the previous two is that we will not trace each philosophy chronologically. My goal is to provide the pedigree for what I will call Covenantal Halakhah. Other philosophies will be explicated for purposes of juxtaposition and elimination. In legal parlance, this section is a brief for Covenantal Halakhah. Optimizing *tzedek* and instilling devotion to God are halakhic objectives, but how should individual halakhot (pl. of halakhah) be crafted, implemented, and interpreted over time to best serve those objectives?

In addition to the elements of any philosophy of law, Halakhah has also inherited what we earlier called an archaic ontology. That archaic ontology, although not without some salvage value, is generally wrong. As we will see, having such an ontology or metaphysics as an underlying substratum to the Halakhah can be pernicious. Thus, in addition to the goals and attendant elements of any philosophy of Halakhah, we will need to identify, when possible, the assumed metaphysics of particular halakhot.

The final element of our discussion of the philosophy of Halakhah involves the scope of the system. There is no autonomous halakhic state today. Since the emancipation of the Jews from their semi-autonomous enclaves, non-Jewish law has been the law of the land. Although we tend to think of emancipation as a nineteenth-century phenomenon, Eastern European and Middle Eastern Jews did not attain political emancipation until after the Shoah and the creation of the modern State of Israel. While Halakhah no longer has the same scope as it historically did, halakhic creativity abounds. We will conclude this book, and *Coherent Judaism*, with several examples of putting Covenantal Halakhah to work so that a coherent Judaism will be a compelling Judaism.

Chapter 11

Turning Torah

The Hebrew word *torah*, in the Torah (i.e., Pentateuch), means *instruction* or *teaching*. The words for teacher, *morah*, and parents, *horim*, share the same root letters. Not until the book of Ezra might *torah* point to the entire Torah (7:10). If *halakhah* should not be translated as law, all the more so should *torah* not be translated as law, notwithstanding the King James Bible translation which does precisely that. Although there may be law in the Torah, there is far more instruction.

Contemporary Bible scholars have recently suggested that what *appears* to be law in the Torah may not have been understood as such by the Torah's initial audience. Cuneiform legal collections, from roughly the same setting as the Torah's laws, were not chiseled for purposes of direct application as much as judicial education and legal training. In other words, scholars now suggest that even the Torah's "laws" were intended as teachings of legal principles and not statutes to be implemented regardless of context or circumstance.[1] The Babylonian Geonim from the early post-Talmudic period similarly viewed Talmudic "law" as legal principles which were not necessarily intended for direct application.[2]

In the first book, we juxtaposed the different theologies undergirding the priestly religion and the Mosaic religion. The priestly worldview imagines that our actions affect God's protective presence, either drawing God toward us through sacrificial offerings or repulsing God from us through violations of the covenant. The Mosaic worldview, however,

---

1 Berman, Ani Maamin, 138-44.
2 Fishman, *Becoming the People*, 36. The same was true for Rabbi Samson of Sens (c. 1150- c. 1230). See Kanarfogel, *Intellectual History*, 29.

understands that God rewards the Israelites for observing the terms of the covenant and punishes them for violations. What allowed rabbinic religiosity to subsume these two conflicting theologies is that the goal of both systems was the same, namely, to keep the Israelites in the Land of Israel. Whether exile was the result of our prior exiling of God's presence through our misbehavior (priestly), or whether it was a divine punishment (Mosaic) mattered less to the rabbis than forging a religiosity that would preserve Jewish identity during exile while hastening redemption through the performance of mitzvot. In other words, the theological foundation was secondary to the religious deed. As the Mishnah says, one blesses over what is essential and brackets the rest (m. Brachot 6:7).

The heart of the priestly Torah commands the Israelites to be holy as God is holy (Leviticus 19:2). After two chapters containing dozens of mitzvot, ranging from the ethical to the ritual to the sexual, the Israelites are provided with the motive clause: "You shall faithfully observe all My laws and all My regulations, lest the land to which I bring you to settle in spew you out" (Leviticus 20:22). And from where do we learn these laws and regulations? According to the Mosaic Torah, from your parents, the ones who share the same root as *torah*. "Take to heart these instructions with which I charge you this day. Impress them upon your children" (Deuteronomy 6:6–7). As for the children: "Honor your father and your mother, as the Lord has commanded you, that you may long endure, and that you may fare well, in the land that the Lord your God is assigning you" (Deuteronomy 5:16).

The overarching goal of the Torah's Halakhah is national security and prosperity. The potential to attain that goal has its seed in the historical memory of the Israelites' origin story. We remind ourselves of that potential through ritual mechanisms to keep despair at bay. God redeemed the Israelites from slavery in Egypt, and the deeds of the ancestors are indicators of what is to come for the children—should we deserve it. In a remarkable mishnah that bears the traces of an ontological halakhah that affects metaphysical reality, we learn that when one despairs of repossessing a lost object, that object no longer belongs to its former owner (m. Baba Metzia 2:1). Despair causes the lost object to become legally ownerless with the consequence that the one who then takes possession of the object acquires legal ownership. The moral of the mishnah is to never despair. The founders of rabbinic religiosity did their utmost to weave that lesson into the ritual lives of the People of Israel.

One of the stations on the road toward monotheism was the conflation of the gods of nature with the gods of history. The three pilgrimage holidays—Passover, Shavuot, and Sukkot—were originally tied to agricultural events that punctuated the annual cycle for an agrarian society. In the Torah, Passover and Sukkot were tied to the exodus and the desert wanderings. Not until the post-biblical period was the harvest holiday of Shavuot linked to the giving and acceptance of Torah. The book of Ruth is, thus, a perfect text for the holiday. Not only is the barley harvest the backdrop for the unfolding drama, but Ruth the Moabite marries into the Jewish people and becomes, from the rabbinic perspective, the model convert—one who accepts the Torah as did the Israelites at Mount Sinai.

For our purposes, the rabbinic Ruth is also a model. Ruth is a Moabite, and that is a serious liability for the Pentateuch. First of all, the eponymous ancestor of the Moabites was the offspring of Lot and his daughter. The folk etymology of his name, *Moav*, means "from father" (Genesis 19:37). The Moabites were both neighbors and adversaries of the Israelites. According to the Hebrew Bible, their King hired a prophet to curse the Israelites, their women seduced Israelite men into idolatry, and their men waged war against Israel. James Kugel, a leading authority on the Hebrew Bible, concludes that "in biblical genetics it is axiomatic that the founder's chromosomes are passed on with unvarying accuracy from generation to generation."[3] Kugel may well have identified the author's motivation to paint Moav as a product of incest and shrewd deceit. Lot's brazen daughter got her father just drunk enough to attain unawareness but not so drunk that he was unable to impregnate her. But there are other biblical voices that reshuffle the chromosomes so that the children are not guilty of the sins of their parents (Ezekiel 18:20). The author of *Ruth* must have been of that school of thought.

The etiology of the Moabites smacks of a realist, ontological worldview. (Legal realism or halakhic realism is predicated on an ontological halakhah.) What Kugel meant by his chromosomal quip is that for the author of the Moabite origin story, there was a conviction that the essence

---

3   James Kugel, "Cain and Able in Fact and Fable: Genesis 4:1-16," in *Hebrew Bible or Old Testament? Studying the Bible in Judaism and Christianity*, ed. Roger Brooks and John J. Collins (Notre Dame: University of Notre Dame Press, 1990), 167-90.

of Moav is, to use a loaded term, depraved. That depravity is passed down through the generations and there is nothing that the Moabites can do to change their essence. The reason why the Moabites act monstrously toward the Israelites is that they were conceived in a monstrous fashion. If this sounds outlandish, a) it is; b) this archaic ontology persists throughout the Hebrew Bible; c) it is the same metaphysics that explains the Catholic dogma of original sin; and d) even within the Hebrew Bible, this archaic ontology was opposed.

Regardless of which text was written earlier, the marriage of Ruth the Moabite by Boaz contradicts the rule in Deuteronomy against marrying Moabites (23:4). The rule was reiterated and seemingly reapplied when the exiled Judeans first returned to the Land of Israel (Nehemiah 13:1). Yet, the book of Ruth not only features what according to Deuteronomy is a forbidden union, it claims that the descendants of this forbidden union include King David and, therefore, the future messiah! (Jesus' lineage is also traced through David, which makes the concepts of immaculate conception and virgin birth reactionary shifts back to a realist worldview to ensure Jesus' essential, ontological purity.) The author of *Ruth* must not share the realist worldview with the author of the etiology story of Moav in Genesis. The author of *Ruth* must be a legal nominalist, at least when it comes to individual identity. But when the rabbis receive this story and make Ruth into the model convert, they do two things. The first is that they harmonize the conflicting texts through midrash and claim that when Boaz convenes the men of Bethlehem to discuss Ruth's fate (Ruth 4:1–2), his first order of business was to qualify Deuteronomy's prohibition. Moabites may not marry the daughters of Israel, but Moabitesses may marry the men of Israel (Yevamot 69a).

The second thing the rabbis did returns us to our biblical tug-of-war between legal realism and legal nominalism. The prohibition against marrying Moabites was referenced repeatedly in the books of Ezra and Nehemiah. Even though the prohibition in Deuteronomy was not originally ontological (because the Mosaic Torah does not operate with such a metaphysics,) the Deuteronomic prohibition was interpreted ontologically by the *priestly* authors of Ezra and Nehemiah. Indeed, the smoking gun for an ontological Jewish identity is found precisely in those texts. Ezra is told that intermarriages with the local populations, including the Moabites, are rampant: "*The holy seed* has become intermingled with the peoples of the land" (Ezra 9:2). Upon hearing such grievous news, Ezra rends his garments, rips out his hair, and sits desolate. Within the Hebrew Bible, there is a perception that Israelite seed is holy and that non-Israelite seed is not. What we see in Ruth is a rejection of that ideology. Nevertheless, the rabbis, and here I can use the term as a reasonable generalization, retained this element of realist metaphysics for purposes of Jewish identity.

For Ezra, there was simply no way to make someone an Israelite.[4] The rabbis, however, had to find a way to legitimize what they considered to be Ruth's conversion.[5] Redemption, through King David's lineage, depended on it. The rabbis had a mechanism on the books, a mechanism no longer applicable in the post-Temple world, that had once been used to ritually purify one who had become ritually impure. The rabbis invested that mechanism with the realist power to purify one who had always been ritually impure. A non-Jew could enter a *mikveh*, a ritual pool, and consequent to immersion be like an Israelite "in all respects" (Yevamot 47b). The person who emerges is, in her essence, a new person. She is called up to the Torah as a daughter of Abraham and Sarah. More radically, were her biological brother to convert, they would be able to marry one another since they are no longer siblings (Yevamot 22a). That is the metaphysical power of an ontological, realist halakhah.

Ruth is our model for yet another reason. She is both a childless widow and a foreigner. As we have seen, she is not just any foreigner, she is a member of an enemy population. What Boaz extends to Ruth, even before his hand in marriage, is protection (Ruth 2:8–9).[6] What we see with Ruth and Boaz is the Israelite tradition of social justice in action. According to other ancient Near Eastern law codes, one was obliged to do no wrong. Only in the Torah was the obligation extended to helping

---

4   We see a similar posture toward non-Jews in both *Jubilees* and the Dead Sea Scrolls. See Christine E. Hayes, *Gentile Impurities and Jewish Identities: Intermarriage and Conversion from the Bible to the Talmud* (New York: Oxford University Press, 2002), 70-91.

5   Although there is no conversion, *per se*, in the Torah, the rabbis turned the Torah's resident alien (*ger*) into a convert. I have written on Ruth in the context of contemporary conversion. See my "Bracketing Belief: *Giyyur* for the Godless," *Conservative Judaism* 66, no. 1 (2014): 83-106.

6   Robert Goldenberg, "How Did Ruth Become the Model Convert?" *Conservative Judaism* 61, no. 3 (2009): 56.

other people, be they natives or aliens.[7] Why? Because we know what is was like to be on the receiving end of oppression as slaves in Egypt. Rabbi Reuven Hammer has pointed out that the Torah's laws not only prevent the Israelites from returning to the conditions of slavery under Pharaoh, but they prevent us from becoming like Pharaoh ourselves.[8]

Legislation

Although the Torah records hundreds of laws, it legislates only a handful. In other words, there are very few moments in the Torah where a situation arises which the extant law fails to address. In those moments, Moshe inquires of God directly, and new legislation is incorporated into the Torah. It is worth emphasizing that the mere existence of such narratives testifies to the need of supplementing the Torah's mitzvot. The Torah was not designed to be an exhaustive legal code. Since we no longer have recourse to divine authority to legislate anew, the Torah provides a mechanism whereby Levitical priests or judges can adjudicate (Deuteronomy 17:8–11). The rabbis later expanded judicial discretion to include the ability to legislate.

Within the Torah, God is the Legislator. On the eve of Passover, two men appeared before Moshe explaining that they were ritually impure from having touched a corpse. They knew that in such a state of impurity, they would not be able to make the Passover offering. They came to Moshe asking for a way to celebrate notwithstanding their ritual impurity (Numbers 9:6–7). Moshe told them to stand by while he asked God. God's answer expands on their question by addressing not only those who are ritually impure, but also those who are on a long journey (verse 10). Both categories are instructed to make the Passover offering the following month and to eat it with matza and bitter herbs (verse 11).

Although the rabbis understood that those who were unable to partake of the Paschal sacrifice on its originally scheduled date were still obligated to eat matza on the first night and refrain from eating leavened

7 Jeremiah Unterman, *Justice for All: How the Jewish Bible Revolutionized Ethics* (Philadelphia: Jewish Publication Society, 2017), 33.

8 Reuven Hammer, "The Impact of the Exodus on Halakhah (Jewish Law)," in *Exodus in the Jewish Experience: Echoes and Reverberations*, ed. Pamela Barmash and W. David Nelson (Lanham: Lexington Books, 2015), 115.

products for the entire week, the Torah's text is unclear (see m. P'sachim 9:3). Indeed, it may have been difficult for those on a long journey to find matza and avoid leaven. But it is clear that there is no prohibition on eating leavened products for the second Passover. Just taste the bread of affliction; just chew on the bitter herbs. No need to clean or observe the dietary restrictions. If you need to sandwich the bitter herbs in bread, it is not forbidden on the second Passover. My suggestion that the Torah might be lowering the barrier for participation is informed by how the rabbis interpreted God's more expansive response. What the rabbis do is breathtaking.

The rabbis imagine a pilgrim who has come to the Temple for the communal celebration of Passover. Upon arrival at the threshold to the Temple courtyard, he stops and cannot continue. Something about the scene in front of him, or the stirrings within, form an insurmountable barrier at that moment. The mishnah tells us that this is the pilgrim who is on a long journey (m. P'sachim 9:2). The men had asked Moshe a question concerning their ritual status. Moshe's response added an element of geography. The rabbis added religious psychology. The Temple was not geographically distant from the pilgrim; the pilgrim was psychologically distant from the Temple at the moment of communal celebration. What both the Torah and the rabbis did was to recognize the distance and to bridge it. We all deserve a second chance.

The second Passover is an instance of legal innovation within ritual law. Civil law, too, required elaboration within the Torah. One law actually underwent two phases of modification. A man, Tzelophechad, died in the wilderness leaving five daughters and no sons. Before the Land of Israel was to be apportioned, the daughters publicly approached Moshe and the entire leadership with the following demand: "Let not our father's name be lost to his clan just because he had no son! Give us a holding among our father's kinsmen!" (Numbers 27:4). As in the previous case, Moshe consulted with God and accommodated their request. Of course, the argument was predicated on the preservation of the father's memory, not on the equal rights of women to inherit property. Nevertheless, one might see this as a step toward the recognition of women's property rights. But, within the biblical context, such a surmise would be premature.

The sequel to this amendment circumscribes women's rights in order to nullify the long-term consequences of female inheritance. The men of Tzelophechad's tribe approached Moshe and the leadership with the following argument. If women who inherit land marry outside the tribe, since their husbands will ultimately inherit from their wives, the wives' property will be transferred to a different tribe (Numbers 36:3). Again, Moshe consulted with God, who found their claim to be just. Thus, the previous law allowing daughters to inherit when there were no sons, was conditioned by the stipulation that the daughters marry within the tribe. This way, the tribe's property will not be diminished (Numbers 36:6).

Although the rabbinic commentary on this passage is both fascinating and presciently sensitive to women's issues, the biblical through line offers a wonderful case study in the philosophy of halakhah.[9] The daughters' claim was that the law of inheritance was unfair to their father. That amendment had the unintended consequence of creating a situation where the tribe's territorial integrity was vitiated. The tribal leadership then claimed that the amendment was unfair to the tribe. The resolution was a second amendment to the original law that addressed both the claim of the daughters, to preserve their father's name through a parcel of land, and the interests of the tribe. It is true that the women's freedom to marry was restricted, but their expressed goal was achieved. What the Torah has offered us is an example of how legal systems should strive to be just when situations arise where a strict application of the law would be unjust. In the third chapter of this book, we will look at a Hasidic comment which understands this case to epitomize the Torah's philosophy of halakhah.

Adjudication and Interpretation

Within the Tanakh, there are very few legal disputes. Perhaps the most famous involves two women who come before King Solomon claiming the same baby. His ruse to divide the baby in two follows no prescribed statute. The narrator describes the Israelites in awe of the King because "they saw that he had within him divine wisdom to execute justice" (1 Kings 3:28). The Hebrew Bible showcases judges' wisdom; they are not consulting statutes to resolve conflict. What we see in the Tanakh is primarily a presentation of laws, some of which include motive clauses.

---

9   Chapter six of my *Torah through Time* brings rabbinic commentary on this passage.

Through critical biblical scholarship, we have been able to infer that some laws are actually interpretations or revisions of earlier laws presented within the Tanakh.

In a concise essay on inner-biblical interpretation, Benjamin Sommer offers a wide array of examples of this phenomenon. His argument is that the rabbis inherited the process or phenomenon of interpretation "from the biblical authors themselves."[10] A particularly poignant example of inner-biblical interpretation relates to the laws of slavery. After the Decalogue in Exodus, the very first issue deals with slaves—appropriately enough for a band of newly liberated slaves. The most conspicuous element within the laws dealing with the Hebrew slave is that he is not a slave, at least not how we understand the word in English. This person serves his master for six years and in the seventh year goes free (Exodus 21:2). Although the same Hebrew term is used for the Israelites in Egypt (*eved*), the person described here is an indentured servant. When he is sent free in the seventh year, Exodus says he will go "without payment." The servant does not have to buy his freedom. He was worked for it.

Later, in Deuteronomy, the slave laws are repeated with several significant differences. The first is that this person is not called a slave/indentured servant; he is referred to as "your Hebrew brother" (Deuteronomy 15:12; see also Leviticus 25:39). The semantic shift, intrinsically significant, has far-reaching consequences for subsequent rabbinic interpretation.[11] The second difference is that when he is set free, he is provided with enough wealth to be able to start anew. Here, the Torah reminds its readers that we, too, were slaves. Not explicitly mentioned is that the Israelites left with much wealth from the Egyptians (Exodus 12:35–36). What Deuteronomy has done to Exodus is something like this: Exodus says the slave does not have to pay. From this, I infer that the master does have to pay. After all, how could the Hebrew master be less gracious toward his own brother than the Egyptians were toward the Israelites?

As we transition to the rabbinic period, it is worth emphasizing that the Hebrew Bible tells the story of the Israelites securing the Land of Israel, being exiled from the Land of Israel, and returning to the Land of Israel. Returning to Jerusalem is literally the Hebrew Bible's concluding

---

10 Benjamin Sommer, "Inner-Biblical Interpretation," in Berlin, *Jewish Study Bible*, 1832.

11 See chapter four in my *Torah through Time*.

line.[12] The commandments laid out in the Hebrew Bible are means to that end—returning to and rebuilding a secure, sovereign Jewish state. Living long on the land that the Lord has given us is the ultimate motive clause. The only thing the Torah tells us to *pursue* is "justice, justice, in order to live and inherit the land that the Lord, your God, is giving to you" (Deuteronomy 16:20). Without double justice, that is justice for both parties to a conflict, we'll neither live nor inherit the land—double jeopardy.

Rabbinic Ethics

One contemporary scholar of rabbinic literature, Christine Hayes, argues that "at the rhetorical level, at least, rabbinic moral interpretation of the Bible does not in general rely on moral principles *internal* to the biblical text."[13] Hayes' rather narrow claim relies on a handful of the Torah's moral maxims that the rabbis rarely quote.[14] But, Hayes confuses principles and maxims. The difference between the slave laws in Exodus and Deuteronomy moves toward a more ethically sensitive position, yet Deuteronomy justifies it by recalling the former Israelite status as slaves. That rationale is a principle frequently invoked, yet Hayes neglects its importance.

Another example from Exodus in which an explicit biblical rationale influences rabbinic interpretation involves the following mitzvah: "You shall not wrong a stranger or oppress him, for you were strangers in the land of Egypt" (Exodus 22:20). The Mishnah uses the verse's two different verbs, wrong and oppress, to distinguish between verbal wronging and financial oppression (m. Baba Metzia 4:10). The biblical verse itself gives no indication that either verb refers to verbal abuse. That expansion of the biblical prohibition against oppressing a stranger is rabbinic. Moreover, the ethical impulse is obvious and is rooted in the verse's motive clause: for you were strangers in the land of Egypt. Generally, not

---

12 Michael Carasik, "Three Biblical Beginnings," in *Beginning/Again: Towards a Hermeneutics of Jewish Texts*, ed. Aryeh Cohen and Shaul Magid (New York: Seven Bridges Press, 2002), 17-18.

13 Christine Hayes, *What's Divine About Divine Law? Early Perspectives* (Princeton: Princeton University Press, 2015), 312.

14 Ibid., 311.

until the Middle Ages are there analyses of mitzvot which discuss moral motivation. "At the root of the mitzvah . . . is the value of always subjugating our impulses to restrain ourselves from inflicting the evil which is in our power to do. Therefore, Torah warned us about this person [the stranger] who is amongst us but without help or support" (*The Book of Education*, Mitzvah 63). Those without a support system are most vulnerable to oppression. Therefore, they require the most protection.

There are also many ethically motivated rabbinic interpretations of biblical verses untethered to either moral maxims or motive clauses. In the Decalogue, for example, there is the prohibition against theft. The rabbis enumerate seven different kinds of thievery including thought thievery (*g'neivat da'at*) –that is, fabricating a false and favorable impression for personal advantage (Mekhilta, Mishpatim 13).[15] Nowhere in the classical rabbinic literature of midrash and Talmud is this ethical extension of biblical law grounded in an explicit moral maxim. To expect an articulated connection between law and ethics is to misread the rabbinic mind and the rabbinic enterprise. In this case, God is truthful, so we are to be truthful (Exodus 34:6 and Yoma 69b). After all, following after God's rabbinically sanctioned ways is one of our primary descriptions of Halakhah.

Often, the connection between biblical ethics and the rabbis is subtle and takes spade work to uncover. That spade work, the intellectual interrogation of the text, is what has attracted so many to Talmudic literature (and repulsed others). Analyzing the Talmud like other philosophical or religious works of the west is a category error. The Talmud is associative not linear. Let me use a relatively well-known midrash as an example of the associative thinking of the rabbinic mind.

Above, we mentioned that the King of Moav hired a prophet to curse the Israelites. After initially refusing, the prophet succumbed to the King's entreaties. What the prophet eventually declared begins with: "How goodly are your tents, O Jacob" (Numbers 24:5). A rabbinic midrash on this verse explains that the prophet was moved to offer such a description because he saw, from atop a mountain overlooking the Israelite camp, that the Israelite tent flaps did not open facing one another in such a way

---

15 This mitzvah is the subject of my essay, "Death by Deception," *Conservative Judaism* 61, no. 3 (2010): 40-54.

that their privacy or modesty would be compromised (Baba Batra 60a). How did the darshan, the author of the midrash, connect the prophet's description of "goodly" to issues of modesty? To my point, the rabbis never provide an explicit answer. The answer takes some spade work.

Perhaps even before the destruction of the second Temple, prophetic passages were designated to conclude (or, perhaps replace) the Shabbat and holiday Torah readings. The readings are called haftarot. The haftarah (sing.) for the Torah portion that includes our goodly tents comes from the prophet, Micah. He is best known for his maxim which concludes the haftarah: "He has told you, O man, *what is good*, and what the Lord requires of you: Only to do justice, and to love goodness, and to walk modestly with your God" (Micah 6:8). What is good? *Ma tov*? How goodly are your tents! *Ma tovu*! Rabbi Yohanan, our darshan, plucks the words from Micah's maxim which emphasizes modesty, and plugs it into the prophetic blessing from Numbers. What makes Jacob's tents goodly? Well, Micah tells us that modesty is good. Therefore, the tents must be positioned modestly.

On one level, this example is a demonstration of rabbinic ethics informed by a moral maxim from the Hebrew Bible. On a deeper level, Rabbi Yohanan's interpretation of Micah is brought in the gemara as *biblical* justification for the following mishnah: "One may not open a door into a jointly held courtyard directly opposite another's door, or a window directly opposite another's window" (m. Baba Batra 3:7). This halakhah in the Mishnah, characteristic of the Mishnah in general, cites no biblical verses. That is the project of the gemara. Nevertheless this Mishnaic halakhah *is* anchored to a biblical moral maxim, that of Micah, but the connection is associative rather than explicit. (More precisely, the Talmud's editors anchor the halakhah to a biblical moral maxim.) Thus, as we excavate examples of the rabbinic halakhic process, one should expect similar subtlety.

Rabbinic Legislation

Throughout the earliest stratum of rabbinic literature dating to the third century, the rabbis of this period, the Tanna'im, used specific legal terms as markers for innovative legislation. These amendments to the Halakhah are called *takkanot*. The rabbis exercised their authority to change Torah law when they deemed it necessary. Later rabbis "betray a tremendous anxiety about legal change."[16] Our contemporary age of anxiety would do well to look back at a specific section of Talmud that deals explicitly with legal change. It offers both a devastating critique and a corrective.

The fourth and fifth chapters of Mishnah Gittin are the Tannaitic focal point of takkanot. These are case studies in the rabbinic philosophy of halakhah. Significantly, chapter four features the term *tikkun olam* for the first time. Although we use the term today to mean social justice for the disadvantaged, originally it had the broader sense of social welfare for all. The reason we find this block of social welfare innovation in the tractate of Gittin (the plural of *get*), is because the list begins with changes to the conditions in which a *get*, a writ of divorce, can be delivered to a wife.

In a stunning example of the potential perniciousness of a realist halakhah, the mishnah offers the following scenario. Shimon and Sara marry. Subsequently, Shimon orders a *get* to be delivered to Sara. Before Sara receives the get from Shimon, he convenes a court in a different place in order to nullify the *get*. He does so before Sara receives her writ of divorce. According to the rabbis' understanding of Torah law, when Sara receives what looks like a kosher *get* is legally meaningless because her husband had already nullified it (m. Gittin 4:2). The gemara spins out the possibility that Sara, who thinks she is now single, impetuously accepts a marriage proposal from the very messenger who delivered the *get*! After all, he does not know that the *get* had been nullified. They marry, and Sara gets pregnant. They later find out that the *get* from Shimon had been nullified. Sara and Shimon are still legally married! Thus, Sara and the messenger are both guilty of adultery, and the fetus, when born, will be stigmatized for its entire life with the legal status of a bastard (*mamzer*) (Gittin 33a).

Rabban Gamliel the Elder fixed the iniquity. He "repaired" the Torah's law, according to the Mishnah, by prohibiting the indecisive husband (or, was his desire to entrap?) from retracting the *get* in a different location.[17] The gemara constructs a debate between Rabban Gamliel and

16 Aaron Panken, *Rhetoric of Innovation: Self-Conscious Legal Change in Rabbinic Literature* (Lanham: University Press of America, 2005), 334. See also Fisch, *Rational Rabbis*, 125–28.

17 The prospect of a despicable husband haunts this chapter of Talmud. See RaSHI's comment on *v'lo amrinan*, Gittin 32a.

his grandson, Rabbi Yehuda HaNasi, where clashing metaphysical orientations lead to different halakhic outcomes. Imagine that *after* Rabban Gamliel's takkanah, the husband goes ahead and convenes a court in a different location to nullify the *get*. His act is in flagrant violation of Rabban Gamliel's takkanah, but is the *get* nullified? Within a realist ontology, the husband said it, it was heard, and the *get* is nullified. This is Rabbi Yehuda HaNasi's position. Rabban Gamliel's artificially constructed retort to his grandson is: what good is the court's takkanah if our directives have no force? The *get*, therefore, is not nullified because the husband's retraction contravened the court's takkanah (Gittin 33a). Although there are other plausible explanations, I believe this dispute showcases a dispute between a realist halakhah (that of Rabbi Yehudah HaNasi) and a nominalist halakhah (that of Rabban Gamliel). For the sake of *tikkun olam*, nominalist halakhah trumps realist halakhah.

Our next example from Mishnah Gittin bears the remnant of a parallel philosophical dispute: "One who stole a beam and builds it into a building—one financially compensates the owner for the value of the beam" (m. Gittin 5:5). In the gemara this position is identified as that of the House of Hillel. The House of Shammai, we learn, insists on destroying the entire building in order to return the beam to its owner (Gittin 55a). As we saw in the first book, scholars have associated Shammai with a realist halakhah.

Could Shammai and his disciples be so literal and formalistic as to insist on the destruction of the building? Yes—it is conceivable. As Yair Lorberbaum has pointed out, strict formalism mimics halakhic realism.[18] Far more plausible, though, is that Shammai and his disciples read the biblical remedy for stolen property—"to return that which was stolen"—as the only way to correct the cosmic disturbance caused by the theft (Leviticus 5:23). Halakhic realists could still amend Halakhah when there were no damaging consequences. Our next mishnah presents us with exactly that scenario and, thus, adds weight to the claim that what is motivating Shammai and his disciples is *not* strict formalism or legal literalism.

In one of the few disputes where the House of Hillel shifts its position to that of the House of Shammai, there is a discussion of a man who

---

18 Lorberbaum, "Halakhic Realism": 55.

is half slave and half free. The Hillelites take a narrow view of the law and decide that he should work for his master one day and for himself the next. Shammai and his disciples look at the *consequence* of such a resolution for the man's marital prospects. He can marry neither a free woman, because he is part slave, nor a slave woman, because he is part free. "Wasn't the world created only for the sake of being fruitful and multiplying, as it says, 'He did not create it to be a wasteland, but formed it for settlement' (Isaiah 45:18)? Therefore, for the sake of *tikkun olam* we force his master to release him, and the former slave must write the former master a promissory note for the value" (m. Gittin 4:5).

The world was created for human habitation. Thus, if there is a way to promote that goal without violating a Torah law, Shammai is willing to work within the Halakhah toward that end. There is no Torah law that prevents Shammai from instituting the takkanah. In some ways, the takkanah is to the man's *disadvantage* because as a free man he is now responsible for his own food, lodging, and medical expenses—costs that are borne by slave masters but not creditors. But as a free man he can marry and fulfill his obligation to be fruitful and multiply. There are no metaphysical consequences from shifting a debt from one instrument to another—the Torah nowhere prohibits it. But, as Lorberbaum has demonstrated, increasing the quantity of divine images, through procreation, most certainly does have a beneficial metaphysical impact.[19]

In the case of the stolen beam, however, the Torah explicitly stipulates that the stolen object must be returned. The lack of an explicit prohibition in the Torah concerning the half slave gives Shammai the latitude to manipulate legal mechanisms. His understanding of the goal of the legal system gives him the motivation to do so. There is a metaphysical opportunity cost for a man being half slave. Thus, in this scenario, Shammai was not acting as a legal literalist but as a halakhic realist. The Hillelites, when presented with a solution that protected the master/creditor *and* improved the marital prospects of the slave/debtor, adopted Shammai's position not out of halakhic realism but of a compassionate and pragmatic consequentialism.

---

19 Yair Lorberbaum, *The Divine Image: Halakhah and Aggadah* [Heb.] (Jerusalem: Schocken Books, 2004), 292–301 and 386–97.

That the Tanna'im were moving away from a realist halakhah is cor-roborated by the Mishnah's silence regarding the House of Shammai's position on the stolen beam—Shammai's dissenting voice was only recorded in the gemara. This general tendency is most transparent in the mishnah following that of the stolen beam. The mishnah discusses the problem of the Roman *sikarikon* (m. Gittin 5:6). During the war with the Romans, *sikarikon* could kill Jews indiscriminately in order to seize their property. After the war was over, and order was largely restored, the rabbis had to develop a process by which the land in the hands of the *sikarikon* could most fairly and efficiently be returned to Jewish owner-ship. At first, the rabbis decreed that a Jew who wished to buy the prop-erty first had to buy it from the original Jewish owner and then go to the *sikarikon* and purchase it from him. This phase of the law attempted to preserve Jewish ownership rights.

Unsurprisingly, particularly after the war, few Jews were in a posi-tion to effectively overpay for property by compensating both the origi-nal Jewish owner and the *sikarikon*. Thus, a subsequent court voted for a significant change. If the original owner did not have the financial where-withal to buy back his property, the new court ruling allowed any Jew to purchase the land from the *sikarikon* and then compensate the origi-nal owner with one quarter of the property's value. Apparently, even this modification was insufficient incentive to get Jews to purchase land from the *sikarikon*. This law exercised the court's power to strip the original owner of ownership.[20] Alternatively, one could say that this law recog-nized the political reality that the original owner, no longer in possession of the property, was empty handed, and that with the purchase of his old property, at least he would recoup some wealth.

Our mishnah continues to demonstrate its ultimate concern, which is to return the land to Jewish ownership. Thus, in the final phase of this law, Rabbi Yehudah HaNasi's court voted that after a year in the *sikarikon's* possession, the original owner forfeits the right of first refusal. Any Jew can immediately buy the property from the *sikarikon* and give one quar-ter of the value to the original owner. As Rubenstein has noted: "But was

---

20 The court exercised the right of eminent domain. It should be noted, however, that the Pentateuch does not give the court this right. The dispute about the biblical basis for eminent domain is also found in the fourth chapter of Gittin, and the two scriptural candidates establishing the right are from Joshua 19:51 and Ezra 10:8 (Gittin 36b).

the new law just? It compels the original owners to sell against their wills and only grants them one-fourth of the value!"[21] As Jeffrey Rubenstein goes on to remark, the self-confidence demonstrated by the sages to change individual laws in order to achieve the goals of the entire system is the antidote for the poison of legal formalism. The subsequent story in the gemara presents rabbinic diffidence as the cause of the Temple's destruction.

Prior to this story, the gemara briefly elaborated on the *sikarikon*. For our purposes, what is most informative is our discovery that the Romans, too, issued three different decrees concerning the Jews and their property. Thus, the three changes in halakhah were, in part, responses to the three changes in Roman law. Although Hayes does not cite this example, it does support her overall thesis: "It seems plausible that takkanot that improved, repaired, and on occasion *overturned Torah law* were largely tolerated in Roman Palestine… because of the highly visible and parallel phenomenon in the surrounding legal culture, namely, edictal modifications of the civil law."[22]

Immediately after that revelation of the legislative parallels between the Romans and the rabbis, the gemara informs its readers through the voice of Rabbi Yohanan that Jerusalem's ruin illustrates the following verse: "Happy is the one who is always afraid, but he who hardens his heart will fall into evil" (Proverbs 28:14, Gittin 55b). The tragic story the Talmud then presents to explain Jerusalem's fall is predicated on a simple error, inviting the wrong man to a banquet—Bar Kamtza rather than Kamtza. The host refused to allow the unintended guest, who turned out to be his enemy, to remain at the banquet under any circumstances. The host hardened his heart. Bar Kamtza's conspicuous ejection from the banquet was humiliating. In attendance were some sages who did nothing to intervene. They hardened their hearts. Our jilted guest sought vengeance against both the host and the indifferent rabbis.

Bar Kamtza devised a plan that could have been easily thwarted. He went to the Roman leader and informed him that a rebellion was being planned. Bar Kamtza said, "Send them a sacrifice and see if they offer it." As our vengeful guest brought the calf to the rabbis to be sacrificed, he

---

21 Jeffrey L. Rubenstein, *Talmudic Stories: Narrative Art, Composition, and Culture* (Baltimore: Johns Hopkins University Press, 2003), 162.

22 Hayes, *What's Divine?*, 307. Italics mine.

made a slight blemish on it rendering it questionably kosher for sacrifice. The rabbis debated how to proceed. They were persuaded not to offer the sacrifice for fear that people might say blemished animals can be offered. They were also persuaded not to kill the perfidious entrapper lest people say that one who causes a blemish on sacrificial animals is to be killed. Their decision not to offer the animal as a sacrifice was interpreted by the Romans as an act of rebellion, and the military was dispatched to quash the nonexistent revolt.

The same Rabbi Yohanan who began the story with a biblical verse, concludes the story by decrying the "humility" of the rabbi who was able to dissuade the others from action. Humility, normally a praiseworthy quality, is associated with Moshe (Numbers 12:3). But, in this new legal climate when God is unavailable for consultation, humility is, as Rubenstein translates it, meekness.[23] Our opening verse from Proverbs contrasts fear, which is good, and hard-heartedness, which leads to evil. In context, what brings happiness is fear of consequences. What brings evil is being hard hearted, which means being hardheaded, that is, stubborn and inflexible to the point of paralysis. A realist halakhah, by definition, is inflexible.

After the Temple's destruction has been narrated, the Talmud's reader flashes back on the dispute about the stolen beam in the previous mishnah. Into what was the beam built? Into a *birah*. That is an uncommon word for *building*, as all the translations I have seen render it. The House of Shammai demanded destroying the entire structure in order to retrieve that beam. Our unusual word, *birah*, in the final books of the Hebrew Bible, means *sanctuary*, the Temple (Nehemiah 2:8 and 7:2, and 1 Chronicles 29:1 and 29:19).[24] The halakhic realism of the House of Shammai brought down the House of God.

The Interpretive Tilt toward Halakhic Nominalism

In our first book, the kitchen of Camp Ramah was the scene of a kashrut violation. We learned, there, that according to the Halakhah, if the

---

23 Rubenstein, *Talmudic Stories*, 151.
24 I am not claiming that the decision to neither sacrifice the animal nor kill Bar Kamtza was motivated by halakhic realism, but the mishnah's foreshadowing of the sanctuary's destruction casts halakhic realism as ruinous.

violation was unintentional *and* the transgression involved no more than one-sixtieth of the volume of the total food volume *and* one cannot taste the presence of the prohibited food, *then* the entire mixture is still permissible to consume. The one-sixtieth rule is flagrantly nominalistic. In a realist system, the mixture would be forbidden regardless of the quantities involved.[25] Indeed, that is precisely the position of a minority voice recorded in the Tosefta (t. Hullin 7:7 vs. m. Hullin 7:5 and Rashi on Hullin 97b, *m'sha'arinan*).

Let's move to Shabbat. We'll begin with disputes that no longer have direct legal implications. Our first case involves someone who was kidnapped at an early age and raised by gentiles. As a young man, he discovers that he is Jewish. According to one Talmudic opinion, he needs to offer a sacrifice for all the Sabbath transgressions he has committed (Shabbat 68a/b). I suggest that the best way to understand this position is not that it is punitive—for how could one merit punishment in such a case? Rather, it is corrective. A Jew violating Shabbat damages the invisible infrastructure of the cosmos according to halakhic realism. Thus, a sacrifice is necessary to rectify the damage regardless of intention.[26]

Another inconsequential dispute for our day highlights the absurdity of halakhic realism when viewed from outside its system. The Mishnah describes a priest's wife who is enjoying a meal that can only be consumed by a priest's family. She is informed that her husband has passed away. Rabbi Eliezer, a halakhic realist, rules that the widow must repay all the priestly food she has eaten since the moment her husband died plus a twenty percent fine (m. Trumot 8:1)! Rabbi Joshua, the nominalist, exempts her from all consequences.

The same mishnah pictures a priest standing and offering sacrifices at the altar. Someone runs toward the priest with flailing arms and informs him that the priest's mother has just confessed to being divorced prior to marrying his father. Since a priest cannot marry a divorcee, his male children do not have the status of priests. Rabbi Eliezer, thus, declares that *all* the sacrifices that the son has ever offered are invalid, while Rabbi

25 Christine Hayes, "Legal Realism and the Fashioning of Sectarians in Jewish Antiquity," in *Sects and Sectarianism in Jewish History*, ed. Sacha Stern (Leiden: Brill, 2011), 131.
26 Yohanan Silman discusses this tension in "Commandments and Prohibitions in the Halakhah: Obedience vs. Rebellion or Repair vs. Destroy," *Diné Yisrael* 16 (1991): 173-201.

Joshua declares them valid. It is theoretically possible to understand these disputes as predicated on legal formalism, on a strict interpretation of the law. But that would be a disservice to the rabbis involved. These disputes are more likely to be the product of clashing metaphysics (realism vs. nominalism) rather than differing styles of interpretation (strict vs. lenient). For the halakhic realist, like Rabbi Eliezer, those "sacrifices" were nothing more than slaughter by a butcher.

Here is a Shabbat case that has had practical consequences. The Torah's prohibition on Shabbat work are enumerated in the Mishnah. There, one of the thirty-nine prohibited categories of work is digging (m. Shabbat 7:2). But, we learn in the gemara that what the Torah actually forbids is digging a hole. Thus, if someone dug a hole for the purpose of creating a hole, that's prohibited. But, if someone dug a hole because she needed dirt, that is not biblically prohibited according to the rabbis (Shabbat 73b). At this point in the dispute, we are introduced to one who insists that digging a hole even for the dirt requires a sacrifice. Although the gemara tries to harmonize the conflicting positions, the most plausible way to interpret this dispute is between a halakhic realist who forbids digging for any reason—intention is irrelevant—and a halakhic nominalist who takes intention into account. The nominalist position won the day in terms of practical halakha (h. Shabbat 1:17).[27]

In 1950, when the Conservative movement justified driving to synagogue on Shabbat for those who did not live within walking distance, their argument included the following nominalist strategy. The Torah forbids kindling fire on Shabbat. The use of electricity and spark plugs, however, are exempt because the Torah's fire prohibition was narrowly defined by the rabbis as work done in the building and maintenance

---

27 The nominalist position of the House of Hillel also won the day, halakhically, in terms of the sequence of blessings for Kiddush, t. Brachot 5:25 and Vered Noam, "Essentialism, Freedom of Choice, and the Calendar: Contradictory Trends in Rabbinic Halakhah," in *Nominalism and Realism in Halakha Revisited: Studies in the Philosophy of Halakha*, ed. Y. Lorberbaum and J. Rubenstein, special issue, *Diné Israel* 30 (2015): 131. Noam also shows, in my reading, how rabbinic nominalism muscles into the rabbinic reworking of the priestly/realist Yom Kippur, 132–34. We also see a shift in the priestly contagion of the altar from the Torah to the rabbis, Exodus 29:37 to m. Z'vachim 9:1.

of the tabernacle (Shabbat 94a and Tosafot).[28] If a later rabbinic court finds sufficient justification for overruling a previous *rabbinic* rule, the Halakhah affords them the power to do so. Therefore, although the rabbis built a hedge around the Biblical prohibition and forbade kindling for any reason, the Conservative movement felt empowered to remove the rabbinic hedge in order to promote synagogue attendance. Had the prohibition on fire been understood by the rabbis in terms of halakhic realism, that is, independent of one's intention for kindling a flame, then the traditional rules of Halakhah would have made it much more difficult to exempt the use of spark plugs. The logic and motivation for the Conservative movement's decision is a ringing rejection of realism:

> We think of Halakhah as an instrument of the people, for the enrichment of the spiritual life of our people and not as an end in itself. . . . The above analysis leads us to the conclusion that riding in an automobile is at most a rabbinically interdicted activity. When this act prevents the fulfillment of the mitzvah of attending public worship it shall not be considered a prohibited act.[29]

There are several passages in the Talmud that are nearly unintelligible without recourse to a realist halakhah. Consider the source for throwing a party for a bar mitzvah boy. Rabbi Hanina claims that someone who is obligated to perform the commandments and does so is greater than one who does so without being commanded (Kiddushin 31a and Baba Kamma 87a.) When a bar mitzvah boy becomes obligated to engage in the commandments, we should throw him a party to celebrate the greatness that he now enjoys that he hadn't when doing exactly the same things before he had turned thirteen. The Tosafot offer a psychological explanation for what seems so counterintuitive. They suggest that when one is obligated, there is a nagging anxiety surrounding the performance of the mitzvah. When there is no such obligation, one can choose at one's convenience whether or not to perform the commandment. Since the reward is proportional to the effort, the one with an obligation is greater than one without.

---

28 Morris Adler, Jacob Agus, and Theodore Friedman, "Responsum on the Sabbath," *Proceedings of The Rabbinical Assembly* 14 (1950): 112–185.

29 Ibid.: 130–1.

A different Tosafot comes closer to a realist halakhah. Tosafot Tukh explains that God has no reason to be pleased with an action He did not command. A realist halakhah, I believe, explains the claim best. It is not necessarily about pleasing God, but about empowering God. When one performs a mitzvah, one adds strength to the divine. The one who does the same deed that is uncommanded is engaging in a metaphysically neutral act.[30] Within a realist universe, intention or one's psychological disposition is irrelevant; so the deed, to be efficacious, must be commanded.

Another of these otherwise unintelligible disputes is about whether the function of law is to promote peace or attain truth. Should judges value compromise and settlement, or should the "law pierce the mountain"? (Sannhedrin 6b) The Talmud offers no dissenting voice to the proposition that the entire Torah was given to instill peace (Gittin 59b). Nevertheless, in our dispute about the function of law, one position is that "one who compromises is a sinner" (Sannhedrin 6b). Even given the rabbinic predilection for hyperbole, compromising is a sin? It may be that, as Chaim Saiman phrases it, "compromise inevitably compromises justice."[31] Another possibility, however, is that this is the statement of a halakhic realist who believes that corrective justice, rather than restorative justice (like restoring the monetary value of the beam), is the only remedy that will correct the invisible infrastructure of our world that would otherwise be compromised by compromise. Ultimately, not only was this worldview largely (but not entirely) rejected, but so was strict legal formalism. After all, according to Rabbi Yohanan, Jerusalem was destroyed because they judged according to strict Torah law (Baba Metzia 30b). Shammai's worldview brought down much more than just his own House.

There have been two unwelcome consequences of halakhic realism. The first involves specific laws that many, including myself, would call immoral. Such laws are relatively easy to identify. The more insidious consequence is the rabbinic tendency to perseverate on picayune details believing those details to have cosmic and divine reverberations. Tannaitic sources say that when judges render a true verdict, they are partners with God in the act of creation. Halakhic realism understands

---

30 Cf. Silman, "Commandments and Prohibitions": 185-92.
31 Chaim N. Saiman, *Halakhah: The Rabbinic Idea of Law* (Princeton: Princeton University Press, 2018), 114.

that when Jews perform mitzvot, God's own potential is realized.[32] If true law complements creation and empowers the Divine, one can readily understand why halakhic disputants might cavil. Those details constitute the difference between affecting reality and legal legerdemain.[33]

Realism is redeemable. As Abraham Joshua Heschel helped us see, the Hebrew prophets' demand for righteousness and justice points to the ways in which we can enhance the divine presence in our midst. Moreover, halakhic realism is internally consistent. That consistency is a prerequisite for any coherent Judaism. "Originally [in tannaitic sources], the provisions of the halakhah and their irrational foundation are inseparably interwoven, to the extent that the halakhah may be regarded as a practical, ritualistic manifestation of the very same conception that found its verbal formulation in the aggadah."[34] Avinoam Rosenak claims that in the rabbinic period, it was the Aggadah that drove the Halakhah.[35] Other approaches to Halakhah risk severing the law from its aggadic roots, making the law an end in itself rather than a means of following after God. We can purge what is irrational, if also immoral, in the Aggadah, but still preserve the fundamental, internal unity. As Hayim Nahman Bialik pointed out a century ago, "A living and healthy Halakhah is an Aggadah that has been or will be. And the reverse is also true. The two are one in their beginning and end."[36]

---

32 Silman, "The Source of Validity": 4.
33 Idel, *New Perspectives*, 171. Arthur Green made this point to me in response to a question of mine during a class on The Zohar in 1994.
34 Jacob Katz, *Halakhah and Kabbalah* [Hebrew] (Jerusalem: Magnes Press, 1984), 12. Cited in Lorberbaum's English rendition of chapter three of his book *Divine Image*, reprinted as "Reflections on the Halakhic Status of Aggadah" [trans. Michael Prawer], *Diné Israel* 24 (2007): 40.
35 Avinoam Rosenak, "Aggadah and Halakhah: Reflections on Tendencies in the Research of Philosophy of Halakhah" [Heb.], in *The Quest for Halakhah: Interdisiplinary Perspectives on Jewish Law*, ed. A. Berholz (Tel Aviv: Hemed Books-Yediot Achronot and Bet Morashah, 2003), 287–94.
36 Originally published in 1917, the essay was translated into English by Sir Leon Simon. Hayim Nahman Bialik, *Revealment and Concealment: Five Essays* (Jerusalem: Ibis Editions, 2000), 47. See also Robert Cover, "Nomos and Narrative," in *Narrative, Violence, and the Law: The Essays of Robert Cover*, ed. Martha Minnow, Michael Ryan, and Austin Sarat (Ann Arbor: University of Michigan Press, 1993), 96. See also Steven D. Fraade, "*Nomos* and Narrative Before '*Nomos* and Narrative,'" in *Legal Fictions: Studies of Law and Narrative in the Discursive Worlds of Ancient Jewish Sectarians and Sages* (Leiden: Brill, 2011): 17-34. Barry Scott Wimpfheimer makes

Rabbinic Interpretations and Judgements

Some of the most well-known rabbinic interpretations demonstrate the rabbis' agility and willingness to interpret a law out of existence. Usually, there is an obvious moral motivation for such textual contortions. Should a son be stoned to death for being a glutton and drunkard? Should a wife be subjected to a humiliating, and possibly lethal, ordeal because of her jealous husband? And how does putting someone to death promote peace? (Although the legal requirements for the court to administer capital punishment were practically impossible to meet, there were those who were convinced of the punishment's deterrent value [m. Makkot 1:10].) In these three cases, the rabbis essentially rejected the law of the Torah because they found it immoral.[37]

The infamous injunction of *eye for an eye* is frequently juxtaposed to Jesus turning the other cheek (Exodus 21:23–5 and Matthew 5:38–9). I have never understood the implicit preference for Jesus' prescription for masochism. Why would anyone turn the other cheek after being hit? Turning the other cheek is an invitation for the perpetrator to continue the abuse (as in Lamentations 3:30). Or, perhaps, it is a posture of defiance signaling that the first slap was ineffective. If the intention, however, was to show deference and humility, the Torah models the posture of "falling facedown" (Leviticus 9:24 Numbers 14:5, et. al.) Regardless of Jesus' intention, his words have often been used to highlight the Jewish God of vengeance versus the Christian God of mercy.

It remains unclear to me how love or mercy is promoted by turning the other cheek, but the proper comparison between what is Jewish and what is Christian should not be the Torah and the New Testament, separated by hundreds of years, but by comparing the Talmud and midrash with the New Testament and the writings of the church fathers. It makes just as much sense to say that the Hebrew Bible is biblical Christianity as it does to call it biblical Judaism. The religions we know of today as Christianity and Judaism began diverging as the Temple was destroyed

---

an even stronger case against the binary opposition of Halakhah and aggadah in *Narrating the Law: A Poetics of Talmudic Legal Stories* (Philadelphia: University of Pennsylvania Press, 2011).

37 Deuteronomy 21:18–21 and Sannhedrin 68b–71a; Numbers 5:11–31 and Sotah 2a–9b; and Sannhedrin chapters 4 and 5.

by the Romans and did not fully separate until the fourth century. The metaphysics of early Christianity is that of the priestly Torah—a vicarious blood sacrifice atones for sins, including original sin, that are transmitted generationally. Participation in that vicarious sacrifice is through the ontological transformation of the eucharist. The metaphysics of rabbinic Judaism, although retaining elements of the priestly Torah, is primarily that of the Mosaic Torah in which teshuvah atones for transgressions; and the messiah, rather than being of immaculate conception, has the most stained lineage conceivable. (We have mentioned Ruth's lineage; Boaz was the descendant of an act of illicit, though righteous, harlotry [Genesis 38].)

When we look at the rabbinic interpretations of *eye for an eye*, what we find is a consistent rejection of a literal reading in favor of an assessment of the value of the loss of an eye (m. Baba Kamma 8:1 and Baba Kamma 83b–84a). There is, no surprise, a dissenting voice from Rabbi Eliezer, but the interpretive burden of reading the expression figuratively is distributed among many of Rabbi Eliezer's colleagues. Strategies range from the textual, usage of the expression *life for life* when it explicitly calls for monetary compensation (Leviticus 24:18), to the logical, what if the person who put out Ploni's eye was himself blind? Or, perhaps in the process of administering a punishment, a graver injury would occur.

The Talmudic conclusion was that since the expression cannot be applied literally in all cases, it must be intended to be applied as a principle of proportionality. After all, they insist, "You shall have one law" (Leviticus 24:22), which means that you shall have one law that applies to all (Baba Kamma 83b). That law, therefore, must be proportionate compensation for damage incurred. In the case of a human death, however, monetary compensation is ruled out. For the spilling of blood, blood must be spilled. Under no circumstances can one buy one's way out of murder. For our purposes, this Talmudic exercise in legal interpretation demonstrates that what are ostensibly biblical laws were read by the rabbis as religious literature.

The cases involving the *eye for an eye* principle fall under the category of criminal law. The interpretive move made by the rabbis by which the perpetrator was liable for financial compensation to the victim required an enumeration and method of evaluation of damages. How does one place a value on an eye? The rabbinic response is fascinating in that it enumerates five different levels of compensation: physical damage, physical pain, medical expenses, opportunity costs of being out of work, and embarrassment. If the terminology of *eye for an eye* is not to be taken literally, then the principle of just compensation, from the rabbinic perspective, must include all five levels.

As we have seen, rabbinic interpretations enlarge the scope of some laws and narrow the scope of others. The rabbis had that discretion. Their discretion was also exercised through their rulings in specific cases. The Talmud describes a situation where the owner of a field has asked his foreman to hire workers for the day at, say, 100 shekels.. The foreman, on his own initiative, hires workers at 75 shekels. The workers come to find out that the owner had expected to pay more for the workers. Are the workers entitled to receive the additional wages? In the American legal system, there would be no question. The workers agreed to 75 shekels, and they are entitled to nothing more. But the response in the Talmud included a quotation from a biblical source that ordinarily has no halakhic weight, *Proverbs*: "Do not withhold good from his men" (Proverbs 3:27 in Baba Metzia 76a). In our case, the foreman is withholding good, in the form of additional wages, from his men and His men.

In nature, there is symbiosis, parasitism, and commensalism. The last term describes a relationship where one profits but the other does not lose. In other words, there is a net gain in the relationship, although the gain is not mutual. The Halakhah promotes that outcome. The principle is reflected in the ruling that when Ploni owns property between the plots of two brothers, the brothers enjoy the right of first refusal for the sale (Baba Metzia 108a). Ploni will receive the market value of his property, but no more, even though the adjacent land is more valuable to the brothers than to anyone else. The Halakhah is willing to prevent an unjustified windfall for Ploni, in order to provide a benefit for others. Goodwill is baked into the Halakhah to promote a society where goodwill is the norm.

In 1991, I graduated from college and rode my bike around several European countries, one of which was Portugal. At that point, I was with two friends, and we were south of Lisbon on our way to the southern coast of the Algarve. As the sun was setting, we saw a cluster of half-built homes where the foundations had been poured, the roof and walls were in place, but there were no windows or doors. Precociously intuiting the

Talmud's principle of commensalism, I suggested we lay out our sleeping bags on the protected foundation since we were doing no harm, and the property was clearly not yet ready for lease. When the owner of the property woke us up with the sun the following morning, it was clear he was unfamiliar with this Talmudic principle.

> If one takes residence in another's courtyard without his knowledge, the rule is that if the courtyard is not usually rented, the tenant need not pay the owner any rent even though the tenant does usually rent a place for himself. For one has benefitted without the other one having lost anything.[38]

The owner of the property, although shocked by our American impudence, did not follow through on his initial threat to call the police. Had Bar Kamtza's host been as reasonable, we might be living in a different world.

While I was in graduate school in Israel, there was a case making its way up to the supreme court. I first read about the case at an early stage, and the newspaper headline called the decision an example of *middat S'dom*, Sodomesque. In Jewish tradition, Sodomesque has nothing to do with sodomy. In the Prophets, Sodom is depicted as the paragon of self-absorption: "Only this was the sin of your sister Sodom—arrogance! She and her daughters had plenty of bread and untroubled tranquility; yet she did not support the poor and the needy" (Ezekiel 16:49). In the rabbinic tradition, Sodomites were not just selfish and unwelcoming, but ingenious at drafting immoral legislation (Sannhedrin 109a/b). In a parody of both Sodomites and one-size-fits-all legal formalism, the rabbis relocated Procrustes' bed to Sodom—all guests were made, one way or another, to fit the available beds. In a chilling scene, when the poor would come to Sodom, every Sodomite would give the poor person a coin with his own name written on it, but no one would give the poor person food to eat. When he died of hunger, each Sodomite would then return to collect his coin.

The example of Sodomesque behavior that the Israeli headline referred to involved the case of a divorced couple, the Nahmanis. Prior

---

38 Maimonides, MT, Robbery and Lost Articles, 3:9 summarizing Baba Kamma 20a–21a.

to their divorce, the couple had frozen some embryos as part of a fertility treatment. After the divorce, it was clear that Mrs. Nahmani could only have biological children through those embryos, but Mr. Nahmani refused to release them. The lower court ruled in his favor, *middat S'dom*—legally correct, perhaps, but morally unjust. The Supreme Court, in 1996, overturned the decision arguing that the woman's "right to realize parenthood took precedence" over the man's "interest in refusing parenthood."[39] To shoehorn this case into our principle of commensalism, whatever harm there may be to Mr. Nahmani is far outweighed by the benefit to Mrs. Nahmani.

Legacies of a Philosophy of Rabbinic Halakhah

Rabbinic Halakhah was the heir to conflicting legal philosophies. Tragically, medieval Judaism too often cleaved the animating aggadah from the halakhah. Moreover, as Saiman has recently noted, once Talmudic positions were codified, they lost their Talmudic context. "Thus shorn of the layered meanings developed through the sugya [a Talmudic thought unit], these rules can be reduced to a list of pedantic regulations."[40] Rules, like modifying the law for the sake of peace, lost some of their prescriptive power by being categorized as deviations from the norm exercised by the ancient giants of the Halakhah. By the time of the middle ages, an inferiority complex had been internalized, and we were nothing more than dwarves standing on the shoulders of giants.

Genesis Rabbah asserts that a world cannot endure by strict justice—it must be alloyed with mercy. The midrash asserts that we know this because the first name of God to appear in the creation story, *Elohim*, represents strict law, like laws of nature which are unyielding. But, that initial creation story is immediately followed by the second which introduces God's four-letter name which represents mercy and compassion (Genesis Rabbah 12:15). For the world to survive, at least with humans, mercy must temper justice. For instance, when prices for certain animals involved in sacrifices became prohibitively high, Rabban Shimon ben Gamliel dramatically reduced the necessary number of sacrifices. The

---

39 Ruth Nahmani v. Daniel Rahmani, September 12, 1996.
40 Saiman, *Halakhah*, 128.

plunge in demand caused the price to plummet (m. Keritot 1:7). This bold act may have been the paradigmatic precedent for the very common use of halakhic mechanisms to have compassions for Jews' finances.

These concepts [of "great loss" and "the Torah protects the assets of Jews"] belonged, at the initial stage of their entrance into halakhic discourse, to the realm of "needs" and "wellbeing" of individuals. Yet, rabbinic authorities found no problem in seeing these needs as integral to halakhic reasoning and as legitimate components of halakhic thinking, and therefore such concepts could be integrated into halakhah without difficulty.[41]

Leviticus makes explicit provisions for those who are of limited wealth to afford the means of ritual purification (Leviticus 14:21–32). The Mishnah says as long as one's intention is pure, the quantity of the sacrifice is irrelevant (m. Menachot 13:11). The halakhic concept of concern for finances is rooted in the Torah. The rabbis have the discretion to deploy their concern or withhold it. One of my recommendations for Covenantal Halakhah is to eliminate the second day of holidays (Passover, Shavuot, and Sukkot). Among my arguments is that doing so would significantly lighten the burden that many of us feel by taking so many days off from work in the fall and spring.

Menachem Fisch suggests that what is binding in the Talmud is their process of deliberation but not their halakhic conclusions.[42] After all, why should we be bound to the *p'shat* of their *drash*? I would add to that their commitment to reading the Torah for its principles rather than its laws, reading literally rather than literally. Consider the following. In the NJPS translation we have: "If the thief is seized while tunneling, and he is beaten to death, there is no bloodguilt in his case. If the sun has risen on him, there is bloodguilt in that case" (Exodus 22:1–2). We learn from the second verse, which specifies *the sun*, that the case in the first verse happens at night. One can speculate that at night, when you find someone breaking into your home, it is too dark to identify them or see if they are carrying a weapon. Thus, in order to protect yourself, you may disable the intruder, even to the point of death, without being held

---

41 Adiel Schremer, *Toward Critical Halakhic Studies* (New York: The Tikva Center for Law & Jewish Civilization, 2010), http://www.law.nyu.edu/sites/default/files/TikvahWorkingPapersArchive/WP4Schremer.pdf .

42 Fisch, *Rational Rabbis*, 53.

criminally liable. Presumably, during the daytime, you can identify both the intruder and any threatening weapons. Thus, the difference between the daytime scenario and the nighttime scenario is one of identification.

With that in mind, the rabbis noticed an unnecessary word in the second verse: *on him* (*alav* in Hebrew). If the sun has risen, it did not only rise "on him," it rose on everyone. Perhaps, the rabbis reasoned, "the sun rising on him" means that he is identified or recognized as if he were in the bright light of the day (Sannhedrin 72a). Thus, if the homeowner recognizes the thief and knows that he has no motivation to injure the homeowner, and the homeowner still kills the thief, the homeowner *is* liable for murder. What makes this literary reading so interesting is that by turning light and night into symbols of known and unknown, it means that a homeowner, *even at night*, must insure that he really is in the dark about the identity and the motivation of the intruder. This interpretation prevents a "shoot first, ask later" mentality that places the protection of property above the sanctity of life.

Constructing Coherence from Rabbinic Halakhah

Halakhic realism boasts that it knows something about the ultimate nature of reality, and Torah laws conform to that knowledge. Greek notions of natural law, in this sense, are similar. What distinguishes real- ist halakhah from natural law is the ethical. Jews understood very early that the predatory violence and bloodshed integral to nature, the ground of natural law, is neither inevitable nor ideal—at least, not on the human plane. While there is certainly overlap between natural law and Torah law, the Torah never falls prey to the naturalistic fallacy which identi- fies that which is natural with that which is morally good. The world *is* built with mercy (Psalm 89:3), but identifying which parts are merciful requires wisdom.

My emphasis on halakhic realism has three primary motivations: 1) it helps us understand much of what seemed unintelligible from the rabbinic world; 2) it is so distant from the secular worldview that most of us in the west take for granted; and 3) I think there is some truth to it. The Hebrew Bible was framed by priests—Genesis 1 at the start and Ezra/Nehemia at the end. I reject their hierarchical notion as it relates to humans, and I have no reason to believe that the shift I feel when Shabbat candles are lit tracks on to changes in the invisible infrastructure of our universe. But, the priestly religion, which bequeaths to us its halakhic realism, predicates God's presence on our behavior. About that, I agree. The god that so many of us rejected is the god who rewards and punishes. That sort of behavior modification may work for children, but not for adults who seek intrinsic gratification.

Would it undermine our quest for coherence if we accepted elements of priestly religion as well as elements of Mosaic religion? Of course, not; as long as those elements themselves are not contradictory. Specifically, we can accept the priestly theology (what the priestly religion says about God) but reject its hierarchical anthropology (what the priestly religion says about different sorts of humans). Actually, in this case at least, we can extract and isolate the insight of priestly anthropology that sees all of humanity in the divine image. That claim, taken seriously, is just as revolutionary now as it was 2,500 years ago.

The laws of kashrut can be updated to allow for *sh'lom bayit*, peaceful relations within the communities in which we live. If the truth can be "modified" for *sh'lom bayit*—even by God!—then we can relax the stringencies surrounding kashrut by continuing to tilt toward nominalism (Genesis 18:13 and Baba Metzia 87a). Ideals of conscious consumption could be promoted more widely as we extend the metaphorical dining room table and redeem the offenses of Bar Kamtza's host.

We saw Rabban Shimon ben Gamliel reduce the number of necessary sacrifices. Since prayer is the functional equivalent of sacrifice, we have a precedent for shortening prayer services that many find prohibitively burdensome. We also have a rabbinic precedent for modifying the language of prayer when we do not believe what our prayer books claim (Yoma 69b). Yet, on so many issues we have been paralyzed into inaction, what Rabbi Yohanan would sneer at as meekness. Indeed, in a powerful essay by a family member of contemporary rabbinic royalty, Haym Soloveitchik has shown that since the Shoah, there has been *added* pressure on the halakhic yoke through novel stringencies.[43]

The House of Shammai brought down the Temple. Rabbi Eliezer was willing to bring down the House of Study, *with the sages in it* (Baba

---

43 Haym Soloveitchik, "Rupture and Reconstruction: The Transformation of Contemporary Orthodoxy," *Tradition* 28, no. 4 (1994): 64-130.

Metzia 59b). A philosophy of halakhah true to the wisdom of rabbinic Judaism will share rabbinic Halakhah's goals of peace, justice, and mercy (Gittin 59b and h. Shabbat 2:3). When achieving those goals demands additional laws, modifying laws, or suspending laws, we must overcome our inferiority complex and deploy rabbinic methodology and discretion to act accordingly. Flexibility is a prerequisite for survival.

Rabbi Simlai taught that the 613 commandments of Torah comprise 365 prohibitions corresponding to the days in a solar year and 248 prescriptions corresponding to the limbs in the human body (Makkot 23b). Our challenge is to make Torah steady like the passage of time, but flexible enough, like our bodies, to keep moving through time. Rabbi Simlai was telling us to be Torah, and if we are not yet, then to become Torah. Turning Torah is not only what we do, it is who we aspire to be.

Chapter 12

Going Baroque

Pill bugs, when prodded, curl up into armored balls. Locomotion is impeded, but protection is enhanced. "Halakhah in Exile is essentially protective halakhah, often on the defensive."[1] From 750 to 1750, the Halakhah became bloated. Arthur Green has characterized the excessive detail of Lurianic Kabbalah as baroque; the same can be said for medieval Halakhah.

Since there will be much Torah in this chapter, we shall begin with a blessing. According to Rav Yehuda in the name of Shmuel, we should bless God for sanctifying us through His commandment to engage in words of Torah. Rav Hamnuna, however, thinks it preferable to start by blessing God for giving us the Torah with which to engage. But Rabbi Yohanan focuses not on what God has done, but on what we continue to need God's help to do: make the words of Torah sweet in our mouths so that the aftertaste will leave us wanting more (Brachot 11b).

The three blessings above, offered by the Amoraim (the later rabbis) of Babylonia and the Land of Israel, were what these great sages would say before or after studying Torah. The earlier generations of rabbis, the Tannaim, recognized that Torah study was a mitzvah, but we have no record of their individual blessings. That suggests that this was one of many examples where personal initiative was the default.[2] Indeed, the first chapter of the Mishnah records a dispute between the disciples of Hillel and Shammai concerning one's *posture* during the recitation of the

---

1   Eliezer Berkovits, *Not in Heaven: The Nature and Function of Halakha* (New York: Ktav Publishing House, 1983), 86.

2   Sifre, Deuteronomy 34.

evening Shema (m. Brachot 1:3). The House of Hillel advocated autonomy within heteronomy—comply with the law in your own way. Perhaps the same was true for the blessing attendant to Torah study. By the end of the Talmudic period, however, a certain degree of homogenization had set in. After recording the blessings of the three sages, the Talmudic editor concludes: "therefore, let us say *them all*" (Brachot 11b). From individual autonomy to the codification of "them all," the medieval halakhic codes canonized the Talmudic editor's penchant for inclusion (M. T., h. Prayer 7:10 and S. A., O. H. 47:2). In the process from Talmud to codes, polyphony was no longer considered harmonious.

Within the Talmud, we see both the accumulation of laws and a tendency toward legal stringencies. For instance, the Mishnah explicitly allows hair decorations for young girls on Shabbat (m. Shabbat 6:6). In the gemara, we learn that a particular sage's father would not permit his daughters to wear such decorations on Shabbat. The gemara wonders why one would forbid what the Mishnah explicitly allows. The gemara responds that the decorations in question were colorful, therefore the girls' father was concerned that his girls might take them out of their hair to show their friends which would run afoul of the Shabbat prohibition against carrying (Shabbat 65a). The story makes me a bit sad for the daughters who were deprived of color on Shabbat. Although in and of itself not a tragedy, when this idiosyncratic and dour stringency became the law of the land within later codes, it represents a defensive withdrawal into a legalistic world shaded by grays (S. A., O. H. 303:20).

The Talmud and Codification

The greatest accomplishment of the Babylonian Geonim was to make "their" Talmud, the Bavli (Babylonian), authoritative over the Yerushalmi (Jerusalem) Talmud.[3] In large measure, this accomplishment was a byproduct of the Geonim's primary literary activity—responding to legal queries from Jewish communities across the Diaspora. Although the Geonim, as a rule, did not accept the Talmudic text as the definitive source of halakhic authority in the face of an opposing, living practice,

---

3   Brody, *Geonim*, 161.

the Bavli was still their reference point.[4] Nevertheless the Geonim saw themselves as bound neither to the ostensible decisions of the Talmud or their own Geonic predecessors.[5] This broad discretion sometimes resulted in "increased stringency in certain aspects of ritual law."[6] For example, although it was the custom in the Land of Israel to read through the Torah once over a three year period, the Babylonian practice of an annual cycle became the norm. Babylonian practices spreading throughout the diaspora is one thing, but Babylonian practices influencing practices in the Land of Israel is another. The celebration of a two-day New Year, even in Israel, seems to have also been the result of Babylonian influence.[7]

It bears repetition that the Geonim did not see themselves as having less authority to determine practical halakhah than the individual voices of the Talmud, including that of the final editor.[8] When Sherira Gaon (d. 1006) was told that Tunisians were adjudicating straight from the Talmud, he was incensed.[9] Hai Gaon (d. 1038) maintained that the most important datum for halakhic validity is the actual practice of the community: "'Go out and see what the people are doing' (Brachot 45a). This is the principle and the basis of authority. [Only] afterward do we examine everything said about this issue in the Mishnah or Gemara."[10] Given the textual dexterity of rabbinic scholars, their "examination" of the Talmud would likely result in an interpretation that conforms with popular practice.

On the level of jurisprudence, laws were categorized according to their purported origins. Those origins, in turn, represented a hierarchy of authority. For the Talmud, the top three levels in this legal hierarchy were Toraitic, a halakhah to Moses from Sinai, and rabbinic. A rabbinic law is that which the rabbis self-consciously legislate themselves. A halakhah to Moshe from Sinai is not written in the Torah but explains the existence of a long-standing tradition. A Toraitic law is found in the Torah. It cannot

---

4   Ibid., 178–79. Fishman, *Becoming the People*, 36.
5   Brody, *Geonim*, 149.
6   Ibid., 64.
7   Ibid., 117–18.
8   Ibid., 165.
9   Fishman, *Becoming the People*, 47.
10 Levin, Otzar ha-Geonim, RH, responsa 117, 62; cited in Fishman, *Becoming the People*, 50.

be overemphasized that what the Talmudic rabbis "found" in the Torah might not be what we, in the light of critical biblical scholarship, consider biblical (b. Kiddushin 49b). Nevertheless, what they designate as Toraitic has halakhic consequences.

Our middle category, a halakhah to Moshe from Sinai, may have been applied differently in the two Talmudim. The editor of the Bavli distinguishes between Toraitic law and a halakhah to Moses from Sinai more sharply than does the Yerushalmi.[11] That distinction may have paved the way for the Geonim to rely on that category to justify contemporary practices that would be impervious to legal challenges by the rabbinic laws found in the Talmud. Again, the words of Hai Gaon, the greatest of the Geonim: "Since we have this [tradition] in our hands as an implemented tradition, it is correct, [and] a halakhah to Moses from Sinai."[12]

This category also served a polemical purpose in the rabbinic struggle against the Karaite Jews who rejected the authenticity and authority of the rabbinic tradition. The Geonim tethered a halakhah to Moshe from Sinai not to the words of the Written Torah via midrash but to Mount Sinai, itself. In the first half of the tenth century, Saadia Gaon "trivializes midrash halakhah, almost completely denying it any creative role in the formation of Jewish—Rabbanite—law."[13] Moshe Halbertal summarizes the Geonic view, one recycled by many throughout Jewish history.

> The view I call the "retrieval model" was espoused by Abraham ibn Daud, who follows a long tradition among the Geonim. In it the halakhic process is understood as the transmission from generation to generation of an orally revealed body of Halakhah. Moses received the entire Law, both written and oral, and at its source was complete and perfect. All of the Halakhah was then transmitted to us through a continuous chain of scholars. Over time, due to forgetfulness and carelessness (and also to harsh political circumstances), this knowledge began to erode. Halakhic reasoning therefore became essential, not merely to organize, justify, and

---

11   Christine Hayes, "*Halakhah le-Moshe mi-Sinai* in Rabbinic Sources: A Methodological Case Study," in *The Synoptic Problem in Rabbinic Literature*, ed. Shaye J. D. Cohen (Atlanta: Scholars Press, 2000), 81.

12   Levin, Otzar ha-Geonim, RH, responsa 117, 62; cited in Fishman, *Becoming the People*, 49. Translation slightly modified. See Fishman, *Becoming the People*, 49–51.

13   Harris, *How Do We Know This?*, 76.

transmit given knowledge, but as a vital tool in the desperate attempt to reconstruct, through argumentation, the lost portions of a once complete body of knowledge.[14]

Disputes, in this model, were a rabbinic Achilles' heel. The Karaites could point to them as examples of errors within the rabbinic transmission process. Logically speaking, who can guarantee that even uncontested traditions are not the result of identical transmission errors by different lines of transmission? Rather than hoisting red flags of uncertainty, the genre of univocal legal codes emerged during the early Geonic period (mid-eighth to tenth centuries). *Halakhot Pesuqot* and *Halakhot Gedolot* both represent digests of practical law, primarily derived from the Talmud, but without the give and take of the multiple voices characteristic of the Talmud. (The purported founder of the Karaites, too, wrote his own univocal legal code.[15]) Both texts seem to be geared toward advanced students, rabbanite and Karaite, as well as provincial judges who had studied the Talmud and were seeking a reference digest.[16] An unintended consequence of these digests, according to later Geonim, was that judges were making decisions based exclusively on those codes without having a thorough grasp of the underlying issues as presented within the Talmud.[17] The irony is that although the Geonim strongly preferred oral traditions to written texts for purposes of adjudicating law, for polemical purposes two of their own wrote reference digests that later became relied upon as a code for adjudicating law.[18]

The genre of practical legal codes took a leap forward with the publication of Rabbi Isaac ben Alfasi's *Sefer Halakhot*. Alfasi (1013–1103) was born in Algeria, studied with Rav Nissim Gaon in Tunisia, and settled in Fez, Morocco. The Rif, as he is known, links the world of the Babylonian Geonim to the Arabic Jews of North Africa and Spain. His practical digest of the Talmud included post-Talmudic legislation and Geonic responsa. In 1088, the Rif moved to Andalucía and became the head

---

14 Moshe Halbertal, *People of the Book: Canon, Meaning, and Authority* (Cambridge, MA: Harvard University Press, 1997), 54.
15 Brody, *Geonim*, 86.
16 Ibid., 217–30.
17 Gideon Libson, "The Age of the Geonim," in Hecht, *Introduction to the History and Sources of Jewish Law*, 204.
18 Brody, *Geonim*, 232.

of the yeshivah in Lucena outside of Cordoba. Talya Fishman recently suggested that one significant difference in the halakhic philosophy of the Geonim and the Rif may be attributable to contemporary Islamic jurisprudence. Fishman notes that the Maliki School of Jurisprudence emphasized submission to religious authority and exclusive reliance on manuals of applied law. When the Almohads overthrew the Almoravids, Maliki ideology extended from Tunisia and Morocco to Andalucía. The Almohad invasion caused RaMBaM's family to flee from Andalucía.

The notion that the Talmud itself is to be studied for applied law is made explicit by Rabbeynu Hananel, one of the Rif's primary teachers in Tunisia where the Maliki School of Jurisprudence held a monopoly from the ninth century forward.[19] Curiously, according to this approach the Talmud's function was to provide practical halakhah even though the bulk of the Talmud is a record of halakhic arguments often without any clear conclusions. If the Bavli's value is practical halakhah, then the Bavli's editorial voice that constructed arguments pointing to a certain conclusion should be considered authoritative. After all, the editorial voice is the latest voice in the Talmud, and there was a Talmudic principle cited by the Geonim that the halakhah should follow the latest authority.[20] This principle originally concerned intra-Talmudic disputes between earlier and later rabbis, pointedly excluding the editorial voice.[21] Although the Geonim did not privilege that editorial voice, they did author codes that eliminated much of the back and forth of the Talmud's legal argumentation. What the Rif does in his Talmudic digest is to isolate that editorial

---

19   Fishman, *Becoming the People*, 69, and Talya Fishman, "The 'Our Talmud' Tradition and the Predilection for Works of Applied Law in Early Sephardi Rabbinic Culture," in *Regional Identities and Cultures of Medieval Jews*, ed. Javier Castano, Talya Fishman, and Ephraim Kanarfogel (Liverpool: Littman Library of Jewish Civilization, 2018), 135. Leonard R. Levy cites J. Schacht, who notes the influence of the Shafi'i School of Jurisprudence in Babylonia and the Arabian Peninsula on the shift from oral traditions to text, in Leonard R. Levy, "The Decisive Shift: From Geonim to Rabbi Yitshak Alfasi," in *Tiferet le'Yisrael: Jubilee Volume in Honor of Israel Francus*, ed. Joel Roth, Menahem Schmelzer, and Yaacov Francus (New York: Jewish Theological Seminary, 2010), 129.

20   Ibid., 117–23. Levy points out that the Rif's conclusion is based on the assumption that the entire Talmud had only one editor. The Geonim do not hold that assumption (ibid., 123–26).

21   Ta-Shma, *Creativity and Tradition*, 163.

voice, apply to it the Talmudic principle of "the halakhah follows the later," and to identify that voice as the declaimer of practical halakhah.

When in Lucena, the Rif taught and handpicked his successor, Joseph ibn Migash (1077–1141). Ibn Migash articulated a line of reasoning he considered implicit in the Epistle of Sherira Gaon from 987, namely, that when the Talmud was written down, the act signified that what was being canonized was not only the text but the practical halakhah contained within.[22] Fishman notes that in Roman legal culture, which had previously informed the lives of North Africans, that which is written becomes official. Fishman suggests that seeing the Talmud as a repository of practical law, a claim rejected by the Babylonian Geonim, might be part of the cultural residue from the Roman Empire's conceptions of writing and law.[23] Ibn Migash, like his teacher, and his teachers before him, saw Talmudic argumentation as a necessary byproduct of arriving at the applied law. As with many manufacturing processes, byproducts are worthless. In the legal philosophy of ibn Migash, the Talmud shifts from being a treasure house of legal thought to an overgrown legal code in desperate need of pruning; and the codes of the early Geonim shift from serving as a handy reference for jurists that gives no succor to Karaites to the ideological manifestation of univocal, rabbinic law. Ibn Migash's philosophy of halakhah was dutifully transmitted to his students, including Maimon, father of Moshe.

The RaMBaM

When RaMBaM writes in his "Introduction" to the *Mishneh Torah* (1178–1180) that his book is the only book of halakhah the reader will need, RaMBaM believes himself to be presenting the authoritative halakhah, culled from the Talmud, without any of the Talmud's distracting argumentation. Halbertal notes the irony that RaMBaM's project of consolidating the halakhah actually generated commentary upon commentary which "broadened the very discourse it was meant to stabilize."[24] The irony is tragic: it signals RaMBaM's failure as a philosopher of halakhah which only exacerbates his failure as a theologian. As pervasively influential as

22 Fishman, "The 'Our Talmud' Tradition,":125–26.
23 Ibid.: 127.
24 Halbertal, *Maimonides*, 364.

RaMBaM has been in the world of practical halakhah, his philosophy of halakhah was rejected, and his theology has been denounced, misinterpreted, and/or ignored. Since the Jewish Enlightenment of the nineteenth century until today, there have been ongoing efforts to rehabilitate aspects of Maimonidean theology, but results to date have been modest.

David Berger makes two points relevant to our discussion of RaMBaM. The first is that RaMBaM, alone among the medieval Talmudists, leverages an ambiguous comment in the Bavli to both marginalize the study of Talmud and promote the study of philosophy.[25] Berger observes how important it was to the Jewish self-image to not be considered inferior to their hosts. To avoid an inferiority complex, Jews in the Muslim world made a special effort to acquire a philosophical education.[26] The first part of RaMBaM's fourteen-book legal code—*The Foundations of the Torah*—is purely philosophical, in order to anchor the subsequent laws to then-prevailing philosophical description of the cosmos.

Like his teachers, including his own father, RaMBaM believed that the Talmud's primary purpose was to present practical halakhah. But, unlike his teachers, he did not privilege the voice of the Talmud's editor.[27] Indeed, he felt empowered to forge his own philosophy of Halakhah, methodology, and practical halakhah.[28] In opposition to the Geonim, RaMBaM did not believe that the revelation at Sinai was comprehensive. What was revealed at Mount Sinai had been transmitted faithfully, and there have been no disputes concerning laws from Sinai. Disputes emerged through the human process of Torah interpretation. RaMBaM's cumulative approach to Halakhah exposes much of the Mishnah as derived law from fallible humans.[29] "Halakhic truth and error are determined, according to Maimonides, by the degree of consistency between the new norm with the norms given earlier, at Sinai."[30] RaMBaM interpreted the norm given at Sinai, to love God, as necessitating the study of

---

25 Sukka 28a and Maimonides, M. T., Foundations of the Torah 4:13. David Berger, *Cultures in Collision and Conversation: Essays in the Intellectual History of the Jews* (Boston: Academic Studies Press, 2011), 47.

26 Ibid.

27 Halbertal, *Maimonides*, 256–58.

28 Ibid., 94.

29 Ibid., 103–4.

30 Ibid., 106.

philosophy. Thus, for RaMBaM, new norms must be consistent with his idiosyncratic interpretations in order to be halakhically true.

Not until the *Guide of the Perplexed* (1190) does RaMBaM explicitly articulate the purpose of the commandments. According to his most succinct and explicit explanation, the mitzvot are to benefit our minds and bodies (*Guide*, 3:27). Less succinctly, "Every one of the 613 precepts serves to inculcate some truth, to remove some erroneous opinion, to establish proper relations in society, to diminish evil, to train in good manners, or to warn against bad habits" (*Guide*, 3:31). RaMBaM understands that the entire sacrificial system was a gracious ruse to keep the Israelites from reverting to idolatry (an erroneous opinion). The acts involved in the sacrificial system are identical to those of idolatry. The only difference is in the intention of the worshipper. The Israelites were not prepared to abandon their form of worship immediately after the exodus, so God allowed them to continue the external form as long as they changed their intention. They were no longer to worship false gods; they were to worship the true God (*Guide*, 3:32). Correspondingly, we see that RaMBaM requires intention when praying (h. Prayer 4:15–6).

In the first book, we noted that RaMBaM claimed that the purpose of the commandments was to "refine us" (*Guide*, 3:26 on Genesis Rabbah 44:1). Although I believe his reading of the Rabbinic midrash was itself a rationalist midrash, his explanation for the purpose of the commandments has been very influential in Jewish thought. RaMBaM's understanding of the legal system's overall goal enables him to level a grave charge against anyone who delays seeking help for one who is in danger on Shabbat. RaMBaM begins by citing the rabbinic midrash on Leviticus 18:5 which says about the commandments, "You shall *live* by them," and not *die* by them (Yoma 85b). RaMBaM then plies open the midrash to implant his own rationale for the commandments: "The laws of Torah were given to bring compassion, lovingkindness, and peace into the world. The heretics who say that violating Shabbat is forbidden [even for one who is dangerously ill] offer an example of what Ezekiel wrote citing God's words, 'I also gave them laws that were not good and statutes that they could not live by (Ezekiel 20:28)" (h. Shabbat 2:3).[31]

---

31 See Menachem Lorberbaum, "Messianic Halakhah?: On the Religious Function of the Philosophy of Halakhah," in *New Streams in Philosophy of Halakhah*, ed. Aviezer Ravitzky and Avinoam Rosenak (Jerusalem: Magnes Press, 2008), 107.

Ezekiel's God gave the Israelites lethal laws; RaMBaM's God gave the Israelites good laws that, under certain circumstances, could be lethal. For RaMBaM, all the mitzvot serve a beneficial purpose, either to perfect the body or to perfect the intellect. But laws cannot be applied mechanically. Often, there are competing values at play. RaMBaM is declaring that when a specific mitzvah undermines the promotion of compassion, lovingkindness, or peace, it may need to be set aside in the interest of the goals or purpose of the halakhic system. RaMBaM brands as heretics those who enforce a single law when it conflicts with the legal system's purpose.

RaMBaM was a radical philosopher but a conservative jurist. What the Torah prohibits, even though the threat no longer be present, cannot be changed (*Guide*, 3:34). Yet, his understanding of the mitzvot as beneficial to our being, and neither the arbitrary whims nor the inscrutable will of a dictator, is crucial to my own understanding of the goal of Halakhah. As Halbertal has emphasized, RaMBaM brings an insight to the halakhic table that is indispensable for any coherent Judaism. Philosophy and science are not only obligatory subjects of study, they are necessary tools to determine halakhah.[32]

The telos of a coherent Judaism, as expressed in the Torah, is to live long on the land that the Lord, our God, has given us. The land, for us, is no longer confined to a thin strip along the eastern Mediterranean Sea. The land is the Earth, both of which are designated by the same Hebrew word, *ha'aretz*. Science is instrumental in that task. For RaMBaM, divine revelation is maximally disclosed through creation. Our comprehension of creation, and how to "work within it while watching over it" (Genesis 2:15) is our primary responsibility. A Halakhah that does not reorient itself to address the urgent needs of our planet is incoherent. If carbon and methane be the new idols, we need new prohibitions on their worship.

Sepharad, Ashkenaz, and the Aggadah of Kabbalah

In describing the halakhic arc from Babylonia through North Africa to Andalucía, our attention was on *Mizrachi* Jewry. In English, this group is sometimes called Oriental Jewry or Middle Eastern Jewry. This group is

---

32 Halbertal, *Maimonides*, 2–3.

often lumped together with Sephardic Jews by prolific American Jewish authors who are nearly all Ashkenazim and have had a tendency to designate all Jewish others as *Sephardic*. *Ashkenazi*, which mean *German*, includes those Jews, and their descendants, who emigrated to Germany, France, and England from the Italian Jewish community that dates to the Roman Empire. *Sephardi*, which means *Spanish*, refers to those Jews, and their descendants, who emigrated to Spain in Roman times and lived through the conquest of the Iberian Peninsula by the Muslim Moors beginning in 711 and the reconquest by the Catholics. Life for Sephardim was intermittently precarious under Muslim rule and increasingly inhospitable under Catholic rule. Ultimately, Jews were served with the Edict of Expulsion in 1492.[33]

Not dissimilar to the Geonic academies in Babylonia, ninth- and tenth-century Ashkenazi academies also responded to legal queries from within their cultural orbit. One of the first luminaries in the Ashkenazi constellation was Rabbeynu Gershom (950–1028), known as the "Light of the Exile." He headed the yeshiva in Mainz, a city on the Rhine River not far from Frankfurt. Although Rabbeynu Gershom was not beholden to the decisions of the Geonim, collecting post-Talmudic traditions was central to the work of the yeshiva.[34] "It was in medieval Europe that *Halakhot Gedolot* achieved its greatest prestige. For these [Ashkenazi] authors, unable to read Arabic and cut off from the living oral traditions, it represented the major repository of the Geonic tradition which they venerated."[35] Perhaps the influence of the Geonim in Ashkenaz helps to explain why Rabbeynu Gershom, when writing the first comprehensive and systematic commentary to the Talmud, chose the Bavli rather than the Yerushalmi. Rabbeynu Gershom's commentary was largely absorbed and ultimately canonized in the running commentary of RaSHI (1040–1105).

Until the first Crusade in 1096, Ashkenazi jurists were primarily involved in clarifying discrete Talmudic units and amassing legal traditions. By the second quarter of the twelfth century, there had been an

33 Zion Zohar, "A Global Perspective on Sephardic and Mizrachi Jewry: An Introductory Essay," in *Sephardic and Mizrachi Jewry: From the Golden Age of Spain to Modern Times*, ed. Zion Zohar (New York: New York University Press, 2005), 4–6.
34 Kanarfogel, *Intellectual History*, 95.
35 Brody, *Geonim*, 232.

intellectual shift to the dialectics of the Tosafot.[36] Each yeshiva offered their own additions (*tosafot*) to seemingly conflicting traditions within the Talmudic corpus. By the mid-thirteenth century, Tosafot creativity had peaked.[37] Just as the early Geonim did not view the Talmud as definitive Halakhah, neither did at least one of the latest Tosafists, Rabbi Samson of Sens (c. 1150–c.1230). The very word *tosafot, additions* in Hebrew, suggests that the Tosafot were adding on to the Talmud. The aphorism of a dwarf standing on the shoulder of a giant, suggesting that small-minded contemporaries can see beyond what the intellectual giants of the past could, originated in the twelfth century and is reported in Jewish sources in the first half of the thirteenth century.[38] Given their sense that Halakhah develops over time and the Ashkenazi privileging of local custom, it is not surprising that writing halakhic codes was not central to the Ashkenazi intellectual effort.[39]

> The early eleventh-century German scholars and their followers—Rashi and the multitude of French and German sages of the twelfth and thirteenth centuries—never thought to produce a central, definitive law book that would put an end, once and for all, to the innumerable controversies over so many details of the law that were current in their countries. On the contrary, these differences of opinion and practice were of major importance to them, because many of them represented old communal, local, or familial customs and traditions, which were by definition much more important than the plain, normative Talmudic text. Contrary to the Geonic-Spanish view of controversy as representing, basically, a mistake, the Northern European attitude was to view controversy in principle as representing various legitimate practices that should all be kept alive together, side by side, in the different places where they were practiced.[40]

One legal principle which emerged in the writings of the Tosafot demands promotion and preservation. In a Talmudic discussion of the laws incumbent upon gentiles, from the rabbinic perspective, it is

---

36 Soloveitchik, "Catastrophe and Halakhic Creativity": 79.
37 Ephraim Kanarfogel, "Progress and Tradition in Medieval Ashkenaz," *Jewish History* 14, no. 3 (2000): 295.
38 See Ta-Shma, *Creativity and Tradition.*
39 For exceptions, see ibid., 189–90.
40 Ibid., 189.

revealed that the laws given to Noah and his family after disembarking no longer apply to Jews whose ancestors stood at Sinai and replaced the Noahide covenant with the Sinai covenant. The specific issue under discussion was feticide. "Whoever spills human blood, for that human shall his blood be spilled" is drashed by the rabbis as, "Whoever spills human blood *in* a human, his blood shall be spilled" (Genesis 9:6 and Sannhedrin 57b). Thus, for gentiles, feticide is murder. For Jews, however, feticide is not only permitted, but when the mother's life is in danger, feticide is mandated (m. Ohalot 7:6). The gemara claims, and Tosafot broadly concurs, that there is nothing permitted to Jews that is forbidden to gentiles. In the case at hand, the Tosafot suggests that if the gentile woman's life is in jeopardy, she too may be able to save her life by aborting the fetus. The larger point is that the ethical standards of the Jews should never be lower than that of the gentiles.[41]

The transition from Ashkenaz to Sepharad is best exemplified by Rabbeynu Asher ben Yehiel (c.1250–1328) and his sons. Rabbeynu Asher was born in Germany and studied under Rabbi Meir of Rothenburg. After Rabbi Meir's imprisonment and death, Rabbeynu Asher led his community for fifteen years until he was forced to leave Germany in 1303. He arrived in Toledo in his fifties, where he continued to write responsa literature and his Tosafot on the Talmud until his death. Rabbeynu Asher never produced a code. His son, Rabbi Yakov, did.

The *Tur*, which first appeared in Spain before 1340, was the most practical of the codes. The Rif's *Halakhot Gedolot* followed the Talmud thus necessitating its knowledge. RaMBaM's *Mishneh Torah* was organized very logically, but contained many laws no longer, or not yet, relevant. The *Tur* of Rabbi Yakov ben Rabbeynu Asher was both organized logically and contained only what was relevant. "The work proved so useful and so popular as a standard authority that it was one of the first books ever printed in Hebrew, appearing in a complete edition in 1475."[42] Its legacy was ensured by the numerous commentaries it generated and by Yosef Caro's adoption of its format for his own restatement of the Halakhah.

---

41 See, for example, Rabbi Meir ben Abulafia, *Yad Ramah*, op. cit.

42 Stephen M. Passamaneck, "Toward Sunrise," in Hecht, *Introduction to the History and Sources of Jewish Law*, 338.

Ta-Shma points out the irony that although the *content* of the Tur is largely from the Ashkenazi Rabbeynu Asher, including some of the halakhic innovations of the Hasidei Ashkenaz, the trend of codification was Mizrachi and Sephardi. Rabbi Yakov's brother, Rabbi Yehuda, more Ashkenazi than Sephardic on this count, rejects the definitive authority of even his own brother's code.

> One, he says, should never blindly follow a book—any book—even though most of it is unequivocally known to be true and reliable. Every book has its faults and mistakes, which, although they may be minor in quantity, are still major from a qualitative point of view and might carry a blind follower into great religious harm.[43]

Outside of the halakhic world of the Tosafot academies, as we saw in the first book, some Jewish leaders were concerned with the pernicious spiritual effects of caviling over fine points of Talmudic law. Bahya ibn Paquda's *Duties of the Heart* (c. 1040) is an early example of a jurist who is compelled to remind us that duties of the limbs are physical manifestations of duties of the heart. On occasion, duties of the heart, themselves, require halakhic innovation. Although adding laws based on customary jurisprudence is expected, there is another source from which laws might be generated: creation. "Bahya does not contemplate creation with the eye of a secular scientist, who seeks to understand nature as an autonomous system. Rather, the purpose of contemplating creation is to realize all that is owed the Creator. . . . We can actually discover new obligations."[44] In other words, contemplating creation fills us with awe and gratitude which in turn motivates us to new forms of service.[45]

Hasidei Ashkenaz also did not "shy away from acknowledging non-talmudic sources of legal authority. Indeed . . . they invoked aggadah in defending certain legal decisions."[46] The status of Talmudic aggadah is unclear in the Middle Ages. Avinoam Rosenak suggests that its status was lowered in the Middle Ages as a result of confrontations with Christians.[47] That seems plausible given what we know about Moshe

---

43 Ta-Shma, *Creativity and Tradition*, 193.
44 Lobel, *A Sufi-Jewish Dialogue*, 188.
45 Bahya, *Duties of the Heart*, 184.
46 Fishman, *Becoming the People*, 192.
47 Rosenak, "Aggadah and Halakhah": 28.

Nahmanides' disputation in 1263 in which he was confronted with the Talmudic aggadah that the messiah had been born on the day the Temple was destroyed. Nahmanides explained that one could understand the statement metaphorically as hope being born in the throes of catastrophe, or one could understand it literally and disregard it since agaadah is not authoritatively binding in the way that halakhah is.

Yair Lorberbaum offers a more nuanced view of Talmudic aggadah that is in no way vitiated in the Middle Ages. The category of rationales for the commandments, while not halakhic, per se, are "quasi-halakhic principles" that have halakhic force.[48] As we saw in the first section on theology, the Hasidei Ashkenaz understood the ravages of the First Crusade as a divine punishment that required penance. The scourge of the Crusades did not balance out the cosmos for the sins of the Israelites; only penance could do that. Furthermore, their theology allowed them to atone vicariously for the sins of others.[49] Their ascetic tendencies and penitential stringencies were recorded in Sefer Hasidim and influenced subsequent legal codes. For instance, the Talmud prohibits appearing naked in front a Torah scroll (Shabbat 14a). Sefer Hasidim prohibits laying a Torah scroll on a bed since the assumption is that people were previously naked on the bed (648). The Shulchan Arukh allows a Torah on the bed but prohibits anyone from simultaneously sitting on the bed (S. A., Y. D. 282:7).

As Talya Fishman points out regarding these particular laws of respecting the Torah scroll, "The sheer density of regulations [in Sefer Hasidim], all novel with respect to earlier legislation, if not sui generis, suggests that the [Ashkenazi] Pietists were attempting to alter something within the cultural or legal status quo."[50] That attempt, which included both innovation and making existing laws more stringent, had a dual influence. Some of the novel content from Sefer Hasidim made its way into subsequent codes, as we have seen. But, more importantly, the license to innovate halakhically and ascribe theurgic or cosmic power to these legal innovations is notable as Kabbalah begins to influence halakhah in the fourteenth century.

---

48 Yair Lorberbaum, "Reflections on the Halakhic Status of Aggadah," *Diné Yisrael* 24 (2007): 56.
49 Soloveitchik, "The Midrash, Sefer Hasidim, and the Changing Face of God": 168–70.
50 Fishman, *Becoming the People*, 200.

In a discussion of kabbalists as legal adjudicators, Moshe Hallamish claims that for some, Kabbalah was at least as authoritative as Halakhah, if only on an unconscious level.[51] The authors of early Kabbalah wrote for a small circle of mystical cognoscenti. But when codified, their pious idiosyncrasies have weighed down the yoke of Halakhah for all Israel. A handful of halakhic innovations emerged with the *Zohar*, but halakhot mentioned in the earlier *Bahir* had already been given a kabbalistic interpretation.[52] Jacob Katz explains the way Kabbalah was able to circumvent standard halakhic argumentation. "Once a detail of the Law was interpreted kabbalistically, it received a metaphysical dignity irrespective of its place in the halakhic hierarchy."[53]

As Israel Ta-Shma points out, "The world of Ashkenazi halakhah assigned a very important place to custom, far beyond that implied by the usual talmudic norm, which treats custom on the lowest rung on the ladder of halakhic importance."[54] Thus when a kabbalist offers a novel halakhic frill that was correlated to the unification of the sefirot, in the world of Ashkenazi Halakhah, that frill becomes "deified;" that new custom unifies, or makes, God. As Katz concludes, "Once a ritual, even if halakhically of little weight, had been kabbalistically interpreted, it assumed metaphysical significance vindicating its implementation."[55] In practice, leveling the halakhic field elevated local custom to the status of Toraitic law, *even if that custom was a product of the kabbalists themselves*.

By the sixteenth century, a rule developed that if there were a dispute about a certain law and the more stringent position was the kabbalistic one, the more stringent position should be adopted.[56] Indeed, Katz has shown that even previously articulated rules concerning the relationship between Halakhah and Kabbalah were ignored in favor of Kabbalah by the author of the Shulchan Arukh, Yosef Caro. "Karo . . . absorbed Zoharic prescriptions and granted them higher status than had

---

51 Moshe Hallamish, "Kabbalists Opposite Adjudicators," in Ravitsky, *New Streams*, 181.

52 Jacob Katz, *Divine Law in Human Hands: Case Studies in Halakhic Flexibility* (Jerusalem: Magnes Press, 1998), 294–95.

53 Ibid., 286.

54 Ta-Shma, *Creativity and Tradition*, 138.

55 Katz, *Divine Law*, 299.

56 Ibid., 292–95.

any halakhist before him. . . . [He] yielded to [Kabbalah] to the utmost extent possible for a halakhist of his stature."[57]

Menachem Me'iri (1249–1310) offers a different model of halakhic philosophy. He was presented with a situation where Jews in France had long been engaged in commerce with local Christians. This was problematic because of Talmudic prohibitions on doing business with idolaters lest we support them in mood, merchandise, or money. Although there had been attempts to circumvent those prohibitions, the Me'iri's approach addressed the issue head on. The Me'iri recognized that Christianity does not conform to what the Talmud considered idolatry. On a technical level, Christ is not an idol for the Christians, but an aspect of their triune God. An idol is an icon representing a distinct deity. Moreover, Christians are bound by moral norms and "restricted by ways of religion."[58] There is nothing intrinsically immoral about Christianity. From the position of a Talmudist, Christianity involves a theological error; and errors, even of a theological nature, are Talmudists' stock-in-trade. Thus, the Talmudic prohibition on dealing with idolaters should not apply to Christians because those Talmudic laws were targeting pagans, who having no fear of divine retribution, were "unconcerned about any sins."[59] In elegant and honest fashion, Me'iri exonerated Jews doing business with Christians *and* created a category for religions, like Christianity, that contradicted Judaism's understanding of monotheism.[60]

Me'iri was influenced by RaMBaM's anthropology—all humans are equally created in the divine image—yet RaMBaM still considered Christianity an idolatrous religion. RaMBaM, however, lived in Egypt where there was little contact with Christians and correspondingly little need to accommodate Jewish-Christian business dealings. Furthermore, Islam, too, considered Christianity to be violating its understanding of strict monotheism. Thus, there was no compelling reason for RaMBaM to reevaluate the Talmudic posture toward "idolaters." As Adiel Schremer has noted, the Talmudic decisions predicated on avoiding great economic loss and showing compassion for Jew's finances were later pressed into

---

57 Ibid., 303–4.
58 Moshe Halbertal, "'Ones Possessed of Religion': Religious Tolerance in the Teachings of the Me'iri," *Edah Journal: Orthodoxy and the Other* 1, no. 1 (2000): 2.
59 Ibid.: 6–7.
60 Ibid.: 11.

service as general principles for legislation.[61] These were undoubtedly significant factors for Me'iri. Nevertheless, as Moshe Halbertal points out, Me'iri was motivated by more than the utilitarian.

The Torah, so the rabbis understand, "is a tree of life . . . and her ways are pleasant" (Proverbs 3:17 and Gittin 59b).[62] Once Me'iri has defined Christianity as a religion whose adherents fear God and accept belief in divine providence, including rewards and punishment, his next move is to radically redraw the circle of "Israel." Halakhah, like many legal systems, differentiates between insiders and outsiders; thus the Talmud differentiates between Israel and idolaters. What Meiri's classification effectively does is "convert" Christians into the etymology of *Israel*, God wrestlers. A less confusing term might be gentiles. As *gentiles*, prohibitions against intermarriage apply, but for most other legal considerations, they are like Israel.

> The Me'iri treated the gentiles of his day no differently from Jews with respect to obligations and rights in the following matters: compensation for property damage, the prohibition on robbery, the obligation to return lost property, the obligation to rescue from harm, granting gratuitous gifts, the obligation to help in loading a beast of burden, the prohibition of excessive profit, the imposition of equal punishment for killing a gentile, the prohibition of delaying payment to a hired worker, the violation of sabbath to save human life, the authorization to sell armaments to a gentile, and the authorization to stable an animal in a gentile's inn. According to the Me'iri, the discrimination that pervades the *halakhah* with respect to these rights applies only to the ancient nations, which "are not restricted by religious practices." In the Me'iri's view, contemporary gentiles are fully equal to Jews in these respects.[63]

Halbertal points out more areas of Talmudic law which the Me'iri renders inoperative vis-à-vis contemporary Christians. His ambitious goal was "to diminish inner hostility and effect a change in consciousness itself."[64] When discussing biblical law, I cited Edward Greenstein:

---

61 Schremer, "Toward Critical Halakhic Studies": 32–33.
62 Aaron Kirschenbaum, *Equity in Jewish Law: Beyond Equity: Halakhic Aspirationism in Jewish Civil Law* (New York: Ktav Publishing, 1991), 151–83.
63 Halbertal, "Ones Possessed of Religion": 3.
64 Ibid.: 11.

"The goal is a modest utopia in which people will bless each other for being kind."[65] In enlarging the circle of Israel, the Me'iri wants to enlarge the borders of the modest utopia. As the Torah and Jesus understood, the best way to disarm an enemy is by showing them care. Animosity tends to be reciprocated, but so does concern. The Torah does not go quite as far as to command us to love our enemies (Matthew 5:44), but we are forbidden from hating them in our heart. We must do whatever is in our power to redress grievances, forgive the past, and turn enemies into friends and neighbors (Leviticus 19:16–18 and Avot d'Rabbi Natan 23:1). There is a sweet irony in the Me'iri's attempt to extend the Torah's ways of pleasantness to Christians through the Halakhah given that Christians have historically held the Halakhah in contempt.

The code which has had the greatest influence on world Jewry is Yosef Caro's Shulchan Arukh, published in 1565, though the impact was felt in the Ottoman Empire before the rest of the world.[66] By 1580, Rabbi Moshe Isserles' comments were interspersed within Caro's own text, and the Shulchan Arukh has included them ever since. (*Shulchan arukh* means *a set table* in Hebrew, and Isserles' work was entitled, *Mapah*, the *Tablecloth*.) Isserles looked askance at Caro's methodology—adopting the opinion of two of the following three jurists: Alfasi, RaMBaM, and Rabbi Yakov the son of Rabbeynu Asher. As Stephen Passamaneck explains, Isserles' motivations to write his work were not only to balance out the lopsided Sephardic representation.

> The usual assessment of Isserles' purpose was that he wishes to give greater emphasis to Ashkenazi views upon the *halakhah*. This opinion is correct up to a point. In ritual matters, the German (and later the Polish) style of ritual did differ substantially from the Spanish. . . . In many other areas of the law, Isserles is as apt to quote a leading Spanish authority as a leading German one. . . . Isserles was as much concerned with providing a more thorough and rounded statement of a given law, *with optional procedures clearly stated*, as he was with giving due weight and consideration to the wealth of ritual practice which had developed among German Jews.[67]

---

65 Greenstein, "Biblical Law," in Holtz, *Back to the Sources*, 100.
66 Zvi Zohar, "Sephardic Jurisprudence," in Zohar, *Sephardic and Mizrachi Jewry*, 174.
67 Passamaneck, "Toward Sunrise," 340. My emphasis.

Optional procedures. For Ashkenazi jurists, local customs are to be preserved and honored. Not only does Isserles present options within the world of halakhah, but his presence on the page of the Shulchan Arukh offers two different philosophies of halakhah. Another philosophy of halakhah that views optional procedures positively, as opposed to the Geonim and Sephardim, relies on a rabbinic notion of revelation. Steven Fraade has analyzed texts from the earliest stratum of rabbinic literature discussing revelation. From the first moment of reception, the process of interpretation began. "When the Israelites stood at Mount Sinai to receive the Torah they interpreted the divine word (as soon) as they heard it."[68] Anticipating Kantian epistemology, the word of God *in itself* is inaccessible to the Israelites; they are only able to process the Word through their idiosyncratic capacities. Moreover, some rabbis understood that the Halakhah, itself, was revealed in a divine fullness that transcended a univocal directive. "Rabbi Yani said, 'Words of Torah were not given as clear-cut decisions.'"[69]

For either of these rabbinic reasons, multiple interpretations might be valid. Although Shammai would have never said such a thing, the Talmud describes disputes between the Houses of Hillel and Shammai as "these and those are the living words of God" (Eruvin 13b). These sorts of rabbinic statements reflect a philosophy of Halakhah that Halbertal calls the "constitutive view."[70] The decision of the majority *constitutes* what the Halakhah will be without making any claim to the truth value of the decisions that were accepted or rejected. Indeed, it is in the Tosafot's treatment of this "these and those are the living words of God" that we see the origins of the constitutive view of Halakhah.

According to a later source, Rabbi Yehiel of Paris, a thirteenth-century Tosafist, explained that contradictory rulings can both be true because "when Moshe ascended to heaven to receive the Torah, he was shown for every construct forty-nine ways to prohibit and forty-nine

---

68 Mekhilta d'Rabbi Ishmael, Yitro, Bachodesh 9. Cited in Steven D. Fraade, "Rabbinic Polysemy and Pluralism Revisited: Between Praxis and Thematization," *Association of Jewish Studies Review* 31, no. 1 (2007): 24.

69 *Midrash on Psalms* 12:7. Cited in Fraade, "Rabbinic Polysemy": 16.

70 Halbertal, *People of the Book*, 63–67.

ways to permit."[71] Thus, it is on the basis of a majority of the scholars in each age to determine the practical halakhah. Nahmanides, educated by French Tosafists, was also deeply influenced by Kabbalah.[72] Nahmanides' students were, therefore, influenced both by the Tosafists' understanding of multiple truths and the mystical notion that within the Torah there is a multiplicity of divine truths. As an Ashkenazi who also wrote kabbalistic explanations for the mitzvot, what would have been inexplicable was if Isserles had not included multiple options in his comments on the Shulchan Arukh.[73]

> The legitimacy of multiple halakhic truths that is at the heart of this Tosafot passage (and that constitutes a cornerstone of Tosafist thought and endeavor) is a fundamentally exoteric concept. [The Tosafot were interested in law not mysticism.] Nonetheless, there were Ashkenazic rabbinic figures in both the pre-Crusade period and the Tosafist period for whom this notion had mystical connotations. Ritva [Rabbi Yom Tov Ashvelli, 1250–1330] understood the importance of this formulation in both exoteric and esoteric [kabbalistic] ways as well.[74]

"Ritba understood revelation as completely open-ended and pluralistic."[75] The sages in each generation are empowered by the Torah to determine their truth, and that truth, as they see it, is from Sinai. Thus, there is a relationship between the mystical notion that the Torah inherently contains and is a partner in generating multiple truths, and the constitutive theory of Jewish law in which a decision of the majority constitutes the halakhah.

---

71 *Hiddushei ha-Ritva, Eruvin*; cited in Ephraim Kanarfogel, "Between Ashkenaz and Sefarad: Tosafist Teachings in the Talmudic Commentaries of Ritva," in *Between Rashi and Maimonides: Themes in Medieval Jewish Thought, Literature and Exegesis*, ed. Ephraim Kanarfogel and Moshe Sokolow (New York: Ktav Publishing, 2010), 252.
72 Ephraim Kanarfogel, "Torah Study and Truth in Medieval Ashkenazic Rabbinic Literature and Thought," in *Study and Knowledge in Jewish Thought*, ed. Howard Kreisel (Beer Sheva: Ben-Gurion University of the Negev Press, 2006).
73 Lawrence Kaplan, "Rabbi Mordekhai Jaffe and the Evolution of Jewish Culture in Poland in the Sixteenth Century," in Cooperman, *Jewish Thought in the Sixteenth Century*, 271.
74 Kanarfogel, "Between Ashkenaz and Sefarad," in Kanarfogel and Sokolow, *Between Rashi and Maimonides: Themes in Medieval Jewish Thought, Literature and Exegesis* 267. The Tosafot passage mentioned is from Tosafot Rabbenu Perez to Eruvin 13a.
75 Halbertal, *People of the Book*, 65.

The principle of majority rule is found in the Talmud, in the story of the Oven of Achnai (Baba Metzia 59a/b). But there the principle is pragmatic. What we have in the fourteenth century is a far bolder claim: the truth of the majority decision is rooted in the divine fullness. As a community, we channel a torah of truth. Ultimately, in the sixteenth-century Kabbalah of Tzfat, we find the image that each individual present at Mount Sinai possesses a discrete and unique understanding of Torah. Through the process of reincarnation, each of us has sparks from those Sinai souls. Only in concert can we reestablish the fullness of the Torah and bring on the messianic age.[76]

The Loyal Opposition

The earliest opponent to halakhic codes was Rabbi Abraham ben David (RABaD) of Posquieres (1125–1198). His critical glosses on RaMBaM's *Mishneh Torah* explicitly denounce RaMBaM's arrogance. After all, he called his code *Mishneh Torah*, the second Torah, and proposed that the Torah of Moshe and the Torah of Moshe ben Maimon were the only two Torahs one needed. Menachem Elon succinctly summarized the RABaD's opposition.

> Rabad's strong disagreement was with Maimonides' method of declaring the law without citing the sources and without setting out the range of opinions on each legal issue–information which is vital to the very essence of Jewish law and to the methodology of halakhic decision making.[77]

Without knowing the Talmudic context of any given law, one is liable to misapply a code that, by definition, is shorn of context. Furthermore, once a law has been codified, it becomes ossified. Rigor mortis is more likely to set in because future decision makers lack a range of positions from which to develop their own responses to the exigencies of their day. As noted above, this healthy instinct against codification, particularly among Ashkenazi Jews, ultimately undermined RaMBaM's effort to

---

76 Gershom Scholem, *On the Kabbalah and its Symbolism* (New York: Schocken Books, 1965), 64–65.

77 Menachem Elon, *Jewish Law: History, Sources, Principles*, trans. Bernard Auerbach (Philadelphia: Jewish Publication Society, 2003), 1224.

write a second Torah. The RABaD's comments, as well as other commentaries, appear alongside the *Mishneh Torah* in most editions.

Let us take one example from the Talmud to see how subsequent jurists contended with a tradition that no longer seemed sensible. One voice in the Talmud, the final voice in the discussion, prohibits consuming meat and fish together for fear of contracting leprosy (P'sachim 76b). RaMBaM understood that such a concern was outlandish and ignored this superstitious suggestion. Rabbi Yakov the son of Rabbeynu Asher, on the other hand, codified the prohibition of eating fish and meat together in his code, the Arba'ah Turim (Y. D. 116). He also mentioned that his father, Rabbeynu Asher, would wash his hands between eating meat and fish. The Shulchan Arukh not only codified the prohibition of consuming meat and fish together, it also obligated us to wash our hands between meat and fish. What RaMBaM relegated to benign neglect, Caro codified. In Isserles' comments on eating meat and fish together, he *extended* the prohibition to include cooking meat and fish together, though he does recognize the legitimacy of not washing hands between courses.

Another commentator of the Shulchan Arukh, Rabbi Abraham Gombiner (c. 1637–1683), offers an insight into Caro's comment without suggesting a modification in the halakhah. Gombiner explains it is possible that in his day, the seventeenth century, the consumption of meat and fish together is "not so dangerous." "We have seen several things mentioned in the Talmud that are dangerous due to an evil spirit or other things. But now there's no harm because nature has changed and, also, everything depends on the nature of the lands" (Magen Avraham on S. A., O. H. 173). The voice in the Talmud that was afraid of leprosy by mixing meat and fish was wrong. In the past, explicitly acknowledging the mistake would undermine the perception of the infallibility of uncontested Talmudic statements. In our day, when infallibility has fallen out of grace, there is no disrespect in acknowledging as much. Nor is there a need, as we have seen in the past, in restricting such fallibility to issues of medicine or science (e.g., P'sachim 94b).

Indeed, given that our fallible Talmudic voice considered the issue of mixing meat and fish to have such grave consequence, I appreciate the prohibition. It would have been a small price to pay to avoid leprosy. But, once we understand the medical error, we would be better served to admit it without resorting to the unfalsifiable claim that nature has changed. This *deus ex machina*, that nature has changed, has been used repeatedly to save the phenomenon for halakhic purposes. I will offer one more example to argue for the retirement of the principle.

Watering is a violation of the general Sabbath prohibition against planting. Without offering the full halakhic history on the topic, I will cite the relevant section of the Shulchan Arukh for our discussion. Although spilling water on the ground on Shabbat is forbidden, it is permissible to urinate on the ground since urine was not considered conducive to plant growth (O. H. 336:3).[78] By the nineteenth century, science had determined that the concentration of acid in urine was not detrimental to plant growth. Indeed, in Israel Lifschitz's (1782–1860) Mishnah commentary *Tiferet Yisrael* he cites contemporary scientists who assert that urine acts like a fertilizer which is "very good" for the earth and ultimately beneficial for plant growth. His conclusion is not that knowledge of such things has advanced, but that nature must have changed.

For traditional halakhists, the prohibition on Sabbath watering is considered biblical. The halakhic rule, first expressed in the Talmud (Beitza 3b), is that when there is an issue of doubt concerning a biblical law, one leans towards the stricter interpretation. One of the leading halakhists in late nineteenth-century Europe, Avraham Bornsztain (1838–1910), in his *Eglei Tal*, did in fact prohibit urination on the ground during Shabbat. Surprisingly, the leading codifier of the subsequent generation, Rabbi Israel Meir Kagan (1839–1933), did not follow suit in his *Mishnah Brurah*. Kagan cites the Shulchan Arukh's allowance without qualification. Only in his footnotes, the *Beur Halakhah*, does he cite the statement of the *Tiferet Yisrael* before dismissing it by saying that no one worries about such things. In what we might call *strategic neglect*, Kagan chooses to ignore the likelihood of violating a biblical prohibition in order to avoid the unpalatable alternatives: the halakhah was wrong, nature has changed, or he believed that people (men) would not change their behavior even after learning of the change in practical halakhah.

Just as there was immediate opposition to Maimonides' attempt to codify halakhah, so, too, for Caro and Isserles's work. Leon Wiener Dow summarized the critiques of three of the leading halakhists in Ashkenaz,

---

78   For the full halakhic history, see Neria Gutel, "'Changes in Nature'—A Halakhic and Ideological Answer to the Conflict between Halakhic Rulings and Objective Reality" [Heb.], *Bekhol Derakhekha Daehu: Journal of Torah and Scholarship* 7 (1998): 81–82.

all students of Rabbi Moshe Isserles: Shlomo Luria (1510–1573), Judah Loew ben Betzalel (1520–1609), and Haim ben Betzalel (1530–1588). They shared a philosophy of Halakhah that precluded using a code for the adjudication of specific cases since each case has its own unique and idiosyncratic details.[79] Wiener Dow also raises the important issue of the role of analogies in legal reasoning.[80] Are all cases available for purposes of analogy? Are there conditions that limit or preclude analogies? When the Me'iri halakhically obligated us to help load the fallen beast of burden of both Jews and Christians (Deuteronomy 22:4), does that obligate us today to stop and assist everyone we see with a flat tire?

In terms of Caro's own goal for his composition, it, too, met the same fate as did the *Mishneh Torah*.

> The four slim volumes that had been published in Venice in 1564–1565 were well on their way to their modern form of ten, heavy, folio tomes laden with commentaries and super-commentaries in the tiniest of prints—rather an ironic fate for a work intended to be a review tool for scholars and a legal primer for young students.[81]

Sixteenth-century Tzfat was the axial age and epicenter of Kabbalah. Although Jewish creativity in all genres pulsed through this mountaintop village, mysticism was queen. We have concentrated on the legal work of Yosef Caro, but he, too, was a spiritual savant. Solomon Schechter called Caro's Maggid Mesharim "a long dream, lasting for nearly half a century."[82] In this waking dream, Caro personifies and channels the Mishnah, vocalizing her spirit for those nearby to hear. Yet, although he promotes halakhah emerging from kabbalistic sources, he refrains from any sort of aggadic framing. As Isadore Twersky has pointed out, "The Shulhan Arukh pruned the *Turim* [of Rabbi Yakov ben Rabbeynu Asher], relentlessly excising midrashic embellishments, ethical perceptions, and theoretical amplifications. . . . This austere functionality comes to the surface

---

79 Leon Wiener Dow, "Opposition to the 'Shulhan Aruch': Articulating a Common Law Conception of the Halakha," *Hebraic Political Studies* 3, no. 4 (Fall 2008): 375.
80 Ibid.: 372–75.
81 Edward Fram, "Jewish Law from the Shulhan Arukh to the Enlightenment," in Hecht, *Introduction to the History and Sources of Jewish Law*, 365.
82 Solomon Schechter, "Safed in the Sixteenth Century: A City of Legists and Mystics," in *Studies in Judaism: Second Series*, ed. Solomon Schechter (Philadelphia: Jewish Publication Society, 1908), 265.

in the virtually complete elimination of ideology, theology, and teleology."[83] In the Shulchan Arukh, as Caro writes in his introduction, he deals with the law, and nothing but the law.

As we saw in the aftermath of the Crusades with the *Sefer Hasidim*, many of the denizens of Tzfat identified as penitents in the wake of the expulsion from Spain. "Life practically meant for them an opportunity for worship, to be only occasionally interrupted by such minor considerations as the providing of a livelihood for their families. . . . Prayer was the main and universal occupation. . . . The example set by them seems to have infected the general Jewish public."[84] Their frequent night vigils did not spread to the entire Jewish community but saying the bedtime *Shema* and the morning *Modeh Ani* did. Inviting the *ushpizin* (guests) into the sukkah and bringing the four species together to shake in a choreographed fashion; having a seder for Tu B'shvat; walking around with the Torah scrolls on Simchat Torah; Kabbalat Shabbat and the post-Shabbat get together, the *Melaveh Malka*; all were kabbalistic innovations from sixteenth-century Tzfat.[85]

Although Isaac Luria did not write halakhah, his comments on the Zohar were influential to subsequent halakhists who granted the Zohar halakhic status.[86] Thus, when Gombiner wrote his commentary on the Shulchan Arukh, Kabbalah's influence radiated outward from the central texts, those of Caro and Isserles, to the margins. The preeminent code of Jewish law was marinated in mysticism, even if much of it was unstated.[87] One of the subsequent works reacting to the Shulchan Arukh explicitly criticized the work for not offering the rationale for the commandments. Thus, Mordekhai Jaffee's *Levush Malkhut* (c. 1600) incorporates both kabbalistic and philosophical explanations for the commandments, though he structures his ten-volume work to correspond to the ten sefirot, not Aristotle's

---

83 Isadore Twersky, "The Shulhan Arukh: Enduring Code of Jewish Law," *Judaism* 16, no. 2 (1967): 332.

84 Schechter, "Safed," 283.

85 Morris M. Faierstein, "Safed Kabbalah and the Sephardic Heritage," in Zohar, *Sephardic and Mizrahi Jewry*, 204–08.

86 Hallamish, "Kabbalists": 198.

87 Jay R. Berkovitz, "Rabbinic Culture and the Historical Development of Halakhah," in *The Cambridge History of Judaism*, vol. 7, *The Early Modern World, 1500-1815*, ed. Jonathan Karp and Adam Sutcliffe (New York: Cambridge University Press, 2019), 367.

four elements. As Kabbalah continues its ascent in the Ashkenazi world, not a single work of philosophy was published from 1620–1720.

Isaiah Horowitz, in his *Two Tablets of the Covenant*, also describes the kabbalistic meaning to the commandments, and he introduces even more rituals.[88] He explains that prohibitions and stringencies need to keep pace with the moral decline of the generations.[89] This notion that kids today just cannot be trusted also made its way into the margins of the Shulchan Arukh.[90] Although the rabbis did their best to accommodate their communities concerning economic hardships, the same was not true on ritual matters. "When its observance was lax, the machinery of halakhah was engaged to foster greater piety."[91] Thus, Halakhah goes baroque.

As we evaluate halakhic trends and philosophies of Halakhah from the Middle Ages, let us begin where the Middle Ages ends, with the supremacy of Kabbalah. There is a consensus among the kabbalists that Halakhah has an ontological component, particularly ritual halakhah. Performing the commandments with the proper mystical intention affects God's very being. Kabbalists do what all the king's horsemen and all the king's men could not do. By invoking a children's poem, I do not mean to belittle the kabbalistic myth. On the contrary, the myth gives us fantastic powers that repair, in some way, our own immature conceptions of God. The God we reconstruct, not through ritual but through righteousness, is a vulnerable deity. To the degree that ritual enhances our righteousness, let it be.

Yet, as I hope to have shown throughout the chapter, ritual accretion characterizes the history of Halakhah. Within the Talmud, after the Talmud, through the codes, and with kabbalistic influence, the Halakhah has become unwieldy. In the Zohar, evil is a product of the left side, *middat ha-din*, breaking away from its equilibrium with the right side, *midat ha-rachamim*. We have been translating *midat ha-din* as the attribute or quality of justice. But it might just as well be translated as the attribute of law. When the attribute of law becomes untethered to the quality of mercy, *midat ha-rachamim*, that which makes law righteous and equitable, then

---

88 Katz, *Divine Law*, 54.

89 See Krassen's translation, *Generations of Adam*, 269.

90 David ben Samuel ha-Levi, *Turey Zahav*, Y. D. 119:2.

91 Edward Fram, *Ideals Face Reality: Jewish Law and Life in Poland, 1550–1655* (Cincinnati: Hebrew Union College Press, 1997), 105.

law becomes an end in itself. Unalloyed mercy may corrupt, but unalloyed law destroys. Lest I be accused of unprecedented blasphemy, here is the precedent: "Rabbi Yohanan said, "Jerusalem was destroyed only because they judged according to Torah law" (Baba Metzia 30b).

Halakhic codes may still be printed for some in the Orthodox world, but scholars like Joseph Telushkin and Elliot Dorff, as well as the denominational movements, have published what I would call guidebooks. They are far less detailed than the medieval codes, and they are framed with reasons and narratives. Readers will either chose autonomy within heteronomy, and exercise their own discretion based on the guidebooks; or they will seek rabbinic counsel knowing that guidebooks, by definition, do not deal with specific details that affect which principle might be determinative in any given case. In America, when we "go out and see what the people are doing," it is often at odds with traditional Jewish practice. Channukah bushes and tattoos might fall under the general prohibition of *chukkat goyim*, imitating the gentiles (Leviticus 18:3). But, what about eating plant-based food at unsupervised restaurants that also serve non-Kosher food? Isn't that a form of conscious consumption that Judaism should recognize and encourage? Our ability to be an *or l'goyim*, a light unto the nations, is in tension with our historical need to keep the non-Jewish world at a safe distance.

A judge has only what her eyes see, and we decide according to the majority of sages. Reform Judaism will challenge the authority of Halakhah, but we all agree that Judaism demands a behavioral response to the miracle of life. In order to allow for new growth, which is desperately needed, our Tree of Life needs to be pruned. Many of the stringencies and accumulated halakhah of the centuries no longer protect the Tree, they just block the sun.

RaMBaM bequeathed us a model of coherent Judaism. We need to update all its terms. What do we believe about God and God's relationship to creation? Answering the latter question demands knowledge of creation that is pursued through the study of science, writ large. One of the things that scientists have told us about the world, for instance, is that although nature changes, it does not change as our ancestors claimed. RaMBaM understood that the Halakhah serves a protective function to guard against idolatry. People used to make gods *out* of gold and silver; now we make gods *of* gold and silver.

After the Shoah, no one should believe that Jews were punished and require penance. Nor does the ostensible moral decline of our generation demand a halakhic response that mirrors previous responses. We should learn from Bahya ibn Pakuda, the Tosafot, and Hasdei Crescas who all saw the Talmud as an expression of principles and values to be applied to changing circumstances. Crescas, in particular, saw the ongoing generation of halakhah as the Jewish corollary to God's continuous creation of the cosmos. "Infinity looms large in Crescas's innovative philosophical, scientific, and theological approaches. . . . The notion of the infinite Torah served as the lynchpin of his halakhic philosophy."[92] Crescas' worldview, influenced by Kabbalah and its myth of the infinite Torah, is similarly rooted in the priestly Torah where human creativity and divine creativity are analogous. In many ways, the next chapter's focus on the authority of Halakhah in modernity is but a distraction from the more important conversation about which Halakhah modernity demands of us. RaMBaM's admonition should be set always before us: those who enforce a single law at the expense of the legal system's overall purpose are heretics.

The Stages of Going Baroque

Talmudic Period

- The rabbinic assumption that nothing is superfluous in Torah invites innovative legislation
- Customs by individual sages become collected and legislated
- Stringencies of individuals become norms

Middle Ages

- Ashkenazi privileging of local customs
- Hasidei Ashkenaz desire to increase opportunities for worship and stringencies of worship to atone for the sins that triggered the Crusades

---

92 Ari Ackerman, "Hasdai Crescas on the Philosophical Foundation of Codification," *Association of Jewish Studies Review* 37, no. 2 (November 2013): 327–28.

- Sefer Hasidim ascribes theurgic power to their legal innovations
- Kabbalistic customs make their way into halakhic codes and because of their supposed theurgic power are granted the highest halakhic authority
- The Shulchan Arukh, which becomes the most influential legal code of Jewish history, is composed by a mystic from Tzfat heavily influenced by Kabbalah
- After the expulsion from Spain, kabbalists in Tzfat innovated many rituals particularly around prayer and the holidays
- The Ashkenazi "co-compiler" of the Shulchan Arukh included additional procedures and was also influenced by Kabbalah
- After the publication of the Shulchan Arukh, popular works were published offering kabbalistic explanations for the mitzvot and continuing to increase ritual mitzvot, such as Horowitz's *Two Tablets of the Covenant*

A P.S. on the printed prayer book by Jakob Petuchowski in "Some Laws of Jewish Liturgical Development":

Once the ordinary worshippers had inherited printed prayerbooks from their parents and grandparents, the particular printed version of the Liturgy in hand assumed a "canonical" status, suggesting to the unlearned that, even if that particular prayerbook was not given by God to Moses on Mount Sinai together with the Torah, it must at least have been composed by the Men of the Great Synagogue, or, failing that, by the Sages of Yavneh at the very latest. . . . Different local communities used to opt for different poetic selections, with preference often given to the products of local talent. But once the printed prayerbook made its appearance, the state of affairs was to change radically. In the first place, a poem, whatever its degree of intelligibility, if printed as part of the standard rubrics of the worship service, assumed the authoritative look of something that "has to be said." In addition, the printer—and who can blame him for that?—also had to be a business man. The more poems of purely local usage he could incorporate in a regional prayerbook, or even in a prayerbook meant for, say, for all of Ashkenazi Jewry, the more copies of that particular edition he was able to sell—without bearing the cost of printing a number of different and much smaller editions for purely local markets. Yet once local various selections were united in a single prayerbook, it did not take long before the *totality* of the printed poems came to be recited by *all* of the congregations in which that particular printed prayerbook was used. We see, then, that the ultimate authority in matters liturgical is the printer.[93]

---

93 Jakob Petuchowski, *Studies in Modern Theology and Prayer* (Philadelphia: Jewish Publication Society, 1998), 164–65. Emphasis in original.

Chapter 13

The Two Branches of a Divining Rod

Ploni Almoni, the generic Joe Shmoe of Jewish literature, visits a Jewish house of worship on Saturday morning. In some places, he might need to sit apart from his female partner. There will be some Hebrew, but the extent will vary greatly. The prayers, themselves, will differ depending on the denominational affiliation of the—what shall we call it?—synagogue, temple, *shul*? But at each venue, Torah will be read, *even though there is no suggestion in the Torah that it is to be read on Shabbat.* From where and when does this universal Jewish tradition come? There's a dispute.

Once the Israelites had crossed the Sea of Reeds, and they were no longer anxiously looking over their shoulders, the reality of their new-found freedom set in. They were in the desert with sand surrounding them on all sides. For three long days they could not find water (Exodus 15:22). According to the rabbis who lived in allegory, three days without life-sustaining water is three days without life-sustaining Torah. Isaiah said so: "Yo! All who thirst, come for water!" (Isaiah 55:1). According to this midrashic reading of survival in the desert, *we* should never go for three days without Torah. Thus, the prophets and elders at that time ordained that Torah should be read every Monday, Thursday, and Shabbat (Mekhilta at Exodus 15:22). Since chronology should never interfere with allegory, or better, since allegory rises above the contingencies of the mundane, the fact that the Torah had not yet been given to the Israelites at Mount Sinai is irrelevant.

In the Talmud, this explanation of Shabbat Torah reading is juxta-posed to an alternative suggestion. The reading of the Torah on Monday, Thursday, and Shabbat was instituted by Ezra the Scribe centuries after Sinai.[1] This is a dispute for the sake of heaven which remains unre-solved. In this dispute about the origin of the universal practice of read-ing Torah on Shabbat, we see a choice between midrash and tradition. In our case, the tradition is from Ezra rather than Moshe, but the basic contours of the dispute are the same.[2] What I want to emphasize is that the midrash halakhah, the biblical source for reading Torah on Shabbat, is from an aggadic passage. Although our medieval thinkers contended that Aggadah is not binding, they never suggested that it is halakhically neutral. The role of rabbinic Aggadah in modern Halakhah will feature prominently throughout this chapter. We begin our examination of hal-akhic responses to modernity from the most traditional segments of Jewish society to best judge how the more culturally familiar Western ideologies of change compare.

To find water in the desert, one uses a divining rod. A divining rod has two branches. Since water is Torah, the two branches are Aggadah and Halakhah. As we enter the halakhic debates of modernity, we begin with a sage who lived in eighteenth-century Prague and had a firm grasp on both branches. Ezekiel Landau (1713–1793) is best known for his col-lection of legal responsa, Noda b'Yehuda. In this collection, he explic-itly addresses the halakhic status of Aggadah. He claims that although aggadot contain the "very essence of religion," they have no role in the determination of Halakhah.[3] As we will see, he doth protest too much.

One of the many questions addressed by Landau is the issue of sport hunting. Landau does not hide his disdain. How can a Jew set out to murder one of God's creatures for pleasure? Landau acknowledges that

---

1   Baba Kamma 82a. Ezra did not ordain, according to this Talmudic source, the Torah reading on Shabbat morning, only for the Shabbat afternoon service. Thus, in the Talmud, the dispute is about Torah reading on Monday and Thursday. Therefore, the only rabbinic justification for reading Torah on Shabbat morning is our anachronistic midrash from the Mekhilta.

2   The Talmud Yerushalmi ascribes this tradition to Moshe (y. Megillah 4:1 and 10:1).

3   Noda b'Yehuda, Mehadura Tnina, YD 161. My thanks to Rabbi Gordon Tucker for bringing this source to my attention. See also Daniel Sinclair, "Fictitious Retractions and False Attributions: The Balance between Truth and Falsehood in Halakhic Discourse," *Jewish Law Association Studies* 22 (2012): 283–84.

neither the halakhic category of causing distress to animals nor conservation of resources suffices for him to rule against sport hunting. After
bringing up the moral, sociological, and direct halakhic issues that he
finds insufficient to steer our gamesman toward more virtuous pursuits
with more honorable people, Landau plots a more circuitous route to
his desired destination. Landau introduces the Torah's most notorious
hunter, one whose skills are singled out for mention (Genesis 25:27). He
claims that in the scene where Esau trades his birthright for a mess of
pottage, the dialogue between the two brothers has halakhic implications:

> Once when Jacob was cooking a stew, Esau came in from the open,
> famished. And Esau said to Jacob, "Give me some of the red stuff to gulp
> down, for I am famished. . . . " Jacob said, "First sell me your birthright."
> And Esau said, "I am at the point of death, so of what use is my birthright
> to me?" (Genesis 25:29–32)

As sensitive readers of the Torah, we notice that the word *famished* is
repeated. Between the repetition and the comically inarticulate demand
to "gulp down red stuff," I am not inclined to read his comment about
being *at the point of death* as anything other than hyperbole. Esau is so
hungry he could eat a horse. Nevertheless, there is a long tradition of
reading Esau's comment as a calculated assessment of his birthright's
worth. According to Rashbam, Ibn Ezra, and others, Esau understands
that hunting is a dangerous line of work. He's out in the forests with lions
and tigers and bears. There is a reasonable chance that he will predecease
his father. Thus, Esau determines that the net present value of the red
stuff may well be greater than the fruits of the birthright which he may
never see.[4]

What does our biblical interlude have to do with our query about
sport hunting? According to Landau, the Torah informs us that hunting
is potentially lethal. It is permissible to put oneself in danger for one's
livelihood. But the Torah forbids us from unnecessarily putting ourselves
in danger—and that would be precisely what our gamesman would be
doing. Hence, sport hunting is forbidden.[5] Note, the prohibition derives
from protecting the hunter, not the hunted. Note, as well, that the

---

4   Manfred Gerstenfeld cites this source in his *Judaism, Environmentalism and the
    Environment* (Jerusalem: Jerusalem Institute for Israel Studies, 1998), 116.
5   Noda b'Yehuda, Mehadura Tnina, YD 10.

method used to prohibit sport hunting required our adjudicator to rely on a rather forced reading of an aggadic passage. In one hand, Landau holds the halakhic branch of the divining rod that says Aggadah is not a factor in finding Torah; while in the other hand, Landau holds the aggadic branch that leads him towards what he understands to be God's will, that is, Torah. The halakhic challenge of modernity is about who holds the divining rod, and how she grips it.

There is one additional element in Landau's responsum that bears mention. In the previous chapter, we saw how economic realities influenced Halakhah. In our responsum, Landau reasons that since hunting is inherently dangerous, professional hunters should not face additional competition for game from sportsmen who hunt merely for "pleasure." Any such competition would increase the time spent in the forest, and therefore the danger, the professional hunter confronts. Landau cites a Talmudic explanation for why people might choose dangerous professions and elevates the explanation to a broad principle that he then applies to the case before him (Baba Metzia 112a citing Deuteronomy 24:15).

Although Landau opposed many of the innovations of the maskilim in Berlin, particularly in the realm of secular education, he shared some of their concerns. On the issue of customs, in distinction to Halakhah proper, Landau saw room for leniency. Daniel Sinclair points out that Landau's approach to Halakhah, in which "only statements in the Talmud and its cognate literature are absolutely binding in halakhic terms," allows him to dismiss certain customs that he finds counterproductive or onerous.[6] But when a student of Landau, Aaron Chorin (1766–1844), became a proponent of religious reform in Hungary and espoused his teacher's views on customs, the traditionalists circled the wagons.[7] Moshe Sofer (1762–1839) was their leader, and as sometimes happens, his followers recalled his rhetoric more than his deeds.

As the founding father of Hungarian ultra-Orthodoxy, Sofer's battle cry was: "The Torah prohibits all innovation!" But, as Sinclair points out, Sofer simply concealed his own innovations, at least those that applied to halakhic methodology. In a private letter, Sofer showed his hand:

---

6   Daniel Sinclair, "Halakhic Methodology in the Post-Emancipation Period: Case Studies in the Responsa of R. Yechezkel Landau," *Leẽla* (1998): 16.
7   Ibid.: 18, and Meyer, *Response to Modernity*, 51.

In any case, in the present era, the normative status of a prohibition [whether it is deemed to be of biblical or Rabbinic origin] must not be allowed to have any effect on its binding nature, and it is good to augment prohibitions. . . . This view should not be revealed to the public because, due to our many sins, many of our coreligionists now claim to be bound solely by biblical law, and they ignore Rabbinic norms, which, they argue, do not emanate from a divine source.[8]

"It is good to augment prohibitions." In practice, that meant promoting rabbinic law to biblical status *and* enshrining custom as halakhah. Sofer was quite explicit that the response to Reform Judaism should be to add stringencies since sick patients, that is, our generation, need more medicine, that is, halakhic stringencies.[9] In his ethical will, Sofer charges his children to remain whole Jews. The Hebrew word for *whole, shalem*, is an acronym for *sh'mot* (names), *lashon* (language), and *malbush* (attire), three reasons why the rabbis tell us Jews in Egypt were redeemed. With his dying wish, Sofer transforms these cultural markers into religious requirements. Needless to say, Moshe Rabbeynu didn't speak Yiddish or wear a black hat. Indeed, according to the experts, even the name *Moshe* was not originally Hebrew—it was Egyptian.[10] Yet, for Sofer's followers, to be a whole Jew required the perpetuation of their contingent circumstances.

As fierce an opponent of Reform Judaism as he was, Sofer's own halakhic decisions were anything but reactionary. Joel Roth cites a responsum of Sofer dealing with a husband who had travelled overseas and went missing. Sofer cites the two relevant principles that he extrapolated from the Talmudic discussion of such a case and renders them both inoperative.[11] The Talmud had been concerned that the husband might be unable to contact his wife and let her know he was alive. Sofer dismisses this

---

8 Cited in Maharatz Chajes, Darkhei Hahoraa; Daniel Sinclair, "Normative Transparency in Jewish Law: Maimonides, R. Moses Sofer and R. Kook," *Jewish Law Annual* 19 (2011): 131.

9 Michael Silber, "The Emergence of Ultra-Orthodoxy: The Invention of a Tradition," in *The Uses Of Tradition: Jewish Continuity in the Modern Era*, ed. Jack Wertheimer (New York: Jewish Theological Seminary of America, 1992), 48.

10 Friedman, *The Exodus*, 32.

11 *Responsa of Hatam Sofer*, Even Ha-Ezer, pt. 1, no. 58. Cited in Joel Roth, *The Halakhic Process: A Systemic Analysis* (New York: Jewish Theological Seminary of America, 1986), 261–62.

concern because of the presence of postal services and newspapers. The second issue was whether he would *want* to contact his wife. Remarkably, Sofer only considers the possibility that the husband had been injured and too embarrassed to contact his wife. Sofer applies the halakhic principle that "times have changed," and, in our times, his injuries would no longer be a cause for shame. Shockingly, given the Talmud's obsession with the recalcitrant husband's refusal to give his wife a *get*, Sofer never addresses the possibility that the Jewish husband abandoned his wife while overseas. In order to protect the wife and allow her to remarry, Sofer not only incorporates technological advances like newspapers, but acknowledges, sincerely or not, that *what was once shameful is no longer*. Sadly, the idea that a woman's leadership role in synagogue ritual, which had also once been a source of embarrassment for men by suggesting their ritual incompetency, seems to remain a source of embarrassment for his community even today.

In the middle of the nineteenth century, in the middle of Europe, a new machine was invented that would forever change the way Jews think of matza: the matza-making machine. This newfangled piece of technology made matza square and uniform rather than circular and idiosyncratic. It did not take long for the question to reach the rabbinic authorities as to whether this soulless machine could be used to create the object of a mitzvah. Rabbi Solomon Kluger (1763–1869), a prominent decisor in the Austro-Hungarian Empire, rejected machine-made matza for a reason related to that given by Landau in his response to sport hunting. Rabbi Kluger discusses the relevant precedents from the Talmud through the codes.[12] Given that there could be no direct precedent prior to the invention of the machine in 1857, Kluger offers analogies from the Talmud. He prefaces the analogies relating to the specific case at hand with a seemingly unrelated case that establishes a foundation for his subsequent deliberations. In the Talmud's discussion of Purim, there is a prohibition against reading the Megillah on Shabbat. The gemara explains the prohibition because the indigent look forward to the reading of the Megillah because of the mitzvah to thereafter distribute gifts to the poor (Esther 10:22). Since the gift giving could not occur on Shabbat, the

---

12 David Ellenson, "Jewish Legal Interpretation: Literary, Scriptural, Social, and Ethical Perspectives," *Semeia* 34 (1985): 98–100.

reading of the megillah on that day was prohibited so as not to dispirit and deprive the indigent. Kluger's passionate language is worth citing: "Behold, the reason for the prohibition against this appears first and foremost to be that it is not within the realm of the upright and the ethical to plunder the poor who anxiously await this [task]. For from the assistance they provide [in the baking of] *matzot*, they earn a significant income for the many Passover expenses which accrue to our people."[13] David Ellenson, who cites this responsum in his discussion of Jewish legal interpretation, offers this analysis.

> It is crucial to note that Kluger grounds his moral objection to the use of a machine for the production of Passover *matzot* in a text taken from the Babylonian Talmud (i.e., Megillah 4b). This is significant for several reasons. First, it indicates that the Talmud itself, the source of Jewish law, embodies moral concerns and makes them, in legal parlance, "actionable." Secondly, it reveals that such concerns are taken up by the Tradition and may be employed by later authorities as legitimate considerations in rendering a contemporary decision.[14]

Technological advances accelerated throughout the nineteenth century, as did the consequences of the Jewish enlightenment and emancipation. On each side of the turn of the twentieth century, halakhic codes were published explicitly geared toward the average Jew whose level of Jewish learning was, well, average.[15] The earlier of the codes, the Arukh Hashulchan, was written in Russia by Rabbi Yechiel Mechel Halevi Epstein (1829–1908). The latter code, the Mishnah Brurah, was authored by Rabbi Israel Kagan (1838–1933) and had far greater influence on twentieth-century halakhic developments. Perhaps the greatest

---

13 Translated by Ellenson, with slight modifications. Ellenson, "Jewish Legal Interpretation": 109.

14 Ibid.: 106. Ellenson suggests that the value which Kluger cited was, crucially, explicit within the Talmud. But, as we saw with Landau's citation of medieval, biblical exegesis, halakhic decisors avail themselves of strictly aggadic sources, as well.

15 Benjamin Brown, "'Soft Stringency' in the Mishnah Brurah: Jurisprudential, Social and Ideological Aspects of a Halakhic Formulation," *Contemporary Jewry* 27, no. 1 (2007): 13.

difference between the two halakhists was that Epstein was a community rabbi living among the people, while Kagan was an ivory tower scholar.[16]

According to Simcha Fishbane, "The majority of nineteenth-century European rabbis felt that stringency and thus stronger boundaries was the solution to guard the observant Jew from the dangers of modernity."[17] Epstein was an exception. He maintained that Halakhah was a process open to change and adaptation. He was relatively lenient, particularly about new discoveries. For instance, Epstein discusses a new method of kindling Channukah lights—paraffin candles. He sees that they enhance the mitzvah of "publicizing the miracle" (Arukh Hashulchan, O. H. 673:1). The Mishnah Brurah, on the hand, does not even mention the possibility of using anything other than oil in the Channukiah.[18]

Another issue in which we see a clear difference between the two codes involves hair coverings for married women. Fishbane points out that Epstein was no crusading feminist, yet he realized that the Talmudic claim that a woman's uncovered hair is provocative (Brachot 24a) has been neutralized by changes in women's fashion.[19] Epstein decries the recalcitrant immodesty of "women these days," but he acknowledges the reality and the consequences thereof. Kagan, once again, ignores the reality altogether. For Kagan, there was only the black and white law. For Epstein, the text was colored by reality.[20]

One final issue of technology that continues to be a dividing line between Orthodox and Conservative Halakhah involves the use of electricity on Shabbat and holidays. In 1903, Rabbi Epstein, using standard halakhic reasoning, ruled that it was permissible.[21] Although Epstein's position was not relied upon, neither was it forgotten. Nearly fifty years later, Rabbi Shlomo Zalman Auerbach (1910–1995) wrote about his

---

16 Simcha Fishbane, *The Boldness of a Halakhist: An Analysis of the Writings of Rabbi Yechiel Mechel Halevi Epstein's "The Arukh Hashulhan"* (Boston: Academic Studies Press, 2008), 20, 53.

17 Simcha Fishbane, "A Response to the Challenge of the Modern Era as Reflected in the Writings of Rabbi Yechiel Mechel Epstein," in *Essays in the Social Scientific Study of Judaism and Jewish Society*, ed. Simcha Fishbane and Stuart Schoenfeld, with Alain Goldschläger (Hoboken: Ktav Publishing House, 1992), 96.

18 Ibid., 101.

19 Arukh Hashulchan, O. H. 75:7. Fishbane, *Boldness*, 22.

20 Ibid., 52.

21 Ibid., 24.

mother's battery operated hearing aid. In order to preserve battery life and silence unwanted white noise, the hearing aid needed to be turned on and off. Rabbi Auerbach permitted it and convinced a number of his Jerusalem colleagues that such button pressing on Shabbat and holidays was not a violation of Halakhah.[22] The halakhic argumentation used by Epstein and Auerbach was parallel.

Although the Mishnah Brurah was relatively more stringent than the Arukh Hashulchan, Kagan did offer something to his readers that symbolized this new age: choice. One of the characteristics of the Mishnah Brurah is that multiple acceptable positions are given "to enable the commoners to rule for themselves."[23] In a fascinating article, Benjamin Brown recognizes this strategy as a concession to the individualism of the day.[24] When laying out the options, Kagan offers the acceptable minimum and the ideal maximum, and he encourages the latter. Brown also shows how Kagan utilized this strategy of "soft stringency" to an unprecedented degree in halakhic literature. In a sense, Brown argues, the soft stringency recognizes the aspirational element in Halakhah and brings it to the fore.[25]

As we have seen repeatedly in this book, what began life as a pious individual's stringency grew up to become a communal norm. Kagan's experiment in individual choice was no exception. "The language of soft stringency that is found in the Mishnah Brurah and other works has come to be taken almost as a hard stringency. What was once only a suggested behavior has been taken increasingly to represent an obligatory normative standard."[26]

Moshe Sofer remains identified with his polemical slogan: innovation is forbidden by the Torah. His great-grandson, however, offers a counterbalancing *cri de coeur*. Moshe Shmuel Glasner (1856–1924) wrote that the Torah was given to the Israelites "to constantly improve

---

22 Ariel Picard, "Meta-Halakhic Considerations in Relationship to the Use of Technology on Shabbat," in *Halakhah, Meta-Halakhah, and Philosophy*, ed Avinoam Rosenak (Jerusalem: Magnes Press, 2011), 128.
23 Brown, "Soft Stringency": 16
24 Ibid.:14.
25 Ibid.: 11.
26 Ibid.: 25.

and perfect it."[27] Glasner's philosophy of Halakhah recognizes that contemporary sages have the power to "adapt the Halakhah to contemporary circumstances. This adaptability was sanctioned by the Written Torah (Deuteronomy 17:9–12), which gave the judges of each generation unlimited discretion to overturn the halakhic decisions of earlier judges. It was to preserve this adaptability that writing down the Oral Torah had originally been forbidden."[28]

In addition to his contribution on the level of philosophy of Halakhah, Rabbi Glasner also makes explicit a principle of the Halakhah that returns us to our nominalism/realism dispute from the Torah. The priestly Torah demands separation. One of the instances of separation is the requirement to not wear clothing made of wool and linen (Leviticus 19:19). The Talmud asks what should happen if one discovers, while one is out and about, that his garment is made from biblically forbidden materials. He should strip immediately upon becoming cognizant that he is transgressing this biblical prohibition (Brachot 19b). After all, in the priestly Torah, his conscious violation of Torah law is punishable by death to counteract the negative cosmic consequences of his ontological onslaught on creation.[29] Given the logic of this archaic metaphysics, it should come as no surprise that the Shulchan Arukh demands that someone who discovers someone else wearing the forbidden mixture must "jump him and tear it off immediately" (Y. D. 303:1).

Daniel Sinclair cites Glasner's response to such a situation as an example of natural law in modern halakhah. Glasner writes: "Parading naked in public is a worse offense than breaking the biblical prohibition . . . since it is an offense accepted as such by all rational people, and anyone who commits it is no longer in the category of those who are created in the image of God."[30] Glasner uses RaMBaM's identification of the divine image with

---

27 Introduction, Sefer Dor Revi'i. Cited in *Jewish Legal Theories: Writings on State, Religion, and Morality*, ed. Leora Batnitzky and Yonatan Y. Brafman (Waltham: Brandeis University Press, 2018), 120.

28 David Glasner, "Rabbi Moshe Shmuel Glasner, The *Dor Revi'i*," *Tradition* 32, no. 1 (1998): 45.

29 Death might be at the hands of a human court or by God (*karet*). Sannhedrin 10a acknowledges that the rabbinic punishment of lashes is an expression of divine mercy for what otherwise would have warranted a death penalty.

30 Translated in Daniel Sinclair, "Feticide, Cannibalism, Nudity and Extra Legal Sanctions: Elements of Natural Law in Three 19th 20th Century Halakhists,"

rationality (*Guide*, 1:7). He then says that rationality trumps Torah law. In our categories, Glasner has implied that since the ontological "laws" of halakhic realism are not amenable to rational critique, when they conflict with common morality, they should be nullified. After all, the Talmud insists that Jews are not permitted to do anything—like parading around naked—that gentiles forbid for themselves (Sannhedrin 59a). When we introduced the Mosaic Torah, we suggested that its philosophy of halakhic nominalism was akin to natural law. Sinclair looks to natural law to resolve "tension between halakhah and universal, rational norms."[31] My suggestion is more radical in that it goes to the root of the problem, which is not irrational laws, but the irrational metaphysics of halakhic realism that instantiates and perpetuates laws that are sometimes immoral.

The process of upgrading prohibitions and increasing stringencies has only intensified in the time since Sofer died. Akiva Schlesinger (1838–1922), a later leader of Hungarian ultra-Orthodoxy, wrote that "every rule in the Shulchan Arukh is equal to the Ten Commandments; and every Jewish custom is equal to the Ten Commandments!"[32] Haym Soloveitchik charts how this process was a response not only to specific reforms but to the phenomenon of political emancipation in general. Soloveitchik makes the point that the protection of Jewish identity fell exclusively to halakhic norms. Until emancipation, Christian antisemitism collaborated with the Halakhah in shielding Jews from gentile influence. When the ghetto walls came tumbling down, Jews could take advantage of new opportunities only to the degree that they acculturated into gentile society. Thus, Halakhah became the sole sociological mechanism to erect and fortify barriers to entry.[33]

The Shulchan Arukh, although a code, is far from univocal. Multiple opinions are sometimes cited by Caro, and then Isserles' additions provide even more options. Frequently, the citation of halakhic texts is complemented by descriptions of communal practice. This mix of textual traditions and communal customs, historically characteristic of codes,

---

Jewish Law Association Studies 20 (2010): 284. See Sinclair's analysis on pages 293–96.

31 Sinclair, "Feticide": 301.

32 Yad Ivri, at the end of Lev Ha-Ivri, vol. 2, fol. 846n23; cited in Silber, "Emergence of Ultra-Orthodoxy," 49.

33 Soloveitchik, "Rupture": 77.

breaks down at the turn of the twentieth century. The Mishnah Brurah marginalizes custom and promotes the halakhic textual tradition to an unprecedented degree.[34] Soloveitchik shows how this trend towards text culture was further exacerbated by the trauma of the Holocaust and the rise of intermarriage in the United States.[35] For our present purposes, I want to focus on the strategy used by the ultra-Orthodox in their halakhic process. It seems they also have their hands on both the halakhic and aggadic branches of the divining rod.

> The Halakhah was often too flexible or ambiguous, at times silent, or worse yet, embarrassingly lenient, which is the reason why the center, while not above harboring a certain sympathy for ultra-Orthodoxy's utopian ends, could not bring itself to legitimize the latter often "unorthodox" means. But if the Halakhah strictly defined did not easily lend itself to the extreme formulations of the ultra-Orthodox, there was no denying that there were traditions in Judaism which did. In the vast storehouse of aphorisms, legends, parables, homilies, scriptural exegesis, moral teachings, and the like which made up the aggadic material of the Talmud, the Midrash, and the Kabbalah, there was no lack of such strongly worded statements. . . . Their tactic was to expand the halakhic process by tapping into the Midrash, Aggadah, Jerusalem Talmud, and Kabbalah.[36]

Michael Silber emphasizes the degree to which the ultra-Orthodox circumvented standard halakhic procedures in their effort to extend the Halakhah.[37] Brown, in a slightly different context, points out that these responses to modernity were also present in traditional Judaism.[38] Motivations will change, as will hermeneutics, but there has never been strict and consistent compartmentalization of Halakhah and Aggadah. Landau claimed there was, but his own decisions undermined those claims. Most Orthodox halakhists might want to resist the explicit incorporation of Aggadah into a halakhic context, but such a restriction would be both innovative and hypocritical.

---

34 Ibid.: 67.
35 Ibid.: 78–82.
36 Silber, "Emergence of Ultra-Orthodoxy," 59–60.
37 Ibid., 61
38 Benjamin Brown, "The Gaon of Vilna, the Hatam Sofer, and the Hazon Ish: Minhag and the Crisis of Modernity," *Hakira* 24 (2018): 156.

In the analyses above, Hungarian ultra-Orthodoxy, represented by Moshe Sofer and Akiva Schlesinger, emphasized the importance of custom. Lithuanian Jewry, described by Soloveitchik, emphasized text culture at the expense of custom. These were two different strategies from two distinct communities. "If for the Litvaks the books and the rabbis were the bedrock of tradition, for the Hungarian and the hasidim it was the home and the community that served this function."[39] Although the Hasidic masters produced relatively few halakhic works, and each Hasidic rebbe had his own idiosyncrasies, several of the rebbes adumbrated a philosophy of Halakhah that is essential for a compelling Judaism.

While Israel Ba'al Shem Tov is considered to be the founding father of Hasidism, Dov Baer Friedman (1704–1772), known as the Maggid of Mezhirech, was largely responsible for spreading the message and ethos of the movement. He left no written work, but his teachings were collected by his disciples and first published in 1780. In this collection, the Maggid explores the reason that there are contradictory positions within the Oral Torah. Maoz Kahana and Ariel Mayse recently analyzed one of the Maggid's sermons which deals with the Talmudic description of the disputes between Beit Hillel and Beit Shammai: "These and those are the living words of God" (Eruvin 13b). The Maggid's sermon is written in "Kabbalese," but from what I understand, in part due to Kahana and Mayse's analysis, the text of the written Torah is protean. In this, there is much rabbinic aggadah that anticipates such a view of the Torah. In my own work on Torah commentary, I refer to this quality of the Torah as *pluripotence*, the power and capacity to take any of many meanings.[40] According to the Maggid, "Each person draws forth from *da'at*, combining the words in this way or that. This one draws love from *da'at* . . . and another draws awe."[41]

In the sefirotic realm, from the sefirah of *da'at* emerge the seven lower s'firot. *Da'at* is mind or awareness. If the halakhic decisor draws down the Torah of *da'at*, of our awareness of the divine mind as embodied in the written Torah, along the left side of the sefirot, the Torah is

---

39   Ibid.: 152.
40   Cherry, *Torah through Time*, 14.
41   Dov Baer of Mezhirech, Magid devarav le-Ya'akov, nos. 58, 86–87; cited in Maoz Kahana and Ariel Mayse, "Hasidic Halakhah: Reappraising the Interface of Spirit and Law," *Association of Jewish Studies Review* 41, no. 2 (2017): 398.

filtered through the attributes of awe and strict justice. If another decisor, or the same decisor at a different time, draws down the Torah through the right side, the Torah is cooled through pools of love and compassion. In this way, both decisions, *even if contradictory*, are the living words of God. Those decisions, which are oral Torah, are both true within the sefirah of *da'at*. Their opposition or antagonism only manifests in our world of action. Perhaps the Maggid is suggesting that the rabbinic method of *drash*, or recontextualizing the written Torah, can offer *us* an equally divine and equally valid expression of oral Torah for our world.[42] In the conclusion, I will *drash* the biblical prohibition on male anal intercourse that may well be an example of what the Maggid is describing.

One of the most radical of all Hasidic masters is Mordechai Joseph Leiner of Ishbitza (1802–1854). The Ishbitzer, as he was known, understood that the prohibition against making molten images included the miztvot. God forbid that the living word of God should become fossilized from our unwillingness, our meekness, to translate God's will anew. The mitzvot are not to be worshipped—that is idolatry. The mitzvot are the means by which we express our worship of God. In the following teaching of the Ishbitzer, he claims that some of the Torah's mitzvot come with an explicit expiration date precisely so we don't confuse the means for the end.

The Ishbitzer is commenting on a case we have previously considered. Five orphaned daughters have no brothers to take possession of their father's property once the Israelites conquer Canaan. "Let not our father's name be lost to his clan just because he had no son. Give us a holding among our father's kinsmen!" (Numbers 27:4). Moshe consults with God, and the law is amended. But with the amendment came an unintended consequence that caused the elders of tribe to complain to Moshe. The amendment was amended, and the curtain drops on the book of Numbers (Numbers 36). Now, the Ishbitzer:

> The whole point is to understand, at every moment, the will of God in the words of the Torah, knowing His will at all times, within the context of that particular time. Thus, light emanates from the words of Torah to the hearts of Israel in order for them to understand the depth of the will

42 Ariel Evan Mayse, "The Ever-Changing Path: Visions of Legal Diversity in Hasidic Literature," *Conversations* 23 (2015): 92.

of God, according to the time. Therefore, this section was written after the completion of the entire Torah, in order to let Israel understand that details emerge from the Torah at all times, at each moment. The words of the Torah are words of advice to let human beings understand what the blessed God wants of us now, and to do it. Therefore, this section was written (at the end), for it too is active only for a specific time.[43]

On a literary level, the Ishbitzer is explaining why the book of Numbers seems to end on such a prosaic note. Moreover, since the next and final book of the Pentateuch, Deuteronomy, is largely a repetition of the prior narrative, in a sense the book of Numbers is the finale to the entire Torah. Yet, the conclusion seems neither climactic nor dramatic. But here the Ishbitzer shifts from the literary to the theological and halakhic. The Torah plays its quiet crescendo with an amendment to an amendment that itself sunsets upon the Israelites' entrance to the Land of Israel (b. Baba Batra 120a). The Ishbitzer is pointing out the laws of allocating property to the tribes as they enter the Land of Israel are only applicable at the moment they enter Israel for the first time. Why, then, do *we* need to know about it? We will never enter the Land of Israel for the first time again. The Ishbitzer claims that the story was written as an example of how Halakhah should be pursued. There could be no clearer illustration that laws, even Torah laws, are historically contingent. *The whole point of the Torah* is to understand God's will in each particular time and place. For the Ishbitzer, that message is the Torah's climactic crescendo.

The image of light emanating from the words of Torah has a history. There is a midrash which pictures God lamenting the Israelites who have abandoned Him and His Torah. Better that they would have abandoned Me, cries God, but kept My Torah. Why? Because by engaging in mitzvot, *the light in the Torah* would return these wayward Jews to God.[44] The Ishbitzer may well be drashing this midrash. Light does not always emanate from every word in Torah. For every season, there is a light.[45] It

---

43   Mei HaShiloach, Masei. See also my analysis in *Torah through Time*, 182–83.

44   Psikta de-Rav Kahana 15:5 on Jeremiah 16:11.

45   Arthur Green translated and commented upon a homily from Rabbi Ze'ev Wolf of Zhitomir who seems to emphasize the role of the tzaddik more so than does the Ishbitzer. Or Ha'Meir 2:25a, cited in Arthur Green, "Hasidism and its Response to Change" *Jewish History* 27, no. 2/4 (2013): 331.

is through engaging in the mitzvot that we are graced with the perception to discern the divine will from the words of Torah that set our hearts aglow.

"The whole point is to understand, at every moment, the will of God in the words of the Torah, knowing His will at all times, within the context of that particular time." Arthur Green points out this theory of each generation being encouraged to reinterpret or change halakhic practice is far more radical than anything that actually happened.[46] (The most serious violation of Halakhah committed by the Hasidim was running late for prayer.) It is unlikely that the Ishbitzer would have written such words had he known Zecharias Frankel (1801–1875) was articulating a very similar philosophy of Halakhah fewer than 300 miles to the west in Breslau. Frankel was a reformer of Judaism, the likes of which I assume the Ishbitzer was blissfully unaware.[47] That ignorance allowed him to express his philosophy of Halakhah without fear that he would be perceived as betraying the tradition and giving succor to the enemy.

Our final European thinker, while not technically Hasidic, is a mystic. In each of our sections, we have engaged the thought of Rabbi Avraham Isaac Kook (1865–1935). There is both an irony and a lesson when it comes to Kook and Halakhah. Within the most traditional enclaves of modern Judaism, there is often an inverse relationship between how radical is the halakhic rhetoric and how tame are the halakhic decisions and practice. Unlike Moshe Sofer, for example, Rav Kook championed the ethos and language of novelty.

> The life of the Jewish people, which is constantly being renewed in the Land of Israel, causes us to renew and exalt our thought processes and our logic. The specific form of this novelty must be felt in all disciplines— in halakhah and in aggadah, in all areas of science and ethics, in our conception of life, and in our *hashkafah*[worldview].[48]

---

46 Green, "Hasidism and its Response to Change": 330–34 and Arthur Green, et. al., *Speaking Torah: Spiritual Teachings from around the Maggid's Table* (Woodstock: Jewish Lights Publishing, 2013), vol. 1, 49.

47 Shaul Magid, *Hasidism on the Margin: Reconciliation, Antinomianism, and Messianism in Izbica and Radzin Hasidism* (Madison: University of Wisconsin Press, 2003), xxii.

48 "Ne'edar ba-Kodesh," in Ma'amrei ha-Re'ayah, 413. Cited and translated, with modifications, in Norman Lamm, "Harmony, Novelty, and the Sacred in the Teachings of Rav Kook," in Kaplan, *Rabbi Abraham Isaack Kook*, 165.

Although Rav Kook's poetic rhetoric is radically progressive, his halakhic decisions were consistently conservative. A halakhic innovator he was not. He ruled against milking cows on Shabbat; against voting rights for women in the Land of Israel; against drinking wine touched by a Jew who does not observe the halakhah of Shabbat; and he ruled that autopsies performed to further medical knowledge may only be carried out on non-Jews. The most well-known permissive ruling associated with Rav Kook involved the *shemittah*, the cessation of agricultural work in the Land of Israel every seven years. Rav Kook did endorse a legal fiction that allowed the early Zionist pioneers to continue their agricultural efforts, but he was anxious to acknowledge that he was no pioneer: "I was not the first one to rule permissively."[49]

Nevertheless, his philosophy of Halakhah, as opposed to his actual decisions, offers us three elements to incorporate into our own coherent model. The first element involves what Daniel Sinclair calls "normative transparency." Sinclair credits RaMBaM, the father of philosophical esotericism, with the demand for transparency when identifying a law as either biblical or rabbinic.[50] Moshe Sofer, as we saw above, disagreed with the tactic in his own writings. Rav Kook expressed sympathy for Sofer's position and motivation in combatting Reform Judaism, but Rav Kook insisted that such a strategy is no longer effective. These days, Kook claims, nonobservant Jews do not ignore Halakhah due to any given halakhah's status within the traditional hierarchy.

In addition to transparency, Rav Kook demands loosening the yoke of halakhah.

> Moreover, it is clear to me that as far as the present generation is concerned, it is important to demonstrate complete transparency in our halakhic rulings. We should permit everything that is permissible from a halakhic standpoint so that it will be understood that what we do is dictated solely by halakhic norms and nothing else. . . . If it emerges that there are practices which are halakhically permissible, but the rabbis do

---

49 *Letters*, 1:334. Cited in Michael Z. Nehorai, "Halakhah, Metahalakhah, and the Redemption of Israel: Reflections on the Rabbinic Rulings of Rav Kook," in Kaplan, *Rabbi Abraham Isaack Kook*, 128. The list of stringent rulings is taken from the same article.

50 M. T., h. Rebels 2:9. Cited in Sinclair, "Normative Transparency": 120–21.

not permit them . . . this is the greatest disservice that we can do to the halakhic cause.[51]

In addition to Rav Kook's advocacy of transparency and loosening the yoke of Halakhah, there is another mystical component of his halakhic thought that continues a thread from what we have seen above with certain Hasidic masters. James Diamond recently discussed Rav Kook's commentary on the first section of RaMBaM's legal code. RaMBaM believed that truth was objective and unitary. To the degree that humans obtained knowledge, they were activating their intellectual soul. The prophet, for RaMBaM, had attained a high degree of intellectual and imaginative perfection such that he was able to translate objective truth into words readily understood by the masses.

Rav Kook, on the other hand, expands on the mystical and Hasidic image that each of us has a unique contribution to understanding the totality of the divine. The twelve Torahs that were copied from the original Torah in the Ark of the Covenant, for example, varied according to the characteristics of each tribe. "Rather than each Torah being an exact replica of the master copy residing in the Ark, conforming to Maimonides' notion of one absolute truth, Rav Kook perceives truth in subjectivity, as the copies tailored to accommodate the respective spirits of each tribe indicate."[52] Diamond's distinction between the two thinkers' metaphysics points toward a qualified pluralism that may be useful toward denominational détente and interreligious respect. "For Maimonides, the prophet must adopt the language of the many to *teach* the truth of the One, while for Rav Kook the language of the many *is* in fact the truth of the One."[53]

The Non-Ashkenazi Sample

Until quite recently, Jewish Studies in North America has largely neglected the Sephardic and Mizrachi experience. Since the vast majority of American Jews are of European descent, there was Eurocentric bias

---

51 Kook, Orah Mishpat 119. Cited in both Sinclair, "Normative Transparency": 140 and Nehorai, "Halakhah," 131.
52 James A. Diamond, "A Kabbalistic Reinvention of Maimonides' Legal Code: R. Abraham Isaac Kook's Commentary on Sefer Hamada," *Jewish Studies Internet Journal* 11 (2012): 11, citing Kook, Orot Ha-RaMBaM, 163.
53 Diamond, "Kabbalistic Reinvention": 32.

to our scholarship. After the Spanish exile in 1492, there was Josef Karo's Shulchan Arukh, some mystics in Tzfat who wore white for Shabbat, and then the Sephardic stage went dark until the Jews of the Arab countries, who are largely Mizrachi, were expelled by their host nations and went to an Israel founded by Ashkenazi Jews.

Fortunately, the non-Ashkenazi experience is now being shared widely by both novelists and historians. In our case, the history and philosophy of Halakhah within the Sephardic and Mizrachi world is so interesting because of its contrasts to the European experience which grappled with emancipation and the enlightenment. The Jews of North Africa and the Middle East were aware of European developments, and the more cosmopolitan, urban Jews were certainly influenced by European fashions. But that influence never translated into an ideological program for the reform of Judaism. Thus, the Sephardic and Mizrachi samples demonstrate a less self-conscious response to modernity than we see with the European traditionalists.

The Shulchan Arukh became the preeminent halakhic work very quickly in the Sephardic world. Yet, there was never an assumption that any work of Halakhah could be authoritative for all future cases. The greatest Sephardic halakhist of the eighteenth century was Hayyim Yosef David Azulai, known by his acronym, HIDA. The HIDA (1724–1806) was born in Jerusalem, eventually settled in Livorno, Italy, and wrote additions to the Shulchan Arukh as well as responsa. The HIDA traveled extensively and believed a halakhist had to be widely educated beyond Jewish texts. He understood that contemporary halakhic practice "depends on the incremental, organic growth and development of Halakhah throughout its entire history. Thus, study of post-Shulchan Arukh halakhic masters was, to him, of greater significance than the creation of error-free Talmudic manuscripts."[54] The Vilna Gaon (1720–1797) considered only Talmudic sources to be halakhically binding, thus error-free Talmudic manuscripts were crucial. As we will see, Sephardic jurisprudence developed in ways that vitiated the force of the Shulchan Arukh, the Talmud, and even the Torah.

---

54 Zohar, "Sephardic Jurisprudence": 179. See also Zvi Zohar, *Rabbinic Creativity in the Modern Middle East* (London: Bloomsbury Academic, 2013), 69–74.

Rabbi Yosef Hayyim (1835–1909) was a leading halakhist and kabbalist in Baghdad. He concurred with the HIDA that it is imperative for a decisor to consider the entire span of previous decisions prior to arriving as a conclusion. Just because a later author might not have the same stature as an earlier halakhic master, the later author may have considered something that escaped the earlier master's attention. Moreover, this was the rationale in the Talmud when senior scholars would invite challenges from their students.[55] Rabbi Hayyim offers another reason to peruse the gamut of halakhic reasoning on a topic before issuing a decision. Particularly when a decision breaks new ground, the support of an earlier minority opinion is valuable. The support of an earlier sage marks the difference between singing solo and having a backup vocalist.[56]

Rabbi Raphael Aharon Ben Shimon was the chief judge of Egypt from 1891–1921. As a result of British colonialism, European clothing was regularly imported into Cairo. Zvi Zohar, in his analysis of several rulings dealing with European garb, notes that when Rabbi Ben Shimon was able to defend his community's innovative practice, he felt that it was obligation to do so. Zohar reports the following case: Jewish tailors in Cairo were selling garments in which linen and wool were sewn together. This combination, as we saw above, is biblically prohibited to wear, but not to manufacture or to sell. Jewish tailors asked Rabbi Ben Shimon how they should respond to Jewish customers who wanted to buy these garments. Rabbi Ben Shimon recognizes that what the tailors are doing is not, in and of itself, prohibited. Furthermore, he recognizes that the tailors' livelihood depends on making garments that are in demand. Of course, there is no problem selling these garments to gentiles. As far as Jewish customers are concerned, Rabbi Ben Shimon responds as follows:

> When a Jewish customer comes in [and expresses interest in buying such a garment], he [the tailor] must announce to him that there is *kilayim* [a biblically forbidden mixture] in it. If he [the customer] refrains—very well. And if he does not heed, but rather intentionally decided to wear the *kilayim*, this is what the tailor shall do to save himself from [transgressing] the aforementioned prohibitions: he himself should not dress the Jewish

55 Ibid., 72–73.
56 Ibid., 80. For an interesting example of this technique and the motivation behind its use, see 82–89.

customer in the garment . . . only give it to him to put it on by himself . . .
or he should give it to his non-Jewish servant to dress him in it . . . and
this suffices.[57]

As we saw above, the Shulchan Arukh demands that we rip a garment of *kilayim* off a Jew, even if the result is public nudity. Rabbi Ben
Shimon tells the shop keeper to hand the customer the clothing but to
refrain from helping him put it on. I am in no position to judge that
Rabbi Yosef Caro was wrong, but I do agree with Rabbi Ben Shimon.
There was no entrapment, a legal term for "placing a stumbling block
before the blind" (Leviticus 19:14). Rabbi Ben Shimon insisted that the
tailor explicitly tell the customer that the article of clothing in which he
is interested is forbidden, thus opening the customer's proverbial eyes. At
that point, the customer chooses. If the customer still wants the clothes,
the tailor steps out of the picture and does not facilitate the transgression.

A thought experiment. Imagine a kosher café where both dairy *and*
meat were served. Customers could buy a kosher hamburger but not a
cheeseburger because halakhah prohibits eating milk and meat together.
Could the same café sell the customer a slice of kosher cheese that she
could then place on her hamburger? One may ask why such a customer
would *want* to eat at this café, but that's a different thought experiment. I
will not venture to guess how Rabbi Ben Shimon would decide the case,
but I would be delighted to be the proprietor of such a café. For those
people who wanted to have a kosher meal, such a café would serve them
in a venue that respected different choices. Keeping kosher can enhance
one's relationship to Judaism; but not keeping kosher in a Kosher café can
enhance one's relationship to Jews.

Ideological Responses in Germany

One of the earliest figures of the Haskalah was Isaac Wetzlar (1680?–
1751). His great contribution to the German Jewish enlightenment was to
advocate for a Sephardic curriculum where secular subjects were valued.
He encouraged, for example, the study of philosophy as well as Hebrew
grammar. He also advocated for the education of girls. Aaron Solomon

---

57 Ben Shimon, Nehar Mitzrayyim, 128a, cited and translated in Zohar, *Rabbinic
    Creativity*, 247.

Gumpertz (1723–1769), a physician, promoted the study of natural science.[58] Thus, when Moses Mendelssohn rose to fame in the second half of the eighteenth century, a culture of secular learning was already beginning to take root amongst German Jewry. Mendelssohn, as we discussed in book 1, agreed with Spinoza that Judaism was essentially law, and since the nation of Israel was no longer a legal entity, there was no conflict for German Jews. They could be loyal to both the national laws of Germany and the ritual laws of Judaism. Since only the state has the power of coercion, should a German Jew abrogate traditional Halakhah, the Jewish community no longer wields the power of enforcement or sanction. Mendelssohn's Judaism accommodated both Kant's insistence on individual autonomy and the political liberalism of the nation state. But the price was dear: "Modern individualism undermines, and would even deny and shatter, the inherent link between Jewish persons and the Jewish people."[59]

"Hand in hand with the reformation of Jewish education went the attempt likewise to adapt the worship service to the new requirements of enlightenment and emancipation."[60] The Jewish Consistory of Westphalia was the first to reshape its services beginning in 1808. "The changes and deletions which it ordained had little to do with theology. The principal interest was to bring order and solemnity into the service."[61] They pursued "decorum"—worshippers were asked not to interrupt the rabbi during the sermon or spit on the floor. But, some of the changes were more substantive. Edifying sermons were instituted for Shabbat services, ideally in German rather than Yiddish. The only liturgical changes were for the sake of brevity. Hebrew remained the language of prayer.

"The most radical innovations were the interior arrangements."[62] The reading table, for example, was relocated from the center of the sanctuary to the front so that the rabbi could deliver his edifying sermons from a raised platform. The leaders justified their adaptations with reference to traditional Halakhah. Although some of their reforms were later adopted by Reformers, these pioneers saw themselves as working within

---

58 Sorkin, "The Early Haskalah", in Sorkin, *New Perspectives on the Haskalah*, 15–25.
59 Verbit, "Emancipation", in Fishbane, *Contention, Controversy, and Change*, 313.
60 Meyer, *The Origins of the Modern Jew*, 132.
61 Ibid., 133.
62 Meyer, *Response to Modernity*, 41.

traditional Halakhah to mold their style of service toward that of their Protestant neighbors.[63] It is not unusual for changes on the ground to occur before ideology catches up.[64]

A decade after the Westphalia Consistory rolled out its relatively innocuous adaptations, Temples in Berlin and Hamburg were emboldened to both imitate and further acculturate. Choirs, organs, some prayers in German, others in transliteration with Sephardic pronunciation, special vestments for the rabbi, and confirmation for teenagers were all continuations of an aesthetic overhaul that could be justified halakhically. But, the new nomenclature of *temple* rather than *synagogue* acknowledged that the members were no longer pining to return to the Land of Israel to rebuild *the* Temple in Jerusalem. Charges of dual loyalty were preempted. Similar changes were made to the liturgy. Crucially, no longer does God favor Israel over other nations. "The reformers' God did at one time command animal sacrifices, but He now desires only prayers and sacrifices of the heart. In place of a *Messiah* to lead Israel back to Palestine He will send *redemption* to Israel—and to all mankind."[65]

In 1818, Leopold Zunz sketched out a program for the academic study of postbiblical Judaism. He sought to use the tools of historical scholarship to better understand Jewish literature in its many forms. The following year, Zunz was instrumental in the founding of The Society for the Culture and Science of the Jews. According to a leading scholar of Reform Judaism, Michael Meyer, "From the first, Zunz identified himself with the strivings of the reform group, and though his enthusiasm faltered from time to time, he continued to favor ritual reforms until the rabbinical conferences of the 1840's."[66] Another founding member of the Society was Isaac Marcus Jost who began to publish his multivolume *History of the Israelites* in 1820. The reformers had no better ally than historians.

Samuel Holdheim, a leading rabbi of early Reform Judaism, injects historicism right into the heart of Judaism: "The Talmud speaks out of the consciousness of its age and for that time it *was* right; I speak out

63 David Ellenson, "Emancipation and the Directions of Modern Judaism: The Lessons of Meliz Yosher," *Studia Rosenthaliana* 30, no. 1 (1996): 107.
64 Ibid.: 99–100.
65 Meyer, *The Origins of the Modern Jew*, 136.
66 Ibid., 151.

of the higher consciousness of my age and for this age I *am* right."[67] Abraham Geiger, a fellow Reform rabbi and scholar, extended the project of historical contextualization but with greater sensitivity toward the tradition. Geiger understood the Talmudic rabbis to be role models not because of how they defined Judaism, but by their commitment to redefine Judaism.[68] His academic work included publishing a textbook in 1845 that distinguished the meaning of the Mishnah from its subsequent interpretations by the Gemara. "Even more radically, Geiger separated the Mishnah, in turn, from the still earlier stratum of the Bible. . . . The cumulative effect of Geiger's critical work was thus to historicize and therefore relativize every sacred text of Judaism, biblical no less than rabbinic. Each reflected its age of origin, none stood above its historical milieu, none could serve as unassailable norm."[69]

The rabbinical conferences in 1844 and 1845 resulted in the split between ideologies that would eventually distinguish Reform and Conservative Judaisms. I have hovered over the period from Mendelssohn to Geiger because it represents, to a degree, the source of my own religious sensibilities. This period saw religious reform and academic study in tandem. In part, it was scholarship in the service of religion. As an academic, I ran up against the wall of what I could teach through historical research; so I became a rabbi in order to share what I believe to be true that transcends rational demonstration. As we saw above, Judaism offers several critiques of rationalism, whether it be the divine void of Rebbe Nachman or the transnaturalism of Mordecai Kaplan.

The pioneer of Conservative Halakhah was Zacharias Frankel (1801–1875). He attended the rabbinical conference in 1845 and decided that the reformers' embrace of historicism and retreat from a commitment to Hebrew were too much. Frankel endorsed certain reforms, but only when those changes served a goal. As Elliot Dorff, the Conservative movement's leading legal theorist and decisor, explains it, "Frankel perceives changes in the law *not* as mere compromises with current practice, but as ways to animate the law and renew its divine spirit—that is, to keep

---

67 Cited in Meyer, *Response*, 83. The statement anticipates the ideology of the Ishbitzer we saw above.

68 Arnold Eisen, "Constructing the Usable Past: The Idea of 'Tradition' in Twentieth-Century American Judaism," in Wertheimer, *Uses of Tradition*, 432.

69 Meyer, *Response*, 93.

the law an effective avenue to God and God's values and ideals."[70] It is helpful, even if not entirely accurate, to think of the distinction between Reform and Conservative approaches to tradition as follows: Reform Judaism maintains traditions that serve religiosity; Conservative Judaism rejects traditions that undermine religiosity.

In the previous chapter, we saw that RaMBaM held a position similar to Conservative Judaism. When a specific mitzvah undermines the promotion of compassion, lovingkindness, or peace, it may need to be set aside to protect the purpose of the halakhic system. RaMBaM, we recall, branded as heretics those who enforce a law to the detriment of the legal system's purpose. The Reformers were quick to cite RaMBaM as a precedent for both their thinking and actions.[71] Early Reform ideologues like Samuel Hirsch (1815–1889) and Geiger held that the ceremonial laws were instrumental in achieving halakhic goals. "For Abraham Geiger, there was a creative spirit inherent in Judaism that produced principles and moral ideals of undying authority. However . . . ceremonial laws were tangible ever-evolving representations of the spirit. No single ceremony was enduringly binding."[72] Reform leaders and maskilim, throughout the nineteenth century, considered ethics and the Talmudic process of recontextualizing Judaism for an unprecedented environments to be primary. According to Eliyahu Stern:

> The enlighteners freed the Talmud from the shackles of its own canonicity, internal contradictions, and economically problematic statements. They turned it from a fiat that was eternally binding into a prototype that could be applied in any context and reinterpreted. . . . The Talmud was not the word of law or a sacred scripture but a style and a method; it was a means by which a religious person could evaluate or assess the nature of a particular situation.[73]

70 Elliot N. Dorff, *The Unfolding Tradition: Jewish Law after Sinai* (New York: Aviv Press, 2005), 51.
71 Meyer, "Maimonides": 4-15 and Jay Harris, "The Image of Maimonides in Nineteenth-Century Jewish Historiography," *Proceedings of the American Academy for Jewish Research* 54 (1987): 117-39.
72 David Ellenson, "Antinomianism and Its Responses in the Nineteenth Century," in *The Cambridge Companion to Judaism and Law*, ed. Christine Hayes (New York: Cambridge University Press, 2016), 277.
73 Stern, *Jewish Materialism*, 45

Let me repeat and juxtapose the words of the scholars upon whom I have relied.

The Tosafist enterprise transformed the Talmudic text from a collection of legal and nonlegal traditions into a prescriptive blueprint for Jewish life. . . . Indeed, by the thirteenth century, northern European Jewish scholars (like earlier rabbis of Sefarad [Spain] and Provence) expressed astonishment that Babylonian geonim could have knowingly deviated from Talmudic teachings.[74]

If for the Litvaks the books and the rabbis were the bedrock of tradition, for the Hungarian and the hasidim it was the home and the community that served this function.[75]

The Talmud of the Litvaks was the Talmud of the Tosafot. The maskilim and Reform leaders returned to the Talmud of the Geonim. The aggadic principle which informed how Reform thinkers read the legal traditions was that the entire Torah was given for the sake of peace (Gittin 59b).

Sh'lom bayit, which may narrowly be defined as *peace in the home*, was broadened into the *peace of the homeland*. The mission of Reform Judaism was to serve as a "kingdom of priests" (Exodus 19:6) preaching ethical monotheism to the nations of the world. In 1885, the Pittsburgh Platform of Reform rabbis in the United States stated that only the moral laws were still binding. "[We] maintain only such ceremonies as elevate and sanctify our lives, but reject all such as are not adapted to the views and habits of modern civilization." The final plank of the Pittsburgh Platform anchored the values of the Protestant Social Gospel to the "spirit of Mosaic legislation" and the demands of the Hebrew prophets for "justice and righteousness"—the *sine qua non* for peace.[76]

The destruction of its ancient temple and political institutions became the starting point of a universal and still unfinished task. Hence the events which had evoked mourning for nearly 2,000 years were in fact providential, not a punishment for sin but a necessary condition for universal priestly activity. . . . In substituting the mission of Israel for

---

74 Fishman, *Becoming the People*, 147–48.
75 Brown, "Gaon of Vilna": 152.
76 Plank eight of the Pittsburgh Platform and Jonathan D. Sarna, *American Judaism: A History* (New Haven: Yale University Press, 2004), 150.

the messianic return, the Frankfurt rabbis thus not only universalized messianism and made room for the human role in historical progress; they also asserted that the special vocation of Judaism – to be a priest people among the nations –could be set aside neither by their daughter faith [i.e., Christianity] nor by the national culture with which they themselves identified.[77]

The Pittsburgh Platform, in an attempt to highlight its enlightened approach to religion, accepted both biblical criticism and biological evolution. The latter, as we saw in the previous book, was the biological parallel to religious evolution. The former, which required rejecting the divine dictation model of revelation, undermined the divine authority of the Torah, allowing the Reform leaders the logical leeway to reject rituals that were no longer conducive to their religiosity. If God was not the author of the Torah, the laws therein and therefrom are not authoritative; since humans made the laws, humans can change them.

Frankel represented the reaction against Reform camp form within. As we have seen, his philosophy of Halakhah bore a strong resemblance to that of the Ishbitzer who was not self-consciously opposing the German Reform movement. Frankel's philosophy of Halakhah also had much in common with a traditionalist rabbi who was responding to Reformers and academics, but did so in Hebrew from Ukraine. Nachman Krochmal (1785–1840) titled his book, published posthumously in 1851, *The Guide of the Perplexed for the Time*. Obviously, Krochmal is gesturing toward the RaMBaM's attempt to accommodate Aristotelian philosophy with halakhic Judaism. Krochmal's muse is the philosopher of time and history, Georg Wilhelm Friedrich Hegel. Krochmal wants to explain, in demythologized language unlike the Ishbitzer, how the Oral Torah is still binding on contemporary Jews. Krochmal cites legal theorists who are grappling with the same sorts of questions, except their source material has no claim to divinity. Thus, Krochmal addresses the historicity of Second Isaiah, for example, but never discusses the Pentateuch.[78] Nevertheless, his philosophy of Halakhah stresses the growth of new

---

77 Meyer, *Response*, 247 and 138.
78 Jay M. Harris, *Nachman Krochmal: Guiding the Perplexed of the Modern Age* (New York: New York University Press, 1991), 156–60.

laws in ways that, rhetorically at least, are opposed to other traditionalists contending with maskilim and Reform.

> It is necessary that law be formulated in general principles, in such a way that particular [issues] that will arise in the future, over the course of time, will be covered by those general principles. . . . Here it is neither necessary nor even possible that these methods for how the particulars are to be extrapolated from the general principles that accompanied the law when it was promulgated be set down in writing.[79]

Just as RaMBaM's *Guide* suggested that the tradition relied on esoteric knowledge that could not be written down, so, too, does Krochmal in his *Guide*. It is true there are rules of legal interpretation in the rabbinic tradition, but Krochmal suggests that there are other rules that are not "possible" to write down which enable scholars to extrapolate from precedent. It is through the legal analysis undertaken in previous chapters that we can bring some of the principles to light. As we conclude our discussion of nineteenth-century philosophies of Halakhah, we have seen that decisors inherit both specific content of their ancestors as well as the methods. God forbid we should become imprisoned in the peshat of our ancestors' midrash.

Twentieth-Century German Jewish Halakhic Thought

As we saw in the first book both Martin Buber and Franz Rosenzweig accepted, and devalued, biblical criticism. These thinkers, neither of whom grew up strictly Orthodox, understood Torah not as a source of halakhic authority but as a paradigm for a theology of response. Buber (1878–1965), akin to Alexis de Tocqueville (1805–1859), was a tourist in a partly alien world. As an enlightened tourist, he was able to see and describe aspects of Hasidism that were transferable to western Judaism. Buber was particularly invested in the distinction between religion and religiosity. Today, we might substitute the word *spirituality* for *religiosity*.

> Religiosity is man's sense of wonder and adoration, an ever anew becoming, an ever anew articulation and formulation of his feeling that,

---

79 Nachman Krochmal, trans. Lawrence Kaplan, in Batnitzky, *Jewish Legal Theories*, 61–62.

transcending his conditioned being yet bursting from its very core, there is something that is unconditioned. Religiosity is the longing to establish a living communion with the unconditioned, his will to realize the unconditioned through action, transposing it into the world of man.[80]

This burning of the eternal, internal flame is discontinuous. That is what it means to be unconditioned. It flares anew, *b'chol yom tamid*, every day always, but every day differently. Every day without precedent. For Buber, revelation of the unconditioned must be transposed into the world of action, but today's action is independent of the action that will be actuated by tomorrow's revelation. Indeed, Buber would be suspicious about the continuity.

> Religion is the sum total of the customs and teachings articulated and formulated by the religiosity of a certain epoch in a people's life; its prescriptions and dogmas are rigidly determined and handed down as unalterably binding to all future generations, without regard for their newly developed religiosity, which seeks new forms. . . . Thus religiosity is the creative, religion the organizing, principle.[81]

The ideology of Reform and its emphasis on personal autonomy meshes well with Buber's existentialist theology. The demands of such a religiosity are far more exacting than one finds in the predictable stability of traditional religion. "I do not believe that *revelation* is ever a formulation of law. It is only through man in his self-contradiction that revelation becomes legislation."[82] The issue is that whatever response Ploni had to revelation, that he then transformed into a pious precedent, is not necessarily the same as Almoni's response or even Ploni's response tomorrow. "I cannot accept into the realm of my will the law transformed by man if I am to hold myself ready for the unmediated word of God directed to a specific hour of life."[83] For Buber, inertia is the root of all evil.[84]

In book 1, we juxtaposed the theologies of Buber and Franz Rosenzweig (1886–1929). The relationship between their theologies and philosophies of Halakhah was refined in a series of letters between the

---

80 Buber, "Jewish Religiosity," in Glatzer, *On Judaism*, 80.
81 Ibid.
82 Martin Buber, Letter to Franz Rosenzweig, in Glatzer, *On Jewish Learning*, 111.
83 Ibid., translation slightly modified.
84 Buber, "Jewish Religiosity," in Glatzer, *On Judaism*, 82.

two thinkers from 1922 to 1925.[85] In *The Star of Redemption*, Rosenzweig indicated that "the human being who is beloved of God responds to the divine love of revelation by turning toward the world in redemptive love."[86] The question that then animates Rosenzweig is how to concretize that redemptive love through action. In a letter during this period, Rosenzweig offers both a description and prescription: "Judaism is not law; it creates law."[87] Sixty years later, Robert Cover coined the alliterative term *jurisgenerative* to describe such a phenomenon.[88]

Revelatory power may still inhere in the mitzvot that have been created throughout Jewish history as a response to God's love. The only way to know if Ploni's performance of mitzvah x offers Ploni an intimation of God's love is by doing mitzvah x. For Buber, the religiosity that generated mitzvah x long ago is now a relic of the past. For Rosenzweig, the mitzvah is what Mendes-Flohr calls an "invitation to all Jews in every generation. This invitation is not a guarantee [of revelation] but it points in faith to the mitzvot's revelatory possibility." Thus, Rosenzweig turns towards traditional mitzvot while Buber turns away. An orientation, however, is not an embrace.

Rosenzweig might agree that Halakhah has a claim on the Jew, but not any specific halakhah within the tradition. Rosenzweig manifested a classical Reform response, with an emphasis on divine disclosure, to the mitzvot. According to the Pittsburgh Platform, Reform Jews "maintain only such ceremonies as elevate and sanctify our lives." Rosenzweig's amendment would be that the only way to know which of those ceremonies fulfills that function is by engaging in the ritual. As Rosenzweig wrote in a 1924 letter, "One hears differently when one hears in the doing. . . . Only in the commandment can the voice of He who commands be heard."[89] But if there is silence, what then? If at first you don't succeed, do you try again? If so, or how long?

---

85 Paul Mendes-Flohr, "Law and Sacrament: Ritual Commandments in Twentieth-Century Jewish Thought," in Green, *Jewish Spirituality*, 2:327–29.

86 Pollock, *Franz Rosenzweig*, 214.

87 Franz Rosenzweig, *Briefe*, 425, dated March 27, 1922. Cited in Mendes-Flohr, "Law and Sacrament," in Green, *Jewish Spirituality*, 332.

88 Robert Cover, "Nomos and Narrative," in *Narrative, Violence, and the Law: The Essays of Robert Cover*, ed. Martha Minnow, Michael Ryan, and Austin Sarat (Ann Arbor: University of Michigan Press, 1993), 109.

89 Franz Rosenzweig, "The Commandments," in Glatzer, *On Jewish Learning*, 122.

While in graduate school, I had the blessing of learning with Rabbi David Hartman at the Hebrew University of Jerusalem. He once said, "When I get sick, I want to live next to a Jew who will bring me chicken noodle soup even if he doesn't feel like it." What if Ploni, Rabbi Hartman's neighbor, had visited the sick before and was uncomfortable? Does Rosenzweig's philosophy give him an exemption? Can't Ploni engage in the redemptive love of the neighbor by writing a check to a charity that will do the leg work for him? After a book-length treatment of Rosenzweig's philosophy of Halakhah, Leon Weiner Dow writes: "The problem is that Rosenzweig's view of revelation—an open gate for each person to encounter God—threatens the stability of the halakhic framework."[90] Arnold Eisen, the former Chancellor of the Jewish Theological Seminary of America, noted the novelty of the debate and the persistence of the debate's terms.

> Both Buber and Rosenzweig *shifted the authority of observance from a commanding God to the individual self* who hears the commandment— exactly where it still lies for the vast majority of non-Orthodox Jews. What is more, both thinkers by the time of their debate *presumed that diverse selves would hear and practice differently:* that Jews are driven to (or away from!) observance by various individual and communal motives and inevitably discover manifold individual and collective meanings in whatever observance they do follow. This, too, is a widespread belief.[91]

Crossing the Atlantic

Although Mordecai Kaplan (1881–1983) was born in the old country (fifty miles north of Vilna), the mature Kaplan was all American. Unlike his father who studied at the vaunted Volozhin Yeshivah, Kaplan studied at Columbia University. By 1914, Kaplan had accepted biblical criticism and was the only faculty member at the Jewish Theological Seminary

---

90 Leon Weiner Dow, *In Your Walking on the Way: A Theory of Halakha Based on the Thought of Franz Rosenzweig* [Heb.] (Ramat Gan: Bar-Ilan University Press, 2017), 271–72. Samuel Hugo Bergman described Rosenzweig's system as "anarchic subjectivism." See *Faith and Reason*, 78.

91 Arnold M. Eisen, *Rethinking Modern Judaism: Ritual, Commandment, Community* (Chicago: University of Chicago Press, 1998), 208. Emphases in original.

teaching it to his students. In a 1969 survey of rabbis ordained by the Jewish Theological Seminary, almost all the respondents who were attracted to Kaplan's thinking agreed that what was most attractive about Kaplan was his honesty in wrestling with the most challenging problems confronting American Jews. "Other faculty were teaching texts, Kaplan was thinking thoughts" and extending them to their logical conclusions.[92]

Like the Reformers, Kaplan understood that biblical criticism undermined the divine authority of Halakhah. Thus, Halakhah is not binding on the Jew. But, to the degree that the Jew wants to live Jewishly, she should voluntarily appropriate as many of the traditional mitzvot as cohere with her modern responsibilities and sensibilities. Although the term *halakhah*, a way of being Jewish, is still tenable, Kaplan thought that the term *mitzvot*, understood as commandments commanded by God, should be retired. He suggested using his translation of *minhag*, which is usually translated as *custom*, but rendered by Kaplan as *folkway*.[93]

> If we were henceforth to designate all "commandments pertaining to the relations between man and God" as *minhagim* or "folkways," we would accomplish a twofold purpose. First, we would convey the thought that they should not be dealt with in a legalistic spirit, a spirit that often gives way to quibbling and pettifogging. . . . Secondly, we would convey the implication that not only should as many "commandments" or folkways as possible be retained and developed, but that Jewish life should be stimulated to evolve new and additional folkways.[94]

Although Kaplan does not cite Rosenzweig, he urges that Judaism should generate law/folkways. Judaism is jurisgenerative, at least in the ritual sphere. The traditional observance and burden of *yom tov sheni* (the second day of pilgrimage holidays), for example, might be replaced with innovations to celebrate *isru chag* (the day following a pilgrimage holiday).

Unlike Buber and Rosenzweig who were European philosophers and theologians, Kaplan was more of a sociologist and philosopher in

---

92 Charles S. Liebman, "Reconstructionism in American Jewish Life," in *American Jewish Yearbook 1970*, vol. 71, ed. Morris Fine and Milton Himmelfarb (New York: American Jewish Committee, 1970): 52–53.

93 Kaplan, *Judaism as a Civilization*, 431.

94 Ibid., 432.

the tradition of American Pragmatism. For Kaplan, Judaism is a civilization; hence, Jews are a people. In large part, this explains why Kaplan, like Frankel, insisted on the importance of Hebrew. It also explains why his attachment to the mitzvot/folkways is predicated not on their ability to invite revelation, but on their function to preserve and promote Jewish identity. As Kaplan writes about many cultural folkways that are not codified in the Halakhah, "they have the effect of deepening the Jewish consciousness and promoting a sense of unity with the rest of Jewry."[95]

I learned Hebrew in Israel as a young adult. One of my early lessons in linguistic dissonance was that the Hebrew word for *religious*, *dati*, was used to designate those who observe Halakhah. A deeply religious Jew was not so described unless he observed (Orthodox) Halakhah. Conversely, simply by observing the Halakhah, regardless of one's inner spiritual orientation, one was considered *dati*, religious. Buber would have identified this as a category error between religiosity/spirituality and religion/rules. Halakhic observance has, indeed, become a central, if not *the* central, axis around which we moderns perceive Jewish difference. Kaplan, the religious functionalist, also keeps the desideratum of halakhic observance clearly in view. "The Torah seeks to translate righteousness into law."[96] For some, righteousness is an end unto itself. For Kaplan, however, God *is* "the power that makes for righteousness."[97] Thus, our ability to enhance the divine (*tikkun olam*) is directly proportional to our willingness to generate righteous *takkanot* (new legal provisions). The connection between the original legal and medieval mystical meanings of *tikkun* meld. "In the present unredeemed and broken state of the world this fissure which prevents continuous union of God and the Shekhinah [two sefirot] is somehow healed or mended by the religious act of Israel."[98]

In medieval mysticism, those religious acts were often ritual. The Hebrew translation for that category of commandments is *between humans and the Place* (*hamakom*), the latter term being a rabbinic name for God. An early aggadic text explains that God is so named because "God is the place of the world, but the world is not God's [only] place"

---

95 Ibid., 452.
96 Kaplan, *The Meaning of God*, 315.
97 Ibid., 297.
98 Scholem, *Major Trends*, 233.

(Genesis Rabbah 68:9). Given the urgent need for new environmental *takkanot*, how felicitous that such Halakhah will fall under the categories of *between humans and the Place* and *healing the world (tikkun olam)*.[99] Such legislation will be religious, righteous, and emerge organically from traditional Halakhah, both in terms of content and method.[100] Kaplan would concur. Although he unyoked Jews from traditional Halakhah, he praised the need for what he called *law mindedness* "if Judaism is to be true to itself."[101]

Conclusions

With modernity, Jews become historically self-conscious. Every text has a context. Every divining rod has two branches, Halakhah and Aggadah. Halakhah is context sensitive. The principles that quicken the Aggadah remain relatively constant within the flux of historical change. Thus, to divine God's will, to seek Torah, requires the ongoing unification of agg-adic principles and halakhic forms. Whether we look to Zelophechad's legacy or rabbinic *takkanot* for social welfare, when times (and contexts) change, sometimes laws must change with them. Sometimes, sages must promote new halakhah to further the goals of the aggadic principles. If I were to disrobe in public because I suddenly realized my robe contained wool and linen, I would be arrested, and Judaism would be shamed. If I were to drive a gas-guzzling, emissions-belching vehicle, should Judaism be any less shamed?

What we have seen in this chapter is sharp rhetoric often combined with compassionate rulings. Sport hunting is dangerous and makes hunt-ing for a living unnecessarily dangerous. Newspapers provide the pretext for women to remarry when their husbands have gone missing overseas. Using a machine for matza deprives manual laborers of needed income. Using battery operated hearing aids on Shabbat is permitted. At the same time, there has been stringency creep under the assumption that sick patients need stronger medicine. In addition, aspirational behavior, what

---

99 Rebecca Cherry first pointed out to me how appropriate the language of *between humans and the place* is for environmental halakhah.

100 Charles Vernoff, "Toward a Transnatural Judaic Theology of Halakhah," *Jewish Civilization* 2 (Philadelphia: Reconstructionist Rabbinical College, 1981): 203.

101 Kaplan, *Meaning of God*, 320.

Brown calls "soft stringencies," have become norms. A particularly unsavory element of stringency creep is the tendency to intentionally obfuscate the lines among traditional halakhic statuses to make everything equally sacrosanct or abominable. Rav Kook stands out as a paragon of honesty and compassion in his insistence on normative transparency and inclination to lighten the yoke of halakhah. Alas, as Marc Shapiro has recently catalogued with depressing thoroughness, within the ultra-Orthodox world, not even the giants are beyond the reach of later-day dwarves who judge the latter's wisdom to be off message. "[Rav] Kook has been the victim of more censorship and simple omission of facts for the sake of *Haredi* [ultra-Orthodox] ideology than any other figure."[102]

There is a Talmudic story about a halakhic realist beating back a prospective convert with a builder's straightedge (Shabbat 31a). That was Shammai whose ontological Judaism could not accommodate deviations; each halakhah was integral to the totality of the Halakhah. Hillel's halakhic nominalism dominated rabbinic Judaism, and RaMBaM did what he could to enhance its stature. Nominalism has continued to spread in modernity, but as we will see in the next chapter, the foul residue of ontological realism persists.

---

102 Marc B. Shapiro, *Changing the Immutable: How Orthodox Judaism Rewrites Its History* (Liverpool: Littman Library of Jewish Civilization, 2015), 145.

Chapter 14

The Shrinking Middle

As William Butler Yeats said, "the centre cannot hold." Yeats wrote the line following World War I. After the planet's first aerial bombardment in Guernica, the London Blitz, the Rape of Nanjing, the siege of Stalingrad, the carpet bombing of Dresden, and the atomic bombing of two Japanese cities, the human conscience had been anesthetized as civilian deaths became normalized. The center had, indeed, collapsed. When the dust cleared and the ashes settled, the center of European Jewish life and creativity had suffered the worst of all. The Nazis were able to mobilize much of Europe in an antisemitic frenzy that drew strength from hundreds of years of Christian supersessionism, xenophobia, and economic envy. Those whom they did not mobilize in their demonic cause, with very few exceptions, were neutralized.

In their noble, but misguided attempts to protect the surviving remnant, halakhists and philosophers of Halakhah have become increasingly defensive and dishonest since the end of the Shoah. Rabbi David Hartman (1931–2013) was among the few, courageous leaders to publicly decry his colleagues' timidity and mendacity. His final books were entitled *From Defender to Critic* and *The God Who Hates Lies*. Hartman blasts the Israeli rabbinate's "attempt to delegitimize three-fourths of diaspora Jewry [as] simply perverse. . . . The desperate and cynical maneuvering to reshape halakhah into a private club for fundamentalists reflects a deep failure to identify with this [entire] people in this moment."[1]

---

1   David Hartman, *The God Who Hates Lies: Confronting & Rethinking Jewish Tradition* (Woodstock: Jewish Lights Publishing, 2014), 175–76.

Lawrence Kaplan zeroes in on the breakdown of the relationship between two of the towering figures in American Orthodoxy, Emanuel Rackman and Joseph Soloveitchik, which illustrates Hartman's point. Both Rackman and Soloveitchik initially shared a similar view that Halakhah is intended to be responsive to specific historical circumstances and to pursue specific values.[2] In 1952, Rackman introduced American Jewry to Soloveitchik, through an article in Commentary Magazine, as one of the "greatest of Orthodox rabbis today." Rackman revealed Soloveitchik's own admission that certain halakhic decisions were not approached with "complete objectivity." Rackman's conclusion is that "in the deepest strata of halakhic thinking, logical judgment is preceded by value judgment, and intuitive insight gives impetus to the logic of argument."[3]

According to Kaplan, the overlap in Rackman and Soloveitchik's halakhic views diminished during the fifties, sixties, and seventies, precisely as the Conservative movement grew to dominate the American Jewish scene. As Rackman became more conscious of Halakhah's role as a *means* to the "fulfillment of God's will," he became increasingly critical of those who would "freeze the Halakhah against further development by ignoring the dialectic which is the very essence of the halakhic process. . . . The dialectic confirms the role of history while allowing for progress."[4] The dialectic in question is the "balancing of the conflicting values and interests which the Law seeks to advance."[5] Rackman details the theory and practice of this teleological balancing act in his 1961 article entitled "The

---

2   Lawrence Kaplan, "From Cooperation to Conflict: Rabbi Professor Emanuel Rackman, Rav Joseph B. Soloveitchik, and the Evolution of American Modern Orthodoxy," *Modern Judaism* 30, no. 1 (2010): 46–53.

3   Emanuel Rackman, "Orthodox Judaism Moves with the Times: The Creativity of Tradition," *Commentary* 13 (June 1952): 548. J. David Bleich, a contemporary philosopher of Halakhah, argues just the opposite in an historically uninformed and hypocritical essay misleadingly called "The Halakhic Process," in *J. David Bleich: Where Halakhah and Philosophy Meet*, ed. Hava Tirosh Samuelson and Aaron W. Hughes (Leiden: Brill, 2015), 25. Although he contends that a *posek* must acknowledge when he is choosing the more stringent position (p. 34), he avoids disclosing that his own stringent preference for insisting that "the law bore through the mountain," was contested on the very same folio of Talmud with an approach of compromise (Sannhedrin 6a/b). Bleich's approach is precisely what Hartman finds so objectionable.

4   Emanuel Rackman, "The Dialectic of the Halakha," *Tradition* 3, no. 2 (1961): 148.

5   Ibid.: 131.

Dialectic of the Halakhah." The "theocentric character" of the Halakhah demands of the rabbis who apply the law not slavish adherence to the statute's language, but devoted pursuit of the law's intent.[6] To repeat: Halakhah is a means to the "fulfillment of God's will," regardless of any particular legal formulation that our ancestors sincerely believed was appropriate for their generation to fulfill the divine will.

Kaplan tells the story of the fallout between Rackman and Soloveitchik in the context of American Judaism. Hartman tells the same story but as a religious philosopher, using the language we have employed throughout. In a chapter entitled "Where Did Modern Orthodoxy Go Wrong? The Mistaken Halakhic Presumptions of Rabbi Soloveitchik," Hartman pinpoints the debate between Rackman and Soloveitchik concerning the plight of *agunot* (women whose husbands refuse to give them a writ of divorce). The heart of the problem is in the ontological realism of Soloveitchik's metaphysical approach to Halakhah. (The approach, known as the Brisker Method, was pioneered by Hayyim Soloveitchik (1853–1918), Joseph Bear's grandfather. It was designed for legal analysis not halakhic implementation.)[7] We saw in an earlier chapter how the Halakhah's demand that the husband speak certain words to establish a *get* aligns with halakhic realism's assumption about the power of words. Issues of personal status also rest in the realm of halakhic realism. Although the rabbinic trend was away from halakhic realism and toward nominalism, Hartman catches Soloveitchik going in the other direction. Hartman cites Soloveitchik's 1975 address to the Orthodox Rabbinical Council of America:

> Not only the *halakhos*, but also the *hazakos* [a prediction based on observed patterns of consistent behavior] which the traditional sages have introduced, are indestructible. For the *hazakos* which the Rabbis spoke of rest not on trenchant psychological patterns, but upon *permanent ontological principles* rooted in the very depth of the human personality—

---

6   This language is adopted from Rackman's 1954 essay, "Can We Moderns Observe the Sabbath: Neither Fundamentalism nor Evasion Offers an Answer," *Commentary* 18, no. 3 (September, 1954). See Kaplan, "From Cooperation to Conflict": 47–8 and David Singer, "Emanuel Rackman: The Gadfly of Modern Orthodoxy," *Modern Judaism* 28, no. 2 (2008).

7   Chaim N. Saiman, "Legal Theology: The Turn to Conceptualism in Nineteenth-Century Jewish Law," *Journal of Law and Religion* 21 (2006).

in the metaphysical human personality—which is as changeless as the heavens above.[8]

Women prefer to be married, regardless of the quality of the partner, than to be alone. That is the operating assumption, the *hazaka*, upon which Soloveitchik rejects Rackman's attempt to find a creative solution for the plight of *agunot*. Rav Soloveitchik, Hartman's esteemed teacher, claims that this piece of Talmudic psychology is not subject to changing social or economic conditions—it is an eternal principle of womanhood. Such a thoughtless comment, itself radically innovative, would be better left neglected were it not for its pernicious consequences. Soloveitchik prefers to "protect" the integrity of the halakhic system rather than the real lives of the *agunot* whose misery testifies to the falsity of Soloveitchik's metaphysical claims. For the record, the claim about women's marital preferences is attributed to one sage, is presented in Aramaic, and, according to Rashi, is a saying among *women* that Resh Lakish is quoting in the vernacular (Kiddushin 41a and Ketubot 75a). Furthermore, to extend halakhic realism from specific mitzvot to all mitzvot is unwarranted and unprecedented. To extend halakhic realism to *hazakot* turns the Talmud into a text of terror, not only for women, and is a desecration of the divine name.

I am not now, nor have I ever considered, becoming a member of the Orthodox community. Soloveitchik was never my teacher. I appreciate his intellect and gifts as a thinker and writer, but he is not my rav. I want to cite Rabbi Hartman at length. It is relatively easy for me to critique Soloveitchik. Hartman's critique, however, carries the whiff of patricide.

> According to Soloveitchik, if you think you are meeting a modern, independent, self-sufficient single woman, dignified about her capacity to cope with reality, you are mistaken: it is an illusion. You are not seeing the real woman, the desperately lonely and abject Talmudic woman that lies at the ontological heart of even the most seemingly capable or contented single modern female. In reality, every powerful, yet-unmarried CEO would prefer a man who has the stature of an ant to the howling pain of singlehood; the professor of history would just as soon live with a cabbage-

---

8   Hartman, *God Who Hates Lies*, 149. Hartman's emphasis. Hartman defines *hazakot* on p. 139.

head or a degenerate. Within this halakhic theology, simply allowing ourselves to acknowledge the reality of what we see is to undermine the foundations of the Torah itself. The Torah can only survive if it is based on what we know not to be true.[9]

Here we see the incoherence of the philosopher, the Jewish philosopher, Soloveitchik, who represents Orthodoxy's most sophisticated attempt to defend Judaism in the modern age. Yet, as clearly as he sees the problems within Orthodoxy, Hartman is incapable of, or unwilling to, offer anything more than a tactic for unobservant Jews. Hartman suggests that for those interested in an "experiential encounter with the Jewish tradition as it is lived, halakhah should be engaged as an open-ended educational framework rather than a binding normative one. . . . The legalistic weight of halakhah should be lifted completely and without theological compunction."[10] Hartman cites Hillel's strategy, according to Rashi, toward the prospective convert (Shabbat 31a): "In the educational process through which Hillel would guide him, he would become 'progressively more accustomed [to the mitzvot].'"[11] But, eventually, our convert will see the incoherence and the lack of compassion in Orthodoxy.

When I was studying in Jerusalem throughout the nineties, I would often see Rabbi Hartman at the Reform-affiliated Kehilat Kol Haneshama, standing at the back of the congregation during Friday night services. The service was egalitarian; the liturgy almost traditional; and the mood was both serious and uplifting. It may have been the most traditional showcasing of Jerusalemites' expression of Reform Judaism. On the other side of the Atlantic, Reform Jews have tended to eviscerate the tradition and salvage a few moral platitudes, like *tikkun olam*, that fit comfortably with the liberal American ethos. Our definition of "coherent Judaism" includes cohering maximally with the tradition; in this sense, Reform Judaism lacks coherency.

In the book of Numbers, there is an attempted coup d'état against Moshe. The leader of the rebels is Moshe's own cousin, Korah. At the turn of the twentieth century, a Hasidic master in Poland explains what rebellion looked like in his own day as well as our own. Rabbi Yehuda

9   Ibid., 151.
10   Ibid., 50–1.
11   Ibid., 174–75.

Leib Alter of Ger (1847–1905), known as the Sefat Emet, notes that the Torah describes Korah's initial action as "taking" (Numbers 16:1). He cites earlier authorities, both ancient and contemporary, to demonstrate that Korah's rebellion was to take himself, and others, away from the customs and traditions of his ancestors. "That was Korah's sin. Korah took, he separated himself. He took a different road that had no connection to the past. He severed the links to the ancestors."[12] Korah's rebellion was one of omission and indifference rather than commission and defiance.

Korah claimed that the entire community was holy (Numbers 16:3). That claim was never refuted—indeed, it was never even challenged. The problem was what Korah took from that claim. He took his own road. It wasn't necessarily a bad road, it just wasn't a Jewish road, a Jewish path, a Jewish way. You can be a bad Jew by eating a bacon double cheeseburger without being a bad person. The problem with the ideology of Reform Judaism is that it validates individual autonomy over communal praxis and solidarity. Reform Judaism encourages bad Jews in the sense that it endorses being Jewish only in ways that are personally meaningful. By definition, what is meaningful to Ploni may not be to Almoni, and what is meaningful to Ploni today, may not be tomorrow.

Given the airtight compartmentalization of subjects within the academy, my doctorate in Jewish thought left me relatively ignorant of Jewish practice. The place to remedy that deficiency is rabbinical school. Before I decided to attend rabbinical school, I had been associating with the Conservative movement as a congregational member, but I did not identify as a Conservative Jew. Ironically, it was by reading the most articulate theologian of Reform Judaism, Eugene Borowitz, that I began to see myself as a Conservative Jew. In a 1963 essay, Borowitz already used the language of *claims* that Judaism has made and continues to make upon Jews.[13] In a later formulation and development of that idea, Borowitz wrote in 1991: "We must think in terms of a *self-discipline* that, because of the sociality of the Jewish people, becomes communally focused and

---

12   Sefat Emet on Numbers 16:1. See also my comments in *Torah through Time*, 136. For Buber and Soloveitchik on Korah, see my *Torah through Time*, 150–52.

13   Eugene B. Borowitz, *Studies in the Meaning of Judaism* (Philadelphia: Jewish Publication Society, 2002), 81–2.

shaped. The result is a dialectal autonomy, a life of freedom-exercised-in Covenant."[14]

I won't go so far as to claim that the term "dialectical autonomy" is incoherent, but the way that Borowitz means it is unintelligible. Ploni can autonomously choose to cede some degree of autonomy to the claims of the Jewish covenant. But, once that decision has been made, until he reverses that decision, he lives in a covenant which, by definition, places limits and makes claims on Ploni's autonomy. One might argue that Ploni is always making the decision to cede autonomy to the covenant, and therefore the dialectic is real. I disagree. Inertia obtains until the energy required for escape velocity is reached. Judaism has always made claims on its members' behavior. What *is* incoherent is *autonomous* Judaism.

As I read Borowitz, then and now, I see that vision of Judaism which requires self-discipline best instantiated not through Reform but through Conservative ideology, although I much prefer his usage of *covenantal* Judaism than either the labels of *Reform* or *Conservative*. Thus, when I chose to attend rabbinical school it was within the Conservative Movement precisely because a Judaism coherent with all previous expressions of Judaism *demands* a certain set of behaviors. Of course, Orthodoxy does, as well. But, the commitment to finding halakhic solutions to specific laws and customs that we now perceive as either onerous or inconsistent with what we believe to be fundamental Jewish values is explicit only within Conservative ideology. The leading figure in Conservative Halakhah, both in terms of articulating its theory and legislating halakhah, is Elliot Dorff. In 2007, I became his student.

Rabbis Borowitz and Dorff penned a series of letters that is very much a contemporary version of the Buber-Rosenzweig letters on Halakhah. These letters were included in Dorff's 2005 volume on the history of Conservative legal theory *The Unfolding Tradition*. Dorff rejects individual autonomy on traditional grounds, and he could have cited his interlocutor. Borowitz himself had written: "I am regularly exasperated by an American Jewry that, wallowing in freedom, prates piously of the sanctity of individual choice and uses it mainly to sanction casual non-observance and flabby ethics."[15] A later Reform ideologue, Dana Kaplan,

14 Eugene B. Borowitz, *Renewing the Covenant: A Theology for the Postmodern Jew* (Philadelphia: Jewish Publication Society, 1991), 288. Emphasis in original.
15 Ibid., 222.

points out another major problem with Reform ideology: "Religious autonomy only works well if each person takes the time to carefully consider her religious choices. For the average American, overworked and overloaded, such careful consideration is rare indeed."[16] Before you can consider your choices, you have to know them. This is where my teacher finds the theory of an autonomous Jewish self, living in covenantal Jewish community, unrealistic.

> My problems with [Borowitz's] theory are, in essence, the reasons why I am a Conservative Jew and not a Reform Jew. First, to be a serious Reform Jew along these lines is a *very* tall order. One must first learn both the Western and the Jewish traditions thoroughly so that one's choices can be informed and intelligent. . . . The amount of Jewish and general education needed for such a theory to work . . . is simply too great for most Jews to master.[17]

Reform has largely abandoned traditional Halakhah; Orthodoxy has largely abandoned the traditional halakhic process. Reform has turned individual autonomy into an idol, an ultimate value; Orthodoxy has turned Halakhah into an idol, a graven image.

Alas, as I have charted with sorrow, the custodians of the halakhic tradition have betrayed their trust to the Jewish people. The faithful remnant that survives on the traditional fringes of Reform and Reconstructionist Jewry are voices in the desert. Similarly, the progressive fringe of modern Orthodoxy, whose representatives I will mention further below, have been marginalized, and in some cases, ostracized. The process of marginalization leaves us with a shrinking middle. Conservative Judaism has fared poorly in the early years of the twenty-first century, at least numerically. Although it is true that there are broad, sociological trends that have contributed to the quantitative decline, my sense is that Conservative Judaism's incoherence is also to blame.

"America's suburban Jewish population more than doubled in the 1950s, with Jews suburbanizing at a rate almost four times that of their non-Jewish neighbors."[18] There goes the neighborhood! The neighbor-

---

16 Dana Evan Kaplan, *The New Reform Judaism: Challenges and Reflections* (Philadelphia: Jewish Publication Society, 2013), 46

17 Dorff, *The Unfolding Tradition*, 466. Emphasis in original.

18 Sarna, *American Judaism*, 282.

hood to which I am referring, however, is the urban, Jewish neighborhood that experienced a devastating exodus of Jewish families. There
goes the *Jewish* neighborhood! Sociologists and historians have told this
story from their perspectives. What we see as students of the philosophy
of Halakhah is the Conservative movement's response. Orthodoxy also
responded—but not halakhically. The Reform movement had already
emancipated itself from halakhic deliberation, leaving only Conservative
Judaism to address the needs, halakhically, of Jews who lived beyond
walking distance to the closest synagogue. To its credit, rather than be
content with a policy of discrete hypocrisy—such as exists to this day in
Orthodox communities where some members drive to synagogue on the
Sabbath and park a block away—the Conservative movement was committed to finding a halakhic resolution.

In 1950, Rabbis Morris Adler, Jacob Agus, and Theodore Friedman
wrote a "Responsum on the Sabbath."[19] Their goal was explicit: "Our program seeks to reintroduce into the lives of our people as much Sabbath
observance and spirit as we may reasonably hope our people will, with
proper education, accept."[20] The authors recognized that if Jews didn't
come to Shabbat services, they would likely become High Holiday Jews.
Without Shabbat services, Jewish education would wither. Thus, the need
to condone automobile travel for Shabbat services motivated them to
find a halakhic solution to the issues attendant to driving on Shabbat.
Many have argued that their halakhic analysis was deficient. Others have
argued that it was unwise to offer official sanction to move even farther
away from a Jewish center. Without dismissing those concerns, I have
appreciated the driving exemption on days when the weather was unusu-
ally wretched—including hot and humid summer days when my wife was
eight months pregnant. I have also extended the exemption to include
Shabbat meals with friends or family who do not live within walking
distance. At the conclusion of their halakhic analysis of using electricity
on Shabbat, they write, "We think of Halakhah as an instrument of the
people, for the enrichment of the spiritual life of our people and not as an

---

19 Rabbi Morris Adler, Rabbi Jacob Agus, and Rabbi Theodore Friedman, *Proceedings of
    the Rabbinical Assembly* 14 (1950): 112–37.
20 Ibid.: 121.

end of itself."[21] They sought to avoid the Halakhah becoming a stumbling block that prevents Jews from celebrating Shabbat.

At roughly the same time, one of the authors, Rabbi Jacob Agus, published an article which begins by taking issue with Kaplan's description of Halakhah as "folkways." Although Kaplan did not ignore the spiritual, he did emphasize the sociological function of the Halakhah. Agus, as we saw above, was explicit about the Halakhah serving as an "enrichment of the spiritual life." In his article, Agus notes that the term *folkways* "lacks the moral quality, which alone evokes a sense of obligation and a feeling of consecration. Why should we strive with might and main to preserve folkways?"[22] I agree with Rachel Adler who argues that it is time to reclaim the term *halakhah*.[23] (And I agree with Agus that *folkways* is uninspiring.) Beyond the terms, lies the goal. According to Agus:

> Halakhah [is] the Divinely inspired and self-imposed disciplines of the Jewish people, undertaken for the purpose of elevating the level of individual and group life to the highest rungs of the ideals of Judaism. In this conception, the ideals of Judaism, insofar as they determine the standard images of the perfect individual and the perfect society, are recognized to be the goal and purpose of the entire halakhic structure, while the ceremonies are identified as instruments, of relative value and significance.[24]

In the previous chapter, we introduced Rabbi Moshe Glasner. His son was the teacher of Eliezer Berkovits (1908–1992), whose philosophy of Halakhah bears a family resemblance. Although Berkovits' most concentrated treatment of Halakhah is in his 1983 book *Not in Heaven: The Nature and Function of Halakhah*, his earlier works adumbrated his more mature theory. In a discussion of ritual laws in a 1959 work entitled *God, Man, and History: A Jewish Interpretation*, Berkovits brings the practical wisdom of Mussar and applies it to ritual law. Berkovits acknowledges that morality is the ultimate value in Halakhah,[25] but ritual law strength-

---

21 Ibid.: 130.
22 Jacob Agus, "Laws as Standards," in Dorff, *The Unfolding Tradition*, 165.
23 Rachel Adler, *Engendering Judaism: An Inclusive Theology and Ethics* (Boston: Beacon Press, 1999), 25.
24 Agus, "Laws as Standards," 170–71.
25 Berkovits, *Not in Heaven*, 19–45.

ens our capacity to rise to the challenge of a higher morality. Most of us are rarely tempted to commit mortal sins, but it is the constant avoidance of peccadilloes and venial sins that reinforces the framework necessary to withstand more enticing temptations.

> To put on phylacteries, to observe the three times of daily prayer, to pronounce a blessing before the enjoyment of the fruits of the earth—these require some submission, some discipline, some sacrifice. However, the self-regarding interests of vital needs and inclinations are not radically challenged. In submitting to the discipline of "ritual laws," the egocentricity of man's organic nature is not directly assaulted. . . . The indirect method deals cunningly with the "evil inclination."
>
> . . . The aim [of the ritual laws] is to teach purely subjective emotions, needs, and desires a new "awareness," one which is foreign to the organic component of the human personality. It is the *awareness of the other*, of an order of being as well as of meaning different from that of organic egocentricity. The purpose of the inhibitive rules is to practice saying "no" to self-centered demands; whereas the fulfillment of the positive commands is the exercise of saying "yes" in consideration of an order different from one's own.[26]

How Maimonidean—*all* the laws were given to ethically purify us (*Guide*, 3:26); some are just more direct than others! Being an observant Jew requires discipline. One needs discipline to master anything, from body building to meditation. Judaism is a discipline that trains one's being to withstand physical temptations and trains the spirit to become attuned to God's presence.[27] Ritual mitzvot do both. A blessing over food makes us wait to eat and makes us think about what we are eating. But, in the same chapter where Maimonides tells us that all the mitzvot were given to refine us, he also says that the details of the mitzvot have no specific meaning. In the first chapter of book 1, I commented that the ethical heart of the Torah (Leviticus 19) is framed by laws of eating and the holidays. I said there, echoing RaMBaM, that those specific details are not sacrosanct, but a communal framework of eating and celebrating

---

26 Eliezer Berkovits, "Law and Morality in Jewish Tradition," in *Eliezer Berkovits: Essential Essays on Judaism*, ed. David Hazony (Jerusalem: Shalem Press, 2002), 25. Emphasis in original.

27 Ibid., 30.

holidays together *is* essential for a moral community. A Judaism that coheres most robustly with its own history requires a similar framework to provide structure for and guidance to the ethical vision at Judaism's heart.

Berkovits, a philosopher of Jewish law, begins his extended meditation on Halakhah by picturing it as "the bridge over which the Torah moves from the written word into the living deed."[28] A contemporary of Berkovits, a Jewish philosopher of law, uses the same image: "Law may be viewed as a system of tension or a bridge linking a concept of a reality to an imagined alternative—that is, as a connective between two states of affairs, both of which can be represented in their normative significance only through the devices of narrative."[29] We will return to this author, Robert Cover, in the conclusion. Suffice it to say at this point that the quotation above is from an essay entitled "Nomos and Narrative," which may well have been a nod to Chayim Nachman Bialik's (1873–1934) classic essay "Halakhah and Aggadah." Bialik begins his essay with botanic imagery describing the intimate relationship between Halakhah and Aggadah: "as flower [seeks its realization] in fruit, so aggadah in halakhah. But in the heart of the fruit there lies hidden the seed from which a new flower will grow." By the end of essay, Bialik yearns for a new Halakhah for our age. "What we need is to have duties imposed on us!" In Cover's words, the imagined narrative is jurisgenerative.

Berkovits predicates his philosophy of Halakhah on several factors. The first is that the Talmud accepts the insights of logical thinking and common sense.[30] The second is that the Talmud is not utopian; it is pragmatic.[31] Berkovits admirably applies his philosophy of Halakhah to gender issues around marriage and divorce. He pleads for the rabbinic leadership to revitalize the Halakhah in accordance with our times. And he highlights an early articulation, offered by Rabbi Abraham the son of Maimonides, that it is incumbent upon each generation's leaders not to emulate the decision of the earlier rabbis, but to use logic and analogy to

---

28 *Berkovits, Not in Heaven*, 1.
29 Robert Cover, "Nomos and Narrative," in Minnow, *Narrative, Violence and the Law*, 101.
30 *Not in Heaven*, 3–8.
31 Ibid., 8–19.

determine what the new decision should be in our specific situation.[32] Yet, what Berkovits could not do himself was to recognize that there has been a paradigm shift as a result of biblical scholarship. There is consensus that the Torah's documents were written by different people over hundreds of years, representing different ideologies, and then stitched together by an editor into the biblical books as we now have them.

To put it delicately, Jewish feminists have grown frustrated with the timid, piecemeal proposals offered by rabbinic leadership. Rachel Adler and Judith Plaskow were among the earliest to throw down the egalitarian gauntlet. In Plaskow's *Standing Again at Sinai*, she notes that as a result of biblical scholarship, the Torah has lost its "sacred authority" and should not be viewed as a "transcript of divine revelation."[33] Plaskow then cites Adler who had earlier offered an illustration of a much larger problem. At Sinai, the women were not addressed (Exodus 19:15). Thus, when the story is chanted in synagogue, "women each time hear ourselves thrust aside anew, eavesdropping on a conversation among men and between men and God."

> As Rachel Adler puts it, "Because the text has excluded her, she is excluded again in this yearly reenactment and will be excluded over and over, year by year, every time she rises to hear the covenant read." If the covenant is a covenant with all generations (Deut. 29:13ff), then its reappropriation also involves the continual reappropriation of women's marginality.[34]

I have a proposal for a reappropriation. I would not want to silence the text itself. Knowing our starting point is crucial to appreciate how far we have come. Rather I would choose three other texts as foils. Almost every Shabbat, after the seventh Torah reader chants the final verses of the weekly portion, the final three lines are repeated. On certain occasions, rather than repeating the final three verses, the final Torah reading, known as the *maftir*, is from a different part of the Torah, altogether. My proposal is that when the Torah portion contains the Decalogue, we read a special *maftir* from Deuteronomy 31:9-13. These verses mandate the priestly rereading of the Torah, every seven years, to all the people,

32 Ibid., 55 and 117-18.
33 Plaskow, *Standing Again*, 15-6.
34 Ibid., 26, citing Rachel Adler, "I've Had Nothing Yet, So I Can't Take More," *Moment* 8, no. 8 (1983): 23.

specifically including women. One could argue that Deuteronomy's ritual "thrusts [women] aside anew" by demanding that they hear their exclusion from the Exodus account of revelation at Sinai every seven years. I prefer to see Deuteronomy as a leap toward including women in the community of the covenant.

In addition, I propose using a technique that the rabbis, or their ideological ancestors, used frequently with Torah portions that left them uneasy. At the completion of the Torah reading on Shabbat and holidays, there is another reading, usually from the books of the prophets that is called a *haftarah*. The haftarah for the Torah portion in which we receive revelation as a community is about Isaiah the prophet experiencing revelation. My proposal is to add to the haftarah the eight verses in which Ezra reads Torah to the descendants of the Judean refugees who had returned from the Babylonian exile. In front of Jerusalem's Water Gate, in 458 BCE, Ezra read to "men, *women*, and all who could listen with understanding" (Nehemiah 8:1–8). I would also excise at least eight verses from the haftarah to prevent the service from becoming further prolonged.

My third proposal is to confront the issue directly. Before the revelation at Sinai, Moshe says to "the people: Be ready for the third day— do not approach a woman" (Exodus. 19:15). It is not unreasonable to interpret this verse as indicating that *the people* were exclusively men. Moreover, the prohibition against coveting your neighbor's wife also seems addressed to a male audience (Exodus 20:14). Without rejecting these possible biblical readings, a contemporary rabbi must point out that these readings are neither necessary nor traditional. In the very earliest layer of rabbinic Halakhah there is the assumption that women were standing at Sinai (m. Shabbat 9:3). In order to be present, they needed to be ritually pure which required them abstaining from sexual relations for two complete days. Thus, on the third day, they would be prepared. This reading is both the Halakhah and included in RaSHI's commentary which makes it common knowledge among traditionally educated Jews. As for the prohibition against coveting your neighbor's wife, since the rabbis were primarily concerned with heterosexual sex, the androcentric phrasing still covered the required partner in crime. The rabbi needs to remind her congregation how progressive our ancestors were if she hopes to recapture that momentum.

Whatever one thinks of my proposal, it falls far short of what Jewish contemporary women deserve. There are elements of biblical and rabbinic Halakhah that reflect the patriarchy from which those laws emerged. All women were created in the divine image, according to Genesis One, just like all men.[35] In Genesis Two, when God forms a second human to be a helpmeet for the first, the Hebrew word for *help* (*ezer*) describes only a superior level of help. (Compare, "I need help cleaning the house," to "I need help with my homework.") Thus, Genesis One is pristinely egalitarian, and Genesis Two begins with woman being in a superior position before she falls into the trap laid by the serpent. At that point, Plonit's "urge shall be for her husband, and he shall rule over her" (Genesis 3:16). A maximalist reading of this male domination would lead to the wife submitting graciously to her husband, as we see in the 1998 Southern Baptist Convention. A minimalist reading might lead to the husband regulating when his wife can indulge her urge for him. Even this minimalist reading is countered by the rabbis. The Halakhah prevents a husband from withholding his marital responsibilities (m. Ketubot 5:6). But even this well-intentioned attempt to mitigate gender discrimination falls short.

> Any halakhah that is part of a feminist Judaism would have to look very different from halakhah as it has been. It would be different not just in specifics but in its fundamentals. It would begin with the assumption of women's equality and humanity and legislate only on that basis. Laws governing the formation and dissolution of marriage and divorce would acknowledge women's full agency, so that the present laws of marriage and divorce would be ruled unjust and unacceptable.[36]

Just as the Me'iri removed Christians from the Talmudic category of idolaters, we need to acknowledge that the Talmud's generalizations about women are not applicable to contemporary women and need to be historically bracketed. That will be the halakhic consequence of privileging Genesis 1's account of humanity for the fundamental proposition of gender equality. We should celebrate that the radical equality of Genesis One can be realized *within* the tradition. Suzanne Last Stone

---

35 Suzanne Last Stone, "Formulating Responses in an Egalitarian Age: An Overview," in *Formulating Responses in an Egalitarian Age*, ed. Marc D. Stern (Lanham: Rowman & Littlefield Publishers, 2005), 54.

36 Plaskow, *Standing Again*, 72.

offers an insight that penetrates to the heart of the halakhic dialectic: "Developments in general society, such as enhanced equality between the sexes, may become a catalyst for halakhic innovation because a posek's [decisor's] historical situatedness leads to the insight that the halakhah's own values as yet have been imperfectly realized."[37]

Consider our own country's Torah. In three minutes, on November 18, 1863, Abraham Lincoln brought the ideals of the Declaration of Independence of the United States closer to realization. In 1776, the men who were created equal were white men, not dark-skinned men from Africa, and certainly not women of any shade. Gary Wills credits the Gettsyburg Address for "cleansing the Constitution . . . by altering the document from within, by appealing from its letter to the spirit, subtly changing the recalcitrant stuff of that legal compromise [i.e., the Constitution], bringing it to its own indictment."[38] Or, as Stone might say, more perfectly realizing its own values. My colleague, Benjamin Edidin Scolnic, also emphasizes the glory of the realization rather than the ignominy of the indictment. In this excerpt, he is speaking of the Torah's laws of slavery.

> To paraphrase this from God's point-of-view: "I'm going to take this people, a people that can only conceive of a society based on a stratified view of human worth and try to bring them My dynamic of freedom. I'll trust that this current formulation of My truth will point beyond itself. The contradiction between the law and its principles will prevent the tradition from becoming rigidified. It may take centuries or even millennia, but the dynamic I am revealing will eventually explode in the consciousness of this people. . . ." God's Will unfolds over time . . . Halakhah is the result of God's Will in relationship with concrete realities.[39]

According to Stone, "Appeals to adopt a new norm or rule of law must be based on arguments that fall within the class of arguments recognized as legitimate bases for legal action within the legal system."[40] Stone and I disagree about what constitutes a legitimate basis for legal

37 Stone, "Formulating Responses," in Stern, *Formulating Responses*, 66.
38 Garry Wills, *Lincoln at Gettysburg: The Words that Remade America* (New York: Simon & Schuster, 2006), 38.
39 Benjamin Edidin Scolnic, "How to Read the Torah's Laws of Slavery," *Conservative Judaism* 47, no. 3 (1995): 40–1; discuss this in *Torah through Time*, 125.
40 Stone, "Formulating Responses," 66.

action. For instance, she is less willing than I to afford being created in the divine image halakhic weight. She argues that the biblical verse plays a "relatively negligible role" in rabbinic Halakhah.[41] Stone is arguing from silence. The paucity of a specific biblical citation is a poor indicator of the influence that the verse's principle embodies. When the rabbis comment on the daughters of Zelophechad receiving land in Israel, they cite a verse from Psalms: "God is good to all, and His mercies are upon all His works" (Psalms 145:9).[42] Does the use of this verse preclude the influence of our verse from Genesis One in which male and female are created in the divine image? We will return to this question, and this verse, below.

Rachel Adler takes a more aggressive stance toward redeeming traditional texts through feminist readings. She wants to reclaim and reread the narrative, the Aggadah, to generate a new nomos. Adler wants to make sure that some of the Torah's 70 faces reflect the other half of God's kingdom. Each new face, after all, has the potential to evoke a new halakhah.

> The alternative tradition she presents must assert its authenticity by grounding itself in narratives the tradition believes it owns and understands. Out of the multipotentiality of those narratives, she must draw meanings that contest the tradition's legal meanings. She must make the law her accomplice in its own destabilization.[43]

A forceful example of the destabilization of a biblical narrative for purposes of public policy, if not Halakhah, is provided by Lauri Zoloth, an ethicist at the University of Chicago. She developed an *Ethics of Encounter* using *Ruth* as her primary text. Just as the rabbis rerooted Ruth in their own soil and made her into a model for the halakhic process of conversion (Yevamot 47a/b), Zoloth reroots Ruth into our American soil where the values of communitarianism and libertarianism engage in subterranean struggle. Zoloth brings the struggle to light and leverages Judaism's harsh critique of libertarianism into a promotion of communitarianism. In Zoloth's reading, "Elimelech is the prudent libertarian" who abandons

---

41 Ibid., 70–73. Cf. Yair Lorberbaum, *Divine Image*.
42 Sifre, Numbers 133. See my *Torah through Time*, 162–71.
43 Adler, *Engendering Judaism*, 51.

his community in the face of famine.[44] Although Elimelech imagines he is protecting his family, the reader sees his decision to move to Moav is immediately followed by his death (Ruth 1:2–3). In the very next verse, death strikes again. The dead were Elimelech's sons, who had matured enough to marry and to be held accountable for their own decision to remain in "a pagan land, a place of stark individualism, [which] offers no social welfare for the needy."[45] Elimelech's widow, who has now lost both her sons, returns to Bethlehem. Only one of her daughters-in-law, Ruth, remains by her side. "The return to the world of justice [in the Land of Israel] begins with the recognition that each person is responsible for the commitment to community."[46]

Ruth is the alien, the loyal daughter-in-law, who works to keep herself and her mother-in-law alive. Ruth's altruistic predisposition is a prerequisite for future leaders of Israel as she enters the community, marries into Naomi's extended family, and becomes the great grandmother of King David. In Zoloth's summary of Ruth, she lays the foundation for an Ethics of Encounter that affords "practical and tangible use in the setting of policy."[47] What Zoloth abstracts from Ruth is deeply relevant as Jews grapple with issues of particularity, identity, and ultimate values.

> [Ruth] links the messianic with the personal and makes the covert but radical claim that it is the face-to-face encounter of the poorest and the most outcast, the female stranger [i.e., Ruth], who makes possible the continuance of the Jewish people and each self. . . . The conscience can be said, then, not to be the speaking of the voice within but rather the hearing of the quiet voice of the other. It is this voice that must precede any claim in the distribution of the scarce resource. This voice, just as clearly as one's "own," must remind us to see each child as our own, each journey and each need as fundamentally shared.[48]

44 Laurie Zoloth-Dorfman, "An Ethics of Encounter: Public Choices and Private Acts," in *Contemporary Jewish Ethics and Morality: A Reader*, ed. Elliot N. Dorff and Louis E. Newman (New York: Oxford University Press, 1995), 224.
45 Ibid.
46 Ibid., 225.
47 Ibid., 233.
48 Ibid., 232 and 236.

Zoloth brings together the narrative of Ruth, rabbinic midrash, and the ethics of Emmanuel Levinas (1906–1995) to forge the parameters of public policy. This model of a constructive conversation among different streams of wisdom, regardless of their headwaters, takes us back to RaMBaM's encouragement to accept the truth regardless of its source. RaMBaM held that studying physics and philosophy was a mitzvah; today we need to add climate science and economics.

Tamar Ross is an academic theologian and philosopher of Halakhah. Ross recognizes the need to accept the truths of biblical criticism as well as revitalize the Halakhah in consonance with the insights of feminism. In Ross's attempt to undermine the frequent argument against using the *description* of halakhic evolution as a *prescription* for further development, she acknowledges the following: "[Since] these far-flung [midrashic] interpretations of Torah have evolved in a certain way, there is likely something of significance to be derived from this particular evolvement."[49] Yes—we derive rabbinic principles and values!

Ross directly confronts non-Orthodox halakhic theories of revelation, which we have articulated above, that seem superficially similar to her own. Like Rav Kook, Ross maintains that what she calls *cumulative revelation* "does not involve devaluing or supplanting the previous norms of tradition. . . . Subsequent revelations [through history and textual interpretation] may transform a former 'hearing' by building upon it, but they cannot skip over it entirely."[50] I find Ross's distinction somewhat overblown. I am not interested in devaluing tradition; but, to claim that new revelations leading to new halakhic interpretations do not "supplant previous norms" is rhetoric over reason. What Ross is describing is essentially continuous revelation, "a sacred force that is present within history, inspiring a vision of liberation that progresses from age to age."[51] That inspired vision, progressing over time, requires form through Halakhah. Ross is more forthright when she later nuances her approach: "A view of divine revelation as an ongoing, accumulating process, even when allowing for the role of future interpretation, does require the believer to

---

49 Ross, *Expanding the Palace of Torah*, 199.
50 Ibid., 207.
51 Ibid., 213–14.

justify the meaning of the text as it was understood in the past as valid at least *for that time*."[52]

Ross mentions several mystical notions that parallel her vision of halakhic development, one of which is the notion that Torah, as we currently have it, will undergo a literal and literary recombination of letters *in the future*. There is another mystical notion, far more radical, expressed by none other than the "No Innovation from Torah" standard bearer, Moshe Sofer. In his Torah commentary on Zelophechad's daughters, he combines a kabbalistic tradition about the rearrangement of letters with Rashi's commentary to explain how the halakhah *has* changed. The Chatam Sofer credits the daughters of Zelophechad not only with changing the laws of inheritance, but, more incredibly, with changing the wording in God's own heavenly Torah! When Moshe brings the daughters' plea to God, the letters in *God's* Torah are reconfigured, and God *then* says, "That's how this section is written before Me in the heavens."[53]

Human actions have the power to rewrite God's Torah. That's the mystical myth. As the rabbis themselves conceded, regardless of their own male privilege, God is not sexist. As we saw above, the oldest rabbinic commentary on our passage confesses that sexist laws are male constructs, because "the Lord is good to *all*" (Psalms 145:9 in Sifre). Notice that the daughters' plea was not based on gender equality (Numbers 27:4). It was the rabbis of the Sifre who changed the terms of the argument by emphasizing gender equality. We see the rabbis thinking with women, and it is the rabbis who reveal *their* discomfort with the disconnect between their vision of an impartial God, good and fair to all, and the law as written which favors men. Stone's search for a specific textual connection to the divine image shows a misunderstanding the rabbinic mind. We have seen how the rabbis, themselves, shifted the conversation; Rashi's comment elevates the women to the status of prophets who can see God's Torah better than can Moshe; and the Chatam Sofer envisions women taking the quill from the quiver, claiming their rights, and rewriting God's Torah. In our midrash in Sifre, their rights flow from the poetry of Psalms which demands, just like father Abraham, "that the Judge of all the earth deal justly" (Genesis 18:25).

---

52 Ibid., 216. Emphasis in original.
53 See *Torah through Time*, 175–77.

As we consider activating the inherent dynamism of Halakhah, there is no shortage of resistance from within the non-Orthodox world. From Reform thinkers, like Borowitz and Adler, we hear that introducing flexibility into the halakhic process is "an unwarranted break" with tradition because the halakhic process is "methodolatrous."[54] I hope to have shown both claims false. Within the Conservative Movement, there are voices increasing in number and volume that are, in Rabbi Joshua Gutoff's words, "against the law."[55] In 1995, Gutoff argued that Conservative Judaism is not halakhic, that there is no such thing as either Jewish law or a halakhic process, and that the Conservative rabbi no longer functions as the halakhic arbiter for his (or her) community. Some of Gutoff's argument involves semantics. Is Halakhah "law" since it is not enforceable?[56] More substantively, what does it mean for a rabbi to have halakhic authority? "Has God really given us authority over those who do not recognize our authority? . . . It is not a desideratum for people to be inquiring of their rabbis what to do; it is a desideratum for them to be inquiring of God and using us as their guides and servants in this inquiry."[57]

For many years, Rabbi Dorff has dealt with the issue of enforceability.[58] In his most sustained work on the philosophy of Halakhah, before taking on the issue directly, he explains his own submission to Halakhah.

> I observe Jewish law (that is, Jewish law has authority for me) both because it is the way *my people* have understood *the demands of God* in the past and do so now and because of its own intrinsic wisdom as a program for satisfying human needs, acting morally, and maximizing human potential in the world as we know it.[59]

In other words, Dorff, and I, observe Halakhah because it is traditionally what Jews have done *and* because its wisdom runs so deep. We feel blessed to call such wisdom our own and to have it as an inexhaustible resource in confronting the unimagined complexities of our

---

54 Borowitz, *Renewing the Covenant*, 281 and Adler, *Engendering Judaism*, 28.
55 Joshua Gutoff, "Against the Law," *Conservative Judaism* 47, no. 3 (1995).
56 Ibid.: 29–31.
57 Ibid.: 32–33.
58 Dorff, *For the Love of God and People*, 166–82.
59 Ibid., 34.

time. Historically, Jews have considered Halakhah to be authoritative. Dorff lays out multiple motives for observing Halakhah and argues that enforceability is only one such motive. Dorff then makes a logical move that I find problematic.

> People have always abided by Jewish laws for many reasons other than enforcement. Therefore, even in a voluntaristic society, where no government officials force Jews to abide by Jewish law, treating Jewish law as fully law makes great sense. This means not only that we should see Jewish law as authoritative but also that we should apply to the rules of Jewish law all of the legal techniques of interpretation and application that Jews have used for millennia to plumb its guidance for our lives.[60]

There are, indeed, multiple *reasons* for observing mitzvot; but, that is not the same as mitzvot being authoritative. Once the elements of enforcement and sanction have dropped out of the constellation of motivations, what remains *may be* compelling, but it is no longer authoritative. Consider the following analogy. The speed limit is sixty-five miles per hour. Even though the speed limit is enforced with sanctions, some people still speed. There are multiple reasons not to speed, from fuel mileage efficiency to increased safety, but without any enforcement mechanism, more people will violate the speed limit. On a practical level, the speed limit is no longer authoritative once the authority behind the law's enforcement has been removed. Thus, for me, a halakhic lifestyle must be intrinsically compelling—and coherence is a prerequisite for adherence.

Returning to Gutoff's critique, his argument was that since Halakhah is not authoritative, Judaism is not halakhic. Gutoff asks: "Has God really given us [rabbis] authority over those who do not recognize our authority?" Of course not. We have no authority over individuals—we have authority over the Halakhah. What we have vis-à-vis individual Jews is influence. If we represent a compelling Judaism, Jews will voluntarily cede a measure of their personal autonomy to be part of our community. The influence rabbis have can be squandered. The autonomy that individuals cede can be reclaimed. Judaism will continue to be halakhic to the extent that Jews allow the Halakhah to make claims on their behavior.

---

60 Ibid., 181.

My two teachers view what is compelling about Judaism from opposite sides of Mount Sinai. The complementary perspectives of Green and
Dorff regarding the primary function of Judaism speaks to theology and
ethics. We begin, with Green, in the Garden of Eden:

> I am suggesting that the silently spoken divine "Where are you?" is the
> essence of revelation. To be a religious human being is to recognize
> that call and seek to respond to it . . . to be aware, to attain the deepest
> understanding we can of the evolving oneness of being, and to live in
> faithfulness to that awareness.[61]

Green starts with theology and moves to religion as a response
to the immanent divine call. "The righteous live by their faithfulness"
(Habakkuk 2:4). As a consequence of our knowledge and awareness of
the One, beyond which there is nothing else, we respond "by our deeds.
This is the part of 'Where are you?' that calls for *com*passion and moral
action."[62] While Green attempts to "reinvigorate" Judaism through a
rereading of the Decalogue, he acknowledges that for him, "the old halakhic rule book fails to work."[63] Yet, he has faith that Bialik's call for a new
Halakhah to emerge from a new Aggadah will be answered.[64] My faith is
that the new Halakhah will grow out of the principles and values of the
old Halakhah as expressed in the old Aggadah. Green, himself, forges the
way with a midrash whose aggadic plea demands a halakhic response:

> The two "commandments" that lie within the "Where are you?" addressed
> to every person—"Become aware" and "Share that awareness"—in our age
> are joined by a third: "Protect My earth! Save it from destruction!"[65]

Prior to God asking the first human "Where are you?" the Lord God
placed the human in the garden to protect it (Genesis 2:15). Before the
question was the expectation. The logical presupposition to living long
in the land is that the land will live long. Only from the rabbinic midrash
does the warning resound: if you spoil the garden, no one will be able
to repair the damage (Ecclesiastes Rabbah 7:13). We rabbis, known for

---

61 Green, *Radical Judaism*, 93 and 95. See also Green's *Seek My Face*, 75 and Ehyeh, 94.
62 Green, *Radical Judaism*, 97. Italics in original.
63 Ibid., 113 and 165.
64 Ibid., 166.
65 Ibid., 154.

our logic, have been derelict in generating new Halakhah to protect the garden.

Elliot Dorff starts with neither with God nor the theological. Although he by no means ignores the divine, Dorff's focus is on refashioning a Halakhah for today's world:

> In more contemporary terminology, the soul of the covenant with God is *tikkun olam*, "fixing the world," where the morals of the Jewish tradition apply directly to this task, and its rituals bring together and identify the community, remind it of its mission and moral obligations, and make life an art. . . . In interpreting and applying Jewish law in our day we must recognize that its goals are moral and theological, and those factors therefore test the mettle of any ruling we make.[66]

Dorff is a self-described "objectivist," in that he emphasizes "publicly observable facts rather than private, personal experiences" in his deliberations concerning Jewish law.[67] His halakhic methodology, therefore, is squarely focused on the promotion of "mercy, kindness and peace."[68] Although Dorff has been instrumental in the modifications and qualifications of existing Halakhah, he also acknowledges that "when we find an opportunity to expand the law to improve our morality, we should take advantage of it."[69]

After many years of deliberation, in 2006 the Conservative Movement's Committee on Jewish Law and Standards offered an exemption for rabbinic prohibitions around sexual intimacy for gay men. The responsum was authored by Rabbis Elliot Dorff, Daniel Nevins, and Avram Reisner. Basing themselves on the Talmudic principle of human dignity, *k'vod habriyot*, they exercised their rabbinic authority by allowing gay men who have no other possibility for a healthy, loving relationship to engage sexually with other men. Yet, what these rabbis did not do was to exempt gay men from the Torah's prohibition on male anal intercourse (Leviticus 18:22 and 20:13). They felt unqualified. Or, even if they felt qualified, they knew that not enough of their colleagues felt

---

66 Dorff, *For the Love of God and Man*, 91 and 225.
67 Ibid., 36.
68 Ibid., 229.
69 Ibid., 232.

qualified to uproot the biblical prohibition.[70] (The Committee on Jewish Law and Standards requires a minimum of six out of the twenty-five voting members to endorse a position.) Rabbi Yohanan might say they felt meek. Knowing full well that giving men the green light to be physically intimate, but maintaining red lines is a half-solution that requires what Dorff calls "wise silence."[71]

Rabbi Gordon Tucker pursued a different path in his attempt to normalize the halakhic status of gay and lesbian Jews. For our purposes, Tucker brings two arguments that merit our attention. The first argument is that Aggadah is an invaluable resource for our halakhic deliberations and needs to be explicitly featured.[72] We have seen that although references to Aggadah have not always been explicit, they have always been present. Steven Fraade has argued that the rabbinic practice of multiple legal interpretations presented side by side was rationalized by an understanding of revelation that accommodated each person's capacity (Mekhilta d'Rabbi Ishmael, Yitro, Bachodesh 9). Reminiscent of Rav Kook's differentiated Torah scrolls for each of the tribes, the rabbis imagined revelation, itself, tailored to each unique individual. Fraade's suggestion is that this aggadah served as the foundational myth. "The Mekhilta [an early rabbinic midrash on Exodus] thereby provides midrashic justification, via Sinaitic grounding, for its own midrashic practice of multiple interpretations."[73]

Ronald Dworkin, an American legal theorist, distinguishes between principles and rules. Both, however, are integral to every legal system. I agree with Tucker that we should be unabashed in our usage of the principles we find in our Aggadah when it comes to interpreting existing rules and generating new ones. I hope to have shown that our rabbis, more often than not, did the very same thing. What Fraade has brought to light suggests that one rabbinic principle is tolerance for multiple opinions. Fraade is careful to distinguish this stance from relativism, but there is an overlap. At a minimum, the rabbis anticipated Kant's epistemological

---

70 Ibid., 235
71 Ibid.
72 Tucker, "Halakhic and Metahalakhic Arguments Concerning Judaism and Homosexuality": 27, https://www.rabbinicalassembly.org/sites/default/files/public/halakhah/teshuvot/20052010/tucker_homosexuality.pdf.
73 Fraade, "Rabbinic Polysemy": 26.

insight that individuals have different perceptions of an object precisely because the object itself is mediated through our senses. The rabbis may also have intuited that since their multiple legal interpretations are the products of their idiosyncratic capacities, their descendants' interpretations will similarly vary.

It is important to acknowledge that these principles are not external to or beyond the halakhic system. Before Dworkin suggested his principles/rules dichotomy, it was articulated by Eliezer Goldman (1918–2002) in reference to Halakhah. "Legal principles, for both thinkers [Goldman and Dworkin], were part of the law but also said things about the law."[74] Some philosophers of Halakhah use the term *meta-halakhah* to describe these overarching legal principles. Noam Zohar argues that such a term is problematic because it suggests a distinction between halakhah and meta-halakhah. "Meta-halakhah does not involve deviating from standard halakhic reasoning . . . it is an organic element of the halakhic discussion itself."[75]

Tucker's second argument in his attempt to normalize homosexuality is to accept the consequences of the Torah's human authorship. As Tucker points out, the refusal to acknowledge biblical criticism when we engage in halakhic deliberation is not just incoherent with what we know to be true, but it is hypocritical since Conservative seminaries teach biblical criticism to their rabbinical students.[76] My contention is that the problem of the *agunah*, the chained widow, should be easier to resolve, thanks to biblical studies, now that we understand the priestly ontology from which the Halakhah derived. We no longer accept the metaphysics which understands that words magically create their own reality. Rather than beat the recalcitrant husband into saying, "Write her a *get*," rabbis should be empowered to have the *get* written on his behalf. There is a halakhic principle that one can obtain benefit in absentia (Gittin 11b). If the *agunah* receives her *get*, the recalcitrant husband won't need to be beaten—that's a benefit. If we benefit theologically from the fruits of biblical criticism, as I believe we do, we should not

---

74 Alexander Kaye, "Eliezer Goldman and the Origins of Meta-Halacha," *Modern Judaism* 34, no. 3 (2014): 324.

75 Noam Zohar, "The Development of Halakhic Theory as the Positive Basis for Philosophy of Halakhah" [Heb.], in Ravitzky, *New Streams*, 49.

76 Tucker, "Halakhic and Metahalakhic": 1.

deprive ourselves of benefitting halakhically.[77] The Talmud Yerushalmi says we will be held accountable for that from which we could have benefited but did not.[78]

Conclusion

Above, I referred to *the shrinking middle* in quantitative terms. But the description runs deeper than the number of Conservative synagogues closing their doors. The meekness of Conservative halakhists in facing the ramifications of biblical criticism is both incoherent and hypocritical. Rabbi Tucker's response to homosexuality was not endorsed by the Committee on Jewish Law and Standards. It remains unclear to me why contemporary Conservative halakhists are inclined to follow the letter of the law slavishly rather than to pursue righteously the goal of Halakhah: to live long on the land that the Lord, our God, has given to us. Of course, when I cite this goal, *the land* is now the entire earth and *us* are all its denizens, regardless of race, religion, or even species. Although like Dorff, I foreground the behavioral aspects of this goal, God's gift through divine grace is not the background to our behavior; it is the foundation. The awareness of living in and through God's grace, as Green says, leads to compassion and peace.

Reform Judaism, while institutional affiliation grows numerically in the United States, slides further away from engaging in distinctively Jewish rituals, studying traditional texts, learning Hebrew, and identifying with Israel. Dana Kaplan explains that "because the clientele that the Reform movement caters to is highly acculturated, they are easily swayed by sociological trends and cultural shifts."[79] The language of *catering to clientele* speaks to the commercialization of Judaism. Kaplan is surely correct that themed bar mitzvas and destination weddings have become increasingly popular among non-Orthodox Jews. Yet, when Kaplan concludes that "every religious group needs a strict theology in order to make serious demands of their adherents," I wonder

---

77 See Roth, *Halakhic Process*, 371–77. Roth argues that a *posek* can use Talmudic criticism to discover a previously unknown peshat which can then be used in halakhic deliberation. I believe the same argument applies to the biblical text.
78 Y. Kiddushin 4:12.
79 Kaplan, *New Reform Judaism*, 141.

how the Reform clientele would respond.[80] There is irony in Kaplan inviting two Reform leaders to write the foreword and afterword to his book, neither of whom endorses his call for a strictly defined theology. On the one hand, having Jews disagree on the same page is entirely traditional. These and those are the living words of God. On the other hand, the call for a defined, single theology is Christian, or as Kaplan, himself, might say, *highly acculturated*. Jews, as a people, have never had a single theology, not in the Torah, not in the Talmud, not in the Aggadah, and not in the Halakhah.

A coherent Judaism, one might argue, could not have a single theology if it seeks to remain faithful to traditional Judaism. To be coherent, Jewish theologies do not need to cohere with one another. RaMBaM failed most spectacularly in his attempt to transform Judaism into a single theology. Jewish theologies need to cohere with what we believe about God and the world. Jewish religion must then flow coherently, or at least without contradiction, from those beliefs. I do not believe in the ontological superiority of Jews, for example; nor do I believe in any ontological distinctions among Jews. When a Cohen recites the blessings on the Torah before all others, I understand that privilege not as a marker of ontological priority, but as an expression of tradition.

Although I reject the ontological anthropology of priestly theology, their theology attracts me. God's presence, or more accurately, my awareness of God's presence is a function of human behavior. I reject the Mosaic theology enshrined in the prayer book. God does not reward or punish. Such a theology can lead to obscene conclusions. What a blessing that the Torah has two different theologies that have shaped the history of Jewish thought! What is coherent today, for me, is the priestly theology and the Mosaic anthropology which mirrors the fundamental equality radically expressed in Genesis 1: all humans are created equally in the divine image.

The very first rabbis understood that we hear revelation, we experience our awareness of God, according to our unique capacities. Those varying experiences of God's presence will evoke different behavioral responses. The rabbis taught us to tolerate different theologies and

---

80 Ibid., 311.

different behavioral responses, what we might call religion or Halakhah. Finally, the rabbis taught us to not tolerate certain behaviors that are anathema to our covenantal consensus. Participation in any covenant makes certain claims on our individual autonomy. The conclusion of *Coherent Judaism* offers a vision of how threads from our covenant can be woven into a compelling Judaism where partners willingly cede their autonomy for the blessings of our covenant.

Conclusion

A Compelling Judaism

Rabbi Shmuel bar Ami said, "From the beginning of the world's creation, the Holy One, blessed be He, yearned to enter into partnership with earthly creatures."
—Genesis Rabbah 3:9

Not just Jews, and not just humans. Although Rabbi Shmuel bar Ami doesn't impute motive to God for creating the world, he does describe a divine craving not just for relationship but for partnership with all worldly creatures. Sovereigns and subjects are in a relationship, but a partnership emphasizes mutuality. In Judaism, partnership is called covenant. The conclusion to *Coherent Judaism* will retrace the elements of a coherent theology and then apply the theology's implications, using our philosophy of Halakhah, to further the goals of our covenant.

Partnership begins in Genesis 1 where God partners with the primordial elements of the earth and the waters to co-create life; further collaboration creates human beings. God then delegates stewardship of all creation to the ultimate co-creation. Fittingly, God leaves all the unfinished work of creation for us "to do" (Gen. 2:3). That work must happen without humans enslaving one another since each of us is created in the divine image. We are God's servants, not servants of servants (Lev. 25:55 and Baba Kamma 116b). For the priestly Torah, recognition of our neighbor's divine image precludes owning his labor in perpetuity, as a slave, *and* precludes dispossessing him of his land in perpetuity.[1] "The land must not be sold beyond reclaim, for the land is Mine; you

---

1   Without venturing a position on who is the neighbor of Leviticus 19:18, only Hebrew slaves are exempt from perpetual slavery (Lev. 25:45–46).

are only strangers and tenants with Me" (Lev. 25:23). The priestly Torah begins with the axiom of radical equality. The ensuing narrative and laws, culminating at the conclusion of Leviticus, establish the political and economic corollaries: no permanent slavery, no permanent debt, and no permanent homelessness. The literary structure of beginning with א and concluding with 'א is called an envelope structure or *inclusio*. The priestly Torah presents a divine envelope—from the radical claim of creation in the divine image in Genesis 1 to the corollaries thereof at the end of Leviticus.

At the apex of the literary ziggurat that forms the iconography of Leviticus, itself, lies the commandment to love our neighbor, the same one created in the divine image (Lev. 19:18). Although ritual purity is fundamental in priestly religion, what nourishes our partnership with God is love expressed through fidelity to the covenant. What drives God away is bloodshed and sexual immorality, both associated in the biblical period with idolatry. Heschel shows us how the Hebrew prophets conflated those three priestly cardinal sins with political and economic injustice. Moral rectitude, not ritual purity, was responsible for maintaining the divine presence in our midst. Priestly aspirations for a life of holiness were lofty: not standing idly by the blood of our neighbor, not hating our kinsfolk in our heart, not taking vengeance, and not holding a grudge. The love of neighbor in Leviticus 19:18 is the culmination of the compassion generated by the self-restraint called for in the preceding verses.

Since each of us is created in the divine image, our behavior towards one another is, at some level, our behavior towards the divine. The priestly insight that God is responsive to our deeds captures the reality that all creatures are implicated in our deeds. As RaMBaM wrote in the twelfth century, we are all one organism. Subsequent Jewish thought, particularly the mystical strands, developed the notion of a God who has needs and responds to human deeds. The Mosaic Torah leans more toward relationship than partnership, but both biblical theologies agree about the centrality of teshuvah, or righting our actions when needed. The Mosaic Torah is explicit that we should reorient ourselves in order to walk in God's ways. The implied optimism is that we can. For the rabbis, doing teshuvah, itself, is following in God's ways.

In the first chapter, I promised we would return to Day Four when "God made the two great lights, the greater light to dominate the day, and the lesser light to dominate the night and the stars" (Gen. 1:16). One Rabbi, Shimon ben Pazi, noticed, or created, a "contradiction" between the parity of the two "great" lights at the beginning of the verse and the subsequent disparity between "greater and lesser." Rabbi Shimon ben Pazi reconstructed the lunar query at the break in our verse: "God, how can two kings serve with one crown?" God seemed to have been fine with power sharing, but the moon was unfamiliar with anything other than monarchy—one ruler. God, peeved at the perceived challenge by the moon to God's novel management structure, told the moon to shrink and that would solve the problem. Hence, the moon became the "lesser light."

The moon did as commanded but then defended herself: "I was asking a good question, not angling to become the greater light." God regretted his hasty response and told the moon that, as compensation, the Jewish calendar would be a hybrid where the months would begin at the new moon. The halakhah dictates that the aggrieved party is to be appeased, and God could see that the moon was not (m. Yoma 8:9). So, God requested that we bring a sin offering *on His behalf* at each new moon. "And there shall be one goat as a sin offering for the Lord" (Numbers 28:15). The peshat of the verse has us bringing a sin offering to the Lord, not for the Lord, but such is the wondrous way of midrash (Hullin 60b).

God, like those in God's image, is imperfect. The Torah describes a God who regrets having made humans and starts over with Noah and his family. Our lunar midrash recognizes that what's done is done. We can only strive to improve in the future, and sacrifices were intended to prompt teshuvah. If God's imperfections require teshuvah, all the more so do ours. As an educator, like the rabbis, I appreciate the rabbinic projection of impatience on to the chief educational officer. Sometimes we educators respond flippantly to our students. Sometimes we parents respond impatiently to our children. But no one is above acknowledging their mistakes, apologizing, and trying to make amends—not even God. Rabbi Shimon ben Pazi heroically held God to account, he spoke truth to Power, and by doing so created a divine role model for teshuvah. As Tikva Frymer-Kensky said, "The *halakhah* [doing teshuvah] is the path of God in the world and the path of the world to God."[2]

---

2   Frymer-Kensky, *Studies in Bible*, 259.

Rabbi Shmuel bar Ami imagines God yearning for partnership with all earthly creatures; Rabbi Shimon ben Pazi gave God the chance to demonstrate it. The Torah, itself, bequeathed to the rabbis the value of synergy: "Five of you will pursue one hundred, and a hundred of you shall pursue ten thousand" (Lev. 26:8). When we are aligned in our pursuit, our power surges exponentially. It leaps. Rabbi Shmuel bar Ami imagines the covenant between God and all earthly creatures to maximize the potential power of the covenant.

Since the destruction of the Temple, God's wisdom and will are accessed through Torah study. As Rabbi Louis Finkelstein (1895–1991) said, "When I pray, I talk to God. When I study, God talks to me." There were other avenues to God, but the rabbis posted warning signs on them. We have accounts from the mystics who craved an unmediated experience of God. We also have scattered scenes throughout rabbinic literature offering glimpses of divine encounters. But the recommended route was Torah study, which, unlike Temple service, was not restricted to Priests in Jerusalem. Thus, divine access was increased but divine contact became mediated.

Rabbis were relatively tolerant of different theologies as long as the mitzvot were observed. In the Torah, as well, we saw the priestly religion coexist with the Mosaic religion since they both agreed that the mitzvot were the means to fulfill their mutual goal of living long on the land that the Lord, our God, has given us. Rabbinic religiosity had the same goal. Just as the Mosaic Torah recontextualized the priestly Torah, and the rabbis recontextualized the Torah, we must recontextualize the goal of the mitzvot: to live long on the whole land that the Lord, our God, has given all of us. The stewardship with which God charged humanity was universal. Our best chance at success is by partnering with those whose values and deeds share an overlapping consensus with our own.

The emphasis on deeds over creeds may have prompted a reaction by our medieval thinkers who emphasized the inner life, whether it be the intellectual rationalism of RaMBaM, the mystical intention of the Hasidei Ashkenaz and kabbalists, or the devotional piety of even those who no longer practiced Jewish observance. Proper intention was absorbed into the Halakhah, as well. If in the rabbinic world, one had to have the intention to transgress, in parts of the medieval world, one had to have the intention to fulfill. The entropy of the priestly world is increased by the Zohar, and once again in Lurianic mysticism. Perhaps the increasing cosmic instability had real-world roots. Throughout the Middle Ages, Christianity had become increasingly inhospitable to the Jews.[3]

RaMBaM did his best to insist on rationality in religion, but his influence on that score was modest.[4] Mysticism crowded out philosophy during the Middle Ages. The kabbalists did acknowledge, taking a page from RaMBaM's *Guide*, that there is an aspect of God which is impenetrable and about which we know nothing, the *Eyn Sof.* Unlike RaMBaM, however, they depicted another aspect of God incorporating the ten sefirot in dynamic unity. The sefirot represent the divine facets responsive to human deeds and intention. Jews have the power to strengthen or weaken the divine. The interdependencies that characterized the biblical creation account come to represent the dynamic interdependencies within God. In the words of Gershom Scholem: "Theogony [the creation of God] and cosmogony [the creation of the world] represent not two different acts of creation, but two aspects of the same."[5]

Medieval mysticism also continues rabbinic Judaism's understating that creation is a unity, a single whole. When the mystics describe a homology between the creation of the world and the creation of God, they bestow a measure of divine immanence to the world. At a minimum, we see a mediated monism through the tenth sefirah which links the supernal and earthly realms. At a maximum, we have the following vision from Moshe de Leon: "Everything is linked with everything else down to the lowest ring on the chain, and the true essence of God is above as well as below, in the heavens and on the earth, and nothing exists outside Him."[6]

Perhaps RaMBaM's greatest success as a religious reformer came from his insistence on the inviolability of natural laws.[7] Neither the phi-

---

3 David Nirenberg, *Anti-Judaism: The Western Tradition* (New York: W. W. Norton & Co., 2013), chapter 7.
4 Maimonides did have undue influence over the early scholars of *Wissenschaft des Judetums*. See Dov Weiss, "The Rabbinic God and Mediaeval Judaism," *Currents in Biblical Research* 15, no. 3 (2017): 369-73.
5 Scholem, *Major Trends*, 223.
6 Sefer HaRimon 47b; cited in Scholem, *Major Trends*, 223.
7 Halbertal, *Concealment and Revelation*, 139; David Berger, "Miracles and the Natural Order in Nahmanides," in *Rabbi Moses Nahmanides (RaMBaN): Explorations in His*

losophers' nor kabbalists' God performs miracles that interrupt the natural order. For Crescas, God's nature overflows with love, and the need to share that love is uncontrollable, i.e., beyond God's control. For Luria, too, there is an element of determinism in the very heart of creation that resulted in the shattering of the vessels. Earlier Jewish thinkers, both philosophers and kabbalists, recognized the inherent necessity of nature's laws; but what we have with Crescas and Luria is the recognition that those laws themselves are beyond divine control. With Luria, God initiated the invitation to relationship. What emerges after that decision to share love, however, is unscripted. Before the shattering of the vessels was *tzimtzum*, the prerequisite for the emergence of another with whom to be in partnership. My midrash of Rabbi Shmuel bar Ami's midrash says, "From yearning to enter into partnership with earthly creatures, the Holy One, blessed be He, began the world's creation."

For the rabbis, we love God by lovingly engaging in God's commandments. For RaMBaM, acquiring knowledge of nature is how we show our love *of* God; for Crescas, deeds of lovingkindness are how we show our love *for* God. Elijah de Vidas (1518–1592), a kabbalist from the Land of Israel, understands love as a cosmic principle that is the vehicle for communion with God: "One's deeds, enthusiastically performed from one's heart and soul, are the outstanding signs of love. . . . [and] Devekut [cleaving to God] grows organically out of love."[8]

The outpouring of love eventually encircles the gentile neighbor. Between German Jewry's *bildung* and Eastern European Jewry's Mussar was the publication of Pinhas Hurwitz's Sefer Habrit in 1797. For a culture that prized Torah study, Hurwitz's conclusions must have been revolutionary. His book was a best seller and correspondingly influential. Hurwitz devoted nearly fifty pages to an extended analysis of neighborly love. Resianne Fontaine offers the following summary:

> Hurwitz's systematic inquiry leads to the conclusion that reason, nature, Torah and tradition all require the love of one's neighbor, and that the

Religious and Literary Virtuosity, ed. Isadore Twersky (Cambridge, MA: Harvard University Press, 1983), 126; and Weiss, "Rabbinic God": 381-83.

8 Pachter, "Concept of Devekut," in Twersky, *Studies in Medieval Jewish History*, 210–11.

obligation to love one's fellow man is prior to anything else, including the pursuit of truth and the [study of and] observance of the Torah.[9]

One can see how such a view could lead into Reform Judaism's celebration of the brotherhood of humanity over the particularism of Jewish ritual. Both Hermann Cohen and Martin Buber understood the love of the other to be prior to the love of God. Rosenzweig flipped the causality: we should love the other as a response to the love of God. For all three, theology and ethics have become conceptually intertwined. In their Germanic fastidiousness, they may have been unnecessarily explicit. I'm not sure whether ethics is prior to theology or not; I *am* sure that the sequence shouldn't matter for purposes of covenant and a compelling Judaism. My experience is that these and those are the living words of God. I have been graced with a divine encounter through the love of another; and I have been graced with a divine encounter that invites my love of others.

My suspicion is that this dispute is rooted in a metaphysical category mistake. There is no fixed sequence because our sensitivity to the sublime is subjective. I disagreed with Rosenzweig that God's love is not constant. What's not constant is our receptivity to God's love. Our openness to God's presence, here and now, there and always, is the Hasidic contribution to a compelling Judaism. What is an illusion is God's absence. Unlike the tactical claim of the Mitnagdim, we do have the capacity to see through corporeality. We can worship through corporeality, as well. "The world (*ha-olam*) is a place of concealment (*he'lem*), for the divinity is hidden within the cloak of corporeality."[10]

The theology of panentheism neutralizes some of the problems of traditional monotheism. Theodicy and providence are no longer challenges to a God who is not altogether distinct from creation. There is no separate, willful God who intervenes in creation to blame for our misfortunes. If someone is looking for a God who does intervene on one's behalf, panentheism is not the right theology. God is neither omnipotent nor omniscient in the sense of knowing the future. Omni-cide is the ultimate theodicy.

---

9   Fontaine, "Love of One's Neighbour," in Baasten, *Studies in Hebrew Language*, 276.
10 Wolfson citing Rebbe Menachem Schneerson of HaBaD, *Open Secret*, 52.

Another implication of this understanding of God emphasizes the unity of creation. Instantaneous creation began the unfolding of creation, and *creatio continua* sustains it every moment. *Creatio continua*, the essence of the rabbinic theology of creation, involves a conspiracy, a breathing together, of all the elements of creation. The Cosmic Conspirator coordinates creation as a unity, *ma'aseh bereshit* in the singular. Darwin's theory corroborated Jewish wisdom on the unity of creation that was explained by divine immanence. A kabbalistic great chain of being sees divine emanations resulting in material creation as the metaphysical prelude to the emergence of humanity through the transmutation of species in nature. Fossils of extinct animals are evidence that either God is not in control of the unfurling of nature's history and/or that God's goals are not thwarted by extinction. The former is an inherent proposition of panentheism. The latter coheres with the rabbinic blessings for God varying creatures and not withholding anything from creation's bouquet.

Among the responses to modern individualism and existentialism has been the emphasis on overcoming the ego. Consider that the word *solipsism* first appears in English in 1836. It means excessive self-regard to the exclusion of others. A decade later came the neologism *self-transcendence*. Self-transcendence, for most of our theologians, involves *hesed*—bringing your love to neighbor, orphan, widow, and refugee. But self-transcendence can also be "the negation or transcendence of self, and the discovery, in the wake of that experience, that it is only God who remains."[11] In our contemporary theology of creation, *hesed* is not isolated to human deeds. Jonas call cosmic *hesed* "cosmogonic eros." God's energy pulses through creation opportunistically, seeking out avenues for freedom, diversity, and awareness.

As we saw in Genesis 1, created agents have both agency and interdependency. Just as all existence is co-existence, all evolution is co-evolution. "Long-term stable symbiosis that leads to evolutionary change is called 'symbiogenesis.' These mergers, long-term biological fusions beginning as symbiosis, are the engine of species evolution."[12] Symbiosis is the antiphonal call of the Deep to the Deep. Within each constellation of corporeality, divine immanence beckons. The entanglement between

---

11   Green, *Heart of the Matter*, 244.
12   Margulis and Sagan, *Acquiring Genomes*, 12.

two of them transcends either of them. At some point in earth's history, and at every moment since then, there was a leap to life. *T'chiyat ha'metim*, often translated as *the resurrection of the dead*, is better understood as the quickening of the lifeless.

We have seen two countervailing phenomena in the history of Jewish thought and nature, the first of which is also veiling. In the priestly environment, entropy reigns. Sacrifices were required to maintain equilibrium. Ontological realism is unyielding; only through the grace of divine mercy is the world prevented from returning to *tohu va'vohu*. In the worldview of medieval mysticism, creation's operations are fixed firmly along the sefirot's left meridian of *din*, uncompromising law. What we see in nature are shocking inefficiencies—one seed out of a billion takes root and terrifying extinction events have punctuated earth history even before our all-too-eager assistance. Nature red in tooth and claw veils the divinity of creation until read with truth and awe. The great reveal is from the other side of the sefirotic chart, the ever flowing, overflowing love that exploits every opportunity to exude.

> Why is [the divine name] *YWVH* introduced into the creation story only in the second chapter? This may be compared to a king who had empty glasses. The king said, "If I pour hot water into them, they'll burst; if I pour cold water into them, they'll contract." What did the king do? He mixed the hot and cold and poured the mixture into the glasses so they remained intact. Thus the Holy One, blessed be He, said, "If I create the world with mercy alone, its sins will overflow; with justice alone, how will the world survive? Hence, I'll create it with both justice and mercy, and then may it endure! That's why the verse says, "YHWH God made the earth and the heaven" (Gen. 2:4).[13]

In the language of rabbinic theology, it's *YHWH* to *Elohim*. In the language of Kabbalah, it's *hesed* to *din*. It's the force that, together with blind law and chance, mediates harmony in the central axis of kabbalistic equilibrium. Kaplan called it transnaturalism; Jonas called it cosmogonic eros. The manifestation of this love, let's call it cosmogonic *hesed*, reveals that we are at home in the universe, neither unwelcome visitors (as in Gnosticism) nor ephemeral epiphenomena (as in nihilism

13 Genesis Rabbah 12:15.

or existentialism). In the language of science, it's convergent evolution to entropy. It's the explanation for why these adaptive structures evolve repeatedly at varying scales and across species. Just as all existence is co-existence, all being is being with God.

Artson's emphasis on relationships is most welcome at this point. Rabbi Shmuel bar Ami identified the divine desire for partnership. We see that motif throughout Jewish literature and exemplified by Heschel's title: *God in Search of Man*. But it's not good for the human to be alone, either. The need is mutual; the results, ideally, are symbiotic. Gravitational pull obtains between two objects. So does eros, and so does divine transcendence. The Shechinah dwells in the inbetween. The consequence, for better and worse, is entanglement.

Our actions, which reveal or conceal the divine presence, have an afterlife. "What we perform may seem slight, but the aftermath is immense. . . . The sun goes down, but the deeds go on."[14] The Divine doesn't directly reward or punish us as a response to our behavior, but our deeds have transnatural consequences—entanglement. Since we are embedded within an interconnected matrix, akin to the intersecting lines of the sefirotic chart, the aftershocks of our deeds will be felt by all.

By virtue of our interconnectedness, we are co-created co-creators. Genesis 1 illustrates this in narrative. In that myth, the author uses the term *bara*, create, for how scientists describe *emergence*: a quality of the whole that is irreducible to its component parts. In HaBaD theology, recycled by Rav Kook, *leaps* describe bursts of new understanding in revelation parallel to emergence within creation. As creation is continuous and builds on itself, so does revelation. Jonas leverages the concept of cosmogonic eros into a philosophic argument for the ontological foundation of ethical behavior. He characterizes our responsibility as a consequence of our conviction that being has value.[15]

> Act so that the effects of your action are compatible with the permanence of genuine human life; or expressed negatively: Act so that the effects of your action are not destructive of the future possibility of such life. . . .

---

14 Heschel, *God in Search of Man*, 284.
15 Jonas, *Mortality and Morality*, 102.

We do not have the right to choose, or even risk, nonexistence for future generations on account of a better life for the present one.[16]

Jonas writes as a philosopher who infers cosmogonic eros from nature. I write as a Jewish theologian who accepts the divine invitation for partnership extended from cosmogonic *hesed*.

Morality and Midrash

After decades of debate, the Conservative movement's legal advisory board, the Committee on Jewish Law and Standards, offered an exemption to gays and lesbians on same-sex intimacy. This decision, at the end of 2006, opened the door for same-sex marriage and admission into rabbinical school for gays and lesbians. The exemption, however, was neither full nor fully honest. Although the members of the committee felt empowered to provide an exemption for rabbinic prohibitions around same-sex intimacy, they were too meek to extend the exemption to the biblical prohibition of male-to-male anal intercourse.[17]

As was pointed out by Rabbi Gordon Tucker at the time, the traditional halakhic distinction between biblical law and rabbinic law is predicated on a theory of revelation that Conservative Judaism rejects. Torah law is not ontologically distinct from rabbinic law. Both were good faith attempts by our ancestors to legislate what they believed to be God's will. The irony is that the Talmudic principle that Rabbis Dorff, Nevins, and Reisner relied on in their legal responsum posits that human dignity trumps even a biblical prohibition (Shabbat 81b). They argued that a life devoid of physical intimacy, for those capable only of same-sex intimacy, is an affront to their dignity. Yet, the authors knew that the members of the Committee on Jewish Law and Standards would be unwilling to follow the letter of that *principle* in order to exempt gay men from the biblical prohibition.[18]

---

16 Hans Jonas, *The Imperative of Responsibility: In Search of an Ethics for the Technological Age* (Chicago: University of Chicago Press, 1984), 11.

17 I previously discussed this issue in "Ethical Theories in the Conservative Movement," in *The Oxford Handbook of Jewish Ethics and Morality*, ed. Elliot N. Dorff and Jonathan K. Crane (New York: Oxford University Press, 2013), 227–29.

18 Dorff, *For the Love of God and People*, 232–38.

In a previous discussion of this legal fiction allowing gay men to be physically intimate while still upholding the prohibition on anal intercourse, I wrote that we are party to a halakhic "charade."[19] Legal fictions are designed to serve a positive function. In a religious legal system, however, they undermine our faith in the honesty of the system as a whole. Furthermore, in this case, as Rabbi Joel Roth wrote in his responsum against that of Rabbis Dorff, Nevins, and Reisner, exempting only rabbinic prohibitions is a farce likely to entrap gay men. Roth's charge, to which I am sympathetic, is that this "permissive" ruling is in violation of the biblical prohibition of placing a stumbling block before the blind.[20] How unrealistic, and cruel, to give gay men permission to be sexually active, but still sexually restricted.

The prohibition in Leviticus states: "Do not lie with a man as one lies with a woman" (Lev. 19:22). I have no doubt that the priestly author of our text, dedicated as he was to a realistic halakhah, would not tolerate anal intercourse under any circumstances. I am not so sure about the rabbis. We have seen that the rabbis drifted away from realism toward nominalism in their halakhah. We have also seen how morality motivated so many of their legal innovations and midrashic readings. Furthermore, there is a rabbinic principle that the Merciful One exempts those whose transgressions are beyond their control (Nedarim 27a). One of the examples used to demonstrate this latter principle is taking a vow that you would have a meal with Ploni next Tuesday. In the interim, your child falls ill, and you change your date. You are exempt from the consequences of violating the vow because of the unforeseen circumstance that prevented you, because of your concern for your child's welfare, from making the lunch date. In this case, not only do we see the principle of "beyond their control" in operation, but the specific case deals with a vow which many rabbis understood to have ontological force.

In chapter 11 ("Turning Torah"), we saw the rabbinic midrash on someone breaking into another's home at night versus when the sun had arisen "on him." The rabbis, noting that when the sun rises, it is not

---

19 Dorff disagrees that this is a legal fiction since studies indicate that a significant percentage of gay men do not engage in anal intercourse. Ibid., 235.

20 Joel Roth, "Homosexuality Revisited." All the teshuvot on homosexuality can be accessed through the Rabbinical Assembly's website: https://www.rabbinicalassembly.org/jewish-law/committee-jewish-law-and-standards/even-haezer#interpersonal.

just "on him" that it rises, learned something from the inclusion of what would have otherwise been superfluous. Similarly, our verse in Leviticus prohibiting male anal intercourse has a seemingly superfluous phrase: "as one lies with a woman." If the verse were to have simply stated: "Do not lie with a man," wouldn't that have been intelligible? To phrase the question more traditionally, what more do we learn from the seemingly superfluous phrase? The last time I asked this question to a group of undergraduates, only recently exposed to rabbinic logic, at least one of them immediately answered, "This prohibition is addressed only to men who 'lie with women.' This prohibition is not directed at gay men—only straight men and bisexuals."[21]

This reading is not a peshat reading, but Judaism is not a peshat religion. I inherited the method of midrash from the rabbis, and I am a faithful heir. In this case, modern literary criticism has opened up our eyes to how prescient some of the rabbis' reading methods actually were. In the words of Moshe Greenberg (1928–2010), a scholar of the Hebrew Bible, "The meaning and significance of a passage (an event, an utterance) may not be realized until activated by later circumstances or contemplation."[22] Stone takes that literary theory and places it in a halakhic context: "Developments in general society, such as enhanced equality between the sexes [or, enhanced equality between sexual orientations], may become a catalyst for halakhic innovation because a *posek's* [decisor's] historical situatedness leads to the insight that the halakhah's own values as yet have been imperfectly realized."[23] In our case, the normalization of gay rights in the United States has activated/catalyzed a new reading of our ancient prohibition. This reading furthers Halakhah's goals of compassion and inclusivity. I believe Moshe would be comforted and God would smile (Menachot 29b and Baba Metzia 59b). It is not good for man to be alone (Gen. 2:18).

---

21 Talal Ayalar, University of San Diego, Jewish Belief and Practice, Spring 2019.
22 Moshe Greenberg, *Studies in the Bible and Jewish Thought* (Philadelphia: Jewish Publication Society, 1995), 239. See also Adiel Schremer, "Toward Critical Halakhic Studies," New York University, The Tikvah Center for Law and Jewish Civilization (2010), 24, https://www.carlyoshea.com/toward-critical-halakhic-studies.html.
23 Stone, "Formulating Responses," 66.

Burden and Analogy

Let us consider another example, this time within the ritual sphere. Jakob Petuchowski points out that "Concern with the need not to 'bother [or burden] the congregation' has atrophied in the course of millennia. The initial framers of the Jewish liturgy seem to have had an awareness of the limited span of attention possessed by ordinary mortals. They also seem to have known that, at any rate on weekdays, Jews, in addition to worshipping their Creator, have to devote themselves to earning a living."[24]

What did the Talmud understand as burdensome? The mere addition of several extra verses in the morning prayer service qualified (Brachot 12b). Rabbi Yehuda, a student of Rabbi Akiva, reported that when his teacher would lead the congregation in service, he would shorten his prayer to avoid burdening the congregation (Brachot 31a). The sentiment was codified (h. Tefila 6:2 and S. A., O. H. 53:11). If several verses were considered burdensome, I would like to suggest that the five extra days of festivals required in the diaspora are unconscionable.

Festivals fall on specific days of the month, and the beginning of each month was established by witnesses testifying in Jerusalem. The system in place to notify distant communities of the new month was undermined by the Samaritans (m. Rosh Hashana 2:1–2). In response, the sages of Jerusalem mandated that communities far enough away to be in doubt concerning the first of the month should celebrate each festival for two days rather than one. During the time of the Talmud, in the fourth century, the mathematics of the lunar cycle were established which precluded confusion about the proper day to celebrate the festival. Yet, it was decided that out of deference to the customs of the ancestors, the second day of the festivals outside of Israel should be preserved (Beitza 4b).

Reformers in both England and Germany pushed for the abolition of the second day in the 1840s. In 1846, the London Tempelgemeinde was the first Jewish institution to actually do so. When Moses Sofer heard about the desire to eliminate the second day of festivals, predictably, he sought to raise the level of the prohibition.[25] Although there was halakhic justification for ceasing customs that developed for reasons no longer relevant, the Orthodox community in Europe rejected any such

---

24 Petuchowski, *Studies in Modern Theology*, 160.
25 See Katz, *Divine Law in Human Hands*, 263–64.

accommodation on this issue.[26] Geiger and Holdheim were among the earliest German Reform rabbis to advocate abolition of the second day, and they were joined by their American colleagues. By the 1860s, Reform congregation that kept two days of the festivals were in the minority.

The Conservative movement addressed the issue in 1933 and then again in 1963. Not until 1969 were there enough rabbis to endorse the authority for individual rabbis to forgo the second day. Rabbis Philip Sigal and Abraham J. Ehrlich were quick to point out that for both students and workers, missing those extra days is "an extreme hardship." Their arguments included both historical data and halakhic issues concerning the holiness of the second day and the permissibility of nullifying a custom. After dispensing with potential objections, they enumerated several motives:

> Our proposed declaration on the Second Day of Festivals will also help restore some semblance of confidence in the machinery of halakhah, in the operation of our Law Committee, and in the realism of our approach to Judaism. Yom Tov Sheni [the Second Day of Festivals], more than anything we can pinpoint, is a severe case of an enactment which the community cannot live with, which the Rabbis of old had the good grace to remove. . . . A declaration on the Second Day of Festivals should be offered because the second day is *halakhically indefensible*. It is not crucial if the declaration utterly fails to increase piety or Jewish observance among those of little devotion. We should act for the sake of those who enjoy and observe one day, but regard the second day as repetitious and burdensome, although they observe it because of their loyalty to halakhah.[27]

Although we must use analogies if we are to remain committed to Judaism, honesty demands that we are as transparent about motivations and the contexts of our analogies as possible.[28] The rabbis didn't want to burden their community with an extra two minutes of prayer, three times a day, every day. The analogy with the Second Day is inexact. On

---

26 Ibid., 294.
27 Abraham J. Ehrlich and Philip Sigal , "A Responsum on *Yom Tov Sheni shel Galut*," *Conservative Judaism* 24, no. 2 (1970): 1257. Emphasis in original.
28 See Mark Washofsy, "The Woodchopper Revisited: On Analogy, Halakhah, and Jewish Bioethics," in *Medical Frontiers and Jewish Law*, ed. Walter Jacob (Pittsburgh: Freehof Institute of Progressive Halakha, 2012), 1-62.

the one hand, the rabbis were concerned with the daily issue of prayer length; on the other hand, the second day of festivals is only five times per year, but it's a day that might otherwise be spent at work or school. Given the expectations of today's marketplace, I believe those extra five days constitute an unnecessary burden on the community. Thus, I find Sigal and Ehrlich's claim that observance of the Second Day of Festival is an extreme hardship is a valid analogy to what we find in the Talmud.

Although the teshuva was endorsed by the Law Committee, it was not unanimous, and very few synagogues have availed themselves of the dispensation. In one of the opposing statements, Rabbi Wilfred Shuchat marshalled several arguments against Sigal and Ehrlich's proposal. Rabbi Shuchat cites a nineteenth-century rabbi, David Luria, who argued that in the case of such an important custom, monetary loss is an unacceptable reason to repeal the custom.[29] What is *important* and what is *unacceptable* is subjective. To parry, I will cite Adiel Schremer:

> These halakhic concepts [of "great loss" and "the Torah shows care for Israel's wealth"] are tools of justification, applied in support of halakhic positions motivated by a concern to prevent the loss of a Jew's property, in cases where that prevention stands in contrast to an existing halakhic norm. To be sure, once these concepts entered the halakhic discourse [in the Talmud] they became so popular, that one is entirely justified in seeing them as "halakhic."[30]

Before taking leave of the Second Day, it is worthwhile returning to the *philosophical* origin of the issue. Historically, the origin of the practice was concern that diaspora Jews should observe the festival on the "right day." That attitude bespeaks a realist worldview where there is a right day, where the inherent holiness of the cosmos shifts to a festival holiness which prescribes certain actions and proscribes others. This perspective on time comes from a priestly worldview and halakhah. But rabbinic Judaism largely rejected this inheritance.

In a scene best remembered for its implications for leadership and governance, Rabban Gamliel summons Rabbi Joshua and demands that he bring his walking stick and purse (m. Rosh Hashana 2:9). The

---

29 Wilfred Shuchat, "Response to a *Responsum*," *Conservative Judaism* 24, no. 2 (1970): 1266.
30 Schremer, "Toward Critical Halakhic Studies," 32–33.

summons to appear fell on a day that, by Rabbi Joshua's calculation, would have been Yom Kippur. Thus, carrying his stick and purse would be prohibited. But Rabban Gamliel had overseen the testimony of eye-witnesses establishing a different beginning to the month. Thus, for Rabban Gamliel, it was just another day. The sources agree that Rabbi Joshua appeared before Rabban Gamliel and that the biblical text that was drashed in connection to this dispute was from the priestly Torah: "'These are the times of the Lord, the festivals, that *you* will invoke' (Lev. 23:4), whether in their correct time or not." This shift from realism to nominalism is both transparent and illustrative of the general tendency of rabbinic Judaism.[31] As always, a dissenting voice confirms the linger-ing presence of halakhic realism. "Rabbi Elazar ben Rabbi Tzadok says: If you don't see [the moon] at the right time, don't sanctify it. They have already sanctified it in heaven" (Rosh Hashana 24a). But as Rabbi Joshua taught, the power to sanctify the moon is not in heaven.

A Contemporary and Compelling Covenant

A contract is between parties, a covenant between partners. The mid-rash imagining God and the Jewish people marrying under the *huppah* of Sinai with the Torah as the ketubah is the quintessential representa-tion of a covenant (Pirkei d'Rabbi Eliezer, 40). The terms of a contract can be updated through reference to the consumer-price index. But a covenant of love involves more than discharging obligations. A covenant represents an ongoing, dynamic relationship between partners where the terms of the contract must change in order to fulfill the purpose of the covenant: to love one another and fulfill each other's needs. What I need from my partner now is different than what I needed on our honey-moon—although there is overlap. Covenantal partners require devotion.

The Hasidic master, Yehuda Leib Alter of Ger (1847–1905), offers a drash bridging devotion and halakhah. He is commenting on a familiar

---

31 If my assumption is correct, the gemara's question and Ritba's interpretation of the scene between Rabbi Akiva and Rabbi Joshua makes more sense (Rosh Hashana 25a). "Who was distressed by Rabban Gamliel's summons—Rabbi Akiva or Rabbi Joshua?" Akiva, the one with realist sensibilities, is the one who is distressed. The nominalist derash, regardless of who spoke to whom in the gemara's story, was a teaching of Rabbi Joshua.

verse from the Torah and the liturgy which has a doubling of the verb *listen.*

> This is the issue of *listen, yes listen.* The doubling means that if you've listened to what's old, you'll listen/hear something new (Deut. 11:11). It's the same issue with our verse in Deuteronomy (5:18). God's great voice never stops because the words are alive, and God is always giving Torah. Thus, according to how one upholds the Torah and mitzvot, one is able to hear/sense novelties at every moment. This is like an infant nursing at her mother's breast. When the infant sucks, milk is expressed. This is also the issue with the midrash of *we will do and we will understand*—One knows through the doing and is able to understand increasingly more (b. Shabbat 88a on Exodus 24:7). When the Torah and the prayer book say, "Happy is one who listens to/obeys Your mitzvot," it really means listening *out* for God's mitzvot (Prov. 8:34). Through this power of listening, sages can draw forth Oral Torah that lies dormant. And then the sages of each generation can broaden the Torah's light at each moment. And so, too, can each individual.[32]

For Bahya, we need to be on the lookout in nature for novel ways to serve God.[33] For our Hasidic tzaddik, the Gerer Rebbe, we need to be listening out for the new Torah that God is always giving. For both Bahya and the Gerer, it's not only the sages who can awaken the sleeping Oral Torah; it is in the power of each individual. Through doing mitzvot, we become attuned and understand increasingly more. As Heschel wrote fifty years ago, "Jewish thought is disclosed in Jewish living."[34]

Judaism's value of protecting life prohibits us from doing anything to unnecessarily put our lives at risk (b. Shabbat 32a). The Talmudic examples are being in a public space where fights are likely to break out and walking among palm trees during strong winds. Those cases cover location and conditions. As the prohibition was codified in the Middle Ages, it was broadened to include anything that posed a mortal danger (h. Murder 11:4–5 and S. A., H. M. 427:8–10). The midrashic mechanism for this prohibition is particularly forced. In Deuteronomy we are warned "to take utmost care and watch yourselves scrupulously so that

---

32 Sefat Emet, Parashat Ekev, 1896.
33 Bahya, *Duties of the Heart*, 184.
34 Heschel, *God in Search of Man*, 282.

you do not forget the things you saw with your own eyes" (9:4). The midrash severs the first part of the verse and reads it in isolation as: "Take utmost care to watch yourselves [your lives] scrupulously." These sorts of strained midrash halakhah are particularly illuminating in that they legislate something about which the Torah is seemingly silent. In these midrashim we can hear the rabbis most clearly. How might this halakhah be applied today?

Once the detrimental health effects of smoking became accepted, rabbis across the denominational spectrum responded. While some, such as the Orthodox Rabbi Moshe Feinstein, prohibited everyone from starting to smoke, he "grandfathered" in those smokers who were already addicted.[35] The Israeli Reform Rabbi, Moshe Zemer, goes further. Not only is smoking prohibited, without exception, it is also prohibited to provide a smoker with a lighter.[36] Zemer has applied the Talmud's prohibition on helping someone commit a transgression and applied it to our case (Avoda Zara 55b).

Health issues around smoking are direct and imminent: it is unhealthful for the smoker and those around her in their lifetimes. I would like to extend Rabbi Zemer's thinking on smoking in two different directions, both involved with economics. First of all, people should not work for tobacco companies. Secondly, people should not own stock in tobacco companies. Employees and investors are either standing idly by the blood of one's neighbor or placing stumbling blocks before the blind (Lev. 19:16 and 14). In an analysis of this issue, Aaron Levine applies Rav Soloveitchik's understanding of the command in Genesis 1 to steward [*kibbush*] the earth: "Fulfillment of this mandate bids man to achieve dignity but along with it to attain a rarefied sense of responsibility."[37] Rav Soloveitchik understands that mastery over nature, the primary meaning of *kibbush* from Genesis, is a prerequisite for humanity to not be at the mercy of nature. According to Rav Soloveitchik, "There is no dignity without responsibility, and one cannot assume responsibility as long as

35 Igrot Moshe, H. M. 2:76.
36 Moshe Zemer, *Evolving Halakhah: A Progressive Approach to Traditional Jewish Law* (Woodstock: Jewish Lights Publishing, 2003), 350.
37 Aaron Levine, *Case Studies in Jewish Business Ethics* (Hoboken: Ktav Publishing House, 2000), 373; summarizing Joseph B. Soloveitchik, *The Lonely Man of Faith* (New York: Doubleday, 1992), 16–20.

he is not capable of living up to his commitments."[38] To enjoy mastery but avoid responsibility is the demise of dignity. But responsibility presumes ability, and smoking is disabling.

> What emerges from the *kibbush* doctrine is a criterion for evaluating the *inherent worthiness* of economic activity. If an economic activity contributes neither to advancing man's dignity nor to his sense of responsibility, it has no rationale for existence. . . . Far from advancing human dignity, the tobacco industry degrades human existence by causing disease, misery, and pain. Its very existence perverts the *kibbush* mandate.[39]

Robert Cover, a philosopher of law who taught at Yale Law School until his death in 1986, brought Jewish law and American law into conversation in his celebrated 1983 article "Nomos and Narrative." In his introduction to that essay, he offers a précis worthy of Bialik's "Halakhah and Aggadah": "No set of legal institutions or prescriptions exists apart from the narratives that locate it and give it meaning. For every constitution there is an epic, for each decalogue a scripture."[40]

In his final essay, published posthumously, he defined mitzvah as an *incumbent obligation*.[41] In this essay, he contrasts the American and Jewish legal systems. To over-simplify, American law is concerned with individual rights, and Halakhah with communal responsibilities. In the conclusion of the essay, he combines *noblesse oblige* and *tikkun olam* to articulate a halakhic posture, much like the *kibbush* mandate.

> The struggle for universal human dignity and equality still proceeds on many levels all over the world. There is no question that we can use as many good myths in that struggle as we can find. Sinai and the social contract both have their place. Yet, as I scan my own—our own—privileged position in the world social order and the national social order, as I attend the spiritual and material blessings of my life and the rather obvious connection that some of these have with the suffering of others—

---

38 Ibid., 16.
39 Levine, *Case Studies*, 374. Emphasis in original.
40 Cover, "Nomos and Narrative," 95–96.
41 Robert Cover, "Obligation: A Jewish Jurisprudence of the Social Order," in Minnow, *Narrative, Violence, and the Law*, 239.

it seems to me that the rhetoric of obligation speaks more sharply to me than that of rights. Of course, I believe that every child has a right to a decent education and shelter, food, and medical care; of course, I believe that refugees from political oppression have a right to a haven in a free land; of course, I believe that every person has a right to work in dignity and for a decent wage. But more to the point I also believe that I am commanded—that we are obligated—to realize those rights.[42]

Cover's final written words exemplify the rabbinic dictum that the righteous, even after their deaths, remain alive (Brachot 18a).

As a graduate student in Israel in 1992, I was introduced to the economic power of *kashrut* during the cola wars. Pepsi was running ads showing the march of evolutionary progress from an ape to a Pepsi-chugging human. One of the organizations providing kosher supervision to Pepsi withdrew its hekhsher, the symbol to consumers that the product is kosher. Evolution, for these ultra-Orthodox rabbis, was *treyf* (not kosher). No hekhsher, no sales. Although I disagreed with their rationale, I applauded their larger vision of extending the designation of what is kosher beyond mere ingredients or the slaughterer's slice of the jugular vein. In the Talmud, kosher means *proper*, and the term is applied to business practices, employee relations, environmental issues, health and safety concerns, animal welfare, waste disposal, modesty, and food consumption. In all of these domains, and more, Jewish practices had to be kosher, i.e., proper. Designating food as kosher predicated exclusively on the ingredients or the moment of an animal's death, while ignoring how the animal lived, or how the employees were treated, or the disposal of manufacturing by-products, or the effects of using the product, or how the product is marketed butchers the term "kosher" and is a desecration of God's name.

At the time, I also noted that Coca-Cola was running television advertisements featuring female dancers in immodest clothing. Their *hekhsher* was not threatened. Then I realized that Coca-Cola had a manufacturing plant in Bnei Brak, an ultra-Orthodox city just east of Tel Aviv. Since Coca-Cola was a pillar of the city's economic base, it seems the ultra-Orthodox rabbinical establishment chose not to bite the hand that fed them. The Pepsi bottling plant was in the secular city of Holon.

42 Ibid., 248.

When Pepsi's *hekhsher* was removed again the following year, the reason offered was scantily clad women in their advertisements. Nevertheless, Coke's hekhsher was not suspended.

A coherent philosophy of halakhah should be organically linked to a theory of creation. The fundamental model for our contemporary theology of creation was articulated by Rabbi Avraham Yehoshua Heschel of Apt (1748–1825) who then sowed it into a philosophy of halakhah.

> Rabbi Berechiyah says in the name of Rabbi Yehudah, "Not a single day goes by without the holy blessed One innovating halakhah in the supernal court" (Genesis Rabbah 49:2). . . . To understand this, we recite [in liturgy]: "Through His goodness He renews, daily, the work of creation." It is known that the holy blessed One created the world through Torah (Genesis Rabbah 1:1). Since the creation of the world was through Torah, the constant renewal of the work of creation must also take place through the renewal of Torah and the halakhot that the tzaddikim innovate in each and every generation, each and every day. . . . Since they are daily engaged in Torah and God's *mitzvot* with integrity, sincerity, awe, and love, the blessed One showers them with straight thinking and human insight to understand how to make analogies and the reasons for Torah and the mitzvot. Through this [intellectual clarity] they innovate new halakhot every day. . . . And through their innovations, the work of creation is renewed each day, always.[43]

According to the Apter Rav, the work of creation is renewed because the tzaddikim, the Hasidic leaders, imitate God by innovating halakhah. Indeed, there is reason to think that when the Apter Rav speaks of innovating new halakhot, he means more than updating the halakhah on the books. He may mean creating new halakhah, *de novo*, to realize the values and principles inherent in traditional halakhah.[44] It is in the spirit of renewing halakhah in order to renew the act of creation that I present the following argument to eliminate beef from our diets.

Cattle chew their cud and have cloven hooves. Anatomically, they are fit for Jewish consumption. So are goats and sheep. Yet the Mishnah

---

43 Avraham Yehoshua Heschel, Ohev Yisrael, *Tol'dot*, 23. Cited and translated by Mayse, with modifications, in "The Ever-Changing Path," 102.

44 In a closely related discussion, Shaul Magid called this *neonomianism*. See his *Hasidism on the Margin*, 211.

prohibits raising the latter in the land of Israel because of *their* consumption requirements (m. Baba Kamma 7:7). The concern is that small livestock consume vegetation that could more efficiently be used to feed people. The Talmud records a scene where a goat is called an *armed bandit* (Baba Kamma 80a). Rashi explains that goats frequently eat vegetation from other people's property. Yet, the mishnah's concern was not with theft, *per se*, but with the relatively poor return on animals versus crops for satisfying the needs of the community. Thus, it seems more logical to call goats and sheep armed bandits because they take resources from the poor who cannot afford the relatively high price of meat. Cattle are, similarly, armed bandits. At this point, my only claim is that the sages responded to a scarcity of resources that privileged the wealthy. Small livestock was still kosher to raise outside the Land of Israel, and the wealthy could import and consume the meat within the Land. Another innovative prohibition prohibits foul odors generated by businesses (m. Baba Batra 2:9). With cattle, it is not the foul odor from their belches and flatulence that does damage, it is the release of methane that exacerbates the greenhouse effect which contributes to global warming. The mishnah's prohibition on injurious manufacturing byproducts should surely apply to raising cattle.

We have already discussed halakhah's health concerns, and the prohibition of needlessly putting oneself, or others, at risk. Although there is evidence that beef consumption contributes to heart disease and colon cancer, I do not believe that the halakhah could prohibit beef consumption on that basis alone. There are simply too many products and activities that carry some risk to prohibit each one. Only the most egregious should be banned. Nor do I think that killing animals is halakhically impermissible. Scientific experimentation, for example, will likely endanger animal subjects. Factory farming raises issues about the ethical treatment of animals, but those issues are procedural, not substantive. They can be addressed, and there are small operations that offer kosher slaughter for pasture-raised cattle. Thus, even the cumulative weight of the concerns for individual human health and animal welfare do not warrant the prohibition of beef consumption. But there are other concerns.

On the human scale, the first analogy is armed banditry. Cattle production requires significantly more water and land to yield the same amount of nutritional value as provided by other crops. I take it as a given that these resources, already scarce in some parts of the world, will become increasingly depleted as the world's population grows. Even this argument, however sound, lacks the urgency to be halakhically decisive.

On a global scale, the issue is dual-belching byproducts. We are currently supporting a farming system that is exacerbating global warming which experts agree is threatening life on our planet. This environmental damage is occurring right now and the need to address the crisis is urgent. Preserving life is an ultimate value, and giving up beef is not life threatening. There are both beef substitutes and other accessible ways to get protein. There is also other animal meat. Cow emissions are disproportionately polluting. Our covenant's primary principle is to live long on the land the Lord, our God, has given us. Thus, we must make immediate changes in our behavior patterns. In a prescient midrash written well over a millennium ago, God warned Adam not to despoil the earth for there would be no one to repair it.[45] Giving up beef is something we can do immediately that is nontrivial. Other changes will, of course, also be required.

This halakhic innovation, I have been told, is both impractical and meaningless. It is impractical because Jews will not give up beef; it's meaningless because even if they did, Jews represent a negligible share of the beef-eating market. Were rabbis to withhold *hekhshers* on beef, I believe many Jews would comply with the intention to boycott beef. Jews may represent an insignificant market share, but Jews also have disproportionate influence in American culture. Doing the right thing does not require certainty that others will follow suit. We aspire to be a light unto the nations, and we reject the inertia of indifference. As Martin Buber wrote in 1923, "Inertia and indifference are called the root of all evil; sin is basically nothing more than inertia."[46]

Lightening the yoke of halakhah cannot be the singular goal of a coherent Judaism. There are occasions when we must show strength by exercising self-restraint (m. Avot 4:1). Our covenant sometimes demands significant sacrifice. "We can, in community with one another, in conversation with religious virtuosi of earlier generations, and in communion

---

45 Ecclesiastes Rabbah 7:13.
46 Buber, "Jewish Religiosity," in Glatzer, *On Judaism*, 82.

with that divine power at work in the world, choose a moral direction."[47] There is no guarantee of a happy ending. There is no *deus ex machina* to save us from ourselves. Our fate and God's rests in our hands.

> I call as witnesses against you today the heavens and the earth. Life and death I place before you, blessing and curse. Choose life so that you may stay-alive, you and your seed. Loving the Lord your God, listening for His voice, and cleaving to Him—For that is your life and the length of your days that you may endure on the land that the Lord swore to give to your ancestors, to Avraham, to Yitzhak, and to Ya'akov (Deut. 30:19–20).[48]

In Pope Francis' 2015 encyclical on the environmental threats to our planet *Laudato Si*, he calls for an "environmental conversion." Given the pope's deep concern for our environment, is there room to review the Church's counterproductive stance toward birth control? Judaism needs no environmental conversion, just an updated version of *kashrut*: kosher 2.0.[49] My suggestion for the Church in no way diminishes my appreciation for Pope Francis leading the religious charge for changing environmental policies and practices. My suggestion for the Church touches on halakhic development, as well.

In a Talmudic discussion of the laws incumbent upon gentiles, we find the claim that the laws given to Noah after disembarking no longer apply to Jews, who replaced the Noahide covenant with the Sinai covenant. The specific case involved feticide. "Whoever spills human blood, *for that human* shall his blood be spilled" is drashed by the rabbis as, "Whoever spills human blood *in a human*, his blood shall be spilled" (Gen. 9:6 and Sannhedrin 57b). Who is a human in a human? A fetus. Thus, for gentiles, feticide is murder. For Jews, however, feticide is not only permitted, but when the mother's life is in danger, feticide is mandated (m. Ohalot 7:6). The Talmud suggests, and the Tosafot broadly concur, that there is nothing permitted to Jews that is forbidden to gentiles. Thus, the Tosafot suggest that if the gentile woman's life is in jeopardy, her life should be preserved by aborting the fetus.

---

47   Louis E. Newman, *Past Imperatives: Studies in the History and Theory of Jewish Ethics* (Albany: State University of New York Press, 1998), 157.
48   This translation follows ibn Ezra and not the New Jewish Publication Society.
49   My daughter, Rina, came up with that term when she was nine years old.

The Tosafot demand that Jews behave no less morally than Christians.[50] Thus the pope's charge in *Laudato Si* raises a halakhic challenge. Indeed, one of the conclusions for students of the history of Jewish thought is just how influential the surrounding cultural, religious, and intellectual contexts have been for Israelites and Jews. Research into ancient Near Eastern texts shows similarities with the literature of the Torah; Hellenistic and Sassanian thought with rabbinic literature; and Aristotelianism, Neoplatonism, and Islamic jurisprudence, philosophy, grammar, and mysticism, with medieval Judaism. Even the Virgin Mary of the medieval Catholic Church finds her counterpart in the emerging role of Shechinah within Jewish mysticism.

In the modern period, Kant was the towering gentile for Jewish thought. Other nineteenth-century thinkers also had their influence on Jewish thought, but the school of American Pragmatism ushered in a new sensibility that proved comfortably familiar to American Jews. William James avoided metaphysics by focusing on the "cash value" of competing propositions—what difference would it make in the real world? That question is a reverberation of rabbinic religiosity where the underlying theology or metaphysics was bracketed because the behavioral prescriptions of both the priestly and Mosaic theologies were nearly identical. For rabbinic religiosity, the mitzvot were the cash value of their mutually exclusive belief systems.

Mordecai Kaplan was a metaphysical minimalist expressly concerned about the function of the mitzvot—their cash value. Kaplan's posture towards theology reflects neither the priestly nor Mosaic theologies, but it captures their mutual presence within rabbinic religiosity. Kaplan offers just enough metaphysics to provide an ontological foundation for Jewish ethics. The acceptance of multiple perspectives within rabbinic Judaism, which becomes even more valorized within the later mystical tradition, is a model for a contemporary, coherent Judaism. The House of Hillel presented a model of mutually engaged fallibilism. Nevertheless, there are still red lines. Here are three examples to illustrate where those lines lie.

The Shulchan Arukh imagines a situation where a Jew has violated a communal norm. But if he wants to pray with the community, as long

---

50 See, for example, Rabbi Meir ben Abulafia, *Yad Ramah*, op. cit.

as he hasn't been banished, he can be counted toward the ten needed for a quorum.[51] Even a murderer who has not been banished can count towards the quorum. Why? Because even when a Jew sins, according to the priestly anthropology, *his holiness endures.*[52] The late nineteenth-century legal codifier, Yehiel Epstein, is faced with a different social reality. He writes in his Arukh Hashulchan that someone who transgresses the entire Torah should not be counted in a prayer quorum, even if has not been banished.[53] That seems reasonable. The Mishnah Brurah, then, retreats to the position of the Shulchan Arukh and specifies that someone like me, who does not transgress the whole Torah but does accept the "heresy" of the human origin of the Written and Oral Torahs, is not to be counted toward the quorum.

I can understand allowing any Jew who wants to pray to be counted toward the quorum, but the Mishnah Brurah's rationale is racist and offensive. A murderer can count, but I don't? Nevertheless, with such silliness I can live. A heretic like me can still pray and be counted towards a quorum in a community of like-minded heretics. More significantly for me, any of those nine other heretics can be women. No red line.

In 1985, a train crashed into a bus killing twenty-two people, twenty-one of whom were on a fieldtrip with their middle school in Petach Tikva. Two weeks afterwards, Yitzhak Peretz, a government minister from the ultra-Orthodox Shas Party, linked the accident to Shabbat violations in Petach Tikva and invalid mezuzas at their school. The same Mosaic theology was utilized again by Christian preachers after the felling of the Twin Towers. They claimed God was punishing America for its acceptance of homosexuality. I reject the Mosaic theodicy. It is offensive, but it does not impinge upon the freedom of society. No red line. However, were the minister to demand changes in the law to prevent Sabbath violations or extra funds to purchase valid mezuzas, then there would be a red line that would require negotiation.

The final example is *agunot*, women anchored to recalcitrant husbands who refuse to give them a divorce. For me, indifference to this behavior is a red line because it violates our covenant's values of freedom and dignity for God's creatures. As Robert Cover wrote, I have an

---

51 O. H., 55:11.
52 Ibid., 55:11:47.
53 Ibid., 55:16.

obligation to help realize those fundamental freedoms for others who need such assistance. I profoundly disagree with the status of women in all forms of Orthodoxy. But concerning the lack of egalitarianism in prayer services, I am prepared to say, "These and those." The red line emerges when gender inequality imprisons women. Just as God releases the captive, so, too, must we.

We are blessed to be living in a period when women's contributions to Judaism, science, and law strengthen our covenant, our knowledge, and our ability to pursue justice and equity. In each of the three books of *Coherent Judaism*, feminist theory has played a crucial role both in helping us understand our history and clearing paths for our covenantal future. As Tamar Ross has reminded us, according to Rav Kook, whatever increases in inclusivity enjoys a corresponding increase in holiness.[54] A coherent Judaism must overturn tradition when its leaders have been graced by "the insight that the halakhah's own values as yet have been imperfectly realized."[55]

A coherent Judaism preserves tradition when it can. Oliver Wendell Holmes wrote, "It is revolting to have no better reason for a rule of law than that so it was laid down in the time of Henry IV."[56] Such a principle could never apply to Judaism because the antiquity of a law is part of its own justification. When I tell the barber to keep my sideburns, i.e., not to cut the corners of my head (Lev. 19:27), I do two things. First of all, I preserve a long tradition that connects me to the history of my people and to the current practice of many Jews. Secondly, it reminds me of the obligation of *tzedakah* (charity). The same chapter in Leviticus obligates us to leave the corners of our field for the poor and the strangers (Lev. 19:9–10).

Of course, it is revolting, to use Holmes' term, to preserve a law if there are pernicious consequences that undermine the goals of the legal system, what RaMBaM called "bad laws." Today, prohibiting gay men from full sexual expression with other gay men is a moral example of a bad law. Another bad law, this time due to its unnecessary burden, is demanding all congregations in the diaspora to observe the second days of festivals. A coherent Judaism, in remedying these bad laws, should be

---

54 Ross, "Feminist Aspects," in Ravitsky, Derekh Ha-Ruach, 732–33.
55 Stone, "Formulating Responses," 66.
56 Oliver Wendell Holmes, "The Path of the Law," in *Philosophy of Law and Legal Theory: An Anthology*, ed. Dennis Patterson (Malden: Blackwell Publishing, 2003), 16.

honest that the traditional halakhic distinction between biblical and rabbinic laws is flawed. There is no fundamental difference. Nor is there an ontologically distinctive day on which to celebrate Shabbat and holidays.

Furthermore, as Benjamin Sommer has pointed out, it makes little sense to always give a rabbinic interpretation of the Torah greater halakhic weight than what we give to the Torah itself. I refuse to be enslaved to the *peshat* of a rabbinic *derash* when the consequence is a bad law. The Pharisees were accused by the Sadducees of being *leniency seekers*, and they were. So be it. If a more just and compassionate halakhah can be obtained by rehabilitating a reading from within our tradition that has been eclipsed or marginalized, that is preferable to straying outside our tradition. According to the Mishnah, that's precisely why the words of minority opinions were preserved (m. Eduyot 1:5). The rabbis knew we would need tools for Halakhah to serve as our bridge "from the written word into the living deed."[57] They gave us those tools. Shame on us if we are too meek to use them.

Finally, there are times when a covenantal Halakhah must be *jurisgenerative*, to use Robert Cover's term, and legislate for the times. There is a long tradition of the desirability of increasing mitzvot and good (*kosher*) deeds. The Zohar says that by doing good deeds, we give God strength (Zohar 2:32b on Ps. 68:35). In some cases, rabbinic encouragement to buy a more eco-friendly car might suffice. At other times, urgency requires the full weight of the Halakhah, including analogies and aggadah, to generate kosher Halakhah.

Yeshayahu Leibowitz was almost right:

> What characterizes Judaism as a system of mitzvot is not the set of laws and commandments that was given at the start, but rather the recognition of a system of precepts as binding, even if their specifics were determined only with time. Moreover, this system of norms is constitutive of Judaism.[58]

Leibowitz and I disagree about what constitutes Judaism. He sees it as a contract—a system of norms. I see it as a covenant. I am unwilling to relegate my relationship with God to the contract's appendix.

---

57 Berkovits, *Not in Heaven*, 1.
58 Yeshayahu Leibowitz, "Religious Praxis," in *Judaism, Human Values and the Jewish State*, ed. Eliezer Goldman (Cambridge, MA: Harvard University Press, 1992), 3–4.

Blessings are said prior to doing mitzvot. As we saw in book 1, Abraham ibn Gikatilla links the tradition of saying one hundred blessings to the hundred sockets of the portable Tabernacle's frame.[59] In other words, the recitation of blessings should build a consciousness of God's indwelling presence, akin to the function of the Tabernacle, throughout the day, every day. The Rebbe of Komarno, Yitzhak Safrin (1806–1874), "took the bold step of condoning the creation of new blessings that fit new or unique occasions. . . . One *must* offer blessings whenever possible."[60] Blessings, and the mitzvot that follow, reveal and strengthen God's presence. As Arthur Green teaches, "Each *mitzvah* is an *opportunity* for encounter between the silent divine presence and the human soul that seeks to articulate it."[61]

"A voice calls in the wilderness: clear a road of God" (Is. 40:3).

The verse lacks a preposition. We don't know if it is a road to God or a road for God. Are we on the move or is God? Yehudah Ha'Levi dissolves the question: "And in my going out to meet You, I found You coming toward me."

The road we clear requires a communal effort. The verse's imperative is in the plural. God cannot do it alone, nor can we as individuals. We exist in covenant.

God's name in this verse is the tetragrammaton, the four-letter name of divine being. In book 1, I suggested YHWH carries the meaning of *let being become.*

The voice we hear in our wilderness, sometimes still and small, and sometimes howling, is a voice uniquely our own. How do we best let being become more free, more diverse, and more self-conscious? How do we best ensure that we live long on the land so that we can partner with God in the ongoing act of creation? Those are the questions of a coherent and compelling Judaism.

אשרי איש שישמע למצותך

---

59 Gikatilla, Sha'are Orah, 17-18.
60 Kahana and Mayse, "Hasidic Halakhah," 406. For the daring novelty of this position, see Langer, *To Worship God Properly*, 85–109.
61 Green, *Radical Judaism*, 97. Emphasis in original.

Glossary*

acosmism	belief that the world as an independent reality is an illusion
agunah/agunot	literally, a chained woman; a woman whose husband refuses to issue her a writ of divorce
Amora, Amora'im	rabbis from the period of the Gemara, third–sixth centuries; Aramaic
Ashkenazi	related to Jews from Europe, specifically France, Germany, and further eastward
autarchy	self-sufficiency
bildung	edification or moral education; German
cosmogony	creation of the cosmos
creatio ex nihilo	creation out of nothing; Latin
derash	recontextualizing a biblical verse. Can be used as a noun or verb. Compare *peshat*.
devekut	literally, clinging or cleaving; term often used in mysticism to describe clinging to God
din	strict, formal justice; one of the ten sefirot
entanglement	the ongoing influence on discrete entities subsequent to their initial encounter
epistemology	the study of how we know what we believe we know
Eyn Sof	Literally, *endless*; in Kabbalah, the aspect of God that is beyond the human ability to imagine or know
Gaon, Geonim	Leaders of the rabbinic academies in Babylonia, seventh–eleventh centuries
Gemara	Later compositional stratum of Talmud following and organized around the Mishnah. Two Gemaras, one redacted in Tiberias but called the Jerusalem Talmud and the other in Babylonia. Authors are called *Amora'im*.

get	a writ of divorce that must be initiated by husband according to halakhah
Gnosticism	theological system positing autonomous and adversarial sources of good and evil
haftarah	a biblical selection, usually from the books of the prophets, chanted in synagogue after the chanting of the Torah portion on Shabbat and holidays
Hasidei Ashkenaz	German Pietists in the Rhineland, twelfth–thirteenth centuries
Hasidism	Jewish revival movement in Eastern Europe, eighteenth century
Haskalah	The Jewish enlightenment, an attempt to update the Jewish curriculum; Europe, eighteenth century
hekhsher	a symbol attesting to a product being kosher
hesed	lovingkindness; one of the ten sefirot
hitbonenut	contemplation on the nature of reality
huppah	a wedding canopy
idealism	a philosophical approach that ascribes ultimate reality to mental processes
impassible	without passions or emotions
jubilee	the year following the completion of seven cycles of the year of release *(shmittah)*
jurisgenerative	that which generates laws. Coined by Robert Cover but earlier described by Franz Rosenzweig.
Karaites	post-Talmudic Jewish group that rejected authority of Rabbanite (rabbinic) Jews and their Oral Torah. Only Bible *(miKRA)* is divine.
kavannah	concentration, intention, devotion
klipot	literally, shells, husks, or peels; that which surrounds and covers the holy sparks in Lurianic Kabbalah
legal nominalism	see nominalism, legal
legal realism	see realism, legal
maftir	the final Torah reading in the Torah service
metaphysics	branch of philosophy dealing with first principles including being and knowing
midat ha-din	the aspect of strict justice
midat ha-rachamim	the aspect of mercy
Mishnah	first composition of rabbinic Halakhah. Compiled by Judah the Prince, c. 220. First compositional stratum of Talmud. Capitalized for entire composition and lower case for a specific unit.

Mitnagdism	Opponents of Hasidism in Eastern Europe, emphasized Talmud Torah
mitzvah, mitzvot	commandment, incumbent obligation
Mizrachi	literally, eastern; ethnic term for Jews from North Africa and the Middle East
modeh ani	a prayer of gratitude said upon arising in the morning
monism	reality's essence is singular; dualities such as mind and matter or God and creation are specious
Mussar	program founded by Rabbi Israel Salanter in Eastern Europe to improve character traits, late nineteenth century
nominalism, legal	philosophy of law in which laws are designated or named without any necessary relationship to the world nor influencing the world
ontology	branch of philosophy dealing with the nature of being
pantheism	reality is divine
panentheism	reality is divine and God is more than the reality we perceive
peshat	the contextual meaning of a word or phrase, usually biblical. Compare *derash*.
Ploni Almoni	Hebrew version of John Doe. Names can also be separated to indicate two people, Ploni and Almoni. The feminine version is Plonit. See Ruth 4:1.
RaMBaM	Rabbi Moshe ben Maimon, Moses Maimonides, 1138–1204, Cairo. Leading Sephardic halakhist and philosopher, wrote Mishneh Torah and *Guide of the Perplexed*.
realism, legal	philosophy of law in which laws track on to the invisible architecture of the world; actions of legal consequence can sometimes affect the world
scientism	science is not only a method for discovering truth, there is nothing real that science cannot study; science can exhaustively describe all of reality
sefirah, sefirot	in medieval Kabbalah, there are ten sefirot that comprise the icon of divine unity
Sephardic	related to Spain or those exiled from Spain in 1492
shefa	overflowing divine blessing
Shema	Deuteronomy 6:4-9 used in liturgy
shmittah	every seven years; the biblical year of release from debts and agricultural labor
siddur	prayer book

sitra achra	literally, the other side; kabbalistic name for the parallel system of evil that operates parasitically on our transgressions; Aramaic
Sufi	Islamic mysticism
Talmud	Mishnah plus Gemara. The magnum opus of rabbinic Judaism. Babylonian Gemara redacted in sixth century, and Jerusalem Gemara redacted in fifth century.
Talmud Torah	the mitzvah of studying Jewish texts
Tanna, Tanna'im	rabbis from the period of the Mishnah, first–third centuries
teleology	the goal, purpose, or end of an act or process
teshuvah	literally, turn or return; to reorient oneself towards God and Halakhah
theodicy	the attempt to explain evil in a world where God is presumed to be all powerful and all good
theogony	the creation of God
theosophy	the inner life of the divine
theurgy	the influence on divine activity through human action
tikkun	amend, repair, restore. As a legal term, tikkun indicates a fix to a legislative problem; when used as a mystical term, tikkun restores a previous state of wholeness.
tohu va'vohu	the initial, chaotic state of creation
Tosafot	literally, additions; school of Ashkenazi Talmudic commentators, eleventh–fourteenth centuries
Tosefta	A larger ideological variant of Mishnah. Capitalized for entire composition and lower case for a specific unit.
treyf	an informal designation of something not kosher
tzadakah	literally, righteousness; often in the form of charity
tzaddik	literally, a righteous man; the sefirah associated with male sexuality in Kabbalah and, later, the leader of a Hasidic group
tzedek	justice, equity
tzimtzum	withdrawal, contraction, or evacuation; first movement of Lurianic Kabbalah to create "space" for subsequent creation
ushpizin	literally, guests; used to refer to the seven lower sefirot representing biblical characters invited into one's sukkah; Aramaic

* Unless indicated otherwise, foreign words are Hebrew

Index of Names and Subjects

conversos, 113–14, 115, 126
Cordovero, Moshe, 119–20, 124, 125, 146, 153, 311
Cosmic God (Wise), 295, 298
cosmogonic eros (Jonas), 214, 278, 280, 321–23, 331, 337, 485–88
cosmogony, 104, 270–71, 322, 335, 336, 338, 508
Cover, Robert, 443, 460, 497, 504–5
Creatio Appellata (Schmitz-Moormann), 336–37
creatio ex nihilo, 259, 508; *bara',* 8, 22, 236–37, 291; *ex nihilo* in rabbinic thought, 252–55, 257–58; Gamliel on, 291; God as cause of creation, 230–31, 233–34, 256–58; leaps and, 220; Mordecai Kaplan on, 190; pre-existing elements in the world, 252–54; in rabbinic theology, 252–55, 257–58, 268, 291; RaMBaM on, 267; resurrection of the dead, 73, 256–58; as volitional creation, 276, 280
creation: agency in, 236; *bara',* 8, 22, 236–37, 244, 291, 487; chance in, 343; choices in, 334; Christian theories of, 283, 284; collaboration in, 236, 237–38, 239–40, 249; construction of the Tabernacle, 11, 240, 264–65; cosmogony, 104, 270–71; as *creatio continua,* 485; deep time, 251; divine transcendence, 265; divinity of, 173; emanation, 274; evolution, 292–93; God in, 230–31, 236, 237–38, 239–42, 244–45, 249–50, 267, 341; as good, 341; Hebrew alphabet, 254; in Heschel's literary organization, 205; historical emergence, 246–47; in Kabbalah, xxiii, 116; language of, 8, 9, 20, 22, 233, 236–37, 254, 291, 292–93; mystical theology of, 263; Nachmanides (RaMBaN) on, 271; natural selection, 287–88; neoplatonism on, 267; parallels with the Temple in Jerusalem, 240–41; and the promise of redemption, 272; repentance as, 21–22; revelation, 289; seed principle (Rabbi Nehemia), 246, 247, 248–49, 258, 343; as self-propelled, 292–93; seventh day of, 35–36, 292–93; Shabbat, 11, 35–36; stewardship (*kibbush*) in, 496–97;

theogony, 104, 271, 482, 511; *tikkun,* 123; unity of, 485; as volitional act, 276–79; work of, 292–93; YHWH, 21, 49, 213–14, 218, 378, 486, 507. *See also* evolution; speciation
Creation narrative: Adam (biblical figure), 16, 17, 55, 119–20, 216, 251, 257, 501; *adam* (humanity), 19, 20n43; construction of tabernacle, 11, 240, 264–65; creation of humanity, 216; dietary restrictions, 13–14; Eve (biblical figure), 17; Garden of Eden, 17, 29, 136, 236n14, 246, 247, 303; *ki tov,* 9, 17n28, 20; language of, 8–9; light, creation of, 8, 10, 254, 479–80; moon, 10, 22, 110, 480; partnership in, 478; Plato's *Timaeus* compared with, 234; Reform Judaism on creation narratives, 297; sun, 10, 22, 230–31, 231n3; time in, 8–10, 10–11, 251; *tohu va'vohu,* 8, 232–34, 253, 258, 486, 511. *See also* Shabbat
creative agency, 258–59
Crescas, Hasdei, 113, 122; creation as volitional act, 276–77; God of, 138–39, 278, 337, 483; influence of, 142, 280; Kabbalah's influence on, 139; known by Spinoza, 142n199; on natural laws, 278; *Or Adonai,* 277n55; on RaMBaM, 269
Critique of Pure Reason (Kant), 154–55
crown imagery, 66, 276, 480
crypto-Jews, 113–14, 126
cud-chewers, land animals as, 14, 16, 20, 499–500
Cumulative revelation, 208–9
Cuvier, George, 283, 318
Cyrus (Persian King), 48

daily offerings, 23
Dan, Joseph, 72, 95, 119, 156, 254
darkness, 235
Darwin, Charles, 166, 187; American opposition to, 294; on competition, 339; on creation, 485; *Descent of Man* (Darwin), 288; natural selection, 227, 250, 285–88, 298–99, 306, 334; on natural theology, 226; origin of species, 251; *On the Origin of Species* (Darwin), 226, 282, 284, 286, 302–3; religious responses to, 250–52,

g'milut chasadim (deeds of loving
kindness), 60–61, 203–4, 278, 337, 483
Gnosticism, 133–34, 341, 486, 509
God: acts of loving kindness (*g'milut
chasadim*), 60–61, 203–4, 277–78,
336–38, 483; in Aristotelian
philosophy, 261–63, 262n5; attributes
of, 19–20, 46n3, 168–72, 176,
189–90, 218, 352, 480; as author of
Torah, 161–62, 184–85, 255–57, 289;
blessings, 62, 67–68, 83, 383, 507; as
cause of creation, 252–53; covenant
with, 34–35, 42–43, 55, 57–58, 68–69,
76; in creation, 8–9, 101, 173–74,
230–31, 235–36, 237–38, 239–42,
244, 249–50, 253, 267, 341; divine
corporeality, 135, 266, 273–74, 392;
evil, 119–20, 254, 341; as God of
Hosts, 73–74; on human suffering,
133–34, 210, 268, 344; *imitatio Dei*,
8, 270–71, 277, 337, 344; immanence
of, 25–26, 99–100, 125, 142, 151, 153,
155, 164, 168, 210, 307–8, 336–37;
impact of human behavior on, 23, 33,
54–58, 60–61, 107, 109, 111, 133–34,
171–73, 201, 351–52, 479, 482, 506–7;
light radiating from, 16–17; Moshe's
consultations with, 16, 356–58;
names of, 122, 213–14, 218, 230, 378,
446–47, 486, 507; in need of man,
54–56, 74, 201, 208; and observance
of mitzvot, 42, 60–61, 73, 112–13,
155, 201, 220, 280, 304, 372–73, 483;
presence in the sanctuary, 23–24; in
process theology, 315–16, 330–31;
RaMBaM on, 102, 131–32, 138, 266,
268–69; sacrifices in Deuteronomy,
35; YHWH, 21, 31, 49, 213–14,
218, 378, 486, 507. *See also Eyn Sof*;
sefirah/sefirot; Shechinah
God in Search of Man (Heschel), 205, 487
God's love: Buber on, 174–75, 178;
commandment to love God, 174–75,
175n111, 178; Heschel on, 200; for
humankind, 176; observance of
mitzvot, 42, 60–61, 73, 112–13, 155,
201, 220, 280, 304, 372–73, 483;
as proof of existence, 138–39; as
reciprocal, 174–75, 175n111
Goldman, Eliezer, 474
Goldsmith, Emanuel, 315

Goldstein, Jonathan, 256, 258
Gombiner, Avraham (*Magen Avraham*),
144, 405, 408
Goodman, Lenn, 324, 325
Goodman, Micah, 135
Gordon, Peter Eli, 173
Goshen-Gottstein, Alon, 16, 332
Gould, Stephen Jay, 5, 234, 287, 312
great chain of being, 290, 291, 310, 485
Great Revolt, 58
Green, Arthur: on body/soul dualism,
331–32; on crown symbolism, 66,
276; on Halakhah, 429, 471–72; on
Hasidism, 147–48, 156, 196, 211–12,
228–29, 325; on immanence, 326–27;
on Jewish feminism, 216; love among
humanity, 213–14, 214n116; on
mitzvot, 201, 215, 507; on modern
Orthodoxy, 195; monism of, 331–32;
Neo-Hasidism of, 211–12, 325; on the
one of Being, 328n30; panentheism
of, 211–12, 215, 328–29; personal
theology of, 103; on role of the
tzaddik, 428n45; on the *sefirot*, 104,
105, 276; on the Temple in Jerusalem,
108; on theology of Abraham Joshua
Heschel, 196, 201, 204–5; on *tohu
va'vohu*, 232; on transcendence,
211–15, 326–27, 329; on yearning for
life, 339–40; YHWH, 213–14, 218
Greenberg, Irving, 194, 210
Greenberg, Moshe, 252, 490
Greenstein, Edward, 39, 401
Gruenwald, Ithamar, 23, 53, 77, 99, 338
Guetta, Alessandro, 166
Guide of the Perplexed (Maimonides),
77, 103; on the divine image,
423–24; Garden of Eden, 92;
kabbalistic literature and, 113; on
prayer, 391; on prophecy, 128–29,
128n145; publication of, 102, 146; on
refinement, 58–60, 128, 137, 391, 459;
style of, 128; translations of, 102, 113
Guide of the Perplexed for the Time
(Krochmal), 440–41
Gumpertz, Aaron Solomon, 434–35
Gutoff, Joshua, 469, 470
Guttman, Julius, 275

Ha'amek Davar (Naphtali Zvi Berlin),
20n43

444–45, 474; blessing on studying
Torah, 383; centrality of, 49, 176;
divinity of, 69, 153, 184–85, 255–57,
289, 297, 304; Elijah Benamozegh
on, 304; feminist readings of,
465–66; God as rock, 337–38,
337n63; heart in the, 348; human
language of, 89–90; importance of,
21, 176; as intermediary between
God and creation, 242; law as legal
principles, 351; laws of inheritance in,
357–58, 427–28, 465, 468; multiple
interpretations, 402–3; peshat, 88,
90; RaMBaM on, 135–36; reading
of, 48–50, 245, 385, 414–15, 461–62;
scientific prescience of, 291; scribes as
keepers of, 48–50, 355, 415; slavery in,
277–78, 359, 464; soul in, 332; tenth
Sefirah, 105; Wisdom as, 243
Torah from heaven, 256
Torah from Sinai, 5
Torah light emanating from, 428–29
Torah study *(Talmud Torah),* 69–70,
81–82, 86, 481
Tosafot, 86–88, 90–91, 114, 372, 395,
402–3, 416, 511
Tosafot Tukh, 372
transcendence, 166, 265, 326–27, 329, 335
transmutation, 251, 284–85, 296–98, 311,
485
Tucker, Gordon, 415n3, 473, 474, 475, 488
Tur (Rabbi Yakov ben Asher), 395–96,
405, 407
turning the other cheek, 374
Twersky, Isadore, 87n7, 114–15, 407–8
Two Tablets of the Covenant (Horowitz),
125, 142n199, 143, 146, 148–49,
164n72, 263, 270, 280–81, 409, 412
tzaddikim, 150, 156, 499, 511
tzedek, 39, 347n1, 349, 511
Tzelophechad (biblical figure), 357,
427–28, 465, 468
Tzfat. *See* Safed Kabbalah
tzimtzum, 511; in Christian theology, 324,
332; determinism, 278–79; as divine
contraction, 278, 279; evil, 119; *Eyn
Sof* and, 278; Godless world depicted
by, 119; God's engagement in, 199,
483; in Hans Jonas's myth, 321–22;
Hasidism on, 213, 220; psychological
aspects of, 122, 153, 213, 220, 326; as

purgation, 278; shattering of vessels,
116, 117–18, 119, 120, 121, 279
tzorekh gavoah, 201, 202–3

ultra-Orthodoxy. *See* Schlesinger, Akiva;
Sofer, Moshe
Uncertainty Principle (Heisenberg), 333
United States: gay rights in, 490; racial
discrimination in, 464
Urim and Tumim, 48, 49
utopianism, 272–73

Vilna Gaon (Elijah ben Solomon
Zalman), 151, 153–55, 432
Vital, Hayyim, 116, 117, 121

water, 10, 22, 236, 327
watering as prohibition on Shabbat, 406
Weinfeld, Moshe, 30, 34
Weise, Christian, 321n5
Welker, Michael, 236
Wetzler, Isaac, 434–35
What is Darwinism? (McCosh), 294
Whewell, William, 288
White, Andrew Dickson, 295
Whitehead, Alfred North, 217, 330–31
Wiener Dow, Leon, 406, 407, 444
Wimpfheimer, Barry Scott, 373n36
wine consumption, 430
Wise, Isaac Mayer, 295–98, 296n29, 30,
303
Wissenschaft des Judentums, 482n4
Wolf, Ze'ev, of Zhitomir, 428n45
Wolfson, Elliot, 33, 116, 124n130,
173n101, 271, 307, 328
Wolfson, Harry, 140
women: *agunot,* 451, 452, 504–5;
associated with moon (tenth sefirah),
110; creation of, in Genesis, 17, 463;
feticide, 395, 502; hair coverings
for married women, 421; inclusion
in Torah reading, 461–62; Jewish
feminism, 207–8, 210–11, 216, 461,
465–66; laws of inheritance, 357–58,
427–28, 465, 468; oaths taken by,
63; Ruth the Moabite, 353–55, 375,
465–66; at Sinai, 461–62; voting rights
for, 430
world to come, 58, 91, 272
worship: acculturation in, 435–36;
decorum, 435; Israelites' worship of

Index of Sources

CPSIA information can be obtained
at www.ICGtesting.com
Printed in the USA
BVHW082131261120
594192BV00009B/23/J

9 781644 693407